福建历史文化双语丛书

总主编 葛桂录

（中英双语版）

福州古厝

林明金 主编

Resurgent Beauty:
Fuzhou's
Ancient
Architecture

社会科学文献出版社
SOCIAL SCIENCES ACADEMIC PRESS (CHINA)

城市文脉传承与建筑瑰宝再生

——《福州古厝》（中英双语版）序言

　　世称福州乃有福之州，钟灵毓秀，气象斐然。福见山水，福在文化，尤其是极具特色的建筑瑰宝福州古厝，雕梁画栋，其艺术设计和建造风格令人叹为观止，凝聚了古代工匠的精湛技艺和独特审美，承载着千年榕城的繁盛文脉，散发着百年文化交汇的历史遗韵。

　　作为福州历史图景的见证者，福州古厝不仅展现了福州地区丰富的建筑艺术，更是中华文明多元一体的生动体现。每一座古厝都承载着一段段历史，每一块砖瓦都诉说着一个个故事，它们是闽人智慧的结晶，也是中华福文化的延续。古厝的每一处细节，都蕴含着深厚的文化内涵和历史信息，它们不仅是汇通当下与往昔的精神津梁，更是传承与创意的情感纽带。

　　让我们静静地翻开这本《福州古厝》（中英双语版），伴随时间的年轮来一场心灵绽放之旅，去领略那些安顿在岁月长河中的建筑艺术与文化瑰宝，去探寻这些古老建筑背后的前尘旧梦与如烟往事，去发现它们所蕴含的深厚底蕴和独特魅力。

　　走进福州古厝，您会被那些精致的空间布局、精美的雕刻装饰所吸引。这些古厝以其独特的建筑风格和艺术风貌，展现了中国传统建筑艺术的博大精深。无论是木雕、石雕还是砖雕，每一件作品都堪称艺术精品，它们不仅体现了工匠的高超技艺，更展现了中华民族的审美情趣和文化追求。

　　福州古厝的建造，不仅体现了古代工匠的智慧和创造力，更蕴含了深厚的哲学思想和生活智慧。从选址、布局到建筑结构和装饰艺术，每一处设计都体现了人与自然和谐共生的理念，展现了古人对天地万物的理解和尊重。我们希望通过这本双语版著述，向世界传递福州古厝的艺术之美、文化之韵和历史之重，让更多的人了解和欣赏福州古厝的故事，体悟这些古建筑的独特魅力。

　　全书分为三篇，各篇自成体系又相互关联，为我们呈现了一个全方位且立体化的福州古厝世界。上篇"溯源：历史与现在"详述福州古厝的历史沿革和发展脉络。从汉冶城到现代福州，从城市的发展变迁到古厝的兴衰荣辱，我们得以一窥福州古厝背后的历史故事和文化内涵，深刻感受到福州古厝作为历史文化遗产的独特价值和珍贵宝藏。中篇"艺术：风格与特色"着重介绍福州古厝的建筑风格和艺术特色。从书院祠堂到琳宫塔庙，从商贾会馆到名庄古寨，每一种建筑形式不仅体现了古代工匠的精湛技艺和卓越才能，更展现了福州人民对美好生活的追求和向往。下篇"漫游：沉浸与品味"带领我们走进福州古厝的实地探索之旅。从梦回闽都的岁月如歌，到城南旧事的藤山余韵，从海丝觅踪的揽古察今，到船政追昔的壮怀激越，我们得以亲身体验福州古厝的魅力所在。我们不仅可以欣赏到福州古厝的美丽风光和独特韵味，更可以感受到福州这座城市的历史文化底蕴和人文精神。

《福州古厝》（中英双语版）的出版，不仅向国内外读者呈现了福州建筑艺术的魅力，更是对福州古厝文化的一种传播和推广。我们希望这本书能够成为连接不同文化背景读者的桥梁，让更多的人了解和欣赏福州古厝的独特价值。福州古厝不仅是福州的历史文化遗产，也是中华民族乃至全人类的共同财富。我们借此得以窥见古代文明的辉煌，感受传统文化的魅力，思考现代社会的希望。

走进一座城市，延续它的城市记忆，体验它所蕴含的历史文化的深度。踏进一座座古厝，理解它们的前世今生，感受它们所承载着的梦想与希望。那么多充满辉煌与温情的古厝故事，唤醒着蒙尘的历史记忆，呈示出福州古厝新旧交融的人文风情，让人徜徉其中而心旷神怡，如同面对丰盛的审美飨宴，也随时随地触发对过往岁月的遐思与对美好未来的向往。

愿这本书能成为您探索和理解福州古厝建筑瑰宝之美、感知历史文化名城福州深厚文脉的起点。

葛桂录

2024年6月10日（端午节）定稿于福建师大外语楼

前 言

　　作为有着两千两百多年建城史的国际历史文化名城，福州不但有山川之胜、园林之美，还有琳宫塔庙、名庄古寨、书院祠堂、西洋建筑等各种风格迥异的古建筑群。这些古建筑于岁月斑驳中矗立，记录着城市的历史变迁，承载着游子的乡愁，也镌刻着族群的文化基因。

　　福州古厝，又称"福州传统民居"，源于宋元时期，盛于明清，是福建省最具代表性的建筑风格之一。这些古厝以木结构为主，多为四合院式布局，错落有致，古朴典雅。从唐宋时期开始，福州古厝便形成了具有地方特色的建筑风格，历经数百年的沧桑岁月传承至今。作为古代中原文化与福建当地文化相融合的产物，福州古厝不仅具有极高的艺术价值，还蕴含着丰富的历史文化内涵。这些古厝见证了福州这座城市的繁荣与发展，记录了福州人民的勤劳与智慧。每座古厝背后都有着动人的故事，诉说着历史的沧桑与变迁。

　　"传统建筑是历史的活化石"。作为福州珍贵的历史文化遗产，福州古厝不仅见证了这座城市的悠久历史和独特魅力，更是福州先民们超凡智慧和卓越才能的结晶。这些古厝以其独特的建筑风格和精美的雕刻艺术，诠释了福州民间工艺的精湛技艺和丰富内涵，成为福建乃至中国历史文化宝库中的璀璨瑰宝。

　　走进福州古厝，你会被这些古建筑的细腻雕刻所震撼，为它们的优雅气质所吸引。每一座古厝都有着自己的故事，它们或悲壮或婉约，仿佛在诉说着福州的历史。在这里，你可以感受到浓厚的历史气息，领略到古人的智慧和才情。

　　福州古厝，饱含了多少人的乡愁、乡情、乡恋。时光斗转，两千多年的沧海桑田和人间烟火，以福州古厝为载体，追忆往昔，仰望未来，氤氲出人间岁月长。古厝的"前世"道不尽，"今生"更精彩，漫步在福州的城区郊野、街头巷尾，享受福文化与闽式生活，守护这闹市中的"桃花源"。

　　《福州古厝》（中英双语版）用双语的方式全面介绍福州古厝的历史、文化、艺术和保护价值，通过大量的图片和文字资料，带领读者深入了解这些古厝的魅力所在，注重对古厝背后故事的挖掘和呈现，让读者更加深入地了解和感受到这些古建筑所承载的历史与文化。本书为福建师范大学外国语学院师生集体创作的成果。葛桂录为丛书总主编，组织并启动丛书的编写。林明金为本册主编，负责全书统稿、审订并补充编写部分内容（完成约8万字）。全书分三篇，每篇既自成体系，又相互联系。上篇"溯源：历史与现在"由胡雯（完成约7万字）、李恩福（完成约6万字）、张铃（完成约3万字）负责编写；中篇"艺术：风格与特色"由张爱珍（完成约6万字）、黄薇（完成约7万字）、陈明达（完成约4万字）负责编写；下篇"漫游：沉浸与品味"由唐炯（完成约7万字）、邱永忠（完成约7万字）、蔡巧英（完成约5万字）负责编写；福建师范大学文学院林婕、吴秀芳、陈紫薇协助修订本书的中文部分。本书系"福建历史文化研究及外译丛书编撰"项目的研究成果之一，由福建师范大学外国语学院资助出版。

上篇
溯源：历史与现在

中篇
艺术：风格与特色

下篇

漫游：沉浸与品味

Contents｜目录

Part One
Seeking the Root: Past and Present

Part Two
Unveiling the Legacy: Styles and Features

Part Three

Rambling: Immersion and Taste

[上篇]

—

Part One

溯源：历史与现在

Seeking the Root: Past and Present

福州古厝

福州地处我国东南部，依山傍海，为山川灵秀之都。这里人杰地灵，人文荟萃，自古就有"东南都会"、"八闽首邑"的美称，是一座声名远播的历史文化名城。福州古厝，泛指福州古建筑，历史悠久，源远流长。从秦汉时期的冶城开始，历代都有很多极具特色的古建筑，包括城池桥梁、寺院宫观、名人故居、传统街区、文教建筑、西洋建筑等。经过历史的洗礼，这些古建筑很多仍保存至今，显示出福州丰富的文化底蕴，向人们诉说着福州辉煌的历史。

————— · ◇ · —————

Located in southeast China's Fukien Province, Fuzhou is a city surrounded by magnificent mountains, beautiful rivers and the sea. As a renowned historical and cultural city with a wealth of talented individuals, it has been known as the "Metropolis of Southeast China" and the "Capital of Bamin" since ancient times. Fuzhou Gucuo generally refers to the ancient buildings in Fuzhou with a long history. Since Yecheng in the Qin and Han Dynasties, there have been many distinctive ancient buildings in Fuzhou, such as cities, bridges, temples, palaces, former residences of celebrities, traditional districts, cultural and educational buildings, and western-style buildings. Many of them have witnessed the vicissitudes of the city while still being preserved today, showing its rich cultural heritage and glorious history.

第一章

城池衙署 安振闽疆

Chapter One
Cities and Government Offices:
Guarding the Territory of Fukien

福州这座历史文化名城内遍布各类城池衙署，它们以极具特色的建筑布局组成了稳固的防御体系，默默地守卫着古城的安全，同时也承载着福州辉煌灿烂的历史文化，作为历史的亲历者亲眼见证了这座古城两千多年来的沧桑巨变。

◎ 汉冶城

明朝诗人王恭《冶城怀古》诗云："无诸建国古蛮州，城下长江水漫流。野烧荒陵啼乌外，青山遗庙暮云头。"这首诗抒发了对无诸建立闽越国、建都冶城这段历史兴废变迁的无限感慨。

《史记·东越列传》记载："汉五年（前202年），复立无诸为闽越王，王闽中故地，都东冶。"（司马迁，1959：2979）无诸为战国时期越国王室后裔，战国中期，楚灭越，越王室后裔率众南迁入闽。战国末年，无诸自行在福建建立闽越国，称闽越王。秦始皇统一六国后，置闽中郡，贬无诸为"君长"。秦末农民起义爆发，无诸率部北上中原，参加反秦战争，后又助汉灭楚，立下功劳。刘邦建立汉王朝后，于高祖五年（前202年）复封无诸为闽越王，治理闽中故地，闽越国便成为汉王朝的异姓诸侯国，仍旧在今福州建立都城，史称东冶或冶。

无诸统治时期，与汉廷保持和睦关系，执行汉初休养生息政策，发展经济与文化，使闽越国逐渐走上封建化的发展道路。无诸还改变了闽越人"处溪谷之间，篁竹之中"、"非有城郭邑里"的原始生活状态，创筑了闽越国都城冶城。无诸创建闽越国、首筑冶城的功绩，受到后人景仰。无诸死后，相传葬于今冶山西面的王墓山（闽越王墓之意），又一说葬于南台大庙山闽越国祖庙后。福建各地建有很多奉祀闽越王的庙、殿、寺，表达了人们对他的怀念。

福州建城，始自无诸。林枫《榕城考古略》记载，"闽之有城，自冶城始"，"其地当在今诸古岭以南、城隍（庙）以北等地也。故今华林寺及乾元废寺（在今钱塘巷）皆指为冶城故址"。（转引自卢美松，2002：548）考古发现的冶城遗址，主要集中在今屏山南麓一带，从北侧的越王山到南侧的冶山和云步山。闽越国时期的大面积遗址发现于越王山至冶山之间。

Spread throughout Fuzhou, various cities and government offices have formed a solid defense system with a distinctive architectural layout. They have long quietly guarded this ancient city, carrying its brilliant history and culture, and witnessing its great changes over the past thousand years.

◎ Yecheng in the Han Dynasty

One of the Ming Dynasty poets, Wang Gong wrote a poem entitled "Reminiscence of Yecheng" to express his infinite emotions towards the historical vicissitudes of Wuzhu's founding of Minyue State and its capital city, Yecheng.

According to *Historical Records of Dongyue State in the Records of the Grand Historian (Shi Ji)*, Wuzhu, a descendant of the royal family of the State of Yue during the Warring States period, was re-nominated as the king of Minyue State in 202 BC, the 5th year of the Han Dynasty, setting Dongye as its capital. After the State of Chu defeated the State of Yue, the descendants of Yue's royal family initiated a migration of people to move south to Min in the middle of the Warring States period. Wuzhu started Minyue State in Fukien on his own, and was called the king of Minyue State at the end of the Warring States period. After unifying China, the first emperor of Qin Dynasty set up Minzhong Commandery and demoted Wuzhu to a chief. At the end of the Qin Dynasty, the peasant uprising broke out, and Wuzhu led his forces northward to the Central Plains to join the Anti-Qin war, and later helped the Han Dynasty defeat the state of Chu. In 202 BC, the 5th year of Gaozu, Liu Bang established the Han Dynasty, and then renominated Wuzhu as the king of Minyue State to take charge of the old places of Minzhong. Later, Minyue State became the kingdom of different surnames of the Han Dynasty and still established its capital in today's Fuzhou, with the name of Dongye or Ye in history.

During his reign, Wuzhu maintained a harmonious relationship with the imperial court of the Han Dynasty. He adopted the rehabilitation policy of the early Han Dynasty, and developed the domestic economy and culture, making Minyue State gradually embark on the road to feudalization. He also improved the primitive living conditions of people there, and created the capital city of Minyue State, Yecheng. Later, he was revered by later generations for his great achievements in founding Minyue State and building Yecheng. Legends claim that Wuzhu was buried in Wangmu (the tomb of the king of Minyue State) mountain in the west of today's Yeshan mountain after his death, and he was also said to be buried in the ancestral temple of Minyue State in Damiao mountain of Nantai. Many temples, halls and palaces in Fukien were built in memory of Wuzhu.

The city of Fuzhou was founded by Wuzhu. It is recorded in Lin Feng's *Archaeological Records of Rongcheng* that the city in Fukien started from Yecheng, which was located in the south of Zhugu Range and the north of Chenghuang Temple. Therefore, today's Hualin Temple and the abandoned Qianyuan Temple(in today's Qiantang Lane)are the former sites of Yecheng(cited in Lu Meisong, 2022: 548). According to archaeological findings, the historical site of Yecheng is mainly at the southern foot of today's Pingshan mountain, covering the area from Yuewang mountain in the north to Yeshan and Yunbu mountain in the south. Large areas of sites in the Minyue State period were found between Yuewang mountain and Yeshan.

"冶山春秋园"中的闽越王无诸雕像
The Bronze Statue of Wuzhu, the King of Minyue State in Yeshan Chunqiu Historical Park

　　1991年底，在冶山福建省建设银行营业大楼建筑工地上，考古工作者发现了一处汉初建筑遗址。红黄色夯土基址厚达90厘米，在基址上残留的护坡砖墙长达1.7米，每块汉砖长44.7厘米、宽33.4厘米、厚3.7厘米，保存完整，硬度较高。同时出土的还有一批板瓦、筒瓦、菱纹铺地砖、方格硬纹陶片等。在一个仅25平方米的考古探方内就出土砖瓦片609块，更有价值的是其中15块板瓦内壁戳印有文字。如"亚"形字，是蝮蛇头部的象形，金文中是"它"字，又释为"虫"、"蛇"，也是"闽"字的初文，是最早的"闽"字。考古工作者在地面上采集到一块汉初板瓦，内壁戳印"郳"字。郳，古国名，即小邾，其上世出于邾，后改邹，在今山东邹县东。战国中，为楚宣王所灭，郳人被迫南迁于楚地（今湖北黄冈市），以国为姓。郳又通作"倪"，即今之倪姓。中国建筑从战国晚期开始，砖瓦上的题字都是正规的印记，所戳之印标明烧造砖瓦的官署和监工姓氏。出土板瓦上的"闽"字应为汉初闽越王的徽记，"郳"字应是烧造砖瓦的监工姓氏（卢美松，2002：548）。

At the end of 1991, archaeologists discovered a historical site from the early Han Dynasty at the construction site of the headquarter building of China Construction Bank Fukien Branch in Yeshan. The red and yellow rammed earth base was as thick as 90 centimeters, and the remaining slope protection brick wall on the base site was 1.7 meters long. Each Han brick, well preserved and hard enough, was 44.7 centimeters long, 33.4 centimeters wide and 3.7 centimeters thick. A batch of slab tiles, tube tiles, diamond-patterned ground tiles, and checkered hard-grained pottery pieces were also unearthed at the same time. Out of the 609 bricks and tiles unearthed in an archaeological excavation area of only 25 square meters, 15 were stamped with characters on the inner layer. For example, the shape of the Chinese character of "Ya"(亚) is a pictogram of a viper's head. In Chinese bronze inscriptions (bell-cauldron inscriptions), it is the character of "Ta" (它), which is also interpreted as "Chong" (虫) or "She" (蛇), thus becomes the earliest character of "Min" (闽). A piece of slab tile in the early Han Dynasty was collected on the ground, with the character stamped on its inner layer. "Ni" (郳), the name of the ancient state, namely "Xiaozhu" (小邾), was born from "Zhu" (邾)in the last life, and later changed to "Zou" (邹), and it was in today's east of Zou County, Shandong Province. During the Warring States period, Ni was destroyed by King Xuan of Chu, and the people of Ni were forced to move south to Chu (now Huanggang, Hubei Province), with the name of the country as people's surname, also known as "Ni" (倪), the current surname. Since the late Warring States period, in Chinese architecture, inscriptions on bricks and tiles have consistently featured formal stamps, indicating the surnames of the officials and supervisors who made the bricks and tiles. According to historian Lu Meisong, the Chinese character of "Min" (闽) on the unearthed tiles should be the emblem of the King of Minyue State in the early Han Dynasty, and "Ni" (郳) should be the surname of the supervisor who baked the tiles(Lu Meisong, 2022: 548).

《史记·东越列传》载："闽越王无诸及越东海王摇者，其先皆越王勾践之后也，姓驺氏。"（司马迁，1959：2979）可知闽越王无诸乃是越族的后裔。为闽越王烧造宫殿祠庙等大型建筑所需砖瓦的郧氏，则是从北方再次南迁的旧贵族，他们担任技术人员，用北方先进的生产技术为建造闽越王宫殿贡献力量。

在福建省建行北面的屏山农贸市场，出土了大量绳纹筒瓦、板瓦片，其中有"万岁未央"、"常乐万岁"、"万岁"文字瓦当，龙凤纹"万岁"瓦当，卷云纹箭镞等，表明这一带有闽越国大型宫殿遗址。在福州地铁屏山站的考古中，发现长达100多米的夯土台基，出土大量汉代大型板瓦、筒瓦及大铁器、陶器等，考古界认为这一带是大面积的汉代王城遗址。

总的来看，考古发掘证明，冶山至屏山一带确实是汉冶城的宫殿区和官署区。对于冶城在福州的说法，以往学界一直有人抱怀疑态度。但从冶山和屏山的考古成果看，尤其是完整的"常乐万岁"瓦当，当属皇室专用。建筑的高等级和高规格，出土的大板瓦、筒瓦等遗物，也显示出汉代王城的规制。应该说，冶城在福州的说法难以推翻。

在以春秋时期冶城遗址与冶山命名并整修而成的"冶山春秋园"内，特地留有一片"考古预留区"，作为将来的考古发掘场地，用以发掘更多冶城从西汉至清代各时期的遗存与大量文物。

冶城初建时规模并不大。宋梁克家《三山志·地理类四》载："闽越王故城，今府治北二百五步。"（梁克家，2003：44）闽越国冶城的范围，北起今华林寺一带的越王山南麓，南至湖东路，东到冶山岭东侧，西至钱塘巷，范围不大。后来，由于无诸的子孙们狂妄自大，据险叛汉，元封元年（前110年），闽越国灭亡，冶城也因此被废弃良久。

晋太康元年（280年），福州置晋安郡，首任郡守严高觉得冶城太小，便将城移建在越王山（今屏山）南的小山阜上，并筑子城。此后，冶城便不断向南、向东拓展。唐末五代，闽王王审知创筑罗城，将子城包围其中，以后又筑南北夹城。明朝初年，大修城池，北跨越王山（今屏山），南边则将乌石山、九仙山二山包围，广袤方十里。清代，随着经济发展、人口增加，城市不断往南扩展，以至和台江、仓山连成一片。至今福州城正继续向闽江两岸、乌龙江乃至长乐沿海拓展。

It is recorded in *Historical Records of Dongyue State in Records of the Grand Historian*, the ancestors of King Wuzhu of Minyue State and King Yao of Dongyue State were both descendants of Goujian, king of Yue, with the surname of Zou (驺) (Sima Qian, 1959: 2979). Therefore, Wuzhu was a descendant of the ancient Chinese nationality of Yue. The Ni (郳) family, who baked the bricks and tiles needed for large buildings such as palaces and temples for the king of Minyue, were old nobles who moved south again from the north. They worked as technicians and contributed to the construction of the palaces of the king of Minyue with the advanced technology of the north.

In Pingshan market, the north of China Construction Bank Fukien Branch, a large number of rope-patterned tube tiles and slab tiles have been discovered. Among them were eaves tiles inscribed with the Chinese characters of "Wansui" (万岁, meaning longevity), "Wansui Weiyang" (万岁未央, meaning longvity neverends) and "Changle Wansui" (常乐万岁, meaning forever happiness and longevity), the dragon-phoenix patterned tiles inscribed "Wansui" and cloud-patterned arrowheads, indicating the historical existence of large palaces of Minyue State. In the archaeological excavations around Fuzhou Metro Pingshan Station, a rammed earth stylobate with a length of more than 100 meters was found, and a large number of big plate tiles, tube tiles, ironware and pottery from the Han Dynasty were unearthed as well. The archaeologists believe that this area was the royal residence of Minyue State in the Han Dynasty.

Archaeological excavations have proved that palaces and governmental offices of Yecheng were gathered in the area ranging from Yeshan to Pingshan. In the past, some people in academia have been skeptical about the idea that Yecheng was in Fuzhou. However, the archaeological discoveries of Yeshan and Pingshan, especially the complete "Changle Wansui" tiles showed that they were exclusive for the royal family. The high-class design and manufacturing of the buildings, and the relics such as large slab tiles and tube tiles also indicated the regulation of the imperial city of the Han Dynasty. Therefore, it is undeniable that Fuzhou is where Yecheng was located.

In the newly renovated Yeshan Chunqiu Historical Park (Yeshan Spring and Autumn Garden), which is named after the site of Yecheng and Yeshan in the Spring and Autumn Period, an archaeological area is specially reserved for future archaeological excavations to discover more remains and relics of Yecheng from the Western Han Dynasty to the Qing Dynasty.

Yecheng City was not large when it was started. According to Liang Kejia's *Geographical Records in San San Zhi (History of the Three Mountains)* in the Song Dynasty, the old place of Minyue State, was 205 bu (step) north to its capital. (Liang Kejia, 2003: 44) Yecheng in Minyue State did not have a wide range, and it extended northward to the southern foot of Yuewang mountain in the area of Hualin Temple, southward to Hudong Road, eastward to the east side of Yeshan Ridge, and westward to Qiantang Lane. Later, Wuzhu's descendants, filled with their undue arrogance, rebelled against the imperial court of the Han Dynasty. In 110 BC, the first year of Yuanfeng, Minyue State fell apart, and Yecheng was abandoned for a long time.

In 280, the first year of Taikang in the Jin Dynasty, Jin'an Commandery was set up in Fuzhou. Yan Gao, the first governor of Jin'an Commandery, felt that Yecheng was too small, so he moved the city to a small mountain in the south of Yuewang mountain (now Pingshan) and built a Zicheng (sub city) as an extension of the old city. Since then, Yecheng has continued to expand southward and eastward. In the Five Dynasties of the late Tang Dynasty, Wang Shenzhi, the king of Min, built Luocheng to surround Zicheng, and later built the North-South Jiacheng. In the early Ming Dynasty, the city was renovated, crossing Yuewangshan (now Pingshan) in the north, and surroundedby Wushi mountain and Jiuxian mountain in the south, covering a vast area of ten miles. During the Qing Dynasty, due to economic development and population growth, the city expanded southward, and later merged with Taijiang and Cangshan areas. Up to now, Fuzhou City has been expanding to both sides of Minjiang River, Wulong River and even the coastal area of Changle.

　　冶山，有著名的欧冶池胜地。《吴越春秋》记载："越王允常聘请欧冶子作名剑五枚，允常传数世至无疆，因灭于楚，乃徙居闽。"欧冶子选中了冶山的池畔铸剑淬火，此地故名"欧冶池"。福州最早称"冶城"，大概也与欧冶子的传说有关。宋熙宁元年（1068年），程师孟以光禄卿出任福州知府，他在知府任上主持修复子城城墙。在清理子城东北部杂树时发现了这个水池，并命人在池边修建了欧冶亭。此外，这里还建有剑池院、喜雨堂、凌云台等。如今，欧冶池成了福州人休憩游乐的好去处。北宋文学家黄裳《欧冶池》诗曰："人随梦电几回见，剑逐云雷何处寻？惟有越山池尚在，夜来明月古犹今。"

　　元代，欧冶池旁边又建了三皇庙、五龙堂。元泰定五年（1328年），朝廷在欧冶池畔立一石碑，上刻"三皇庙五龙堂欧冶池官地"，明确将这一带的池塘、土地、建筑物列为官产，予以保护。

欧冶池今景
Today's Ouye Pool

There is a famous resort called Ouye Pool in Yeshan. According to *Wu Yue Spring and Autumn Annals*, Yun Chang, the king of Yue hired Ou Yezi to forge five famous swords, and passed it down for generations to Wujiang. After being defeated by the State of Chu, people in the State of Yue moved to Min. Ou Yezi chose the poolside of Yeshan to cast swords, so this place is named Ouye Pool. Yecheng, the earliest name of Fuzhou, is probably related to the legend of Ou Yezi. In 1068, the first year of Xining in the Song Dynasty, Cheng Shimeng, the Minister of Imperial Household, took the post of Prefect of Fuzhou and was in charge of repairing Zicheng's wall. In clearing the weed trees in the northeast of Zicheng, he found this pool and ordered to build the Ouye Pavilion beside it. There are also Jianchi Courtyard, Xiyu Hall, Lingyun Platform, and so on built in this area. Today, Ouye Pool becomes one of the best relaxing places for people in Fuzhou. Huang Shang, a famous poet in the Northern Song Dynasty, wrote a poem Ouye Pool to show his love for this pool.

In the Yuan Dynasty, Wulong Hall and Sanhuang Temple was built next to Ouye Pool. In 1328, the 5th year of Taiding in the Yuan Dynasty, the imperial court set up a stele by Ouye Pool, bearing the inscription of "Sanhuangmiao Wulongtang Ouyechi Guandi" (三皇庙五龙堂欧冶池官地, meaning the official land of Ouye Pool, Wulong Hall and Sanhuang Temple), and identified the ponds, lands and buildings in this area as government properties for protection.

泉山摩崖题刻
Quanshan Cliff Inscriptions

　　清道光八年（1828年），官府重新疏浚并扩大欧冶池，不久后还立了"欧冶子铸剑古迹碑"。1983年，福建省财政厅拨款重建欧冶池，疏通池塘和水源，池岸砌石，周边新建喜雨轩、剑光亭、池心亭、石舫等建筑。

　　冶山虽小，然而摩崖石刻却有50多处，如"独秀峰"、"剑胆琴心"、"玩琴台"、"山阴亭"、"洛社遗风"等，镌刻时间久远，书法风格各异，构成了石刻上的历史，为我们研究福州历史提供了真实可考的依据。

　　在冶山的最高处，人们有一个惊人的发现，这里曾是唐代福州最大的马球场，由唐代福州刺史裴次元所建。"唐裴刺史毬场故址"八个大字镌刻在一块巨石上。这是中国首次通过考古发掘出土的唐代马球场遗迹，为研究古代体育史尤其是马球运动发展史提供了重要的实物依据。同时，这项通过海上丝绸之路传来的体育娱乐活动，也充分展现了唐代福州对外交往的繁荣景象，见证了唐代福州文化生活与休闲娱乐的丰富多彩。经测量，现存的福州马球场遗址面积有1万多平方米，约有两个足球场大。站在马球场遗迹旁，不难想见唐代福州人在马球场上豪迈奔放、策马奔腾的热闹场景。

唐代马球场遗址旁的马球浮雕
Relief Wall of the Polo Field in the Tang Dynasty

In 1828, the 8th year of Daoguang in the Qing Dynasty, the government redredged and expanded Ouye Pool and soon set up the sculpture of Ou Yezi beside it. In 1983, the Fukien Provincial Department of Finance allocated funds to rebuild Ouye Pool, by dredging its water source, laying stones along the pool deck, and building Xiyu(love for rain)Pavilion, Jianguang (light of the sword) Pavilion, Chixin (heart of the pool) Pavilion and stone boats around the pool.

Although Yeshan is small, there are more than 50 cliff inscriptions in it, such as "Duxiu Peak" , "Jiandan Qinxin" (courage of a warrior and the soul of a musician), "Wanqin Platform" , "Shanyin Pavilion" and "Luoshe Yifeng" . Those inscriptions of different calligraphy styles present a long history and provide verifiable evidences for people to study the history of Fuzhou.

People made a surprising discovery that the area at the top of Yeshan mountain was once the largest polo field in Fuzhou in the Tang Dynasty, built by Pei Ciyuan, then Fuzhou's governor. The eight Prominent characters of "Tang Peicishi Qiuchang Guzhi" (唐裴刺史毬场故址, meaning the former site of Inspector Pei's Polo Field) were engraved on a huge stone. This was the first time that China has unearthed the remains of the polo field of the Tang Dynasty through archaeological excavation, providing important evidence for the study of ancient sports' history, especially the development of polo. At the same time, this sports and entertainment activity brought by the Maritime Silk Road also witnessed the rich cultural life, colorful recreational activities and leisure entertainment in Fuzhou in the Tang Dynasty, showing the prosperity of Fuzhou's foreign exchanges in those days. The existing site of the polo field in Fuzhou covers an area of more than 10000 square meters, about the size of the two football fields. Standing beside the polo field, it is not difficult to imagine the lively scenes of the bold and unrestrained people of Fuzhou in the Tang Dynasty galloping on the polo field.

冶山春秋园门口
The Entrance of Yeshan Chunqiu Historical Park

　　1983年，冶山欧冶池等古迹被列为福州市级文物保护单位。2021年2月初，由福建历史上首座王城所在地——冶城遗址开发而成的遗址公园"冶山春秋园"正式开园。公园四周绿树葱茏，鲜花盛开，与文物古迹交相辉映，重现了各个时期的古城文化风貌。汉冶城作为福州最早修筑的城池，以及闽都两千多年历史文化的重要见证者，静静地诉说着闽都政治文化中心——福州城发展与变迁的历史往事，传递着博大精深的闽越文化。"冶山春秋园"也成为当今福州人发思古之幽情和散步休憩的绝佳去处，人们在这里缅怀历史、放眼未来。

◎ 镇海楼

　　镇海楼位于福州城北居中的屏山之巅，是福州古城的最高楼，为中国九大名楼之一。镇海楼始建于明洪武四年（1371年）。当时，明太祖朱元璋委任驸马都尉王恭为福建行省参政，兼任福建最高行政长官。王恭到福建后，为了镇压反叛、防御外敌入侵，开始了规模宏大的修筑福州城墙的工程。

　　原有的福州城，经历了汉代冶城、晋代子城、唐代罗城及南北夹城，到宋代熙宁年间（1068—1077年），程师孟知福州，建造楼阁，疏浚护城濠和内河，架设桥梁，兴建起一座超越历代规模的福州城。然而好景不长，福州城垣在元末被毁。王恭根据福州城的历史和具体的地形地貌特点，将福州城墙的北段从屏山脚下迁移到海拔72米的屏山上，并建筑城楼，称为样楼。样楼即福州城其他各座门楼的标准样板，这座样楼后定名为镇海楼。样楼借鉴了各城楼的优点，经过精心设计修建而成。在福州城北屏山上建镇海楼，就是在城北设置了一道人造天险。这里是福州城的最高处，也是福州城绝佳的地理位置。站在屏山之巅的城楼上，全城山川形胜尽收眼底，城市动静也了如指掌，这便于控制城市，攻守自如。

　　镇海楼坐落于福州城南北中轴线的北端正中，往南看，山下左右两侧分别是衙门、坊市、民居、河道，再远处则把乌山、于山环抱于城墙之内。整个福州城将三山两塔包揽其中，方圆十余里，藏风聚水，乃风水绝佳之地。

In 1983, Ouye Pool in Yeshan and other historical sites were listed as major historical and cultural sites protected at the municipal level. At the beginning of February 2021, Yeshan Chunqiu Historical Park officially opened, which was developed on the site of Yecheng, the first imperial city in Fukien history. Surrounded by green trees and blooming flowers, this park glitters with cultural relics and reproduces the cultural scene of the ancient city in various periods. As the earliest city built in Fuzhou and an important witness of its history and culture for more than 2000 years, Yecheng quietly tells the history of Fuzhou as the political and cultural center of the capital of Fukien, and passes the profound culture of Minyue State. At present, Yeshan Chunqiu Historical Park is an excellent place for people in Fuzhou to relax, remember the past and look forward to the future.

◎ Zhenhai Tower

Situated on the top of Pingshan mountain in the north of Fuzhou and built in 1371, the 4th year of Hongwu in the Ming Dynasty, Zhenhai Tower was the highest building in the ancient city of Fuzhou and one of the nine famous buildings in China. At that time, Zhu Yuanzhang, the emperor Taizu of the Ming Dynasty, appointed Wang Gong, his son-in-law and Commandant, the chief executive of Fukien Province, taking in charge of the political affairs. After Wang Gong arrived in Fukien, he began the large-scale construction of Fuzhou city wall in order to suppress the rebellion and to defend against the invasion of foreign enemies.

The original Fuzhou City has gone through Yecheng in the Han Dynasty, Zicheng in the Jin Dynasty, Luocheng and North-South Jiacheng in the Tang Dynasty. In the Xining period of the Song Dynasty (1068-1077), Cheng Shimeng was in charge of Fuzhou. He built towers, pavilions and bridges, dredged the moat and the inland river, making the city's scale far exceed that of the previous dynasties. However, the good times did not last long, and the city walls of Fuzhou were destroyed at the end of the Yuan Dynasty. Wang Gong moved the northern section of the Fuzhou city wall from the foot of Pingshan mountain to the Pingshan mountain with an elevation of 72 meters, and built a city tower as Yang Lou (the sample building). It drew on the advantages of various city towers and was carefully designed and built. As the standard sample of different gatehouses in Fuzhou, Yang Lou was later named Zhenhai Tower. On the top of Pingshan mountain, the tower actually set up an artificial danger in the north of Fuzhou, and occupied the highest place and the best geographical location of Fuzhou City. Standing in the tower on the top of Pingshan, you can overlook all the mountains and rivers and be well-informed about everything in the city, which makes it easier to control the city by launching an attack or defense.

Zhenhai Tower is located in the middle of the north end of the North-South central axis of Fuzhou City. Looking south, government offices, lanes, markets, folk houses and rivers are on the left and right sides down the mountain. In the distance, Wushan and Yushan are both surrounded by the city wall. Covering a vast area of more than ten miles, the entire city of Fuzhou is surrounded by three mountains and two pagodas, making it a Fengshui treasure land.

从样楼到定名镇海楼，其名称颇有深意。从镇海楼向闽江、海口方向极目远眺，一江如带，出了闽江口，则是波涛汹涌、激流奔腾的大海。清代学者谢章铤《重建镇海楼碑记》写道："镇海楼者，建北城之标，障北山之望……且夫楼以镇海名，工在楼，意实在海。嗟乎！海风叫啸，海水飞扬，登斯楼也，其忍负中流砥柱之心哉！"（转引自福建省炎黄文化研究会、福建省作家协会，2016a：138）登上镇海楼，对陆上、水上、海上交通便有了一种掌控感。此外，突出于城市天际轮廓线的镇海楼也成为进出闽江口航船的重要航标。即将入港的船只可以遥望府城制高点的城楼，以此作为进出闽江口航船的"准望"，找到进港的方向。正因为如此，镇海楼便有了保护航海安全、抗击台风侵扰的实际功用。又因为镇海楼是砖石结构建筑，在当时以土木结构建筑为主的福州城内实为罕见。它以大石砌成，坚固牢靠，历狂风暴雨而不倒，与福州城内在风雨中飘摇的那一片片低矮木屋相比，镇海楼更显示出其镇海之功。

"越王山拥海潮流，山上嵯峨镇海楼"（明·车大任《登镇海楼》）是对镇海楼雄姿的真实写照。当时的老百姓也将镇海楼视为一座坚不可摧、颇具传奇色彩的风水楼，在它身上寄托了驱邪避灾、护卫海疆的美好愿望。因此，"样楼"后来改名为"镇海楼"，名副其实，是民意所向。直到现在，镇海楼依然是福州人民的精神寄托。

镇海楼于明洪武年间修成之后，历经沧桑。清咸丰十年（1860年），镇海楼遭雷击焚毁，数月后重建，楼宽缩减三尺。清光绪十六年（1890年），镇海楼整体坍塌，两年后重修，恢复原有规制。1933年，光绪年间重建的镇海楼毁于大火。同年，国民革命军第十九路军发动"福建事变"，在镇海楼原址修建了军事碉楼。1946年，镇海楼原址上的军事碉楼被改造为纪念福建乡哲、国民政府主席林森的纪念堂。1970年，林森纪念堂因故被拆。2006年，福州市文物部门按明代镇海楼原式样重修。2008年4月28日，历经一年多，镇海楼复原工程竣工，结束了福州镇海楼那一段有记无楼的历史。

Both names, Yang Lou and its final name Zhenhai Tower, have profound meanings. Gazing at the Minjiang River and the entrance of the sea in the distance from Zhenhai Tower, you can first see a belt-like river, and then a rough sea out of the Minjiang River Estuary. Xie Zhangting, a scholar in the Qing Dynasty, described in his *Inscriptional Records of Rebuilding Zhenhai Tower* the splendor of the sea and the excitement he felt when he was on the top of Zhenhai Tower. (cited in Fukien Yanhuang Culture Research Association and Fukien Writers Association, 2016: 138) You have a sense of control over land and sea traffic when you climb to the top of the tower. In addition, Zhenhai Tower, which protrudes from the urban skyline, becomes an important navigation mark for ships entering and leaving the Minjiang Estuary. Ships that are about to enter the port can look from afar the tower at the commanding height of the city, which can be used as the "reference point" for their coming in and going out of the Minjiang River and finding the direction to enter the port. Therefore, Zhenhai Tower has the practical function of ensuring navigation safety and fighting typhoons. Built by large bricks and solid stones, it was quite different from many buildings made of clay and wood in Fuzhou at that time. Compared with the low-rise wooden houses, the indestructible Zhenhai Tower survived a lot of storms and faithfully performed the duty of guarding the sea.

The lines of "Yuewang mountain embraces the sea, and the steep Zhenhai Tower stands upright on the top of the mountain" from Che Daren's *A Poem of Zhenhai Tower* portrays vividly the majesty of Zhenhai Tower. At that time, the people also regarded the tower as an indestructible and legendary Fengshui building, and placed on it the best wishes of exorcising evil, avoiding disasters and protecting the sea. Therefore, Yang Lou was later renamed Zhenhai Tower, which was worthy of the name and in line with the public opinion. Up to now, Zhenhai Tower is still the spiritual sustenance of Fuzhou people.

Built in the Hongwu years of the Ming Dynasty, Zhenhai Tower went through the vicissitudes of history. In 1860, the 10th year of Xianfeng in the Qing Dynasty, the tower was destroyed by lightning strikes. It was rebuilt several months later, and the width of the building was reduced by three chi. In 1890, the 16th year of Guangxu in the Qing Dynasty, the entire building collapsed. Two years later, it was rebuilt and the original regulations were restored. In 1933, the Zhenhai Tower was destroyed by fire. In the same year, the 19th Route Army of the National Revolutionary Army launched the "Fukien incident" and built a military blockhouse at the original site of the tower. In 1946, the blockhouse was transformed into a memorial hall to commemorate Lin Sen, a sage in Fukien and the chairman of the national government in China. In 1970, Lin Sen Memorial The hall was demolished for some reason. In 2006, the Department of Cultural Relics in Fuzhou rebuilt the Zhenhai Tower by restoring its original style in the Ming Dynasty. On April 28, 2008, the restoration project of Zhenhai Tower was completed, ending the history of only records but no building of the tower.

2018年，福州市屏山公园围绕"绍越开闽 镇海通津"主题开始改造，位于屏山上的镇海楼成为"屏山十八景"中一处重要景点。原址重建的镇海楼飞檐翘角，十分壮观。楼体分上下两层，现存建筑均按明代制式格局复原，为重檐歇山顶，施以斗拱，屋面为陶制筒瓦和板瓦，两侧辅以汉白玉石雕的栏杆。楼高21米，地基深24米，楼宽45.6米，连接镇海楼的城墙厚1.73米。为了再现当年屹立于屏山之上的壮观景象，重建镇海楼时，设计人员根据屏山周边楼宇的建设现状，果断将基座提高了10米。这一提高使得镇海楼更加雄伟，作为福州城的地标更加突出和显眼。因此更准确地说，镇海楼的高度应再加上这10米，为31米。

如今，镇海楼内部已经成为生动再现福州历史、展现福州古厝文化的博物馆。镇海楼基座这个巨大的地下空间，被设计成极有特色的"福州历史文化名城展示馆"。这是一座集中展示福州两千两百多年历史文化的高科技现代化展馆，建筑面积1600平方米，以福州城的历史为主线，分"闽在海中"、"闽越都城"、"晋代郡城"、"唐代州城"、"宋元路城"、"明代府城"、"清代会城"、"近代城台"、"当代辉煌"九个展区。展厅地面使用地形地貌沙盘，别出心裁的同时突出了福州特有的地理特征。展厅上方的牌坊则刻有福州别称，时空走廊上则悬挂着福州著名的中国近现代名人照片。这些名人中有开眼看世界的林则徐、晚清重臣沈葆桢、启蒙思想家严复、黄花岗七十二烈士之一的林觉民、文学家冰心等。馆内共有700多件文物，其中有300多件为三级文物，著名的冶山遗址出土的汉代瓦当、怀安窑青瓷博山炉等十分引人注目。

镇海楼二层及以上为福州古厝展示馆，门口悬挂"福州古厝展示馆"七个镏金大字。展厅墙上挂有软木画《古厝精粹》，这是福州很有特色的非遗工艺品。展厅两侧的观赏台上摆放有20个颇具福州特色的古典建筑模型，有著名的水榭戏台、林则徐故居、小黄楼等，通过实物和史籍记载，全方位地展示福州古厝的历史。

整座镇海楼的展厅通过声、光、电等现代化表现手法，将福州市的历史与文化表现得淋漓尽致，使观众如同身临其境，它是福州历史文化和人文风貌的浓缩版。

In 2018, Pingshan Park in Fuzhou was renovated around the theme of "continuing the State of Yue and starting the State of Min, guarding the sea and heading for the waterway", and Zhenhai Tower on the top of Pingshan thus became an important scenic spot of the "18 scenic spots of Pingshan". The rebuilt tower in its original site is spectacular with its overhanging eaves. Restored according to the pattern of the Ming Dynasty, the two-story building has a double-eaved gable roof with a corbel arch. The surface of the building is made of ceramic tube tiles and slab tiles, with white marble railings along its two sides. The tower is 21 meters high, 24 meters deep, and 45.6 meters wide, and its wall is 1.73 meters thick. In order to reproduce its magnificence, the project raised the base of the tower by 10 meters according to the construction status of buildings around Pingshan, which made the tower prominent as the symbol of Fuzhou City. To be more precise, the 10 meters should be added to the height of Zhenhai Tower, which is 31 meters actually.

Today, the interior of Zhenhai building has become a museum that reproduces vividly the history of Fuzhou and displays the ancient house culture of Fuzhou. The huge underground space of Zhenhai Tower's base is now the Exhibition Hall of the Historical and Cultural City of Fuzhou. This is a high-tech modern exhibition hall focusing on the history and culture of Fuzhou for more than 2200 years, with a building area of 1600 square meters. Taking the history of Fuzhou as the theme, it is divided into nine exhibition areas, namely "Fukien in the Sea", "Capital City of Minyue", "County City of the Jin Dynasty", "State City of the Tang Dynasty", "Prefectural Ciry of Song and Yuan Dynasties", "Prefectural City of the Ming Dynasty", "Provincial Capital of the Qing Dynasty", "Modern City Tower" and "Contemporary Glories". Topographic and geomorphic sand tables are used on the ground of the exhibition hall, highlighting the unique geographical characteristics of Fuzhou. The archway above the hall is engraved with Fuzhou's alternative name, and photos of Chinese modern celebrities in Fuzhou are hung along the Space-Time Corridor. Among these celebrities are Lin Zexu, who opened his mind to the world; Shen Baozhen, an important minister in the late Qing Dynasty; Yan Fu, an enlightenment thinker in China; Lin Juemin, one of the 72 martyrs of Huanghuagang Uprising, and Bing Xin, a famous writer. Among more than 700 cultural relics on display in the museum, more than 300 are Grade 3 ones. The famous tiles of the Han Dynasty in the site of Yeshan, and the celadon Boshan furnace from Huai'an kiln are all eye-catching.

On the second floor of Zhenhai Tower and above is the Exhibition Hall of Fuzhou Ancient Buildings. At the entrance, we can see a plaque with seven gold-plated characters of "Fuzhou Gucuo Zhanshiguan" (福州古厝展示馆). On the wall of the exhibition hall, there is a cork painting called Essence of Ancient Houses, which is a distinctive intangible cultural heritage of Fuzhou. On the viewing areas on both sides of the hall, there are 20 classical architectural models with Fuzhou characteristics, including those of Shuixie Xitai (Waterside Stage), Lin Zexu's former residence and Xiaohuang building (Little Yellow Tower). The history of Fuzhou's ancient houses is displayed in an all-round way through physical objects and historical records.

As the epitome of Fuzhou's history and culture, the exhibition halls of the entire Zhenhai Tower display vividly the history and culture of Fuzhou through modern means of sound, light and electricity, so that the audience can immerse themselves in it.

在镇海楼右前侧，有一组排列成神秘图案的石缸石柱，这就是著名的"七星缸卦阵"。清乾隆年间（1736—1795年），有人给镇海楼算过"命"，说它三次遭雷击、两次遇大火的原因，是越王山山形尖锐，属火星之相，建筑物应作卷棚式圆形，而不宜再用棱角屋脊。为了避免大的火灾，就建了七组由六根小石柱围起来的石缸，人称"七星缸"，象征北斗七星按天象排列组合，成斗勺状。古人以为，斗勺盛水，可伏火灾。建七星缸，正是人们为了防避火灾而表达的一种良好愿望。如今的镇海楼依然保留古代的七星缸卦阵，说明福州不忘历史、保存历史并走向未来。

站在镇海楼外，抬头看10米高台上新建的镇海楼：城门式高台，二层楼阁，外观为歇山顶加腰檐，雄伟壮观。两只巨龙压着翻滚海浪的大型浮雕石刻"双龙盘海"栩栩如生。在浮雕石刻的正上方，匾额上"镇海楼"三个大字熠熠生辉。作为福州古城的最高楼以及标志性建筑之一，镇海楼将过去与现在紧密地连接起来，饱含着福州人对海晏河清、风调雨顺的美好生活的向往和不懈追求。

镇海楼外观
Zhenhai Tower

On the right front of Zhenhai Tower, there is a group of stone cylinders and columns arranged in mysterious patterns, forming the famous Seven Star Cylinder Bagua Array. During the reign of Emperor Qianlong of the Qing Dynasty (1736-1795), someone told the fortune of Zhenhai Tower, talking about the reasons the tower was struck by lightning three times and was caught in fire twice, believing it was the sharp mountain shape of Yuewang mountain that belongs to the Martian phase, and suggesting a round rolling shed instead of an angular roof should be applied to the building. In order to avoid the fire, seven stone cylinders were built surrounded by six small stone columns, known as "Seven Star Cylinders". It symbolizes the dipper-shaped arrangement and combination of the seven stars of the Big Dipper according to the celestial phenomena. The ancients believed that the dipper could contain water and fire, so Seven Star Cylinders expressed their good wishes of preventing fire. Today, the ancient Seven Star Cylinder Bagua Array is still retained in Zhenhai Tower, which shows that Fuzhou would always remember the past, preserve the history and look ahead.

Standing outside Zhenhai Tower, we can look up at the newly built tower on a 10-meter-high platform. It is a two-story magnificent tower with a gate-type platform, in the appearance of the peak of the mountain and the waist eaves, with the large lifelike relief stone carvings of two giant dragons pressing against the rolling waves. The three big characters of "Zhenhai Lou" (镇海楼) on the plaque are shining right above the relief stone carvings. As the highest and one of the landmark buildings in the ancient city of Fuzhou, Zhenhai Tower closely connects the past and the present, and is full of Fuzhou people's unremitting yearning and pursuit for a better life of clear water and good weather.

◎ 闽安巡检司衙门

在福州闽江出海口，有一个叫"闽安镇"的地方，那是福州对外交往的门户，也是保卫福州安全的军事重镇。"闽安镇"即"安镇闽疆"之意。闽安镇著名的文化遗址是闽安巡检司衙门，是国内唯一的海防军事衙门，也是福州对外交往的水上检查衙署。

闽安巡检司衙门始建于唐代，宋代天圣七年（1029年）设监镇卫，元代称巡检司衙门，明洪武二年（1369年）仍建闽安巡检司衙门。清代重建，改称协台衙门，是清代闽台军事防御指挥机关，管理水师，又厘海关，是福建省南北盐馆总卡。

闽安巡检司衙门位于今福建省福州市马尾区亭江镇闽安村城里街（闽安小学边），为明末清初建筑，占地面积1768平方米，由前埕、门楼、照壁、门厅、正厅、后堂及两侧厢房、三个天井等建筑组成。正殿面阔五间、进深四间，周以封火山墙，为硬山顶穿斗式木构架，保存完好。

"闽安巡检司衙门"正门
Front Door of Min'an Inspection Department Yamen

◎ Min'an Inspection Department Yamen

Located at the estuary of the Minjiang River in Fuzhou, Min'an Town is a gateway of Fuzhou's external relations and a military town to protect Fuzhou, and its name means "An Zhen Min Jiang", guarding the territory of Fukien. The famous cultural site in Min'an Town is the Min'an Inspection Department Yamen(government office), the only military office for coastal defense in China, and the water inspection office for Fuzhou's external relations.

Min'an Inspection Department Yamen was built in the Tang Dynasty. In 1029, the 7th year of Tiansheng in the Song Dynasty, the position of Jian Zhen Wei (the town guard) was set up, and it was called Inspection Department Yamen in the Yuan Dynasty. In 1369, the second year of Hongwu in the Ming Dynasty, Min'an Inspection Department Yamen wasre built, and it was renamed Xietai (assisting Taiwan) Yamen in the Qing Dynasty. As the military defense headquarters of Fukien and Taiwan in the Qing Dynasty, it administered the Navy and the Customs, and it was also the general North-South Salt taxation department of Fukien Province.

Min'an Inspection Department Yamen is located in today's Chengli Street next to Min'an primary school, Min'an Village, Tingjiang Town, Mawei District, Fuzhou City, Fukien Province. Built in the late Ming and early Qing Dynasties, it covers an area of 1768 square meters and consists of the front courtyard, the gate building, the screen wall, the entrance hall, the main hall, the rear hall, the wing rooms on both sides, and the three patios. As a well-preserved wooden frame of gabbled roof and column-and-tie construction, the main hall is five-room wide and four-room deep, and surrounded by fireproof walls.

福州闽安镇为福建省第一门户，在历史上曾是海关口岸和军事重镇。东汉时，交趾（今越南）的贡品要先运到福州，再转运至京城洛阳，便是通过闽安镇完成的。福州港的船舶亦经此远至东洋、南洋。景福二年（893年），王潮占领福州，在闽安镇设立税课司衙门，负责往来福州港对外贸易船只的课税。福州对外贸易北至新罗，南至南洋群岛的三佛齐，西南至天竺（古印度）等国家。宋天圣年间，在闽安镇设巡检司，作为监镇衙门，置使臣一员，负责巡察沿海各县政事、巡捕海匪、缉私及设关课税等事务。

宋朝梁克家所著《三山志》记载："天圣七年，本路转运司奏：'闽县界有闽安镇，枕居海门，为舟楫往来冲要之地，宜用使臣一员监纳商税，兼沿海县分巡检，仍于本城及屯驻、驻泊指挥内抽差军级员寮六十人，往彼巡防，量给衣甲器械。'"（梁克家，2003：304）

而后历朝沿袭此规制。嘉祐三年（1058年）蔡襄奏请朝廷，教习官兵水师，修造船只，缉捕海寇。此时闽安巡检司已有巡海兵员60人。元代闽安复置巡检司，明代闽安巡检司由官兵世代驻守，水师多数官兵熟悉海上的各种情况，有丰富的航行和海战经验。

闽安镇历来以经济和商业贸易著称于世，清顺治十五年（1658年）以后，历代沿袭设置的巡检司、盐馆卡、海关等机构不断完善。闽安水门道沿江有众多码头，是货物、海产的集散地。镇中心为商业区，鼎盛时期有米行、茶行、酒库、鱼行、木材行、典当行、钱庄银楼、布匹丝绸行、餐饮店、打铁店、旅馆等各类商行商店300多家，还有"牙店"进行大宗货品的交易。每当海外船舶到来之时，闽安番商云集，舟车辐辏，一片繁荣景象。

As the first gateway of Fukien Province, Min'an Town of Fuzhou was historically a port of customs and an important military town. In the Eastern Han Dynasty, the tributes from Jiaozhi (now Vietnam) were first transported to Fuzhou and then to Luoyang, the capital city, through Min'an Town. Ships from the port of Fuzhou also went as far as Dongyang (Japan) and Nanyang (Southeast Asia). In 893, the second year of Jingfu, Wang Chao occupied Fuzhou and set up a tax department office in Min'an Town, in charge of the taxation of foreign ships to and from Fuzhou. Fuzhou's foreign trade extended to Xinluo in the north, Nanyang islands such as Sanfoqi in the south, and Tianzhu (ancient India) in the southwest. During the Tiansheng period of the Song Dynasty, an inspection department was set up in Min'an Town as the Yamen of the town, and a post of the envoy was set up for inspecting the political affairs of the coastal counties, arresting the pirates, suppressing smuggling and imposing taxes.

According to Liang Kejia's *Geographical Records* in *San Shan Zhi* (*History of the Three Mountains*) in the Song Dynasty, the Transportation Secretary in the 7th year of Tiansheng has ever reported Min'an Town's important position for ships to travel, advised setting up an envoy to supervise the taxation and sending 60 military personnel to patrol the coastal counties (Liang Kejia, 2003: 304).

The following dynasties continued carrying out the regulation. In 1058, the third year of Jiayou, Cai Xiang petitioned to the imperial court to train the officers and sailors to build ships and arrest pirates. At this time, Min'an inspection Department had already 60 coastal soldiers. In the Yuan Dynasty, an inspection department was reset in Min'an Town, and since the Ming Dynasty, the officers and soldiers of Min'an Inspection Department were stationed there for generations. Familiar with various conditions at sea, most of the Navy soldiers had rich experience in navigation and naval warfare.

Min'an Town has always been famous for its economy and trade. After 1658, the 15th year of Shunzhi in the Qing Dynasty, the inspection departments, general departments of salt taxation, Likin tax departments, customs and other institutions established in successive dynasties have been improved continuously. There were many riverside wharfs along Shuimen Road in Min'an, forming a distribution center for goods and seafood. The town center was a commercial district, with more than 300 shops in its heyday, such as rice shops, tea shops, wine stores, fish shops, timber shops, pawn shops, money houses, jewelry shops, cloth and silk shops, catering shops, iron shops, hotels, and so on. There were also "tooth shops" for the trade of bulk commodities. When overseas ships arrived, a lot of foreign merchants, boats and carriages gathered together in Min'an Town, rendering the trade in full swing and the whole town prosperous.

闽安镇的迴龙桥是贯通福州海外贸易必经之路的重要桥梁。该桥始建于唐，又名沈公桥，宋端平年间郑性之重修，清康熙、嘉庆、道光及民国期间又多次重修。迴龙桥横跨邢港南北两岸，全长66米，结构别致，四墩五孔。桥墩为罕见的船形外观，花岗石平梁结构，石护栏36根护卫两侧，外观优美。柱顶雕刻有独特的宝奁、海豹与官印，为我国古桥石雕仅见，系唐代原构件。迴龙桥作为福州著名的古代通海大石桥，自唐代保留至今，体现了我国唐宋石刻的精湛技艺，对中国的桥梁文化有很高的研究价值，也见证了"海上丝绸之路"福州段的历史与发展。

闽安为闽江口进入福州的咽喉，地势险要，为历代兵家必争之地。每当朝代变更、外敌入侵，这里便成了海防重镇，水战、陆战的战场。因此，自唐至清历代在这里驻有重兵，设水师、建炮台、修寨城、立烟墩，军事海防建设相当齐备。

闽安江面狭窄，闽江之水自马尾至闽安，两岸群山夹峙，闽安镇枕居海门，成为舟船从海上进入闽江的重要地点。此形胜之地使闽安镇自古以来便成为闽江口的军事要冲。闽安江段低潮时江面仅330米，驻防军在江边拉一条横江铁链直至对岸的石龙山麓，平时铁链沉江底，有敌来犯时由驻军士兵用磨轴车推拉卷紧，铁链即横在江面阻挡敌船。明朝嘉靖年间，日本倭寇来犯，这里成了拱卫福州、阻止敌寇侵犯的主战场。当时这里烟墩林立，军事设施完备，倭寇四次攻打福州，均在闽安门被歼。抗倭名将戚继光在这里垒石构筑松门水寨、乌猪寨、高山寨、东高寨四座城寨，墙高25米、厚11米，驻扎精兵，历时五年，连战皆捷，歼敌无数，保卫了福州的安全。

Built in the Tang Dynasty, Huilong Bridge, also known as Shengong Bridge in Min'an Town, is an important bridge in the history of Fuzhou's overseas trade. It was rebuilt by Zheng Xingzhi in the Duanping period of the Song Dynasty, and rebuilt many times in the Kangxi, Jiaqing, Daoguang periods of the Qing Dynasty and the Republic of China period. Huilong Bridge spans the north and south banks of Xinggang, with a length of 66 meters and a unique structure of four piers and five holes. Its pier has a rare ship shape, with a granite flat beam structure. There are thirty-six beautiful stone guardrails protecting both sides of the bridge, and on the top of their columns are carved seals, dressing cases and official seals, which are unique in Chinese ancient bridge stone carvings and are all the original components of the Tang Dynasty. As a famous ancient stone bridge across the sea in Fuzhou, Huilong Bridge has been preserved well since the Tang Dynasty. It not only reflects the exquisite skills of stone carving in the Tang and Song dynasties, shows great research value for Chinese bridge culture, but also witnesses the history and development of Fuzhou, as an important part of Maritime Silk Road.

As an important place from the estuary of Minjiang River into Fuzhou and with a dangerous terrain, Min'an Town has been of great military importance of all dynasties. Whenever the dynasties changed and foreign enemies invaded, it became an important town for coastal defense and a battlefield for warfare on land and water. Therefore, the town has been heavily guarded from the Tang Dynasty to the Qing Dynasty. The Navy was established, and the fortresses, walled cities and beacon towers were also built there, forming a complete system for military and coastal defense.

A narrow body of river water flows along Min'an Town. The water of the Minjiang River flows from Mawei to Min'an, with the mountains standing against each other on both sides of the river. The town sleeps at the sea gate and becomes an important place for boats to enter the Minjiang River from the sea. With superior geographical conditions, Min'an Town has been a military hub at the mouth of the Minjiang River since ancient times. In times of low tide, the Min'an section of the river is only 330 meters wide. The garrison pulled an iron chain across the river to the foot of Shilong mountain on the opposite bank. At ordinary times, the iron chain was sunk at the bottom of the river. When the enemy came, the soldiers pushed and pulled the iron chain tightly with a roller mill, blocking the enemy ship across the river. During the Jiajing period of the Ming Dynasty, Wokou assaulted Fuzhou, and Min'an Town became the main battlefield to defend Fuzhou and prevent the invasion of the pirates. At that time, there were numerous beacon towers and complete military facilities. The Wokou attacked Fuzhou four times and were all wiped out at the gate of Min'an Town. Qi Jiguang, a famous anti-Japanese general, built in the town the following four walled cities of Songmenshui, Wuzhu, Gaoshan and Donggao, with 25-meter-high and 11-meter-thick walls. By stationing elite troops in the town, he won a series of battles in a five-year period, annihilated countless enemies, and protected the city of Fuzhou.

清初，民族英雄郑成功把闽安作为抗清和收复台湾的根据地。他在闽安巡检司内设置军事指挥部，率领40万大军十四年间多次攻守闽安镇。现在闽安江边还有"郑爷鼻"的地名，指的是江边突出部的山岗以及下面的港湾，那是当年郑成功操练水师的地方。当时，这个军港先后驻扎有郑成功的水师大军五路，人数数万，战船数百艘。郑成功大军正是以这里为出发点之一跨海东征，终于在清顺治十八年（1661年）收复台湾，迫使荷兰驻台湾总督揆一投降，被荷兰侵占长达三十八年之久的台湾终于重新回到了祖国怀抱。郑成功水师在闽安构筑的炮台和驻扎的遗址今仍保存，似乎在向人们诉说当年郑成功的辉煌业绩。

清朝为了加强海防力量，顺治十五年（1658年）重建闽安城。闽安城墙用石头垒砌，周长1850米，故闽安镇又有石头城之称，十分坚固。同时在闽安设总兵府，设水师9个营汛，辖24个塘，分五营四哨。闽安邢港还建有较场演武厅。清康熙元年（1662年），闽安水师官兵多达5000余人。闽安总兵府辖本标左营、右营、烽火营，现在闽安镇仍有左营、右营的地名。

清康熙年间收复台湾后，为保卫台湾不受外国侵略，特在闽安镇城里街设置闽安协台衙门，这是清朝的军事指挥机关驻地。作为军事指挥机关，闽安协置左、右营将士戍守台湾，清朝的总兵、巡抚、都督、总督不断进驻闽安镇，在闽安协台衙门任职的副将（二品）以上官员中负责涉台事务的多达120名。

亭江考古挖掘出的红夷大炮
Hong Yi Cannon discovered from an archeological excavation in Tingjiang

At the beginning of the Qing Dynasty, Zheng Chenggong, a national hero, took Min'an Town as a base for fighting against the Qing Dynasty and recovering Taiwan. He set up a military headquarter in the Min'an Inspection Department, and led the troops of 400000 soldiers to defend Min'an town and attack the enemies many times during a fourteen-year period. Now, there is still a place called Zheng Yebi along the Min'an River, which is the hill of the protruding part of the river where Zheng Chenggong's training division was located and the estuary below. At that time, five routes of his naval force were successively stationed on this naval port, with tens of thousands of naval divisions and hundreds of warships. Zheng Chenggong's army took this place as one of the starting points, made a cross-sea expedition eastward, and finally recovered Taiwan in 1661, the 18th year of Shunzhi in the Qing Dynasty, forcing Kuiyi, the Dutch governor of Taiwan to surrender. Taiwan, which had been occupied by the Netherlands for thirty-eight years, finally returned to its homeland. The fort built by Zheng Chenggong's navy in Min'an Town and the site of its garrison are still preserved today, telling people about Zheng Chenggong's brilliant achievements in those years.

In order to strengthen the coastal defense, the Qing Dynasty rebuilt Min'an Town in 1658, the 15th year of Shunzhi. The walls of Min'an Town were made of solid stones, with a circumference of 1850 meters, so the town was also known as the stone town. At the same time, the general military office was set up in Min'an, with nine naval divisions in charge of 24 dykes, divided into five battalions and four sentinels, and a martial arts hall was also set up in Xinggang in Min'an Town. In 1662, the first year of Kangxi in the Qing Dynasty, there were more than 5000 officers and soldiers in the navy in Min'an Town. The general military office of Min'an Town governed the battalions of Zuoying, Youying and Fenghuoying. Now, there are still places called Zuoying and Youying in the town.

After the reunification of Taiwan in the Kangxi period of the Qing Dynasty, Min'an Xietai Yamen was set up in Chengli Street of Min'an Town in order to protect Taiwan from foreign invasion, and then became the military command center of the Qing Dynasty. As a military command center, it set up the left and right battalions to guard Taiwan. The commanders in chief, governors, military governors and inspectors of the Qing Dynasty were constantly stationed in Min'an Town. In Min'an Xietai Yamen, there were up to 120 officials with the position of deputy general (the second grade) and above who had ever dealt with Taiwan affairs.

在衙门的天井中，有一块《英军犯顺厦门报警》碑。碑文大意是：道光二十一年七月（1841年8月），英军挑起战端，攻陷厦门。闻警后，闽安镇协孙云鸿不顾资金短缺，发动僚属、乡绅募捐，开濠筑坎，改造水门炮台7座，以抗击英军入侵。这块石碑为我们提供了鸦片战争时期闽安协台衙门和闽安人民为反抗侵略而英勇斗争的史实。

从闽安出发的戍台将士，有的为国捐躯后归葬闽安。在闽安镇虎头山有一处清军墓地，是国家级文物保护单位，里面埋葬着135名福建戍台将士的遗骸。

清同治十三年二月（1874年3月），日本以"牡丹社事件"为借口发兵侵略台湾，船政大臣福建人沈葆桢奉命援台，负责台湾防务，兼理各国事务。6月，沈葆桢率领闽安镇水师左、右营和马尾船政水师等27个营及大批陆军精锐近万将士乘军舰赴台，终于迫使日军撤离台湾。在戍台战役中，一些闽安水师将士为国捐躯，后归葬闽安。闽安的清军墓地彰显了他们为保卫祖国宝岛台湾共击外来侵略的民族精神。现如今，这里已辟为公祭广场，每年举行一次公祭活动。

在抗日战争中，为阻止日寇从海上入侵福州，国民政府命令福建省用石头、舰船封填闽江口。闽安千余名石工不分昼夜开山取石，还将坚固无比的石头城拆除，用以沉船堵江。历时两年多，工程才完成。填江石料达500余万吨，布设水雷400余枚，有效地阻止了日寇的海上进攻，捍卫了福州城。

如今，闽安镇作为国家级经济技术开发区（马尾区）的重要组成部分，驶上了经济发展的快车道。这里拥有福州新区、自贸试验区、"21世纪海上丝绸之路"核心区、生态文明先行示范区等"四区叠加"的优势。两岸先进制造业、电子商务合作和金融合作项目不断催生，国内第一家中国-东盟海产品交易所也位于此地。交易往来频繁，闽江口经济圈初步形成。在城市建设上，闽安镇高楼林立，桥梁密布，绿树成荫，花团锦簇。同时，这里文化发达，人杰地灵，英雄辈出，国家级、省级和市级文物保护单位比比皆是，军事堡垒、戍台遗址星罗棋布，经济与文化发展齐头并进。

In the courtyard of the Yamen, there erects a stele of "The Alarm of the Invasion of Xiamen by the British Army", writing that in August of 1841, the 21st year of Daoguang in the Qing Dynasty, the British army captured Xiamen. After hearing about the alarm, Sun Yunhong, the adjutant general of Min'an Town, in spite of the shortage of funds, called in his subordinates and the squires to raise funds, excavate the trenches, build barriers, and renovate seven watergate batteries to prepare for resisting the British invasion. This stele provides us with the historical facts of the heroic anti-aggression struggle of Min'an Xietai Yamen and the Min'an people during the Opium War.

Some of the soldiers who set out from Min'an to guard Taiwan died for the country and were buried back in Min'an. There is a cemetery of the Qing Dynasty's troops in Hutou mountain, Min'an Town, and it is now a national-level cultural relics preservation unit, and a resting place for the remains of 135 Fukienese soldiers.

In March, 1874, the 13th year of Tongzhi in the Qing Dynasty, Japan used the "Peony Society Incident" as an excuse to send troops to invade Taiwan. Shen Baozhen, the Minister of Shipping of Fukien Province, was ordered to help Taiwan and to take charge of Taiwan's defense and other affairs. In June of the same year, he led 27 battalions to Taiwan by warships and finally forced the Japanese army to withdraw from Taiwan. Among the battalions were the left and right battalions of the navy of Min'an Town and the navy of Mawei shipping administration, and a large number of elite officers and soldiers of the army as well. In the battle of defending Taiwan, some officers and soldiers of Min'an Navy sacrificed their lives for the country and were buried back in Min'an Town. The cemetery of the Qing army in Min'an Town demonstrates their national spirit of fighting jointly against foreign aggression to defend the motherland's treasure island of Taiwan. Now, it has been turned into a square for public memorial ceremony, with public memorial service held once a year.

During the Anti-Japanese War, the national government ordered Fukien Province to block the estuary of the Minjiang River with stones and ships in order to prevent the Japanese from attacking Fuzhou from the sea. Day and night, more than a thousand stoneworkers in Min'an Town cut into the mountains for quarrying, and dismantled the solid stone town for sinking the ships and blocking the river. It took more than two years before the project was completed. More than 5 million tons of stones were filled in the river, and up to 400 mines were laid, which effectively defended Fuzhou City by preventing the Japanese's attack from the sea.

At present, as an important part of the state-level economic and technological development zone(Mawei District), Min'an Town has moved onto the fast lane of economic development. It enjoys the advantages of "Four Areas", which include Fuzhou New District, Pilot Free Trade Zone, Core Area of the Maritime Silk Route and Ecological Civilization Pilot Zone. Cross-strait advanced manufacturing industry, e-commerce and financial cooperation projects have been constantly blooming. The first China-ASEAN Marine Product Exchange in China is also located here. The economic circle of Minjiang Estuary has been initially established with the flourishing trade. In terms of urban construction, Min'an Town is full of high-rise buildings and bridges, and dotted beautifully with trees and flowers. With a lot of outstanding people, many cultural relic preservation units at the national, provincial and municipal levels, and military fortresses and garrison sites scattered all over the place, Min'an Town enjoys a developed culture and a booming economy as well.

　　闽安镇、闽安巡检司与闽安协台衙门作为牢不可破的福州古戍台和古战场，以及国内唯一的海防军事衙门，忠实地捍卫着福州城，为福州古城的安全提供坚实的保障，见证了福州明清时期反侵略的历史，记录着马江上的风云变幻，也诉说着闽台之间血脉相连的密切关系，以及福州对外贸易与交往的历史轨迹。它们通过辉煌的历史和现在，沟通着福州与世界的经济交流，激励人们以更昂扬的斗志去创造美好的未来。

As the indestructible ancient garrison, the ancient battlefield of Fuzhou, and the only coastal defense military Yamen in China respectively, Min'an Town, Min'an Inspection Department and Min'an Xietai Yamen faithfully defended Fuzhou City and guaranteed the safety of the ancient city of Fuzhou. They have witnessed the history of Fuzhou's anti-aggression struggles in the Ming and Qing Dynasties, recorded the changes in the Majiang River, told the blood tie between Fukien and Taiwan, and presented the history of Fuzhou's foreign trade and external relations as well. Through their glorious past and present, they link up the economic exchanges between Fuzhou and the world, and encourage people to create a better future with higher morale.

第二章

寺院庙宇：交通中外

Chapter Two

Chinese Temples: Communicating

China to the World

福州具有深厚的历史文化底蕴，坐拥众多宏伟壮观、神圣威严的寺院庙宇。这些古老的寺院庙宇不仅是各类宗教信仰的汇集之地，也汇聚着福州悠久的历史文化。它们保留了众多宗教文化遗存与各个朝代沿流至今的各类文物，成为福州古城的象征，也是福州古厝的历史宝库。这些庄严恢宏的殿堂庙宇，与山、林、水等清幽怡人的自然景观融为一体，成为福州古厝文化的璀璨明珠。

◎ 开元寺

开元寺是福州现存最古老的佛寺之一，位于福州市中心地带鼓楼区开元路，为福建省重点文物保护单位。史籍记载，南朝梁太清三年（549年）始建。外山门"萧梁古刹"四个大字向人们诉说着它那近一千五百年的悠久历史。

开元寺原称"灵山寺"，后改称"大云寺"，唐初又名"隆兴寺"，唐开元二十三年（735年）重修后改为今名。开元二十六年，皇帝下诏，命天下诸州以纪年为名，各建一寺，开元寺正是当时福州保留下来的寺院。寺额"开元寺"三字，为唐代书法家欧阳询所书，笔力遒劲，结构紧凑，堪称书法一绝，今尚存。

福州开元寺正门
The Main Gate of Kaiyuan Temple in Fuzhou

A city with profound history and culture, Fuzhou has many magnificent and sacred temples. These ancient temples are not only places for converging different religious beliefs, but also for convergence of Fuzhou's long history and culture. As the symbols of this ancient city and historical treasures of ancient buildings in the city, they have preserved many religious and cultural relics from past dynasties. Integrated with the quiet and pleasant natural landscapes such as mountains, forests and water, these majestic and solemn temples are the brilliant pearls of Fuzhou ancient houses.

◎ Kaiyuan Temple

Located in Kaiyuan Road, Gulou District, the central area of Fuzhou, Kaiyuan Temple is one of the oldest existing Buddhist temples in Fuzhou and a key cultural relics preservation unit in Fukien Province. According to historical records, it was built in 549, the 3rd year of Taiqing in the Southern Liang Dynasty. The four characters of "Xiaoliang Gucha" (萧梁古刹) on the temple's main gate tell its long history of nearly 1500 years.

Kaiyuan Temple was initially called Lingshan Temple, and later renamed Dayun Temple. In the early Tang Dynasty, it was also known as Longxing Temple. In 735, the 23rd year of Kaiyuan in the Tang Dynasty, it was renamed Kaiyuan Temple. In the 26th year of Kaiyuan, the emperor ordered all the states in China to build a temple of their own named after the chronology. Kaiyuan Temple was the one built in Fuzhou at that time and preserved till now. The three characters of "Kaiyuan Si" (开元寺) on the temple's plaque were written by Ouyang Xun, a calligrapher of the Tang Dynasty. This masterpiece of calligraphy still exists today with its vigorous strokes and compact structure.

开元寺所在地为福州九山之一的芝山。芝山，得名于当年盛产灵芝，故寺名原称"灵山寺"，是南无消灾延寿药师佛著名的道场。俗话说："芝山不见山，有刹开元古。"药师佛是健康之王、消灾之王、吉祥之王、长寿之王，正因为它与民众的健康关系密切，故自古以来香火鼎盛、绵绵不绝，民间盛传药师佛的灵验事迹亦是数不胜数。其中便有21世纪初，开元寺斋堂前因雷击而枯死多年的龙眼树竟然老树发新芽，在树桩里长出一朵直径达20厘米的灵芝。枯木出灵芝，被视为吉祥之兆。

开元寺弘扬药师佛消灾延寿的宗旨，救死扶伤。前住持宝松和尚曾在开元寺创办福建佛教医院，后继者为提润法师。他们用中草药及自制秘方治病救人、治疗癌症，声名远播海内外。福建省佛教协会因此任命提润法师为省佛教中草药医院筹委会主任，并由他出资，在寺内创办全国首家佛教中草药肿瘤门诊，求医者络绎不绝。提润法师还走出山门，到全国各地乃至海外的东南亚、美洲地区为癌症病人消灾祛病，带去健康。

开元寺曾为皇家寺院、宗庙，因此规模宏大，其面积当年约占城区的十分之一。唐代，福州开元寺是官方接待各国来闽僧人之所。日本真言宗祖师空海大师、日本天台宗祖师圆珍大师、印度密宗高僧般若怛罗大师等均在开元寺或学习、交流佛学，或传教、翻译经文。

空海大师，俗姓佐伯直，幼名真鱼，后亦名遍照金刚、弘法大师。他出生于774年，卒于835年，出生地为日本赞岐国多度郡屏风浦（今日本香川县善通寺市）。空海大师自幼聪慧好学，进入日本培养官吏的教育机关"大学寮"明经科学习中国儒家经典，22岁在奈良东大寺戒坛院受戒成为正式僧侣，法名空海。

为学法深造，汲取中华佛教经典精义，唐贞元二十年（804年），30岁的空海随日本第十七批遣唐使藤原葛野麻吕走海路入唐求法。然船只在途中被风暴吹离航道，在与惊涛骇浪的殊死搏斗中漂流了34天，最后到达福州长溪县赤岸镇（在今福建霞浦）。当时，因为日本使团的文书凭证在另一艘失散的副大使船上，他们没有凭证，难以取信于当地守官。关键时刻，空海运用他娴熟的汉文代遣唐大使藤原葛野麻吕向福建主政官写了《为大使与福州观察使书》。其诚恳的态度、充足的理由、纯正的汉文打动了刚上任的福州观察使兼刺史阎济美，他们最终被允许上岸，并被一路护送入住福州开元寺。

Kaiyuan Temple is located in Zhishan, one of the nine mountains in Fuzhou. Zhishan got its name from Lingzhi, a kind of ganoderma lucidum, so the temple was originally called Lingshan Temple. It is a famous Taoist temple of Namo Disaster-Eradicating and Longevity-Extending Medicine Buddha. It is said that people could see no mountain but the ancient Kaiyuan Temple in the Zhishan area. Medicine Buddha is the king of health, auspiciousness, longevity and disaster elimination. Closely related to people's health, the temple has attracted many people to worship and pray since ancient times. There are also countless efficacious stories of the Medicine Buddha. It is said that at the beginning of the new century, the longan tree in front of Zhaitang (Vegetarian Canteen) in Kaiyuan Temple, which died long ago due to lightning strikes, sprouted unexpectedly again. A Lingzhi with a diameter of 20 centimeters grew in its tree stump, which was regarded as an actual auspice.

Kaiyuan Temple carries forward the spirit of Medicine Buddha to eliminate disaster, prolong life, save the dying and heal the wounded. Monk Baosong, the former abbot of Kaiyuan Temple, founded the Fukien Buddhist Hospital in the temple, and his successor Master Tirun continued his work. They enjoyed a widespread reputation at home and abroad by curing the sick and treating cancer with Chinese herbal medicine and self-made secret prescriptions. Therefore, the Buddhist Association of Fukien Province appointed Master Tirun as the director of the Preparatory Committee of Fukien Buddhist Hospital of Chinese Herbal Medicine. Master Tirun funded in Kaiyuan Temple the first Buddhist tumor clinic of Chinese herbal medicine in China, with an endless stream of health seekers. He also went to various parts of China and even Southeast Asia and the Americas to help cancer patients cure the disease and regain their health.

Once a royal and ancestral temple, Kaiyuan Temple was a large-scale one, with an area accounting for about one-tenth of the urban area in those days. In the Tang Dynasty, Kaiyuan Temple served as the official reception place for monks from various countries to Fukien. Master Kukai, the founder of the Japanese Shingon Sect, Master Enchi, the founder of the Japanese Ten Dai Sect, and Master Prajnatara, the Indian Tantric Monk, all studied, preached, exchanged knowledge of Buddhism and translated scriptures in Kaiyuan Temple.

Master Kukai, commonly known as Zuobozhi, was named Zhenyu when he was young, and later was also known as Bianzhao King Kong and Master Hongfa. He was born in Byobugaura, Dodu Prefecture, Saki State, Japan (today's Zentsuji City, Kagawa Prefecture) in 774 and died in 835. Kukai was smart and eager to learn since he was young, and entered the Department of Mingjing in the Japanese educational institution called Daigaku Ryou to study Chinese Confucian classics. At the age of 22, he was ordained in kaidan-in, a place for monastic vows in Todaiji Temple in Nara and became a real monk named Kukai.

In order to study further the dharma and the essence of Chinese Buddhist classics, in 804, the 20th year of Zhenyuan of the Tang Dynasty, the 30-year-old Kukai followed the 17th Japanese Kentoshi (envoy to China), Fujiwara no Kadanomaro, to seek the dharma. However, the ship was blown off the channel by the storm, and drifted for 34 days in the fierce struggle with the sea and finally reached Chi'an of Changxi in Fuzhou (now Xiapu in Fukien Province). At that time, the documents of the Japanese envoys were placed on another lost Deputy Ambassadorship, so it was difficult to win the trust of the local guard. At that moment, Kukai, with proficient Chinese, wrote a letter to the chief of Fukien Province on behalf of Japanese Kentoshi Fujiwara no Kadanomaro. The letter moved Yan Jimei, the newly appointed Inspector and Governor of Fuzhou with its sincere attitude, sufficient evidence and idiomatic Chinese. At last, they were allowed to go ashore and were escorted all the way to Kaiyuan Temple in Fuzhou.

空海入福州开元寺认真学习佛法。恰逢当时来华不久的印度密宗高僧般若怛罗大师正在开元寺传教、深研。大师常年主讲密宗，空海认真听取讲演。后来，曾在印度那烂陀寺修行的般若三藏来到福州，空海投其门下虚心请教梵文。空海刻苦钻研、融会贯通，佛法精进，同时与寺僧惠灌等人也建立了深厚友谊。

空海在福州开元寺求法期间，得到时任观察使阎济美的多方关照。空海因随身无官方文书，又系私费留学僧，本未被列入去长安的名单中，但在阎济美的争取下，获得了去长安学习的机会。空海在福州期间写下的《灵源深处离合诗》、《请福州观察使入京启》、《为大使与福州观察使书》三篇作品，成为考察空海与福建关系的流传了一千多年的珍贵文书。《灵源深处离合诗》云："磴危人难行，石崄兽无升。烛暗迷前后，蜀人不得过。"如今，福州开元寺内因此诗得名的"灵源阁"仍巍然屹立。

空海获得准许进京的批文之后北上长安，他博览内经外典，遍访诸寺名僧。公元805年，他到青龙寺东塔院往谒唐密法脉传人惠果大师，请求传法。惠果大师喜道："吾待汝久，来何迟矣。"从惠果大师那里空海受胎藏界和金刚界曼荼罗法，并受传法阿阇黎的灌顶。惠果大师圆寂后，空海奉唐宪宗之命为惠果撰写碑文，享受极高的荣耀。

唐元和元年（806年），空海大师搭乘遣唐使判官高阶远成的船舶回到日本，他带回200多部、500多卷佛典，还有大量佛像、法器。其清单登记在《御请来目录》中上奏天皇。他归国后讲授《大日经》，创立了影响力很大的密宗分支真言宗，拥有上至天皇、名僧，下至黎民百姓的千百万信徒，被天皇赐谥"弘法大师"。空海善于诗文书画，尤以书法最为著名。他对汉字之篆、隶、真、行、草五体皆精通，被唐德宗授予"五笔和尚"的雅号，在日本有"草圣"之称。他根据汉字的草书发展完善了日本文字平假名，对日本文字的形成贡献巨大。他还效仿唐朝在日本设立教育机构——综艺种智院，招请老师讲授佛教、儒学、道教的内容，对日本后世的教育发展也产生了深远影响。

Kukai studied Buddhism carefully in Kaiyuan Temple. The Indian Tantric Master Prajnatara, who had just come to China, was also preaching Tantra and studying Buddhism in the same temple at that time. Kukai seized the chance and joined his lectures. Later, Master Prajna Tripitaka, who had practiced in Nalanda Temple in India, came to Fuzhou. After being permitted by Master Prajna Tripitaka to learn Sanskrit under his guidance, Kukai made a rapid progress in understanding Buddhism through a comprehensive and hard study, and also built deep friendship with Monk Huiguan and others.

During his stay at Kaiyuan Temple, Kukai got the care from Yan Jimei, the then inspector. At the beginning, Kukai was not included in the list of people who could go to Chang'an, because he had no official documents with him and was only a monk studying abroad at private expense. But with Yan Jimei's help, Kukai finally got the opportunity to study in Chang'an. He wrote the following three works during his stay in Fuzhou, *The Acrostic in the Depths of Lingyuan*, *The Invitation to the Inspector of Fuzhou to Beijing*, and *The Letter to the Ambassador and the Inspector of Fuzhou,* which have become valuable documents spread over 1000 years investigating the relationship between Kukai and Fukien. Today, Lingyuan Pavilion, named after *The Acrostic in the Depths of Lingyuan*, still erects in Kaiyuan Temple.

After obtaining the approval to enter Beijing, Kukai went north to Chang'an, where he read the scriptures from around the world and visited famous monks in various temples. In 805, he visited Master Huiguo, the successor of Esotericism in the Tang Dynasty, in the Yard of East Pagoda of Qinglong Temple, and asked him to pass on the Dharma. Master Huiguo said happily, "I have been waiting for you for a long time. Why are you late?" Kukai conceived from Huiguo the Mandala Dharma in the Tibetan and Diamond realms, and received the Enlightenment of the legendary Buddhist Teacher. After the death of Huiguo, Kukai was ordered with great honor by Emperor Xianzong of the Tang Dynasty to write the inscriptions in memory of him.

In 806, the first year of Yuanhe in the Tang Dynasty, Kukai returned to Japan on the ship of Kentoshi Takashina no Tonari. He brought back over 200 Buddhist scriptures with more than 500 volumes, a large number of Buddhist statues and musical instruments used in Buddhist services. The list of the articles was put in *The Catalogue of Imperial Invitations* to present to the emperor. After returning to Japan, Kukai taught Mahavairocana Tantra and founded the influential branch of the Tantric School, the Shingon Sect, with millions of followers from the emperor, famous monks to the ordinary people. So he was conferred the title of "The Grand Master who Propagated the Dharma" by the emperor. Kukai was also good at poetry, calligraphy and painting, and was most famous for his calligraphy. He was proficient in all the five scripts of Chinese characters (seal, official, regular, running hand and cursive), so Emperor Dezong of the Tang Dynasty awarded him the title of "Monk of Five Scripts". Known as "Sage of Cursive Script" in Japan, Kukai improved the Japanese Hiragana according to the cursive script of Chinese characters, and made great contributions to the formation of Japanese characters. Following the example of China, he set up Shugei Shuchiin, an educational institution in Japan, and hired teachers to teach Buddhism, Confucianism and Taoism, leaving a profound impact on the educational development of later generations in Japan.

如今，福州开元寺为纪念日本空海大师入唐居住的这一段历史专门设立了空海大师纪念堂。作为空海大师入唐驻锡首刹，又是日本佛教真言宗祖庭，每年都有不少日本和世界各地人士与真言宗僧侣前来福州开元寺参观、拜谒。

除了空海，唐代日本遣唐大使藤原葛野麻吕、书法大师橘逸势、天台宗寺门派宗祖圆珍大师，宋代日本东大寺重建圣人重源上人、诗僧庆政上人等，都与福州开元寺结下了不解之缘。

福州开元寺供有五代后梁贞明四年（918年）所铸的千年特大型铁佛——阿弥陀佛。佛身高5.96米、宽4米，重10万斤以上，叠掌盘足于莲台之上，外披泥贴金。这是中国最早、最大、最重的古代特大型宗教造像铁铸件，是体现古代福州冶铸技术的重要遗迹类实物，也象征着中国佛教中心的南迁。

关于铁佛的故事很多，其一是据说1941年日本军队侵占福州，想把铁佛搬到日本，可铁佛太大无法搬动，日军便在铁佛旁搭了架子，想带走佛头。然而第一个日本兵刚爬上去，就摔了下来；再一个人上去，也是摔落在地。日军心惊，以为佛祖显灵，只好打消此念头，铁佛因此得以完整保存至今。

铁佛殿
Iron Buddha Hall

与铁佛合称开元寺"双璧"的是宋代刊刻的佛教经典《毗卢大藏经》。北宋年间，开元寺曾大量刊刻佛经，设有经局，专门从事印经及染黄纸的生产加工。《毗卢大藏经》又称《毗卢藏》、《开元寺大藏经》、《大藏经》福州开元寺本，北宋徽宗政和二年（1112年）始刻，历时四十载才基本完成。全藏以《千字文》为序，收经1451部，共6132卷，是私家刻藏之始。由私家刊刻雕印佛教全集，这在中国印刷史和佛教刻经史上都是有巨大影响的历史事件。《毗卢大藏经》先后由日本僧人带回日本，至今保存完好，成为日本的"国宝"。

Today, Master Kukai Memorial Hall has been set up in Kaiyuan Temple, in order to commemorate the history of his stay in China. As the first temple where Master Kukai stayed in China and also the ancestral temple of Japanese Buddhism, Kaiyuan Temple is visited and paid homage to every year by many monks of the Shingon Sect and people from Japan and all over the world.

In addition to Kukai, many Japanese sages forged an indissoluble bond with Kaiyuan Temple in Fuzhou. Among them were Japanese Kentoshi Fujiwara no Kadanomaro, a calligraphy master Tachibana no Hayanari, founder of the Japanese Ten Dai Sect, Master Enchi, poet monk Keisei, and Chogen, the master in charge of Todaiji Temple's reconstruction in the Song Dynasty.

Kaiyuan Temple was dedicated to Amitabha, a thousand-year-old giant Iron Buddha in 918, the 4th year of Zhenming of Later Liang (Five Dynasties). The Iron Buddha is 5.96 meters tall, 4 meters wide, weighing more than 50 tons. With his palms folded and his legs crossed on the lotus platform, the Buddha is covered with golden paint. As the earliest, largest and heaviest iron-cast statue of ancient religion in China, it is an important relic of smelting and casting technology in ancient Fuzhou, and also a symbol of the southward movement of China's Buddhist center.

There are many stories about the Iron Buddha. It is said that in 1941, the Japanese army invaded Fuzhou and wanted to move the Iron Buddha to Japan, but it was too big to move, so they set up a shelf beside the Buddha trying to take its head. However, when the first Japanese soldier climbed up, he fell down, and another fell down again when he went up. The Japanese army was shocked and thought that the Buddha had shown his power, so they had to give up. Thus, the Iron Buddha has been completely preserved to this day.

Another treasure of Kaiyuan Temple is the complete collection of the Buddhist Classic *Pilu Tripiṭaka* published in the Song Dynasty. During the Northern Song Dynasty, Kaiyuan Temple published a large number of Buddhist scriptures and set up a Sutra Department, which was specialized in the production and processing of sutras and yellow paper. *Pilu Tripiṭaka*, also known as *Piluzang*, *Kaiyuan Temple Sutra*, and *Version of Kaiyuan Temple*, was engraved in 1112, the second year of Zhenghe of Emperor Huizong in the Northern Song Dynasty, and it took 40 years to complete the work. With *The Thousand Character Classic* as the preface, the whole collection includes 1451 scriptures with 6132 volumes, marking the beginning of a private engraving collection. The engraving and printing of complete works of Buddhism by private publications is a historical event in the history of Chinese printing and Buddhist Scripture. *Pilu Tripiṭaka* was brought back to Japan by Japanese monks. It has been well preserved and has become a national treasure of Japan.

开元寺于1979年重修，现占地面积3000平方米，呈坐北朝南向。主体建筑大雄宝殿面阔三间、进深七柱，穿斗式木构架，双面坡硬山顶。沿中轴线有外山门、内山门、药师殿（灵源阁）、大雄宝殿（铁佛殿）、毗卢藏经阁等。寺内还有宋代八角七层、高7.5米的仿阁楼式实心石塔，以及宋代石槽、观音阁、宝松和尚纪念楼、明旸法师图书馆、提润和尚纪念楼、四面佛阁、108罗汉堂等珍贵文物和各式建筑。

开元寺办有佛教老年安养院，免费安置贫困老人数十位。还创办了福建省开元佛教文化研究所，从事佛教文化和与海内外各国的佛教文化交流研究，办有刊物《21世纪禅文明》。

开元寺作为福州现存的最古老的佛寺之一，见证了福州悠远绵长的对外交流历史，尤其是与日本深厚的历史文化渊源，如今更是成为中日民间交往的重要场所，继续致力于中日民间友好与文化交流。

◎ 西禅寺

西禅寺位于福州市西郊祭酒岭山脉怡山之麓。怡山形如飞凤落坡，因此又名"凤山"。相传，南朝炼丹士王霸居此炼丹成药、点石为丹。每逢灾年，他便卖药换米以拯济百姓。后来，王霸蝉蜕而去、羽化成仙。为了纪念他，人们便在他的住处建寺，这便是西禅寺的前身。至隋朝末年，该寺废圮。

唐代，大安禅师（793—883年）来到怡山兴建寺院。大安禅师在福建黄檗山出家，后至江西参拜百丈怀海禅师，又在湖南沩山住了三十年，接任沩山密印寺住持。受当时福建观察使李景温邀请，大安禅师来到怡山兴建寺庙，寺院规模建置悉经大安禅师等人筹划。大安禅师在怡山从者甚众。咸通十四年（873年），唐懿宗赐大安"延圣大师"号，并赐西禅寺紫袈裟和《开元寺大藏经》。当时，西禅寺香火鼎盛，有僧人三千。大安圆寂后，谥号"圆智大师"，葬于楞伽山（今祭酒岭）。灵骨塔内有唐刻《塔内真身记》石碑，该石碑于1953年出土，是西禅寺的珍贵历史文物。五代后梁开平三年（909年），慧稜法师住持西禅。后唐长兴三年（932年），慧稜圆寂，葬于怡山方丈室后。今寺内尚有慧稜禅师纪念塔及碑记，同样也成为西禅寺古老历史的见证。

Rebuilt in 1979, Kaiyuan Temple now covers an area of 3000 square meters and faces south. As the main building, the Grand Hall is three rooms wide and seven columns deep, with a wooden frame of columns and tie construction and gabbled roof of two sides. Lined along the central axis are the Outer Gate, Inner Gate, Medicine Buddha Hall(Lingyuan Pavilion), Grand Hall(Iron Buddha Hall), Depositary of Pilu Tripiṭaka and so on. Inside the temple, there are also many precious cultural relics and various buildings, including a solid stone tower with octagonal seven floors and a height of 7.5 meters in the Song Dynasty, a stone trough from the Song Dynasty, Guanyin Pavilion, Monk Baosong Memorial Building, Master Mingyang Library, Monk Tirun Memorial Building, Four-faced Buddha Pavilion, and 108 Luohan Hall.

Kaiyuan Temple started a Buddhist nursing home for the elderly, which resettled dozens of poor old people for free. It also founded the Kaiyuan Buddhist Culture Research Institute of Fukien Province, which has been engaging in the research of Buddhist culture exchanges at home and abroad, and established a journal called *Zen Civilization in the 21st Century*.

As one of the oldest Buddhist temples in Fuzhou, Kaiyuan Temple has witnessed Fuzhou's long-term exchanges with foreign countries, especially the profound historical relationship between Fuzhou and Japan. Now, it has become an important place for Sino-Japanese non-governmental exchanges, and has been committed to Sino-Japanese cultural exchanges, telling the stories of "Lands apart, sky shared" and marking the deep friendship between China and Japan.

◎ Xichan Temple

Xichan Temple is located at the foot of Yishan mountain of Jijiuling mountain range in the western suburb of Fuzhou. With the shape of a flying phoenix falling on the slope, Yishan Mountain is also known as Fengshan. It is said that the alchemist Wang Ba of the Southern Dynasty lived here and made pills of immortality. In the disaster years, Wang Ba sold medicine for rice to help the poor people, and later became immortal. In order to commemorate him, people built a temple in his residence, which was the predecessor of Xichan Temple. At the end of the Sui Dynasty, the temple was abandoned.

In the Tang Dynasty, Zen Master Da'an (793-883) came to Yishan to build a temple. After becoming a monk in Huangboshan, Fukien, he went to Jiangxi to pay homage to Zen Master Baizhang Huaihai, and then lived in Weishan in Hunan for 30 years, serving as the abbot of Miyin Temple in Weishan. At the invitation of Li Jingwen, the then Fukien Inspector, Da'an came to Yishan to build a temple, and carefully planned the scale and construction of the temple with others. In Yishan, he had a lot of followers. In 873, the 14th year of Xiantong, Emperor Yizong of the Tang Dynasty granted Da'an "Master Yansheng" and bestowed Xichan Temple the purple cassock and the Kaiyuan Scripture. At that time, there were about 3000 monks in Xichan Temple, with a lot of worshippers. After his death, Da'an got the posthumous title of "Master Yuanzhi", and was buried in Lengjia Mountain (today's Jijiuling). In Linggu Tower, the stele called Record of Real Body of Buddha carved in the Tang Dynasty and unearthed in 1953 is a precious historical relic of Xichan Temple. In 909, the third year of the Kai Ping era of the Later Liang in the Five Dynasties Period, Master Huileng was the abbot of Xichan Temple. In 932, the third year of the Chang xing era of the Later Tang in the Five Dynasties period, he passed away and was buried behind the Abbot's Office of Yishan. There are still a tower and inscriptions in memory of Master Huileng in the temple, witnessing its ancient history.

大安奉命所建寺院，初名"清禅寺"，不久改名"延寿寺"，五代后唐长兴四年（933年）闽王王延钧奏请改名"长庆寺"。五代末，寺院遭南唐兵毁坏，建筑物多被焚毁。北宋天圣年间（1023—1032年）僧宗元重修，景祐五年（1038年）敕号"怡山长庆禅寺"。当时福州城内有南禅、东禅、北禅三大寺，合此为四。此寺又地处城西，故名"怡山西禅长庆寺"，俗称"西禅寺"，相沿至今。

西禅寺自建立起屡毁屡修。清光绪二年（1876年），住持微妙禅师赴京，光绪皇帝赐《龙藏》一部、康熙御书《药师经》一部。回来后，微妙禅师觉得祖庭破旧，便多方集资对西禅寺进行重修。微妙禅师主持新建了藏经阁，重建大雄宝殿、法堂、天王殿等30多座殿堂，形成如今西禅寺的规模和格局。抗战期间，日军飞机轰炸西禅寺，寺院受到极大破坏，后该寺监院证亮等人多方努力募款修复，基本上恢复了原有的格局和风貌。

历史上，西禅寺名僧辈出，海内外信徒无数。雪峰义存的弟子、青原下六世法嗣慧稜曾在此住持弘法，其门下有新罗国龟山和尚等三名弟子。西禅寺名僧有大安、慧稜、宗元、元至、微妙等。该寺在我国台湾地区和海外均极负盛名，新加坡双林寺、马来西亚双庆寺以及越南的南普陀寺、二府庙、观音寺等寺院都属于西禅寺的下院，因此每年有许多海内外高僧和信众来此参谒登临。

新中国成立后，对西禅寺又屡加修复新建，重筑了玉佛楼，新建了报恩塔等建筑，千年西禅寺焕发了新光彩。

如今的西禅寺占地面积60000平方米，主入口大门坐西朝东，沿中轴线有照壁、前埕、天王殿、大雄宝殿、法堂、华严三圣佛殿等建筑，庄严规整。主体建筑大雄宝殿坐北朝南，面阔五间、进深四间，穿斗式减柱造木构架，重檐歇山顶。整体建筑画栋雕梁，风格古朴恢宏，大佛色相庄严，笑对人间，给人以一种平和与亲切之感。

大雄宝殿后通往法堂前庭，埕中有石柱撑起一个大石球，人称"姻缘石"。石球中有一小孔，据说如有求男女姻缘者，焚香礼佛后以眼观看石孔便可见神奇影像，可以促成姻缘的结合。

The temple Master Da'an was ordered to build was originally named "Qingchan Temple", and then "Yanshou Temple". In 933, the fourth year of Changxin in the Late Tang (Five Dynasties), the temple was destroyed by the soldiers of the Southern Tang Dynasty, and many buildings were burnt down. During the Tiansheng period of the Northern Song Dynasty (1023-1032), the monk Zongyuan rebuilt it, and in 1038, the fifth year of Jingyou, it was named "Yishan Changqing Temple". At that time, there were the following three temples in the city of Fuzhou: Nanchan Temple, Dongchan Temple, and Beichan Temple. Along with this rebuilt temple, there were altogether four. Located in the west of the city, the temple was named "Yishan Xichan Changqing Temple", commonly known as "Xichan Temple" till now.

Since its establishment, the Xichan Temple has been destroyed and rebuilt many times. In 1876, the second year of Guangxu in the Qing Dynasty, the abbot Zen Master Weimiao went to Beijing. Emperor Guangxu gave him a *Longzang* and Emperor Kangxi's imperial book of *Medicine Master's Sutra*. Upon returning home, Weimiao found the ancestral hall very shabby, so he raised funds from various sources to rebuild Xichan Temple, and presided over the reconstruction of more than 30 halls and palaces, including the Grand Hall, the Lecture Hall, and Hall of the Heavenly Kings, and built the Depository of the Sutra, forming the present grand scale of Xichan Temple. During the Anti-Japanese War, the Japanese aircraft bombed the temple, and made it greatly damaged. Later, Zheng Liang, the supervisor of the temple and many other people raised funds to repair and restore its original structure and style.

In history, there have been many famous monks in Xichan Temple, with countless believers overseas. Huileng, a disciple of Xuefeng Yicun and the sixth generation of the Qingyuan Dharma, once lived here to promote Buddhism. He had three disciples including Monk Guishan of Silla. Among the famous monks of Xichan Temple were Da'an, Huileng, Zongyuan, Yuanzhi and Weimiao. Xichan Temple is extremely famous in Taiwan and overseas. Shuanglin Temple in Singapore, Shuangqing temple in Malaysia, Nanputuo Temple, Erfu temple and Guanyin temple in Vietnam, and many other temples are all subordinates of Xichan Temple. Therefore, a lot of eminent monks and believers from home and abroad visit and pay homage to the temple every year.

After the founding of the People's Republic of China, Xichan Temple was repaired and restored again and again, and new buildings, such as the Jade Buddha Tower and Bao'en Tower were also built. At present, with a one-thousand-year history, Xichan Temple is taking on a new look.

The present Xichan Temple covers an area of 60000 square meters. Its main entrance gate faces east, and along the central axis, there are solemn buildings such as Screen Wall, Front Yard, Hall of Heavenly Kings, Grand Hall, Lecture Hall and the Hall of Three Holy Buddhas of Huayan Buddhism. As the main building, the Grand Hall faces south and is five rooms wide and four rooms deep, with a bucket-type timber frame column, and double-eaved hip-and-gable roof. With carved beams and painted rafters, the whole building appears simple and magnificent. The Giant Buddha looks solemn with a smile, impressing people with a sense of peace and kindness.

In the courtyard that connects the Main Hall and the front court of the Lecture Hall, there is a large stone ball called Yinyuan Stone, which is supported by a stone column and has a small hole in it. It is said that when those who long for marriage burn incense and worship the Buddha, they can see a magical image in the hole, which makes good marriages.

法堂之外有新建的华严三圣佛殿，富丽堂皇。大殿中有释迦牟尼大佛、骑狮文殊、驮象普贤，高大宏伟，令观者肃然起敬。

三圣殿右侧为观音阁，阁中一尊千手千眼观世音佛像重达29吨，用黄铜铸成，全国少见。

玉佛楼，1985年新建，供有坐卧大白玉佛各一尊，坐像高2.95米，卧身长3.7米，为国内之最。

报恩塔，于1987年新建，塔高67米，共15层。塔内大厅，外造九廊，八角飞檐，塔尖直入云霄，是西禅寺里最高的佛塔，也是国内最高的石塔。

报恩塔旁的五百罗汉堂，由福建侨胞捐资新建而成，是西禅寺内最大的佛教建筑，占地1000多平方米。外观雄伟壮观，金碧辉煌。殿内五百名罗汉千姿百态，神情各异，栩栩如生。

在西禅寺塔林中有三座大塔，最左为当代谈禅法师预备的未署名墓塔，中为慧稜禅师塔，上刻"稜禅师之塔"字样，右为微妙禅师塔。

寺内的文物除了唐代开山祖师大安禅师塔内真身铭碑和五代慧稜禅师塔及碑铭外，还有"白龟吐泉"遗址、唐代七星井、弘一法师放生池碑等。西禅寺内还有一座藏经楼，康熙御笔《药师经》就藏于其中。此外，还藏有其他珍贵经卷，如刺血缮写的《法华经》等。

五百罗汉堂
500 Luohan Hall

Outside the Lecture Hall, there is the newly-built magnificent Hall of Three Holy Buddhas of Huayan Buddhism. There are Shakyamuni Buddha, Wenshu Pusa who is riding a lion and Puxian Pusa who is carrying an elephant in the hall, leaving the audience in awe of their grandeur.

Guanyin Pavilion is on the right side of the Hall of Three Holy Buddhas of Huayan Buddhism. In the pavilion, there is a 29-ton brass statue of Guanyin Buddha with thousands of hands and eyes, which is rarely seen in China.

In the Jade Buddha Building, newly built in 1985, a sitting white jade Buddha and a lying one are worshipped. The sitting Buddha is 2.95 meters tall and the lying one is 3.7 meters long, which are the tallest and longest Buddhas in China.

Bao'en Pagoda, newly built in 1987, is 67 meters high with 15 floors. There is a hall inside the pagoda, and nine corridors with octagonal cornices outside, with the top of the pagoda upthrust against the sky. It is the highest pagoda in Xichan Temple and the tallest stone pagoda in China.

The 500 Luohan Hall next to Bao'en Pagoda was built with donations from Fukien overseas Chinese. It is the largest Buddhist building in Xichan Temple, with more than 1000 square meters. Inside the magnificent and resplendent hall, there are 500 life-like Luohans in different poses and with various expressions.

There are three large pagodas in the Pagoda Forest of Xichan Temple. The leftmost is the unsigned tomb pagoda prepared by the contemporary Master Tanchan, and the middle is the Master Huileng Pagoda, with the words "Pagoda of Master Huileng" engraved on it, and the right is the Master Weimiao Pagoda.

The cultural relics in the temple include the real body inscription of Master Da'an in the Tang Dynasty, and the pagoda and inscriptions of Master Huileng of the Five Dynasties, as well as the site of "Baigui Tuquan" (white turtle spitting the spring), the Seven-star Well of the Tang Dynasty, and the monument of the release pond of Master Hongyi. There is also a Depository of the Sutra in Xichan Temple, in which the Emperor Kangxi's imperial book of *Medicine Master's Sutra is* preserved. In addition, there are other precious relics such as the *Lotus Sutra* written by Ci Xueshan.

西禅寺旧有古荔三百多株，为此寺的特殊象征。唐慧稜法师曾在法堂前后种植四株荔枝，现仍有一株尚存，俗名"天洗碗"，历经千年而犹存，弥足珍贵。在报恩塔边的花园中，有一株高3米的荔枝树，盘根错节，枝干粗壮，旁有一石刻"宋荔古迹"。历代咏西禅寺荔枝的诗句不少，如清代的朱彝尊有诗云："露比三霄冷，浆同十酒甘。倒囊元止渴，勿药定祛痰。"据说，当年赵朴初先生首访西禅寺时也曾赋诗一首："百柱堂空观劫后，千年象教话当时。禅师会得西来意，引向庭前看荔枝。"

住持智水、监院证亮重修西禅寺时，另开辟寄园和放生池，并在寄园种植荔枝数百株，以延续西禅寺荔枝闻名于世的传统。到了盛夏，寺内蝉声阵阵，荔枝红熟。西禅寺荔枝，皮光而薄，味清而甘，自唐以来，每当荔枝成熟时节，便有很多文人墨客前来品尝和赋诗。现在，西禅寺年年举办荔枝会。各地名人、雅士、高僧均来此吟诗作画抒发感想、切磋学问，留下了很多名句、对联、诗词和逸事，如"来啖荔枝，此地合留苏子带；闲翻贝叶，真源参彻柳州诗"，"宏法大雄，胜迹重开存宋荔；安禅贞志，空门高讽隐诗僧"；等等。"怡山啖荔"已成为西禅寺一道亮丽的风景，吸引游客，饮誉海内外。

西禅寺以其悠久的历史、匀称的布局、美丽的自然景观，以及宏伟的古代建筑，尤其是众多崭新的佛教建筑而著称于世。由于它在台湾及东南亚地区有很多下院，在海内外也产生了重大的影响。宋代名相、福建人李纲《西禅斗车堂》诗云："杰阁雄楼杳蔼间，佳辰良夜共跻攀。斗回曲柄临华栋，月涌清光出远山。急景行将悲婉晚，此身难得几时闲。世间百事何时了，且对金尊一解颜。"这首诗表达了人们对西禅寺的赞赏和景仰。如今的西禅寺除了专注弘扬佛法外，还在赈灾、扶贫、助学（如希望工程）、宣传中华文化等许多方面做出了优异的成绩，获得广大信众和人民群众的一致赞扬。

千年古刹西禅寺作为东南亚地区众多佛寺的祖庭，凭借其独特的寺庙殿堂、建筑园林与塔影湖光，不仅创造出一种古朴端庄的历史场域，也时刻散发着强大的文化魅力。它与城市里鳞次栉比的高楼大厦和谐相处，在呈现出新旧交错、古今融合的独特风貌的同时，也体现着其深厚的历史价值与文化底蕴。

There are more than 300 ancient lychee trees in Xichan Temple, which are the special symbols of the temple. Master Huileng in the Tang Dynasty once planted four lychee trees around the Lecture Hall. One of them, commonly known as "Tianxi Wan", has survived for thousands of years and still exists today. In the garden beside Bao'en Pagoda, there is a 3-meter-tall lychee tree with tangled roots and strong branches, with a stone carving "Song Lychee" (lychee of the Song Dynasty) beside it. For example, Zhu Yizun in the Qing Dynasty wrote a poem praising lychee's sweetness and its efficacy in quenching thirst and dispelling phlegm. It is said that when Mr. Zhao Puchu first visited Xichan Temple, he also wrote a poem to describe the great appeal of lychee trees to the masters in the temple. There are also many poems praising the lychees of Xichan Temple in the past dynasties.

When the abbot Zhishui and the supervisor Zhengliang rebuilt Xichan Temple, they started a Ji Garden and a release pond, and followed the tradition of the world-famous litchi in Xichan Temple by planting hundreds of lychee trees in the garden. In the middle of summer, the high-pitched buzzing sound of cicadas can be heard again and again in the temple, and the lychees are all red and ripe. With a light and thin skin, the lychees in Xichan Temple have a clear and sweet taste. Since the Tang Dynasty, many scholars have come to the temple for tasting the lychees and writing poems for them when the lychees were ripe. Now, the Lychee Festival is held annually in Xichan Temple. Celebrities, scholars and eminent monks from all over China come here to chant poetry and paint pictures to express their feelings and to learn from each other, leaving many famous sentences, couplets, poems and anecdotes. As a beautiful scene in Xichan Temple, "Eating lychee in Yishan" attracts a lot of tourists and enjoys a good reputation at home and abroad.

Xichan Temple is famous for its long history, symmetrical layout, beautiful natural landscape, magnificent ancient buildings and many new Buddhist buildings. With many subordinate courts in Taiwan and Southeast Asia, the temple has also had a significant impact home and abroad. Li Gang, a famous prime minister in the Song Dynasty, wrote a poem called *Douche Hall of Xichan Temple* to express people's appreciation and admiration of Xichan Temple. In addition to promoting Buddhism, Xichan Temple has contributed a lot to disaster relief, poverty alleviation, student aid, the Hope Project, and promotion of Chinese culture, thus winning high praise from the public and a great mass of believers.

As the ancestral temple of many Buddhist temples in Southeast Asia, Xichan Temple, a millennium temple, not only creates a quaint and dignified historical tone, but also exudes strong cultural charm by virtue of its unique halls, pavilions, towers, gardens and ponds. As a beautiful example of when historic and modern architecture meet, Xichan Temple complements and integrates with the rows of high-rise buildings in the city, showing its profound historical value and cultural heritage.

西禅寺俯拍图
Overhead View of
Xichan Temple

◎ 涌泉寺

涌泉寺，又称华严寺、国师馆、鼓山白云峰涌泉禅院、涌泉禅院等，位于福州市鼓山镇鼓山（海拔925米）山腰，依山傍谷。唐建中四年（783年），山中建有华严寺，会昌年间（841—846年）废圮。因寺前有一股被称为罗汉泉的泉水涌出，得名涌泉寺。罗汉泉与现天王殿下的龙潭相通。

涌泉寺海拔455米，在鼓山半山腰白云峰麓。五代后梁开平二年（908年），闽王王审知延请雪峰寺名僧神晏法师任住持，称其为"国师"，并给予大量资助，馆徒达千百人。根据清人所修《鼓山志》，王审知施予鼓山涌泉院田产财物无数，仅僧田一项就有84000亩。

宋咸平二年（999年），赐额"鼓山白云峰涌泉禅院"。咸平六年，赐御书一百二十卷。皇祐三年（1051年），赐御书二轴。至和元年（1054年），赐《新乐图》三卷。明清时期，涌泉寺经多次重修、重建和扩建。康熙三十八年（1699年），皇帝御赐题写"涌泉寺"寺名匾额；五十三年（1714年），赐给涌泉寺御藏书四橱。乾隆七年（1742年），再赐涌泉寺御藏七千二百四十卷。

◎ Yongquan Temple

Yongquan Temple is also known as Huayan Temple, Master Teacher Hall, Yongquan Zen Temple in Baiyun Peak of Gushan Mountain, Yongquan Zen Temple, etc. Nestled in the valley, it is located on the mountainside of Gushan Mountain (925 meters above sea level) in Gushan Town, Fuzhou City. In 783, the 4th year of Jianzhong in the Tang Dynasty, Huayan Temple was built in the mountains, and was destroyed in the Huichang period (841-846). The temple got its name from Luohan Spring in front of the temple, which was connected with Dragon Pond of the Hall of Heavenly Kings.

455 meters above sea level, Yongquan Temple is at the foot of Baiyun Peak on the hillside of Gushan Mountain. In 908, the second year of the Kai Ping era of the Later Liang in the Five Dynasties Period, Wang Shenzhi, King of Fukien, invited Master Shenyan, a famous monk of Xuefeng Temple, to serve as the abbot, and conferred on him the title of Master Teacher. There were thousands of monks and disciples in the temple who were greatly funded by the country during that period. According to *The Records of Gushan* compiled by people in the Qing Dynasty, Wang Shenzhi donated a lot of properties and fields to Yongquan Temple, including 84000 mu(about 14000 acres)of monk's field alone.

In 999, the second year of Xianping in the Song Dynasty, the temple was conferred the plaque of Yongquan Zen Temple in Baiyun Peak of Gushan Mountain. In the sixth year of Xianping, 120 volumes of imperial books were given to the temple. In 1051, the third year of Huangyou, and in 1054, the first year of Zhihe, two scrolls of imperial books and three volumes of music books were also given respectively to the temple. During the Ming and Qing dynasties, Yongquan Temple was repaired, rebuilt and expanded many times. In 1699, the thirty-eighth year of Kangxi, the emperor granted the temple an engraved plaque of Yongquan Temple. In 1714, the 53rd year of Kangxi and in 1742, the seventh year of Emperor Qianlong's reign, the emperor bestowed on the temple four collections of imperial books and 7240 volumes of imperial books respectively.

涌泉寺
Yongquan Temple

涌泉寺建筑布局奇特，素有"进山不见寺，进寺不见山"之称。现有建筑基本上属于明嘉靖年间（1522—1566年）的布局，于明清两代先后建成。新中国成立后该寺曾多次修建。该寺建筑规模宏大，占地25亩，有大小殿堂25座，槛廊连缀，浑然一体。主入口大门坐西朝东，沿中轴有放生池、前埕、天王殿、大雄宝殿、法堂、钟鼓楼、客堂、斋堂等建筑。主体建筑大雄宝殿坐北朝南，面阔七间、进深八间，穿斗式减柱造木构架，重檐歇山顶。殿内释迦牟尼三世佛端坐其中，只披汉装，不着梵服。两旁十八罗汉法相庄严，神情各异。大殿天花板上保留着清光绪八年（1882年）绘制的带有佛教色彩的图案242幅。大殿后侧保存有清康熙年间（1662—1722年）铁铸的"西方三圣"像，每尊重达1吨多，外表贴金。像前有一张康熙时用铁丝木制成的长供桌，据说历经多次火劫，至今仍完好无损，被称为镇寺之宝。

涌泉寺天王殿前两侧有两座千佛陶塔，原系福州城门镇梁厝村龙瑞寺之物，1972年移置鼓山涌泉寺天王殿之前。陶塔共两座，形制相同，左边一座称"庄严劫千佛陶塔"，右边一座称"贤劫千佛陶塔"。双塔用陶土分层烧制累叠而成，高约7米，八角九层。塔身细部为仿宋代木构楼阁建筑风格，自下而上逐层缩小。因施釉，外表呈铜色，部分呈绿色。两座塔上各塑有1038尊佛像，因而称"千佛陶塔"。八角塔檐另塑有僧人、武将像各36尊，悬挂陶制塔铃72只。塔座上塑莲瓣、侏儒、舞狮，并刻有铭文。塔上题记记载了布施者与工匠的姓名，以及烧制的时间——宋元丰五年（1082年）。

在涌泉寺法堂后的山上，有神晏国师塔。有塔座，塔身呈圆馒头形，形制古朴，系用花岗岩砌造。神晏为涌泉寺开山之祖，后梁开平二年（908年）来鼓山任住持。后晋天福四年（939年）六月示寂。闽王于闽侯县桐口大嘉山为其建舍利塔，后周显德五年（958年）移建今所。

Yongquan Temple has a unique architectural layout, and people can see no temple upon entering the mountain and no mountain while entering the temple. Built in the Ming and Qing Dynasties, the existing buildings maintain the layout of the Jiajing period of the Ming Dynasty (1522-1566). Reconstructed many times after the founding of the People's Republic of China, the buildings in this area cover 25 mu, with 25 large and small halls, and the sills and corridors are connected together. The gate of the main entrance faces east, and along the central axis, there are buildings such as the release pond, the front courtyard, the Hall of Heavenly Kings, the Main Hall, the Lecture Hall, the Bell and Drum Tower, the Guest hall, and the Vegetarian Canteen. As the main building facing south, Main Hall is seven rooms wide and eight rooms deep, with a bucket-type timber frame column, and double-eaved hip-and-gable roof. Buddha Shakyamuni Ⅲ sits in the middle of the hall, wearing only Chinese clothes instead of Buddhist clothes. The eighteen Luohans on both sides are solemn with various expressions. On the ceiling of the main hall, there are 242 Buddhist patterns painted in 1882, the 8th year of Guangxu in the Qing Dynasty. At the back of the main hall, there are iron-cast statues of Three Saints of the West in the reign of Emperor Kangxi of the Qing Dynasty, each weighing more than one ton and standing upright. There is a long offering table made of iron wire wood in the same period. It is said that the table has survived many fires and remained intact, so it was regarded as the treasure of the temple.

There are two Thousand Buddha Pottery Pagodas on front sides of the Hall of Heavenly Kings in Yongquan Temple. Originally from Longrui Temple, Liangcuo Village, Chengmen Town, Fuzhou, they were moved to the front of the Hall of Heavenly Kings in Yongquan Temple in 1972. There are two pottery pagodas with the same shape and structure, the left one is called Grandeur Misfortune Thousand Buddha Pagoda and the right one Puxian Misfortune Thousand Buddha Pagoda. As octagonal nine-storied pagodas made of layered fired clay, the two pagodas are both about 7 meters high. The body of the pagodas follows the architectural style of the wooden pavilion of the Song Dynasty, and draws in upward layer by layer. Because of the glaze paint, most parts are copper, and some are green. There are 1038 figures of Buddha on each of these two pavilions, so they are called Thousand Buddha Pottery Pagoda. There are also 36 monks and generals statues on the eaves of the octagonal pagoda, and 72 ceramic bells are on the eave corner. The pedestals of the pagoda are decorated with lotus petals, dwarfs, lion dances and inscriptions. The inscriptions record the names of the aim givers and artisans, and the year of its establishment, 1082, the 5th year of Yuanfeng in the Song Dynasty.

On the mountain behind the Lecture Hall of Yongquan Temple, there is the Shen Yan Guoshi Pagoda. Made of granite, the pagoda has a pedestal, with its body in the simple shape of a round steamed bun. As the founder of Yongquan Temple, Shenyan served as the abbot of Gushan Mountain in 908, the second year of Kaiping in the Later Liang Dynasty. He died in June in 939, the fourth year of Tianfu in the later Jin Dynasty. The King of Min built a stupa for him in Dajia mountains, Tongkou, Minhou County. In 958, the 5th year of Xiande of the Later Zhou Dynasty, it was moved to the present site.

涌泉寺为台湾许多寺庙的祖庭。清乾隆年间，台湾寺庙住持多来自福州鼓山涌泉寺和西禅寺。《南部台湾志》载："本岛的佛教，传自福州鼓山、西禅二丛林。康熙、乾隆年间，奉佛的官绅建立寺刹，延请二丛林道德崇高的出家人到台湾住持寺刹。"（转引自卢美松，2017：575）

光绪二十四年（1898年）鼓山涌泉寺善智、妙密两位禅师赴台湾弘法，在基隆东郊月眉山发起修建灵泉禅寺，灵泉禅寺后来成了台湾佛教月眉山派的大本山，这是台湾第一座具有丛林规模的禅刹。光绪九年（1883年），理明禅师和宝海禅师在台湾共同发起修建凌云寺，凌云寺后来成了台湾佛教观音山派的大本山。可知，台湾佛教四大法脉中的两大法脉——月眉山派、观音山派均出自鼓山涌泉寺。由于台湾地区佛教与福州的寺院关系密切，清代台湾多数僧侣都要渡海赴鼓山涌泉寺等大丛林受戒，以表明自己的正统。受戒时间为每年农历四月初八和十一月十七日，受戒回台后，所有佛教礼仪均依主庙之制。台湾日据时期，台南开元寺的住持几乎都在鼓山涌泉寺受戒。

东南亚佛寺也与涌泉寺关系密切。光绪十一年（1885年），鼓山涌泉寺住持妙莲及本忠、善庆两位禅师，应马来西亚槟城华侨邀请，前往弘扬佛法。光绪十七年（1891年）妙莲禅师在槟城创建极乐寺，作为福州鼓山涌泉寺的廨院，妙莲禅师为首任住持。光绪三十年（1904年）妙莲禅师还进京请得《龙藏》两部，其中一部藏于极乐寺中。同年，妙莲禅师返回鼓山，由本忠禅师继承法席，组织念佛莲社，成为南洋群岛最早的莲社。本忠禅师之后，极乐寺住持均由鼓山涌泉寺一系僧人传承。

涌泉寺藏经楼内保存有许多珍贵的佛经，包括明本《南藏》、《北藏》以及清版《龙藏》等众多经卷，还保存有中国、印度以及东南亚等地不同文字的贝叶经、血写经书675册。印经楼中保存有明末以来佛经、佛像、雕版1万余方，弘一法师曾用鼓山原雕版印赠日本各大寺。

涌泉寺方丈室（又称"圣箭堂"）前有一株铁树，相传为闽王王审知与神晏法师亲手种植，距今已一千多年。铁树、铁锅、铁丝木供桌被称为涌泉寺的"三铁"，雕版、血经和陶塔则被称为"三宝"，它们都是国宝级文物。

Yongquan temple is the ancestral temple of many temples in Taiwan. During the reign of Emperor Qianlong of the Qing Dynasty, most of the abbots of Taiwan temples came from the two forest monasteries of Yongquan Temple of Gushan and Xichan Temple in Fuzhou. According to *The Annals of Southern Taiwan*, Buddhism of Taiwan was spread from Gushan Mountain and Xichan Temple, and during the reign of Emperor Kangxi and Qianlong, the officials and gentry who worshipped Buddhism established temples in Taiwan and invited monks with high moral from the above two forest monasteries to serve as abbots in Taiwan's temples (cited in Lu Meisong, 2017: 575).

In 1898, the 24th year of Guangxu, two Zen Masters, Shanzhi and Miaomi of Gushan Yongquan Temple, went to Taiwan to promote Buddhism. They initiated the construction of the Lingquan Temple on Yuemei Mountain in the eastern suburb of Keelung. Later, Lingquan Temple became the main temple of Yuemei Mountain Sect of Taiwan Buddhism, which was the first large Buddhist temple in Taiwan. In 1883, the 9th year of Guangxu, Master Liming and Master Baohai of Yongquan Temple started together the construction of Lingyun Temple, which later became the main temple of Guanyin Mountain Sect of Taiwan Buddhism. Two of the four main lineages of Taiwan Buddhism, the Yuemei Mountain Sect and the Guanyin Mountain Sect, both came from Yongquan Temple in Gushan. Because of the close relationship between the temples in Taiwan and Fuzhou, most of the monks in Taiwan in the Qing Dynasty had to go across the sea to Yongquan Temple to be ordained to show their orthodoxy, and the ordination was often carried on the 8th of April and the 17th of November of the lunar calendar. After returning to Taiwan, they conducted all the Buddhist rituals following the system of the main temple. During the Japanese occupation, almost all the abbots of Kaiyuan Temple in Tainan were ordained at Yongquan Temple in Gushan.

Buddhist temples in Southeast Asia are also closely related to Yongquan Temple. In 1865, the 11th year of Guangxu, Master Miaolian, the abbot of Gushan Yongquan Temple, along with Master Benzhong and Master Shanqing, promoted Buddhism at the invitation of overseas Chinese in Penang, Malaysia. In 1891, the 17th year of Guangxu, Miaolian established Jile Temple in Penang as the branch of Gushan Yongquan Temple in Fuzhou, and he served as its first abbot. In 1904, the 30th year of Guangxu, he also went to the capital city to ask for two books of *Longzang*, one of which was kept in Jile Temple. When Miaolian returned to Gushan in the same year, Benzhong took his place and organized the Buddhist Lotus Society, which was the earliest Lotus Society in the islands of Southeast Asia. After Benzhong, all the abbots of Jile Temple were the monks of Yongquan Temple in Gushan.

There are many precious Buddhist scriptures preserved in the Depository of the Sutra in Yongquan Temple, including the Ming Dynasty's editions of *Nanzang* and *Beizang*, the Qing Dynasty edition of *Longzang*, and 675 volumes of the Bayeux and blood scriptures from China, India and Southeast Asia as well. In the Printing Building, there are more than 10, 000 cubic meters of Buddhist scriptures, Buddha statues and Buddhist engraved wooden blocks since the late Ming Dynasty. Once Master Hongyi printed and presented the original engravings of Gushan to the major temples in Japan.

There is a sago cycad tree in front of the Abbot's Room (also known as Shengjian Hall) in Yongquan Temple. It is said that the 1000-year-old tree was planted by Wang Shenzhi, the king of Fukien, and Master Shenyan. The sago cycad tree (tie shu), the iron pots, and the iron wire wooden tables are called the Three Iron Items of Yongquan Temple, and the engraved wooden blocks, the blood scriptures and the pottery pagodas are regarded as the Three National Treasures of the temple.

涌泉寺"喝水岩"一带的灵源洞有宋以来的摩崖石刻300多段。鼓山摩崖题刻为国家级文物保护单位，真、行、草、隶、篆诸体俱备，为天然的石刻书法宝库，也是研究历史的珍贵资料。

喝水岩的由来与涌泉寺祖师神晏法师有关。传说，当年神晏法师在此诵经，洞下涧水汩汩流淌，神晏法师大喝一声，流水顷刻便止住了。自此，洞水改道，从东侧半山观音阁石壁涌出，原来的溪涧不复出现流水，哗哗的流水声自然也就没有了，"喝水岩"因此得名。喝水岩旁有一天然石柱，上刻有宋徐锡之《喝水岩》诗："重峦复岭锁松关，只欠泉声入坐间。我若当年侍师侧，不教喝水过他山。"清新隽永，别有新意。喝水岩周边最早的题刻为宋代庆历六年（1046年）蔡襄所作，此外还有李纲、赵汝愚、朱熹、张元幹、沈葆桢等历代众多名人题刻。

喝水岩一带有灵源洞、弥勒阁、国师岩、忘归石、石门、水云亭等胜景，也是石刻集中之地。在灵源洞口有一石砌方门，门上有明代本山住持元贤所书"灵源深处"石匾。

元贤（1578—1657年）为佛教禅宗曹洞宗的代表人物，福州鼓山为曹洞宗的重要道场。明清鼎革之际，元贤主持鼓山，大振曹洞宗纲，开创曹洞宗鼓山寺一系，形成"鼓山禅"。清顺治十五年（1658年），元贤法嗣道霈禅师继承主持鼓山涌泉寺，鼓山成为东南大法窟，兴盛一时。此后又有恒涛大心禅师、惟静道安禅师、圆玉兴五禅师等传法于鼓山。涌泉寺名僧有神晏、永觉、为霖、古月、虚云、圆瑛和妙莲等。

涌泉寺除了弘扬佛法，在禅学上有所发展外，还热心慈善活动，如施粥救饥，具棺收葬饿殍，修路造桥等。清康熙七年（1668年），福州水部门外的河口渡河狭舟小，竞渡者众，往往船翻人亡，鼓山涌泉寺僧成源见状便募集巨款，建成台江河口万寿桥。桥建成后，"往来纷如，不俟舟楫，信步而趋，人莫不利"（《河口万寿桥记》碑刻）。

There have been more than 300 cliff inscriptions in Lingyuan Cave in the area of Heshui Rock (Yelling at Water Rock) of Yongquan Temple since the Song Dynasty. As the national cultural relics preservation units, cliff inscriptions in Gushan cover all the five scripts of Chinese characters(regular, running hand, cursive, official and seal). It is a natural treasure house of stone carving calligraphy and provides precious materials for history research.

The origin of Heshui Rock is related to Master Shenyan, the founder of Yongquan Temple. It is said that when Shenyan chanted scriptures here, the water under the cave made loud noises, so he yelled at the water and the water stopped flowing immediately. Since then, the stream has changed its course, gushing out from the stone wall of Guanyin Pavilion on the eastern side of the mountain. Without water in the original stream, the noise went away naturally. Hence the name of Heshui Rock. There is a natural stone column beside the Heshui Rock, on which is engraved the fresh, meaningful and creative poem entitled *To Heshui Rock* by Xu Xizhi of the Song Dynasty. In the poem, the poet wrote that there could be no water in the range upon range of mountains, and if he had been there, he would have advised the master not to yell at the water to divert the stream. The earliest inscriptions around Heshui Rock are those of Cai Xiang in 1046, the 6th year of Qingli in the Song Dynasty. There are also many inscriptions of celebrities in the past dynasties such as those of Li Gang, Zhao Ruyu, Zhu Xi, Zhang yuangan, and Shen Baozhen.

In the area of Heshui Rock, there are a lot of scenic spots, such as Lingyuan Cave, Maitreya Pavilion, Guoshi Rock, Wanggui Rock, Stone Gate and Shuiyun Pavilion. It is also an area where the cliff inscriptions are concentrated. At the entrance of Lingyuan Cave, there is a square stone gate, with a stone plaque of "Lingyuan Shenchu" (灵源深处) on it written by Yuanxian, the Abbot of this temple in the Ming Dynasty.

Yuan Xian (1578-1657) was a representative of Caodong Sect of Zen Buddhism, and Gushan in Fuzhou was an important place for this sect's rites. At the time of the great revolution of the Ming and Qing Dynasties, Yuan Xian took charge of the affairs in Gushan, greatly invigorating the principles of Caodong Sect, starting a Gushan Temple system of Caodong Sect and forming "Gushan Zen". In 1658, the 15th year of Shunzhi in the Qing Dynasty, Yuanxian's dharma heir, Master Daopei carried on Yuanxian's work and administered Yongquan Temple, which became a big Buddhist Temple in southeast China and flourished for a time. Later, Master Hengtao Daxin, Master Weijing Daoan, and Master Yuanyu Xingwu also passed on the doctrines in Gushan. The famous monks of Yongquan Temple included Shenyan, Yongjue, Weilin, Guyue, Xuyun, Yuanying and Miaolian.

In addition to promoting Buddhism and developing Zen, Yongquan Temple was also engaged in charity activities, such as providing porridge to save the hungry, burying the dead in coffins, and building roads and bridges. In 1668, the 7th year of Emperor Kangxi's reign of the Qing Dynasty, the river outside Fuzhou's Ministry of Water was narrow and small, but there were many people crossing the river, resulting in a lot of deaths. Seeing that, Monk Chengyuan of Yongquan Temple raised a large amount of money to build the Wanshou Bridge at the mouth of the river in Taijiang. According to the inscriptions of *Wanshou Bridge at the Mouth of the River*, after the completion of the bridge, people could walk along the bridge to cross the river instead of relying on the boats, so everyone benefited a lot from the bridge.

"闽刹之冠"的涌泉寺作为台湾众多寺庙的祖庭，凭借高大雄伟的塔楼殿阁、美丽精致的水榭亭台与清新隽永的摩崖题刻屹立在石鼓名山，诉说着一段段深沉的历史往事。如今鼓山涌泉寺已经成为游览观光胜地，是外地游客来榕的必游之处。这座香火旺盛的千年古寺在香客络绎不绝的祭拜中，持续传递着中国传统历史的深远意义与福州古厝文化的重要价值。

Yongquan Temple, the top temple in Fukien and the ancestral temple of many temples in Taiwan, stands on the famous Gushan mountain, telling the profound past with its tall and majestic halls, pavilions and pagodas, beautiful and exquisite waterside pavilions, and elegant and delicate cliff inscriptions. Nowadays, the Yongquan Temple in Gushan has become a tourist attraction and a must-see place in Fuzhou. This thousand-year-old temple, along with its endless worshippers, continues to pass on the profound significance of Chinese history and the important value of Fuzhou ancient buildings' culture.

第三章

名人故居：积厚流光

Chapter Three
The Former Residence of Celebrities:
From the Past to the Present

中国历史文化悠久，其间出现的名人不胜枚举，因此中国的名人故居无论是数量还是类型都很丰富。名人故居是以建筑形式存在的重要文化载体，经过时间长河的洗刷，记录并保留下了历史名人生活的痕迹、风采，其历史文化价值巨大。福州人才荟萃，名人故居颇多，保存下来的亦不在少数。

三坊七巷建筑群是福州著名的古街坊，始建于西晋末年，唐安史之乱后，这里逐渐成为以士大夫阶层、文化人为主的居住街区。

◎ 陈季良故居

三坊七巷中，文儒坊19号是海军抗日名将陈季良的故居。该宅第最早由陈氏八世祖陈兆盛于明崇祯十五年（1642年）购置，虽然陈家几经起落，这宅子也曾几易其主，但主体建筑变化不大，一直延续到现在。

故居见证了陈氏几代人的发展，保存了原来的建筑格局。比较来看，在马鞍墙波动如海的三坊七巷历史文化街区中，这个占地面积只有1500多平方米的院落与其他大户人家相比并不算大，但是"山不在高，有仙则名；水不在深，有龙则灵"。幼年的林则徐便跟随其母（陈氏十三世祖姑母陈帙）及其娘舅长居于此。后来，此地又诞生了著名的爱国将领、海军上将陈季良。

故居的整个院落为典型的福州民居布局，一院一花厅。主院落前后三进，一进面阔三间，主体建筑坐南朝北，穿斗式木构架，封火山墙为高高的马鞍墙，与周围的街区、三坊七巷乃至整个福州的历史文化景观融为一体。

位于文儒坊19号的陈季良故居
the former residence of Chen Jiliang in No.19 of Wenru Lane

China has a long history, during which there are countless celebrities. Therefore, as an important cultural carrier in the form of architecture with great cultural value, the former residences of celebrities in China are rich both in quantity and style. With time going by, it has recorded and preserved the traces of historical celebrities living here. Fuzhou (the capital city of Fukien Province) is full of talents, and there are many former residences of celebrities, most of which have been well preserved.

Three Lanes and Seven Alleys, an architecture complex, is the most famous urban historic conservation area in Fuzhou. It was originally built in the late Western Jin Dynasty. After the An Shi Rebellion in the Tang Dynasty, it gradually became a residential area dominated by officials and intellectuals.

◎ The former residence of Chen Jiliang

Located in No.19 of Wenru (means "men of literature and writing" in Chinese) Lane in Three Lanes and Seven Alleys, the former residence of Chen Jiliang, a famous naval officer fighting against Japanese aggression, still shines. This mansion was purchased in 1642 during the Ming Dynasty by Chen Zhaosheng, the eighth ancestor of the Chen family. Although the Chen family went through several ups and downs and the mansion was lived by several owners, the main structure of it has not changed much.

The mansion witnesses the development of several generations of the Chen family, and its original architectural layout has been preserved. Compared with other residences in Three Lanes and Seven Alleys, this courtyard, which covers an area of only more than 1500 square meters, is not that large. But just as the saying goes, "mountains are famous for living saints and waters gains miraculous for residing dragons", it is still glittering today for Lin Lexus and Chen Jiliang's living here.

The whole mansion has a typical Fuzhou residential layout, with one courtyard and one flower hall. From the front door to the back door, the main courtyard has a three-story structure perpendicular to the vertical axis, with each story having three rooms. The main building faces north and has a post-and-beam wooden frame structure with high saddle wall. The exterior wall, which is used to separate the space and resist the wind and fire, is in the shape of a saddle, so it is also known as a Saddle Wall. This mansion is integrated with the surrounding blocks, including the Three Lanes and Seven Alleys, and even the entire history of Fuzhou.

　　宅院虽然经过后人修整，但是其清式建筑特色仍非常鲜明：雕饰上的镂花移木、飞禽走兽栩栩如生，虽由人作，宛自天开。纹饰古朴的灰塑，高高翘起的屋脊，以及檐下弯弯的截水脊，都是清代建筑的典型特征。

　　细节决定品质，也许正是由于陈季良将军有高雅的涵养和对品质的追求，才能设计出独具特色的花厅。在这里，所有门、窗、壁板、地板甚至楼梯、橡板全都采用昂贵的楠木并经过完美的艺术加工而成，大方而明快。一楼会客厅内的椅、桌、茶几、书橱等全是红木制成，统一而协调。楼前庭院东北角的一座六角亭为陈季良将军亲自设计并修建，雕制精美。亭周围种有各种花树，亭旁原有一座假山、一口鱼池。

　　陈季良在中国近代史上留下了浓墨重彩的一笔，他在"一战"后最惨烈的海空战——江阴海空战中宁死不屈，英勇献身。走进文儒坊，在陈季良故居前久久伫立，我们会知道何为文儒、何为大丈夫。

◎ 林觉民、林徽因和冰心故居

　　来到杨桥东路17号，这栋素朴不显的宅第跟三坊七巷其他名人官邸一般地灵人杰，先后居住了林觉民、林徽因和冰心三位历史名人。

位于杨桥东路17号的林觉民、冰心故居
the former residence of Lin Juemin and Bingxin in No.17 Yangqiao Road

Although this mansion has been repaired by later generations, its Qing style architectural characteristics are still preserved. For instance, the lifelike carved flowers and animals on the carving move wood, the gray sculptures with ancient patterns, the curved intercepting ridges under the eaves are typical features of architecture in Qing Dynasty.

Out of the pursuit for quality, Chen Jiliang designed a unique flower hall, in which all doors, windows, wallboards, floors, even stairs and rafters were made of expensive nanmu through perfect artistic processing, generous and lively. The chairs, tables, tea tables, bookcases, etc., in the reception hall are all made of mahogany, unified and coordinated. With exquisite carving, the hexagonal pavilion at the northeast corner of the courtyard was designed and built by Chen Jiliang himself. There were all kinds of flowers and trees growing around the pavilion. Besides the pavilion, there was a rockery and a fish pond.

Chen Jiliang left a remarkable legacy in modern Chinese history. He would rather die than surrender in the Jiangyin Sea and Air Battle, which was the most tragic sea and air battle after the First World War. Wandering in Wenru Lane and standing in front of the former residence of Chen Jiliang for a long time, we will understand what a literary scholar is and what a great man looks like.

◎ The former residence of Lin Juemin, Lin Huiyin and Bing Xin

Located in No. 17, Yangqiao Road in Three Lanes and Seven Alleys, this simple and unsophisticated mansion is inhabited by Lin Juemin (famous revolutionist in Qing Dynasty), Lin Huiyin (an architect in the Republic of China) and Bing Xin (a famous writer in Modern China) successively.

该故居为清代建筑，坐西朝东，四面封火墙。前门临后街，门头房曾作为"万升桶石店"。主体建筑三进，占地面积694平方米，大门改在杨桥路。

进入院子后，入眼的是敞开式正堂。正堂的两旁是几间不大的居室。院子有些狭窄而拥促，房间重重叠叠，不见开阔的宅院，抬起头便是几尺见方的蓝天。穿过狭窄的过道，便是林觉民与陈意映生活过的居室。小小的一间房子藏在整个院落的一个角落，房间的墙上挂着两幅画像。一幅是林觉民，一脸的豪情与英气。另外一幅是陈意映，面庞敦厚、慈善。

林觉民《与妻书》中有一段写道："吾真真不能忘汝也！回忆后街之屋，入门穿廊，过前后厅，又三四折，有小厅，厅旁一室，为吾与汝双栖之所。初婚三四个月，适冬之望日前后，窗外疏梅筛月影，依稀掩映。吾与汝并肩携手，低低切切，何事不语？何情不诉？"此书信中所描写的"双栖楼"至今犹在，且仍保存原状。而楼下那棵梅花亦欣欣向荣，见证了林觉民与陈意映的鹣鲽情深。

林徽因是林觉民的堂哥林长民的女儿，林氏家族同居此宅，是理所当然。但是冰心和林家并无渊源，为何也居住在此？这是有故事的。

林觉民追随孙中山先生参加革命，黄花岗之役惊天地、泣鬼神，林觉民以24岁的年纪从容就义，壮烈牺牲。革命失败后，清廷开始追捕革命党人，林觉民的岳父暗地里通知亲家赶紧逃亡。林觉民的父亲为保全家人忍痛出售宅邸，逃至乡下避祸。

林宅的买主姓谢，名銮恩。谢銮恩是住在三坊七巷南后街的望族。辛亥革命后不久，谢銮恩的儿子即当时烟台海军学堂监督谢葆璋罢官回乡，带着家人住进杨桥巷17号的房子。而谢葆璋的女儿谢婉莹，就是后来著名的女作家冰心。

冰心晚年在《我的故乡》中记述："具有很典型的福州民宅特点，除中轴建筑外，左右两旁还有许多自成院落的房屋，每个院落都有水井；北院之西还横亘着一列坐西朝东的双层楼房，楼房之西为花园。"

如今，这栋曾经有过三进院落的大宅邸已不复从前规模。宅第的第一进院落、北边小院与花园，已经不敌时代的变迁，被分割并改建成楼房、辟建成马路，幸好第二进及第三进院落仍然维持旧时模样，供人缅怀。

故居虽在闹市，但安静得很。古之书香门第，大抵如此。

This mansion was built in the Qing Dynasty, facing east and surrounded by exterior walls. Lying in the downtown with its front door facing the street, it used to be an outlet to sale barrels and chests. Covering an area of 694 square meters, the main building has a three-story structure perpendicular to the vertical axis and the main gate has been moved to Yangqiao Road.

After entering the courtyard, the open main hall comes into view. On both sides of the main hall are several small bedrooms. The yard is narrow and crowded. Looked up, the blue sky has been shaped quadrilateral by the quadrangle. Through the narrow aisle, there is the room where Lin Juemin and Chen Yiying (Lin's wife) once lived. It was a small room with two portraits hanging on the wall hidden in a corner of the whole courtyard. Among the two portraits, one is Lin Juemin, gentle and confident, and the other is Chen Yiying, pretty and lovely.

In Lin Juemin's *To My Beloved Wife*, he worte, "I really can't forget you and the mansion where we spent life together. Enter the gate, through the hallways, and pass the front room and back room, there is a small living room. Next to the small living room is a bedroom, and that is where you and I lived. Three or four months after we got married, it was just around mid November when sparse plum branches cast shadows under the moonlight outside of the window, each reflecting on the other. You and I were walking side by side, holding hands, whispering our deepest thoughts. Those were the happy times we spent together and this house was a place that held our unforgettable memories." The bedroom where Lin Juemin and his wife lived described in this letter still exists today and remains unchanged along which the plum blossom tree downstairs is also thriving, witnessing the deep love between Lin Juemin and Chen Yiying.

Lin Huiyin was the daughter of Lin Changmin, Lin Juemin's cousin. It is reasonable for the Lin family to live in this mansion. However Bing Xin had no relationship with the Lin family. Why did she live here? This is a story.

It is said that Lin Juemin followed Dr. Sun Yat Sen to participate in the Huanghuagang Uprising, a rebellion against Qing government. Though failed, this rebellion, which could be called a successful failure, shocked the world. What made us sad was that Lin Juemin died calmly and heroically in the battle at the age of 24. After the failure of this revolution, the Qing government began to hunt down revolutionaries, so Lin Juemin's father-in-law secretly informed his in-laws to flee. In order to save his family, Lin Juemin's father reluctantly sold this mansion and fled to the countryside.

The buyer of Lin's mansion was Xie Luan'en who was a famous family living in the South Back Street in Three Lanes and Seven Alleys. Shortly after the Republican Revolution of 1911, Xie Luan'en's son, Xie Baozhang, the supervisor of Yantai Naval Academy at that time, quit his job and returned home, taking his family to live in this house. And Xie Baozhang's daughter, Xie Wanying, was later the famous female writer known as Bing Xin.

In her later years, Bing Xin wrote in *My Hometown* that "it is a typical Fuzhou residential house which has a main hall in the axis and other rooms on the left and right sides, each of which has a water well. To the west of the north courtyard, there is also a row of double-storey buildings sitting west to east, in the west of which is a garden."

This large mansion, which once had three courtyards, is no longer the same size as before. The first courtyard, the north courtyard and the garden of the mansion have been changed over times. They have been divided and rebuilt into buildings and roads. Fortunately, the second and third courtyards still maintain their old appearance for people to remember.

The former residence is located in the downtown area, yet it is very quiet. This is generally true of ancient scholarly or aristocratic families.

◎ 严复故居

郎官巷20号的院落是严复故居。严复1920年底回到福州，直至1921年病逝前一直居住在这里。尽管严复于此居住的时间并不长，但这是他落叶归根的地方。

郎官巷严复故居是当时福建省督军兼省长李厚基为严复购置的。整座故居占地面积609平方米，采用清式结构，坐北朝南，主座与花厅两座毗连。门内三面走廊，前设有插屏门。大厅面阔三间，正间分前后厅，左右边间为前后厢房。主座前廊西有小门通花厅。故居建筑在细节处理上有仿西方建筑纹饰的栏杆、宽广的天井等，是晚清中西合璧建筑的典范。

步入故居，率先映入眼帘的是"有王者兴必来取法，虽圣人起不易吾言"这副楹联，笔墨之间彰显出严复在沧桑岁月中的智慧与坚守。

除了郎官巷宅院之外，严复早年在福州还有一处故居，即坐落于阳岐村伯仲山麓的祖居。

因严氏迁闽始祖严怀英曾为唐朝朝请大夫，所以阳岐严复故居又被称为"大夫第"。故居历经严氏家族几代营建，现存为明末清初建筑。占地面积745平方米，共两进（严复幼时即居于第二进西披榭），由前后厅堂、左右厢房、前后天井、左右披谢、门廊等组成。

他在《梦想阳岐山》中所说的"门前一泓水，潮至势迟迟"，便是指这座故居门前的岐江。岐江穿村（上岐、下岐）而过，不远处即为连接古驿道的宋代古桥——午桥，两岸有翠竹、丹荔和龙眼树，景色宜人。

位于郎官巷20号的严复故居
the former residence of Yan Fu in No.20 of Langguan Alley

◎ The former residence of Yan Fu

Yan Fu's former residence is located in Langguan Lane, No.20. Yan Fu returned to Fuzhou at the end of 1920 and lived here until his death in 1921. Although Yan Fu didn't live here for a long time, it was his final resting place.

This mansion was purchased by Li Houji, the governor of Fukien Province at that time. Facing north, the whole mansion covers an area of 609 square meters, adopts the Qing style structure, and the main hall is adjacent to two flower halls. There are three corridors inside the door, and there are screen doors in front. The hall is surrounded by three rooms, and the room in middle is divided into front and rear halls. The left and right side rooms are front and rear wing rooms. There is a small door to the flower hall in the west of the front porch of the main block. Also, there are railings imitating western architectural patterns and broad patios, which is a model of Chinese and Western architecture in the late Qing Dynasty.

Stepping into the mansion, the first thing to come into view is the couplet, "the king would come to me if he would like to make a career and I would not change my mind even though the saint had different idea from me". From his words, we can feel Yan Fu's wisdom and persistence in his career.

In addition to this mansion, there is another former residence of Yan Fu in early years in Fuzhou, which is located at the foot of Bozhong Mountain in Yangqi Village.

Yan Huaiying, the first ancestor of the Yan Family who moved to Min area (Fukien Province today), once served as minister in the imperial court, so this mansion is also known as "Da Fu Di(the mansion with a minister living in it)". This mansion has been built by the Yan Family for several generations, and now it has been preserved as a house built in the late Ming and early Qing Dynasties. It covers an area of 745 square meters and has a three-story structure perpendicular to the vertical axis, including front and rear halls, left and right wing rooms, front and rear patios, etc.

In *Dream of Yangqi Mountain,* Yan Fu mentions that "there is a quiet and slow river in front of the door". The river mentioned in his words is the Qijiang River in front of the mansion. The Qijiang river passes through the village including Shangqi village and Xiaqi village to connect Wu Bridge --- an ancient bridge built in the Song Dynasty. The scenery along the riverside is pleasant with emerald bamboo and longan trees on both sides.

1921年10月27日，带着对家国的满腔深忧远虑，严复在福州三坊七巷的郎官巷与世长辞，从此在故乡阳岐的鳌头山长眠。

午后的阳光斜打在大夫第的门前，照耀在郎官巷巷头，使经年的古厝隐隐现出一种庄重智慧的光影。到严复故居瞻仰，我们感受到先生科学与爱国的思想仍在闪耀光芒。严复一生都处在中华民族危机日益深重的艰难时期，他始终心系国家和民族的前途，抱有强烈的爱国情怀，发出"物竞天择，适者生存"的呼喊，提倡"鼓民力、开民智、新民德"，以期救亡图存。他是中国近代精通"西学"的第一流人物，一生翻译了200多万字西方著作，他所提出的"信、达、雅"翻译三原则为推进中国翻译事业做出了不可磨灭的贡献。

时光轻拂，这些经历岁月沧桑的名人故居如今依旧静静地停留在原地。他们的主人用自己的人格魅力为故居增添色彩。当我们站立在故居门前，仿佛又一次看见故居的主人们在这里度过恬淡的岁月，时空在此重叠，我们在同一缕风中感受着同一段时光。

On October 27th, 1921, with full of worries about his family and country, Yan Fu finally passed away in Langguan Alley, buried in the Aotou Mountain in Yangqi, his hometown.

With the sun casting down the door of this mansion, this ancient house flicker with a solemn and wise light. When visiting Yan Fu's former residence, we felt that his scientific and patriotic thoughts were still shining. Yan Fu has been in a difficult period of increasingly serious crisis in the Chinese nation all his life. He has always been concerned about the future of the country and the nation, issued the cry of "nature will select the fittest for survival", and advocated "encouraging the people's strength, opening the people's intelligence, and rebuilding people's morality". With a strong sense of patriotism, he devoted his life to saving the nation from untold miseries. As a master in western learning, he translated more than two million words of Western works in his life. His three translation principles of "faithfulness, expressiveness and elegance" have made indelible contributions for the spread of western literature in China.

With time going by, the former residences of celebrities which have experienced the vicissitudes of time are still quietly in place. The charming characters of their owner made them shine through the ages. When standing in front of these former residences, we can still feel the quiet years spent by the original owners here as if time and space have overlapped here.

第四章

传统街区：穿越古今

Chapter Four

Traditional Cultural Blocks:
Crossing the Ancient and the Modern

历史与文化在城市长期发展中积淀，以传统街区的形式留存下来。传统文化街区是人类文明的延续，是城市历史延留的风貌，也是地域独特性的体现。古老的街区经过岁月的洗礼，在今天诉说着昨天的故事。福州历史悠久，留存下来的历史街区不少，在今天仍在熠熠生辉。

◎ 三坊七巷

在福州古城的中心，坐落着遐迩闻名的三坊七巷历史文化街区。它兴起于晋、完善于唐、至明清鼎盛，是"非"字型街区，东临八一七北路，西至通湖路，南达吉庇巷、光禄坊，北接杨桥路，是中国都市为数不多的"里坊制度（把全城分割为若干封闭的"里"作为居住区，商业与手工业被限制在一些定时开闭的"市"中）活化石"。

整个街区以南北向的南后街为中轴，自北向南依次辐射十条支巷，形成纵横交错、极其规整的街区格局。其中，向西辐射的三条支巷连接通湖路，称"三坊"，即衣锦坊、文儒坊、光禄坊；向东辐射的七条支巷连接八一七北路，称"七巷"，即杨桥巷、郎官巷、塔巷、黄巷、安民巷、宫巷、吉庇巷。整个街区占地40余公顷，现存明清时期建筑200多座，素有"中国明清建筑博物馆"之称。

走进三坊七巷，明风清韵扑面而来。在三坊七巷建筑群中，明式建筑有着大量遗存。这一时期的建筑风格，上承宋代营造法式的传统，下启清代官修的工程作法，以规模宏大、气象雄伟、用材较大为主要特点，其建筑风格较为严谨，整体也较为古朴雄浑，直到晚明才逐渐趋向繁琐。这一时期的主要代表是位于宫巷的林聪彝故居和位于黄巷的郭伯荫故居等，这些建筑在布局上气势恢宏，庭院深深，活动空间宽广。建筑本身上则梁柱硕大，做工虽古朴却不失细腻，配以各种精美雕刻，浑然一体。

"三坊七巷"在清朝达到鼎盛。这一时期"三坊七巷"的传统建筑受建材日渐匮乏等各方面的影响，逐步扩大了砖石材料的选用范围，同时也更加重视装饰，对一些外露的构件如斗拱、雀替、垂花柱、卷棚等进行了大量繁复的修饰。与明代建筑相比，清代在传统民居建筑上虽缺少了一些力度感和纯朴感，但是在建筑装饰艺术方面更具有表现力。

The history and culture of a city have accumulated in the long-term development and preserved in the form of traditional blocks. The traditional cultural block is the continuation of human civilization and the embodiment of the unique regional characteristics. As a city with long history, Fuzhou has many traditional cultural blocks still shining today.

◎ Three Lanes and Seven Alleys

In the center of Fuzhou, there is a well-known traditional cultural block called Three Lanes and Seven Alleys. Originated in the Jin Dynasty, perfected in the Tang Dynasty and reached its peak in the Ming and Qing Dynasties, it was adjacent to Bayiqi North Road in the east, Tonghu Road in the west, Jibi Alley in the south, and Yangqiao Road in the North. Built in the shape of "非", it is called " the living fossil of the Li-fang Unit System." The Li-fang unit system is a form of urban construction design, as well as a management policy in social order. In this system, the whole block has been divided into several closed areas called "Li" as residential areas, and open areas called "Fang" as commercial stores.

The whole block takes the South Back Street as the central axis, radiating ten lanes from north to south, forming a crisscross and extremely regular block pattern. Among them, three branches radiating to the west to connect Tonghu Road are called "Three Lanes" including Yijin Lane, Wenru Lane and Guanglu Lane. And there are also seven branch lanes radiating eastward to connect Bayiqi North Road called "Seven Alleys" including Yangqiao Alley, Langguan Alley, Ta Alley, Huang Alley, Anmin Alley, Gong Alley and Jibi Alley. The whole block covers an area of more than 40 hectares, and preserves more than 200 architectures belonging to Ming and Qing Dynasties. Therefore, it is known as the "Museum of Architecture in the Ming and Qing Dynasties of China".

Walking into the block, you will have a strong impression of the architectures with Ming and Qing Dynasty styles, especially the style in Ming Dynasty. The architectural style of this period is the continuation of Song Dynasty in which architecture is a combination of decoration and structure. Also, the architectural style of Ming Dynasty is characterized by large scale and great momentum, which became the typical architectural features in the later Qing Dynasty. The main representatives of the Ming Dynasty in this block are Lin Congyi's former residence located in Gong Alley and Guo boyin's former residence located in Huang Alley. They are magnificent in layout, deep in courtyard and wide in activity space. For the architecture itself, the beams and columns are large with simple but exquisite workmanship.

Three Lanes and Seven Alleys reached their peak during the Qing Dynasty. Due to deficient materials, architecture in this period began to adopt brick and stone in building. At the same time, more attention was paid to decoration, and a large number of complex modifications were carried out on some exposed components such as bucket arches, sparrows, hanging columns, and rolling sheds. Compared with the buildings in Ming Dynasty, the traditional folk houses in Qing Dynasty lacked some sense of strength and simplicity, but were rich in expressing decoration art.

三坊七巷传统民居
Folk Houses in Three Lanes and Seven Alleys

到了近代，福州成为中国重要的通商口岸。自开埠以来，外部世界带来的冲击对传统文化影响很大，再加上西洋和南洋的福州人回归故土，西方的思想迅速进入这片既传统又开放的领地。福州的近现代西式建筑主要分布在闽江沿岸的通商口岸一带，"三坊七巷"内并不多，如叶氏古民居的对外门面、刘冠雄故居的后花厅等。

鸟瞰三坊七巷，白墙瓦屋，曲线山墙，布局严谨，匠艺奇巧，不少还缀以亭、台、楼、阁、花草、假山，融人文、自然景观于一体。许多民居的漏花门窗采用镂空精雕的手法榫接而成，丰富的图案雕饰，精巧的石刻桂础、台阶、门框、花座、柱杆，集中体现了福州古民居特色。

经过保护与修缮，这些建筑群在今天持续焕发生机。马鞍墙是三坊七巷屋面极具特色的墙头风格。它两侧对称，呈流线型，翘角伸出宅外，状似马鞍，墙头和翘角皆泥塑彩绘，独具特色。在修复这些古建筑的时候，马鞍墙得以保存，并加入了能够体现福州特色的现代元素——波涛状的海洋线条。从空中俯瞰三坊七巷，屋顶就像万顷波浪般延伸铺展开来，甚是壮观。

此外，位于衣锦坊的水榭戏台经过多次改建与修缮至今仍在使用，讲述老福州故事的戏曲仍在上演，诉说着古宅的悠悠往事。

In modern times, Fuzhou became an important trade port in China. Since the opening of the port, the outside world has had a great impact on traditional culture. In addition, with more Fuzhou people abroad returning to this city, western ideas have rapidly entered this traditional and open city. The modern western-style buildings in Fuzhou are mainly distributed in the commercial ports along the Minjiang River; few of them lie in Three Lanes and Seven Alleys, like the former residence of Ye Family and Liu Guanxiong's former residence.

Looking down from above, what comes to the eye are tile-covered houses with white walls, exterior walls with curved brick, rigorous and ingenious. Many of them are also decorated with pavilions, platforms, flowers and plants, and rockeries, integrating human and natural landscapes. Many of the doors and windows of resident houses are made of hollowed mortise and tenon with fine carving. Besides the doors and windows, there are still exquisite stone steps, door frames, flower seats and columns, which reflect the characteristics of resident houses of ancient Fuzhou.

With protection and repair, these architectures are constantly rejuvenated today. Among them, the Saddle Wall gets its name for the similar shape of saddle, and it is a distinctive wall style of the roof for the architectures in Three Lanes and Seven Alleys. It is symmetrical on both sides and is streamlined. The warped corner of it extends out of the house, like a saddle. The wall and the warped corner are painted with unique clay sculpture. When restoring these ancient buildings, the Saddle Wall was preserved, and based on this, a modern element, wavy ocean lines, was added into the Saddle Wall. Looking down, the Saddle Wall is like a vast expanse of waves, which is very spectacular.

Also, the Shuixie Stage used for performing in Yijin Alley is still in use after renovation and repair. The opera telling the story of ancient Fuzhou is still on stage, tells people the long history of the ancient house.

除了特点鲜明的建筑群，许多历史事件也在三坊七巷留下印记，记录了它的千年沧桑。

文儒坊最初是一条穿过小山包的林荫道，因坊内住户个个以"鸿儒"自居，于是名为"儒林巷"。宋代，国子监祭酒郑穆在此安居，里人学风日盛，巷人引为自豪而改称"文儒坊"。文儒坊历代文儒辈出，明清时期更是成为文武官员聚居之地。

郎官巷是七巷中最短的一条巷，只有100余米。郎官是古时为皇帝出谋划策的谋士，也是朝廷重要官职的候补人选。北宋时这条巷子里住着一个叫刘涛的人，其子是郎官，孙辈也接连做郎官，郎官结队成行，满巷生辉，于是巷子便被称为郎官巷。

安民巷的由来据说与唐末的黄巢有关。黄巢率领的农民起义军占领了福州以后，为了安抚百姓，就在这条巷口张榜"安民"。最后，这条在当时作为城乡接合处的无名小巷就与"安民"结下了不解之缘。虽宋元时历经多次更名，最终仍以"安民巷"传于民间。

黄巷是因聚居黄姓人家而得名。晋代中原战乱，人们为躲避战争而迁徙入闽，有一黄姓家族落户于此，便有了"黄巷"名字的由来。唐朝末年，崇文馆校书郎黄璞退隐归居黄巷。黄巷在历代多住儒林学士，因此成为文化名人和社会名流的集居地。

漫步三坊七巷间，更为惊叹的是它的文化底蕴。近代诗人陈衍有诗曰："谁知五柳孤松客，却住三坊七巷间。"（《畏庐寄诗题匹园新楼次韵》）三坊七巷自形成起便是贵族和士大夫的聚居地。特别是到了清代中后期，以林则徐、沈葆桢、严复、陈宝琛、甘国宝、林纾、林旭、林白水、郁达夫、冰心、林觉民、林徽因、王冷斋、黄乃裳等为代表的历史人物扎堆涌现，成为中国近代星空里的璀璨繁星。因此，人们说："三坊七巷一条街，半部中国近代史。"

坊巷长深，文化久远。经过岁月洗礼的三坊七巷吸引着来往行人的驻足观望和细细品味。

◎ 朱紫坊

朱紫坊与三坊七巷隔街相望，记录着福州千年历史，承载着古城乡愁。

In addition to the distinctive architectural complex, many historical events have also left their marks on Three Lanes and Seven Alleys, recording the vicissitudes of thousands of years.

Wenru (educated person) Alley was originally a tree-lined road through the hills. Because the residents in this alley all regarded themselves as 'Hongru(educated person)", it was renamed "Rulin (a place gathering educated person) Alley". In the Southern Song Dynasty (420 - 479), Zheng Mu, the Chancellor of the National Academy, lived here. From then on, the atmosphere of learning was flourishing. People in this lane were proud of it and changed its name to "Wenru Alley". In Wenru Alley, there lived many celebrities. In the Ming and Qing Dynasties, it even became a place where civil and military officials lived.

Langguan Alley is the shortest among the seven alleys, only more than 100 meters. Lang Guan was a counselor who advised the emperor in ancient times and was also a candidate for important official positions in the imperial court. In the Northern Song Dynasty, a man named Liu Tao lived in this alley. His son was Lang Guan, and his grandchildren were also Lang Guan. Known for the "Lang Guans" here, this alley was full of glory. Therefore, the lane was called Lang Guan Alley.

It is said that the origin of Anmin Alley is related to Huang Chao (the leader of peasant uprising) in the late Tang Dynasty. After the peasant uprising led by Huang Chao occupied Fuzhou, in order to pacify the people, he put up a banner read "An Min" at the entrance of this lane. Finally, this anonymous alley, which was the intersection of urban and rural areas at that time, formed an indissoluble bond with "An Min". Although it was renamed many times in the Song and Yuan Dynasties, it was finally spread to the people as "Anmin Alley".

Huang Alley is named after the family of Huang. In the Jin Dynasty, because of the war in the Central Plains, people migrated to Fukien to avoid the war. Among them, there was the Huang family who settled here. For Huang's family living here, this alley got its name as Huang Alley. At the end of the Tang Dynasty, Huang Pu, a civil official in imperial court, retired to live in Huang Alley. And in the past dynasties, many scholars lived here, so it gradually became a gathering place of scholars and social celebrities.

Walking in the Three Lanes and Seven Alleys, what is more amazing is its cultural heritage. Modern poet Chen Yan wrote that "Men with great soul lived in Three Lanes and Seven Alleys." Since its formation, it has been the gathering place of nobles, scholars and officials. Especially in the middle and late Qing Dynasty, historical figures represented by Lin Zexu, Shen Baozhen, Yan Fu, Chen Baochen, Gan Guobao, Lin Shu, Lin Xu, Lin Baishui, Yu Dafu, Bing Xin, Lin Juemin, Lin Huiyin, Wang Lengzhai, Huang Naishang and so on emerged and became the bright stars in china's modern history. Therefore, people say that "one street in Three Lanes and Seven Alleys covers half of Chinese modern history".

Through the ages, long and deep lanes as well as alleys reflect the long history of Fuzhou, attracting pedestrians to stay, enjoy and appreciate.

◎ Zhuzi Lane

Carrying the history and nostalgia of Fuzhou, Zhuzi Lane and Three Lanes and Seven Alleys face each other across the street.

朱紫坊形成于唐代，距今有一千一百多年历史。其名称始于宋代。传言坊内住着朱敏功四兄弟，即朱敏功、朱敏中、朱敏元、朱敏修，"昆仲四人，皆登仕版"，"朱紫盈门，因以为名"。就是说朱敏功四兄弟各自为官，分别着朱红色和紫色官服。依宋朝官制，三品以上官员着紫色官服，五品以上官员着朱红色官服。朱家朱紫盈门，所以称"朱紫坊"。

朱紫坊面临安泰河，当时因河上有三座桥，故又名"三桥巷"。安泰河、三桥、朱紫坊组成的"河–桥–坊"格局是朱紫坊历史文化街区最具特色的空间格局，内部空间较完整地保存了从唐到明清时期的坊巷弄结构，道路具有明确的等级划分，主次分明。从河坊公共空间到巷弄半开放空间再到私密空间，人们的活动被有机联结起来，构成了朱紫坊诗情画意的空间意象。

朱紫坊背靠于山，又临安泰河。"山"和"水"的和谐交融，使朱紫坊成为货物流通的重要码头。有了安泰河，商人们可以把各种商品货物运到四面八方，两岸居民因之可以安宁地生活，文明之风蔚然而起。

朱紫坊学府林立，不仅有州学、府学、庙学、县学、督学署等古代各级官办学校与教育机构，还有书院、私塾等私立学校，如宋太平兴国年间创建的孔庙，明正德年间巡按御史沈灼建的一峰书院，清代设立的提督福建学院署等。这里学子云集，弦歌不绝，一片儒雅之风。

位于鼓楼区安泰街道的朱紫坊
Zhuzi Lane in Gulou Strict

With a history of more than 1100 years, Zhuzi Lane was formed in the Tang Dynasty and got its name in the Song Dynasty. It was said that there were four brothers, namely Zhu Mingong, Zhu Minzhong, Zhu Minyuan and Zhu Minxiu, they were all senior officials wearing red and purple uniforms in the imperial court. According to the song Dynasty's official uniform regulations, officials above the third rank wore purple robes, and officials above the fifth rank wore red robes. The Zhu family had many officials, so they were called "Zhu Zi Lane".

Zhuzi Lane faces the Antai river. There were three bridges across the river at that time, so Zhuzi Lane was also known as "Sanqiao (Three Bridges) Lane". The "River-Bridge- Lane" pattern in which the structure of lanes from the Tang Dynasty to the Ming and Qing Dynasty has been well preserved is composed of Antai River, Sanqiao and Zhuzi Lane, and this is the most distinctive spatial pattern of Zhuzi Lane. In this pattern, the whole space is clearly divided. From the public space to the semi open space and then to the private space, people's activities are organically combined, forming the poetic spatial image of Zhuzi Lane.

Zhuzi Lane backs on Yushan mountain and faces the Antai river. The harmonious blend of mountain and water makes Zhuzi Lane an important wharf for the circulation of goods. With Antai River, merchants can transport all kinds of commodities and goods to all directions. As a result, residents on both sides can live a rich life in peace, which made it possible and a trend to pursue for knowledge .

As a result, Zhuzi Lane has numerous academic institutions. There are not only ancient official schools and educational institutions at all levels, such as state schools, temple schools, county schools, and inspector's offices, but also private schools such as academy and home school. For example, the Confucius Temple built in Song Dynasty, the Yifeng Academy built by Shen Zhuo in the Ming Dynasty, and the Fukien Academy Office set up in the Qing Dynasty, attracted students from all over China.

朱紫坊文教发达，辐射周边。如鳌峰坊受其影响，办起了著名的鳌峰书院。说到鳌峰书院，坊间还流传着民族英雄林则徐避雨遇良缘的故事。朱紫坊名儒郑大谟是林则徐的岳丈。传说，少年林则徐奉舅父之命从文儒坊母家到鳌峰坊的鳌峰书院送文章，途经朱紫坊时赶上下雨，就在郑宅屋檐下避雨。郑大谟慧眼识人，与他交谈甚欢，便招林则徐为女婿。

自宋代起，安泰河两岸种植许多榕、柳、樟等树木，至今秀冶里河墘巷和朱紫坊沿岸的老榕树仍盘根错节、枝繁叶茂，须如垂帘，浓荫似盖，蔚为奇观。这里的古榕无一例外地向河面倾斜，两侧树木在安泰河上交错相拥，形成一条绿荫拱廊，清静幽雅。

坊内浓荫似盖，流水潺湲，闹中取静，故而吸引许多富商世家、文人雅士在此定居。沿河的庭院花厅，以植榕为风，以引水造园为常，各具特色，其中以"芙蓉园"最具代表性。

芙蓉园位于花园巷，在其历代主人中，有南宋理宗时的参政知事（副宰相）陈韡，有明代万历内阁首辅（宰相）叶向高（他一生两次为相，人称"独相十三载"），有曾任承天府同知的谢汝韶（他在辖区内推行"一条鞭法"，该措施成为张居正改革的主要内容）。今天，芙蓉园重新开放，这个经历了一个世纪沧桑的古老花园，正在以一种现代的方式开放。

此外，朱紫坊还是近代中国海军将领的聚居地，不少海军人物居住在这里，故有"海军一条街"之称。街区内有以海军耆宿萨镇冰、"中山舰"舰长萨师俊为代表的萨家大院，以海军名将方莹为代表的方家大宅，还有江南造船所所长、福州船政局局长陈兆锵故居，民国海军运输舰队司令张日章宅院，等等。这些杰出人物为古老的街区留下不少人文景观和传奇故事。

今天的朱紫坊，有小桥流水的古典浪漫，也有创新求变的现代活力。

悠悠老福州，翩翩坊巷情。作为老福州的历史缩影，朱紫坊从古老走向现代，从过去走向未来，承载着每一个福州人浓浓的乡情，融入骨血，深入人心。

Zhuzi Lane was well-developed in culture and education, which also had a positive impact on surrounding areas. For example, Aofeng Lane was affected by it and established the famous Aofeng Academy. When it comes to Aofeng Academy, there is a famous love story happened in raining of national hero Lin Zexu. It is said that a famous scholar called Zheng Damo, who was later Lin Zexu's father-in-law, lived in Zhuzi Lane. One day, young Lin Zexu was ordered by his uncle to send articles from his mother's home in Wuren Lane to Aofeng Academy. When he passed through Zhuzi Lane, it happened to rain. So he took shelter under the eave of Zheng's mansion. Zheng Damo had a good conversation with him and knew he would make a career, so he recruited Lin Zexu as his son-in-law.

Since the Song Dynasty, many banyan, willow, camphor and other kinds of trees have been planted on both sides of the Antai river. With luxuriant branches and leaves, the old banyan trees along are still intertwined. They are all inclined to the river, like a hanging curtain. The trees on both sides of Antai River crisscross each other, forming a green arch, quiet and elegant.

The lane is covered with thick shade formed by the trees, and under the shade flows clear water, quiet and slow. Therefore, it attracts many businessmen and scholars to settle here. They planted banyan and took advantage of water to build gardens. Among them, Lotus Garden is the most representative one.

Lotus Garden is located in Huayuan Alley of Zhuzi Lane. Among its owners, there are Chen Wei, the Political Governor(Deputy Prime Minister)in the LiZong period of the Southern Song Dynasty, Ye Xianggao, the Chief Assistant(Prime Minister)in the Ming Dynasty, Xie Rushao, who once served in imperial court to implement a whip policy in his jurisdiction in the Ming Dynasty. Now, Lotus Garden is reopened, and this ancient garden, which has undergone a century of vicissitudes, is being opened in a modern way.

In addition, Zhuzi Lane is also the residence of modern Chinese naval generals. Many naval figures live here, so it is also called "Naval Street". For example, here once lived Sa's family represented by Sa Zhenbing, the navy general, and Sa Shijun, the captain of the Zhongshan fleet, the Fang's family represented by the famous navy general Fang Ying. And here also lies the former residence of Chen Zhaoqiang, director of the Jiangnan Shipyard and Fuzhou Shipping Bureau, and the residence of Zhang Rizhang, commander of the naval transport fleet of the Republic of China. These outstanding figures have left many cultural landscapes and legends for this ancient block.

In today's Zhuzi Lane, we can see classical romance of small bridges and flowing water, as well as the modern vitality of innovation and change.

The older the city is, the deeper the lane will be. As a microcosm of ancient Fuzhou, Zhuzi Lane is walking from the ancient to the modern and from the past to the future. Carrying strong nostalgia of Fuzhou people, it has already become an inseparable part of them.

◎ 上下杭

"天上有银河，地上有上下杭。"上下杭起源于汉朝，形成于大庙山南麓沿岸，如今位于福州城外台江区中南部，呈"二横三纵"的倒"日"字形街区布局。

"杭"其实是从"航"音衍化而来，是码头的意思。远在北宋时，上下杭还是闽江水域，而后，水域随着泥沙淤积形成两个大沙滩，船沿着沙滩向上航行或向下航行，于是人们便称其为上航、下航。后来，沙滩逐渐形成陆地，分别称"上杭街"、"下杭街"，合称"上下杭"。

上下杭早期以水陆交通为主，是来往船只装卸货物的码头，由此成为物产集散的枢纽。又因其南部星安河通向闽江，云集了省内外广大商贾与物资，于是逐渐为福州商贸的发源地。五口通商之后，上下杭更是成为马可·波罗笔下的国际商港。"百货随潮船入市，万家沽酒户垂帘。"（宋·龙昌期《三山即事》）可见百年前福州上下杭的繁华景象。

由此，上下杭的建筑独具特色，主要体现在街区内建筑形式在传统民居建筑的基础上加入了少量西方元素。街区内就有不少采用西式风格建筑的会馆，如兴安会馆、建宁会馆、寿宁会馆、南郡会馆等。

会馆是双杭的一大人文奇观。清末，上下杭聚集了众多商业大佬，他们以家乡的县籍为单位纷纷兴建同乡会馆，多达14座，上下杭由此被称为"福州传统商业博物馆"。这些会馆通常是馆庙结合，奇特地融合了西洋和东方建筑的精华，内有厅堂、戏台、酒楼，有的还设了书斋、花园，集交易、聚会、住宿于一体。但由于年久失修以及新中国成立后功能置换，建筑内部空间遭到极大损坏，会馆大多已经面目全非，现多用于民居、教育，仅保有部分建筑外立面。

除会馆外，在闽商文化影响下也产生了诸多宗教建筑与宗祠。这些建筑大多受地方重视，保留完好。曾氏祠堂坐落在下杭路196号，由"唐宋八大家"之一曾巩的后人、福州第一大纸行创业者曾文乾购造，是福州较有代表性的家祠建筑之一。

如今上下杭繁华航运不再，但古桥、古河、古树和古建筑有幸保留了不少。

◎ Shangxia Hang

As the saying goes, "there is a milky way in the sky, and there is Shangxia Hang on the earth". Shangxia Hang, originated in the Han Dynasty, was formed along the south foot of Damiao mountain in the south central part of Taijiang District outside Fuzhou City. It enjoys a block layout of "日(sun)" because it has two streets in the transverse and three streets in the portrait.

In Chinese, the pronunciation of "Hang(杭)" is similar to "hang(航)", which means wharf. As far back as the Northern Song Dynasty, Shangxia Hang was still the waters of the Minjiang River. Then, the waters formed two large beaches with the siltation of the sand. Ships sailed up or down along the beach. Sailing up means Shang Hang and sailing down means Xia Hang in Chinese, so the two beaches got the name as Shang Hang and Xia Hang. Later, the two beaches gradually formed a land, which was called "Shanghang Street" and "Xiahang Street", and collectively called "Shangxia Hang".

In the early period of Shangxia Hang, it was mainly used as a dock for ships to load and unload goods. And because the Xing'an River in the South of it drained into the Minjiang River, it was very convenient in transportation so it gathered a large number of merchants and materials inside and outside Fukien Province here, therefore gradually became the birthplace of Fuzhou's commerce and trade. After the five ports were opened to trade, Shangxia Hang became an international commercial port described by Marco Polo. In Long Changqi's (a poet in the Song Dynasty) poem, he depicted that "there are various goods enter the market with boats, and there are tens of thousands of stores in the street". From this single poem, we can get a glimpse of the prosperous scene of Shangxia Hang a hundred years ago.

Influenced by western culture, the architectures in Shangxia Hang own unique western style, and this is mainly reflected in the architectural form which combines the Chinese architectural style and western architectural style together. For example, there are many guild halls with western style in it like Xing'an Guild Hall, Jianning Guild Hall, Shouning Guild Hall, Nanjun Guild Hall, etc.

The guild hall is a cultural wonder of Shangxia Hang. In the Late Qing Dynasty (1840 - 1911), a large number of business tycoons gathered here. Taking county as a unit, they built as many as 14 guild halls for their fellow villagers. Therefore, Shangxia Hang got the name of "The Traditional Business Museum of Fuzhou". With theatres, restaurants, gardens and even study rooms in it, these guild halls combine the function of halls and temples together, in which people can negotiate trade and take a rest. However, due to long-term disrepair and functional replacement after the founding of the People's Republic of China, the internal space of these guild halls have been greatly damaged, and most of them have been beyond recognition, only few of them are preserved.

Besides guild halls, many religious buildings and ancestral halls are also built under the influence of western culture. Most of them are well preserved and valued by the local government. For example, the ancestral hall of Zeng family purchased and built by Zeng Wenqian, the descendant of Zeng Gong, the founder of Fuzhou's largest paper shop, is located at No.196 in Xiahang Road and still well preserved today, becoming one of the representative ancestral halls in Fuzhou.

Nowadays, the prosperous shipping in Shangxia Hang is no longer available, but many ancient bridges, rivers, trees and buildings have been fortunately preserved.

星安桥建于清朝，是旧时驶入福州城的重要航道之一，桥周围聚居了众多渔民人家。夜晚从桥上四顾，万家渔火闪烁，如今只能从斑驳的桥体去追寻往事。

星安河颇有南京秦淮河的感觉，河面上每间隔一定时间就会放"雾"，营造出一种仙境的感觉。曾经川流的商船再也无法驶入这里，通江达海的喧嚣退变为小桥流水的悠闲，也别有一番风味。

大庙山的石刻、登高石、钓龙台，这些象征着古代上下杭建筑的地标在建筑本体损毁后仍能供人们回想古风余韵。始建于清朝之前的三通桥与星安桥经多次改建，仍发挥河流两岸通行的功能。大庙山石刻等遗存经过历史的沉淀已经成为福州第四中学校园文化的外延。

在上下杭还有座观音庵，建得晚些，为清朝建筑，红色墙体，墙面书写"唵嘛呢叭咪吽"六字大明咒。芸芸众生，佛度有缘人，虔诚的信徒诵念着经文，把整个街区衬托得分外祥和。

在上下杭，不仅有古韵悠长的街巷、中西合并的老建筑，还有潮流时尚的金银里步行街。

紫岩馆是卖紫砂壶的店，又是喝茶的地方，旧时商贩们热情的叫卖声仿佛回荡在耳边，你或许还能细数出那些鼎鼎有名的商人。他们不仅秉承诚信经商的理念，而且重义尚利、兼济天下、取财有道、兴帮为务，体现出榕商文化精神特质和价值取向，开创了上下杭地区商贸的鼎盛局面。民国时期每天有上千担茶叶从上下杭输往世界各地，如今每条街上仍开着茶馆，每天茶香四溢。

上下杭处于三坊七巷的光环之下，显得有些寂寞。漫步在上下杭，穿梭于砖楼间，偶尔抬头还能看到西洋铁艺窗台。在这里你看得见历史，也触摸得到故纸堆外有温度的生活。旧时双杭酒楼林立，而如今时光变迁，繁华褪尽。承载着福州商帮文化的上下杭，荣耀已成过往，但情怀仍在，榕城故事在这里继续发生着。

One of them is the Xing'an bridge built in the Qing Dynasty. With many fishermen living around it, it was one of the important channels for ships from other places to enter Fuzhou in ancient times. At that time, looking around the bridge at night, we could see thousands of fishing fires sparkling. Now, all these fishing fires have gone and we can only trace the past through the mottled bridge.

Xing'an river left people the same feeling as the Qinhuai River in Nanjing left people. On both rivers, the "fog" would be released every certain time, during which ships could not across the river, creating a feeling of fairyland. Nowadays, the bustling scene of the river is no longer available, but the calmness and leisure of the small bridge and the flowing water still have a different flavor.

The stone carvings, climbing stones and fishing dragon platforms (a small mountain) in Damiao mountain, which are of symbols of ancient Shangxia Hang, still serve as the carrier for people to recall the old times in Shangxia Hang. Santong bridge and Xing'an bridge, which were built before the Qing Dynasty, have been rebuilt many times, and still play the role as transportation hubs for people on both sides of the river. The stone carvings of Damiao mountain have become the extension of Fuzhou No. 4 Middle School.

There is also a Guanyin (a Bodhisattva in ancient Chinese tale) nunnery built in the Qing Dynasty in Shangxia Hang. The exterior wall of it is painted in red, the same color with the Forbidden City. There are six characters from the Daming mantra (the mantra of Guanyin) written on the wall, which is read as "Ma Ma Ba Mi Hong(唵嘛呢叭咪吽)". With loyal believer murmuring the mantra, the whole block seems to be more quiet.

In Shangxia Hang, there are not only streets and alleys with ancient architectures, but also the pedestrian street full of modern atmosphere called Jin Yin Li Pedestrian Street.

In it, Ziyan Pavilion is a shop selling purple clay pots and also a place to drink tea. When drinking a cup of tea in it, you would hear the enthusiastic cries of traders and even remember those famous merchants. They not only adhered to the business philosophy of integrity, but also attached importance to benefit the world at the same time. During the period of the Republic of China, thousands of tons of tea were transported from here to all parts of the world every day. Today, tea houses are still open on every street. The fragrance of tea is everywhere in Shangxia Hang.

Under the halo of Three Lanes and Seven Alleys, Shangxia Hang is not that famous. Walking here and occasionally looking up, you will see the iron window sill in western style, through which you can feel the warmth of life. With time going by, the prosperity faded away and the glory of Shangxia Hang, which carries the culture of Fuzhou merchants also faded away. However, spirits never die and the story of Fuzhou continues to take place here.

第五章

文教建筑：诗书继世

Chapter Five

Cultural and Educational Architecture:

Poetry and Books Unfolding the World

福州是一座历史文化名城，悠久的历史孕育了海纳百川、底蕴深厚的闽都文化，因此也造就了黛瓦相连、百年沧桑的古建筑群。福州自古以来文教昌盛，人文渊薮，文庙则是福州文教的重要建筑见证。至近代，"五口通商"后，福州逐渐成为西方教会学校发展的重点地区。从儒家孔孟思想到西方教会教育，中西思想交流碰撞出的火花在保留下来的古厝中得以体现。

◎ 福州孔庙

福州孔庙位于福建省福州市鼓楼区圣庙路10号。现存建筑建于清咸丰元年至四年（1851—1854年），坐北朝南，南北中轴线长约116米，东西长约65米，总占地面积为7552平方米，总建筑面积约4000平方米。

福州孔庙是古代文化教育的殿堂，作为福州市区现存最大的清晚期官式建筑，文庙主体建筑大成殿具有清代建筑古朴典雅的特点，用材硕大，保存完好。这在全国上千座孔庙里是罕见的，有很高的科学、艺术和历史价值。旧时，孔庙被列为"圣地"，东西宫门均立有下马碑，上书："文武官员至此下马"。

而大成殿为孔庙的主体建筑，陈列有古代祭孔礼器、乐器及历代名人遗物等。1961年9月，福州孔庙被福州市人民委员会公布为第一批市级文物保护单位；1996年9月2日，被福建省人民政府公布为省级文物保护单位。2006年5月25日，福州文庙被国务院公布为第六批全国重点文物保护单位。孔庙是了解古代文化教育的珍贵实物资料。

孔庙的主要建筑

孔庙建于贯穿南北的中轴线上，以大成殿为核心，南北依次为二进院落，采用沿中轴线左右对称的传统建筑布局方式。由南往北依次有棂星门、前埕、大成门、庭院、月台和大成殿；在两侧则有廊庑、乡贤祠、名宦祠和东西庑等，其建筑充分体现了清代官式建筑的风格。

As a famous historical and cultural capital city, Fuzhou's long history has given birth to its profound culture of inclusiveness in Fukien. The ancient buildings complex with black tiles are closely linked to the century-old vicissitudes of life. Since ancient times, Fuzhou has witnessed Confucian Temple as an important architectural symbol of Fuzhou's prosperous culture and education; during modern times, with "five ports of trade", Fuzhou gradually became the key area of the development of western church schools. From thoughts of Confucius and Mencius to western church education, the sparks of the collision between Chinese and Western thoughts are well reflected in the ancient buildings remained.

◎ Fuzhou Confucian Temple

Fuzhou Confucian Temple is located at No.10, Shengmiao Road, Gulou District, Fuzhou City, Fukien Province. The existing buildings were built in the first year of *Xianfeng* Emperor of the Qing Dynasty to the fourth year (1851—1854). The north-south central axis is about 116 meters long and about 65 meters long from east to west. It covers a total area of 7, 552 square meters and a total construction area of about 4, 000 square meters.

Fuzhou Confucian Temple is a palace of ancient culture and education. Fuzhou Confucian Temple is the largest official building in the late Qing Dynasty existing in Fuzhou. The main building of the Confucian Temple, *Dacheng* Hall, has the characteristics of being simple and elegant in the Qing Dynasty, with large materials well-preserved. It is rare among thousands of Confucian temples in the country with high scientific, artistic and historical value. In the old days, Confucian Temples were listed as "holy lands", with dismounting tablets standing in all the east and west palaces, which warned that "civil and military officials cannot ride till here".

Dacheng Hall is the main building of the Confucius Temple, displaying some ancient ritual vessels, musical instruments and relics of famous people. In September 1961, it was announced as the first batch of municipal cultural relics protection unit by Fuzhou Municipal People's Commission; on September 2, 1996, it was announced as the provincial cultural relics protection unit by Fukien Provincial People's Government. On May 25, 2006, Fuzhou Confucian Temple was announced as one of the sixth batch of national key cultural relics protection units by the State Council of the People's Republic of China. The Confucian temple is a precious tangible location to gain insights into ancient culture and education.

The Main Building of the Confucian Temple

The Confucian temple is built on the central axis, with *Dacheng* Hall as the core, in a symmetrical traditional architectural layout, from south to north with *Xinglin* Gate, Front Cheng, *Dacheng* Gate, courtyard, platform and *Dacheng* Hall one by one; on both sides, there are veranda, hometown celebrities temple, famous officials temple and two siderooms, which fully embodies the style of official architecture in the Qing Dynasty.

泮宫门

泮宫门，亦称圣贤门。泮宫即学宫，周代诸侯的学校前有半月形的水池，名叫泮水，诸侯的学校就称泮宫，以在泮水边建学宫而名。孔子有"素王"之称，历代由"宣尼公"晋封到"文宣王"，被树为"百世文官表，历代帝王师"。明清科举制度规定，学童考进县学为新进学员，须入学宫拜谒孔子，叫作入泮或游泮。而许多文庙的泮宫楼上也撰有楹联："海国闽疆东南重镇，典章文物邹鲁遗风。"

棂星门

棂星门，亦称先师门。相传，棂星为天镇星，即天上文曲星。孔庙庙门以"棂星"命名，意谓孔子应天上星宿而降。现存石构件为明代所建，六柱三开间，对称布局，每根柱脚配两块旗杆石，前后对夹。东西两翼墙上题有各长2.62米、宽0.73米，用花岗岩雕刻的楷书阴文"江汉秋阳"和"金声玉振"八字。门前增修了三级台阶，使棂星门和街道中间隔开了一小段距离。

大成门和金声门、玉振门

大成门是孔庙第二进院落的正中大门，现存系清末建筑。大成门古称戟门，面阔五间，进深二间。中三间屋面高出两边间，有青石抱鼓石三对，石檐柱八根。大成门左内侧竖着《咸丰元年重建福州文庙碑记》石碑二方，通高2.68米、宽0.84米、厚0.21米，郭柏荫撰文并书写190字碑文，刘永松篆书碑额，工匠为蒋学心。站立二碑前静心凝视，阴刻的碑文会逐渐地凸显出来，呈现阳文碑刻的奇异效果。

大成门与金声、玉振两门，系引申自孔子思想，集古代圣贤学说之大成。孟子说："孔子之谓集大成。集大成也者，金声而玉振之也。"（《孟子·万章下》）这是盛赞孔子"德开天地"、"道冠古今"，并与孔庙中心大成殿相呼应。

泮池和月台

泮池在大成门内、大成殿拜庭前方，作半月形，南岸半圆，北岸平直，可通潮汐。中间纵贯一座石桥，桥长约20米，中稍拱突，石板横铺，护以栏杆。栏柱雕石像，象征着太平景象。桥板七十二条，隐喻孔门七十二贤人。整体风格端重，人行桥上，有雍容端庄之感。月台又叫露台、拜亭，在大成殿前面、泮池北面，是高出地面1米的台式石建筑，为古代文武官员绅士祭孔时跪拜及歌舞之地。

Pan Palace Gate

Pan Palace Gate, also known as Saint Gate, is the school palace. In front of the vassal school of the Zhou Dynasty, there is a half-moon-shaped pool called *Panshui*. The school of the vassal is called *Pan* Palace, which is intended to build the school palace by the water side. The Sage *Kongqiu*, known as "the King of Integrity", promoted from "*Xuan Ni* King" to "*Jin Xuan* King" through many dynasties, was recorded as" the good example of all civil officials, the teacher of all emperors of all dynasties ". Therefore, the imperial examination system of the Ming and Qing Dynasties stipulated that new students who entered the county school must visit the palace and pay homage to *Kongqiu*, called *Pan* Palace-entering or *Pan* Palace-Visiting. And many couplets were written in *Pan* Palace upstairs in many Confucian Temples: " the important town in southeastern Fukien; seals and cultural relics with Zoulu *heritage*."

Lingxing Gate

Lingxing Gate is also known as the *Xianshi* gate. According to legend, *Lingxing* is the sky town star, that is, the sky literary star. Confucian temple gate named after "*Ling xing*" means that The Sage *Kongqiu* fell from the sky. The existing stone components are built in the Ming Dynasty, with six columns and three open rooms, with a symmetrical layout, each column foot with two flagpole stones, front and back clip. The walls of the east and west wings are inlaid 2.62 meters long and 0.73 meters wide, with granite carved couplets in regular *Yin* script of "*Jianghan Qiuyang*" and "*Jinsheng Yu Zhen*". In front of the door, three additional steps were repaired, with the Lingxing gate and the street separated by a short distance.

Dacheng Gate, Gold Sound Gate and Jade Vibration Gate

Dacheng Gate is the central gate of the second courtyard of the Confucian Temple, which is an existing building in the late Qing Dynasty. *Dacheng* Gate, also called halberd Door in ancient times, is five rooms wide, two rooms deep, with middle three roof high above both sides, and three pairs of drum-embracing bluestones, eight stone-eaves columns. On the left side of *Dacheng* Gate are two stone tablets of *Essay on the Reconstruction of Fuzhou Confucian Temple in the first year of Xianfeng Emperor*. It is 2.68 meters high, 0.84 meters wide and 0.21 meters thick. *Guo Baiyin* wrote a 190-word inscription and *Liu Yongsong*'s stone script of seeking craftsmanship. Standing in front of the two tablets calmly, the *Yin* inscriptions will gradually appear, presenting the miraculous effect of the *Yang* inscriptions.

Dacheng Gate, Gold Sound Gate and Jade Vibration Gate are named from the "completion" theory of ancient sages. As Mencius said, " Confucius is the master, with golden sound and jade vibration." This is to praise the Confucius "who opened heaven and earth with integrity", and "who set a moral example for ancient and modern times", echoing with *Dacheng* palace, the center of the Confucian Temple.

Panchi and Platform

*Pan*chi was in front of the *Dacheng* temple, half-moon shaped, south bank semicircular, north bank straight, linking to the tide. In the middle of a stone bridge, the length of the bridge is about 20 meters, with the middle of slightl arch protrusion. Stone slabs spread horizontally on the top, with fences as the protection. Stone statues are carved on the column, symbolizing the scene of peace. There are 72 bridge boards, representing the 72 wise disciples of Confucius. If walking on the bridge, one has a sense of grace and dignity. The platform is also called terrace and worship pavilion. In front of *Dacheng* Hall and in the north of *Panchi*, it is a platform with stone one meter above the ground, where ancient civil and military officials kneel and dance when worshiping Confucius.

大成殿及两庑

大成殿为孔庙的主体建筑，是祭祀孔子的正殿。大成殿雄踞于高出埕面1.46米的石台基上，面阔七间、进深四间，重檐歇山顶，穿斗式木结构辅以石柱，有石檐柱22根、石内柱8根。石柱硕大，按花岗岩每立方米2.8吨计，石内柱每根重达约9吨，石檐柱每根重8吨有奇，当年施工艰难由此可见一斑。殿中上部藻井顶部有一精美的古星象图，星座金光熠熠。

大殿内安放着新制的青石雕刻孔子坐像，高25.51米，基座厚1.18米。孔子塑像两边分别安放孔子最出色的四名弟子的青石雕刻坐像——复圣颜子、宗圣曾子、述圣子思子、亚圣孟子，通高3.45米。东、西、北三面绕孔子坐像立着七十二贤人青石雕刻造像，形态各异、栩栩如生。殿内的儒家青石群雕造像，在表现技法上注重质感和比例，形神兼备，雕刻精美洗练。同时展示了儒家现实生活气息的境界，形象丰满圆润，气质浑厚，衣饰简素，具有轻快流畅的特色。

文庙内的正殿"大成殿"供奉被尊为"万世师表"的孔子。大殿上方悬挂着清朝历代皇帝的题词匾额，有康熙皇帝御书"万世师表"，雍正皇帝御书"生民未有"，嘉庆皇帝御书"圣集大成"等，金碧辉煌，尽显隆恩。

孔庙陈列的文物

大成殿内陈列的文物分为祭孔的礼器、乐器、舞器（均为清康熙年间仿古制做成），儒家经典著作，历代名人的遗著遗物三大部分。

礼器

礼乐文化是儒家学说的主要内容之一，后代统治阶级以之作为规定。儒家制定的礼教秩序，用以约束人际关系，称为礼治。孔子要求人们守礼并要用乐来配合。"礼严肃形于外，乐和顺存于内。"礼有乐配合，增强了礼的教化作用。

礼器是古代贵族在举行祭祀、宴飨、征伐及丧葬等活动时使用的器物，有不同的等级、规制。公元前478年，孔子逝后的第二年，鲁哀公命将其故居改建为庙，用于收藏孔子生前所用的衣、冠、琴、车、书之类。汉高祖十二年（前195年），以太牢（猪、牛、羊各一）祭礼孔子，开历代帝王祭孔的先河。北魏孝文帝太和十六年（492年）始规定，每年春秋二仲（二、八月）举行祭孔大典，即"大祭"，又称"丁祭"，并由皇帝颁定祭孔祀仪，包括祭典程序、祭奠规格、乐舞编制、主持官员以及服饰、舞具和供品等。

Dacheng Hall and Two Verandas

Dacheng Hall is the main building of the Confucian Temple, the main hall of ancestor worship. *Dacheng* Hall is located 1.46 meters above the stone platform. Seven wide rooms, four deep rooms, and double eaves rest on the mountain top, through the bucket type wooden structure paved with stone columns, with stone eaves in column 22, stone inner in column 8. The pillar is huge, with a granite column weighing 2.8 tons per cubic meter, the stone inner column weighs about 9 tons each, and the stone eaves column weighs 8 tons each. This shows the difficult construction of that year. On top of the upper part of the temple is a beautiful ancient star image, with golden light of the constellation.

Inside the hall is a newly carved bluestone of seated-statue Confucius, 25.51 meters high with 1.18 meters-high base. On both sides of the statue are the four outstanding disciples of seated statues of carved bluestone: Yan Zi, Zeng Zi, Si Zi and Mencius, with an average height of 3.45 meters. In the three sides of east, west and north around Confucius standing 72 sage bluestone carving statues, in different lifelike forms. The Confucian bluestone group carved statues in the hall focused more on texture and proportion in the expression techniques, both in shape and spirit, exquisite carving and washing. At the same time, it shows the realm of the Confucian real life atmosphere. The images are of plump and round, rich temperament and simple clothes, with light and smooth feature.

The main hall of the Confucian Temple "*Dacheng* Hall" is dedicated to Confucius, " the role model of all dynasties ", and above the hall there are inscribed tablets of the emperors of the Qing Dynasty. Hanging on the above are the tablets " the role model of all dynasties " written by the Qing Dynasty Kangxi Emperor, "The chosen one never witnessed before" written by Yongzheng Emperor, "Master of Achievements" written by Jiaqing Emperor honored by the long grace of all emperors.

Cultural Relics Displayed at Confucian Temple

There are about 500 pieces of cultural relics displayed in *Dacheng* Palace, which are divided into three parts: ritual vessels, musical instruments and dancing instruments(imitating the ancient period of Kangxi Emperor of the Qing Dynasty), the classics of Confucius and Mencius, and the relics of celebrities in all dynasties.

The Ritual Apparatus

Musical Rite is one of the main contents of Confucianism. The subsequent ruling class took it as a regulation, and its numerous rites were used to restrain interpersonal relationships, called etiquette management. As Confucius advocated, when people keep the etiquette, they should use music to cooperate. "Rites are serious outside, and music exists harmoniously inside." Music cooperates with rite, thus enhancing the educational role of rites.

The ritual instruments are used for different occsions with different hierarchy. In 478 BC, the second year after Confucius' death, Duke Lu decided to erect his former residence as Confucian temple, which includes something like the "clothes, crown, chariot and book" used by Mr. *Kong Qiu*.

In the 12th year of Emperor *Gaozu* of the Han Dynasty(195 BC), "*Tailao*(pig, cow, sheep each) were offered as the sacrifices to Confucius", setting a precedent for successive emperors to worship Confucius. In the 16th year of Emperor *Xiaowen* of the Northern Wei Dynasty(492), the ceremony was held every year(February and August), which is also called "Grand sacrifice" or "*Ding* sacrifice". And the emperor decided the ceremony, including the ancestral procedures, memorial specifications, music and dance, official presiders, costumes, dancing utensils and offerings, etc.

大成殿内所陈列的礼器有铜尊（含铜牺尊）、铜壶、铜豆、铜爵，以及竹木祭器和木雕祭器等，工艺精致，风格迥殊。其中，云雷尊为初献（第一次奠酒）楚酒之用，以表示神自天而降之意；象尊用于亚献（第二次奠酒），以表示大而有德之意；牺尊形如牛状，用于终献（最后一次奠酒），表示以农立国、永不忘本之意。此三次奠酒总称为"三献礼"。其余各器均作盛五谷、酱料、果品之用。

乐器与舞器

祭孔乐舞也属古代礼仪形式的组成部分，为公元前6世纪流行于鲁国的《韶乐》。乐以颂扬孔子功德为主要内容，其格律是对我国周代雅颂乐歌诗体的承袭。殿内陈列有成套编钟和编磬，还陈列各种吹奏乐器。这些吹奏乐器合奏起来相当幽雅柔和，并且所有陈列的器乐均有其实用价值。

乐舞分为"文舞"与"武舞"。明代以来祭孔典礼固定为六个程序，即迎神、初献、亚献、终献、撤撰、送神等。祭典中使用的乐舞依随释祭仪程固定为六个乐章，其思想内容上集中反映了一个"德"字，表现形式上突出体现了一个"礼"字。舞容庄重文静，又不失抒情之美，以崇颂孔子的功德，显耀统治者的治定功成。除此之外，殿中两旁还陈列着清代文武官员的礼服和文武舞蹈用的道具。

历代名人的遗著遗物

封建时代，文庙府学是培养人才的地方，凡考中秀才者必须先入泮宫，进大成殿拜谒孔子。历朝历代福建各地孔庙培养出来的举人、进士很多。比较著名的有唐代文学家、诗人欧阳詹，宋代政治家、思想家曾公亮，宋代状元、政治家梁克家，明代文学家王慎中，明代史学家何乔远，明代进步思想家李贽，明代书法家张瑞图，明末清初民族英雄郑成功和爱国将领施琅，清初理学家、文渊阁大学士李光地等。

The ritual vessels displayed in *Dacheng* Hall include bronze statues, bronze pots, and bamboo and wood carving sacrifices, with exquisite craftsmanship and different styles. *Yunlei* statue is for the first sacrifice to hold *chu* alcohol, to show the meaning of gods from the sky; the elephant statue is for the second sacrifice of holding alcohol, to show the great and moral level; the animal statue is for the final sacrifice, to establish the country via agriculture by never forgetting the origin. These three times' alcohol sacrifice are always called "three gifts". The rest of the utensils are used to hold grain, sauce, fruit.

Musical Instruments and Dancing Instrument

Music and dance of sacrificing to Confucius is an integral part of the ancient ceremonial form, and it is *Shao music*, which was popular in the state of *Lu* in more than 500 BC. Music took the form of praising the merits and virtues of Confucius as the main content. Its meter is the inheritance of the poetic style of the Zhou Dynasty. The hall displays a complete set of bells and rock, with a variety of playing instruments. All these musical instruments played together are quite elegant and soft, with practical values.

The form of sacrificial dance is divided into "literary dance" and "martial arts dance", as the affiliated etiquette form. Since the Ming Dynasty, the sacrificial ceremony has been arranged into six agendas: "greeting the god", "first offering", "second offering", "final offering", "removal of writing", "seeing off the gods" and so on. The music and dance used in the ancestral ceremony followed six ritual procedures. Its ideological content well reflects the Chinese character--- "virtue", and its expressive form prominently reflects the Chinese character --- "ritual". The dance idea inherited the aesthetic concept of "Harmony" advocated by *Kong Qiu*. The dance form belongs to the ancient "dance of virtue", solemn and quiet, which does not lose the lyrical beauty of the dance. It praises the merits of *Kong Qiu* and shows the achievements of the ruler. In addition, the costumes and dance props of the civil and military officials in the Qing Dynasty are also displayed on both sides of the hall.

Relics of the Celebrities of All Dynasties

In feudal times, the Confucian Temples were places to cultivate talents. Those who passed the first level of imperial examination*(Xiucai)*must first enter the *Pan* Palace and pay homage to Confucius. Throughout many dynasties, quite a few of excellent scholars*(Juren and Jinshi)*were cultivated from Confucius temples in Fukien.

The most noticeable and famous are those celebrities, including the writer and poet *Ouyang Zhan* of Tang Dynasty, the politician and scientist *Zeng Gongliang* of the Song Dynasty; the champion(called *zhuangyuan*)and politician *Liang Kejia* of the Song Dynasty; litterateur *Wang Shenzhong* of the Ming Dynasty, the historian *He Qiaoyuan* of Ming Dynasty, the progressive thinker *Li Zhi* of Ming Dynasty; the calligrapher *Zhang Ruitu* of Ming Dynasty; the national hero *Zheng Chenggong* of the late Ming and early Qing Dynasty; the patriotic general *Shi Lang*; the Neo-Confucianist and scholar *Li Guangdi* of early Qing Dynasty, etc.

福建在历史上曾被誉为"海滨邹鲁"、"理学名邦"，尊孔重教之风在八闽大地盛行。为了迎接世界遗产大会在福州召开，2020年福州文庙进行了一系列展陈改造提升工程，新增了"邹鲁名邦 文脉流芳——福州古代教育史展"、"科举鳌首 大魁天下——福州历代状元展"、"识礼明仁 闻乐知德——礼乐文化展"三个展览，有助于人民更深入地了解孔庙背后蕴含的历史文化。如今，福州孔庙已成为福州热门的旅游胜地，不少游客来此处游玩，切身感受孔孟文化，考生及其父母也会到此祈求考试顺利。

◎ 华南女子文理学院

华南女子文理学院原名华南女子大学，系美以美会于1908年在福州创办的一所教会女子大学。为民国时期十三所基督教教会大学之一，与金陵女子大学齐名，在欧美及东南亚各国有很大的影响力。

成立与发展

1859年，女传教士娲标礼和娲西利在美国巴尔的摩中国妇女布道会的支持下，建立了福州毓英女子寄宿学校。在此后的数十年间，外国教会主要是基督教会相继在福州及其附近地区建立了一些以初等教育为主的女子学校。

八国联军侵华和《辛丑条约》的签订，使中国完全沦为半殖民地半封建社会。为了进一步从思想上对中国妇女进行控制，吸引更多的女子信教，扩大教会在中国尤其是华南地区的影响力，教会开始对妇女实施多层次教育。1904年在美国洛杉矶召开的美以美会的年会上，女传教士程吕底亚呼吁在福州建立一所女子大学，美以美会会督詹姆斯·福特对此表示支持，并于同年10月20日到达福州，会同程吕底亚等人对创办女子大学一事进行实地调查与具体商讨。

他们从福州的地理与文化的角度考察，均认为有设立高级女校、提高女子教育水平之必要。一些教会人士还认为，福建系中国的教育中心之一，又是基督教美以美会的发祥之地，福建的基督教徒约占全国基督教徒的七分之一，其中有不少是妇女，因此在福建省城设立一所女子大学，以培养一批高级女教牧人员具有十分重要的意义。

Historically, Fukien was once known as the "seaside *Zou Lu* with rich culture", "the famous state of Neo-Confucianism", with the popular practice of respecting Confucius and valuing religion in Fukien. In 2020, in order to hold the world heritage conference in Fuzhou, Fuzhou temple was updated for a series of exhibition projects, *"The famous state of seaside Zou lu with rich culture—an exhibition of the ancient education history", "The best talents out of the imperial examination—an exhibition of champions of Fuzhou in different dynasties", "Knowing etiquette and benevolence and gaining music and virtue—an exhibition of rites and music culture"*. These three exhibitions help people get a deeper understanding of the temple behind the history and culture. Now, the Confucius Temple in Fuzhou has become a popular tourist resort. Many tourists can experience the Confucius and Mencius culture by visiting here. The parents and examinees will also pray for a smooth and successful test here.

◎ Hwa-Nan Women's College of Arts and Sciences

Hwa-Nan Women's College of Arts and Sciences, formerly known as South China Women's University, is a missionary women's university founded in Fuzhou, China, by the Christian Methodist Episcopal Church Women's Sermon Association in 1907. It is one of the 13 Christian church universities in Old China. It is as famous as Nanking Women's College and enjoys a wide prestige in Europe, America and Southeast Asian countries.

Establishment and Development

In 1859, the female missionaries *Biaoli Wa* and *Xili Wa*, with the support of the Chinese Women's Sermon Church in Baltimore of the United States, established Fuzhou *Yuying* Women's boarding school. In the following decades, foreign churches, mainly Christian churches, have successively established some primary education-oriented girls' schools in Fuzhou and its nearby areas.

After the failure of the Boxer Rebellion Movement, China was completely reduced to a semi-colonial country. In order to further strengthen the ideological control of Chinese women, attract more women to believe in religion, and expand the influence of the church in China, especially in southern China, the church began to implement a more multi-level education for women. At the annual meeting in Los Angeles of America, Lydia Cheng, a female missionary, called for the establishment of a women's university in Fuzhou. James Bertz Ford, President of the Christian Methodist Episcopal Church supported this proposal, and after arriving in Fuzhou, together with Cheng Lydia and others, he carried out field investigation and specific discussion of establishing women's university.

From the perspective of geography and culture in Fuzhou, they all believed that it was necessary to set up senior girls' schools to improve women's education. Some church members also believed that Fukien was one of the educational centers of China and the birthplace of the Christian Church of America. The Christians in Fukien accounted for about one-seventh of all national Christians, many of whom were women. Therefore, it is of great significance to set up a women's university in Fukien Province to train a group of senior female pastoral staff.

1905年5月18日，美以美会代表大会在上海召开，会议决定在福州创建一所华南地区的女子大学。1907年5月，华南女子大学正式成立，1908年1月程吕底亚被任命为第一任校长。学校校址选在福州仓山梅坞岭后。教会人士普遍认为，这是一个寓布道于办学、实施女子教育的好地方。这所大学也是当时在上海以南唯一一所为妇女创设的大学。

抗战期间，福州、厦门等地的一些学校陆续迁往闽北山区，华南女子文理学院也内迁至山城南平，以教会所办的剑津中学为校址，教育教学活动继续进行，直至抗战胜利后才迁回福州。

解放后，人民政府于1951年4月接办这所学校，并将之与另一所著名的教会大学福建协和大学合并，定名为"福州大学"。又经数次合并调整，1953年9月改称"福建师范学院"，至此结束了从华南女子大学到华南女子文理学院总计四十五年的历史。

规模与建筑

华南女子文理学院初创时期，租赁民房作校舍。经多年经营，逐步形成了一所占地40余亩、规模较大、设施较齐备的新式学校。同教会在其他地方所办的学校一样，该校教舍也盖得富丽堂皇，引人注目。

华南女子文理学院的建筑师是来自美国爱荷华州（Iowa）苏城（Sioux）的毕齐（Wilfred W. Beach）。毕齐设计的最为著名的作品之一，是美国爱荷华州苏城的晨边学院（Morningside College）卢思义楼（Lewis Hall）。根据Tiothy T. Orwig的《晨边学院：一个世纪的历史》一书，毕齐将卢思义楼的设计图做了修改，设计了华南女子文理学院的马莲彭楼。

其主体建筑于1911年12月奠基，1925年全部建成，主要包括办公室兼教室的彭氏大楼、可容纳150名学生的谷莲堂宿舍、为纪念程吕底亚修建的立雪楼宿舍以及家事实习室、科学馆、图书馆、礼堂以及其他学生宿舍、教员宿舍等多栋建筑。校内还有网球场、篮球场等运动场所，图书馆藏有中、英文书籍三万余卷，报刊数百种。校舍的建筑风格以西式为主，其规模同当时国内一些著名的大学相比毫不逊色。时至今日，走进华南女子文理学院旧址，仍可一睹当年主要教学楼——彭氏楼、谷莲楼和程氏楼的风采。

华南女子文理学院的中间主楼为马莲彭学院，俗称彭氏楼，现名胜利楼，由马莲彭为纪念其女儿捐款修建。该楼于1911年12月12日奠基，1914年启用。但在1941年2月9日突然起火，大楼上部坍塌。抗战胜利后基本修复，为三层框架结构，建筑面积2790平方米。

On May 18, 1905, the Methodist Episcopal Church Congress was held in Shanghai, which decided to establish a women's university in South China in Fuzhou. In May 1907, South China Women's University was formally established, and in January 1908, Cheng Lydia was appointed as the first president. The school site is selected at the back of Meiwu Ridge in Cangshan, Fuzhou. Church people generally believed this was an ideal place to preach during women's education. The university was also the only university consisting of women around south of Shanghai at the time.

During the Anti-Japanese War, some schools in Fuzhou, Xiamen and other places successively moved to the mountainous areas of northern Fukien, and South China Women's Arts and Science College also moved to Nanping, the mountainous city. Taking *Jian Jin* Middle School run by the church as the school site, the education and teaching activities continued until they moved back to Fuzhou after the victory of the Anti-Japanese War.

After liberation, the people's government took over the school in April 1951, and merged it with another famous church university — Fukien Concord University, and named it "Fuzhou University". In September 1953, it was renamed "Fukien Normal University", thus ending the 45-year history from South China Women's University to Hwa-Nan Women's College of Arts and Sciences.

Scale and Construction

At the beginning of South China Women's University, it relied on rented private houses as school buildings. After many years of management, it has gradually formed a new school covering an area of more than 40 *mu*, with large scale and more complete facilities. Like the schools run by the church elsewhere, the teaching premises of the South China Women's University were magnificent and conspicuous.

The architect of South China Women's University is Wilfred W. Beach, from Sioux City, Iowa. One of the most famous works is the *Lu Siyi* Building(Lewis Hall)of Morningside College in Sioux City, Iowa, USA. According to Tiothy T. Orwig's book, *Morningside College: A History of a Century,* Beach modified the design of the *Lu Siyi* Building and designed the Malian Payne Building of South China Women's University.

The foundation stone of its main building was laid in December 1911 and was completed in 1925. The main buildings include the Payne's office and classroom building, the *Gulian* Hall dormitory(which can accommodate 150 students), the Snow Building dormitory(built to commemorate Cheng Lidya), the family practice room, science hall, library, auditorium, student dormitory, faculty dormitory and many other buildings. There are also tennis courts, basketball courts and other sports venues. The library contains more than 30, 000 volumes of Chinese and English books, and hundreds of newspapers and magazines. The architectural style of the school building was mainly western style, and its scale was no inferior to some famous universities in China at that time. Today, walking into the former site of South China Women's College of Arts and Sciences, you can still see the main teaching buildings, including Payne Building, *Gulian* Building and *Cheng* Building.

The middle main building of Hwa-Nan Women's College of Arts and Sciences is *Malian* Payne Hall, commonly known as the Payne's Building, now known as *Shengli* Building because Mr. J.D. Payne donated to build in memory of his daughter. The cornerstone was laid on December 12, 1911, and it was opened in 1914. But on February 9, 1941, a fire burst out and the upper part of the building collapsed. After the victory of the War of Resistance against Japan, it was basically restored as a three-story frame structure with a construction area of 2,790 square meters.

右侧为谷莲堂宿舍，俗称谷莲楼，又名谷氏楼。该楼是美以美会哥伦比亚河支会为纪念前任支会主席劳拉夫人（Mrs.Laura Granston）而认捐修建的，于1914年正式启用。现名和平楼。

左侧为程吕底亚宿舍（Lydia A.Trimble Hall），俗称程氏楼。1922年为满足学生人数的增加而兴建，1925年落成。建楼资金来自学生及校友捐款，为纪念第一任校长程吕底亚建校功绩而命名，现名民主楼。谷氏楼与程氏楼均为三层砖木结构，建筑面积均为2720平方米。

课程与管理

在课程教学上，学校开始只设预科班。在1914年2月，开设了大学一、二年级的课程。1916年，有五位学生完成二年级的课程。

首任校长程吕底亚认为，要充分发挥这所学校的作用、扩大社会影响，就必须多招学生，增加班级，提高教育层次。于是1917年，华南女子大学开设了大学四年级全部课程。1921年1月，华南女子大学首批三名学生修完大学本科课程顺利毕业。1925年初，程吕底亚辞职，由美以美会在中国的教育副秘书卢爱德继任校长一职。

从20年代初开始，我国出现了颇具规模的"收回教育权运动"，教会学校受到极大冲击。在此大背景下，1927年国民党政府对教会学校采取了一些限制性措施，规定凡教会学校均应向中国政府注册登记，校长一职应由中国人担任。接着，新成立的福建教育改造委员会决定对包括华南女子大学在内的私立学校实行教育改造，改校长制为委员制。华南女子大学推举陈淑圭、王世静、李美德、黄惠珠、黄惠贞组成校务委员会，由陈淑圭任主席，这五人都曾在美国获得学士和硕士学位。另聘请卢爱德和华惠德担任顾问。

1928年，福建省各级学校奉命取消委员制，恢复校长制。教会学校也经历了同样的变更，原有的五人委员会宣告解散。不久，华南女子大学因不符合普通大学须设有三所学院的规定而改名为"私立华南女子文理学院"，由王世静担任院长，但实际权力仍掌握在教会手中，学校的重大问题均须由教会决定。制改后，华南女子文理学院的文科设国文、英文、教育、史地四个系，理科设生物、数理、化学三个系。

On the right is the Granson Hall Dormitory, commonly known as *Gulian* Building, also known as Gu's Building. The building was built by the Columbia River Branch of the Christian Methodist Episcopal Church in memory of the ex-president, Lady Laura(Mrs. Laura Granston), now known as the *Heping* Building. It was officially opened in 1914.

On the left is Lydia Cheng Hall dormitory, commonly known as Cheng's Building. It was built in 1922 to meet the needs of the increasing number of students, and was completed in 1925, with donations from students and alumni, and was named to commemorate the achievements of the school's founder, the first president(Miss Lydia Trimble). Both Gu and Cheng buildings are three-story brick-and-wood structures, with a construction area of 2720 square meters.

Curriculum and Management

In the teaching curriculum, the school began to set up only preparatory classes. In February 1914, college courses for freshmen and sophomores were offered. In 1916, five students completed all courses of the second year, including four to the United States or Canada, and one to Shanghai Christian Medical University.

Cheng Lydia, the first-appointed president, believed that to give full play of the school's role and expand its social influence, it is necessary to recruit more students, increase its classes and improve the level of education. So, in 1917, South China Women's University established all the courses for the fourth grade. In January 1921, three students graduated from South China Women's University for the first time. In early 1925, Cheng Lydia resigned and was succeeded by Lu Aide, the deputy secretary of education of the Methodist Episcopal Church in China.

Since the early 1920s, there had been a large-scale " movement of recovering the right to education " in China, which has greatly impacted church and school education. Under this context, the 1927 *Kuomintang* government took some restricted measures against church schools. It stipulates that all church schools should be registered with the Chinese government, and the position of presidents should be held by the Chinese people. Then, the newly established Fukien Education and Reform Commission decided to implement educational reform for private schools, including South China Women's University, by changing the principal system to the committee member system. South China Women's University elected *Chen Shugui, Wang Shijing, Li Meide, Huang Huizhu* and *Huang Huizhen* to form the university administration committee, with *Chen Shugui* as the chairman. Five of the Council received Bachelor's and Master's degrees in the United States, and hired Lu Aide and Hua Wade as counselors.

In 1928, schools at all levels in Fukien province were ordered to cancel the committee member system and restore the principal system. Church schools also changed, and the original five-member committee was disintegrated. Soon after, South China Women's University was renamed "private Hwa-Nan Women's College of Arts and Sciences College" because it did not meet the requirements of having three colleges. *Wang Shijing* was the dean, but the actual power was still in the hands of the church, and the major issues of the school must be decided by the church. After the reform, South China College of Women's Arts and Sciences has four departments of Chinese, English, education and history, and three departments of biology, mathematics and chemistry.

华南女子文理学院
South China College of Women's Arts and Sciences

　　在近半个世纪的岁月里，这所学校的所有教育教学活动都是紧紧围绕传播宗教思想、培养女教人员和虔诚的教徒这一总目标来进行的。为了有效地实现教会的培养目标，这所学校十分重视管理，有针对性地选择各种教育内容。在学校管理方面，该校建立了比较严密的三级教育管理体制，加强师资的选配、管理，并注重对学生的管理。

　　在具体的教育活动中，一方面，该校十分重视宗教内容和英文教学，在课程设置和课外活动中，宗教灌输和宗教活动始终居首位，使学生接受宗教意识的熏陶和宗教思想的渗透。另一方面，英文教学也是重要的教学环节。教会人士认为，在教会学校中加强英语教学可以训练中国人的智力，消除学生的排外情绪，促进东西方之间的了解，有助于培养适合政治活动和经济活动的新式人才。

　　同时，学校对学生的社会教育给予比较多的关注，是该校教育的一大特色。学生每逢星期日都到周围农村的主日学校担任义务教员。社教活动以妇女儿童为主要服务对象，主要目的是鼓励和指导学生对服务事业的研究和选择，加强学生对服务人生的信仰，从实地经验中认识服务的意义和价值。同时，在妇女中开展扫盲，促进健康，培养（妇女）服务的人生观与宗教信仰，使其能应付困难，抵御不良潮流，努力进行社会改革与服务事业。

For nearly half a century, all the educational and teaching activities of the school had been centered around the general goal of spreading religious ideas and cultivating women and devout believers. In order to effectively achieve the training goal of the church, the school attached great importance to strengthening management and chose various kinds of educational content accordingly. In terms of school management, the school had built a relatively strict three-level education management system, enhancing the selection and management of teachers and students.

In the specific educational activities, on one hand, the school attached great importance to the religious content and English teaching. In the curriculum and extracurricular activities, religious indoctrination and religious activities have always been listed in the first place, so that students can accept the influence of religion and the infiltration of western thought. On the other hand, English teaching is also important. Church people believed that strengthening English teaching in church schools can train the intelligence of Chinese people, eradicate students' xenophobia, promote the understanding between the East and the West, and help cultivate new talents suitable for political and economic activities.

At the same time, the school paid great attention to the students' social education, which is a major feature of school education. Students attend Sunday schools in the surrounding countryside. Taking women and children as the main service object, the main purpose of social education activities was to encourage and guide students' research and choice of service causes, strengthen students' belief in service life, realizing the significance and value of service from practice. At the same time, it was to eliminate illiteracy among women, promote health, cultivate(women)service outlook on life and religious beliefs, enable them to cope with difficulties, resist the deteriorating trend, and strive for social reform and service cause.

总而言之，这所学校的创办可看作我国近代女子高等教育的发端。其教育教学方面的一些内容，体现了西方新式教育系统的进步性，对传统的中国文化形成了一定的冲击，对于启迪中国妇女更深入地认识外部世界、接受新的科学成果具有积极的意义。在这所思想控制较为严格的女子大学里，也出现了革命思想和爱国思想的萌芽。辛亥革命爆发时，该校的一些师生积极参加红十字会，以实际行动支持革命军。辛亥革命胜利后，孙中山先生莅临福州，该校学生踊跃参加了欢迎孙中山先生的大会。

1996年，因建造三县洲大桥，华南女子文理学院差点儿被拆，幸得福建师大与一些有识之士力保，最终促使大桥引桥部分略作移位，这座福州市区外观最漂亮、保存也最为完整的民国建筑才得以留存。历经风雨的华南女子文理学院，如今已成为福建师范大学仓山校部办公场所，被师大学子亲切地称为"老校部"，不断有包括师大人在内的许多访客前来参观，追忆百年师大的沧桑与荣光。

◎ 马高爱医院

如今说起福州的马高爱医院（Magaw Memorial Hospital），也许没有多少人能够记得。我们来到仓山对湖路与上三路交叉口，感受着历史留下的温度，让思绪徜徉：百年之前，在这片土地上建起了中国最早的妇孺医院，它是福建医科大学附属协和医院的前身之一——马高爱医院。

马高爱医院在光绪三年（1877年）由西格尼·特拉斯克小姐（Miss Sigourney Trask）创办，选址在福州仓山区岭后路一片被称为"开心谷"的墓地，与华南女子文理学院隔街相望，并以捐资者巴尔的摩的一位女信徒的名字命名。这是中国第一家妇女和儿童专门医院，当地人也称之为"岭后妇孺医院"。

据说，最初的马高爱医院是一座简易的两层砖楼，仅用屏风把女医生的住所与病人隔开。这座楼在宣统二年（1910年）前后因台风倒塌，后于民国元年（1912年）重建，是当时全国最大的妇女儿童医院。在这里，外科、产科、手术室、药房、病房、实验室、办公室和教学室等一应俱全，设有独立的门诊部，同时还配有现代化的洗衣房、电梯、排球场和网球场等。

In a word, it should be objectively pointed out that the establishment of this school is the beginning of modern women's higher education in China. Some contents of its education and teaching reflected the progress of the new knowledge system of western education, with a certain impact on the traditional Chinese culture. It had a positive significance for enlightening Chinese women to have a deeper understanding of the external world and accept new scientific achievements. In this women's university with more strict ideological control, there is also the bud of revolutionary thought and patriotic thought. When the Revolution of 1911 broke out, some teachers and students took an active part in the Red Cross and supported the revolutionary army with practical actions. After the victory of the Revolution of 1911, Dr. Sun Yat-sen came to Fuzhou. The students of the school enthusiastically attended the conference to welcome Dr. Sun Yat-sen.

In 1996, due to the construction of the *San Xian Zhou* Bridge, South China College of Women's Arts and Sciences was almost demolished. Fortunately, Fukien Normal University and some people of insight defended it, and finally the lead part of the bridge was slightly displaced, and the most beautiful building of Old China in Fuzhou, was luckily retained. After wind and rain, South China College of Arts and Sciences has been preserved. Now, it has become the office of Cangshan Campus of Fukien Normal University, which is affectionately called "Old Campus" by the students of Fukien Normal University. The visitors including many graduates from Fukien Normal University visit here to recall the vicissitudes and glory of Century-old University.

◎ **Magaw Memorial Hospital**

Now, speaking of the Ma Gaoai Memorial Hospital(Magaw Memorial Hospital)in Fuzhou, perhaps not many people can remember. When I came to the intersection of *Duihu* Road and *Shangsan* Road in Canhshan District, I felt the history and let my thoughts wander around. A hundred years ago, the earliest women and children hospital in China was built on this land, and it was also one of the predecessors of the Union Hospital affiliated to Fukien Medical University—Magaw Memorial Hospital.

Ma Gaoai hospital, in the third year of *Guangxu* Emperor(1877), was founded by Miss Sigourney Trask, located in a place called "happy valley" cemetery in *Linghou* Road of Cangshan, opposite to south China Women's Liberal and Arts College across the street. And it is named "Magaw Memorial Hospital" after a female believer of donor---Baltimore. It is the first specialized hospital for women and children in China, also known as "*Linghou* Women and Children Hospital".

It is said that the original Ma Gaoai Hospital was a simple, two-story brick building, using only screens to separate the female doctor's residence from the patient. The building collapsed in the second year of *Xuantong* Emperor(1910 AD)due to a typhoon, and was later rebuilt in the first year of the Republic of China(1912 AD). It was the largest women and children's hospital in China at that time. Here, surgery, obstetrics, operating room, pharmacy, wards, laboratories, offices, and teaching rooms are all available, with an independent outpatient department, and a modern laundry, elevator, volleyball and tennis courts.

　　重建的马高爱医院大楼为砖混结构，两层带地下室，占地840平方米，呈八字型单外廊平面。外廊位于八字型的"内院"一面，为标准的券廊式结构。建筑外侧立面则造型简洁，除了简单的檐口线脚和半圆形券窗外，没有其他装饰。底层主入口处设有门廊三间，呈新古典主义风格。楼前是宽敞的空地，白色的水泥道路旁种了棕榈、玫瑰、竹子、芭蕉等各种花草树木。

　　此后不久，医院再次扩建。在紧挨医院的东南面买了32间中式房子，粉刷翻新后可收治五六十个病人，成立了福州第一所隔离医院。马高爱医院为近代福州带来了一大批优秀的医学、医务工作者。

　　民国25年（1936年），马高爱医院同中华基督教会创办的"圣教妇孺医院"合并。由于是联合办院，故名为"福州基督教协和医院"（Willis F.Pierce Memorial Hospital），由医院董事会进行管理，并迁往城内太平街"圣教妇孺医院"原址，聘请美国建筑师范哲明为新医院的建筑师。1936年6月26日，在福州太平街破土动工，1938年正式投入使用。新址落成后，马高爱医院的大部分设备被搬到新医院，只在岭后路留下一家诊所。

　　马高爱医院迁出后，原建筑拨给华南女子文理学院附属高级中学使用，作为教学综合楼。华南女子文理学院附中在原来三层楼平屋顶上加盖了一层，增加的一层采用相同的红砖砌筑，木三角桁架坡屋顶四面出檐，小青瓦屋面。

　　1951年，华南女子文理学院附属高级中学和鹤龄英华中学、陶淑女子中学合并，成立福州第二中学，1952年更名为福州大学附属中学，1953年迁往原寻珍女子中学校园。原建筑改归福建师范大学（由原福州大学更名，不是现在的福州大学）教育系使用，后又归福建师范大学数学系等使用。

　　非常遗憾的是，1997年，因上三路拓宽，马高爱医院建筑被拆毁。

　　时至今日，马高爱医院建筑虽已被拆毁，但是与之相关的人物、事迹依然留存于世，在民间广为流传。

西格尼·特拉斯克小姐

　　1874年10月5日，毕业于美国纽约女子医药大学的西格尼·特拉斯克小姐（Miss Sigourney Trask），作为海外妇女传教会的第一批医学传教士，从圣弗朗西斯科乘船驶向中国，在茫茫大海上漂泊了整整一个月后才抵达福州。她从美国和香港地区带了一些西药，在教堂设了一家小诊所，开始给妇女儿童看病，每周两次。教会指定特拉斯克小姐负责建造第一家妇女医院，即马高爱医院。

The rebuilt Ma Gaoai Hospital is a brick-and-concrete structure, two floors with basement, covering 840 square meters. It is an eight-shaped single outer corridor design, with the outer standard colonial voucher corridor in the "inner courtyard" side. The exterior facade of the building is simple, with no other decoration except for the simple cornice line foot and the semicircular voucher window. The main entrance to the ground floor has three porches, presented in a neoclassical style. In front of the building lies a spacious open space, and along the white cement road are planted a variety of plants including plam trees, roses, bamboo, banana trees, and more.

Shortly thereafter, the hospital expanded again. 32 Chinese-style houses were bought on the southeast side of the hospital, with treatment of 50-60 patients after painting and renovation simultaneously, with the establishment of the first quarantined hospital in Fuzhou. Ma Gaoai Hospital has brought a large numbe. of excellent medical workers to modern Fuzhou.

In the 25th year of the Republic of Old China(1936 AD), Ma Gaoai Hospital and the "Holy Church of Women and Children Hospital" founded by the Chinese Christian Church were merged. Because it is a joint hospital, it is named "Fuzhou Christian Union Hospital(Willis F.Pierce Memorial Hospital)", which is managed by the board of the hospital and moved to the original site of "Holy Women and Children Hospital" on Taiping Street, and hired American architect *Fang Zheming* as the architect of the new hospital. On June 26, 1936, ground was broken on *Taiping* Street in Fuzhou, and it was officially put into use in 1938. After the new site was completed, most of the equipment of Ma Gaoai Hospital was moved to the new site, leaving only one clinic on *Linghou* Road.

After Ma Gaoai Hospital was moved out, the original building was allocated to the Senior High School affiliated to South China Women's College of Arts and Sciences as a teaching complex building. The Affiliated High School of South China University of Arts and Sciences has one more layer on the original three floors; the additional layer uses the same red brick masonry, with a wooden triangular truss hip roof with eaves on all sides and a small green tile roof.

In 1951, the Senior High School affiliated to South China Women's College of Arts and Sciences, *Heling* Anglo-Chinese Middle School and *Tao Shu* Girls' Middle School were merged to form Fuzhou No.2 Middle School. In 1952, it was renamed the High School affiliated to Fuzhou University, and in 1953, it moved to the former Xunzhen Girls' Middle School. The building was changed to the Department of Education of Fukien Normal University(renamed by the original Fuzhou University, not current Fuzhou University), and then returned to the Department of Mathematics of Fukien Normal University.

Unfortunately, in 1997, the building of Ma Gaoai Hospital was demolished due to the widening of ShangSan Road.

Today, although the building of Ma Gaoai Hospital has been demolished, the deeds of the related characters still remain in the world and are widely spread among the people.

Miss Sigourney Trask

On October 5, 1874, Miss Sigourney Trask, who graduated from New York Women's Medical University, sailed to China as the first medical missionaries of the overseas women's missionary society for a whole month before arriving in Fuzhou. She brought some western medicine from the United States and Hong Kong, set up a small clinic in the church, and worked as a doctor for women and children twice a week. The church appointed Miss Trask to build the first women's hospital, Ma Gaoai Memorial Hospital.

西格尼·特拉斯克医生为这家医院的第一任院长，院内有六名外国医生和一名护士。医院收治的第一个病人在这里治愈了五年不能行走的病痛。根据1891年的文献，当年马高爱医院的病人总数达6215人，开出处方6975张，医生出诊1088次。

陈芝美（1896—1972年）

马高爱医院同圣教妇孺医院合并后成立的福州基督教协和医院，由医院董事会进行管理。董事会由各教会和教会学校负责人组成，在医院内办公。医院运转的经费大部分由教会供给，小部分为业务收入及传教士在美国募集的捐款和物资。

值得一提的是，当时医院董事会的董事长叫陈芝美。当时福州有一所非常出名的教会学校，叫鹤龄英华中学，而陈芝美正是英华中学的首任华人校长，他为英华中学的发展做出了极大的贡献。而这所学校也是国民政府主席林森、华侨领袖黄乃裳、空气动力学专家沈元、数学家陈景润等名人的母校。

信宝珠（Cora Eliza Simpson，1880—1960年）

1907年福州迎来了一位美国护士，她有一个优雅的中国名字——信宝珠，有着"中国护士会之母"的称号。民国元年（1912年），正是她在福州创办了在中国注册的第一所护校——佛罗伦萨·南丁格尔护理和助产士培训学校（Florence Nightingale School of Nursing）。学校位于麦园路，隶属于马高爱医院。这所护校即为今福建省卫生职业技术学校的前身。

光绪三十三年（1907年）信宝珠来到福州，就任马高爱医院护士长。她发现，当地病人很多，却没有护士，照顾病人的工作被当作苦力，被人瞧不起。在中国医学会秘书菲律普·高士兰（P. B. Cousland）医生的支持下，信宝珠开始创办护士学校。护士学校于1907年开始教学，1909年颁发了第一份毕业文凭。

从1909年夏天起，信宝珠连续几年在福州鼓岭组织召开全国护士协会筹备会议，1912年拟定了统一的护士培养计划，涉及学校的注册、课程设计、教材、测试以及文凭等。1912年，福州的南丁格尔护校成为在中国护士协会注册的首家护士学校。

民国11年（1922年）信宝珠应聘担任中华护士会总干事，民国33年（1944年）离职返美。民国35年（1946年），第15届中华护士学会全国会员代表大会追认她为荣誉总干事。1960年，信宝珠病逝于美国密歇根州的切尔西。

Dr. Sigurney Trask was the first president of the hospital, with six foreign doctors and a nurse. The first patient admitted to the hospital was cured, ending the pain of not walking for five years and received the Gospel. According to the patient records of 1891, the total number of patients in Ma Gaoai Hospital reached 6, 215, with 6, 975 prescriptions and 1, 088 home visits.

Chen Zhimei (1896-1972)

After the merger of Ma Gaoai Hospital and "Holy Education Women and Children Hospital", Fuzhou Christian Union Hospital was formed. After completion, it was managed by the board of directors of the hospital and composed of the heads of the church and church schools, who work in the hospital. Most of the funds for the hospital operation were provided by the church, with a small amount of business income and donations and supplies raised by missionaries in the United States.

It is worth mentioning that the chairman of the hospital's board at that time was called *Chen Zhimei*. At that time, there was a very famous church school in Fuzhou, called Heling Anglo-Chinese Middle School, and *Chen Zhimei* was the first Chinese principal of Anglo-Chinese Middle School. Chen Zhimei had made great contributions to the development of Anglo-Chinese Middle School. The school is also the Alma mater of celebrities including *Lin Sen*, president of the Kuomingdang government of Old China, Chinese leaders overseas *Huang Naishang*, aerodynamics Shen Yuan and mathematician *Chen Jingrun*.

Xin Baozhu (Cora Eliza Simpson 1880-1960)

In 1907, Fuzhou welcomed an American nurse, an elegant Chinese name, Xin Baozhu, with the title of "Mother of the Chinese Nurses Association". In the first year of Old China(1912), it was this American who founded the first Florence Nightingale School of Nursing in Fuzhou, located in Maiyuan Road, which was affiliated to Ma Gaoai Hospital, the predecessor of today's Fukien Health Vocational and Technical School.

In the 33rd year of Guangxu Emperor(1907), *Xin Baozhu* came to Fuzhou and served as the head nurse of Ma Gaoai Hospital. She found that there were many local patients but no nurses, and that the care of patients was treated as coolies and looked down upon by others. With the support of Dr. Philip Cousland, the secretary of the Chinese Medical Association, Xin Baozhu began to establish a nursing school. The nurse school began teaching in 1907, and the first diploma was issued in 1909.

Since the summer of 1909, Xin Baozhu has organized a preparatory meeting of the National Nurses Association in Guling, Fuzhou, for several consecutive years. In 1912, she formulated a unified training plan for nurses, such as curriculum design, teaching materials, school registration, testing and diploma. In the same year, the Nightingale Nursing School in Fuzhou became the first nursing school registered by the Chinese Nurses Association.

In the 11th year of Old China(1922 AD), Xin Baozhu applied to serve as the director-general of the Chinese Nurses Association, and in the 33rd year of the Republic of Old China(1944 AD), she left and returned to the United States. In the 35th year of the Republic of China(AD 1946 AD), the 15th National Congress of the Chinese Nurses Association decided to ratify her as the honorary Director-General. In Chelsea, Michigan, she passed away in 1960.

许金訇（Hü King-eng，1865—1929年）

许金訇，与金韵梅、康爱德、石美玉一样，是我国最早留学海外习医并回国行医的杰出女性之一。

许金訇出生于福州南台岛（今仓山区）的一个牧师家庭。她的父亲是基督教美以美会的早期信徒。幼年时，父母没有按习俗给许金訇缠足，还送她到教会办的寄宿学校读书。许金訇幼年入毓英女塾读书，并以优异成绩毕业。

当时，马高爱医院正缺人手，许金訇被邀请去当助手，由此立下了成为一名女医生的人生志向。由于她聪慧好学、任劳任怨，对病人充满爱心，医院女院长特拉克（Sigourney Trask）十分欣赏，并通过海外妇女布道会费城分会资助她到美国接受更加全面的医学教育。

光绪十年（1884年）秋，许金訇入读俄亥俄卫斯理大学（Wesleyan University，Delaware，Ohio）。四年后毕业，再入费城宾夕法尼亚女子医学院（现在属于德雷塞尔大学）攻读博士学位，并于1892年进入费城综合医院（Philadelphia Polyclinic）实习。光绪二十一年（1895年），许金訇回到福州，出任新建的和新田妇幼医院（Woolston Memorial Hospital，也译为"娲氏纪念医院"，位于乌塔附近）院长。

民国16年（1927年），和新田妇幼医院被毁，许金訇携妹妹许淑訇离开福州前往新加坡。民国18年（1929年）因脑溢血病逝于新加坡，葬于实龙岗比达达利坟场。

Hü King-eng, 1865-1929

Hü King-eng, Like Jin Yongmei, Kang Aide and Shi Meiyu, is one of the first outstanding Chinese women to study in medicine abroad and return to China. Hü King-eng was born in a priest family in *Nantai* Island(now Cangshan), Fuzhou. Her father was an early believer of the Methodist Episcopal Church. When she was young, her parents did not bind Hu King-eng's feet and sent her to a church-run boarding school. Hu King-eng entered Yuying Girls' School when she was young and graduated with honors.

At that time, Ma Gaoai Hospital was short of staff, and Hü King-eng was invited to be an assistant, thus setting a life ambition to become a female doctor of western medicine. Due to her intelligence and conscientiousness, and full love for patients, the female president of the hospital, (Sigourney Trask), appreciated Hü King-eng and helped her with the Philadelphia branch to receive more comprehensive medical education in the United States.

In the autumn of the tenth year of Emperor Guangxu(1884), Hü King-eng enrolled at Wesleyan University in Ohio, graduated four years later, and then entered Pennsylvania Women's Medical College of Philadelphia for a doctorate(currently belonging to Drexel University)and then began his internship at Philadelphia General Hospital in 1892. In the 21st year of *Guangxu* Emperor(1895 AD), Hü King-eng returned to Fuzhou and served as the dean of the newly built *He Xintian* Women's Hospital(also translated as " Woolston Memorial Hospital ", located near Wu tower.)

In the 16th year of Old China(1927), *HeXintian* Women and Children's Hospital was destroyed, Hü King-eng and her sister Hü Shu-eng left Fuzhou for Singapore. In the 18th year of Old China(1929), she died of cerebral haemorrhage in Singapore and was buried in The Bidadali Cemetery.

福州
古暦

第六章

西洋建筑：海纳百川

Chapter Six

Western Architecture: Inclusiveness

Like Rivers into the Sea

漫步福州，走在仓山区的老建筑之中，可以感受充满历史沧桑感的西洋建筑。这些仍留存于世的西洋建筑见证了那个时代福州风云变幻的历史，是一片颇有历史价值且带有欧洲风格的老建筑群。这些西洋建筑隐匿于繁华中，成为一道独特风景。

◎ 美国领事馆

美国领事馆作为福州领事馆群中保存最完好的一栋，久负盛名。其主体为砖木结构的两层楼房，外墙白色，门窗高大，采光和通风条件极佳。清咸丰四年（1854年），美国首任驻福州领事颛士格立（Caleb Jones）在此走马上任，开始了中美文化交流的全新历程。民国时期，美国领事馆馆址用途不断发生改变，在湖路建两座洋楼作为馆舍，之后，曾改为福州卫生学校图书馆，员工宿舍也拆改为学生宿舍。

1840年鸦片战争以后的福州历史，既是近代中国人在西方文明冲击下的抗争史，也是一部中西方文化相互碰撞、认同、融合的交流史。1844年英国领事踏上福州的土地，在给福州人民带来剥削压迫的同时，也带来西方先进的科学技术。这其中就包括了迥然不同的建筑风格和西式的建造技术。

领事馆具有外交特权，在彰显领事国威严的同时，也代表着领事国在国际上的形象。所以我们会看到各国的领事馆建筑大都采用本国当时的建筑风格，一些领事馆建筑的设计图纸也由本国建筑师完成。可以肯定地说，领事馆建筑是西方建筑样式和风格在中国传播的典型代表。

现存的福州美国领馆旧址位于仓山区麦园路84号。根据美国国会图书馆所藏的1868年的历史地图，该建筑当时是医生司徒沃特（Dr.J.A. Stewart）的住宅。他也是英国圣公会差会派遣到中国的第一位传教士。从地图上可以清晰看出，建筑坐北朝南，大门朝南开，对称布置，在南面中部还凸出了一个弧形出龟。

美国政府于咸丰四年正式向福州派出领事颛士格立，并设立领事馆。经过美国领事再三挑选，最终将美国领事馆的馆址选在了烟台山的麦园路84号，与英国领事馆仅隔着一条乐群路，距离当时的万国俱乐部（Foochow Club）——乐群楼也只有短短的100米。

In Fuzhou, walking in the old buildings of Cangshan District, you can feel the western buildings full of the vicissitudes of history. These western buildings remained here witnessed the historical changes of Fuzhou in that period, leaving behind the old buildings of considerable historical values with a European style. These western buildings are the unique scenery hidden in the prosperity of cities.

◎ American Consulate

As the best-preserved consulate in Fuzhou, the American Consulate does not live up to its reputation. The building is a two-story building with white exterior walls, tall doors and windows, and excellent lighting and ventilation conditions. In the fourth year of *Xianfeng* (AD 1854) Emperor, the first American consul in Fuzhou, began a new journey of Sino-American cultural exchanges. From the beginning of Old China, the US Consulate changed constantly, and two houses were built on Lake Road. Later, the US consulate was changed to Fuzhou Health School Library, and the staff dormitory was demolished into student dormitories.

The history of Fuzhou after the Opium War in 1840 is not only the history struggle of modern Chinese under the impact of western civilization, but also the exchange history of the collision, recognition and integration of Chinese and Western cultures. From the moment the British consul set foot on the land of Fuzhou in 1844, he brought exploitation and oppression to the Fuzhou people in time, but also brought advanced western science and technology. This includes the very different architectural styles and western-style construction techniques.

The consulate building is undoubtedly the representative of the forces of various countries in China, not only showing the majesty of the consular states, but also representing the international image of the consular state. So we will see that most of the consulate buildings in various countries are close to the architectural style of the local buildings at that time, and even the designing of some consulate buildings are also completed by the local architects. It is certain that the consulate architecture is a typical representative of the spread of Western architecture in China.

The existing site of Fuzhou American Consulate is located at 84 *Maiyuan* Road, Cangshan District. According to the 1868 historical map of the Library of Congress, the building is the residence for a missionary and doctor(Dr. J.A. Stewart). He was the first missionary sent to China by the Anglican Church. It can be clearly seen from the map that the building faces south, symmetrically arranged, protruding in the south and middle of the building.

In the fourth year of Xianfeng(AD 1854), the United States government officially sent consul Mr. Caleb Jones to Fuzhou to set up a consulate. After repeated selection by the American consul, the site of the American Consulate was finally selected at 84 *Maiyuan* Road in Yantai Mountain, only one road from the British Consulate, and only 100 meters to World Foochow Club, located in *Lequn* Building at that time.

当时在福州的洋行贸易主要以英美洋行为主，来榕的教会也多以英美居多，因此在烟台山一带的外籍人士也以英美籍为多。可能是当时的美国领事考虑到距离英国领事馆近一些能够方便处理事务，才把领事馆的最终地址设在了这里。不过，不像英国领事馆位于烟台山北面，能够眺望闽江、监视船只活动，美国领事馆由于比较迟才建造，已经很难找到地价和地段均适宜的建馆基地了，只能选择在看不到闽江的烟台山南面。

美领馆旧址位于福建省卫生健康监督所的北面，由于地势从入口处逐渐升高，从麦园路并不能看见馆舍。其西面紧邻槐荫里，临街有近3米高的围墙，附近又有大榕树的枝叶遮挡视线，因此从槐荫里只能勉强看见建筑的屋顶。隔着槐荫里对面为福州高级中学（原鹤龄英华中学）。

美领馆旧址有3米多宽可行车的大门，直接朝向北侧乐群路，但是出于管理需要长期紧锁。从乐群路和槐荫里的交叉路口可以望见美领馆旧址的三层以上部分，乐群路对面就是英国领事馆旧址，现在是福建省军区福州第七离职干部休养所烟台山点。

2005年福州卫生学校搬走，实际上还留下一部分教室和宿舍楼，其余部分包括美领馆旧址都归属福建省卫生健康监督所。这两个单位的门牌号都是麦园路84号，从麦园路的同一个大门进入，但内部通过铁围栏隔离，并不相通。这部分教室和宿舍属于福建卫生职业技术学院仓山校区，教室已经废弃不用，宿舍楼给实习生使用。

美国领事馆旧址
The Former Site of the American Consulate

At that time, the foreign trade in Fuzhou was mainly the British and American, and most of the churches and many foreigners in Yantai Mountain were British and American. It may be that the American consul took into consideration the proximity of the British consulate and the convenience of handling affairs, and thus set the final address here. However, unlike the British Consulate, which is located in the north of Yantai Mountain, by overlooking the Minjiang River to monitor the activities of ships, it is difficult for the US Consulate to find a cheap and suitable construction base due to the late construction, only to choose the south of Yantai Mountain, where you cannot see the Minjiang River.

The former site of the American Consulate was located in the north of the Health Supervision Institute base of Fukien Provincial Health Department. As the terrain gradually rises from the entrance, the pavilion cannot be seen from *Maiyuan* Road. The west is close to *Huaiyinli*, and the wall is nearly 3 meters high against the street, and the branches of large banyan trees near it block the sight, so the roof of the building can only be barely seen from the *Huaiyinli*. Across the *Huayinli* is the original "Heling Anglo-Chinese Middle School", which has been changed to Fuzhou Senior High School.

The former site of the American Consulate has a gate more than 3 meters wide, which allows cars to run to the north side, but it is locked for a long time due to management needs. From the intersection of *Lequn* Road and *Huaiyin Li*, you can see just above the third floor of the former American Consulate. Opposite *Lequn* Road is the former site of the British Consulate, which is now the Yantai Mountain Station of the Seventh Fuzhou Cadre Recreation Center of the Fukien Military Area .

In 2005, as Fuzhou Health School moved out, some classrooms and dormitory buildings were left, including the former site of the US Consulate, for the Health Supervision Office of Fukien Provincial Health Department. The doors of these two units are 84# *Maiyuan* Road, respectively, entering from two gates of *Maiyuan* Road, separated by the iron fence, which is not connected. The classrooms had been suspended and the dormitory buildings were used for interns, all belonging to the Cangshan Campus of Fukien Health Vocational and Technical College.

美国领事馆旧址的地势自南向北逐渐升高，这种地形的变化既是对建筑形体的限制因素，又是建筑形体产生的灵感源泉。建筑师巧妙地利用地势相差悬殊的特点，将建筑设计成自西向东的掉层式空间布局——建筑的一层被设计成局部地下室。从西面看，建筑只有两层；而从东面看，建筑却又是三层。从建筑的一、二层均可直接走到室外地面。这样一来，建筑的东西向都拥有良好的采光。而采光面较弱的一层南北向则布置了室外楼梯，丰富了建筑立面。缺少采光的一层西面可以用作储藏室，使空间得到充分利用。

为了消化高差，踏步、坡道等过渡性空间是必不可少的，还能与地形相结合形成错落有致的景观。踏步、楼梯等能对建筑的流线形成导向，让人清楚建筑的平面格局，使美领馆旧址的内部空间和外部空间因地面高度的变化产生动态性，形成具有特殊意味的动态空间。

美国领事馆旧址注重对山地原有环境的维护，强调建筑与各山体地段的融合。以对山地自然环境的最小改变为出发点，充分利用山地等高线，尽量保持山地原有的地形和地貌，使建筑空间与山地空间之间呈现耦合性关系。这表现出对自然的谦卑，易于营造富有人情味、与自然亲和的建筑环境。

美领馆旧址是烟台山"万国建筑博览馆"建筑群的重要组成部分，其建筑造型和立面特征等在当时具有代表性，并具有不可复制的独特性。其外观既有大气的造型，又有众多精彩的细部。整体立面重点突出而又协调统一，庄重而又不失细腻，体现了设计者的非凡匠心。立面设计整体上运用新古典主义建筑语言，局部及细节上又采用了"新艺术运动"倡导的处理手法。屋顶是组合式四坡屋顶与平屋顶的结合，每个立面的坡屋顶天际线变化活跃，建筑内部的空间分隔都反映在屋顶上。

建筑的整体造型自底层到顶层，以不同的材质划分为两段——地下层与底层构成基座部分，二、三层组成上部，下部厚重敦实，上部细腻轻巧。其中，又以南立面最为精彩，东立面次之。

南立面西侧由7根两层通高的柱子组成两层的柱廊空间，其中又分为西段的门廊部分和东段的出龟部分。西段的门廊部分，中间两根为仿塔斯干柱式，柱身长度与直径的比大约为10∶1，两端为方形柱。柱廊由下至上做了三段式过渡处理，从底层厚实的基座过渡到中部轻盈的列柱，再到顶部的额枋和新古典主义式的齿状装饰的檐口。

The terrain of the former site of the consulate was gradually rising from south to north. This change of the terrain was not only the limiting factor of the architectural body, but also the source of inspiration for the body. The architect cleverly took advantage of the current situation of the great terrain height difference to design the building as a space layout from west to east. The first floor of the building was designed as a local basement. From the west, the building had only two floors, while from the east, the building has also three floors. From the first and second floors of the building people can walk directly to the outdoor floor. In this way, both the east and west directions of the building, have good lighting. And the first north-south floor was equipped with outdoor stairs, to enrich dimensions of the building facade. The west side of the floor that lacks light can be used as a storage room to make full use of the space.

In order to reduce the height difference, the transitional space such as steps and ramps will be essential with the combination of the terrain to form a scattered landscape. Steps and stairs can promote a guide to the streamline of the building, and let people make clear the plane pattern of the building, so that the internal space and external space of the former site of the American Consulate will be dynamic due to the change of the ground height, thus forming a dynamic space with a special meaning.

The former site of the American Consulate focused on the maintenance of the original environment of the mountains and the integration of the buildings and various mountain areas. With the minimum change of the image of the natural mountain environment as the starting point, it made full use of the mountain contours, try to maintain the original terrain and landform of the mountain. And the coupling relationship between the building space and the mountain space can be demonstrated to show the humility to nature, creating a human and friendly architectural environment with nature.

The former site of the American Consulate is an important part of the "World Architecture Expo Hall" architectural complex in *Yantai* Mountain. Its architectural shape and facade characteristics represent the architectural art of that time, and its uniqueness cannot be copied. Its appearance has both atmospheric shape and many wonderful details; the overall facade focus is coordinated, unified, solemn and delicate, reflecting the extraordinary ingenuity of the designer. The facade design on the whole uses the neoclassical architectural language, and adopts the processing technique of the New Art Movement in part and details. The roof is a combination of a mixed four-pitched roof and a flat roof. The sloping roof skyline of each facade is active, and the spatial separation inside the building is reflected on the roof.

The overall shape of the building is from the bottom to the top, which can be divided into two different sections. The underground floor and the first floor form the base part. The second and third floors form the upper part, with the lower part thick and solid and the upper part delicate and light. Among them, and the south facade is the most wonderful, and the east facade is the second wonderful.

On the west side of the south facade, seven two-story columns form a two-story colonnade space, which is also divided into the porch section of the western section and the protruding section of the eastern section. In the porch part of the western section, the middle two columns are shaped like the Tas dry column, and the ratio of the column body length and diameter is about 10: 1 with both ends being square columns. The colonnade is a three-section transition process from the bottom to the top, from the thick base on the bottom floor to the light columns in the middle, to the top frontal bar and the neoclassical tooth-like decorated cornice.

建筑的三层外廊做了形式简单的水泥栏杆，栏杆横截面为菱形。二层外廊前还有六级台阶，增强了建筑的气势。东侧突出弧形出龟，中间为仿塔斯干柱式，两端为方形柱式，柱顶部为弧形额枋，再往上有齿饰的檐口和西式的女儿墙，均为弧形。东西两部分各自对称，外廊凹凸变化，错落有致。特别是两层柱廊空间有着明显的新古典主义风格——列柱显示出强烈的秩序感和威严，并采用仿山花的希腊复兴样式，以及新古典主义特征最明显的齿状装饰。

东立面底层外廊有四个石砌拱券，外廊两端的角柱上有楔形扶壁，砌到顶端时带有斜砌式收口，最终形成小斜坡，形式比较灵活自由。扶壁不仅起到稳固墙体的作用，同时也提升了建筑转角的厚重感。二、三层部分后退形成室外平台，有梭形栏杆。

底层为拱券式门窗，二层和三层开矩形门窗，二层的窗户明显比三层的高很多，均是双层木百叶门窗。三层窗户上部有弧形条带样式的窗楣，中间一个锁心石的造型颇有趣味。二、三层白色外墙与一层的石拱廊形成强烈的材质对比，而石拱廊的虚和白墙的实又产生空间对比，丰富了东立面的表现力。而一层凸出的石拱廊内光线较暗，二、三层白墙因直面阳光而较亮，通过光影明暗的对比，更拓展了东立面的空间感。

美国领事馆旧址见证了福州近代历史的发展，见证了中西方文化在福州的交流与融合，反映了福州近代社会、经济、文化的兴衰变化，是研究福州城市发展史的重要实物遗存，具有很高的史学价值。

◎ 汇丰银行

在有"万国建筑博物馆"美称的烟台山历史文化街区里，有英式、哥特式、罗马式以及一大批中西结合的建筑。谈及英式建筑，便不得不提到汇丰银行福州分行旧址。汇丰银行福州分行旧址坐落在仓山区梅坞路，现为仓山区文化馆，平时为市民免费提供文化娱乐大餐，是全国文物保护活化利用的优秀案例。

The three-story outer corridor of the building has simple cement railings, with a diamond-shaped cross-section. There are also six steps in front of the second-floor outer corridor, which enhance the momentum of the building. The east side is of the protruding arc turtle, with the imitation of Tuscan Order in the middle, square column on both ends, arc forehead bar on top of the column, and then up with arc-shaped tooth decoration cornice and western parapet. The two parts of the east and west are symmetrical, with the outer corridor's concave and convex changes, scattered regularly, especially the two-story portico space of an obvious neoclassical style. It has both the strong sense of order and majesty shown by the columns, the Greek revival style of imitating mountain flowers, and the most obvious neoclassical tooth decoration.

There are four stone arches on the ground floor outer porch of the east facade. There are wedge-shaped buttresses on the corner columns at both ends of the outer porch, with inclined closure, and finally form a small slope, which is quite flexible and free. The buttresses not only stabilize the wall, but also enhance the weight of the corner of the building. The second and third floors step back to form an outdoor platform with spindle railings.

The east facade is of the doors and windows with internal functions, and the ground floor is doors and windows. The second and third floors are of the rectangular doors and Windows, with the second floor's windows obviously much higher than that of the third floor, with double wooden louver doors and windows. The upper part of the three-story window has a curved strip style window lintel, and an interesting locking stone in the middle. The white exterior walls of the second and third floors form a strong material contrast with the stone arcade on the first floor, while the emptiness of the stone arcade and the reality of the white wall produce the contrast of space, enriching the performance of the east facade. The space in the protruding stone arcade on the first floor is not so bright, and the white walls of brighter light in the second or third floors. Through the contrast of light and shadow, the sense of space on the east facade is increased.

The former site of the American Consulate had witnessed the development of the modern history of Fuzhou, the exchange and integration of Chinese and western cultures in Fuzhou, and reflected the rise and fall of social, economic and cultural development of modern Fuzhou. It is an important historical material for the study of the development history of Fuzhou city, which is of higher historical value.

◎ Hong Kong & Shang Hai Banking Corporation

In Yantai Mountain Historical and Cultural Block, known as the "Museum of International Architecture", there are English, Gothic, Romanesque and a large number of buildings combining Chinese and Western architecture. When it comes to British architecture, it is the former site of HSBC Fuzhou branch. The former site of HSBC Fuzhou Branch is located in *Meiwu* Road, Cangshan District. It is now Cangshan District Cultural Center, which usually provides free cultural entertainment for the citizens, an excellent case of the protection and utilization of cultural relics in China.

汇丰银行是当今世界三大银行之一，也是中国近代银行发展史上具有代表性的外资银行。汇丰银行正式成立于1864年，全称是"香港上海汇丰银行有限公司"。最初由英、美、德等国一些在远东经营多年且当时在世界经济中占有一定地位的资本家集资合股经营，是一家股份制银行。后来随着美国等国家由于各种原因而退出，汇丰银行便成为英国商人独自出资开办的银行。

汇丰银行广设分支机构，扩大营业范围，并积极开展存款等以往洋行未曾重视的业务领域。1866年8月14日，香港立法会对汇丰银行的各项业务做出明确规定，之后逐步操纵中国金融市场。

港英政府1866年第五号法令规定，汇丰银行"在获得（英国）财政部的同意下，可在伦敦、印度、槟榔屿和新加坡或中国皇帝或日本将军府所辖领土内，设有英国领事或副领事之处，开设银行或设立分行。但设立只经营兑换、存汇业务的分理处（不能发行钞票），则不必经财政部同意"。一般由一个分行管辖其经营所在地附近的几个分支机构，包括福州、西贡等地在内的地区分行属香港管理。至1894年，汇丰银行在与中国有贸易往来的地方、有华人居住的地方都设立了分行，其分支机构基本上涵盖了中国主要的贸易和人员往来区域。

福州的开埠是福建城市近代化的起点。随着对外贸易发展，对资金融通的需求大增，外国银行和本国银行相继设立，传统的金融机构也开始了近代化转型，共同促进城市经济的发展。银行与钱庄之间保持着千丝万缕的联系，体现了传统与近代的复杂关系。福建城市金融近代化是从外国银行设立开始的。开埠之初，尚无专门的近代金融机构，银行业务均由洋行兼理。

19世纪60年代后，福建开始出现独立的外国银行。汇丰银行福州分行于清朝同治时期（1867年）建立，地址在南台大岭顶汇丰弄1号，时为英资汇丰银行在福州设立的分理处，由Gilman and Co.公司代理。1868年升级为分行，经理是英国人沃克（F. G. Walker），属上海汇丰银行管辖，抗战结束后归香港地区管辖。

HSBC is one of the three major banks in the world and a representative foreign bank in the history of modern China. HSBC bank was formally established in 1864, with the full name "Hong Kong and Shanghai HSBC Bank Limited". At first, some capitalists in Britain, the United States, Germany and other countries had operated in the Far East for many years to occupy the position in the world economy, which was a joint-stock bank. Since then, as the United States and other countries withdrew for various reasons and involved interests, HSBC has become a bank independently funded by British businessmen.

HSBC had set up many extensive branches for its business scope, and actively developed the deposit and other business areas that the colonial banks and foreign banks had not valued before. On August 14, 1866, the Legislative Council of Hong Kong passed the HSBC Act, which clearly stipulated the business of HSBC, and then gradually manipulated China's financial market to meet the local trade needs of China as its own business objectives.

The Act V of the Colony Government of Hong Kong of 1866 states that HSBC " may, with the consent of the(UK)Treasury, establish banks or branches, in London, India, Penang Island and Singapore or within the territory of the Emperor of China or the General Office of Japan. However, the branch establishment of only exchange and deposit business(no right of printing and issuing money)requires no consent of the Ministry of Finance." Usually, a branch has jurisdiction over several branches institutions near where it operates. Regional branches, including Fuzhou, Saigon and other places, were managed by Hong Kong. By 1894, HSBC had established branches in main trade areas where Chinese lived.

The opening of Fuzhou is the starting point of the modernization of Fukien city. With the development of foreign trade, the demand for financial financing has increased greatly. Foreign banks and domestic banks have been set up successively, and the traditional financial institutions have also begun to transform in the modern direction to jointly promote the development of urban economy. There are close links between modern banks and old-style Chinese private banks, reflecting the complex relationship between troditional and modern times. The modernization of Finance in Fukien began with the establishment of foreign banks. At the beginning of the opening, there were no specialized modern financial institutions or banks, with all banking businesses managed by foreign banks.

After the 1860s, independent foreign banks began to appear in Fukien. HSBC Fuzhou Branch was established during the *Tongzhi* period of Qing Dynasty(1867)at HSBC Lane 1, as a branch of Gilman and Co. Company. Until 1868, it was, with bank manager F. G. Walker, under the jurisdiction of Shanghai HSBC and then under the jurisdiction of Hong Kong after the end of the Anti-Japanese War.

汇丰银行福州分行作为较早在福州设立的外资银行，是国内外均认可的金融机构，对19世纪末20世纪初福州的对外交流起到重要作用。汇丰银行福州分行作为外汇指定银行，对外经营业务包括侨汇、进出口外汇，对内经营业务包括办理榕沪和榕津地区间木材、笋干及茶叶等贸易的押汇。存款业务仅面向怡和、天祥两家英资洋行，英国圣公会，中华基督教卫理公会及教会所属各学校、医院等公共机构。

1915年以后汇丰银行的海关税收业务改由中国银行办理，但该行仍然办理侨汇、买卖外汇及国际押汇业务。其中结售外汇较多，并承办吉隆坡、槟城和新加坡等地联行委托，直接以国币解付侨汇业务。

汇丰银行福州分行的设立对于福州金融业的近代化客观上起了引导作用。近代福建沿海共有三个开放口岸，其中福州作为土特产贸易中心，占开港以来贸易总值的50%以上。辛亥革命后，福州的金融业在原有基础上继续发展，金融机构近代化趋向日益明显。在民国前期，基本上建立起近代金融体系。

从20世纪30年代起，银行扩大业务范围，逐渐加强与工商业的联系，日渐成为城市金融业主体。而钱庄、当铺等旧式金融机构渐趋衰微，成为新式银行的补充形式。近代拆借市场、汇兑市场、货币兑换市场等随着外国银行的设立相继出现在福州，旧式钱庄等金融组织也逐渐进入金融市场，进而开始近代化的历程。

1942年，受国内抗日战争影响，汇丰银行福州分行迁往重庆，抗战胜利后又迁回福州复业。1945年，中美特种技术合作所（SACO）驻扎福州期间，曾在汇丰银行顶层搭建观察哨，监视闽江之上日本船只的活动。当时在SACO服役的艾尔斯沃斯·史密斯（Elsworth Smith）在执行任务期间拍摄了一批照片，并由其子兰迪·史密斯（Randy Smith）公布在互联网上，照片中可以看到汇丰银行及顶层观察哨的旧影。

汇丰银行福州分行原属上海汇丰银行管辖。1949年5月，中国人民解放军解放上海，汇丰银行福州分行同上海失去联系，便转归香港总行领导。同年8月，香港总行函该行停止营业。1949年8月中国人民解放军解放福州，9月该行同上海行取得联系，10月20日正式停业。

As a foreign bank established in Fuzhou in the early stage, HSBC Fuzhou Branch is a financial institution recognized both at home and abroad, which has played an important role in the opening up of Fuzhou in the late 19th and early 20th centuries. As a designated foreign exchange bank, The Fuzhou Branch of HSBC's foreign business includes overseas remittance, import and export foreign exchange, and its internal business exchange like Fuzhou-Shanghai wood trade, Fuzhou-Tianjing wood trade, dried bamboo shoots and tea trade. Deposit business is only provided to two British foreign banks of *Yihe* and *Tianxiang*, the Anglican Church, the Chinese Christian Methodist Church and the schools and hospitals affiliated to the church.

After 1915, the customs tax business of HSBC was handled by Bank of China, but the bank still handled overseas Chinese currency exchange, foreign currency exchange trade and international exchange business, especially more foreign exchange settlement. Meanwhile, it is also entitled by the Kuala Lumpur, Penang, Singapore and other local banks to directly pay overseas Chinese exchange business in national currency.

The establishment of HSBC Fuzhou Branch has objectively played a guiding role in the modernization of financial industry in Fuzhou. There are three open ports in modern coastal Fukien, among which Fuzhou, as a local specialty trade center, accounts for more than 50% of the total trade. After the Revolution of 1911, Fuzhou finance continued to develop on the original basis, and the modernization trend of financial institutions became increasingly obvious. In the early period of Old China, the modern financial system was basically established.

Since the 1930s, banks have expanded their business scope, gradually strengthened the connection with industry and commerce, and increasingly become the main body of the urban financial industry. And the old financial institutions such as old-style private banks and pawnshops are gradually declining, becoming a supplementary form of the new banks. With the establishment of foreign banks, loan business market and currency exchange market appeared in Fuzhou, and financial organizations like old banks gradually became involved in these financial markets with the transition of modernization.

In 1942, influenced by War of Resistance against Japan, HSBC Fuzhou Branch moved to Chongqing. After the victory of the Anti-Japanese War, it moved back to Fuzhou to resume business. In 1945, when Sino-American Special Technology Cooperative Organization(SACO)troops were stationed in Fuzhou, they set up observation posts at the HSBC floor to monitor the activities of Japanese vessels above the Minjiang River. Elsworth Smith, who was then serving in SACO forces, took a number of photos during the mission and were posted on the Internet by his son Randy Smith, showing old images of HSBC and the top observation posts.

HSBC Fuzhou Branch was originally under the jurisdiction of Shanghai Bank. In May 1949, the Chinese People's Liberation Army liberated Shanghai. HSBC Fuzhou Branch lost contact with Shanghai, and its ownership right was transferred to the leadership of the Hong Kong head office. In August of the same year, the head office sent a letter urging the bank to stop operations. In August 1949, the Chinese People's Liberation Army liberated Fuzhou. In September, the bank contacted the Shanghai bank and officially closed its business on October 20.

现在去到汇丰银行福州分行旧址，我们还能看到以前的痕迹，内部仍旧保留原先的样貌。办公楼是一座典型的柱廊式建筑，外部立面为白色，有两层坡顶。整座大楼地面有两层，地下还有一层，共七个房间。屋内的摆设带有浓厚的西式浪漫气息。建筑由砖、木和钢材等材料构成，屋顶为较陡的双坡式风格。屋顶四面倒水，是西式的封檐，檐口挑出不起翘。

建筑为砖木结构，立面分上、中、下三部分，线条丰富，外墙为红砖砌筑，富有世纪之风。底层是连续的半圆拱券，二层开平窗，窗间做壁柱装饰，檐部线条较多，并有方齿形饰物。采用板条抹灰的做法，外墙砖墙承重，内墙不承重。当时一楼是人们往来的厅堂，二楼是银行办公的地方，银行的发票、档案等材料都存放在地下层。

院中的停车场，最早是汇丰银行的网球场，也是福州第一个网球场，在当时还掀起了一股网球热。

汇丰银行的旧有作用被取消之后，这栋建筑仍然在发挥其他作用。1947年，汇丰银行福州分行旧址供福州私立塔亭护士学校办学。1952年，护士学校被政府接办，银行原址转为福州市第二医院职员宿舍。1992年，汇丰银行福州分行旧址、独立厅被列为市级文保单位。

2009年，汇丰银行经过修复，正式挂牌成为仓山区文化馆。2013年1月，汇丰银行福州分行旧址作为烟台山近代建筑群的一部分，成为福建省省级文物保护单位。2020年，包括汇丰银行福州分行在内的福建省四个文物建筑保护利用案例入选国家文物局《文物建筑开放利用案例指南》。

现在的仓山区文化馆利用汇丰银行福州分行旧址建筑打造非遗展陈场所，以及用于社区公益文化体验及廉政文化传播的活动中心。仓山区文化馆充分利用旧址的功能，设立办公室、活动室、排练厅、美术室、书法室等11个活动室，主要承担群众文化艺术活动，还配套进行文化艺术创造、文艺精品创作等。

此外，这里还针对青少年儿童开展音乐、书法、闽剧表演、油纸伞制作、茶艺等公益免费活动。针对成年人开设古筝培训班等，接受培训的市民已达上千人。接下来，仓山区文化馆还将开展常态化的文艺演出，并计划打造一个小茶艺室，为市民提供学习、了解福州非遗项目——茉莉花茶传统窨制工艺的场所。

Now when we go to the former site of HSBC Fuzhou Branch, we can still see the traces of the previous history, and the interior retains its original appearance. The office building at the former HSBC site is a typical colonial colonnade building with a white exterior facade and a two-story sloping roof. The whole building has two floors above the ground and one floor underground, with a total of seven rooms. The decoration inside the house has a strong western-style romantic atmosphere. The building consists of materials such as brick, wood and steel, with a steeper sloping roof. The roof is water-poured style on four sides, which are of western-style sealed eaves with no tip.

The building is a brick and wood structure, and the facade is divided into three parts: upper, middle and lower, with rich lines. The outer wall is red brick masonry, rich in century style. The bottom floor is a continuous semi-circular arch voucher, and the second floor open window, with pilasters decoration between windows, more eaves lines, and square tooth ornaments. Using the practice of slat plastering, the external brick wall is load-bearing, and the inner wall is not load-bearing. At that time, the first floor was the hall where people traveled, and the second floor was where the bank worked. Bank invoices, files and other materials were stored in the basement.

The parking lot in the court, former HSBC tennis court, is the first tennis court in Fuzhou, which set off a tennis sensation at that time.

After HSBC's old role was banned, the building still played its other role. In 1947, the former site of HSBC Fuzhou Branch was run for Fuzhou Private Tating Nursing School. In 1952, the nurse school was accepted by the government, and the original site of the bank was converted into the staff dormitory of Fuzhou Second Hospital. In 1992, the former site of HSBC Fuzhou Branch and the independent office were listed in the municipal cultural protection unit.

In 2009, HSBC bank was restored and officially listed as the Cangshan District Cultural Center. In January 2013, the former site of HSBC Fuzhou Branch, as a part of the modern Yantai Mountain architectural complex, was announced as a provincial cultural relic protection unit in Fukien Province. In 2020, four cases of the protection and utilization of cultural relics buildings in Fukien Province, including Fuzhou Branch and the Independent Department of HSBC Bank, were selected into *The Case Guide for the Open Utilization of Cultural Relics Buildings* issued by the State Administration of Cultural Heritage.

The current Cangshan District Cultural Center uses the former building of HSBC Fuzhou Branch as a center of community public welfare cultural experience and the dissemination of upright culture, forming an intangible place of exhibition. Cangshan District Cultural Center makes full use of the functions of the old site, and set up 11 activity rooms, such as activity room, rehearsal hall, art room and calligraphy room, mainly undertaking mass cultural and artistic activities, through supporting cultural and artistic creation, literary and artistic fine works creation.

In addition, free public welfare activities such as music, calligraphy, Fukien opera performances, oil-paper umbrellas, tea art and other free activities are also carried out for teenagers and children. For adults, musical instrument *guzheng* training has also been launched, including thousands of citizens. Next, the Cangshan District Cultural Center will also carry out regular cultural performances, and plans to build a small tea room for citizens to learn about the Fuzhou intangible cultural heritage of jasmine tea.

◎ 泛船浦天主教堂

"走马仓前观走马，泛船浦内看番船。"这副民间对联巧妙结合了福州的地名，也凸显了泛船浦教堂的历史地位。

"番船浦"为古地名，今称"泛船浦"，位于仓山区东北部，包括闽江大桥以南，观海路、朝阳路以北地段。《藤山志》载："番船浦之名，由明弘治十一年（1498年）邓太监来闽督泊，贪受贿赂，将该地租与番人停泊船只，因名。"古代这里河道深、江面阔，番船（外国船只）便在这里停泊。当时，这里桅杆林立，船舶密集。福州话"番"与"泛"谐音，"番"带有"洋"的意思，故改称"泛船浦"更文雅、贴切、自然，指停泊众多中外大小船只的江浦，也更生动形象。

泛船浦教堂现全貌
The Church in Full View

◎ Fanchuanpu Catholic Church

As Fuzhou's old folk couplet goes, "see horses riding in a racecourse in *Cangshan* and boats around the *Fanchuanpu* Church." By skillfully combining names of places of Fuzhou, this folk couplet highlights the historical status of *Fanchuanpu* Church.

With *Panchuanpu* as an ancient place name, it is now called *Fanchuanpu*, located in the northeast of *Cangshan* District, including the south of the *Minjiang* River Bridge, north of *Guanhai* Road and *Chaoyang* Road. As *"Tengshan* Biography" contained: " The name of *Fanchuanpu*, in 11 years of Hongzhi Emperor(1498)of Ming Dynasty, eunuch Deng came to Fukien to supervise the ship, because of bribery, rented the land and foreigners berthing ships, hence the name. " In ancient times, the river was deep and wide, so foreign ships(called *"Fanchuan"* by Fuzhou native)moored here. At that time, there were so many masts and so many ships. In Fuzhou dialect, "pan" and "fan" are homophonic, with "foreign" meaning. So, the name of " *Fanchuanpu* " is more elegant, accurate and vivid, which refers to surface of the river, a wide water region for Chinese and foreign ships to berth.

近代由于"洋务运动"，这里不仅外国船多，中国船也不少。福州辟为通商口岸后，这里洋行和仓库也很多，如英国的怡和、太古，美国的美孚等，这些洋行还雇用了一些广东人当买办，他们多集中住在临江大路前街，即今粤华路。这里还有福建最早的邮政局和海关等近代化机构。解放后，这里大多数房屋成为仓库。

作为福州西洋古厝，泛船浦教堂建筑风格极具特色，它位于泛船浦新民街北、海关巷东，始建于清朝同治三年（1864年）。民国22年（1933年）重建，占地8400平方米，建筑面积1253.7平方米。在1848年到1936年的八十余年间，泛船浦天主堂是福州教务最为兴旺的教堂之一。教堂最早租用民房，或利用旧式民房改建，虽保留原来建筑的外貌，但内部装饰西化，是完全西式的建筑。

走进泛船浦教堂，巍峨的建筑立于眼前，便有一种庄严肃穆的感觉。教堂主堂北端建有20多米高的钟楼，楼顶竖立近3米高的十字架，号称"江南第一大堂"。泛船浦教堂至今仍为福建最大的天主教堂，也是福建省、福州市的天主教总堂，为福建省级文物保护单位。

康熙至道光年间，清政府实行禁教，闽浙总督驱逐外国天主教传教士，宫巷天主教堂被查没，改为关帝庙。福州成为通商口岸后，传教士接踵而来，恢复了传教工作。同治三年发还旧时没收的教产，福建省通商总局以泛船浦民田抵换宫巷原天主堂。

民国21年（1932年）秋泛船浦天主教堂重建，于次年9月落成。此次重建耗资17万银圆，设计师是法国人，因此教堂混合了哥特式和法国式（罗马式）建筑风格。教堂为砖木结构，坐南朝北，面对闽江，气势恢宏，外墙用青砖砌造。正面中央为哥特式塔楼，堂身整体为十字型，两边有弧状耳室一对，塔楼尖顶十字架离地约31.2英尺。入口门窗框为石制，哥特式尖券，两侧和祭坛上部的窗门装有彩色花玻璃，前沿三间玻璃绘有八幅彩色圣像。侧立面墙上有仿哥特飞扶壁式立壁柱，尖塔状装饰。

塔楼原高36米，上面装有法国进口大钟，昔日钟楼报时声扬十余里；堂身呈十字形，长60.2米、宽19.52米，面积为1371.4平方米。厅内采用拱状天花，每个柱头放射出四条拱形方木，在拱顶交会，可容3000余人。

In modern times, due to the "Westernization Movement", there were not only many foreign ships, but also many Chinese ships here. After " Five Port Trade " in Fuzhou, there were many foreign shops and warehouses here, such as Jardine and Swire in Britain, and Mobil in the United States. These foreign banks also employed some Cantonese buyers, and most of them lived in the front street of *Linjiang* Road, namely today's *Yuehua* Road. Here are also the earliest post office, customs and other modern institutions. After liberation, most of the houses here became warehouses.

As an ancient house of Fuzhou, *Fanchuanpu* Church has a distinctive architectural style. Today, *Fanchuanpu* Church is located in the north of Xinmin Street and east of Customs Lane.

It was built in the third year of *Tongzhi* Emperor of the Qing Dynasty(1864). In the 22 years of Old China(1933), it was rebuilt, covering an area of 8, 400 square meters, with a construction area of 1, 253.7 square meters. From 1848 to 1936(more than 80 years), The Catholic Church was one of the most prosperous churches in Fuzhou. The church first rented houses, or used old houses for reconstruction, which is to retain the appearance of the original building, with a completely western-style the interior decoration.

Walking into the *FanChuanpu* Church, with the towering buildings in front of you, there is a solemn feeling. At the north end of the main hall, there is a bell tower more than 20 meters high, and a cross nearly 3 meters high on the roof. In the past, with the tower clock ringing more than ten li, known as "the first church of Jiangnan", it is now a Fukien provincial cultural relic protection unit. It is still the largest Catholic church and the heahquarter of Catholic Church in Fukien.

During the reign of Emperor *Kangxi* to *Daoguang* of the Qing Dynasty, as the Qing government banned religion, the governors of Fukien and Zhejiang expelled foreign Catholic missionaries. The Catholic Church of Palace Lane was banned and confiscated into Guandi Temple. After Fuzhou became a treaty port, the missionaries came one after another and resumed their missionary work. In the third year of Emperor *Tongzhi* (1864), the confiscated old church assets were returned, and Fukien Provincial State Administration of Trade exchanged the folk land for the original Catholic Hall of Palace Lane.

In the 21st year of Old China(the autumn of 1932), the Catholic Church was rebuilt and completed in September 1933. The reconstruction cost 170, 000 silver coins and was designed by French, giving the church a mixture of Gothic and French(Romanesque) architecture. The church is a brick-and-wood structure, facing southern Minjiang River. The exterior wall is made of blue bricks magnificently; the front center is of the Gothic tower, and the whole hall is of Cross Shape, with chambers like a pair of curved ears on both sides; the spire of the tower cross about 31.2 feet from the ground. The entrance doors are framed in stone, with Gothic pointed coupons, and the sides and the upper windows of the altar are equipped with stained flower glass, and the three glass windows are painted with eight colored images on the front edge. The side facade wall imitates the Gothic flying buttress pilasters, with the spire shape decoration.

The tower was originally 36 meters high and contained French imported bells. When the bell rang, the voice spread more than ten li; the church body is a cross, 60.2 meters long, 19.52 meters wide, with the area of 1371.4 square meters. The church can accommodate more than 3000 people, and each column embedded 4 arched square wood, in the arch-pattern intersection.

教堂内左右并立11根直径约为1米的欧式水泥柱，堂顶呈拱形穹窿，缀以星辰。内设大小五个祭台，正中大祭台供奉该堂主保玫瑰圣母，旁边的小祭台从东到西分别供奉耶稣的养父圣若瑟、圣母玛利亚、圣女德兰。墙壁上的采光窗户镶着五彩玻璃，左右两边小祭台侧面的采光玻璃各雕刻一幅彩色教会圣人像。教堂第二层是一个长20米、宽6米的唱经台，与大祭台遥相对望。

设计上，教堂的拱状天花实际上不承受屋顶重量，拱顶内部的三角屋架才是真正的受力体，屋面荷载通过三角屋架传向墙、柱、地面。这种西式正统的肋骨拱顶从未在本地出现过。

2008年，因道路建设需要，泛船浦教堂的神父楼不得不进行迁移。百岁神父楼重达1600吨，想要挪动并非易事。福建省政府考虑到其为历史文物，经有关方面多次讨论，最终选择整体平移的方式来迁移该建筑。在多方不懈的努力下，历时一个多月平移80.7米后，10月6日安全抵达指定位置，并实现逆时针方向90度"转身"，由原东西朝向变为南北朝向，最终与主教堂平行。

随后，教堂又陆续建成下沉式广场、教区牧灵中心、圣母圣心亭等建筑，形成现在泛船浦教堂的整体模样。这是国内首次进行古建筑物定点90度旋转，创下了"整体旋转移位"保护文物的先例。在神父楼整体平移之后，还对其破旧部分进行了修缮，经过修缮的神父楼具有更多的功能。

只有走进泛船浦教堂，才能感受到它抽丝剥茧般显现的风情万种。在这里，古老的欧式建筑藏在街巷烟火中，萦绕着欲说还休的历史故事。从空中俯瞰，泛船浦如同一个壮观而精美的巨型十字架矗立江边，展现出它固有的沉稳与庄严。触摸每一个建筑细节，便会发现这里所经历的风云无声而有力、沧桑而壮观。

青砖砌成的拱顶和花窗，在光线中呈现斑驳陆离的美感。当阳光透过五彩的玻璃照进教堂的时候，对心灵而言无疑是最大的洗礼。高耸的塔尖，古典的拱门，似乎有一种魔力让人一下子就喜欢上这里。

教堂如今免费开放，无需门票，每逢节假日当地的居民以及游客都会来这里游玩。教堂因独具特色的建筑外观，也成为诸多电影的取景地，如《地下航线》（1959年）以及《我的早更女友》（2014年）等。这里亦成为新人拍摄结婚照的胜地，见证了很多份甜蜜。在福州关于泛船浦教堂流传着这样的说法：如果在福州拥有爱情，那么一定要去仓山看一眼那些老洋房，那门那窗，那小阳台和木质的楼梯转角，感受泛船浦天主堂那份独特的气息。

Inside the church, there are 11 European cement columns with a diameter of about 1 meter, and the roof is an arched vault, decorated with stars. There are five tables in the middle of the church, the main altar to Patron Saint, Our Lady of the Rosary(OLR), next to several small tables from east to west respectively to Jesus's adoptive father Joseph, the Virgin Mary, Saint Del. The lighting windows on the wall are inlaid with colorful glass, and on two sides of the altar are carved with a colorful image of the church saint. The second floor of the church is a 20-meters long and 6-meters wide singing table, far away from the altar.

In design, the arched ceiling of the church does not actually bear the weight of the roof, and the triangular roof inside the vault is the real bearing body. The roof weight is conveyed and distributed to the wall, columns and the ground through the triangular roof. It is worth mentioning that this western orthodox rib vault has never appeared locally.

In 2008, the priest building had to move for road construction. The 100-years-old priest building, about 1, 600 tons of heavy body, is hard to move. Considering that it is a historical relic, Fukien provincial government chose the overall movement to relocate the building after many discussions by the relevant parties. On October 6, with the unremitting efforts in many aspects, after more than a month of movement of 80.7 meters, it safely reached the designated position, and rotated 90 degrees in a counter-clockwise way, from the original east-west direction to the north-south direction, and was finally paralleled to the main church.

Subsequently, the church has built a sunken square, the parish priest center, the Virgin Sacred Heart Pavilion and other buildings. That is the overall appearance of *Fanchuanpu* Church. It is the first time ancient buildings rotated in China at 90 degrees, setting a precedent for "overall rotation and displacement" to protect cultural relics. After the overall rotation of the priest building, the dilapidated part of the building has been repaired and renovated to be more multifunctional.

Only by walking into this ancient house in Fuzhou, can you feel a variety of western architecture. Here are the ancient European buildings hidden in the streets to tell the colorful historical stories. *Fanchuanpu* church is like a spectacular and exquisite giant cross, standing by the river. Overlooking from the air, you can feel its inherent calmness and solemnness. If you look at every architectural detail, you will find that the history experienced here is silent and powerful, and the vicissitudes of life are spectacular.

The vaults and flower windows made by blue bricks present a mottled beauty in the light. When the sun shines through the colorful glass into the church, it is undoubtedly the biggest purification for the heart. With towering spire and classical arch, there is always a magic for people to like here suddenly.

The church is now free for both local residents and travelers to visit especially on holidays and festivals, which can be reached by bus near the church. The unique architecture has also become the setting for many films, such as *The Underground Route* (1959) and *Meet Miss Anxiety* (2014). Here also becomes holy land for the sweet couple to take their wedding photos. In Fuzhou there is a popular sentence about this church: by visiting Fanchuanpu Catholic Church can one feel true love in the unique atmosphere of old houses.

在满眼的现代建筑群中，泛船浦是一个独特的标志，屹立在闽江边，看滚滚江水流逝，听岁月波涛喃喃。而作为历史悠久又保存完好的西洋古建筑，泛船浦教堂具有极其重要的人文价值和建筑价值，也必将继续作为福州的名片之一为世人所知。

In the visible modern buildings complex, *Fanchuanpu* church is like a unique symbol, standing by *Minjiang* River, listening to the waves of the years in the murmuring. Having such a long history and such a well-preserved Western ancient architecture, it has extremely rich cultural and architectural significance, and will also continue to be known to the world as one of the business cards of Fuzhou.

艺术：风格与特色

Unveiling the Legacy: Styles and Features

福州古厝

伫立在时光斑驳之中的福州古厝，见证了这座城市历史的发展与变迁，承载着游子深深的乡愁，同时也记录着族群的文化基因。作为一座拥有两千两百多年建城历史的国际历史文化名城，福州不仅拥有壮丽的山川、美丽的园林，还拥有众多古建筑，包括宫殿、塔庙、名庄古寨、书院祠堂以及西洋建筑等风格迥异的建筑。这些古建筑在历史的熏陶下，不仅传承了中华民族的本色，还逐渐形成了自己独特的风格，展现出鲜明的地域性、时代性和族群性特征。

———— · ◇ · ————

Fuzhou's ancient dwellings bear witness to the passage of time, recording the city's historical changes, carrying the nostalgia of expats, and inscribing the shared cultural heritage of diverse communities. As an internationally renowned city with a history spanning over 2, 200 years, Fuzhou captivates visitors not only with its picturesque mountains, rivers, and enchanting gardens, but also with a plethora of ancient architectural complexes, each exuding its own distinctive style. From the grandeur of palaces to the serenity of temples, from renowned mansions to ancient villages, and from prestigious academies and ancestral halls to exotic western-style buildings, these architectural treasures have been shaped by the currents of history. They not only embody the essence of Chinese culture but have also developed their own unique styles, reflecting regional, temporal, and ethnic characteristics.

第七章

书院祠堂：传文树德

Chapter Seven

Academies and Ancestral Halls:
Spreading Culture and Cultivating Virtue

◎ 书院文化

福州作为"八闽雄都、神州名府"有着七千多年的文化积淀和两千两百多年的建城史，历史遗存丰富，人文底蕴深厚（钱江、涂洪长、王成，2021）。"三山鼎峙，一水长流"的福州城，钟灵毓秀，人才辈出。根据《中国历代州府进士、状元总数排行表》的统计，福州府以进士4100人排名第一，以文人雅客而闻名的苏州府和杭州府都只能甘拜下风。现今福州籍中国科学院院士共计51人，位列全国第三。福州府更是曾出现"一榜三鼎甲、三科三状元"的全国罕见的科举奇观，以"一县七里三状元"在中国科举史上冠绝一时（佚名，2020c）。

福州教育质量突出的原因有三。其一，自古以来福建就是"八山一水一分田"，山多田少，人们无法大规模从事农业生产。幸运的是，闽人聪颖，笃志好学，从儒入仕，得心应手。其二，世人都道："蜀道难，难于上青天，闽道更比蜀道难。"闽地多峻岭，出入较为不便，人们甘守一方土地，钻研学问，终老一生。其三，福建自古就是兵家不争之地，人们安居乐业，聚族而居。宗族可共享教育资源，并集全族之力供养子弟读书，待其光宗耀祖、衣锦还乡。

螺洲孔庙：朝圣之地

螺洲孔庙坐落于今仓山区螺洲镇吴厝村，是目前福州保存较完好的孔庙之一，被列为福州市级文物保护单位。它由螺洲乡民于南宋宝庆至景定年间（1225—1264年）筹建，明朝成化年间因遭遇强台风而损毁。成化十年（1474年）由吴叔和主持重建，明正德十六年（1521年）和明隆庆二年（1568年）再度进行修缮，明万历二十二年（1594年）重修并塑有孔子像及颜渊、曾参、孔伋和孟轲四配像。明朝年间曾有这么一则轶事：依明朝律法，只有县级以上行政单位才能修建孔庙，而螺洲孔庙却为村制，官府发现后便下令拆除。乡里的陈秀才当仁不让："有闻建孔庙者，而未闻有拆孔庙者。兴而复拆，不敬更大，不敢从事，恭候官宪遣工拆之。"（清·俞樾《俞楼杂纂》）官员执事听罢只得悻悻而归，螺洲孔庙才得以保存至今。清朝年间，对螺洲孔庙也曾两度进行维护，清嘉庆五年（1800年）依律重修，道光元年（1821年）由陈若霖等捐资修建，以慰乡里。

◎ Academy Culture

With more than 7, 000 years of cultural accumulation and 2, 200 years of city history, Fuzhou, the glorious capital of Fukien Province and the renowned capital of China, is endowed with a rich historical past and a profound humanistic heritage(Qian Jiang, Tu Hongchang, Wang Cheng, 2021). Fuzhou is encircled by three mountains and a long stream of water, taking pride in its beauty and talents. Meanwhile, Fuzhou Prefecture topped the list with 4, 100 metropolitan graduates, according to the "Ranking list of the total number of metropolitan graduates and champions of the state in China". Despite being well known for their literary men, Suzhou and Hangzhou Prefectures paled in comparison to Fuzhou. Besides, 51 academics nowadays come from Fuzhou who are members of the China Scientific Academy, which places it third in China. It was an honor for Fuzhou Prefecture to break the record for the Chinese imperial examinations with "Three champions within seven miles of the same county" and experience a unique occurrence of "Top three scholars in the same imperial examination from the same place and one champion in three examinations" (Anonymous, 2020c).

By and large, three primary factors contribute to Fuzhou's outstanding educational standards. First off, since ancient times, Fukien has been blessed with 80% mountain, 10% water, and 10% farmland, making it impossible for locals to participate in large-scale agricultural production. Fortunately, the locals were born brainy and aspired to study, becoming learned men or authorities. Second, as the proverb goes, "While traveling through Sichuan's winding lanes was challenging, reaching Fukien was even more challenging." As Fukien is almost entirely mountainous, it is exceedingly difficult to travel in and out. People were therefore prepared to settle down and continue studying till they passed away. Finally, Fukien was a region which troops did not fight over in the distant past, allowing clan members to live and work in harmony. Hence, they would gloriously return home in remembrance of their forefathers since the clans could finance scholars at full stretch and share educational resources.

The Temple of Confucius in Luozhou: Place of Pilgrimage

The Confucius temple in Luozhou, designated as a Fuzhou-level cultural relic conservation unit, is one of Fuzhou's best-preserved temples. It is located in Wucuo Village, Luozhou Town, Cangshan District. The temple was constructed by villagers between the years 1225 and 1264, but during the Chenghua period of the Ming Dynasty, it was severely damaged by a typhoon. Wu Shuhe rebuilt it in 1474, and it underwent renovations in 1521 and 1568 before being restored in 1594 with five statues of Confucius, Yan Yuan, Zeng Shen, Kong Ji, and Meng Ke. Only governmental bodies at the county level or higher were allowed to erect Confucius temples in accordance with the laws of the Ming Dynasty. Because the Confucius temple in Luozhou was built by local residents, the authorities gave the order for its destruction. However, Scholar Chen replied wittily, "I have heard of individuals who erected Confucius temples, but I have not heard of anyone who tore them down. It would be more insulting to leave this newly-built temple in ruins. Therefore, the choice is yours." (Yu Yue, *Yu Lou Za Zuan*, Qing Dynasty) And then, the officials were forced to leave with a long face, but the Confucius Temple in Luozhou has been preserved up to this date. Under the laws of the Qing Dynasty in 1800, the Confucius Temple was well-maintained and renovated twice. For the benefit of his hometown, Chen Ruolin financed the construction of the temple in 1821.

出于维护封建统治的需要，孔子的儒家思想倍受推崇，全国各地都兴建孔庙。中国的首座孔庙位于孔子的故乡——山东省曲阜市，由鲁哀公在公元前478年下令在孔子故居处按照皇宫的规制修建，岁时奉祀。自汉代以降，孔子和儒学深受统治阶级推崇。汉武帝推行"罢黜百家，独尊儒术"的政策后，儒学义理独享北斗之尊。隋唐开科取士以来，儒家的"四书五经"更是成为士子们学而优则仕的必读书目。时至唐朝太宗年间，皇帝诏令天下州县皆立孔庙，自此孔庙依托官学而兴盛一时。除了曲阜阙里孔庙和衢州孔庙外，其余孔庙的兴建往往依托于地方学校的普及而展开（于亚娟，2013：4）。古语云，"仓廪实而知礼节"。闽地远离中原战火，自给自足，在粮食问题解决以后，人们转而重视教育，因而孔庙在此也得到大力推广。

螺洲，古称"百花仙洲"，东临福厦路，西南濒临乌龙江，北接盖山镇，南面与五虎山相望（福州市仓山区政协委员会，2003：12）。螺洲虽只是由几个小村落组成的聚居地，却建造了福建全省唯一的村一级文庙，这在全国也是极少见的（福州市档案馆，2014：30）。孔庙的设立意在劝学先贤，教导人们崇文尚礼。螺洲文风昌盛，文人辈出，有"三部尚书"陈若霖、末代帝师陈宝琛等，也不乏折冲之臣，如被毛主席盛赞为"虎穴藏忠魂"的吴石中将。

螺洲孔庙占地面积约1048平方米，三进院落，主建筑有棂星门、泮池、拱形步云桥、大成门、天井、大成殿、倒朝房等（王刚，2018）。孔庙的棂星门是一座由六根圆形花岗石柱、十一条石梁、十二块石坊组成的三开间石牌坊，门额浮雕有双龙抢珠、丹凤朝阳等，圆柱上刻有飞龙盘绕、鲤跃龙门等纹饰，至今保存完好（陈炘、陈弓，2006：586）。棂星门是孔庙特有的建筑形制，于明太祖洪武十五年（1382年）以后才出现。棂星原为灵星，又称天田星，掌天下所有的田地。皇帝在祭天之前需先祭天田星，祈求国家风调雨顺、国泰民安。祭孔如祭天，足以说明孔子和儒学在封建帝王心目中举足轻重的地位。孔庙门额上精巧的浮雕和石柱纹饰题材丰富、寓意深远，象征着贤才逢明时能够发愤图强，一路连科而飞黄腾达。

Confucianism was highly valued, so Confucius temples sprang up all throughout the land in an effort to uphold feudal authority. The first Confucius temple in China is located near Confucius' birthplace of Qufu in Shandong Province. In order to make sacrifices to Confucius, the Duke of Lu transformed his home into a palace-like temple in 478 BC. Confucius and his Confucianism thereafter have been highly revered by the ruling class since the Han Dynasty. In particular, it started to play an extremely significant role after Emperor Wu of the Han Dynasty issued the policy of paying the highest homage to Confucianism while rejecting all other systems of thought. In order to promote academic brilliance, the Four Books and Five Classics of Confucianism were made required reading for scholars after the Sui and Tang dynasties' establishment of the imperial examinations. Emperor Taizong of the Tang Dynasty ordered that Confucius temples be built in every state and county, and from that point on, Confucius temples flourished based on official schools. The rest of them, with the exception of the Confucius Temples in Queli(part of Qufu), and Quzhou, were typically influenced by schools(Yu Yajuan, 2013: 4). As the proverb says, "Etiquette is learned after the storehouse is solid." Locals have attached great importance to education and constructed numerous Confucius temples after they kept out of the line of fire and were self-sufficient.

In the past, Luozhou was called "Baihuaxianzhou". It is situated between Fuxia Road and Gaishan Town to the east and north, with the Wulong River to the southwest and Wuhu Mountain to the south(Fuzhou City, Cangshan District, People's Political Consultative Committee(ed.), 2003: 12). Even though Luozhou is simply a town made up of several small villages, it has constructed the sole village-level Confucius temple in Fukien Province, which is incredibly uncommon in the nation(Fuzhou City Archives, 2014: 30). The Confucius Temple was built to encourage learning and respect literacy and manners. In Luozhou, the literary scene has been thriving and people have been intelligent, such as Chen Ruolin and Chen Baochen, who were the heads of three ministries and the last feudal emperor's instructor. Even the fearless lieutenant general Wu Shi has earned Chairman Mao's high praise who was from Luozhou as well.

Confucius temple in Luozhou covers an area of about 1, 048 square meters, with a trio of yards and main buildings such as the Lingxing Gate, the Pan Pond, the arched Buyun Bridge, the Dacheng Gate, the patios, the Dacheng Hall, the Daochao Room(Wang Gang, 2018: Par 5). The well-maintained Lingxing Gate is a three-door stone archway composed of six round granite columns, eleven stone beams, and twelve stone plaques. There are double dragons battling for a pearl and phoenixes rising in the sun served as carvings on the head molding and flying dragons coiling around and carps leaping over the dragon gate served as ornaments on the columns, which have been well-preserved until now(Chen Xin, Chen Gong, 2006: 586). After 1382, the Lingxing Gata, a distinctive architectural design, first appeared in Confucius temples. The Lingxing, known as the Tiantian star, was in command of all fields worldwide. Before praying to heaven and honoring it, the emperors had to sacrifice animals to the Tiantian star. Thus it can be seen that Confucius and Confucianism were crucial to feudal emperors throughout the period when he was revered as a deity. Besides, a high-flying profession is symbolized by the exquisite head molding and embellishments on the stone pillars, which are filled with themes and symbolic meaning.

　　螺洲孔庙虽小，但礼制齐全。棂星门内的广场中心建了一个约15平方米的迷你半月形泮池，形似一方砚台。作为文房四宝之首的砚，承载着仕子们中举登科的美好愿望。泮池上横跨着一座三孔石拱桥，名曰"步云桥"，顾名思义，取平步青云、步步高升之意。时至今日，每逢升学考试，学子们便会效法古人，前往孔庙祭拜。

　　跨过大成门，便是孔庙的主殿大成殿。何谓大成？孟子曰："孔子，圣之时者也。孔子之谓集大成。"（《孟子·万章下》）大成殿面阔五间，进深七柱，穿斗式木构架，单檐歇山顶，鹊尾脊，两旁施马鞍墙（陈炘、陈弓，2006：586）。中国南方的民居普遍采用穿斗式木构架，取材方便，构架灵活，屋顶轻巧，安全稳定。单檐歇山顶的规制较高，故宫的太和门和天安门都是使用此种坡屋顶，古时只有五品以上官员才被允许在住宅的正堂使用。大成殿正脊两端鹊尾高翘，宛若腾飞之姿，象征着扶摇直上、大有作为。大殿正脊与两侧对称的马鞍墙形成横纵之势，错落有致。马鞍墙是封火墙（又称"风火墙"）的一种，在福州地区颇为流行。这些高耸的围墙呈流线型，高低起伏，翘角外伸，因形似马鞍而得名。孔庙马鞍墙的翼角处绘有云纹样式，设计简洁，造型轻盈。因"云"和"运"读音相似，就意味着好运，这正是广大士子们的心之所向。马鞍墙除了具有较高的美学价值外，还具有分割空间、勾勒边界和御风防火的实用价值。

　　大成殿为敞开式、半开放格局，孔子与四配颜渊、曾参、孔伋和孟轲端坐其中，东西两侧立有形态各异的先贤先儒雕像，文脉威仪，至今不减。《史记·孔子世家》记载："孔子以诗、书、礼、乐教，弟子盖三千焉，身通六艺者七十有二人。"（司马迁，2005：1440）孔子所教的七十二贤人，德厚流光，成为后世的典范。孔子身着绿色长袍，手持竹简，和颜悦色；复圣颜回和述圣孔伋坐东朝西，宗圣曾参与亚圣孟轲坐西向东，他们或洗耳恭听，或挟策读书，克恭克顺。孔子周围设有七十二贤人的部分立像，塑像形神兼备，栩栩如生。孔子坐像的横梁前从左至右依次高悬着"圣集大成"、"万世师表"和"与天地参"三块金光煌煌的匾额，分别由清朝嘉庆帝、康熙帝和乾隆帝御笔亲题，孔子的地位不言而喻，古来圣贤无人能出其右。大成殿的后堂是祭祀孔子父母的崇圣殿。孔子不仅自己恪守孝道，还常教育世人尊敬父母。子曰："今之孝者，是谓能养。至于犬马，皆能有养；不敬，何以别乎？"（《论语·为政》），足见孔子对父母的崇敬之心，身为表率。

Although the Confucius temple is not a large-scale one, it is as complete with all buildings as larger ones. Inside the Lingxing Gate, a small inkstone-like half-moon pond that is about 15 square meters in size has been constructed in the middle of the yard. The inkstone, the most valuable of the four study jewels, carries candidates' good wishes to achieve success in the imperial examinations. The bridge across the pond is a three-hole arch stone one, named Buyun Bridge. As its name suggests, it refers to attaining academic excellence gradually. Students today would imitate the example of the ancients to worship Confucius when exams were approaching.

The Dacheng Hall, the temple's main hall, is seen after passing through the Dacheng Gate. How to explain Dacheng? Confucius, who personified the philosophy of all schools, was a saint, according to Mencius. (Mencius, *"Wan Zhang II"*) The Dacheng Hall boasts a column and tie construction, a gable and hip roof with a single eave and a magpie-tail ridge, and it is enclosed by saddle walls on both sides. Moreover, it is five rooms wide and seven columns deep (Chen Xin, Chen Gong, 2006: 586). The column and tie construction has been widely used in folk houses in the southeast of China for a few different reasons. In the beginning, it is simple to obtain wood; besides, wood is adaptable, stable, and safe; additionally, its roof is light and thin. Gable and hip roofs with single eaves, which were once used in the Taihe Gate of the Forbidden City and Tiananmen Gate, were a high-standard specification, and officials of the fifth rank and above were only permitted to employ them in the main hall of their dwellings in ancient times. The magpie-tail ridges that rise on either end of its main ridge appear to be flying upward and stand for great success. Its main ridge and the symmetrical saddle walls establish a horizontal and vertical trend. Overall, saddle walls are a type of firewall that are very common in Fuzhou neighborhoods. Particularly, these high walls, which look like horse saddles, are sleek and undulating with outward warps. If you look closely, you will see the clean and airy cloud pattern on the saddle walls, which have an inverted roof ridge. Scholars are always fond of the meaning behind the word "cloud", because its pronunciation in Chinese is close to the pronunciation of good luck. Along with its great aesthetic value, its usefulness has been emphasized in terms of defining borders, dividing space, and providing protection from wind and fire.

Confucius is seated in the Dacheng Hall, which is a partially open layout. Beside his four successors Yan Yuan, Zeng Shen, Kong Ji, and Meng Ke, statues of other wise men in various shapes stand on the east and west sides as well. Years later, those who seem dignified continue to be the same. According to the Historical Records of Confucius, Confucius taught poetry, calligraphy, ritual, and music to 3000 students, including 72 sages who were proficient in six arts. (Sima Qian, 2015: 1440) In particular, the 72 sages were morally upright to serve as examples for future generations. Confucius is seen in the temple holding a bamboo book with grace when dressed in a green robe. While Zeng Shen and Meng Ke are seated in the west, facing the east, Yan Hui and Kong Ji are seated in the east, facing the west. And they are attentively listening or reading with great respect. What's more, the standing statues of the 72 sages are placed around the statue of Confucius, and they all seem to be full of life. Three golden plaques inscribed by the Qing Dynasty's Emperor Jiaqing, Emperor Kangxi, and Emperor Qianlong are located above the statue of Confucius and read from left to right, "The greatest saint embodying the philosophy of all schools", "The tutor of all generations", and "Justifiable principles". Confucian dominance in Chinese history thereby has been confirmed by these imperial inscriptions. The Chongsheng Hall, where Confucius' parents are worshiped, is located behind the Dacheng Hall. Confucius not only practiced filial piety by himself but also advised others to respect their own parents. Confucius once said, "Even animals are prepared to assist their parents, let alone human beings." (*The Analects of Confucius*, "Wei Zheng") As a result, this is a wonderful example for individuals.

螺洲孔庙历经沧桑、饱经风霜，但师道尊严，乡民们尊孔敬孔之心一日不曾衰减，焚香礼拜、三牲供养从不间断。现如今螺洲孔庙依旧沿袭着昔日的传统，青少年在节日里需前往孔庙祭祀行礼，以倡笃志好学之风。

林浦濂江书院：文脉传承

福建在唐代以前一直被视作化外之地。唐朝大历七年（772年），时任福建观察使李椅在闽兴办教育，扩建学舍，鼓励入学。唐德宗年间的福建观察使常衮，重视教育，增设乡校，亲自讲授，讲学论道之风盛行一时，为福建的文教发展奠定了基础。隋唐科举制度的发展使朝廷选贤任能不再以门第论，从而改变了"上品无寒门，下品无势族"的不良官场风气。时至宋代，民康物阜，儒学复兴，理学盛行，尊师重道蔚然成风。书院形成了独具特色的人才培养模式：它既是培养士大夫的摇篮，也是学术研究的阵地。福建书院从唐五代单一的读书、教授子弟生徒，变成奉祀、讲学、授徒、研究学术、著述兼而有之的场所，因而在建筑结构上也有全面的考虑和安排（何绵山，2016：328）。宋末元初，社会动荡，战乱连连，不少书院惨遭损毁。元朝的统治阶级清醒地意识到自己"武功迭兴、文治多阙"的先天不足，虽崇儒尊朱之风未改，但忙于被甲执兵，无暇书院建设，书院教育一度陷入低谷。明朝是秦汉之后思想最为活跃开放的一个朝代。福建是朱子理学的发祥地，因而福建的士林学子更加热衷于钻研理学。虽然学校教育和科举考试都取得了突飞猛进的发展，却仍无法与宋朝比肩。清承明制，官办书院取得了长足发展。书院聘请通今博古的经学家和理学名儒讲授指导，造就了诸多匡时济世的人才（何绵山，2016：332）。

濂江书院坐落于福州市仓山区城门镇林浦濂江村，又称文昌宫，是福州唯一一座保存良好、办学未曾中断的古书院。林浦背倚山势险峻的九曲山，北瞰江水秀逸的闽江，负阴抱阳，藏风聚气，实乃风水宝地。林浦水光山色，风景宜人，和儒家寄情山水的旨趣与礼乐相成的理想不谋而合（金银珍、凌宇，2010：308）。只有如此清幽雅致的环境才能孕育出以林元美为首的"七科八进士"和以林瀚父子为首的"三代五尚书"。明朝时期，素有"南林北许，国中旺族"之说，闽中望族首推林浦林氏。林浦历来文风昌盛，人文荟萃，学子勤勉，人才辈出。据史料记载，仅宋、明、清三朝，林浦就先后出过18位进士、3位祭酒，实居全国之冠（福州市档案馆，2014：40）。

The Confucius Temple in Luozhou has endured storm and stress, and the locals have continued to pay homage to Confucius in recognition of his tremendous dignity. Accordingly, they continuously offer three animals while burning incense. Children attend the temple and participate in rituals during festivals today since the custom has persisted.

The Lianjiang Academy in Linpu: Inheriting Culture

Before the Tang Dynasty, Fukien was regarded as an uncivilized region. Li Yi, who was sent to supervise Fukien in 772, established education, increased the number of schoolhouses, and promoted learning. Furthermore, Chang Gun, another administrator, developed new schools, gave education a higher priority, and even taught in person. At that period, learning was commonplace, which contributed to the development of cultural and educational system in Fukien. By and large, the imperial examinations in the Sui and Tang Dynasties corrected the problematic official practice of having no powerful family at the bottom and no impoverished family at the top when choosing employees for the imperial court. By the time of the Song Dynasty, since the people were well-off, Confucianism had been restored and Neo-Confucianism had taken hold, and reverence for instructors had become fashionable. Subsequently, the academies created a special system for developing talents that served as both the breeding ground for academics and the hub of academic inquiry. In the Tang and Five Dynasties, the function of academies in Fukien changed from teaching and studying to a combination of worshipping, lecturing, recruitment, academic research, and writing, and thus they needed an extensive layout of architectural construction(He Mianshan, 2016: 328). Afterward, the majority of academies were tragically destroyed during the period of social turmoil and fighting between the late Song and early Yuan dynasties. The Yuan Dynasty's governing class was aware of its inherent shortcomings—strong military power and weak civilization. They honored Confucianism and Master Zhu, but their attention was diverted by military campaigns. Hence, they were ignorant of academies, and education declined. Fortunately, after the Qin and Han Dynasties, the Ming Dynasty was the most energetic and progressive. Scholars in Fukien were keener to brush up on Neo-Confucianism because it was the home to Master Zhu's doctrine. As a result, education and imperial exams made a huge breakthrough, but they were still not able to surpass those of the Song Dynasty. Following in the footsteps of the predecessors, the Qing Dynasty made significant advancements in public academies. So learned scholars who were steeping in Neo-Confucianism were hired to teach and guide students, cultivating many talents who built up the country(He Mianshan, 2016: 332).

The Lianjiang Academy is located in Lianjiang Village, Linpu, Chengmen Town, Cangshan District, Fuzhou City, and also known as Wenchang Palace. In addition, it is the only properly maintained academy in Fuzhou that has been operating without interruption. It stands against precipitous Jiuqu Mountain, facing the stunning Minjiang River. In general, it is a Chinese custom to embrace Yang against Yin in order to store up Qi(a term in Feng Shui). Linpu boasts its spectacular and breathtaking scenery, which coincides with Confucianism's ideal of engaging with nature and taking pleasure in the combination of etiquette and music(Jin Yinzhen, Ling Yu, 2010: 308). Both Lin Han, the head of five ministers from three generations, and Lin Yuanmei, the leader of eight metropolitan graduates from seven imperial examinations, hailed from such a tranquil and elegant area. It is stated that Xu from the north and Lin from the south were two of the most prestigious families in China during the Ming Dynasty. With a solid foundation of culture and education, Linpu has been a gathering place for gifted individuals and conscientious students. According to historical records, there were 18 metropolitan graduates and 3 directors of the imperial academy, which was rare even all over the country during the Song, Ming, and Qing Dynasties(Fuzhou City Archives, 2014: 40).

潇江书院始建于唐朝，因宋朝的理学大家、闽学创始人朱熹及其得意门生黄榦曾在此开堂讲学而声名鹊起。朱熹自幼精研孔孟之学，是南宋最负盛名的理学家和教育家，是孔子、孟子以后最卓越的儒学弘道者、实践者，世人皆尊称其为朱子。朱子是唯一一位非孔子亲传弟子，却能配享孔庙、位列大成殿的贤人。其人为官清正，大兴文教，惠及万民。朱熹对潇江书院的贡献表现在，他为不同学派和不同地域的执教者和求学者创造了很多互动机会，互邀讲学、相互切磋，重现了"百花齐放，百家争鸣"的学术盛况。

现存的潇江书院主体建于清朝，占地面积为764平方米，建筑精巧，环境清幽。书院四周土石墙垣护卫，呈"品"字形排开，营造出层次丰富的空间感。书院门口白墙照壁上刻有"潇江书院"四个清逸隽秀的大字，给人端庄肃静之感。一入门墙，小庭幽院，自成一方天地，读书人的雅趣展露无遗。庭院前立着略显斑驳的青石短围屏，内外两侧分别用楷书题刻"文光射斗"和"潇水龙腾"。"文光射斗"表达了师长的殷切希望，即期待学子们笔下生辉，科举名列前茅。"潇水龙腾"意指潇江的水土孕育出才高八斗、出类拔萃的人才，犹如鱼跃龙门，功成名就。庭院中央立有一方古老的笔洗石臼，古来不知多少风流才子在此洗笔涤砚、摛藻绘句。石臼上阴刻"知鱼乐"三字楷书，意在劝导学子们善于体会物情，既要博闻强识，又要修身养性，以达天人合一的境界。

书院照壁
The Screen Wall of the Academy

The Lianjiang Academy was built during the Tang Dynasty and has become famous for Master Zhu and his prized pupil Huang Gan, both of whom used to teach there. Master Zhu has kept delving into Confucius' and Mencius' philosophy ever since he was a young boy and became the creator of Neo-Confucianism in Fukien. As a result, he was addressed respectfully by Master Zhu, who was the most distinguished ideologist, educator, advocator, and practitioner of Confucianism after Confucius and Mencius. Master Zhu thus has been an exception who was worshipped in the Dacheng Hall of the temples of Confucius but not personally instructed by Confucius. Moreover, he, an honest and upright official, developed culture and education, benefiting the entire country. Most importantly, Master Zhu has made a great contribution to the Lianjiang Academy by creating more opportunities to exchange ideas and interact with scholars from different schools and regions, reviving the cultural prosperity.

The main body of the extant Lianjiang Academy was built in the Qing Dynasty with exquisite artistry and a tranquil setting, covering an area of 764 square meters. The academy is encircled by earthen and stone walls that are shaped like Chinese character "Pin", creating a rich gradation of space. Additionally, the four enormous regular scripts of its name are engraved with dignity and quietness on the white screen wall at the entrance. Going through the wall, the small-scale courtyard is a private space, displaying the elegance of the scholars. In the front of the courtyard, there is a short stone screen that is stained with moss and has two idioms etched on the inner and outer sides with "Full of wit" and "Water of magnificence" respectively. The inscription of "Full of wit" encapsulates the teachers' passionate wish for their students to prosper in the imperial examinations and become good writers. In the meanwhile, "Water of magnificence" is literally translated into "best talents from Lianjiang". In addition, there is a historic stone mortar in the center, where academics and students once washed their pens and inkstones and created their masterpieces. Three characters of Zhi Yu Le are inscribed on the stone mortar to instruct pupils to be adept at comprehending things. They were expected to be knowledgeable and nurture their brains and bodies at the same time in order to reach the unity of heaven and men.

濂江书院为双层杉木结构楼房，穿斗式木构架，单檐歇山顶。屋顶飞檐翘脊，形似飞鸟振翅，灵秀轻盈。飞檐翘角的构造能够有效增加书院内部的采光，满足授课、讲学的光线需要，还能凸显建筑动态的美感。檐角上采用南方传统的雕塑工艺——灰塑进行装饰，极大地丰富了檐角的色彩感，增加了屋面的立体感。作为灰塑纹样的卷草纹，线条流畅、虚实相生、自由灵动，象征着书院传承，薪火不熄，文脉赓续。濂江书院的外檐装饰古朴，体现了儒家追求庄重质朴、反对土木之奢的文雅情趣。在色彩和装饰上除偏向清新淡雅外，还注重象征意义的表达（金银珍、凌宇，2010：318）。

书院楼前及两侧设有楼廊，梁架木雕，典雅美观。楼廊上的梁柱朱漆覆面，梁枋、雀替和托架上的纹饰经描金处理，花样丰富但不琐碎，结构精巧，雕法细腻，在静谧中洋溢着生机。廊内的六扇朱红雕花隔扇大门古朴、庄严，以虚间实的万字纹透雕隔心，做工精良。隔扇大门既有门的联通与隔断作用，又兼有窗的通风与采光用途。隔扇门中的隔心更是其点睛之笔，隔心纹样在光线下呈现出变幻莫测的光影效果，令人叹为观止。可以说，隔扇大门集实用功能、艺术学与美学于一体，是古人智慧的结晶。

书院主楼为文昌阁，正厅为朱熹讲学处，称朱子厅，右厢为朱熹住处，为朱子祠（福州市档案馆，2014：46）。朱子厅正门前高悬着朱熹亲题的“文明气象”黑漆匾额，笔法遒劲有力，两侧楹联为："三台平步上，百尺举高头。"匾额、楹联中所蕴含的中华文化底蕴深厚，集书法、文教、装饰于一体，以凝练的语言、精微的义理提升了古建筑的内涵，反映了人们崇文重教、尚德明礼的传统。厅内正中供奉着朱熹的画像，画像中的朱子一袭蓝袍，儒雅亲善，为人师表。朱熹像后设有圆形木制藻井，上圆下方，样式简洁，藻井正中雕刻着倒悬的花瓣，四周饰以贴金纹样。古人讲究师法自然，推崇天圆地方，因而产生了上圆下方的穹顶装饰。厅内井然有序，整齐地摆放着师生的书桌和文房四宝等，仿佛时光倒流，回到了那个坐不窥堂、笃学不倦的年代。右厢朱子祠内，一张简朴的黑漆卧榻横置其中，古色古香的太师椅列于两侧。朱熹乐育英才，桃李满天下，前来谈书论道者不计其数。朱熹时常与孜孜不倦的学子们讨论至深夜，而朱子祠内的摆设也展现了他诲人不倦的教育热情。

濂江书院至今依旧书声琅琅，教育文化传承千年未曾中断。匾额、楹联激励着学子们上进、立志、虚心、敬业，也因此成就了林浦人文渊薮、成绩斐然的文化局面。

The Lianjiang Academy is a double-layered cedar structure with a single eave, a gable and hip roof, and a column and tie construction. The cornices and ridges of the roof resemble the wings of a flying bird, light and graceful. Additionally, their designs can efficiently improve internal lighting to satisfy educational demands and highlight the dynamic beauty. Traditional sculpture techniques, namely clay sculpture, are used to decorate the eaves, dramatically enhancing their color and giving the roof a more three-dimensional appearance. The scrolling grass design, which is smooth, adaptable, and agile, symbolizes the cultural lineage it has inherited. The exterior finish work is additionally straightforward and tidy, emphasizing Confucianism's goal of seriousness and simplicity. In general, its ornamentation and coloring with symbolic meaning are understated(Jin Yinzhen and Ling Yu, 2010: 318).

There are hallways with exquisitely carved wood and attractive beams in front of the structure and on both sides. The beams and columns are covered with vermilion lacquer and sparrow braces. Meanwhile, brackets on the beams are painted golden, and their patterns are diversified, well-designed, and exquisite. Generally, all seem vibrant and vigorous. Additionally, six vertical partition doors that allow for connection, separation, ventilation, and natural lighting are elegant and plain with a typical "Wan" pattern in the middle. The quintessence of the doors' centers which produce unpredictable light and shadow, are remarkable to observe. Overall, the vertical partition doors integrate aesthetic elements into functions and are thought to represent the ancients' wisdom.

The main building of the academy is Wenchangge, whose main hall was named after Master Zhu. The Zhu Zi Hall is a place where Master Zhu lectured at one time. Master Zhu used to reside in one of its rooms, known as Zhu Zi Shrine, which is separate from the main hall(Fuzhou City Archives, 2014: 46). In the front of the main entrance of the Zhu Zi Hall, there is a black-lacquered plaque inscribed by Master Zhu with a gorous brushwork. The couplets on both sides read, "Platforms ahead, success attained". The plaques and couplets, which incorporate calligraphy, culture, education, and decoration, embody a rich cultural heritage of Chinese origin. Additionally, they all exhibit the custom to respect culture and education, stress morality and decorum, and convey the connotation of the historic building through sophisticated language and deep meanings. The figure of Master Zhu, appearing classy and affable in a blue robe, is placed in the center of the room. Behind the portrait, it is equipped with a round wooden caisson ceiling with a round top and a square bottom in an uncomplicated style, and the ceiling is decorated with carved pendant pedals with gold foil painting in the middle. Because the ancients valued nature, they created a doom with a square bottom to imitate nature. Moreover, the hall is spic-and-span with tidy desks and four study treasures on the desks, which seems to take us back to the old times when pupils concentrated on reading. On the right side of Master Zhu's Shrine, a simple black lacquer couch is placed in the middle and the antique palace armchairs are lined on both sides. Since Master Zhu took pleasure in training scholars all over the country, they were attracted by his great reputation, and he frequently engaged in arduous discussions with students until midnight. In general, his dedication to teaching is evident in the design of his chamber.

The academy is still filled with the sound of reading and the culture of education has been passed down continuously for a thousand years. The plaques and couplets have been encouraging students to be forward-thinking, aspirational, modest, and devoted. As a result, Linpu has been blessed with exceptional accomplishments.

◎ 祠堂文化

魏晋南朝时期，北方汉人大批入闽。隋唐时，大量外来人口进入福建，他们或随军入闽，或因避乱和仕宦入闽，使福建人口持续增长（何绵山，2016）。移民们多是举族南迁，共同择一安身之所，在此繁衍后代，因此同姓者聚族而居的现象屡见不鲜。他们有着共同的归属感和认同感，祠堂的建立为他们创造了公共活动空间和精神寄托之所。祠堂是家族后嗣供奉、追思先祖的祭祀之地，是亲族们商讨家族事宜，承办生辰庆典、婚礼、寿宴、葬礼等的场所。祠堂以血缘为根基，将道德、礼仪和信仰融合为一，教导族人们精诚团结、崇尚孝道、遵守伦理、光前裕后。闽学宗师朱熹提出了有关宗族祠堂与祭祀礼仪的具体思想，强调建祠的重要性，满足人们报本反始之心、尊祖敬宗之意，对祠堂的营造影响深远（朱楠楠，2011：49）。因而，福建各地大规模地兴建宗族祠堂，弘扬朱子精神。

祠堂的规模和建制取决于家族人丁繁衍的数量、社会地位和族人成就的高低。人丁兴旺的家族为了后世寻根问祖和精神传承的需要，通过建祠来增强家族的凝聚力。此外，儿孙满堂的家族往往有着更为雄厚的经济实力，可集众人之力大举兴建祠堂。根据古代典章制度选集《礼记》的规定，只有皇室、诸侯和士大夫才能建造宗庙祭祖。时移世易，南宋理学家朱熹通过礼学著作《家礼》，推动了民间祠堂的发展，形成了营建祠堂的热潮。明清时期，虽祠堂遍天下，但其规制上下有等：高门大户，建祠考究，门楼宏伟，厅堂开阔，用材上等，雕梁画栋，匾额、楹联一应俱全；身微力薄之家，勉为其难，建祠简易，厅堂局促，装饰简陋。家族祠堂的修建是文化昌明、人才兴盛的表现。才学兼优的宗族子弟饱读诗书，通文达理，入仕为宦；或发家致富，富甲一方，造福桑梓。族人们在祠堂中开辟专门的空间展陈先贤的丰功伟绩，颂扬功德，鞭策后人。在宗族中，祠堂举足轻重，其建筑形制、平面布局、装饰设计和内部陈设是家族历史、宗族势力和功名成就的缩影，是家族礼法和文化传承的活化石。

螺江陈氏宗祠：文典之家遗风

螺江陈氏宗祠是一处始建于明嘉靖后期（约1556年）的祠堂建筑，坐落于福州市仓山区螺洲镇店前村，最初是陈氏家族"第一位进士"六世祖陈淮创建的家庙，直至清康熙十六年（1677年）方扩为宗祠。嘉庆二十四年（1819年），"三部尚书"陈若霖出资重修宗祠，后由末代帝师陈宝琛于宣统年间屡次修缮，才基本奠定了总面积达1710平方米的现有规模（福州市档案馆，2014：27）。

◎ Ancestral Temple Culture

Throughout the Southern Dynasties, a sizable population of Han migrants from the north poured into Fukien. Soon after that, a large number of people traveled to Fukien with the army to flee from brutal conflicts or take up positions of local authority, which led to an increase in the population of Fukien during the transition from the Sui Dynasty to the Tang Dynasty(He Mianshan 2016:7). It has been conventional to gather people sharing the same family name and reproduce, in that most of the immigrants moved south with their clans to choose an identical place to settle down. Subsequently, they built ancestral halls to establish a communal area and claim a spiritual homestead because they all shared a strong sense of belonging and identity. Specifically, ancestral halls were places to memorialize and worship their ancestors and venues to discuss family issues and host weddings, birthday banquets, and funerals. Generally speaking, ancestral halls incorporated morality, etiquette, and beliefs based on blood, instructing the clan to unite, uphold filial piety, abide by ethics and honor the future. Additionally, Master Zhu, the founder of Neo-Confucianism, put forward specific theories regarding clan ancestral halls and rituals and emphasized the significance of constructing ancestral halls to appease people's desire to repay the origin and respect their ancestors, which exerted a profound influence on the construction of ancestral halls(Zhu Nannan, 2011: 49). As a result, Ancestral halls flourished throughout Fukien in order to promote the spirit of Master Zhu.

The size and standard of ancestral halls are influenced by the population, socioeconomic class, and accomplishments of clans. Accordingly, families with a large population constructed ancestral halls to reconnect with their history, pass along family spirit, and fortify ties. Additionally, large families with numerous descendants had the financial resources to build elaborate ancestral halls. As time went by, traditions had changed a lot. *The Book of Rites*, a collection of ancient laws and customs, states that only the royal families and dukes were permitted to build ancestral halls for devotion. Nevertheless, the masterpiece of Master Zhu, *the Rites of family*, broke the boundary between civilians and officials, stimulating the development of folk ancestral halls. So, ancestral halls were thriving far and near during the Ming and Qing dynasties, but only wealthy families were able to afford halls with grand entrances, large interior spaces, high-quality materials, exquisitely carved beams and pillars, well-written plaques, and couplets. Contrarily, poor families struggled to build ancestral halls plainly and crudely. It is known to all that ancestral halls are a sign of cultural prosperity and thriving talent who excelled in business and office circles to help fellow compatriots. Evidently, clansmen created an exclusive area for them to showcase their achievements and educate the future generations. On the whole, ancestral halls have played a pivotal role in the clans, epitomizing family history, clan power, and attainment. What's more, they have been witnessing family rituals and cultural heritage.

The Ancestral Hall of Chen's Family in Luojiang: Erudition

The ancestral hall of Chen's family was set up in the late Ming Dynasty(about 1556) and is located in Dianqian Village, Luozhou Town, Cangshan District, Fuzhou City. It was originally established by Chen Huai as a clan temple, who was one of the sixth generation of Chen's family and its first metropolitan graduate. Afterward, it was expanded to an ancestral hall in 1677 and funded by Chen Ruolin in 1819, who used to be the leader in three different ministries. Finally, Chen Baochen, the teacher of the last feudal emperor, restored it multiple times throughout the Xuantong period of the Qing Dynasty, expanding it to a total space of 1, 710 square meters(Fuzhou City Archives, 2014: 27).

祠堂坐北朝南，采取中轴对称的形式，渐次排列照壁、祠堂埕、门楼、天井、仪门、中天井、正大厅、后天井及后座大礼堂、大戏台等建筑。大殿前有回廊，两侧有厢房。其整体结构保存较为完整，具有浓郁的福州地方特色（福建省政协文史委员会，1998：48）。照壁上的浮雕栩栩如生，瑞兽麒麟脚踏八宝神器——葫芦、团扇、宝剑、莲花、花篮、渔鼓、横笛、玉板，疾步回首，鬃毛飞扬。古人云："麒麟出没，必有祥瑞。"麒麟照壁既彰显门庭，又寓意吉祥。照壁之上、屋檐之下的水车堵装饰带惟妙惟肖地刻画出郭子仪七子八婿拜寿的故事。郭子仪在唐朝受封为汾阳王，出将入相，长寿富贵。七子八婿皆贵显朝廷，子孙满堂，多子多福，是福禄寿的象征。

祠堂为两进单层结构。第一进门楼由四扇三间房组成，门楼上方悬挂着金字匾额"螺江陈氏宗祠"，为晚清重臣左宗棠所题。两侧的楹联"冠带今螺渚，诗书古颍川"，由文华殿大学士李鸿章执笔题写。楹联不仅指出了陈氏家族的谱系渊源，还把汉魏时期盛产风雅之士的颍川与螺洲相提并论，愈加彰显出螺洲陈氏族人卓尔不群的品质和诗礼传家的优秀家风。门楼通过匾额和楹联凸显祠堂的文化底蕴，其雕镂彩绘也向世人展示了家族的雅致匠心。檐下的瓜筒端头精雕细刻成花篮状，表面用金粉和红、蓝、绿三色彩绘进行修饰，简约中蕴藏精致，增强了空间表现的艺术效果。在柱头和梁枋交接处，近似三角形的木雕构件称雀替。门楼上雀替的幅面较大，轮廓曲线别致，造型精美，用镂雕工艺雕刻成莲花样式，色彩艳丽，内涵丰富。

进祠门即为祠堂前院，院中为前天井，两侧为东西廊。隶书横匾"百代羹墙"为第一进和第二进的界墙，中有大门，两边为仪门，上方分别有"入孝"、"出悌"石匾（福州市仓山区政协委员会，2003：48）。天井是被主体建筑包围而没有屋顶的空间，用以排除屋面雨水，实现宗祠内部的采光通风（朱楠楠，2011：97）。宗祠建筑的外墙高大坚固，为保证私密性，墙体上基本不对外开窗，内部只能通过天井通风采光。天井西侧现被开辟为红色文化教育基地，展出家族历史名人的先进事迹。"百代羹墙"的"羹"意指教育，寓意家族要世代重视教育，以教育为本。入孝、出悌的训诫来自《论语·学而》篇，意在教诲后代在家须孝敬父母，外出要敬爱兄长。陈氏后裔确也秉承祖训、恪守家风。据统计，螺洲陈氏家族明清时期进士共有21人，举人则多达108人，其中不乏官位显赫的忠臣良将。

The ancestral hall of Chen's family stands the north and faces the south, taking the form of symmetry in the central axis. And it was composed of the screen wall against the gate, the open area in front of the ancestral hall, the gate tower, the patio, the ceremonial door, the middle patio, the main hall, the rear patio, the auditorium, and the grand opera stage, etc. Furthermore, there is a corridor in front of the main hall and compartments on both sides. Hence, the overall structure is relatively complete with strong local characteristics(Fukien Provincial Committee of Political Consultative Conference(ed.), 1998: 48). The lifelike relief carving on the wall depicts the beast Qilin trampling on the eight sacred weapons—lotus, gourd, fan, sword, flower cage, fish drum, horizontal flute, and jade plate while turning to look back with a rapid step and flying hair. As the old saying goes, "When Qilin appears, there must be good fortune." Therefore, Qilin on the screen wall against the gate was a symbol of nobility and auspiciousness. Moreover, it is depicted that Guo Ziyi's seven sons and eight sons-in-law celebrated his birthday as ornaments on Shuichedu beneath the eaves, who was recognized as the prestigious general with fortune and longevity. Apart from it, he was a fruitful man and his sons and sons-in-law all held important posts in the court, standing for blessing, wealth, and a long-life expectancy.

The ancestral hall is a single-story structure with two patios. The first one consists of four doors, above which hangs a plaque in golden letters "The Ancestral Hall of Chen's Family in Luojiang", which was inscribed by Zuo Zongtang, a grand minister of state in the late Qing Dynasty. In addition to that, the couplet on both sides read, "Superior in Luozhu, Erudite from ancient Yingchuan", which was inscribed by Li Hongzhang, a grand secretary of the Wenhua Palace. The couplet was used to infer the family's genealogy, and Luojiang was compared to Yingchuan, a region rich in tasteful and kind people during the Han and Wei dynasties. This comparison highlighted the exceptional clansmen from Chen's family in Luozhou as well as the outstanding family manners and etiquette. On the whole, its couplets and plaques have been conveying an abundance of historical and cultural heritage, and its carvings and paintings have been witnessing delicate craftsmanship. What's more, the end of the gourd tubes under the eaves are finely carved into the shape of flower baskets, and their surface is decorated with golden powder and red, blue, and green painting, which look ravishing and enhance the artistic effects. At the intersection of the pillars and beams, the wood carving which resembles a triangle is called a sparrow brace which is large in size, attractive in outline, and delicate in shape. Besides, they are engraved into lotus with openwork carving, colorful and rich in connotation.

There is a front patio behind the gate, and the east and west corridors are set on either side respectively. Additionally, the plaque in official script, named Baidai Gengqiang, is the boundary between the first patio and the second one. Moreover, there is the main entrance in the middle and ceremonial doors on both sides, above which are stone plaques for "filial piety" and "brotherhood" respectively(Fuzhou City, Cang Shan District, CPPCC Committee(ed.), 2003: 48). The patio is a space surrounded by the main building without a roof and is used to remove rainwater and let in light and ventilation(Zhu Nannan, 2011: 97). Since privacy needs to be ensured, there are few windows on the lofty and fortified walls. For the sake of light and ventilation, a patio hence was constructed inside. Plus, the west side of the patio is now used as a base for red revolutionary culture to display meritorious deeds of the historical figures from the family. Moreover, Geng from Baidai Gengqiang referred to education, emphasizing the importance of education. Likewise, filial piety derived from *Analects* was expected to instruct them to pay homage to their parents at home and look up to brothers outside. Overall, its clansmen have been complying with family instructions. For that reason, there were 21 metropolitan graduates, and 108 provincial graduates, most of whom were loyal officials during the Ming and Qing Dynasties according to statistics.

正大厅是祠堂的主体部分，是祭祀祖先和处理本族事务的活动中心。祠堂屋顶为悬山单檐，屋面曲折，翼角飞翘，檐部轻盈，灵动自然；檐头瓦当设计优美，行云流水，古朴大方。大厅面阔五间、进深六间，抬梁和木柱粗大，外涂黑漆，地面用正方形的块石铺就，两侧设封火墙（黄荣春，2009：155）。祠堂正厅高大开阔，梁柱浑圆，构件精美。厅内正中横置着一张精雕细刻、层次分明的深色案桌，案桌上摆放着一个造型独特的黄铜香炉与一对精雕细琢的铜制烛台，一对1米多高的黄蓝彩绘大赏瓶分立于案桌两侧。除了作为雅赏的器物外，花瓶的"瓶"谐音"平"，寓意阖家平安，这也是对族人平安健康的期许。案桌之后为螺洲陈氏家族的大型神主龛与列祖列宗的牌位，共计有1000多个，用万字纹隔扇窗进行分割保护。正上方悬挂着道光皇帝在刑部尚书陈若霖70岁生日时钦赐的"福寿"鎏金雕花匾额，两侧为宣统皇帝赠太傅陈宝琛的寿联，为中国知名书法家爱新觉罗・启功所题写（福州市档案馆，2014：28）。正厅四面高悬着"巾帼十杰"、"革命一家"、"立祠先祖"等数十幅称颂先贤的金字牌匾和强健儒雅的书法题词，令人肃然生敬。

厅前中天井两侧的东西回廊上挂着历代先贤的肖像，以供后世瞻仰。一侧廊前摆放着清正廉洁、执法严明的"三部尚书"陈若霖的执事牌，另一侧廊前放着内阁学士兼礼部侍郎陈宝琛的执事牌，威严肃穆。天井四周遍布红底金字祠匾："兄弟叔侄同馆翰林"、"同光双御史"、"清代三武将"、"父子将军"、"两院双院士"，尽显"文典之家"的风范，起到垂范百世、敦促教化的积极作用。作为螺洲望族之一的陈氏家族，通过诗礼传家的家风鼓励子孙读书养性、读书养德，因此陈氏子弟中贤良辈出。他们入仕为官，不忘桑梓，也带动螺洲社会形成一股勤学、好学、乐学之风，促使当地民众奋力向学。在这种良好风尚的熏陶下，螺洲文风鼎盛，赢得"人儒之乡"的美誉。时至今日，为一睹帝师之乡的风采而到螺洲观光的游客络绎不绝。他们不只叹服于建筑的精良，更对螺洲地区的人文精神和文脉传承充满赞许和向往。

Its main hall, the major part, is a place, where clansmen offered sacrifice to ancestors and grappled with family issues. From the perspective of design, an overhanging gable roof with a single eave is lively, energetic, and lifelike with a curving roof, soaring corners, and lightsome eaves. Correspondingly, the tile ends are plain, natural, and well-designed. Additionally, a hall is five rooms wide and six rooms deep, with thick black painted beams and wooden pillars, a stone floor, and firewalls on both sides(Huang Rongchun, 2009: 155). What's more, rounded beams and exquisite components are placed in the lofty and broad main hall, where a refined and layered dark-colored table stands. There is a brass censer with a distinctive shape, a pair of peculiar bronze candlesticks on the table and a pair of yellow and blue painted vases with the height of more than one meter beside the table. Apart from appreciation, the Chinese pronunciation of vase is the same as that of safety, so vases denote safety for the entire family, which clansmen all look forward to. In addition, more than one thousand memorial tablets were arranged in the massive shrine behind the table, which were protected by partitioned windows with a traditional pattern. On the upper part of the shrine is a gilded plaque with the title of happiness and longevity, which was given by Emperor Daoguang of the Qing Dynasty for the 70s birthday of Chen Ruolin, the Minister of Justice. Likewise, a couplet on both sides was bestowed by Emperor Xuantong to celebrate Chen Baochen's birthday, and inscribed by Qigong, a Chinese renowned calligrapher(Fuzhou City Archives, 2014: 28). On all sides of the main hall, there are dozens of golden plaques and strong and elegant calligraphy in praise of the sages, such as "The Ten Great Women", "The Revolutionary Family" and "The Ancestors of the Ancestral Shrine", inspiring pnofound esteem among people.

There are portraits of sages from the family hung on the corridors of the patio, which future generations convey their deep reverence for. In front of the corridor on one side is the deacon's plaque of Chen Ruolin, the "Ministers of Three Ministries", who was whitehanded and straight-forwarded and enforced the law strictly. Similarly, there is another solemn plaque belonging to Chen Baochen, both the secretary of the Grand Secretariat and the deputy minister of the Ministry of Rites. All around the patio, there are a great many plaques in golden letters: "Brothers, uncles, and nephews in the same Hanlin academy", "Censors of two courts", "Three military generals of the Qing Dynasty", "Generals of father and son", "Double academicians of the two academies". Overall, these plagues display erudition and enlighten the upcoming generations. As one of the prestigious families in Luozhou, the clan has been encouraging learning and cultivating virtue through the family style, and therefore men of talent have come out in succession, who boosted the development of their hometown. At the same time, the clan has made a far-reaching impact locally on diligence and passion for learning. As a consequence, Luozhou has featured a prosperous culture and abundant talent and has been hailed as the town of talents. To this day, there is an endless stream of tourists visiting Luozhou to get a glimpse of the hometown of the emperor's teacher. Afterward, they not only marvel at the outstanding architecture but also adore and complement its humanistic spirit and cultural heritage.

下杭路曾氏祠堂：商帮文化缩影

上下杭地处福州市台江区中部偏南区域，位于福州城市的中轴线上。在古汉语中，"杭"通"航"，有渡河之意。自明朝中叶伊始，中国与琉球贡舶贸易（即朝廷准许前来进贡的外国使节随车马、船舶捎带货品来中国进行的商贸交易）的中心转移至位于闽江口的福州，再加上由闽江口溯流而上的朝贡船停泊在城南的码头比较方便，福州城的商业也渐渐南移，靠近闽江的上下杭逐渐发展起来。1844年福州开埠后，水运便捷的上下杭更是以优越的地理位置成为货物集散的枢纽，并慢慢发展成辐射全省、沟通省外乃至东南亚地区的商品集散地（陈瑗，2014）。清末民初，上下杭的商帮文化逐步发展壮大，物产繁盛，富贾云集，整个街区充满浓厚的商业气息。

位于下杭路196号的曾氏祠堂的创始人曾文乾（又名曾尊椿），是家财万贯的福州纸行大户。曾文乾早年随父亲由长乐迁入福州，开创"曾长兴"土纸行。他天资聪颖，极具经商天赋，不仅经营纸货，还做起了土特产生意，赚得盆满钵满。马江海战期间，曾文乾低价收购纸货，囤货居奇，使"曾长兴"一跃成为台江纸行之首。在那个四方离乱的年代，曾文乾不忘家国大义，热心公益；发家之后，不忘桑梓，积极为族人营建祠堂和编修族谱，造福子孙。

曾氏祠堂建于民国14年（1925年），坐北向南，原有两进。首进临街为商行，以供出租。二进为祠堂正厅，依次有门厅、回廊、祠厅。祠厅面阔三间，进深七柱，穿斗式木构架，周围是封火山墙。大木架横梁跨度大，石柱上有题刻、楹联多处（福州老建筑百科，2024）。临街商行前的祠埕由石板铺就，面积宽广，视野开阔。祠埕东侧的商行前建有一座万字纹雕花长廊，供人们遮阳避雨、休闲小憩。穿过祠埕，一堵高大的门墙映入眼帘，门墙正中题刻着"南丰衍派"四个大字，展现了曾氏家族的历史渊源。福州《三山志》记载，福州曾氏祖籍江西南丰，唐末随王审知入闽，从永泰再迁长乐（佚名，2021b）。

进入门墙内，一方天井，别有洞天。南方多雨，祠堂天井通过四面檐口的斜角将屋面雨水排出，因而被称为"四水归堂"。中国古人修建屋舍，讲究风水。古语云："山管人丁，水管财。"像曾氏这样的商贾之家最忌讳财富外流，而"四水归堂"则寓意财源广聚、延绵不断，所以方正的祠堂天井正好满足了聚财的风水需求。由于祠堂开间不大，进深较大，不设窗户，正厅难免采光不足，天井的采光作用就尤为重要。且祠堂正厅进深大，气流易阻滞，而天井的设计既能藏风聚气，又能吐故纳新，形成良好的生态内循环，促进空气的流通。

The Ancestral Hall of Zeng's Family on Xiahang Road: the Epitome of Commerce

Shangxiahang is located in the central and southern area of Taijiang District, Fuzhou City, and on the central axis of Fuzhou City. In ancient Chinese, Hang was the equivalent of sail, indicating crossing the river. Since the middle of the Ming Dynasty, the center of tribute trade between China and Ryukyu(the trade transaction between the court and the foreign envoys who came to pay tribute with their carriages and ships to bring goods to China)has been moved to the mouth of Minjiang River. Because it was expedient to moor at the wharf in the south of the city for tribute ships going upstream from the mouth of Minjiang River, the commerce of Fuzhou city gradually moved southward, and Shangxiahang near Minjiang River steadily came to thrive. After Fuzhou's port opened in 1844, Shangxiahang's strategic location allowed it to quickly develop into a hub for the transportation of goods that connected the province with neighboring provinces and even Southeast Asia(Chen Yuan, 2014). In the late Qing and the early Republic of China, the merchant culture of Shangxiahang expanded and developed over time. Because of this, the entire neighborhood was drenched in a vibrant commercial atmosphere when men of business and riches congregated and commodities were prosperous.

Zeng Wenqian(known as Zeng Zunchun), the founder of the ancestral hall of Zeng's family on No. 196 Xiahang Road, was a well-off paper manufacturer. He moved to Fuzhou from Changle with his father at an early age and launched the business of clay paper, called Zeng Changxing. Because Zeng Wenqian was gifted in running businesses for both paper and local produce, he succeeded in making a pile. During the Ma Jiang naval war, Zeng Wenqian bought paper goods at a lower price and then hoarded them, making "Zeng Changxing" the top-notch enterprise in Taijiang District. In that era of turmoil, Zeng Wenqian had a deep affection for his motherland and family and he was a man of public spirit. Hence, he zealously set up the ancestral hall and compiled the family tree for the sake of his clansmen.

The ancestral hall facing the south was built in 1925. There used to be two patios, and its frontal one was a commercial house frontage for rent. The other one is its main body, including a foyer, a corridor, and a main hall successively. It is three rooms wide and seven columns deep, with the column and tie construction and firewalls around. Particularly, the large wooden frame boasts a wide span of beams, and couplets are engraved on the stone pillars (Fuzhou Old Architecture Encyclopedia: Par 2). In front of the commercial house, the open area paved by stone slabs is capacious with an expansive view. Meanwhile, there is a carved long corridor with a traditional Chinese pattern before the commercial house where the public kick back and relax and a shelter is offered to escape from the sun and rain. A towering wall subsequently comes into sight with the inscription of "Nanfeng Yanpai", which reveals the origin of Zeng's family. As stated in Sanshan Zhi, the Zeng had rooted in Jiangxi and then immigrated to Fukien with Wang Shenzhi in the late Tang Dynasty, afterwards shifting from Yongtai to Changle(Anonymous, 2021b).

There is a patio with diverse scenery behind the gate. Since it rains a lot in the south, the patio drains off the rainwater from the pitched roof through bevel angles of the eaves, which is called "Four Waters to the Hall". There is an ancient proverb of Feng Shui saying, "Mountains are in charge of people, while water is in command of wealth." Therefore, a merchant family like the Zeng's would undoubtedly avoid the outflow of wealth from the perspective of Feng Shui. "Four Waters to the Hall" signifies amassing a fortune, so a square patio precisely satisfies the demand. As the ancestral hall without windows was not broad and deep enough, it was extremely crucial to enable the light to pass through and the air to circulate. Furthermore, due to its depth and the difficulty in ventilating it, the patio not only serves to both hide the wind and collect qi, but also exhales the old and inhales the new, promoting good ecological circulation.

祠堂的正厅现已被改造成"苍霞人家"生活馆，分"百年苍霞"、"纸褙棚屋"、"改造旧城"、"情系冷暖"、"世纪搬迁"、"喜迁新居"、"共建共享"、"接续奋斗"和"宜居福地"九大板块进行展陈，向游客展示了苍霞的蜕变重生之路。虽然祠堂正厅的功能业已改变，但正厅的建筑风貌还是得到了较好的保存和还原。厅内梁枋上的木雕、梁头雕刻装饰、雀替和垂花瓜柱主要采用透雕和镂雕相结合的手法，题材以自然界的花草鸟兽为主，造型生动逼真，构图巧妙，惟妙惟肖。祠堂里除了两组"双狮戏珠"的雕饰和梁上的描金花饰外，其他的雕饰均保留了木头原来的色泽和质感，古朴自然。大厅正中，一个纹饰繁复的雕花梁柱极为引人注目，当中嵌有"瓜瓞箕裘"四字楷书，寓意家族兴盛、后继有人、事业蒸蒸日上。垂花瓜筒也与别的宅院祠堂截然不同，造型新颖，上部为鱼鳞鱼身，下部为花叶繁盛的柱头，丝丝入扣，衔接巧妙。正厅中的金字楹联也得以完好保存，向世人展示着富商之家的家风家训和纸行掌舵人曾文乾对子孙后代的殷切希望。祠厅正中的长联"道尊万年永昌世代望达朝廷功崇翼戴 泽贻千载广毓贤良忠以襄赞孝克显扬"，不仅表达了建功立业的渴望，更强调了克己复礼、忠良贤孝的期许。抗战胜利后，曾氏后人在祠堂办了"四端中学"（福州四中的前身），并将三座祠堂房产划归校产。曾氏后人默默践行祖训，通过兴办教育惠及民众。

Presently, its main hall has been transformed into the "Cangxia Family" living museum, which exhibits urban transition in nine sections by modern technology, including "100-year history of Cangxia", "paper shacks", "urban renewal", "the warmth of human nature", "relocation after one century", "moving house", "building and sharing", "arduous efforts", and "habitable blessed land", showing visitors the transformation and rebirth of Cangxia. Although its major function has been altered, its architectural style has been properly conserved and restored. In terms of decoration, the combination of openwork carvings and piercing carvings has been decently applied to the small tie-beams, the end of the beams, the sparrow braces, and short floral-pendant columns. Besides, themes of ornaments predominantly refer to plants and animals with vivid images and ingenious composition. Except for the two sets of carvings of "two lions competing for a pearl" and the gilded flower decorations on the beams, the rest are still retaining the original color and the texture of the wood, plain and natural. In the middle of the hall, it's exceedingly eye-catching to spot an intricately decorated carved beam with the inscription of "Guadie Jiqiu" in regular script, signifying the prosperous family and thriving business. Moreover, the short floral-pendant columns look delicate and innovative with fish scales on the top and bloom on the bottom. Besides, the golden couplets were kept in good condition, indicating the family tradition and ardent anticipation for future generations of the affluent family. Precisely, the long couplet in the main hall reads, "Prospering for thousands of years and conducive to the court, blessing for hundreds of years and praising for filial piety", denoting the aspiration for fulfillment, self-discipline, and fidelity. After the Sino-Japanese war, the descendants of the Zeng's family established Siduan Middle School(the predecessor of Fuzhou No 4. Middle School) and donated three of their properties as school ones. Consequently, the posterity virtually achieved their ancestral motto for the benefit of the people through education.

第八章

琳宫塔庙：敬天护民

Temples and Churches: Worshipping the
Heaven and Protecting the People

◎ 华林寺

佛教是福建境内最有影响的宗教。佛教文化在福州市传播与发展的历史悠久，影响范围广。据资料记载，福州市最早的寺庙建于西晋太康三年（282年），发展至宋朝时佛教的传播进入全盛期。清代后期，受外来宗教冲击，佛教的发展受到影响，寺庙数量的增长也逐渐缓慢。尽管如此，佛教寺院如今在福州依然是晨钟暮鼓、香火鼎盛。这当中便有一座国宝级寺院，它就是位于屏山南麓的华林寺。华林寺建立距今已逾千年，是我国长江以南地区现存的最古老的木构古建筑。1982年成为第二批全国重点文物保护单位。

华林寺有三大特点。特点一，悠久古朴。经放射性同位素碳-14测定，该寺距今已有一千年以上的历史，是长江以南最古老的木构建筑。据专家考证，华林寺始建于北宋乾德二年（964年）。闽国灭亡后，福州郡守鲍修为了祈求郡境安宁，拆除闽王宫殿，并用拆下来的材料建成华林寺前身——越山吉祥禅院。明正统九年，即1444年，御赐匾额"华林寺"，寺名从而沿用至今。

寺院经历过三次香火旺盛的高峰期。在名声最为鼎盛之时，华林寺的僧众们修建了多间木构平房，收容了许多无家可归之人。遗憾的是，由于风灾虫害和"文革"中的"破四旧"等行为，寺庙和文物多有损毁。

1988年，人们在仅存的大殿四周修建了新的配殿、走廊、石板甬道和山门，这才显露出完整的寺庙模样。大殿的主要架构虽经历代重修，却保持原汁原味，大小构件仍为千年前的原物，没有繁复华丽的装饰彩绘，没有飘逸轻盈的飞檐翘角，尽显五代时期古朴、雄浑、苍茫之气。

修建后的华林寺，是一所无香、无僧也无佛像的寺庙。大殿内部空荡荡，正中间摆着木制模型，呈现出大殿原来的模样。模型两侧摆放着一些建筑残件，有千年以上的历史。

◎ Hualin Temple

Buddhism is the most influential religion in Fukien. Buddhist culture has been spreading and developing in Fuzhou for a long time with wide influence. Records show the earliest temple in Fuzhou was built in the third year of the Taikang reign in Western Jin Dynasty (A.D. 282). The spread of Buddhism reached its heyday in Song Dynasty. Till the late Qing Dynasty, the development of Buddhism was affected and limited by the coming of foreign religions, with the increase of the number of temples slowing down. Nevertheless, the Buddhist temples in Fuzhou are still attended by numerous worshippers. Among these temples is Hualin Temple, a national-treasure class temple located at the south piedmont of Pingshan Mountain in the north of Fuzhou City. Built over 1000 years ago, Hualin Temple was the oldest timberwork construction in the south of the Yangtze River in China. In 1982, Hualin Temple was listed among the second batch of major historical and cultural sites protected at the national level.

Hualin Temple boasts of its three features, the first being long in history and simple in style. Tested by radio carbon 14 (14C), the temple shows a history of more than 1, 300 years, being the oldest timberwork construction in the south of the Yangtze River in China. Experts hold that the Hualin Temple was built in the second year of the Qiande reign (A.D. 964) in the Northern Song dynasty, when the Kingdom of Min perished. Bao Xiu, magistrate of Fuzhou Prefecture, pulled down the palace of the King of Min and used the materials to build the Auspicious Buddha Hall, the predecessor of Hualin Temple, for the peace of his county. In 1444, or the ninth year of the Zhengtong reign (A.D. 1436-1449) in Ming Dynasty, an inscribed plaque with the name of the Hualin Temple was granted by the emperor and the name was used till now.

Hualin Temple experienced three heydays, during which the monks of the temple built many wooden one-storey houses to shelter numerous homeless people. Unfortunately, many parts of the temple and the cultural relics were destroyed by natural disasters and human misdeeds.

In 1988, new side halls, corridors, stone paths, and the gate were repaired or rebuilt around the surviving hall, which made the temple complete. For all the reconstructions in history, the framework of the main hall preserved its original features, its components being the 1, 000-year-old originals. There are no complex and flowery decorations and paintings, nor elegant cornices and upturning angles, but just the simple, vigorous and vast flavor of the Five Dynasties (A.D. 907-960).

The restored Hualin Temple is one without incenses, monks or Buddha statues. In the center of the empty main hall is the wooden model of the temple in its original appearance. On both sides of the model are placed some construction relics, all with about 1, 400 years' history.

特点二，用"材"珍贵。整个大殿面积574平方米，高15.5米。面宽虽仅有三开间，但用材硕大，甚至超过了宋朝《营造法式》所规定的最高等级规格。大殿有18根立柱，柱子以上全由斗拱支撑，不用一根铁钉，却能牢牢固定。这保留了部分南朝风格，在唐宋以后不多见，很多手法甚至是没有记载的孤例。如果单以建筑年代排序，华林寺大殿在中国古建筑中位列第七，而前六名都保存在气候干燥的高原地区。长江以南潮湿多雨，木构建筑要想存留难上加难，也更显珍贵。因此，华林寺可以说是研究我国古代建筑的珍贵实物资料。

特点三，见证历史。华林寺对日本镰仓时期也就是12世纪末的建筑风格产生巨大影响。当时日本名僧俊乘坊重源三次来宋朝求法。其中一次是为建造日本奈良的东大寺大佛殿专门到福建考察。华林寺大殿让他叹为观止，于是将这种建筑风格移植到日本，在日本各地开花结果。可以说，华林寺是中日建筑交流史的实物见证。

◎ 泛船浦教堂

基督教堂也是福州极具代表性的宗教建筑。1840年鸦片战争以后，中国被迫签订了一系列不平等条约。其中，1842年的《南京条约》规定福州为五口通商的城市之一，对外开放。开埠不仅使福州成为近代贸易口岸之一，也使当地涌现出大量用于行政、居住、宗教、文教、卫生、商业等的近代西式建筑。

1847年，美国基督教公理会国外布道会传教士杨顺来到福州，拉开了基督教在福州传播的序幕。此后，卫理公会和英国圣公会也陆续派遣传教士来闽。这些基督教派在传播圣经的同时，也将西方宗教建筑即教堂引入福州。

泛船浦教堂是福建省规模最大的天主教堂，创建于1868年，原为双层木结构。1932年，在旧堂的旁边建造新座堂，同时将旧堂拆除，改建成双层、二十四开间的新主教府，包含主教堂和神父楼，占地18亩。"文革"期间，泛船浦天主教堂受到冲击，后被福州市蓄电池厂占用，直至1986年底归还，同时复堂，1996年被列为省级文物保护单位。

The second feature is using rare and valuable materials. The 15.5-meter-high main hall covers an area of 574 square meters, with just three bays in width. The gigantic materials went beyond the highest standard prescribed by *The Building Formulas* in the Song Dynasty. There were altogether 18 pillars, and what was above the pillars was supported by dougong (wooden square blocks inserted between the top of a column and a crossbeam), all fixed together without using a single nail. Its style preserved part of the style of the Southern Dynasties, but was rarely used after the Tang and Song Dynasties. Many skills were even unrecorded isolated examples. Among China's ancient constructions, the Hualin Temple ranks the seventh in terms of the time of construction, with all the first six constructions preserved in dry plateau areas. The wet and rainy climate in the south of the Yangtze River makes it hard to preserve timberwork constructions, which makes Hualin Temple especially valuable for the study of China's ancient constructions.

Hualin Temple's third feature lies in its witnessing communication. Hualin Temple had great influence on the the construction style of Japan's Kamakura period (around the end of the 12th century). Shunjobo Gencho, a famous Japanese monk visited the Song Dynasty three times for the Buddhist doctrines. He visited Fukien once for the construction of Todai-ji Temple's Hall of Great Buddha in Nara, Japan. Greatly impressed with the main hall of Hualin Temple, he transplanted its style to Japan and made it flourish there. Hualin Temple is thus said to be a concrete witness of the history of Sino-Japan communication in architectural construction.

◎ Fanchuanpu Catholic Church

Christian churches deserve the representative of Fuzhou's religious constructions. Since the First Opium War in 1840, China was forced to sign a series of unequal treaties, among which was the Treaty of Nanjing in 1842, setting Fuzhou as one of the five cities opening to the outside. The Treaty not only made Fuzhou one of the trading ports in the modern times, but also fostered the numerous western-styled constructions for religion, administration, culture and education, medical services and business.

In 1847, Stephen Johnson, a commissioner of American Board of Commissioners for Foreign Missions (ABCFM) arrived in Fuzhou, marking the start of the spread of Christian religion in Fuzhou. Later, the Methodist Church and the Church of England both sent their commissioners to Fukien. While spreading the Christian doctrines, these sects brought western religious constructions, namely churches, to Fuzhou.

主教堂为砖混结构，哥特式单塔楼，堂身呈十字形，长60.2米、宽19.52米，建筑面积1254平方米。可容纳2000多人，气势雄伟，内部造型独特。教堂内顶部为拱形穹隆，缀以星辰，两侧和祭坛上部的窗门装有彩色花玻璃，教堂主楼北端有20多米高的钟楼，报时的声音方圆十里都能听见，当年号称江南第一大堂。

泛船浦教堂在福州之所以出名，还因为它是一座行走的教堂。2008年，由于教堂的神父楼位于规划的南江滨大道中央，不得不进行迁移。神父楼先平移80.7米后，再进行90度转向。大楼转身要比平移困难，必须从神父楼的东南角和西北角分别牵出三根拇指粗的钢绞线来牵引拉动。

施工人员撬动上百个液压千斤顶，将重达1500吨的神父楼略微撑起后，在弧形轨道上均匀摆放数百个滚轴，帮助神父楼作90度旋转，随后再向南平移35.96米，终于到达指定位置，由东西朝向改为南北朝向，面朝闽江而立，变成了望江楼。

◎ 闽越王庙

除了寺院、教堂外，福州还有很多道观和清真寺等宗教建筑。这里重点谈谈用作民间信仰的庙宇。这类庙宇供奉和祭祀的对象十分庞杂：有的是远祖族源（图腾崇拜）；有的在历史上对人民有贡献而被人民立庙纪念；有的历史上确有其人，死后被人们神化；还有民间造出来的各类土神及古代神话、演义故事中的神灵。

闽越王庙是为了纪念八闽始祖——汉闽越王无诸兴建的庙宇。福建最早的先民是闽族人，到了战国中期，公元前306年楚国伐越，勾践的六世孙越王无疆兵败，越国王室后裔四散迁徙，分别来到"瓯"（今温州地区）和"闽"（今福州地区）。在福州的这一支与闽族融合，称为"闽越族"。

无诸为勾践的十三世孙，他在闽建国，自立为闽越王。秦朝末年，公元前209年，陈胜、吴广揭竿起义，天下响应，无诸随诸侯起兵攻秦。秦亡后，楚霸王项羽分封诸侯，无诸未列其中，他对此极为不满。楚汉战争爆发后，无诸率闽中子弟佐汉击楚，为汉朝的建立立下功劳。汉高祖五年（前202年），刘邦封无诸为闽越王，治闽中故地，人称"汉闽越王"。无诸班师回闽后统一八闽各部，并在冶山一带建立国都——冶城，正式开启了福州两千两百年的建城史。

The cathedral is a masonry-concrete single-tower building in Gothic style. It is 60.2 meters in length, 19.52 meters in width, and 1254 square meters in area with the capacity for more than 2, 000 people. It is magnificent in appearance and unique in inner design. The inner top of the cathedral is an arched dome, decorated with stars. Windows on both sides and over the altar are decorated with colored mosaic glasses. The northern part of the cathedral is a bell tower of more than 20 meters in height, the bell toll from where could be heard more than 5 kilometers away. It was then called The Largest Cathedral in the south of Yangtze River in China.

Fanchuanpu Church gains its fame in Fuzhou also as a "walking church". In 2008, the Priest's House of Fanchuanpu Church had to be moved to make room for the newly planned South Riverside Avenue. The Priest's House was first moved 80.7 meters horizontally, and then turned 90 degrees. It was more difficult to turn the building than to move it, and three thumb-thick steel cables were linked with the southeast part and the northwest part of the house to direct the moving.

More than 100 hydraulic jacks were used to lift the over 1, 500-ton Priest's House, and then hundreds of rollers were set on curve tracks to help its turning. Then the house was moved 35.96 meters to the south horizontally before reaching its present location. The original east-facing riverside building thus became a south-facing river-overlooking one.

◎ Temple of Min-Yue King

Besides the Buddhist temples and Christian churches, there are numerous Taoist temples and mosques in Fuzhou. Moreover, it is also worth mentioning the temples of folk faiths and religions, which are great in numbers and various in types. Most of them are for worshipping remote ancestors and sources of families (including totems); some of them are in memory of those figures with great contributions to people and history; some are honoring figures who were real in history but divinized after death; while some are worshipping local gods or those immortals in fairy tales and legends.

A typical example is the Temple of Min-Yue King in memory of Wuzhu, Min-Yue King in the Han Dynasty, the first ancestor of Fukien people. Fukien's earliest settlers were Min people. In the middle of the period of Warring States (306 B.C.), when Chu Kingdom started invading Yue Kingdom, Wujiang, Yue's King, was defeated and Yue's royal offspring began migrating to Ou (today's Wenzhou in Zhejiang Province) and Min (today's Fuzhou). Those coming to Min (today's Fuzhou) mixed with Min people, thus making the Min-Yue people.

Wuzhu was the 13th-generation grandson of Goujian, the founder of Yue Kingdom. He established his own kingdom in Min and called himself Min-Yue King. At the end of the Qin Dynasty (209 B.C.), the peasant revolution by Chen Sheng and Wu Guang was supported all over the empire. Wuzhu led his army and joined the revolution against the Qin Dynasty. After the Qin Dynasty was destroyed, however, Xiang Yu, the King of Chu and the leader of the revolution, forgot to grant Wuzhu title and fief, which greatly annoyed Wuzhu. When the war between Chu and Han broke out, Wuzhu led his Min people in support of Han against Chu and made great contributions to the foundation of the Han Dynasty. In the fifth year of Gaozu reign in the Han Dynasty (202 B.C.), Liu Bang, the founder and the first emperor of the Han Dynasty, made Wuzhu the King of Min-Yue to govern Fukien. After Wuzhu returned to Fukien and united all its parts, he established the capital of his kingdom near Yeshan Mountain and called it Ye City, thus beginning the over 2, 300 years' history of Fuzhou City.

无诸在福建开疆拓土，发展生产，促进了福建的发展。在他死后，闽越国慢慢由盛转衰，更加激起了人们对无诸的怀念。因此，人们就在八闽各地，尤其是无诸曾经留下足迹的地方兴建闽越王庙，四时祭祀（福州市茶亭原有的祖庙就是奉祀无诸的）。在钓龙台（今福州四中）曾建有闽越王庙，人称大庙，山亦名大庙山。此庙在抗日战争时被毁。

福州郊县现在仍有一些纪念无诸的庙宇，如闽侯洋里乡仙洋村就有闽越王庙。仙洋村距离闽侯县城近50公里，该闽越王庙始建于明代，现存建筑为清代重修。庙宇为重檐歇山顶，飞檐翘角，周围土筑封火墙，正中大门上方镶嵌石匾，上刻"仙洋正境"四字。

走进庙宇，首先经过的便是戏台。戏台为单檐歇山顶，抬梁木构架。戏台两侧绘有四幅清代壁画，讲述"三英战吕布"、"葭萌关张飞挑灯战马超"、"周文王渭水访贤"等戏文故事。壁画记载的故事大多出自《封神榜》和《三国演义》这两部在民间流传颇广的小说，画工不俗，寓意深刻，是现存难得的古代壁画。

据说，壁画在"破四旧"时曾遭遇过一场"浩劫"，被红卫兵用白灰涂抹遮盖，戏台也被改为办公场所。"文革"结束后，村民用布蘸水、沥干，将壁画上的白灰一点点儿擦干净，恢复了壁画的旧貌。现今，壁画上还有一些白斑点，就是当时村民清洗壁画留下的痕迹。

从戏台旁的木梯拾级而上，在戏台后灰壁上墨书有自清同治十三年至民国31年（1874—1942年）间庙内演戏的时间、班名、剧目等文字记录，共19条。这些记录，长的存世超过百年，短的也经历了七十余年的时光，保存尚算完好，可以说是研究福州地区民间戏剧文化的珍贵史料。

除了戏台外，闽越王庙还有正殿、阁楼等建筑。正殿面阔三间、进深二间，抬梁穿斗式木构架，单檐歇山顶。殿内主祀闽越王，是仙洋村先辈从福州城内的闽越王庙分香而来。殿后是双层木构阁楼，设有回廊，重檐歇山顶，构筑奇巧，很有特色。

闽越王庙的殿内保存有清代楹联两副、横匾八块，颇为珍贵。其中，正殿上方一块书写着"讚禹之绪"的牌匾最为珍贵。该牌匾据说是清代洋里乡贤、举人陈政桂所撰。"讚禹之绪"典出《诗经·鲁颂·閟宫》"有稷有黍，有稻有秬。奄有下土，缵禹之绪"句，歌颂的是周朝的始祖后稷。《史记·殷本纪》引《尚书·汤诰》篇，称大禹、皋陶、后稷为"三公"，评价他们"久劳于外，其有功于民，民乃有安。"

Wuzhu explored Fukien, expanded his territory, promoted production and thus fostered Fukien's development. After his death, Min-Yue Kingdom declined gradually, which aroused people's missing him. As a result, temples of Min-Yue King were built all over Fukien, especially where Wuzhu had been to, for worshipping him all year round. There used to be an ancestral temple in Chating, Fuzhou to worship Wuzhu. There was another temple of Min-Yue King, also called Da Miao (Big Temple), which was built at Diaolongtai, Nantai Island but later destroyed in China's War of Resistance against Japanese Aggression (the small hill there was thus called Damiao Hill).

Some other temples of Min-Yue King were built in Fuzhou's suburbs and counties. There is one in Xianyang Village, Yangli Country, Minhou County, 50 kilometers from Minhou's county town. It was first built in the Ming Dynasty, and the surviving building was what was rebuilt in the Qing Dynasty. The temple has a gable and hipped roof with multiple overhanging and wingspan eaves. Firewalls were built around it. A stone tablet was set above the main gate, on which was carved "Xianyang the Right Place".

Entering the temple, one may first pass by the theater stage, which has a gable and hipped roof with single eave and post-lintel construction. On both sides of the stage were painted four wall paintings, showing stories about the operas, most of which were taken from two popular legendary novels, *The Legend of Deification* and *The Romance of the Three Kingdoms*. These surviving ancient paintings were excellent in skills and deep in morals, which makes them especially valuable.

It is said that the wall paintings experienced a "disaster" during the Great Cultural Revolution, when they were covered with lime, and the stage was used as the office. After the Revolution ended, villagers used wet cloth to remove the lime bit by bit and restored the paintings. Nowadays, white spots can still be found on the paintings, which are traces of villagers' cleaning work.

If visitors take the wooden stairs beside the theater stage and go up, they will find on the grey wall behind the stage 19 records that showed the plays put on the stage from the thirteenth year of the Tongzhi reign in the Qing Dynasty till the thirty-first year of the Republic of China (1874-1942), including the time, the name of theatric company, and the name of the play. The history of these records, ranging from 70 years to more than 100 years, is well preserved, which makes them valuable historical materials for studying the culture of folk operas in Fuzhou.

Besides the theater stage, the temple of Min-Yue King also had constructions including the main hall and the attic. The main hall, measuring three bays in width and two bays in depth, has the timber frame of post-and-lintel construction and column-and-tie construction and the gable and hipped roof with single eave. The hall mainly worships Min-Yue King, and the incense was brought by the ancestors of Xianyang Village from the temple of Min-Yue King in the city of Fuzhou. The two-storey timber attic behind the hall is exquisite in design and construction with double-eaved gable and hipped roof and the cloister.

In the hall of the temple of Min-Yue King are preserved two pairs of couplets and eight horizontal tablets written in the Qing Dynasty. The most precious is the tablet hanging above the hall, on which was written "Zan Yu Zhi Xu" by Chen Zhenggui, a village sage and successful candidate in the imperial examination. The four characters, probably taken from *The Book of Songs*, eulogized Hou Ji, the ancestor of the Zhou Dynasty. *Historical Records* by Sima Qian praised Yu, Gao Yao and Hou Ji as "Three Lords of the state" for their "hardworking, benefiting the people and bringing them peace".

无诸是越王勾践的后裔，而勾践正是大禹的后代。无诸起义讨秦、佐汉击楚、开拓闽疆、汲取先进的汉文化，并获得"讚禹之绪"的评价比肩先贤，这是对他一生功绩最大的褒扬和认可。

◎ 螺洲天后宫

福建有两位女神，即莆田的妈祖和古田的临水夫人。妈祖林默娘和临水夫人陈靖姑生前济世救人，死后一个成了海上保护神，一个成了妇幼保护神。福州也有一位家喻户晓的女神——螺仙洲主。东晋史学家干宝著录的笔记体志怪小说集《搜神记》记载，在侯官有个叫谢端的农民，为人忠厚善良、勤劳上进，却因贫穷一直单身。一天，他下地时发现一只硕大的田螺，就捡回家去养在水缸中。说来也奇怪，从此以后，谢端每天回家都有热饭热菜吃。他心中疑惑，问遍邻居却无人承认。有一天，谢端假装下地务农，半路悄悄折返回家。只见水缸中的田螺爬到地上，从田螺壳里变出一位美丽的姑娘。她熟练地刷锅、淘米、烧火、煮饭……被谢端撞破后，姑娘告知身份，但因天机泄露，不得不返回天庭。谢端为了答谢田螺姑娘的恩德，特地为她造了一座神像，逢年过节烧香拜谢。

位于福州市螺洲镇店前村的天后宫，同时祭祀妈祖、临水夫人和螺仙洲主三位女神。一庙同时祭祀三位女神，这在福建的寺庙里较为少见。螺洲天后宫始建于明中叶，清嘉庆二十二年（1817年）和同治元年（1862年）分别由陈若霖和陈景亮进行两次大修。"文革"期间，寺庙内外建筑均有严重损毁。1994年以后，旅港族人多次捐资进行重修，才有了今日形貌。

天后宫现存建筑占地585平方米，坐北向南，前临乌龙江，由门楼、天井、大殿、后殿等组成。宫庙为双层门楼，上层屋顶为歇山顶，燕尾脊上有双龙戏珠立体雕塑，翘角顶左右皆为丹凤欲飞的造型。门楼为牌楼式木构架，中部由四柱三层斗拱、双悬钟构组，两侧配建双柱低栏的庑房。庙门两边侧壁是圆形透窗。国公帽外墙前有叠涩，突显出明清时期古朴的建筑特色。镶有门钉的大门两侧悬有清末代帝师陈宝琛亲笔题书的楹联，门楼旁立有记录清嘉庆年间陈若霖等重修天后宫的捐资以及天后宫历史沿革的石碑。

Wuzhu was the descendant of Goujian, the king of Yue, who was the descendant of Yu. Wuzhu revolted against the Qin Dynasty, assisted the king of Han to defeat the king of Chu, explored the territory in Fukien, and learned from the advanced culture from Han people. The four characters "Zan Yu Zhi Xu" for eulogizing Hou Ji's contributions to Emperor Yu were written in the temple of Min-Yue King, comparing Wuzhu to Hou Ji, which was a great praise and recognition of his achievement.

◎ Luozhou Goddess' Palace (Tianhou Temple)

Fukien has two well-known goddesses, namely Putian's Lin Moniang (Mazu) and Gutian's Chen Jinggu. They both cured the sick and saved the dying, and after their death, the former became Goddess of the sea while the latter became Goddess of women and children. There is another famous goddess in Fuzhou who is known to all, the Snail Girl. It was recorded in *In Search of the Supernatural* by Gan Bao, a historian in the Eastern Jin Dynasty, that there was a farmer called Xie Duan in Houguan County in Fukien. He was kind and hardworking, but remained single because of poverty. One day, he found a huge snail when working in the field, and then brought it home and kept it in the water vat. It was strange that Xie Duan found hot meals waiting for him every day after that. He was doubtful and asked every neighbor who helped him do that, but no one admitted. Then Xie pretended to go work in the field one day, but returned secretly and found a beautiful girl emerging from the snail shell. She cleaned the pot, washed the rice, lit the fire and cooked the meal. When discovered, she told Xie her identity. However, she had to return to heaven because the heavenly secret was exposed. In order to thank the Snail Girl, Xie built a statue for her and worshipped her on New Year Day and important festivals.

The Goddess' Palace located at Dianqian Village, Luozhou Town in Fuzhou worships the three goddesses mentioned above: Lin Moniang, Chen Jinggu and Fairy Snail. It is rare in Fukien that a temple should worship three goddesses. The Goddess' Palace was first built in the middle of the Ming Dynasty and then underwent two major repairs in the 22nd year of the Jiaqing reign (1817) and the first year of the Tongzhi reign (1862) in the Qing Dynasty, by Chen Ruolin and Chen Jingliang respectively. The inner and outer construction of the temple was severely damaged during the Great Cultural Revolution. After 1994, it was rebuilt and repaired many times with funds donated by clansmen in Hong Kong and restored to what it is now.

The surviving construction of the Goddess' Palace covers an area of 585 square meters, facing the south with Wulongjiang River running before it. It consists of a gatehouse, a yard, the main hall and a rear hall. The temple has a two-storey gatehouse, with the gable and hipped roof. On the swallow-tail ridge set the sculptures of two dragons playing with pearls. The upturning angles were carved into phoenixes ready to fly. The gatehouse was a decorated archway with a timber framework. The middle part is the three-storey bucket arch supported by 4 pillars with double hanging bells. On both sides were built lower verandas supported by two pillars. Round windows were set in the sidewalls on both sides of the temple. On the external side of the cap-styled walls were built corbels, a simple construction feature of the Ming and Qing Dynasty. On both sides of the studded gate hang couplets written by Chen Baochen, the teacher of the last emperor of the Qing Dynasty. Beside the gatehouse stands a monument, which records the donation during Chen Ruolin's repair work in the Jiajing reign as well as the later history and changes of the temple.

天后宫整体为二进，分前后殿。大殿（即前殿）门阔三间，进深五柱。走进门楼，在前天井的两侧边廊上有两个神龛，龛内分别为千里眼金将军和顺风耳柳将军。大殿中央供奉妈祖神像。大殿两侧上方悬有"慈航普渡"和"寰海安澜"两方庙匾。殿厅里的四根立柱上有两副颂扬天后的楹联。神龛前造有对称的金色双凤木雕。厅梁上高挂着一对精美的六角宫灯和绣有"金玉满堂"人兽图案的红色锦帘。整个大殿金碧辉煌，美轮美奂。后殿祀有螺仙洲主，左右配祀临水夫人和珠疹夫人的神像。殿两侧墙壁上绘有临水宫三十六夫人壁画。两殿之间的后壁上绘有临水夫人祈雨斗法以及观音在"白花桥上赐子"的壁画。

The Goddess' Palace consists of two parts, namely the front hall (the main hall) and the rear hall. The main hall is three bays in width and five bays in depth. There are two shrines at the corridors on both sides of the front yard, and in the two shrines are worshipped General Jin (Qianliyan or Thousand-Mile Eye) and General Liu (Shunfeng'er or Wind-Accompanying Ear), both fairies in Chinese legends. In the middle of the main hall stands the statue of Mazu (Goddess of the sea). Two tablets hang over the two sides of the main hall, on which were written "Ci Hang Pu Du" (salvation through charity) and "Huan Hai An Lan"(blessing for safety and peace at sea). There are two pairs of couplets on the four pillars of the hall, eulogizing the goddess. Before the shrine is the golden symmetric double-pheonix wood carving. Over the beam of the hall hang a pair of delicate hexagonal palace lamps and a red brocade curtain, on which were embroidered "Jin Yu Man Tang" (gold and jade fill the hall). All the decorations make the main hall splendid and magnificent. Fairy Snail is worshipped in the rear hall, with the statues for Lady Linshui (Chen Jinggu) and Lady Pearl set on her sides. On both sides of the hall were paintings about Lady Linshui, and on the rear side of the wall between the front hall and the rear hall were paintings showing Lady Linshui's praying for rain and Goddess of Mercy's blessing people with children on the White Flower Bridge.

第九章 商贾会馆：内哺外联

Chapter Nine
Commercial Lodgings and Clubs:
Connecting the World

◎ 柔远驿

在台江区新港街道琯后街旁，柔远驿静静矗立。明清时期，以它为中心的一带是福州城市生活里的一道风景线，华夷杂处，商贾云集。如今，它的四周高楼林立，车水马龙，而驿馆旧址则人迹罕至，被淹没在都市的喧嚣与骚动中，等待有心人翻开这百年履痕上所记载的中外交流史。

柔远驿是官方的正式名称，俗称"琉球馆"，是明清两朝为接待琉球使团而建的馆舍。从琉球到中国的海上航线以到达福州最为便捷，故明政府指定福州为琉球朝贡使的入境口岸。清袭明制，福州仍是中国与琉球交往的唯一口岸。琉球国的进贡船在闽安镇经巡检司检验封仓后入福州内港河口，贡品储存在"进贡厂"，然后再择期前往京城进贡给皇帝。为了方便琉球国的使者、通事、商人、船员等的住宿和生活，清政府在"进贡厂"之南特设"柔远驿"。

柔远驿始建于明成化八年（1472年）。后因各种天灾人祸多次重修，但基本保持了原有的功能和格局，甚至多有扩建，面积不小于6000平方米。如此大的空间，并不完全是为了对藩国表示优待，而是因为每次朝贡的人数和物品着实不少。从贡使到水手，标准队伍都在百人以上。在这些人当中，只有不超过20人可以进京，包括琉球正副使和主要随从，以及官方派遣的要入国子监读书的留学生。另有存留通事等16人，他们住在琉球馆，处理有关事务，为期一年。其余人员或进行商业买卖，或学习交流，等贡使进贡结束从北京回来再一起返回琉球。

清代林枫《榕城考古略》载："柔远驿明曰怀远，以为琉球诸藩国馆寓之所。内有控海楼，明正德间建，俗名琉球馆。"柔远驿取自《尚书·舜典》中的"柔远能迩"，寓意优待远人，以示朝廷怀柔之至意。

大厅的梁上则悬挂着"海不扬波"鎏金匾额。据说这是古代经常出海的人们所钟爱的吉言，祈愿风平浪静、平安无事。

◎ Rouyuan Station

At Guanhou Street in Taijiang District, Fuzhou, Fukien Province, stands Rouyuan Station, which used to be a commercial center of early modern Fuzhou during the Ming and Qing Dynasties. Today, in contrast to the hustle and bustle around it, the site is quiet and unfrequented, waiting to be discovered by those who are interested in the century-old history of China's friendly exchanges with foreign countries.

Rouyuan Station, commonly known as "Ryukyu Embassy" is the official name designated by the government. During the Ming and Qing Dynasties, Fuzhou was designated as the sole port of entry for tributes from the Ryukyu Kingdom to China. To visit the emperor in Beijing, Ryukyuan emissaries first obtained an official trading certificate for their ships from the provincial police station. After sailing about five miles upstream, they arrived at the Maritime Customs Office in Min'an Town. Skilled pilots then guided the ships to the dock, where the larger vessels remained until their return journey the following year. Meanwhile, the small boats transported the tribute emissaries, crew, cargo, and luggage to Rouyuan Station located south of Jingong-chang, which served as the living quarters for visiting envoys, sailors, merchants, scholars, and others.

Originally constructed during the reign of Emperor Chenghua of the Ming Dynasty in 1472, Rouyuan Station underwent multiple renovations throughout its history due to various natural and man-made calamities. With its basic structure left intact, it now covers an area of about 6, 000 square meters. Such spacious space was provided not only out of generosity, but out of necessity to accommodate all the incoming Ryukyuans. Each tribute ship held hundreds of Ryukyuans ranging from emissaries to sailors. The emissaries would first visit the local dignitaries and present gifts. In late September or early October, they set out to Beijing, accompanied by an entourage of about twenty people under the escort of Chinese military ships. A small group of students also followed them to Beijing and pursued studies at the National Academy. The rest of the corps would stay at Ry ū ky ū kan and take charge of all kinds of official business until the emissaries returned in the following year.

As is recorded in Lin Feng's *Archaeological Sketch of Rongcheng* of the Qing Dynasty, Rouyuan Station was originally called "Ry ū ky ū kan" and served as the residence for envoys from the Ryukyu Kingdom and other vassal states. The name "Rouyuan" was derived from the phrase "Rouyuan Neng Er" *The Book of History* "Soothing Station for Those Coming from Afar". On the black lacquered gate roof of the main entrance of Rouyuan Station, a large inscribed board reads "No Waves Scatter on the Ocean", expressing the wish for uneventful, peaceful and secure sea journeys.

琉球馆不仅是供琉球使节住宿的驿馆，同时也是中琉通商贸易的中心。明清"海禁"未开时，随贡贸易是中琉贸易的唯一形式。每当琉球贡舶来时，福州台江河口地区一派繁荣景象。开馆贸易一般是在贡使启程入京后，由存留通事提出申请，地方官批准后，方可在固定区域进行。据《闽书》记载，当时从琉球进口的货物有金、银、铜、锡各种制品，玛瑙、象牙、香料、中药材、磨刀石、硫黄、马刀，以及各种海味干货、日用品等。这些商品很多来自暹罗、爪哇、满剌加等南洋诸国。而琉球人带走的货物，是来自中国各地的木材、铁器、瓷器、漆器、丝绵、细绢、缎匹、药材、茶叶、白糖、沉香、徽墨等。它们也可能通过琉球中转，销往其他各国。因此，琉球在福州进行的随贡贸易，可以说是以琉球为超级中间商的中国与海外诸国的国际贸易。柔远驿将福州与整个东亚海域世界联系在了一起，推动了福州的港口发展和城市繁荣。

琉球馆也是明清时期中琉两国人民文化交流的重要枢纽。开始朝贡没多久，向中国派遣留学生的活动就开始了。留学生分两种：一种是官方派遣的公费留学生，叫"官生"，多为琉球王室、贵族子弟，他们会被送到北京、南京的国子监学习，相关费用由中国政府承担；一种是自费的留学生，叫"勤学生"，他们多在福州学习汉语以及各种职业技能，风水、地理、算命、儒学、医学、律法，音乐、戏剧、绘画，制糖、制漆、制伞……几乎无所不学。学成归国后，一些人成为琉球各个行业领域的开拓者和领头人。例如，在教育领域，曾两次在福州学习的程顺则归国后奏请琉球国王尚敬，在久米村孔庙东西两庑建立"明伦堂"，招收王府及久米村子弟进行汉学教育，传播儒家学说；在天文历法领域，史籍记载，在福州学习历法的琉球人金锵归国后成为琉球国第一位编制历法的天文学家；在医学方面，康熙二十七年（1688年），琉球人魏士哲来福州，师从黄会友医师学修补兔唇，归国后成功地为国王尚贞的孙子尚益治好缺唇。因此，在中琉文化交流的进程中，柔远驿发挥了难以估量的积极作用。

琉球馆还是难民安置和遣返中心。除上述正式入境的人员，福建还有很多"非法入境"者，他们大多乘坐因遇到海难漂到中国海岸的琉球船只。不管在何处被发现，根据规定，当地官府都要把这些难民护送到福州，登记后暂住柔远驿。遣归难民时，原船经修理能用者，乘原船回归，经修理不能用者，搭贡船、接贡船回归，有时还雇用商船护送。这类难民不在少数，仅在中国第一历史档案馆编著的《清代中琉关系档案选编》（中国档案出版社，1993—2002年）中，就有370余条关于漂流到中国的琉球民间船只的正式记录。

Besides being a residence for envoys, Rouyuan Station also serves as a center for trade between China and the Ryukyu Kingdom. During the Haijin(海禁, literally "sea ban", a ban on maritime activities imposed during China's Ming dynasty and again at the time of the Qing dynasty), the Rouyuan Station was still open for trade. In order to do so, the tribute envoys first presented a trade application to the provincial government of Fukien. Once approved, the so-called Qiu merchants(Qiushang 球商)were allowed to enter the Rouyuan Station for trade. Their main task was selling the commodities brought by the tribute ships, and in turn to purchase Chinese goods according to Ryukyuan needs.

According to the *Book of Fukien*, imports from Ryukyu included Products made of gold, silver, copper and tin as well as agate, ivories, spices, medicine, knives, sulphur, swords, dried seafood and daily commodities. These products did not all come from Ryukyu. Most of them were from Siam, Java, Malacca, and Japan. This indicates Ryukyu's role as an intermediary trader. In other words, it is a trade between China and other countries with Ryukyu as a middleman. As noted in the *Dynastic Record of the Ming Dynasty*, Ryukyu connected China with the rest of the world and earned great profits from being a middleman.

Ryūkyūkan used to be an important hub of cultural exchange between Chinese and Ryukyuan people during the Ming and Qing Dynasties. Soon after the tribute system began, the Ryukyu Kingdom started to send students to China. There were two types of students: the first type, called official students, were the descendants of the Ryūkyūan royal families. They were sent to the National Academy in Beijing and Nanjing, with their expenses covered by the Chinese government. The second type, known as self-funded students, or diligent students, covered their own expenses. Most of them studied in Fuzhou, learning Chinese and various skills, from feng shui, geography, fortune telling, Confucianism, medicine and law, to music, theatre, painting sugar making, lacquer making and umbrella making. After their return to Ryukyu, they became pioneers and leaders in a variety of fields. For instance, Tei Junsoku, who had studied twice in Fuzhou, requested King Shō Kei to establish the Minglun Hall on both sides of the Confucius Temple in Kumemura, where he enrolled students in Chinese education and spread Confucianism. Kinsho(金锵)became the first astronomer in Ryukyu to compile a calendar. Gi Shitiici(魏士哲/ギシティーチ), who came to Fuzhou in 1688 to learn lip repair from a Fuzhou physician called Huang Huiyou, successfully performed the surgery for the grandson of King Shō Tei, Shō Eki, under general anesthesia. The above shows that "Ryukyu Embassy" kan played an immeasurably positive role in the cultural exchange between the two countries.

Ryūkyūkan is also a center for the settlement and repatriation of refugees. Apart from the official arrivals, there were many Ryukyuan refugees, most of whom were shipwrecked and drifted to the south coast of China. Once they were found, the local authorities were required to escort them to Fuzhou, where they were registered and temporarily housed in the Rouyuan Station. When repatriated, some refugees returned on their own ships that were usable after repair, some returned on tribute ships, and others were escorted by merchant ships. There are over 370 official records of Ryukyu ships that drifted to China in the *Selected Archives of Sino-Ryukyu Relations in the Qing Dynasty*.

在明清两朝持续五百余年的中琉交往中，福州是绝大部分来访的琉球人居住、生活的城市。据学者高良仓吉考证，明清两代在此居停的琉球人有20万之多。琉球人生活在福州，不同于其他外国人会被严格管制，日常几乎可以随意出入馆驿，行迹遍及城市各处。耳濡目染之下，除了学习到各种知识技能，也把福州的日常习俗带了回去，从而影响了琉球方方面面的生活和文化，并在很多著述中保留下来，成为今天学者研究福州城市历史的宝贵材料。

光绪元年（1875年），日本强迫琉球王国停止向清朝朝贡、断绝与清朝的外交关系，并提出吞并要求。在琉球和清朝方面交涉无果的情况下，1876年，中琉断交，福州柔远驿作为琉球使者驻地的功能消失。今柔远驿的规模不到原来的十分之一，于1992年修复，占地面积约600平方米。如今，柔远驿被辟为福州对外友好关系史博物馆。建筑为坐北朝南的穿斗式杉木结构的双层楼房，一进三开间，馆舍四周有白墙黛瓦的封火墙围绕，避免火烧连营。

进门后有插屏，再后为天井，天井中有些许传统的假山、盆景。天井两侧为偏厅及披榭，天井后为大厅。厅中陈列着传统座椅，两侧为两间厢房。二楼还有三间房。主厅后方还有个后院。

五间房被辟成三个展厅，分别展示古代闽人"以海为田"的过往、古代福州与琉球交往的历史、今日福州与冲绳县友好往来的情况。一楼西厢房是第一展厅，展示的是有关海外交流历史的文字和图片介绍。二楼陈列有中琉和中日友好交流的展品，古代琉球国的赠品多在楼上展出。一楼东厢房为第三展厅，主要展示日本冲绳县那霸市自1981年与福州市缔结友好城市关系后文化、教育、经贸等方面的交流与合作，特别是赠送福州市的纪念品，例如冲绳的漆盘和那霸市的芭蕉布及茶具、丝织品等。

In the Sino-Ryukyu exchange that lasted about 500 years during the Ming and Qing dynasties, an estimated 200, 000 Ryukyuans once lived in Fuzhou. Unlike other foreigners who were subjected to strict control, the Ryukyuans were able to travel all over the city freely. They learned knowledge and skills and also brought back with them the daily customs of Fuzhou, which influenced every facet of life in Ryukyu and were preserved in a number of writings that have become valuable materials for the current study of Fuzhou.

In 1875 during the reign of Emperor Guang Xu of the Qing Dynasty, Japanese authorities stopped Ryukyu from paying tribute to the Qing Dynasty, closed the Ryukyu Embassy in Fuzhou, and demanded annexation. When the negotiations between Ryukyu and China failed in 1876, diplomatic relations between the two were broken off and the Rouyuan Station no longer served as a residence for Ryukyuan emissaries. Refurbished in 1992, the Rouyuan Station now covers an area of about 600 square meters, less than a tenth of its original size, and is made a museum displaying the history of Fuzhou's friendly exchanges with foreign countries. Built in chuan-dou style, it is a two-storied building of cedar wood structure. Sitting North to South, it has three openings in one room, surrounded by four whitewashed walls to prevent fire from spreading.

Following the main entrance is a spirit screen and then a courtyard with a few rockeries and bonsai. The courtyard, flanked by a side hall and a wing room, is connected to the master residence. It boasts traditional wooden furniture, with two wing rooms on the first floor and three rooms on the second floor. Behind the master residence lies a backyard.

Step into the hall on the first floor, turn to the east and west wing rooms to read, and then step up the dark red lacquered wood stairs to the second floor. In the spacious and connected halls upstairs, there are also real objects and photos showing the friendly relations between China and Ryukyu. There is a "Fuzhou Foreign Friendship Relations History Museum" which displays precious historical materials of many Chinese and foreign friendly characters such as Zheng He in China, Marco Polo in Italy, and Monk Kukai in Japan. Upstairs and downstairs, there are also many objects of friendly exchange such as stone tablets, books, and clothing from Ryukyu, which are very precious. For example, photos of Guan Gong and Tianhou Palace of Ryukyu(Okinawa)and the "Shi Gandang" stele are still preserved. Many of them were souvenirs from Naha City in Ryukyu to the Fuzhou Friendship Delegations in the 1980s, most of which were lacquer plates, as well as "basa cloth", tea sets, silk fabrics and so on. A large number of objects and pictures in the exhibition hall also show the general influence of Chinese culture such as Fuzhou food culture and Fukien tea culture on Ryukyu. As stated in the concluding remarks of the exhibition hall: "The Fukien culture represented by Fuzhou culture has had a profound impact on the Ryukyu Kingdom."

◎ 古田会馆

　　会馆是明清至民国时期出现的一种新的公共建筑类型。《辞海》中"会馆"的释义为："中国旧时同乡或同业的人在各城市设立的联络机构，主要以馆址的房舍供同乡、同业聚会或寄寓。"明清时期，福州上下杭一带商贸发达，汇集了14家商会、260多家商行，店铺林立，商贾云集，成为商帮会馆的一处集中地带。据史料记载，明清以来福州最多时有60多所会馆，仅台江上下杭一带就有16所。这些会馆集商业活动、乡亲联谊、文化教育、信俗娱乐、住宿仓储等多种功能，是生动反映中国社会由封建经济向商品经济演进的一面镜子。

　　在福州的诸多会馆中，古田会馆面积不算大，不足700平方米，却是建造最精致、保留最完整、最具代表性的会馆。福建有两个古田，一个是举行过古田会议的龙岩上杭古田，还有一个是宁德古田。宁德古田位于闽江中游，旧属福州府，为"福州十邑"之一，是连接闽江上下游的水路要冲。当年，古田商人将生意扩大到福州，经营特色乡土产品。眼看建宁会馆、闽清会馆、兴安会馆等纷纷拔地而起，他们急于想要建立一个属于自己的会馆。

　　清光绪二十四年（1898年），古田米帮中的一位名叫陈必光的商人采取了关键性举措，他购置了位于台江区白马路和同德路交会处的一块土地，打算在此兴建会馆。然而，米帮人少，加上资金短缺，导致项目进展迟缓。五年后，陈必光离世。古田商帮于是推选同乡魏明然接任工作。在魏明然的协调下，米帮成为主要的出资者，同时还赢得红柚帮、茶帮、柴帮等商帮的慷慨捐助。历经十年的努力，会馆终于在1913年全面竣工。会馆的主院落建筑群包括门楼、戏楼、天井、钟鼓楼、拜亭、正殿等部分。1914年，会馆进一步购置了西跨院，主要用于客房和商务洽谈。1996年，古田会馆被授予省级文物保护单位的荣誉称号。2007年，会馆经过全面修复后免费对外开放。

　　建成后的古田会馆主要有三大功能。其一，作为祭祀场所。会馆门匾上方书"天后宫"，可确定祭祀主神为妈祖。馆内石楹联书"慈航普度观音偈 孝水流芳曹女碑"，可推测观音、曹娥也在祭祀之列。其二，作为商务场所。谷口、黄田两镇的米商，平湖镇、凤埔乡的红柚商等都在会馆囤货、洽谈业务，运送木材的工人也以会馆为落脚点。其三，作为庆典场所。会馆设有戏台，形成"戏台—酬神、娱神—人神共娱"的娱乐体系，以祈福、纳吉、攘灾为目标，常举办迎神赛会、聚餐等集体性活动。

◎ Gutian Guild Hall

Huiguan, often translated as guild halls, were central institutions of guilds of merchants or trades, either found in their hometown, or in foreign provinces, where they served to bring together immigrants from the same region. Guild halls had on the one hand administrative purposes, and on the other served as centers for social activities, entertaining the guild members by theatre plays or carrying out ceremonies, for instance, for common ancestors (*zushi*) or protective deities or "saints"(*shenqi*, 神祇). Being organizational centers for guilds, they also had the task of formulating rules for their business branch, and registering all members and their shops or workshops. Members of the guild had the right to borrow money, were supported financially and were accompanied through all important stages in their lives, including the funeral. Last but not least, members found judicial assistance by the guild halls which was of particular importance when they lived in another province, with different legal customs. Guild halls were found in all important cities of late imperial China. Alone in Fuzhou, there were more than 60 guild halls during the Ming and Qing Dynasties, with 16 located in Shangxiahang, Taijiang District.

Gutian Guild Hall sits to the south, surrounded by red walls, covering an area of 690 square metres.

It's worth noting that two Gutian Guild Halls are located in Fukien, one is Gutian in Shanghang, Longyan, where the Gutian Conference was held, and the other is Gutian in Ningde. The latter was formerly part of the Fuzhou Prefecture(Hok Ciu Hoo 福州府), and was a major waterway linking the upper and lower reaches of the Minjiang River. Gutian merchants expanded their business to Fuzhou, dealing in local products. Seeing that Jianning Guild Hall, Minqing Guild Hall and other guild halls were springing up, they were eager to establish a guild hall of their own.

In 1898, a rice merchant called Chen Biguang came forward. He bought a piece of land at the intersection of Baima Road and Tongde Road in Taijiang District, but he was unable to "pay the huge sum of money for construction and had to delay it". Five years later, Chen died. The Gutian merchants thought there was no time for delay and elected their fellow countryman Wei Mingran to preside over the matter. Under the mediation of Wei, the whole project took around a decade years to complete, with the rice group paying most of their share, and the continuous donations from the red yeast group, the tea group and other merchant groups.

The main courtyard, completed in 1913, consists of an entrance, a theatre, a patio, a bell tower, a pavilion and a hall. The west courtyard, purchased in 1914, is mainly comprised of reception halls and guest houses. In September 1996, Gutian Guild Hall was identified as the Key Provincial Cultural Relics Protection Unit. In 2007, it was refurbished and subsequently opened to the public.

The Hall served three functions. First, it was a site of worship. A large inscribed board on the main gate reads "Tianhou Palace", identifying Mazu as the main deity. Guanyin and Cao'e are also included in the rituals. Second, it was a trade center. Rice merchants from the towns of Gukou and Huangtian, and grapefruit merchants from the towns of Pinghu and Fengpu, stocked up and negotiated business here. Workers who transported timber also stopped over here. Third, it was a gathering place for celebrations. The guild hall was built with a theatre designed to entertain the gods, with the aim of praying for good fortune and warding off disasters. There were folk activities such as welcoming gods and having communal meals.

古田会馆之所以被称为最具代表性的福州会馆，主要体现在以下三个方面。

首先，就建筑形态而言，古田会馆既呈现了本土化特色，又吸收了西式建筑元素。一方面，古田会馆继承了古田地区特有的祠庙建筑形态特征，具有浓厚的乡土文化气息。会馆门楼采用传统的牌坊式设计，五山跌落，庄严雄伟。主大门门额上嵌有"古田会馆"青石横匾，再往上为双龙青石浅浮雕"天后宫"直匾，体现"馆庙合一"的建筑性质与功能。左右两侧旁门门额分别书"应运"、"朝宗"字样。门楼的墙脊分为三层七段，下方边框装饰有精美的道教题材彩画和泥塑，凹折处塑有卷书屏。两侧突出的墀头上也有丰富的装饰图案。

此外，会馆屋脊线条的弯曲弧度十分夸张，呈半月形，动态感强。大殿为单檐硬山式，简洁大气，与两侧马鞍墙的柔美线条形成了强烈的对比。跨院屋顶为内落水形式，朴素简洁，雨水顺着屋顶内侧坡面从四面流入天井中，象征"四水归堂"。这样的设计体现了商人"财不外流"的心理。

另一方面，受到省城和近代西方建筑风格的影响，古田会馆参考、吸收了福州地方传统民居立面造型的设计特点，建筑整体高大雄伟，具有典型的江城文化特质。同时，建造者迎合近代建筑中流行的中西结合的做法，在立面造型中融入西式建筑元素。例如，主院落两侧的封火墙分为前后两部分：后半部分为巨大的如浪曲线的马鞍墙，线条柔美、律动、流畅，这是典型的明清时期福州民居建筑的造型风貌；前半部分墙体采用西式几何形表现手法，墙顶外侧建有砖砌女儿墙，墙高0.47米，每隔3米建砖柱，并随着建筑的起伏变化逐级升高。

其次，在建筑格局上，会馆由主院落和西跨院两部分并联构成，形制类似官式大厝中的主厝与护厝。主院落即"主厝"，是会馆的核心部分，主要用作祭祀。西跨院为"单护厝"，是会馆的从属部分，主要用作接待和议事等商务活动。西跨院与主院落仅一墙之隔，在西跨院二进门东侧开一边门与主院落相通。

主院落面阔15.7米，会馆大门正对插屏门，起挡煞、纳福、聚气的作用。插屏门后边便是戏楼，正面朝北，进深两间，面阔一间。戏台和门楼间设有1.5米宽的通道，通道两头接两侧看台走廊，形成回廊。拜亭面阔一间，结构上大胆采用扛梁减柱造，仅正面有两根八角形青石柱，后侧减柱，与大殿空间融为一体，形成了一个宽敞的大开间。大殿面阔五间、进深四间，采用穿斗减柱构造，共16根立柱。其中前殿与正殿明间各减两根中柱，左右次间各减一根金柱。这种结构设计使正殿空间开放通透，视野更加开阔。

The Gutian Guild Hall is considered the most representative guild hall in Fuzhou mainly for three reasons.

Firstly, in terms of architectural style, the Gutian Guild Hall embodies both local features and Western elements. On the one hand, it inherits the unique features of the ancestral temples in Gutian. The main entrance of the Hall is a Paifang, a traditional Chinese architectural arch, inlaid with a horizontal plaque of "Gutian Guild Hall" and a straight plaque of "Tianhou Palace". The inscribed boards read "Chao Zong" (meaning "worshipping ancestors") and "Ying Yun" (meaning "as the occasion demands") on each side of the entrance. The entrance ridge is divided into three layers and seven sections, and the lower border decorated with exquisite Taoist paintings and clay sculptures. The protruding corbels on both sides also have a rich array of decorative patterns.

The ridge of the Hall has an exaggerated half-moon shape with a strong sense of dynamism. The main hall has a hard hill roof, forming a strong contrast with the soft lines of the saddle-shaped walls on both sides. The roofs of the west courtyard are designed to bring rain into the patio from all sides along the slopes. This symbolizes the "return of the four waters to the hall", reflecting the merchant's belief of "wealth not flowing out".

On the other hand, Gutian Guild Hall draws on the façade form of traditional dwellings in Fuzhou, rendering itself lofty and majestic, and also incorporates into it some Western elements. For example, the firewalls on both sides of the Hall are divided into two parts: the front part and the rear part. The rear part is a huge saddle-shaped wall with soft and smooth lines, which is common in Fuzhou dwellings during the Ming and Qing dynasties. The front part adopts the Western geometric design, with a parapet built along the edge of the wall. The parapet is 0.47 metres high, with brick columns built at 3 metres intervals, and rises with the undulating changes of the wall.

Secondly, concerning the layout of the Hall, the main courtyard is laid in parallel with the west courtyard. The main courtyard, being the core of the Hall, is mainly used for rituals, while the west courtyard, being a subordinate part of the Hall, is used for receptions and business negotiations. The west courtyard is only separated from the main courtyard by a wall, with a door opening on the east side of Ermen(the second gate)to connect with it.

The main courtyard is 15.7 metres wide. The main entrance is followed by a spirit screen that serves to ward off evils and gather good fortune. Behind the spirit screen is a theatre, facing north, with a depth of two rooms and a width of one room. There is a 1.5 metres wide passage between the entrance and the theatre, with its ends connected to the stands on both sides, forming a cloister. The pavilion, with a width of 1 room, is built in post-and-lintel style. With only two octagonal bluestone columns at the front, it connects with the hall and creates a large space in between. The hall is built in chuan-dou style, with a width of five rooms and a depth of four rooms. With a total of 16 columns, the hall has two middle columns removed from the main room and one column removed from the two wing rooms respectively. This removal is intended to render visitors a feeling of spaciousness.

西跨院面阔一间，是一个全封闭式的两进三天井的狭长院落。前后院由一狭窄的通道相连贯通。这种空间结构布局有利于夏季通风排湿，冬季保暖御寒。主楼为双层木结构。楼上为客房，供往来商人、学子居住休息。楼下一进为议事厅，二进为餐厅、厨房。庭院采用开放式环廊设计，中为天井，利于通风与采光。天井中种植花树，自成小园，温馨惬意。

再次，彼时各地同乡商会为了彰显自身雄厚的实力，多斥重金打造会馆。其中室内装饰艺术则是最直观可感的部分。古田会馆的建造耗银近2万两，其中室内装饰部分占总造价的近一半。会馆建筑装饰中所有裸露的木构件都使用红色大漆刷突保护，在重点雕刻构件上采用贴金手法。髹漆和贴金工艺的应用，不但对会馆建筑的木质结构有防腐、防蛀、防潮的保护作用，同时也使建筑整体更加华贵、金碧辉煌。

在装饰雕刻上，古田会馆题材丰富、工艺精湛，浓缩了中国传统民族文化的精髓，反映出古田商人的价值追求和生活愿景。例如，戏台正面有两块正方形青石浅浮雕台裙，便是这种精神的具体体现。其中一块刻着水塘中央两只白鹭在盛开的莲花丛中自由自在地漫步，一只白鹭用嘴触碰着坐于莲叶之上的一只青蛙，青蛙受到惊吓呈欲跳之势，寓意"路路清廉"；另一块刻着盛开的梅花枝头，有两只美丽的喜鹊正在其中欢乐地嬉戏，寓意"喜上眉梢"。

2021年4月，修复后的古田会馆被开发为宣传诚廉文化的新窗口。展馆按照"台江诚廉文化四大优势、台江五大名商诚信主题故事、福州家风家训六大特点、福州诚信建设七个第一"的主题划分板块。在保存古厝风貌、不损伤文物的前提下，古田会馆还利用投影灯、触屏、轮播屏等数字技术丰富展陈内容，并设置展柜展示台江商贸、家风家训、名人遗墨等方面的文物。展柜文物与会馆正堂仿古场景相结合，使参观者沉浸式体验福州会馆文化、诚廉文化的深厚底蕴。

With a width of 1 room, the west courtyard is a long, narrow one with two entrances and three patios. A corridor connecting the front and back yards is designed to clear dampness in summer and keep warm in winter. The main building, a two-storied timber structure, consists of guest rooms upstairs for merchants to rest in, and a reception hall, a dining room and kitchen downstairs. A central patio is used for ventilation, decorated with flowers and trees.

Thirdly, as for design and ornamentation, Gutian merchants spent a lot of money on the interior decorations of the Hall in order to reveal their economic strength. The total cost of the Gutian Guild Hall is nearly 20, 000 taels of silver, with interior decorations accounting for nearly a half. All the exposed wooden parts of the building are painted with red lacquer and all the major carvings are carefully gilded. This not only protects the wooden structures from corrosion, moth and moisture, but also renders the Hall elegant and glorious.

The carvings in Gutian Guild Hall are rich in variety and exquisite in craftsmanship, embodying the essence of Chinese traditional ethics and reflecting Gutian merchants' vision of life. For example, two square pieces of bluestone are carved in shallow relief in the front of the theatre stage. One depicts two egrets strolling freely in the middle of a pond, one of which touches a frog sitting on a lotus leaf with its beak, and the frog is frightened and ready to jump, signifying "free from corruption". The other piece is engraved with a branch of plum blossom, in which two beautiful magpies are frolicking happily, representing "radiant with happiness".

In April 2021, the Gutian Guild Hall was refurbished and developed as a new channel to promote the culture of integrity. Four distinctive thematic galleries are set, equipped with digital technology such as projectors, touch screens, etc., allowing visitors to witness the prosperity of guild halls in Fuzhou and appreciate the traditional virtues represented by Fuzhou people.

第十章

名庄古寨：芳华悠远

Chapter Ten

Fortified Manors of Yongtai: Timeless Splendor

Chapter Ten

福建有土楼、土堡、围屋等多种乡土民居形式，展现出地理、文化的多样性。福建土楼以居住为主，三明土堡以防御为主，而位于闽中戴云山区的永泰庄寨则居住和防御功能并重。永泰庄寨是"原生态"的土、木、石结构，以各姓家族创建为特点，建立在河边阶地、山间盆地、丘陵的山坡和台地上，形成集生产、生活、军事防御、文化传承诸功能于一身的小单元。

所谓"庄寨"，内为庄，外为寨。庄，强调文化诉求；寨，强调防御功能。在庄寨的建筑设计上，则强调"庄寨一体"。庄寨的外部由夯土墙和铳楼组成防御性围护结构，内部是围绕厅堂等级鲜明的堂横式院落。厅堂是整个庄寨内部空间的核心，围绕厅堂的是等级分明的居住空间，采用"四梁扛井"的独特建筑结构，精致的木雕、彩绘、灰塑、挂瓦墙等令人称奇，时人叹为"山岭奇构"。与防御森严的外表不同，庄寨内部则充满生活气息，展现了儒家文化对理想居所的向往。

据考证，永泰庄寨在明清时总量超过2000座，现今保存比较完好的仍有152座。下面介绍较具代表性的谷贻堂、绍安庄、积善堂和爱荆庄。

◎ 谷贻堂——富得"流油"

1860年，是清咸丰十年。在这一年，举世瞩目的圆明园被毁，中国由此加速沦为半殖民地半封建社会。但在东南一隅的重山之中，黄氏家族运转的齿轮却并未受到影响。霞拔乡的黄孟钢尊崇程朱理学，笃信风水命理。在东洋及同安等地坐拥大量良田的他，在锦安村选中一块厝地，同年开建谷贻堂。

这座大宅为土木结构，筑在半山。正座七开间，两边各有一条过水的设计，形成一种双重对称的布局。其中，两个并排的房间被安排在一起，形成横向的空间布局，下方设有书院，通过建筑设计收到良好的采光效果。至今，谷贻堂的主体建筑基本保存完好，占地面积为1727平方米，建筑面积为2650平方米。这座建筑也被乡里人称为"长万（自然村村名）旧厝"。

长万旧厝坐落地风景秀美，青瓦卷檐掩映在绿树丛中。初春时节，自溪边向高处眺望这座大宅，悠长的石径自溪边逶迤而上。屋厝的背景是青山如黛，前景是李花如烟似雾，此情景宛如一幅水墨山水画。

Fukien Province is home to various forms of vernacular architecture, such as earth buildings, earth castles, and walled villages, reflecting its geographical and cultural diversity. Fukien's earth buildings are primarily used for residential purposes, while earth castles in Sanming are designed for defense. The fortified manors of Yongtai, or Zhuangzhai in the Daiyun Mountain area of central Fukien, serve both as residence and defense. They are constructed from earth, wood, and stones by multiple family clans on river terraces, basins, hillsides, and plateaus in Mount Daiyun of central Fukien and are used for production, living, military defense, and cultural inheritance.

Zhuangzhai's architectural style blends the cultural aspirations represented by "Zhuang" and the defensive functions of "Zhai". The external structure of Zhuangzhai is made up of a rammed-earth wall and a turret, creating a defensive perimeter. Inside, there is a courtyard with halls and separate living spaces, with the hall serving as the core of Zhuangzhai. The living spaces are arranged in a hierarchical manner around the hall, with two sets of beams intersecting vertically and horizontally. Adorned with exquisite wood carvings, colorful paintings, clay sculptures, and hanging tile walls, they leave the viewer in awe of their splendor. Despite its formidable defensive appearance, the interior of the Zhuang exudes a lively atmosphere, showcasing Confucian ideals of a dwelling.

According to research, there were over 2,000 Zhuangzhai in the Ming and Qing dynasties, with 152 still relatively well-preserved today. This section will focus on Guyi Manor, Shao'an Manor, Jishan Manor and Aijing Manor.

◎ Guyi Manor: A Living Proof of Wealth

In 1860, the infamous destruction of the Old Summer Palace plunged China into chaos, accelerating its transformation into a semi-colonial and semi-feudal society. Despite the turmoil, the Huang family maintained their way of life in the serene mountainous areas in southeastern China. Huang Menggang, a devoted follower of Confucianism and the Cheng-Zhu school, and a believer in feng shui, owned extensive fertile lands in Dongyang and Tong'an. He selected a plot of land in Jin'an Village and embarked on the construction of Guyi Manor.

Constructed from earth and wood, the manor is perched halfway up the mountain. The front hall comprises seven bays, flanked by a pair of adjacent pavilions and two horizontal buildings. Beneath the main structure is a study room and a back hall. The main building of Guyi Manor has been well-preserved, occupying an area of 1, 727 square meters with a building area of 2, 650 square meters. Later, the villagers also referred to it as the "Old Manor of Chang Wan, " named after the natural village where it is located.

Set amidst picturesque surroundings, the Old Manor of Chang Wan is a sight to behold, with its tiled roofs and upturned eaves nestled among verdant trees. When viewed from high up during early spring, the grand estate comes into view with a meandering stone path that stretches up from the stream, against the backdrop of blue-green mountains and the foreground of plum blossoms, creating a stunning landscape that resembles a traditional Chinese ink wash painting of mountains and rivers.

谷贻堂最富传奇之处在于它的风水传说。永泰庄寨有一大特点，就是对建筑风水极致讲究。在位置坐落、环境营造以及构造细节中，风水及其补救措施都运用到极致。专家认为，中国两大民建风水流派是赣派和闽派，而永泰庄寨可以作为闽派风水运用的代表。谷贻堂恰是赣、闽两个风水流派结合的产物。据传，当年黄孟钢认识了一名常在嵩口（明清时期永泰的重要渡口和集市所在地）行走的江西赣州地理先生，花了大本钱才学得赣州真风水术。而他起的屋厝，全由自己择址，自己布置风水。

话说谷贻堂所在的厝地，在黄孟钢看来，虽然水绕山环是块吉穴，但门前陡立，深十多丈。他忧心溪水不上堂，财气不旺。于是，在他布局下，谷贻堂与正门中开的普通四合院式民居迥然不同：正门并不与大厅相对，而是朝向西北，门外砌了183级石阶通向溪边，寓意引水入宅。厝内与厅相对的是一面横屋围墙（回照），大厅两侧设有通向书院的木梯，廊边镶木板，为水车拖箱状。下第二埕高丈余，中无台阶，但两旁架有木梯。黄孟钢意在将屋宇化成水车，木梯化成水车轮。人从木梯上行走咚咚作响，似水车轮转动抽水不止，寓意财源不竭。

谷贻堂确实没有辜负主人的一番"用心"。黄家的富庶四乡皆知。老人言，黄孟钢每年田租能收4000担稻谷，家中囤的山茶油能装满二三十个油榡（木制容器）。俚语说："上和（长万附近的村落）出水流，到此变成油。"还有人说，黄家的茶油多得可以用来带动水车臼米，正应了那句形容——富得流油。

谷贻堂的建造不仅讲究风水，构筑水准也高人一筹。整座建筑形态灵动飘逸，空间布局合理，毫无拥挤感。装修装饰也是精益求精，屋脊翘角比例适宜，飞扬有度，超凡脱俗，在古建筑中罕见。围脊处置得当，高矮相宜，上刻寓教于乐、通俗易懂的图案，给后人以教诲。正堂上的木雕奇思妙想、巧夺天工，填补了装饰艺术的空白，特别用心。在连续多年的建造中，大厅的屏风、墙壁、枋木窗格全镶嵌了精美的花草木雕；屋脊、女儿墙上，处处都有泥塑彩绘，人物形象栩栩如生。据说，精工细造延续多年，直到工匠雕无可雕、绘无可绘方才停工。

谷颐堂的设计理念也别具匠心。推开木栅栏构成的大门，左右各是一个"才（财）"字，合上则成为一个"本"字，寓意"开门迎财，关门见本"。谷贻堂后人表示，这是老祖宗要子孙记得：本分做人，生财有道。

The most legendary part of Guyi Manor lies in its feng shui. Like other Zhuangzhai in Yongtai, its site selection, orientation, environment, and construction strictly follow feng shui principles. The two major schools of Chinese geomancy are the Jiangxi School and the Fukien School, with Yongtai serving as the center of Fukien School's geomantic study. Guyi Manor is a combination of both schools. Legend has it that Huang Menggang met a geography master from Ganzhou, Jiangxi who often traveled to Songkou(an important ferry and market in Yongtai during the Ming and Qing dynasties)and spent a lot of money learning Ganzhou's feng shui philosophies. He then used his knowledge to select the location and arrange the manor according to feng shui principles.

Surrounded by rivers and mountains, Guyi Manor was located in a favorable position. However, the manor was situated 30 meters higher than the creek, which could weaken its prosperity. Therefore, Huang Menggang came up with a unique layout - instead of having the main entrance facing the hall, it faced northwest. The entrance was connected to the creek by 183 stone steps, symbolizing water inflow into the house. Opposite the hall was a transverse building wall with wooden ladders on either side leading to the study. The sides of the corridor were lined with wooden boards designed to resemble a water wheel. The second courtyard was about 3 meters high, with no steps in the middle, but ladders on both sides. The intention was to transform the house into a waterwheel, with the ladders representing the wheels. People walking on the ladders would make a creaking sound like the turning of the waterwheel, pumping water without stopping, and bringing endless wealth.

Huang Menggang's efforts were not fruitless. The Huang family was widely known for their prosperity in the town. Their lands yielded four thousand tons of rice every year, and the camellia oil stored in their home could fill up twenty to thirty wooden oil containers. There was a local proverb that went "water flowing from the nearby village turns into oil when it reaches here." Some even claimed that the Huang family's camellia oil was so plentiful that it could drive water mills and grind rice. In short, the family was wealthy.

Besides feng shui, Guyi Manor also excels in architectural structure. The manor has an elegant shape, with a reasonable spatial layout. The building has an elegant shape, with a well-planned layout that avoids any sense of crowdedness. The proportion of the roof's raised angles is just perfect, making it a rare sight among other ancient buildings. The eaves are appropriately designed and decorated with educative and easy-to-understand patterns, offering lessons to future generations. The wooden carvings on the main hall are cleverly designed and exquisitely crafted. Over years of construction, the screen walls and window frames of the hall were all inlaid with exquisite flower, plant, and wood carvings, while the roof and parapets were painted with vivid and lifelike figurative images. It is said that the meticulous work lasted for years, until the craftsmen had nothing left to carve or paint.

The design of Guyi Manor is also ingenious. The main gate, constructed with a wooden fence, bears a "财"(prosperity)character on each side that forms a "本"(principle)character when closed, representing the idea of welcoming prosperity while holding on to one's principles. The descendants of Guyi Manor explained that their ancestors wanted future generations to remember to lead an honest and principled life and find a legitimate way to make a living.

◎ 绍安庄："福建的布达拉宫"

绍安庄，当地人称"福建的布达拉宫"，是由黄孟钢的长子黄学书从1892年至1899年花了七年时间建造而成。绍安庄建在周坑村的最下游，也就是"水口"位置，既锁住了风水，也担负起护卫整个村庄的重任。

绍安庄形制威严。据资料，其面宽约45米，总进深约41米，墙体内占地1700多平方米，共有106间房。说它是"福建的布达拉宫"，皆因绍安庄建在村庄南面的山坡上，面溪背山，依山而筑。庄寨后楼的屋脊与寨前小溪水平面的落差达30余米，仰望则高台层层、屋檐重重。从空中看，更是层层叠叠、气势恢宏，极像一座小型的布达拉宫。

寨子的后部，一座青山高高耸立，左右方有凸出的支脉，自然形成"龙虎砂"。锦安溪在流经寨子前方时呈环抱状。因此，站在溪流的对岸看绍安庄，整体上感觉寨子就像稳坐在一把太师椅上，很大气，也很霸气。

距溪涧约50米处，是用巨型鹅卵石垒成的高5米多的基墙。之所以说是基墙而非石墙，是因为绍安庄正面的这一部分是整座庄寨的承台，在此之上才夯筑厚实的土墙。据说，庄寨主人当年单是筑基砌墙就采光了门前两条小溪的卵石，花费了整整十年的光阴。石墙上部的土墙高有四五米，土墙上部原有40多个斗形窗和射击孔，现在多被住户改成了通风和采光更好、更宜居的方窗。

要进入绍安庄正门，必须沿着寨边一条由乱毛石砌筑的三段坡道拾级而上，共有18级台阶。站在正门前的平台上，透过寨门可见正堂高大威严。若从庄门后的门楼进入，则须穿过天井、攀爬两组七级踏跺才能到达正堂。从正堂的后轩往后，又要经过五级如意踏跺才能进入后楼。如此算来，大门前基脚和后楼顶之间的高度差达16.5米。若从锦安溪水面算起的话，高度差则达到30余米。这样大的内高位差，在数千座永泰庄寨中都属罕见。

绍安庄大门的设计也颇值一提。门洞外观呈拱形，由整块条石拼砌而成，厚约1米。门洞装有硬木厚门，非常坚固。顶部设有灌水孔，如遇山贼侵扰，可往孔内灌水以防火攻。大门后部是方砖浆砌的方形门洞，顶上为整块条石制成的门顶框，彰显着主人的豪富。大门后即是门楼，门楼明间为门厅，甚为简约。伫立其间，视线从门厅穿过拥有两个层台的大天井即可看到正堂。门楼的精妙之处在二楼。这层楼厅通过内走廊可以通达庄内各处，将内眷与男主人在正堂上的活动联系起来。此处与正堂地面几乎同等高度，在楼厅里可以与正堂的人平视交流，最适宜作为正堂演戏时的看台。

◎ Shao'an Manor: Fukien's Potala Palace

Shao'an Manor, known locally as "Fukien's Potala Palace, " is a majestic mansion constructed by Huang Menggang's eldest son, Huang Xueshu, from 1892 to 1899. Set at the river mouth in Zhoukeng Village, it commands the surrounding feng shui and serves as a guardian for the entire village.

Shao'an Manor boasts an imposing architectural style. According to records, it has a width of 45 meters and a total depth of 41 meters. It covers more than 1, 700 square meters, with a total of 106 rooms. Situated on the southern slope along the stream, its roof ridge stands over 30 meters above the water, creating a magnificent visual effect when viewed from above. Due to its grandeur, it has earned the nickname "Fukien's Potala Palace."

At the back of the manor stands a towering green mountain, with protruding branches on both sides. When the Jin'an Creek flows through the manor, it bends into a circle. Therefore, when viewed from the opposite bank of the creek, the manor seems to be sitting on a high-backed armchair, giving off a grand and imposing atmosphere.

About 50 meters away from the creek is a 5-meter-high foundation wall built with giant cobblestones. It is the bearing platform of the entire manor, with thick earth wall built on it. Legend has it that the manor's owner spent a decade gathering all the pebbles from the nearby creek to construct the impressive wall. The earth wall on the top of the stone wall measures about four to five meters in height, and there were originally more than 40 slot-shaped windows and shooting holes on the top of the earth wall. However, many of these openings have been replaced by residents with square windows that provide improved ventilation and better natural lighting, creating a more comfortable living space.

To enter the main gate of Shao'an Manor, one must ascend three sections of irregularly paved stone steps along the manor, totaling 18 steps. Standing on the platform in front of the gate, one can glimpse the imposing main hall. If entering through the gatehouse behind the main entrance, one must cross the courtyard and climb two sets of seven steps to reach the main hall. To enter the rear hall from the rear veranda of the main hall, one must also cross five steps. Taking all this into account, the height difference between the foundation of the main gate and the roof of the rear hall is 16.5 meters, or over 30 meters if measured from the surface of Jin'an Creek. Such a significant difference in internal elevation is rare among the thousands of Yongtai manors.

The design of the Shao'an Manor gate is also noteworthy. The arch-shaped gateway is constructed from whole pieces of stone that are about one meter thick. The gateway is equipped with a solid hardwood door with water holes at the top so that water will be poured into the holes in case of fire attacks launched by bandits. Behind the main gate is a square brick and mortar gate, with a stone frame made of whole pieces of stone on top, showcasing the owner's wealth. Behind the main gate are the gatehouse and the hallway, which feature simple design. Standing there, one can see the main hall through the large courtyard with two terraces. The ingenuity of the gatehouse lies on the second floor. The hall allows people to access every room of the manor through an internal corridor, connecting the living spaces of those living in the manor. As it is almost at the same level as the main hall, people can communicate on an equal footing, making it the best viewing platform for performances in the main hall.

大天井两侧的厢房分为上下两部分，各有两开间，根据地势高低和位置不同，自然分出了不同的功能区。下层厢房就是"下书院"，用作处理与外界相关的一般事务；上层厢房的采光、通风都比较好，离正堂也近，作为子弟读书的场所。两侧厢房的雕饰也有所不同：上厢房与正堂的官房、"六扇间"一样雕饰华丽；下厢房则乏善可陈，直接素面示人了。

踏上天井的第二层台，会发现埕边有一道宽约1米的凸起，连接着两边厢房尽梢的横同。一般人可能会有疑惑：它起什么作用呢？其实，它有很重要的用途。一是可以将雨水拦蓄起来，通过特设的排水孔有序地排到寨外，构成"四水归堂，水流钱在"的格局。二是形成一条明显的左右通道，不受雨天积水的影响，方便左右通行。三是起到隐形的礼仪墙的作用。这种设计与谷贻堂相似。

从上天井踏步而上，经过七级垂带踏跺就到了正堂。正堂的整体风格大气、敞亮、简朴、端庄。正中竖着一面高高的太师壁，抬头仰望，可以看到太师壁上的一副凤凰插把和厅头的一块老匾。凤凰是人们心目中的瑞鸟，代表着幸福、吉祥，象征着美满、和谐以及权力。还有一种说法：凤凰会传书，象征着学运昌盛，多出读书人。凤凰造型的插把在永泰的清代庄寨里不算少，主要寓意华贵、进取。在这块匾额之下，是一方装饰精美的神龛，下沿和龛楣雕饰着四季花；两边长条格屏上分别装饰有"松鹤延年"和"竹鹿同春"的图案，造型生动，髹以金漆，甚是华美。

太师壁上方是一面贺寿匾，主书"极婺联辉"，这是古时候祝寿的常用贺词。其中"极"指南极仙翁，"婺"指婺女星，只有夫妻双方均长寿健在方才如此祝颂。仔细辨认，题写这块匾的秦绶章是当时清朝的二品大员，即钦命工部右侍郎、福建学政。从送匾人的身份也可以看出，绍安庄的主人交游甚阔。

绍安庄的雕饰虽然不如谷贻堂、积善堂，但也可圈可点，且雕刻形象更贴近实像。正堂两边的官房都是四扇开高门，高门带有雕刻精美的花窗。上绦环板多饰木芙蓉，象征着荣华富贵；下绦环板分别饰有琴棋书画和"连年有余"、"喜鹊登梅"、"菊蝶贺寿"等图案；版心则饰有"四季瓶花"，象征四季平安，还有蝙蝠衔如意结，象征福寿如意。雕刻精细，刀法纯熟，形象自然。

The wing rooms on both sides of the impluvium are divided into two floors, each with two rooms. They are divided into different functional areas due to differences in terrain and location. The lower floor wing room is used for handling external affairs, while the upper one serves as a study room as it has good lighting and ventilation and is close to the main hall. The decorations of the two rooms also differ: the upper room is as splendidly adorned as the official rooms in the main hall, while the lower room is comparatively simple.

Upon the impluvium is a protrusion about one meter wide along the courtyard edge, connecting the crossbeams at the ends of the two wing rooms. It serves three purposes: firstly, it collects rainwater and drains it through specially designed drainage holes, symbolizing keeping fortune within the manor; secondly, it forms a passage that allows people to walk between the wing rooms on both sides on rainy days; thirdly, it serves as an invisible ceremonial wall, reminiscent of the design of Guyi Manor built by the manor owner's father.

Ascending seven steps from the upper platform of the impluvium, one arrives at the main hall, which is distinguished by its simplicity, dignity, and spaciousness. Dominating the center of the hall is a tall and impressive vertical plaque, featuring a phoenix-shaped door handle and an old plaque hanging at the entrance. In Chinese culture, the phoenix is an auspicious bird that represents happiness, good fortune, harmony, and power. The phoenix can also deliver letters, symbolizing academic success. Therefore, many Yongtai manors feature a phoenix-shaped door handle, symbolizing fortune and ambition. Below the plaque lies a delicate altar adorned with flower carvings, while the long screens on either side showcase vivid images of pines, cranes, bamboo, and deer, all gilded with gold paint.

Hanging above the plaque is a banner that reads "Jiwu Lianhui", a common congratulatory phrase used to wish elderly couples a long and prosperous life. "Ji" refers to the Old Man of the South Pole, an immortal being, and "Wu" refers to the star Wunv, both of which symbolize longevity and good fortune. The calligraphy on the banner was done by Qin Shouzhang, a high-ranking official of the Qing Dynasty who served as the Right Assistant Minister of the Ministry of Public Works and the Education Commissioner of Fukien Province. The identity of the person who presented the banner indicates that the owner of Shao'an Manor had a broad social network.

The carvings of Shao'an Manor may not be as impressive as those found in Guyi Manor or Jishan Manor, but they are more realistic and certainly worthy of attention. The main hall features four tall gates on either side, each with ornate windows boasting exquisite carvings. The upper lintels are adorned with wooden hibiscus, symbolizing wealth and prosperity, while the lower lintels are decorated with an assortment of patterns such as musical instruments, board games, calligraphy, painting, and other congratulatory motifs that represent good fortune, longevity, and prosperity. The center panels showcase flowers in vases, symbolizing peace throughout the year, and bats holding a good luck knot in their mouths, which represent good fortune and longevity. The carvings are exquisitely crafted with attention to details and natural depictions.

与装饰性相比，绍安庄更注重建筑的功能性。首先，它充分利用地势，对不同层级进行了相应的巧妙设计，使庄内各处的采光和通风都非常理想，地面也很好地保持了干燥。其次，布局很科学，内庄和扶楼之间以大通沟相隔，又与多座过雨楼和四通八达的楼廊以及16条木梯道相连，形成一个密集的内部交通网络，方便通行。大通沟上方还可以设置晒台，扶楼可以设置仓房和加工作坊，非常方便主人在庄内生活。

安保方面，除了坚墙厚垒外，庄内西南角和东北角各建有一座三层高的碉楼，分别瞭望庄寨外围两个方向。碉楼是四坡攒尖的屋顶，屋顶下由圆木檩条平铺，其上覆土，最厚处达1米多，土上再盖瓦，以防火攻或火患。

绍安庄的设计考虑周全，为了确保在寨堡遭围攻时寨内仍有水源可用，在东北一侧碉楼的地下一层还挖有一口月牙似的水井。水井砌成弓形也别有寓意：后山形如虎，张弓以镇之，永葆平安。在西南角楼里，还可以见到一种奇异的设施：一方可变换角度、可伸缩的瞭望窗，平时拆下倒扣还可作为小方桌。

绍安庄良好的安保性能曾经在实战中得到检验。1938年，民生凋敝，土匪猖獗，绍安庄多次遭到土匪侵扰。然而面对坚固的寨防工事，土匪只能悻悻而退。最危险的一次是，当地一个非常霸道的土匪头子顺着一根长竹竿攀爬到屋檐下，准备翻进庄内，此时防守人果断地打出一发土炮击中了他，他应声倒在寨脚。随后，众土匪纷纷仓皇退去。

值得一提的是，绍安庄主人黄学书是谷贻堂主人黄孟钢的大儿子。一般人认为，"富二代"起厝建造绍安庄应该是轻而易举的。但事实上，1890年绍安庄初建时，黄学书已50岁，届知天命之年。而父亲对这个长子似乎寄望很高，要求严苛。虽有老父资助，但建寨的资金并不充裕。传说绍安庄在建时曾因钱银不足一度要停工。黄学书暗暗发愿：绍安庄顺利建成后，一定要创设一种生活仪式，让子孙永远铭记这段艰苦的日子。至今绍安庄内仍保留着一个特殊传统：在每年正月初一和十五，厝内各房都要煮食地瓜米，忆苦思甜，铭记今日生活的来之不易。绍安庄断断续续建了相当长的时间才完工，仅周边的基墙就前后垒砌了好多年。如果说建筑有性格，那绍安庄就是那位厝主人稳重、周全性格的投射。

Compared to its decorative features, Shao'an Manor prioritizes the functionality of its architecture. Firstly, it makes full use of the terrain and employs clever design for different levels, resulting in ideal lighting and ventilation throughout the manor and keeping the ground dry. Secondly, its layout is scientifically arranged. The inner manor is separated from auxiliary buildings with a large drainage, and connected through multiple rain pavilions and interconnected corridors as well as 16 wooden staircases, forming a convenient internal network. Sunbathing platforms can be set up above the ditch, while the auxiliary buildings can be used as warehouses and workshops. All of these amenities make it extremely convenient for the owner to live within the manor.

In terms of security, in addition to sturdy walls, there are two three-story watchtowers built at the southwest and northeast corners of the manor, overlooking the two directions outside the manor. The watchtowers have four sloping roofs with upturned eaves, and the roofs are covered with circular wooden rafters and soil that is over a meter thick, with tiles on top to guard against fire attacks or accidents.

Shao'an Manor boasts a meticulous construction system. To guarantee a continuous water supply within the manor during a siege, a crescent-shaped well was excavated on the underground level of the northeastern watchtower. The well's arched shape has a symbolic significance: the mountain behind the manor resembles a tiger, and the arch is drawn to subdue it, ensuring safety and tranquility. Additionally, the southwestern watchtower features a unique installation: a square observation window that can change angles and extend, and can even be detached and inverted into a small square table.

The well-designed fortifications of Shao'an Manor were put to the test in real combat. In 1938, the manor was repeatedly attacked by bandits amid widespread poverty and rampant banditry. However, most bandits retreated in frustration when confronted with the strong fortress defense. The most dangerous encounter was when a particularly ruthless bandit leader climbed up the roof with a long bamboo pole, attempting to breach the defenses of the manor. The defenders promptly fired a homemade cannon, hitting the bandit leader and causing him to fall at the base of the fortress. Witnessing this, the other bandits fled in panic.

It's worth mentioning that Huang Xueshu, the owner of Shao'an Manor, was the eldest son of Huang Menggang, the owner of Guyi Manor. It is commonly assumed that building a manor would have been effortless for Huang Xueshu as he inherited his father's wealth. However, reality told a different story. When Shao'an Manor was initially constructed in 1890, Huang Xueshu was already fifty years old. His father, a strict man who had high hopes for his son, did not provide sufficient financial support, and the construction had to stop at one point due to a lack of funds. Later, Huang Xueshu vowed that after he completed the construction of Shao'an Manor, he would set a special tradition to remind his descendants of these difficult days. This explains why on the first and fifteenth day of the lunar new year, people living in the manor will cook a plain meal to reflect on past hardships and cherish the sweetness of life. The construction of Shao'an Manor progressed intermittently, with the foundation walls alone taking many years to be built. If we were to attribute character to architecture, Shao'an Manor would be a reflection of its middle-aged homeowner - steady, thoughtful, and thorough.

◎ 积善堂：巨石垒成的八卦楼

积善堂位于永泰县霞拔乡锦安村长万自然村，又称长万新厝。起建者黄学猷是黄孟钢的次子，自幼聪慧，天资过人，在成长中显示出非同一般的计数和经营能力。相传他13岁就开始替父亲记账、管家，小小年纪已可以将算盘顶在头上盲打，而计算结果从来无误。他很快在经营上成为父亲的左膀右臂，由他打理的账本至今还保留在积善堂中：条目清晰、书写工整，令人赞叹。

1905年，黄学猷从父亲那分得千担地租，在祖宅谷贻堂不远处择了一块地起建自己的大宅——积善堂。积善堂的外观呈现少有的八角形，坐乾向巽，整体建筑布局依照八卦的形态建造。它蕴含了起建者的期望：希望子孙世代开基立业，万事亨通，荣华富贵。寨墙基础用锦安溪的巨石垒砌，前高约7米，后高约2.5米，两旁高约1.5米，上筑土墙。据传，当时锦安溪上下游五公里的石头都被抬尽；而单是付给从四邻乡村雇来捡取基础垫层小碎石的女人的工钱，最多时一天就要发掉九石莱（传统的度量单位，用于量稻米）的稻米。

积善堂装修装饰处处精美。屋脊翘角平直，简约古朴。屋面高矮处置得当。所有木雕均工艺精湛，花式极尽繁复。据说，一班木雕工匠吃住在积善堂，精雕细琢整整用了三年。正厅左右房间的16扇门和窗棂均镂刻或镶嵌花鸟等吉祥图案，全厅窗棂上下各镶一块花草图案浮雕。浮雕的松梅吉祥图，镂雕的雀替和梁架，状如莲花的斗拱，每一处都有美好的寓意，也彰显了主人不凡的审美情趣。

大厅的梁架结构还有一个与众不同的地方，即厅堂梁框采用一种叫"四梁扛井"的结构，运用十字形受力原理消减梁柱压力，此乃永泰工匠的独创。在过去的永泰，只有家族中有人考取了较大的功名，起屋建厝时才可以如此上梁。但据后世人回忆，黄学猷一生中只考取过秀才。其"资历"并不足以让积善堂拥有"四梁扛井"，这种"规格"在当时是有僭越之嫌的。可是细究黄学猷的用意，或者可以这样理解：他坚信在他的后世子孙中，必然有人能成功入仕、光耀门楣。

◎ Jishan Manor: Octagonal Building Constructed with Stones

Jishan Manor, also known as Changwan Manor, is situated in Changwan Village, Yongtai County. Its proprietor, Huang Xueyou, was the second son of Huang Menggang. From an early age, he displayed exceptional intelligence and remarkable aptitude in accounting and management. At the tender age of 13, he took charge of record-keeping and household management for his father. He could effortlessly manipulate the abacus, performing calculations accurately without even looking at it. He quickly became his father's trusted aide in business operations. The meticulously maintained account books, with their clear entries and immaculate handwriting, are still preserved in Jishan Manor, garnering admiration from later generations.

In 1905, Huang Xueyou had an inheritance from his father and started the construction Jishan Manor nearby Guyi Manor. The exterior of Jishan Manor features a rare octagonal shape, and its positioning follows the arrangement of the Bagua, with the main entrance facing the Qian direction(associated with Heaven)and the back or rear of the manor facing the Xun direction(associated with Wind). The design embodies the builder's aspirations for future generations to make notable contributions and enjoy wealth and prosperity. The foundation of the walls is built with enormous stones from the Jin'an River. The front wall is approximately 7 meters high, the rear wall is around 2.5 meters high, and the side walls are about 1.5 meters high, with earthen walls constructed on top. Legend has it that all the pebbles within a 5-kilometer stretch of the Jin'an River were collected for the construction. Women hired from neighboring villages to collect these pebbles were generously compensated with nine barrels of rice in a single day.

Jishan Manor is adorned with intricate and meticulous decorations, showcasing exquisite craftsmanship. The roof ridges exhibit graceful curves, reflecting a simple and antique style, while the varying building heights add visual interest to the overall design. The creation of the wooden carvings involved a dedicated group of craftsmen who spent three years meticulously crafting each piece with lavish detail. The 16 doors and window frames in the rooms on both sides of the main hall are all intricately carved or inlaid with auspicious patterns of flowers and birds. The window frames in the main hall are adorned with a relief sculpture of flowers and plants. The sculptures portray auspicious elements such as pine and plum. The painted decorative panels, beams, columns, and lotus-shaped dougong brackets further enhance the aesthetic allure of the manor. Every detail carries a positive message and exemplifies the homeowner's refined aesthetic taste.

The structure of the beams in the main hall has a distinctive feature. It utilizes a cross-shaped load-reducing technique to alleviate pressure on the beams and columns, which is an innovative creation by the craftsmen of Yongtai. In the past, in Yongtai, it was necessary for someone in the family to have achieved a significant official position before such a beam structure could be used in house construction. In the past, only when someone in the family achieved a significant official position could they use such a technique in the construction of their residence. However, Huang Xueyou only passed the entry-level academy exam and was not qualified to adopt the technique. Yet it showed that he firmly believed that among his future descendants, there would certainly be someone who would succeed in the imperial examination and bring honor to the family name.

心志颇高的黄学猷，还请了木匠师傅将《朱子家训》中的一段用欧体金字精心镂刻在了四扇木屏上，并将这四扇木屏端端正正地镶放在厅堂正中，用以训示家人："黎明即起，洒扫庭除，要内外整洁。既昏便息，关锁门户，必亲自检点。一粥一饭，当思来处不易。半丝半缕，恒念物力维艰。宜未雨而绸缪，毋临渴而掘井。自奉必须俭约，宴客切勿流连。器具质而洁，瓦缶胜金玉。饮食约而精，园蔬愈珍馐。……祖宗虽远，祭祀不可不诚；子孙虽愚，经书不可不读。"这段文字截取了《朱子家训》中的精华部分，也反映了黄学猷起建积善堂的初心与对儿孙后代的期望。

然而，圣训素来知易行难。在半殖民地半封建社会的陋习影响下，黄学猷的儿子染上了鸦片毒瘾。未经几时，家业就被败尽。刚刚兴建几年的积善堂，原本还要继续装潢，也就此仓促收尾，那些精美富丽的木雕故事再没有了续篇。而许多已经镂刻完工的窗棂被堆放在后屋，主人已无心去安装。

如今来到积善堂，看着大厅梁架的雀替上镂雕的精美云纹，望着两侧的书院仅用木板钉上的窗框，可叹积善堂这部岁月之书，半部繁花似锦，半部落叶凋零，如今读来令人唏嘘。光阴如箭，百年犹如一瞬。庄寨无声，却镌刻着历史，警示了后人。

◎ 爱荆庄

在上千座永泰庄寨中，爱荆庄因独特的名字和文化内涵而享誉天下。爱荆，就是"爱妻"的意思。爱荆庄的主人十分敬爱妻子，以寨堡庄名来表彰她的贤惠和功劳，形成了具有一定社会影响力的女绅文化，爱荆庄也因此被专家誉为"古代村落女绅文化的活载体"。

爱荆庄位于永泰县同安镇洋尾村，于道光十二年（1832年）建。寨主人名叫鲍美祚，为人忠厚，言语不多，与人交往宁亏不争，是个地道的老实人。他的妻子李氏，俗称美祚嫲，是富泉乡巴蕉人，生在财主家庭，从小接受良好的教育，有经济头脑。至今，同安乡间依然流传着这对夫妻同心同德、持家有道，最终建起了一座传世大庄寨的佳话。

Huang Xueyou invited a skilled carpenter to carve a selected passage from *The Family Instructions of Zhu Xi* in ornate golden characters onto four wooden screens. They were then carefully placed in the center of the main hall, serving as a family. The engraved passage reads as follows: " Get up at dawn and sweep the courtyard, ensuring cleanliness inside and outside. Rest early at night. Check personally that the doors and windows are properly shut. When you eat, remember that food is the product of hard work. When you put on clothes, keep in mind that materials do not come by easily. One should repair the house before it rains and not start digging a well when he already feels thirsty. Be thrifty in satisfying your own needs, but generous in hosting a reception. Utensils used in the house should be plain and clean. Earthenware is better than those made of jade and gold. Meals need not be sumptuous; finely prepared, simple vegetables can be better than rare delicacies. Do not construct extravagant mansions; do not try to gain fertile farmland. Matchmakers and sorceresses are agents of vice. Pretty maids and a charming wife need not be a blessing. Do not judge by physical appearance when hiring servants. It is well with you even if your wife and maids look plain without make-up. Even if ancestors are far removed from us, we should offer sacrifices with reverence. Even if your children are slow-witted, you should still instruct them in the Confucian classics." This excerpt captures the essence of *The Family Instructions of Zhu Xi* and represents Huang Xueyou's expectations for his future generations when he built Jishan Manor.

However, as the old saying goes, it is easier said than done. As China was reduced to a semi-colonial and semi-feudal society, Huang Xueyou's son was reduced to an addict, squandering family fortune in no time. Consequently, the construction of Jishan Manor was suspended in a hasty manner. The captivating and exquisite wood carving stories were left in obscurity. Many intricately carved window frames were piled up in the back room, as the owner had lost all interest in installing them.

Entering Jishan Manor, one will notice that the beams are carved with intricate patterns, while the window frames of the adjacent academies remain unfinished, merely held together by wooden boards. Jishan Manor resembles a book, chronicling the ebb and flow of time: its initial chapters brimming with splendid moments, and the latter chapters marked by decline. Though the manor may not utter a word, it carries the weight of history, serving as a cautionary tale for generations to come.

◎ Aijing Manor

Among thousands of Yongtai manors, Aijing Manor stands out for its unique name and cultural significance. Aijing translates to "beloved wife, " reflecting the deep respect and admiration the owner had for his wife. The name of the manor was chosen to honor her virtues and contributions, giving rise to a distinct female gentry culture that had significant social influence. It is recognized by experts as a living embodiment of ancient village gentry culture.

Built in 1832, Aijing Manor is situated in Yangwei Village, Tong'an Town, Yongtai County. Its owner, Bao Meizuo, was renowned for his integrity, simplicity, and peaceful nature. He was a man of few words, preferring harmony over conflict in his interactions. His wife, Mrs. Li, commonly known as Meizuo Ma, hailed from Bajiao Village in Fuquan County. Coming from a prosperous family, she received a quality education from an early age and displayed remarkable business acumen. Even to this day, tales of the couple's harmonious relationship and their joint efforts in constructing the manor continue to be widely shared in Tong'an Town.

知书达礼、智慧善良的美祚嬷一嫁到鲍家，便瞅准商机发展养殖业。她数次典当嫁妆，购买猪崽。偏偏母猪都不产崽，众人皆视眼前之利要杀猪，而美祚嬷始终不答应。她觉得，因为不生崽而杀猪不仁不义。母猪终不负她所望，胎胎十三崽。从此家境开始慢慢脱贫，并于道光十二年买置福坪厝全座十五营，建爱荆庄土堡。

熟读《四书五经》的美祚嬷，秉持着"仁者以天下万物为一体"的信念，把"仁心"推广到万物。在建寨时，专门为她家的黄牛、水牛建有专用的"套房"——牛栏、专用的道路——西南牛道、专用的澡池——牛汶池，还建有狗洞、猫窝。用孟子的话说，就是"恩足以及禽兽"（《孟子·梁惠王》）。

也许是"万物有灵"，也许是"养殖有方"，此后，水牛、黄牛迅速繁殖，杉树拔节而长，油茶硕果累累，水稻也比别人家的高产……由此家道日隆。据记载，农田有240处，山场合计21处，水牛、黄牛超过100头。农田、油茶、山场分布整个三洋，并建有自己的"油行"。

虽有万贯家产，美祚夫妇依然克勤克俭、粒谷必珍，奉行"与天地自然和谐共处"的思想。1832年建爱荆庄时，庄里所有木材取自自家山场，且只取适龄木材。所有建筑材料都是就地择取，既经济又省工。爱荆庄以"简朴"为主调，摒弃奢华。尽管美祚嬷勤俭持家，对乡邻却慷慨大方、乐于施济。即使在缺衣少食时，也留下"美祚嬷把一碗饭让给乞丐吃，而自己饿一晚"的美谈。

美祚嬷不仅善于经营财富，更注重文化教育。建寨的时候，他们就特意在吉利的东南方向楼上建了五间书斋，专门为家中子女的教育而设。为了支持教育事业，他们还划出一块名为"公轮田"的土地，提供必要的粮食，用来资助老师和教育项目。美祚公夫妇极为重视教育，他们不仅尽力邀请优秀的教师，还亲自参与到教学中去。对于那些学业有成的学生，无论是学文还是习武，他们都提供奖励，优秀的学生可以得到田地的租金作为奖赏。在对孩子的学习管理上，他们制定了严格的规则，设置了戒尺和家法杖用于惩罚不良行为和鼓励学习。而教育的核心在于培养德行、亲近民众，并追求至善。在这样的教育理念下，家族中不论是文才还是武艺，人才层出不穷。爱荆庄伬唱文化也因此远近闻名。

Upon marrying into the Bao family, the knowledgeable, courteous, and virtuous Meizuo Ma immediately took charge, identifying business opportunities and developing the livestock industry. She pawned her dowry multiple times to purchase piglets, hoping to breed them. However, none of the gilts gave birth. While others saw the immediate profit in slaughtering the pigs, Meizuo Ma refused their proposal, thinking it was cruel and unjust to kill the pigs simply because they were not reproducing. As the saying goes, "Good deeds bring good rewards." Finally, the gilts gave birth to thirteen piglets. From then on, their family gradually emerged from poverty. In 1832, they purchased the entire fifteen camps of Fuping Village and established Aijing Manor.

Meizuo Ma, deeply knowledgeable in the *Four Books and Five Classics*, the esteemed texts of Confucianism, embraced the concept of treating all living beings with benevolence. During the construction of the manor, she made special arrangements for oxen and water buffaloes, providing them with dedicated facilities such as cowsheds, pathways, and bathing pools. She even went as far as setting up dog dens and cat beds. In the words of Mencius, this exemplified the notion that "benevolence extends to animals."

Perhaps it was the belief in the inherent spirituality of all living things, or perhaps it was their exceptional farming methods. Whatever the reason is, the water buffaloes and oxen multiplied rapidly, the cedar trees grew tall and robust, the tea-oil trees yielded abundant fruits, and the rice harvest surpassed that of others. The family thrived, as historical records indicate: they possessed 240 farmlands, 21 expansive mountain fields, and over 100 water buffaloes and oxen. Their agricultural lands, tea-oil plantations, and mountain fields extended throughout the entire Sanyang region, and they even started their own oil business.

Despite their considerable wealth, the couple maintained a diligent and thrifty lifestyle, embracing the principles of moderation and living in harmony with nature. When Aijing Manor was built in 1832, they sourced all the timber from their own mountain fields, selecting only mature trees. Local materials were used for construction, ensuring cost-effectiveness and reduced labor. Aijing Manor exuded a simple and unassuming style. While Meizuo Ma managed the household with frugality, she displayed generosity and a willingness to assist her neighbors. Even during times of scarcity, Meizuo Ma would offer a beggar a bowl of rice, often skipping her own meals.

Meizuo Ma made significant contributions beyond just financial matters; she also placed great importance on culture and education. She constructed five studies on the southeastern side of the manor and allocated a specific area of land as an incentive for those aspiring to serve the public. She held high expectations for her descendants' study of Confucianism, and the study rooms were equipped with a "disciplinary ruler" and a "family punishment cane." The "disciplinary ruler" was used to discipline those who fell short of Confucian standards, while the "family punishment cane" was employed for disciplining those who displayed disobedience, engaged in theft, or instigated fights. Meizuo Ma often offered calm guidance, stating, "The path of learning lies in cultivating moral integrity, being close to the people, and striving for the ultimate good." Under their tutelage, a multitude of talented individuals emerged from Aijing Manor and gained recognition throughout the region. Eight descendants achieved academic acclaim or were admitted to prestigious academies and martial arts institutions. Diverse talents emerged, with some excelling in the arts and martial arts, while others pursued higher education at renowned academies. The cultural heritage of Aijing Manor, encompassing folk songs and storytelling, also garnered widespread fame.

特别值得一提的是，美祚嬷尤为注重对女性的保护。封建社会重男轻女现象非常严重，溺女成为常态。宅心仁厚的美祚嬷注意到这一现象，竭尽全力收养一些贫穷人家无力抚养的女孩（童养媳）。收养的女童白天劳作，夜晚和家族中的女孩一起读书认字，美祚嬷亲自传授礼仪和妇德。女孩们常常于夜晚时分在庄寨二楼读书的书斋，也被乡人称为"媳妇斋"。这在当时的社会是相当不容易的。现在庄内还保存着一本清代出版、"媳妇斋"使用过的教材《女三字经》。这些女童中有的与爱荆庄的子孙有了感情，成为合格的"准儿媳"而留下，其他的则嫁出去。

不仅如此，美祚嬷还规定，子孙不可随意遗弃妻子（那时农村遗弃妻子不受约束），对于寡居的媳妇，除非她自己愿意改嫁，不然任何族人不能觊觎她的家产或欺侮她。因此，乡里人觉得爱荆庄门槛高、嫁到爱荆庄不易，便有了"铁门槛"之说。"铁门槛"在某种程度上来说，不仅是替贫穷人家养育女儿，减少了她们被溺的风险，还帮她们提升了能力与社会竞争力，使她们因此大受欢迎。

美祚嬷的美好德行为她赢得了"女绅"的称号，也获得了美祚公的尊敬和爱护。美祚公不仅将对妻子的感情书写在大门门楣上，取名"爱荆庄"，也在细节上处处留心。建寨时，他为不便出入厅堂的美祚嬷等人修了一排美人靠，作为休息、聊天、纳凉、赏花的场所。同时，在美人靠上方辟有二层花台，花台上种有各种花卉。在后厅走廊设美人靠，这在永寨庄寨是唯一的。族谱语："美祚公今年已八十有二载，举案齐眉……"可以说，美祚公与美祚嬷是封建社会性别平等意识的积极践行者，爱荆庄也因此成为"古代村落女绅文化载体的孤本"。

从建筑而言，爱荆庄是土木石混合结构。正面东西宽79.2米，前后深64.5米，尾埕140平方米，占地面积5248.4平方米，有房屋361间。整个寨堡分两部分，外围建筑以防御为主，内里是以人居为主的标致四合院。它的建筑风格体现在以下三方面。

第一，完整、巧妙的防御体系。爱荆庄寨堡的外围是一座设计巧妙、布局合理，外防匪、内防火的易守难攻的堡垒式建筑，外墙底部全用乱毛石（夹土石）垒砌，高约4米，右边前后两处最高有5米左右。在右边的西南角（正面的西边）和左边的东北角（即东北面）各建有一座下石上土的碉楼，亦叫铳（枪）楼。碉楼两边都高出寨墙一半以上，是用来瞭望整个寨堡的外围。一座瞭望西南向，一座瞭望东北向。

It is noteworthy that Meizuo Ma placed significant importance on the protection of women, particularly in a feudal society where gender discrimination and mistreatment of daughters were prevalent. She adopted girls from impoverished families who were unable to provide for them and imparted them with etiquette and virtues. These girls would engage in labor during the day and gather in the study pavilion on the second floor for studying. It was really a rare sight in the old society. Some of these adopted girls were married to the descendants of Aijing Manor, others were married off and left the manor. Today, *"The Three-Character Classic for Women"*, the textbook used by those adopted girls, is still well-preserved in the manor.

In addition, Meizuo Ma imposed strict rules on her descendants, prohibiting them from abandoning their wives, a behavior that went unchecked in rural areas at the time. Any family member who coveted the property of widowed daughters-in-law or mistreated them faced severe consequences, unless the daughters-in-law chose to remarry of their own accord. This unwavering stance led the local community to perceive Aijing Manor as having an exceptionally high threshold, making it challenging for women to marry into the family. It not only helped raise these women, but also equipped them with the skills and capabilities to thrive in society. Consequently, these women earned widespread admiration, popularity, and respect within the community.

Meizuo Ma's exemplary virtues earned her the esteemed title of "Female Gentleman" and garnered immense respect and affection from her husband. In a testament to his deep love, he inscribed the name "Aijing Manor" on the lintel of the main gate, showcasing his admiration and devotion. During the construction of the manor, he arranged a row of resting pavilions for Meizuo Ma who found it inconvenient to enter the main hall. These pavilions provided serene spaces for relaxation, conversation, seeking respite from the heat, and reveling in the beauty of the surrounding flowers. Above the pavilions, a two-tiered flower terrace was built, adorned with various blossoms. According to the genealogical records, "Meizuo Gong is now eighty-two years old and still keeps a harmonious and equal relationship with his wife." It can be said that Meizuo Gong and Meizuo Ma were pioneers of gender equality in feudal society, and as a result, Aijing Manor became a unique carrier of the culture of female gentry in ancient villages.

Aijing Manor is constructed with earth, wood, and stone. It measures 79.2 meters in width from east to west, 64.5 meters in depth from front to back, with a backyard of 140 square meters. It covers a total area of 5,248.4 square meters and consists of 361 rooms. It comprises of two parts, with the outer perimeter primarily built for defense and the inner area consisting of separate rooms for residential purposes. It features three distinct architectural styles.

Firstly, it boasts a sophisticated and ingenious defense system. "Aijing Manor" is characterized by its well-designed and strategically laid out fortress-like structure, offering formidable protection against both bandits and fires. The bottom of the outer walls is constructed using a combination of random rubble stone, also known as dry stone, reaching a height of approximately 4 meters, with certain sections on the front and rear right sides reaching around 5 meters. Situated at the southwest and northeast corners are two watchtowers constructed with a combination of stone and earth. These towers extend beyond half the height of the fortress walls and serve as elevated vantage points, enabling surveillance and control over the entire perimeter of the fortress. While one tower overlooks the southwestern direction, the other oversees the northeastern direction.

碉楼下部石墙开有10厘米×20厘米左右的瞭望洞，上部土墙开有内大（50厘米）外小（15厘米）、高约60厘米的观察窗。同时还埋有许多等距离的毛竹管作为铳（枪）洞，有斜直下的，有横向的，能从不同角度打击来犯之敌。这些瞭望洞如今被很多住户改造为采光用的方窗。

进出寨堡的大门有四个，东一、西二、南一（为正门）。南正门为进庄大门，宽1.7米、高2.43米，全青石门框，石材厚度为0.18米，呈马蹄形，上宽0.42米，下宽0.50米。门楣上方直接用毛笔在墙面书写大字行楷——"爱荆庄"。这三字入笔坚实，运笔刚劲，字的结构紧实刚正、稳健圆润、气势恢宏，字里行间透露着一种傲气和端庄。

第二，精致、典雅的"祠宅合一"式民居。爱荆庄的内院由正座、书院、下座、后座组成主体建筑，还有东西两边的厢房，这是明清时期我国东南地区完美的四合院形式。房屋的东西两边按中轴对称。

爱荆庄的正座最具特色，高大、雄伟。厅宽5.8米，深（含廊面）9.1米，可排下八张八仙桌请客，捧盘人还能进出自如。正座廊柱高7.65米，廊柱的直径为38厘米，廊柱上方是带有官式建筑的斗拱结构（有待古建筑专家考证）。次廊柱直径为35厘米。正厅上部为穿斗式结构，廊柱上挑的两边有雕花的楼桁套。雕花桁套的规格，正厅为60厘米×35厘米，下厅为60厘米×25厘米等，精致美观。

内院宅屋所有门框上都雕刻着精美的门楣，雕刻有"寿"字的线穗式样。宅院内上部开设的小窗有圆形的、菱形的、扇形的，玲珑典雅。宅屋正座、下座及书院所有窗扇均为雕花，"文革"中遭受严重破坏，但还有个别完整窗扇对开。窗扇上设三框，上、中框为雕花，底框为人物镂空雕刻，皆栩栩如生、惟妙惟肖。

正厅的外屏更具特色，它建在厅面两边的后冲柱之间。爱荆庄家族内的一位前辈说："厅屏上有一幅巨大的镂空雕刻，高3米、宽2.2米。上截为上八洞的仙，下截为下八洞的仙。镂空雕刻得栩栩如生。"可惜20世纪90年代外屏被文物偷盗者撬走了。同样遗憾的是，厅堂上的丁帽座鎏金麒麟，以及外屏下案几上部的雕刻也被人撬走。现存案几的底座十分精美。

The lower part of the watchtowers features observation holes measuring approximately 10x20 centimeters, while the upper part consists of an earth wall with an observation window that is big inside(50 centimeters)and small outside(15 centimeters), reaching a height of approximately 60 centimeters. Additionally, numerous bamboo pipes are embedded at equal intervals, serving as gun ports. These gun ports are designed at various angles, allowing for attacks on incoming enemies from different directions. Many residents have converted these openings into square windows to allow for natural light to enter.

The manor is equipped with four gates: one in the east, two in the west, and one main gate in the south, which serves as the entrance to the entire estate. The main gate has a width of 1.7 meters and a height of 2.43 meters, featuring a solid and impressive green stone doorframe. The stone used for the doorframe is approximately 0.18 meters thick and shaped in a distinctive horseshoe design, with a width of 0.42 meters at the top and 0.5 meters at the bottom. Above the lintel of the gate, the name "Aijing Manor" is artistically inscribed onto the wall using a brush, in a bold and upright regular script. The strokes of the three characters are firm and dynamic, showcasing a robust and dignified structure, as well as a commanding and majestic presence. The characters radiate a strong sense of pride, while their composition and spacing exude an air of elegance and grandeur.

Secondly, Aijing Manor showcases a refined and graceful integration of ancestral halls and residential buildings. The inner courtyard comprises the main structures, such as the main hall, study hall, lower hall, and rear hall, along with wing rooms on both the east and west sides. This symmetrical arrangement along the central axis exemplifies the ideal quadrangle courtyard design commonly found in the southeastern region of China during the Ming and Qing dynasties.

The main hall of Aijing Manor is notable for its grandeur. It has a width of 5.8 meters and a depth of 9.1 meters(including the corridor), accommodating eight banquet tables with ease. The columns stand at an impressive height of 7.65 meters and have a diameter of 38 centimeters. The upper part of the hall features a unique bracketing structure, possibly following an "official style, " while the secondary columns have a diameter of 35 centimeters. The upper section showcases a through-bracket design with intricately carved brackets measuring 60x35 centimeters in the main hall and 60x25 centimeters in the lower hall, adding to its exquisite beauty.

All the doorframes in the residential courtyard are adorned with exquisitely carved lintels featuring the auspicious motif of "shou"(longevity). The upper windows of the houses are designed in various shapes, including round, diamond, and fan-shaped, displaying elegance and delicacy. The windows of the main hall, lower hall, and study are all intricately carved. Many of the window panels were damaged during the Cultural Revolution, but a few managed to remain intact. These panels consist of three frames, with the upper and middle frames showcasing intricate carvings, while the lower frame features lifelike, meticulously crafted hollowed-out figures.

The outer screen, located between the rear columns on each side of the hall, is particularly notable. According to the ancestors of the Aijing Manor family, the screen showcases a large and intricately carved openwork design, measuring 3 meters in height and 2.2 meters in width. The upper section depicts celestial beings from the Eight Immortals, while the lower section portrays celestial beings from the Lower Eight Immortals. The carvings are exceptionally lifelike. Regrettably, in the 1990s, the artwork was stolen by thieves, including the gilded carved qilin on the ceremonial table in the hall and the carvings on the upper section of the screen's base. Only the exquisitely crafted table base remains.

爱荆庄下层楼没有设置窗户，只有一个位于中间的双开门。门的东西两侧各有一间房。东边房供一些常客聊天喝茶，类似现代人的会客厅。西边房用来放一些家庭常用的器具。

讲究的石材和巧妙的铺设也是爱荆庄内院极具特色的装潢之一。各个部位所用的石材（条石）都是经过琢磨加工，有一定规格、相对光洁平坦的细花青石。最具特色的是正厅前的压廊石，包括东西官房，只用五块条石，宽度均为0.6米。正中间一块最长，达2.95米，两边对称，从中间到两边分别是长2.2米和2米的条石各两块。廊下的塍先用四块青石板垒砌，再用已打磨好的石框套砌，美观雅致。而正中间正厅的那块踏步石条是用整条石板铺设的，踏步石条两边用整块的石板斜铺。小孩在斜铺的石板上可作滑梯玩耍，石板已磨得异常光滑，人站在上面很难站稳。

第三，宅院厅内具有特色的"祠宅合一"布设。厅堂是全屋的核心，是庄厝族人追宗敬祖的地方。一般的宅屋只有一个厅屏，屏下一案几，几上摆有香炉、烛台，供插香烛用。而爱荆庄则建有内屏和外屏，内屏与外屏之间设有公婆龛，有供桌，桌上摆放祖宗和族人的灵牌等。外屏也设有案几或大桌，逢年过节爱荆庄的族人们会在正厅的案几或大桌（大樟树做的）上摆茶酒（三茶五酒）、干果和蔬菜（五果六菜）、肉品（鸡鸭猪等）、各种米制品（九层粿、糖粿、白粿、糍、米粽等）等祭品，还准备香、烛、炮、钱纸、金银纸、元宝纸来举行祭祀。最主要的祭祀日是端午节、七月半、冬至、春节这几个传统节日，各家各户都端着祭品来祭祀。红白喜丧也是在正厅堂里做的，这些活动现在依旧，从未停止。这种"祠宅合一"的建筑为研究我国东南地区的民间宗教活动、民俗历史文化保留了难得的实物资料。

一座座庄寨是世事变迁的映照。品读它们，就如同品读一部在漫长岁月中写就的厚重史书。岁月长河流淌，永泰山林间留下了让人叹为观止的建筑奇观，更留下了数不胜数的美谈。作为一类少为人知的建筑形式，彰显中国传统家族生存智慧的永泰庄寨也进入了国际视野，既将中国民间乡土社会解决人地关系的智慧传递给世界，又向世界讲述更充实、更丰富的人类社会发展演进的故事，同时将永泰传统村落可持续发展的实践推向世界。

The lower section of Aijing Manor does not have windows facing the upper hall. It features a central double-door entrance with a room on each side. The east room serves as a gathering space for socializing and enjoying tea with guests, resembling a modern-day living room. The west room is designated for storing everyday household utensils and items.

The architecture of Aijing Manor's interior courtyard is characterized by the use of exquisite stone materials and clever craftsmanship. Each section is meticulously constructed with finely polished bluestone strips of specific dimensions, providing a sleek and flat surface. Particularly noteworthy are the lintel stones in front of the main hall, as well as the east and west chambers, which consist of just five 60-centimeter-wide strips. The central strip stretches up to 2.95 meters in length, flanked by symmetrical strips measuring 2.2 meters and 2 meters on either side. The sills beneath the corridor are skillfully assembled using four precisely cut bluestone slabs, elegantly framed with polished stone borders. Additionally, the central step stone in the upper main hall is crafted from a single stone slab, while the sides are inclined using complete stone slabs. These stone slabs, worn smooth by children who enjoy sliding on them, present a challenge for anyone attempting to maintain their balance when standing upon them.

The layout of Aijing Manor's main hall is noteworthy for its fusion of ancestral worship and household activities. Serving as the central space, the hall is where the Aijing family pays homage to their ancestors. Unlike typical homes with a single screen, Aijing Manor features both an inner and outer screen. Between them, a shrine is dedicated to the grandparents, complete with an ancestral altar for displaying ancestral tablets. The outer screen is equipped with a table or large desk. On festive occasions, such as the Dragon Boat Festival, Ghost Festival, Winter Solstice, and Spring Festival, the residents gather in the main hall around the table or desk(made of preserved camphor wood). There, they present offerings including tea, alcoholic beverages, dried fruits, vegetables, meats, various rice delicacies, as well as incense, candles, firecrackers, paper money, and paper ingots for ceremonial purposes. The main hall also serves as the venue for important life events like weddings and funerals, preserving these traditions to this day. This unique architectural concept of combining ancestral worship and residential functions provides valuable material evidence for studying southeastern China folk religious practices and cultural heritage.

Each Zhuangzhai is a reflection of the ever-changing course of history. Exploring them is like delving into the pages of a profound historical chronicle crafted over time. As time flows on, Yongtai stands adorned with architectural marvels that inspire awe and hold captivating tales. As a lesser-known form of architecture, Zhuangzhai serves as a testament to the wisdom of traditional Chinese family and find their place on the global stage. They not only share the wisdom of maintaining a harmonious relationship with nature, but also weave a deeper and more enriched narrative of social development and evolution. Lastly, they promote the sustainable development of traditional villages in Yongtai to a global audience.

第十一章

Chapter Eleven

国际社区：异域风韵

International Communities: Exotic Styles

◎ 领事旧影

作为四大文明古国之一的中国，地大物博、物产丰饶，是令欧洲心生向往的东方大国。工业革命后，英国用鸦片敲开了中国的大门，让江河日下的清政府陷入了被动求和的局面。1842年，英国与清政府签订了中国近代史上第一个不平等条约——中英《南京条约》，福州成为五个通商口岸之一，允许英国人在此设驻领事馆。

一座福州城，半部近代史。倘若说三坊七巷是近代文儒大家、仁人志士的聚居地，那么烟台山则是近代福州走向国际的前沿阵地。1842年，随着古城福州被迫沦为五个通商口岸之一，烟台山也随之翻开了新的历史篇章。烟台山位于闽江南岸，海拔41.6米，素有"苍山烟霞、高丘低江"的美誉（仓山区文化体育和旅游局，2021）。正是得益于依山傍水、得天独厚的区位优势，外国人对烟台山情有独钟：1844年至1903年期间，外国人在福州大兴土木，英、美、法、日等国先后在烟台山设立了15个领事馆，兴建教堂、学校、医院和洋行。此后，烟台山成为外国人集中的居留地，建筑呈现异域风情，有"万国建筑博物馆"之称（刘可耕、吴旭涛，2021）。近百年来，烟台山上异国建筑鳞次栉比，囊括欧洲各时期的建筑风格，哥特式、罗曼式、巴洛克式、洛可可式建筑随处可见。整个烟台山有近百处近代建筑文物，烟台山近代建筑群在2006年5月成为国务院公布的第六批全国重点文物保护单位（闽声传媒，2020）。烟台山是近代福州门户开放的缩影，中西交融的历史使烟台山散发着独特的魅力，百年的繁华沧桑借由这些建筑一一呈现出来。

◎ **Consulates**

China, as one of the four ancient civilizations, was a great country in the East that Europeans have constantly longed for. However, the crippled Qing Dynasty begged for peace with Britain after the British invaded China with opium after the industrial revolution. In 1942, the Qing government signed the first unequal treaty in modern Chinese history with Great Britain, named the Treaty of Nanking. Fuzhou was opened as one of the five ports for mercantile pursuits as expected and a consulate was allowed.

It's said that Fuzhou represents modern Chinese history. Although three lanes and seven alleys were home to erudite intellectuals with lofty ideas, Yantai Mountain served as the frontline for Fuzhou to communicate with the world. The old city of Fuzhou was forced to become one of the five ports for mercantile pursuits(a new chapter of history was gradually opened in Yantai Mountain after the Treaty of Nanking) in 1842. Yantai Mountain is located on the south bank of Minjiang River with an altitude of 41.6 meters, which is well-known for its "the haze of Cangshan, high hills, and a low river"(Cultural, sports and Tourism Bureau of Cangshan District, 2021). Thanks to its unique location, foreigners were attracted to Yantai Mountain. Consequently, foreigners constructed a large number of buildings in Fuzhou between 1844 and 1903. For instance, a few countries set up 15 consulates in Yantai Mountain and built churches, schools, hospitals, and foreign banks, including Britain, the United States, France, and Japan. Since then, Yantai Mountain has become a concentration of residence for foreigners, and its architecture has taken on an alien style, with its name of "Museum of Universal Architecture"(Liu Kegeng, Wu Xutao, 2021). During the past hundred years, exotic buildings have lined up on Yantai Mountain, involving European architectural styles of all periods, such as Gothic, Romanesque, Baroque, and Rococo, which can be spotted everywhere. There are roughly 100 modern architectural relics in the modern architectural complex of Yantai Mountain, making Yantai Mountain modern architectural complex the sixth batch of national key heritage conservation units announced by the State Council in May 2006(Min Sheng Media, 2020). Yantai Mountain is the epitome of the opening-up of Fuzhou, whose fusion of the East and the West gives rise to a unique charm, and whose prosperity and vicissitudes of a century are embodied in these buildings.

在《南京条约》签订之际，道光皇帝出于政治考量不愿将福建省城福州辟为通商口岸，但面对英国咄咄逼人的姿态，彼时积弱积贫的清廷无力反抗，最终只能委曲求全。为了避免福州社会动荡，洋人被禁止在福州城内设立领事馆，最终选择在烟台山设立领事馆。在外国人眼中，烟台山山麓遍植梅花，万物凋敝之时唯有暗香疏影可慰严寒。更重要的是，烟台山毗邻闽江，地势较高，可以监控烟台山与城区之间的互动，又可以远眺海关埕闽江江面上的船只活动，因此洋人也乐于在此设立领事馆（李夕汐，2015：18）。福州开埠后，首任英国驻福州领事李太郭（G.T.Lay）于1944年抵榕，被安排住在城外鸭姆洲的民房。几经波折，于次年在仓前山设立了英国领事馆，此为各国在福州设立领事馆之始。

在英国率先在榕设立领事馆后，其他领事馆的建设也受到当时英国维多利亚建筑风格的影响（李夕汐，2015：22），在设计平面和外部构造上如出一辙。从建筑平面看，以简单的矩形为主，根据不同的使用需求分为组合式和对称式。组合式就是在矩形主体的基础上附加一个多边形角楼，通过科学合理的设计增加使用空间；对称式则体现了政治建筑的严谨性，在布局上追求中轴对称，增加布局的巧妙性，大多数领事馆的建筑都采用对称式平面（林诗羽，2020：22）。从19世纪末烟台山的全景图中可以清楚地看到，西式建筑在福州传统建筑群中鹤立鸡群，非常高大。

这些西式建筑大多采用两至三层的外廊式布局，四坡木屋顶，并在正立面设有开放性柱列空间，体现西方人追求高贵、休闲的生活方式（李夕汐，2015：21）。在福州，外廊式建筑有其独特的价值。福州地处亚热带沿海地区，春季多雨，夏季闷热，冬季湿冷。带有外廊的建筑，春日可躲连绵阴雨，夏日可避炎炎烈日，冬日可享和煦暖阳。

领事馆建筑不仅西式风格浓郁，中式特色也展露无遗。建筑多选用砖、木、石作为建筑主材。福建盛产青砖、红砖和花岗岩，外形美观，质地坚硬，抗风化和防水能力强，建造的房屋经久耐用。福建多山，青松翠竹，绿树成荫，林木资源极其丰富。三种主材都取材方便，造价适宜，洋人对此也青睐有加。因而，中西合璧的建筑风格构成烟台山的空间底色，成为烟台山最大的亮点。

美国领事馆：中美友谊的见证

地处仓山区麦园路84号的美国驻福州领事馆旧址，始建于清朝咸丰四年（1854年），首位领事颛士格立（Caleb Jones）便是在此走马上任，开启了中美文化交流的新历程。

At the time of the Treaty of Nanking, Emperor Daoguang was reluctant to open up the provincial capital of Fukien as a port of commerce due to political factors, but the Qing court with shaky dominance was unable to stand against the aggressive British and eventually submitted to them. In order to avoid social unrest in Fuzhou, foreigners were forbidden to establish consulates downtown and Yantai Mountain became the second thought. Additionally, the plum blossoms were planted everywhere at the foot of Yantai Mountain so that there was full of strong fragrance when others withered in chilly winter. What mattered most was that the higher terrain enabled them to oversee the interaction between Yantai Mountain and the downtown as well as the ship activities in Customs, for Yantai Mountain is adjacent to Minjiang River(Li Xixi, 2015: 18). After its opening-up, the first British consul of Fuzhou, G.T. Lay, arrived in Fuzhou in 1944 and was housed in a bungalow on Yamu Island outside the city. Afterward, the British consulate was set up in Cangqian Hill the following year after several twists and turns, which was the beginning of the establishment of consulates in Fuzhou.

The rest of the consulates were profoundly influenced by the Victorian architectural style of the British consulate in Fuzhou at that time(Li Xixi, 2015: 22), and thus their design and external structures looked alike. As regards the flat shape, they are mostly simple rectangular shapes, which are divided into a combined pattern and a symmetrical one in accordance with varying needs. The combined type refers to a polygonal corner tower attached to a rectangular main body to expand space by a scientific and reasonable design. On the other hand, the symmetrical type reflects the rigor of political architectures, pursues the symmetry of the central axis and enhances the skillfulness of the layout. Consequently, a symmetrical plan was widely adopted by consulates(Lin Shiyu, 2020: 22). From the panoramic view of Yantai Mountain in the late 19th century, it is obvious that western-style architectures were remarkably lofty among traditional buildings. Most of these buildings featured a two-story or three-story exterior veranda style, a hipped wooden roof and open columns on the front façade, symbolizing their noble and leisurely Western lifestyle(Li Xixi, 2015: 21). Considering Fuzhou is situated in the subtropical coastal zone with excessive rain in spring, muggy weather in summer, and clamminess in winter, the architectures with exterior corridors have their unique value. Accordingly, people in a building with an exterior corridor can avoid the continuous rain in spring as well as the blazing sun in summer and enjoy the warm sun in winter. Apart from the noticeable western elements, Chinese components are ubiquitous, including bricks, wood, and stones. Fukien is affluent in green bricks, red bricks, and granite, all of which are appealing in appearance, hard in texture, durable in construction and strong waterproof. Besides, Fukien is blessed with numerous mountains and abundant forests where pines and bamboo trees thrive. Most importantly, it was effortless to fetch these materials and their price was reasonable, so foreigners fancied them a lot. As a consequence, the combination of Chinese and Western elements shaped Yantai Mountain, becoming its highlight.

American Consulate: the Witness of Intercultural Friendship between Chinese and Americans

The former site of American consulate was located on No. 84 Maiyuan Road, Cangshan District, Fuzhou, which was built in 1854. It was here that the first consul, Caleb Jones, took up his post and started a new course of cultural exchange between China and the United States.

美国领事馆
American Consulate

　　美国领事馆依北高南低的山势而建。设计师因地制宜，突破中轴对称的建造传统，独具匠心地将建筑的一层设计为局部地下室。从西侧望去，建筑为一幢两层小洋楼，而从东面看却是三层。这既确保了洋楼的良好采光，又形成了层次丰富的立面结构。

　　领事馆是国家的象征，也是宣扬国威、彰显文化、昭示自我的政治名片。美国领事馆办公楼不讲究中轴对称，设计灵活自由、独具匠心，这与美国一直标榜的自由民主之风不谋而合。领事馆造型层次分明，用不同的材料将洋楼分割为上、下两部分。底层为排列整齐的石砌墙体，敦实厚重、坚实稳固。经历了岁月的洗礼和风雨的侵蚀后，石质的墙缝里长满了青苔，看起来略显沧桑。二层和三层为翻新后的白色砖墙，清新素雅。上下墙体的颜色和材质形成鲜明对比，不仅毫不突兀，反而相映成趣。屋顶形式随建筑主体造型的变化而不同，由中式青瓦坡屋顶和平屋顶组合而成，每个立面的形态迥然相异。

The former American consulate was erected in a mountainous area with high north and low south. For this reason, designers broke the routine of axial symmetry based on local conditions and devised a partial basement on the first floor. As a consequence, the structure has two stories when viewed from the west and three stories from the east, providing good lighting for the structure as well as creating a beautifully layered façade.

As is widely known, consulates are a symbol of national power and seem like a political card to promote national prestige, culture, and self-expression. Hence, the American consulate in a flexible form was in line with the liberty and democracy that the United States has advocated. Specifically, architects made the most of diverse substances to divide the building into the upper part and the lower one with a distinctive feature. In terms of each floor, sturdy and massive stone walls are carefully organized throughout the ground floor. Even yet, it appears a little dated when the stone walls are covered in moss from years of wind and rain erosion. In addition, it has been renovated with white brick walls on the second and third floors, fresh and elegant. Despite the stark contrast between the upper walls and its lower counterparts, it is not inconspicuous but rather intriguing. Moreover, because it blends Chinese tile roofs and flat roofs, the contour of the roof changes depending on the design of the main building, and each façade has a unique shape.

由于受到地势限制，领事馆底层的西面和南面部分被厚重的石砌墙体所遮蔽。南面不规则地砌筑着一堵厚实的墙体，上面架设着白色的石质楼梯，通往洋楼二层的内廊。地下室的西侧和西南侧结构较为封闭，为提高空间利用率，此处被作为仓储之用。地下室的东面则修筑了一条石砌拱券式外廊，廊内的雾霾蓝拱券式门窗与外廊呼应，相得益彰。伫立于二层东侧的外廊平台，顺着蜿蜒的山势极目远眺，视野开阔。建筑的二层和三层均采用南北向内廊式结构，与底层外廊式结构共同构筑了层次丰富的立体空间格局。

美国领事馆突破了中轴对称的传统，采用组合式建筑格局。西侧的主体为矩形内廊，东侧原为一个多边形角楼，现将东西侧打通，共同构筑出宽阔的内廊空间。东西立面各有一开间，以方形仿罗马塔司干柱分割。建筑南立面的通高仿罗马塔司干柱，柱基较薄，柱体粗壮，凸显了领事馆的庄严和肃穆。东开间的外墙凹凸变化、错落有致，为威严的领事馆增添了些许明快。三层的外廊设置了形式简洁的梭形水泥栏杆，通透开敞，立于此间，神清气爽、怡然自得。领事馆的门窗设计别出心裁，东立面底层为拱券式门窗，二层和三层嵌有矩形门窗，均是双层木百叶门窗。木百叶门窗既保证了建筑的私密性和美观性，又使人时时感受到光影的律动。

新中国成立后，美国领事馆被撤销。该建筑虽几经易主、多番修缮，仍是目前福州地区领事馆建筑中保存最完好的一幢，见证了历史上中美文化的交融和碰撞。

俄国领事馆：战斗民族的严谨性

清朝同治四年（1865年），俄国首位副领事德理（A.M.Daly）来榕赴任，次年在福州仓山（今公园路39号）建造领事馆（闫茂辉、朱永春，2011：152）。俄国领事馆由办公楼和领事府邸两栋洋楼构成，而今办公楼业已拆毁，仅领事府邸保存完好，于1952年收归政府使用，现为福州第九中学。

领事府邸为坐西向东的二层砖木结构建筑，占地面积213.8平方米，建筑面积396.7平方米。外墙为砖墙并粉刷，四坡屋顶（闫茂辉、朱永春，2011：152）。烟台山领事馆大多用砖筑成，牢固结实、冬暖夏凉。中式坡屋顶造型美观，防水性能好，能很好地适应福州的亚热带季风性气候，深受外国人喜爱。

The ground level is largely hidden by substantial masonry walls in the west and south due to the limitation of the terrain. In particular, a thick wall that is haphazardly constructed leads to the interior hallway on the second floor in the south and has a white stone staircase. In order to maximize space, the basement's west and southwest sides are more enclosed and it used to serve as a storage area. In addition, there is an arched stone corridor outside the basement in the east, which the hazy blue arched wooden windows and doors echo and complement. Standing on the eastern platform of the second floor, one can see down the undulating hill. Apart from it, north-south oriented inner corridors were used on the second and third floors, resulting in a complex three-dimensional spatial pattern. Instead of the axial symmetry, the U.S. Consulate uses a hybrid architectural design that features a polygonal corner building on the east side and a rectangular inner corridor on the west. But in modern times, both sides have been smashed together to provide a larger interior room. Additionally, the eastern room and the western room are separated by Roman Tuscan columns. On the south side, the two-story Roman Tuscan columns are massive and their bases are narrow, underlining their solemnity. Simultaneously, brightness has been added to the stately consulate by the concave and convex exterior walls on the east side. Besides, the outer corridor of the third floor is decorated with simple shuttle-shaped concrete railings, where you feel refreshed and relaxed. Uniquely, there are arched doors and windows on the ground floor, but rectangular windows and doors on the second and third floors, all with double wooden shutters. The wooden shutter guarantees beauty and privacy while providing a constant flow of light and shadow.

After the founding of the People's Republic of China, the U.S. consulate was closed. Although the building has changed its ownership several times and has been restored many times, it is still the best-preserved consulate building in Fuzhou, witnessing the collision and integration of Chinese and American cultures.

Russian Consulate: the Rigor of the Russian National Character

A.M. Daly, the first Russian vice-consul, arrived in Fuzhou in 1865 to begin his duties. The consulate thereafter was set up in Cang Shan, Fuzhou(now on No. 39 Park Road)in the following year(1866)(Yan Maohui., Zhu Yongchun, 2011: 152). The Russian Consulate originally consisted of two buildings, the office building and the consul's residence, but now the office building has been demolished. Fortunately, the consul's mansion, which is now known as Fuzhou No. 9 Middle School and was handed back to the government in 1952, has remained intact.

The consular residence is a two-story brick building facing east with painted brick walls and a four-pitch roof, covering an area of 213.8 square meters and a gross area of 396.7 square meters(Yan Maohui, Zhu Yongchun, 2011: 152). Brick walls, which are strong and durable, warm in winter and cool in summer, are mostly used in the construction of consulates in Yantai Mountain. Besides, Chinese sloped roofs are popular among foreigners because they are stunning, watertight, and withstand the subtropical monsoon climate.

俄国领事馆严格按照中轴对称的传统布局，东西立面造型相仿，南北立面对称，体现了政治建筑的严谨性。东立面设有入口外廊，廊内两侧并立着纤细的爱奥尼柱，柱身有24个凹槽，柱头有一对向下的涡卷装饰。立柱的使用增强了建筑的线条流畅感，凸显了设计的质感。建筑东立面，采用两层联拱券门窗叠起的形式，中轴对称，每侧开两个券窗。建筑南立面采用两层联拱券叠起的形式，每层开四个联拱券，中间开方窗，两端开券窗。东侧拱券较大，窗也较大（闫茂辉、朱永春，2011：152）。窗沿和门洞上精美绝伦的脚线设计，增加了建筑的艺术美感。

随着时代的变迁，各国的领事馆逐渐退出历史舞台。经过岁月的洗礼，曾经风光一时的万国建筑已呈破败衰景。2010年3月，官方正式提出了关于烟台山历史文化风貌区保护与改造项目的动议，拉开了对烟台山历史建筑维护和修缮的序幕。2014年10月，福州市出台了《烟台山历史文化风貌区、公园路历史建筑群、马厂街历史建筑群保护规划》，正式开启了烟台山的复苏之路。这些历史建筑被活化再利用，成为集人文、餐饮、交流和休闲于一体的旅游胜地。百余年后，烟台山"万国风尚"的传统得以传承，历史质感和现代美感在这里相映成趣。

◎ 国际社区

鼓岭地处福州市东郊双鼓横断山脉，群山连绵，东南与亭江白庙村交界，南与鼓山风景区相连，西与鳝溪农场接壤，北与宦溪乡毗邻。距福州市中心约12公里，南北长7公里，东西宽6公里，面积约24平方公里，是福州的第一道屏障（佚名，2021a）。鼓岭与江西庐山、浙江莫干山、河南鸡公山并称全国四大避暑名山，素有"左海小庐山"之称。

鼓岭平均海拔近800米，最高海拔998米，即使炎天暑月，依然凉爽宜人。自福州被辟为通商口岸以来，西方传教士接踵而至，奈何福州夏日酷暑难耐，他们只得费尽心机寻找消暑之地。1886年英国医生连尼（Dr. Thomas Rennie）在鼓岭营建了第一幢避暑别墅，此后各国人士竞相仿效。至1935年鼎盛时，已有来自二十多个国家的侨民建造了约350幢风格迥异的避暑别墅。此外，还兴建了教堂、医院、运动场、游泳池、万国公益社等公共建筑。鼓岭别墅被誉为鼓岭"四绝"之一，建筑多依山而建、随山就势，形成错落有致的空间层次感。每逢夏日时节，鼓岭上山风徐来、鸟虫鸣唱，不仅外国人相继前往避暑，福州城内的达官贵人、文人墨客也欣然前往，鼓岭俨然成了一个季节性国际社区，令人心驰神往。

The Russian Consulate is constructed based on the conventional axis symmetry, with bilateral symmetry on the north and south facades and corresponding patterns on the east and west facades, reflecting the strictness of political architecture. The entrance hallway is located on the east façade and flanked by two thin Ionic columns. Particularly, each column has 24 grooves and 2 embellishments that scroll downward. The columns accentuate the design artistically and make smooth lines. As for its architectural features, the building boasts four double-layered arches on each story on the south façade, while there are double-layered arched windows and doors with a symmetrical central axis on the east face and two arched windows on each side. On the south façade, there are unusual rectangle windows in the center and arched windows at both ends(Yan Maohui, Zhu Yongchun, 2011: 152). The beautiful and exceptional design of the footings on the window margins and doors improved its visual qualities.

The consulates gradually disappeared as time went on. As a result, after some time, the magnificent exhibition of foreign architecture started to deteriorate. The official motion on the preservation and renovation of Yantai Mountain's historical and cultural landscape was officially proposed in March 2010, which started the process of maintaining and restoring the historic structures in Yantai Mountain. "The Protection Plan for Yantai Mountain" issued by the government on march 2014 has represented a milestone on Yantai Mountain's route to recovery. Through adaptive reuse, the historic structures have been transformed into a tourist destination that combines human interaction, dining, communication, interaction, and leisure. More than a century later, Yantai Mountain has continued the legacy of "the universal style", and the area now reveals its historical inheritance and contemporary beauty.

◎ International Community

Guling is situated in the Shuanggu transverse mountain range in the eastern suburbs of Fuzhou, facing rolling hills. It's adjacent to Baimiao village of Tingjiang in the southeast, Gushan Mountain in the south, Shanxi Farm in the west, and Huanxi village in the north, and approximately 12 kilometers from the city center. Moreover, it's said to be the first barrier of Fuzhou with 7 kilometers long from the north to the south, and 6 kilometers wide from the east to the west, spanning an area of around 24 kilometers(Anonymous, 2021a). Guling is referred to as "Little Lushan Mountain in Zuohai" and is one of the four most well-known summer mountains across the nation, along with Jigong Mountain in Henan, Moganshan Mountain in Zhejiang, and Lushan Mountain in Jiangxi.

Guling has a favorable climate even in the sweltering summer thanks to its elevation, with the approximere height of 800 meters and the average height of 998 meters at its top. Western missionaries began to come to Fuzhou in quick succession after it was made a commercial port, but they laboriously looked for a summer resort where they might escape the stifling heat. The first summer residence in Guling was erected by a British physician Dr. Thomas Rennie in 1886, and other foreigners soon followed. Nearly 350 vacation homes in a variety of styles were built during its heyday(around 1935)by expatriates from more than 20 different nations. Additionally, new structures sprang up like mushrooms, including churches, hospitals, sports facilities, swimming pools, and public buildings like the Universal Community Association. Thus, Guling villas are regarded as one of Guling's "Four Uniques". Moreover, most buildings are embraced by mountains, forming a staggered spatial hierarchy. In order to escape the summer heat, not only foreigners but also dignitaries and erudite scholars from Fuzhou City traveled to Guling when the breeze was blowing and birds and insects were chirping. Guling has been a fascinating seasonal international community as a result.

宜夏别墅：东西方文明的交流中心

鼓岭最负盛名的宜夏别墅建于1919年，位于宜夏村的后浦楼，它的前身是鼓岭医院。该别墅的建筑样式将西洋风格和福建元素相融合，形成独具鼓岭特色的建筑风貌。这是一幢单层木石结构建筑，外立面采用整砌和乱砌相结合的方式，以花岗岩为主材砌成。白色素水泥、宽勾缝的西式毛石墙体，承载着中式小青瓦构筑的四坡顶，中西交融的建筑风格跃然入目。工匠们就地取材，厚实的花岗岩造型不但外形美观，且具有坚硬、耐磨和抗压的特性，确保了别墅的稳定性和安全性。由于福州地理位置特殊，鼓岭风大、雨多、雾浓，石料建造的房子性能卓越：冬暖夏凉，防风防潮。别墅不仅在石墙上预留了类似四叶草造型的通风孔，用以保证室内的干燥与通风，地下的排水和通风系统亦十分科学，完美地解决了排水和空气对流的难题。

该建筑面宽25米、进深36米，规模不算宏大，占地面积约390平方米。医院原建有三个病区，一间有良好照明的手术室、一间浴室，以及为护士、仆人们准备的房间（福州老建筑百科，2019a）。在当时封闭的山区条件下，医院设施先进、配备齐全，促进了当地卫生保健事业的发展。洋楼四周绿树成荫、苍翠挺拔，空气清新，非常适合病人疗养和康复。

宜夏别墅
Yixia Villa

Yixia Villa: Exchange Between Eastern and Western Cultures

The most renowned Yixia Villa in Guling is situated in Houpu Lou of Yixia Village, which was once known as Guling Hospital and was built in 1919. The villa's distinctive architectural features result from the fusion of Western and Fukien components. Regarding the structure's design, it is a one-story wooden and stone building with a mixture of neat and haphazard masonry on the facades, mostly built of granites. The four-slope roof is made of tiny Chinese green tiles and is supported by Western-style masonry walls with large white cement joints, combining Chinese and Western architectural forms. In effect, thick granites are not only good-looking but solid, wear-resist, and pressure-proof, ensuring their stability and safety. Guling is windy, rainy, and foggy due to Fuzhou's unique geographic location. Consequently, the stone houses provide excellent performance in Guling, because they are warm in winter and cool in summer and they are windproof and moisture-resistant as well. The villa features four-leaf clover-shaped ventilation openings in the stone walls, underground ventilation and scientific drainage, which completely address the issues of drainage and air convection.

The building, which spans an area of around 390 square meters with 25 meters in width and 36 meters in depth, is not very large. The hospital was originally built with three wards, an operating room with good lighting, a bathroom, and rooms for nurses and servants(Fuzhou Old Architecture Encyclopedia, 2019a). In the secluded mountain, the hospital was advanced and well-equipped to promote the development of local health care at the time. The house was virtually enclosed by lush greenery and filled with fresh air, which was an optimum place for convalescence and rehabilitation.

宜夏别墅选用质量上乘的旧材料和历史构件进行修复，采用传统工艺和技术，以求再现彼时的历史风貌。别墅外残缺破损的青石板路选用当地石材——鼓岭青，用传统的方式铺就，从触感到色泽都力求还原历史。外廊铺陈赤色斗底砖，开阔通透，夏日里凉风习习、舒适宜人，是休闲纳凉的好去处。外廊上整齐地摆放着三套质地古朴的桌椅，供人们休闲娱乐。室内宽敞明亮，功能分区明确，一切井然有序。室内的家具陈设尽可能地复刻百年前的西式传统风貌：高悬的美式大吊灯散发着柔和的光晕，温柔地照在质地温润的木制家具上，仿佛时光凝结，一切如旧。屋内的橘色皮质双人沙发、黄色的木制餐椅、展示柜上的十字架摆件、倚立在侧的自鸣钟，无一不在静静地诉说着那段尘封已久的往事。

随着鼓岭的旅游开发，宜夏别墅不断推陈出新，终年展陈鼓岭历史文化名人的生平事迹，重现历史，唤醒人们的集体记忆。别墅也因具有特殊的历史价值，继续发挥着"东西方文明交流中心"和"中美人民友谊屋"的沟通桥梁作用。别墅还为游客们提供正宗的咖啡西点，使其浸润在西式文化中，获得更加真实的文化体验。宜夏别墅也因此吸引了不少慕名而来的游客驻足参观，共赏美味。别墅在修旧如旧的基础上赋予建筑新的生命力，增强了建筑的空间活力。

万国公益社：旧时社交会所

万国公益社始建于1914年至1915年间，是一座远近闻名的西式社交会所。会所原为一幢坐北朝南的单层木石结构厅堂式建筑，外墙设计就地取材，用青色、黑色和白色的石料垒砌而成，经过岁月的摧残，墙面显得古旧粗糙。建筑外立面中西合璧，屋顶采用双坡顶和四坡顶为主的中式坡屋顶造型，以福建常用的灰瓦为主，上压镇石。北立面显示出西式建筑特征，窗户以白色木门窗为主，双开百叶状，内墙体由不同颜色的石头砌成，石灰勾缝，是明显的波希米亚风格（寻文颖，2013：7）。万国公益社面阔七开间，中间五开间前设有开阔的外廊，粗大的方形毛石柱并立其上，风格古朴简约。首尾两端的两开间呈封闭状，饰以白色双开木制百叶窗户，作通风换气之用。

万国公益社内部空间极具福州民居特色，厅内宽敞，木质屋顶，屋内大梁上装有中式吊顶。室内包括一座有240个座位的礼堂、三个"委员会"房间、更衣室、男女卫生间、浴室、厨房以及一间食品储存室（福州老建筑百科，2023a）。为了丰富广大侨民的业余生活、满足大众的社交需求，万国公益社不时举办各类社交、文艺活动，也组织各项文体比赛，吸引了更多的外国人来此兴建别墅、消暑度假。这样兴盛的场面一直延续到20世纪40年代，随着外国人相继回国，万国公益社也逐渐冷清衰败。

In order to properly restore its original appearance, the villa was meticulously renovated with high-quality old materials and historic components in traditional methods. In particular, the damaged stone path to the building was reclaimed from Guling Green, the local stones, and was paved in the traditional way to reconstruct the original one. The outer corridor where red tiles have been laid is spacious and breezy, and thus it is a great place to ease off and cool off in summer. Besides, the exterior passage provides visitors with three sets of antique tables and chairs for relaxing. Meanwhile, the interior that is roomy and bright is structured with clear divisions. Most importantly, the furniture is modeled after the traditional Western design of a century ago as closely as possible. By and large, it seems that all remain the same as they were back in time. The American chandeliers are glowing with a soft halo, gently spilling over the wooden furniture. In addition, dust-laden stories have been told by the orange leather sofas, the yellow wood dining chairs, the crucifix on the cabinet, and the chime clock leaning on the cabinet.

With the development of tourism in Guling, Yixia Villa has been exhibiting the life stories of historical figures to revive history and activate collective memory throughout the year. Additionally, the villa continues to act as a link between China and the West, a hub of interaction between Eastern and Western civilizations, and the witness for friendship between Chinese and Americans because of its unique historical significance. Additionally, the villa provides visitors with authentic coffee and pastry to immerse themselves in Western cultures and gain a truer cultural experience as well, hence attracting an increasing number of people to enjoy the delicacies. All in all, it has given new life to the building and increased its spatial vitality when restoring the old as the old.

Universal Community: Former Social Clubhouse

Built between 1914 and 1915, the universal community is a prominent Western-style social club far and wide. It was initially a single-story wooden and stone hall-style building, facing the south, whose exterior walls have been made of local materials, including green, black and white stones. However, the walls look old and rough after the ravages of the years. The roof is constructed of double-sloped and four-sloped roofs with gray tiles frequently used in Fukien and weighted down on the top, resulting in a fusion of Chinese and Western architectural styles on the building's facades. Nevertheless, it is a Western style on the north façade. To be specific, most of the windows are white wooden ones with double-opening louvers, and the interior walls are made of different colored stones with lime joints in an apparent Bohemian style(Xun Wenying, 2013: 7). The universal community is seven-room wide, with an open corridor in front of the middle five rooms. And thick stone columns stand side by side in a simple and ancient style on the corridor. Furthermore, the two rooms at both ends are closed and decorated with white double-opening wooden louvers for ventilation.

Its interior is highly distinctive of local folk houses with a large hall, a wooden roof, and a classical Chinese ceiling over the beams. Furthermore, its auditorium used to accommodate nearly 240 people, and there were committee rooms, dressing rooms, male and female toilets, bathrooms, a kitchen, and a food storage room(Fuzhou Old Building Encyclopedia, 2023a). To spice up expatriates' lives and meet their social needs, they constantly held assorted social and cultural activities and organized various sports and cultural competitions in the universal community, which drew more foreigners to settle down, construct villas, and spend their summers. These flourishing scenes continued until the 1940s when foreigners returned to their home countries one after another, and the universal community gradually declined.

2012年，当地居民不忍万国公益社就此荒废，遂对其进行改造和修缮：拆毁原后墙与挡风墙，在其后接筑混凝土结构的祠厅，原前廊被加建水泥靠椅，左侧山墙后侧的阶梯部分也被填补（福州老建筑百科，2023a）。现今的万国公益社已失去了旧有的风貌，室内空间被置换成展示区，辟为"开放福建"、"友好福州"、"鼓岭故事"、"国际社区"等板块展览。万国公益社传承鼓岭文脉的使命从未间断，各类优质音乐会和艺术展层出不穷。与此同时，鼓岭也成为众多侨民的乡愁：曾经风华正茂的他们早已是耄耋老人，改革开放后在儿孙的陪伴下重返鼓岭，与当地乡民们一起忆往昔、品乡情。近年来，更有侨民的后人来此处追思先辈，忆古惜今。

加德纳纪念馆：剪不断的乡情

鼓岭的加德纳纪念馆并非加德纳在鼓岭的故居，而是后人在加德纳别墅附近建造的一幢单层三开间建筑。纪念馆延续了鼓岭地区流行的美式外立面造型与中式四坡屋顶结合的建筑风格，大小不一的深色石料不规则地垒砌着，宽大的勾缝处用素色石灰进行填充，形成了鲜明的色差对比。白漆饰面的木制百叶门窗是鼓岭建筑的一大特色，纪念馆以双开门窗居多，但鼓岭风大雾浓，因此门窗极少全部敞开。纪念馆的四周地势平坦，外廊上的围墙较矮，看起来更为宽敞通透。围墙上立着细长的圆形木柱直通檐口，檐口上挂着一排喜庆的红色灯笼。外廊的拐角处摆放着一个简易的木质秋千架，勾起人们对当年侨民们悠闲生活的回忆。

Locals refurbished and repaired the universal community in 2012 because they could not bear to see it abandoned. Accordingly, the original back wall and windbreak were demolished, and a concrete hall was constructed behind it. Besides, concrete benches were set up in the former front corridor, and stairs on the left wall were filled(Fuzhou Old Architecture Encyclopedia, 2023a). Although the present universal community has lost its original appearance, the interior has been replaced with an exhibition area including "Opening up Fukien", "Friendly Fuzhou", "Guling Story "International Community", "International Community" and other modulars. Overall, it has never ceased inheriting the cultural heritage of Guling for the universal community, for there have been numerous quality concerts and art exhibitions. At the same time, Guling has become the nostalgia of the expatriates. Because of this, the once-young and vivacious individuals who are now elderly were joined by their children on their return, reminiscing and catching up. Even the descendants of expatriates visit this site, remembering the past and valuing the present.

Gardner Memorial Museum: the Endless Nostalgia

The Gardner Memorial is not the former residence of the Gardners in Guling, but a building with a single story and three rooms close to Gardner's villa. The memorial hall adopts the American façades coupled with a Chinese-hipped roof which have been populer in Guling. Besides, its walls are made of irregular dark stones and wide fissures covered with plain lime, creating stark color contrast. Aside from that, it is a typical local feature to install wooden louvered doors and windows with white lacquer, and the memorial hall is no exception. However, it is so foggy in Guling that most doors and windows are rarely wide open. Since the memorial hall is surrounded by the flat terrain and the exterior wall is shorter, it seems more spacious and airier. Moreover, thin round wooden pillars leading to the eaves stand on the parapet, where rows of festive red lanterns are hanging. Besides, a simple and lovely wooden swing is placed at the corner of the outer corridor, reminding people of leisurely days.

加德纳展示馆
Gardner Memorial Museum

纪念馆尽可能地复原百年前中西结合的生活原貌。第一间陈列室布局紧凑，家具不多，入门处放置一张铺着碎花台布的复古餐桌，四张略显斑驳的木椅整齐地围绕在餐桌四周。方桌上的花瓶、仿真面包和甜点等带有浓郁的生活气息，使百年前优雅闲适的侨民生活生动地展现在后人眼前。餐桌旁的墙面上挂着一部老式棕色旋转号盘电话，做工精细。第二间展室更为狭长，因家具陈设较多，略显局促。一张古朴简洁的中式楠木床放置在屋内最显眼的地方，物品摆放齐整。木床边上是一套中式雕花梳妆台，台面正中摆放着色彩鲜艳、造型独特的美式茶具。梳妆台旁放着一架质朴的旧式钢琴，虽置于中式楠木家具中却不显突兀，反而愈加提升了室内的庄重典雅之感。展室的墙面上专门辟出一处照片区，挂着加德纳后人重返鼓岭时的留影，详细记录了他们的"寻根之旅"。最后一间开间参照旧照片中的陈设，摆放了百余件民国时期的旧物，包括留声机、报纸、摇椅、时钟和各式工艺品等。加德纳家族中的后人也捐赠了曾在鼓岭生活过的先人的遗物，缅怀过往岁月。现馆内采用实物、电子影像和AR技术等还原了侨民的生活细节，架设了中西交流沟通的桥梁。

加德纳家族中的密尔顿·加德纳（Melton Gardner）与鼓岭有着深厚的缘分，他对鼓岭魂牵梦萦的故事至今仍广为流传，并被记录在《啊，鼓岭！》一书中。书中的主人公密尔顿在鼓岭度过了永难忘怀的童年时光，结识了与自己年纪相仿、勇敢仁厚的郭小山。在辛亥革命爆发之际，密尔顿恋恋不舍地离开了鼓岭，并与小山约定重聚。小山为了践行自己的诺言，历经万难前往加拿大，却为救工友而不幸客死异乡。密尔顿三次北上寻人，却无功而返。得知小山的死讯后，倍受打击，一心只想重返"故里"探视，却终生未能如愿。临终时，密尔顿对"Kuliang"的声声呼唤让人动容。几经波折，在中国留学生钟瀚的帮助下，密尔顿的遗孀才得以重返鼓岭，实现他毕生的夙愿。

随着国内革命战争爆发，外国侨民陆续归国，鼓岭遂复归寂静山乡本色。近年来，鼓岭为了传承历史基因、赓续鼓岭文脉、延续中西友谊，着手更新文化景观，发展旅游业。鼓岭业已形成集主题公园、文化民宿、度假酒店于一体的大型综合体，打造出独具吸引力的城市名片。

The memorial museum restores the old life as much as possible when the East met the West. In general, the first showroom is compact in size and does not arrange too much furniture. There is an antique dining table covered with a scrappy tablecloth right at the entrance and four slightly mottled wooden chairs beside the table. Furthermore, the graceful and easygoing expatriate life of a century ago is vividly revealed ahead of future generations by the retro vase, the artificial bread and deserts, which are full of life. Next to the dining table hangs an old brown rotary dial telephone set, exquisitely crafted and long-lasting. Compared with the first room, the second one looks even narrower and slightly more confined due to more furniture. A vintage and simple Chinese nanmu bed is prominently positioned in the room with well-organized bedding. Alongside the wooden bed stands a traditional Chinese dressing table, where a brightly colored and uniquely shaped American tea set is in the center of the table. Additionally, A rustic old piano is placed by the side of the dressing table, which does not stand out among the Chinese nanmu furniture, but enhances its sense of grace and dignity. On the wall of the exhibition room, there is a photo area with pictures of Gardner's descendants when in Guling, detailing their "roots-seeking visit to Guling". The third room is adorned with more than a hundred old items from the Republican era, including photographs, newspapers, rocking chairs, clocks, and various artifacts based on furnishings in the old photos. Likewise, the Gardner's descendants have also donated relics of their ancestors who used to live in Guling, in remembrance of the past years. The museum now makes full of objects, electronic images, and AR technology to restore the details of their lives, building a bridge of communication between the East and the West.

Melton Gardner, a member of the Gardner family, had a deep affection for Guling, and his story with Guling is still widely spread and recorded in the book "Ah, Kuliang!". Milton spent his childhood in Guling, where he met Guo Xiaoshan, a courageous and benign boy of his own age. However, Milton left Guling reluctantly and promised to reunite with Xiaoshan at the outbreak of the Xinhai Revolution. To fulfill their promise, Xiaoshan went to Canada and underwent difficulties, but he disastrously died in a foreign country to save his workmate. Afterwards, Milton went north three times to look for him, which turned out to be a wild goose chase. After learning of his death, Milton was devastated and eagerly wanted to return to his Guling, but was unable to do so for the rest of his life. Therefore, Milton's call to "Kuliang"(Guling)towards the end of his life is very touching. After several twists and turns, Milton's widow was able to return to Kuliang and realize his lifelong wish with the help of Chinese student Zhong Han.

Guling's tranquil and mountainous character returned with the start of the civil war and the exodus of foreigners to their home countries. In order to pass on its historical roots, cultural heritage, and friendship between China and the West, Guling has begun to revitalize its cultural landscapes and grow tourism in recent years. Guling, which has developed into a sizable complex of amusement parks, cultural lodges, and resort hotels, has established itself as a distinctive and alluring city card.

◎ 教会学校

自 1842 年福州开埠以来，带着宣教使命的西方传教士纷至沓来，但西方宗教思想的传播受到公众的强烈抵制。西方传教士独辟蹊径，希望通过教育的方式来传播宗教思想。学校可以为传教提供固定的场所并带来稳定的学习者，且对各种思想较为包容，从而为布道提供了更为宽松的环境。此外，中国人素有尊师重教的传统，对于知识的学习甘之若饴，不易对宣教人员产生抵触情绪。近代以来，教会学校的兴办固然是一种文化侵略的手段，具有一定的局限性，但从客观上也提高了民众的文化水平，促进了福州近代教育事业的发展。

教会学校草创时期，学校大多面临校舍简陋、规模较小、人数有限等问题，学习内容也较为局限，以识字和阅读圣经为主。20 世纪初期，教会学校进入了蓬勃发展时期，办学促教的活动如火如荼地展开。从客观上看，日薄西山的清政府在 1906 年正式废除了持续一千三百多年的科举考试，建立了仿造西方公学的新式教育制度，这为当时教会学校提供了绝佳的发展契机。从主观上看，传教士们不断探索合适的办学方式，学校的办学条件逐步改善，也吸引了更多本地学子前往求学。而鸦片战争后社会剧变，局势动荡，民不聊生。其间中华民族的自我意识不断觉醒，"师夷长技以自强"的心态也促进了西学的发展。

鹤龄英华书院：近代人才的摇篮

鹤龄英华书院（Anglo–Chinese College）原位于福州市仓山区鹤龄路，后改名为鹤龄英华中学，是 1881 至 1952 年间基督教卫理公会（美以美会）创办的一所私立教会中学（福州老建筑百科，2021d）。以鹤林英华书院为首的教会学校采用近代西方办学模式，在承认中国伦常和文化的前提下大力宣扬基督教文化，所教授的课程包括宗教、数学、天文、地理、伦理、哲学等。

书院的主楼鹤龄楼是建于 1868 至 1881 年间的一幢两层券廊式建筑，原为有利银行大楼。随后，经各方协调，书院逐步扩建，形成配套完善的校区，其中还包括西式的钟楼和礼堂。遭逢近代动荡的局势和岁月的侵蚀，现今书院的主楼不复存在，但 1905 年所建的力礼堂和美志楼在今福州高级中学内得以幸存和修复，并仍在使用。

◎ Church Schools

Western missionaries flocked to Fuzhou after its port opened to trade in 1842. The public in Fuzhou, however, staunchly opposed Christian notions. Western missionaries instead adopted a novel strategy to propagate religious ideals through education. Generally, schools offered a more comfortable setting for preaching because they could supply a set location for sermons, attract dependable students, and were more accepting of different viewpoints. Besides, Chinese people have a long-standing tradition of valuing teachers and have been open to learning, making them less likely to resist missionaries. In modern times, church schools were a vehicle of cultural aggression and had special restrictions, but objectively they leveled up public literacy and encouraged the establishment of modern education in Fuzhou.

Most church schools underwent a series of issues in their early years, including inadequate instructional content confined to the Bible and literacy, plain and unappealing structures, small sizes, and few pupils. In the early 20th century, church schools embraced a real boom for education. From an objective point of view, the crippled Qing government abolished the imperial examinations in 1906, which lasted for more than 1300 years. Subsequently, a new education system was created modeled on Western public schools, which provided a golden opportunity for the development of church education. From a subjective point of view, the missionaries kept exploring suitable ways to run schools, and their conditions were gradually improved and appealed to more local students. In addition, society remained turbulent and changed drastically following the Opium War, where the bulk of the population was living in poverty. In consequence, Chinese self-awareness was invariably aroused, and the belief of "learning from foreigners to strengthen ourselves" was conducive to the expansion of Western education.

Heling Anglo-Chinese High School: the Cradle of Modern Talents

Anglo-Chinese College was a private church high school run by the Methodist Church between 1881 and 1952, which was previously located on Heling Road in Cangshan District, Fuzhou, and subsequently renamed Heling Anglo-Chinese High School, (Fuzhou Old Building Encyclopedia, 2021d). At the end of the Qing Dynasty, the church schools adopted the Western models and actively promoted Christian culture while respecting Chinese ethics, history, and scripture. under the direction of Heling Ying Hua College, The courses taught involved religion, mathematics, astronomy, geography, ethics, philosophy, etc.

The Healing Building, the school's primary structure, was constructed between 1868 and 1881. It was a two-story colonnaded structure that was once the Youli Bank. Afterward, the school was steadily developed through cooperation into a well-equipped campus with a bell tower and an auditorium in the Western architectural style. The Li auditorium and the Meizhi building, both built in 1905 and currently in use at Fuzhou Senior High School, have survived and been renovated. The main building, however, no longer exists due to the upheaval and years of erosion.

力礼堂又名英华礼堂，现为福州高级中学体操馆。该礼堂是一幢平面呈十字形的哥特式教堂建筑，外立面用红砖垒砌而成，屋顶坡度陡斜，以小青瓦屋面覆之。礼堂四周的门窗呈拱形、带尖顶，给人一种神秘感。礼堂内部设计简洁，高大空旷。美志楼为坐北朝南的三层西洋式建筑，砖木结构，占地面积535平方米，券廊式风格（福州老建筑百科，2021d）。洋楼四面外廊宽阔，中央开间为出入楼道，左右对称地分布着拱形门窗。美志楼现作为福州高级中学的图书馆继续使用。

鹤龄英华书院是一所人才辈出的知名学府，培养了许多胸怀天下的济世之才，如著名数学家陈景润，"中国化工之父"侯德榜，中华民国国民政府主席林森等。

魁岐福建协和大学：自由崇学之风

"协和大学闽江东，世界思潮此汇通；高山苍苍，流水泱泱，灵境产英雄；萃文化，作明星，明星照四方。无远弗届，真理是超；乐群众于一堂兮，作世界大同之先声；协和协和，大德是钦！"福建协和大学的校歌气势磅礴，响彻闽江两岸。这所始建于1915年的教会大学，不遗余力地践行着校歌中的校训宗旨，秉承着教化和培育博古通今、放眼世界的人才的使命，培养了不少出类拔萃的人才。

福建协和大学原租用仓前观井路的茶行，后于1922年春迁入魁岐乡。新校区背倚鼓岭、面瞰闽江，大小几十座校舍屹立于江东，晨曦暮霞，水光山色，美不胜收，被人们称作世界上最好的十所大学之一（谢必震，2004：13）。校区是由大名鼎鼎的美国建筑设计师亨利·墨菲（Henry Killam Murphy）规划设计的，他也曾主持燕京大学和岭南大学等知名学府的设计。墨菲对中国的宫殿式建筑很感兴趣，潜心钻研，深谙其精髓。他的设计兼顾东西方文化，融汇东西方建筑技艺，形成独具特色的建筑群。中国建筑讲究"山环水抱"、"前有照后有靠"的风水之学，因而协和大学选址于群山掩映的丘陵地带，层林叠翠，悠悠烟水，鸟语花香，风光旖旎。墨菲因地制宜，采用嵌入式布局，将校区建于山体之间，把无限的自然风光收于有限的校园之中，突破自然和建筑的物理界限，体现了人与自然和谐共生的中国传统理念，收到扩大视觉空间、提升园区美感的效果。

The Li auditorium, also known as Ying Hua auditorium, is now the gymnasium of Fuzhou Senior High School. The auditorium is a cross-shaped Gothic church structure with a red brick façade and a steeply sloping roof covered in a tiny tile roof. The windows and doors around the auditorium are arched with spires, with a sense of upward mystery. In addition, the inner auditorium is plain, lofty and vacant. On the other hand, the Meizhi Building is a three-story brick structure facing south in the style of a colonial voucher corridor, covering an area of 535 square meters(Fuzhou Old Architecture Encyclopedia, 2021d). It features broad outer corridors on all sides, with a central opening for access to the building and arched doors and windows symmetrically distributed on the left and right. The Fuzhou Senior High School library is currently housed in the Meizhi Building.

It has trained a myriad of talents with a global vision, such as the famous mathematician Chen Jingrun, the "Father of Chinese Chemical industry" Hou Debang, and Lin Sen, the Chairman of the National Government of the Republic of China.

Fukien Christian University in Kuiqi: the Pursuit of Freedom and Curiousness

"Fukien Christian University is located in the east of Minjiang River, where the world's thoughts converge. The mountains are lush and green, and the water is stunning and clear; hence cultivating talents. Acquire knowledge, and be a pillar of our nation, shining all around. Wherever you go, the truth follows you. Altogether, be pioneers of a harmonious world. Fukien Christian University, Fukien Christian University, the highest morality deserves admiration." The school song of Fukien Christian University was majestic and resounded on both sides of Minjiang River. This Christian university in Fuzhou, established in 1915, has made every effort to uphold its credo. Additionally, it has adhered to its objective of educating and developing talents who were informed about the past and the present and who were open to the world, cultivating many distinguished talents for the homeland.

In the spring of 1922, Fukien Christian University was relocated from Guanjing Road in Cangqian to Kuiqi Village. Numerous school buildings of all sizes can be seen on the new campus, which is situated next to Minjiang River and the foothill of Gushan Mountain. Because of the spectacular views of the waterside landscape in the morning sun and evening twilights, it has been regarded as one of the top 10 colleges in the world(Xie Bizhen, 2004: 13). More significantly, the campus was conceived and created by renowned American architect Henry Killam Murphy, who was also in charge of Yanjing University and Lingnan University. Murphy indulged in Chinese palatial architecture and boned up on it to grasp its essence. He combined Eastern and Western architectural methods in his design to produce a singular architectural complex, taking into account the cultural distinctions between the East and the West. Fukien Christian University is situated in a hilly area surrounded by mountains filled with lush forests, flowing water, chirping birds, and delicate flowers, because Chinese architectures are based on the Feng Shui philosophy of "surrounded by mountains and water" and "light in front and support at the back". Murphy built the campus between the hills in an embedded layout to take advantage of the local topography and to break down the barriers between nature and architecture by allowing the endless natural scenery to blend into the campus setting. All of these have mirrored the traditional Chinese idea of peaceful cohabitation between man and nature, expanded the visual field, and improved the aesthetics of the campus.

鼓棹闽江之中，便可看见巍峨矗立的两座雄伟建筑，那就是协和大学的文学院和理学院（谢必震，2004：13）。文学院和理学院的设计不落窠臼，建筑主材选用洋人素来钟爱的砖和石，墙身结合了中国传统的梁柱、斗拱、匾额、窗棂等结构，屋顶设计上选用了棱角分明的单檐歇山顶，中西设计风格完美融合。文、理学院的外立面均为青石整砌墙体，方正规整，给人稳重大气之感。其余楼层皆为砖木结构，单檐歇山顶，上覆晶莹琉璃瓦，造型别致，匠心独运。坡屋顶上翘起的檐角处设有瓦制角兽，形态各异，使建筑充满了生气，也体现了中国"天人合一"的文化内涵。屋顶之下，外墙立面上设置了许多方形玻璃窗，确保室内采光充足、空气流通。大门采用在中国传统民居中广泛应用的屏门，造型丰富，装饰精美，雕刻考究。墨菲的建筑从来不会缺少细节上的刻画，窗棂位置的楼面上也雕刻了类似青铜器上的古典图式（胡阔，2011：40）。

协和大学是近代西方文化传播的载体，是培育英才的摇篮。协和大学的青年学子们不仅学习了知识、增长了见识，还涵养了自己的价值观、人生观和世界观。在这个世外桃源中，学子们可以远离城市的喧嚣、不问世俗的纷争，一心向学。协和大学配备了先进的教学设备，师生之间灵活互动，学生们很少会有"学海无涯苦作舟"式的精神压力。中国古来就有"仁者乐山，智者乐水"的儒学义理，纵情于山水之间不仅能够起到促学的作用，还能培养宽广的胸襟和胸怀天下、兼济苍生的使命感。协和大学的莘莘学子不仅有着精益求精的学术追求和拨乱济危之志，对于自由恋爱也充满向往。传统的封建礼教束缚了人们的思想，限制了人们的自由，而随着教育水平的提高，人们终于有了挣脱封建礼教枷锁的勇气和底气。据毕业生回忆，在波光粼粼的江畔，在碧草如茵的草地上，在绿意盎然的林边，随处可见意气风发的青年学子并肩携手、共赏芳华。

福建协和大学是近代中西方文化交流的成果，她强调人的全面发展，注重健全人格的养成，鼓励体育精神，提倡创新和动手能力，这些至今仍然是极有价值的（福州日报社，2021：139）。

Those who take a boat ride in Minjiang River can see two imposing structures which are the Faculty of Arts and the Faculty of Science of Fukien Christian University(Xie Bizhen, 2004: 13). The design of the Faculty of Arts and the Faculty of Sciences is unconventional and is built primarily with bricks and stones, which were popular among foreigners at the time. The structures, on the other hand, use classic Chinese elements like beams, arches, plaques, window lattices, and the gable and hip roof with a single eave which is sharp-edged, creating a harmonious fusion of Chinese and Western architectural styles. Additionally, the façades of the first floor are all composed of square and regular green stones, with a sense of stability and generosity. Nevertheless, the rest of the floors are made of bricks and wood with a gable and hip roof with a single eave covered with crystal-glazed tiles, chic and unique in shape. The sloping roof boasts tiled corner beasts in different forms, making it full of life and reflecting the Chinese cultural connotation of "the unity of heaven and man". Under the roof, many square glass windows are installed on the façades to ensure sufficient light and air circulation inside the buildings. The main doors adopt screen gates, which are widely used in traditional ancient dwellings and are richly shaped, beautifully decorated, and elaborately carved. Murphy's architecture never lacks detailing, and classical bronze-like patterns are carved on the surfaces of window lattices(Hu Kuo, 2011: 40).

Fukien Christian University is a carrier of modern Western cultures and a cradle for excellence. Young students from the university not only acquired knowledge and expanded their horizons, but also developed their values, outlook on life, and worldview. In this paradise, students could get away from the hustle and bustle of the city, not care about worldly strife, and concentrate on their academic learning. The university was equipped with advanced teaching facilities, and the interaction between teachers and students was flexible, so students rarely had to suffer from the crushing stress of learning. Coincidently, Confucianism has promoted the philosophy of "The benevolent find joy in mountains, while the wise find joy in water." since ancient times in China. Furthermore, indulging in the mountains and water not merely fostered learning, but also cultivated a broad-mindedness and a sense of mission to help others. What's more, the students not only had a strong ambition to pursue academic excellence and help people in danger, but aspired for free love Although the traditional feudal rituals bounded people's minds and restricted their freedom, they ultimately dared to free themselves from the shackles with the improvement of education. According to the graduates' recollections, you could see the spirited young students held hands and enjoyed the beauty together along the sparkling riverside, on the turquoise grass, or on the lush green forest.

Fukien Christian University is the fruit of cultural exchanges between the East and the West, and it is nowadays exceedingly valuable to underscore the all-round development of the human being, the cultivation of a sound personality, the encouragement of sportsmanship, the promotion of innovation, and hands-on skills(Fuzhou Daily News, 2021: 139).

第十二章

建筑装修：雕梁画栋

Chapter Twelve

Architecture and Decoration:
Exquisite Carvings and Paintings

福州有着两千两百多年的建城历史，漫步街头，"三山两塔一条街"的古城格局依稀可辨：明清建筑星罗棋布，历史街区古韵悠长，近代开埠交融中西……福州古厝彰显出建筑的智慧，镌刻着城市的年轮，勾连起文化的血脉。

福州古厝的布局具有强烈的轴线性。每一处院落都有一个正院。而正院又有一条明确的中轴线，正院内的各个建筑空间沿这条轴线严格对称，依次布置大门、门厅、天井、前厅、天井、后堂、后院。各进院落左右对称，布局严谨，总体呈纵向长方形。对于官宦、商贾而言，一个正院往往不足以容纳庞大的家族，故多在正院两侧平行设置侧院。相较于正院，侧院不具有强烈的礼仪性，主要用于满足家庭内部成员的日常生活起居。不难看出，这种建筑布局不仅体现了中国古代建筑讲究平衡、对称的设计手法，也反映出封建社会森严的等级观念。

◎ 沈葆桢故居

位于福州宫巷26号的沈葆桢故居是一座典型的明清时期官宦宅邸。它建于明代天启年间，数次易主。清同治年间，时任江西巡抚沈葆桢将其购置、修葺后居住于此。故居建筑面积约2747平方米，为四进大院，每进均有高墙堵隔。

三坊七巷鸟瞰图
Aerial View of Three Lanes and Seven Alleys

With a history spanning over 2, 200 years, Fuzhou boasts a rich heritage of urban development. As you wander through its streets, you can still catch glimpses of the ancient city layout with its iconic "Three Mountains, Two Pagodas, and One Street." The city is adorned with a multitude of Ming and Qing architectural marvels, while its historic neighborhoods exude a timeless charm. Fuzhou's cultural tapestry is further woven with the interplay of Eastern and Western influences from its bustling port era. The ancient houses of Fuzhou, known as "guzhu", showcase the ingenuity of the southern region and serve as living testaments to the city's vibrant past, preserving the cultural legacy that runs deep within its veins.

The traditional dwellings in Fuzhou are symmetrical along a central axis. Each dwelling has a main courtyard where the axis is based, and the other buildings are arranged along this axis: main entrance—hallway—patio—hall—patio—master residence—backyard. For a large family, side courtyards are often set up on either side of the main courtyard to serve the everyday living of family members. This layout not only reflects the traditional concept of balance in housing design, but also mirrors the rigid hierarchy in Chinese feudal society.

◎ Shen Baozhen's Former Residence

Located at No.26, Gong Lane, Fuzhou, the former residence of Shen Baozhen is a typical official residence built in the reign of Emperor Tian Qi of the Ming Dynasty. It had changed hands many times over the years and was finally purchased and refurbished by Shen Baozhen, who was then the provincial governor of Jiangxi, during the reign of Emperor Tong Zhi of the Qing Dynasty. Covering a floor area of about 2, 747 square metres, the residence consists of a tetrad of courtyards, with high walls separating each other.

故居坐北向南，周围筑有封火墙。建筑沿中轴线自南而北依次为门头房、厅堂、正座、藏书楼。门头房在正门东侧隔墙外，穿斗式构架，左右为带花格门窗的房间，供守门、轿夫等仆役居住。

第一进为外大厅，为待客和婚丧喜庆所用，面阔五间，廊长13米，纵深17米，采用减柱造木构架。厅前为宽敞庭院，厅堂宽敞明亮。厅正中高悬黑底金字抱柱联："文章华国 诗礼传家"。厅堂左右两廊用以安放主人的各种官职的仪仗执事牌。大厅的梁架、斗拱古朴规整，基本保留了明代建筑原貌。

第二进厅堂为"明三暗五"式，与第一进间隔一面高墙，中辟石框门，两旁厢房分别为前后房，为主人居住之处。

第三进面阔五间、进深七柱，穿斗式木构架，双坡顶。前有大天井，中分前后厅。前厅堂上配饰挂屏，窗棂皆镶楠木板，正中一副对联："子孙贤，族乃大；兄弟睦，家之肥。"左右两边隔有厢房，为家人居住之所。后厅庭院过道建有覆龟亭用于遮雨，与倒朝楼相接。

第四进为双层楼阁，用作藏书楼。后天井中轴亦建有覆龟亭，宽2米，石铺过道，两侧设有美人靠。左右天井栽种花木，自成一小园，供主人游憩。

故居是沈葆桢为官后所购置。其母病逝，他丁忧守制时就居住于此。光绪五年（1879年），沈葆桢病故。他为官二三十年，除了这座房子，没有留给家人其他不动产。如今，故居建筑基本保存完整，2006年被列为国家级文物保护单位。

◎ 陈氏五楼

福州古厝的平面布局追求"矩形"构图。传统的院落一般建设周期较长，往往不是一次性建设完成，多是随着主人家的财力和人口的逐渐增加分次加建完成。典型建筑为陈氏五楼。

陈氏五楼位于仓山区螺洲镇，是清代大儒、帝师陈宝琛的故居。该建筑始建于清光绪年间，由赐书楼、还读楼、北望楼、晞楼和沧趣楼组成，故被称为"陈氏五楼"。陈氏五楼内亭台楼阁相映成趣，集南方私家园林风格和北方庭院风格于一体，兼容少许西式元素，是福州著名的古典园林建筑。

The residence is situated north to south, surrounded by firewalls. The buildings along the north-to-south central axis are the entrance, the hall, the master residence and the library. The Daozuofang ("reverse-facing" rooms), built in chuan-dou style, is located on the east side of the main entrance and used to accommodate servants such as doorkeepers and carriers.

In the outer courtyard lies a hall used for receptions and celebrations. The hall is five rooms wide and seventeen metres deep, with a large inscribed board on the beam that reads "article for the glory of a country; morality passed down from generation to generation". The corridors on both sides of the antehall are used to house the owner's official plates.

The second courtyard, separated from the first one by a high wall, consists of a hall and two wing rooms where the owner lives. Upon arrival at the courtyard, guests could only see three entrances; upon departure from it, they would notice the two hidden side entrances.

With a width of five rooms and a depth of seven columns, the third courtyard is comprised of a patio and a master residence that are arranged along the central axis. All the buildings adopt the chuan-dou style with double-pitched roofs. The master residence is divided into the front and rear parts. The front part is decorated with guapings (挂屏, a screen attached to a wooden panel or set in a frame for hanging), with Nanmu (楠木, Phoebe zhennan) panels set in the windows. A couplet in the middle of the room reads "if descendants are virtuous, the family will grow; if brothers live in harmony, the family will thrive." Located on both sides of the master residence are the ells, where family members live.

The rear courtyard is composed of a pavilion, two patios and a two-storied library. A corridor paved with stones connects the pavilion to the library, with long benches set on both sides for people to rest. The patios are decorated with plants and rockeries.

In 1879, Shen Baozhen passed away, leaving nothing but the residence to his family. Most of the residences remain intact even after 150 years. In 2006, it was listed as the National Cultural Relics Protection Unit.

◎ Chen Baochen's Residence ("Five Houses of Chen")

A traditional residence in Fuzhou is generally built over a long period, with new courtyards added with the growth of family wealth and the increase of family members. The formal residence of Chen Baochen is a good example.

Built during the reign of Emperor Guang Xu of the Qing Dynasty and located in the town of Luozhou, the Residence consists of the Book House, the Reading House, the Beiwang House (beiwang meaning "looking to the North"), the Dawn House and the Fun House, also called "Five Houses of Chen". The residence embodies the features of both the classical garden in southern China and the courtyard in northern China, and also borrows from Western designs.

陈氏"望族"之说是从陈若霖开始的。陈若霖是清乾隆期间进士，乾隆、嘉庆、道光三朝重臣，官历湖广总督、四川总督、刑部尚书等。他为官刚正不阿的形象深入人心，人们对他的评价堪比包公。儿子陈景亮是道光年间举人，官至云南布政使。孙子陈承裘为咸丰年间进士。曾孙一辈最光彩，以陈宝琛为首，兄弟有六人中举，并有三个进士。

陈宝琛一生大致可分为三个阶段。第一个阶段是37岁之前，科举及第后在京为官，36岁就已经是内阁学士兼礼部侍郎。第二个阶段是37—61岁，由于得罪了慈禧，被借故连降五级，谪居在家，回到家乡福州做乡绅。第三个阶段是62—87岁，再次入朝为官，并成为溥仪的老师，被授予太傅衔，人称"末代帝师"。

现存的陈宝琛故居就是他回乡后兴建的。今天的螺洲已经不是百年前的乡村，但他精心营造的五楼基本还是当年模样。

赐书楼用来存放御赐的图书。该楼是清代典型的穿斗式楼阁，内部豪华、典雅，房中陈设更居五楼之冠。陈宝琛罢官乡居时，与夫人王眉寿的住房便设在此楼。如今，这里设有陈氏家风家训馆，全面展示了陈氏家族优良的家风家训。

还读楼用于收藏御赐图书之外的其他书籍，名字取自陶渊明《读山海经》中的"既耕亦已种，时还读我书"，曾是福州最大的私人图书馆。楼中藏书丰富，大多是陈宝琛自己收藏的民间善本、珍本。为了有利于楼上藏书，还读楼底层的所有木柱都以石柱垫托，楼体完全开敞，将前后院空间连为一体，使得整体建筑更为通风、防潮和防虫。如今还读楼已成为"陈岱孙纪念馆"，用于展示他可贵的为学之道、为师之道、为人之道。

陈宝琛回乡隐居长达二十多年，建沧趣楼以自娱，"沧趣"二字便含有归隐之意。沧趣楼为庭园风貌，楼前有鱼池，池水引自乌龙江，周围有假山和凉亭。楼内则贮藏了大量陈宝琛收集的古玩，如金石、书画等，是福建省内最大的一座私人博物馆。如今，沧趣楼被开发为螺洲镇名贤文博馆，呈现不同时期有代表性的螺洲名人。

北望楼为辛亥革命后陈宝琛回乡期间所建，取名"北望"，有"丹心朝北阙"的含义。楼内曾悬挂溥仪盛服临朝的巨幅照片，并陈列祭器等物，寄托了他的遗老情怀。北望楼是一个独立的院落，由南北两楼相对组成，有回廊曲径、修林茂竹、清池流水，精巧生趣，也被称为"小姐楼"。

The prosperity of the Chen clan can be traced back to Chen Ruolin. He had been the governor-general of Huguang, the governor-general of Sichuan and then the minister of Justice. He was known for his uprightness and was often compared to Bao Zheng. Chen Jingliang, son of Chen Ruolin, was listed as juren (举人, a qualified graduate who passed the triennial provincial exam) during the reign of Emperor Dao Guang of the Qing Dynasty and promoted to buzhengshi (布政使, a second-grade official position) of Yunnan. Chen Chengqiu, grandson of Chen Ruolin, was jinshi (进士, "advanced scholar", a graduate who passed the triennial court exam) during the reign of Emperor Xian Feng of the Qing Dynasty. The great-grandsons of Chen Ruolin, led by Chen Baochen, were all selected as juren, among which three were jinshi.

The life of Chen Baochen can be roughly divided into three stages. In the first stage, he was selected as jinshi and became Grand Secretariy and deputy minister of Rites. The second stage was marked by his return to Luozhou after being relegated five grades due to an offence to Empress Dowager Cixi. Following the collapse of the imperial order and the establishment of the Republic of China in 1912, Chen, at the age of 62, went back to the court and served as a tutor of the former emperor, Puyi, who was allowed to stay in the Forbidden City for more than thirteen years under the "Articles of Favorable Treatment". Chen Baochen continued to serve Puyi after he was finally expelled from the Forbidden City in 1924.

The residence of Chen Baochen was built over the years when he stayed in Luozhou and most parts of it still remain intact today.

The Book House is used to store the books bestowed by emperors. Built in the chuan-dou style, the house boasts the most luxurious and elegant furnishings among the five houses. After relegated and sent back to Luozhou, Chen once lived here with his wife Wang Meishou. Today, it is developed as a museum displaying Chen's family education and values.

The Reading House was once the largest private library in Fuzhou. Most books are the rare versions collected by Chen himself. To better protect the books, all the wooden pillars on the first floor are supported by stone columns. The front and rear yards are joined together to form a large open space in between so as to keep the house dry and free of insects. Now, the house has become the memorial hall of Chen Daisun, where visitors can appreciate his way of learning, of being a teacher and of being a human.

Chen Baochen returned to Luozhou at the age of 37 and lived in seclusion for more than 20 years. The Fun House, where he used to entertain himself, is a classical garden decorated with rockeries, pavilions and a fish pond with water drawn from the Wulong River. The main hall houses antiques, precious stones, calligraphy and paintings collected by Chen and is the largest private museum in Fukien. Now, the House is turned into a museum presenting representative Luozhou celebrities over the history.

The Beiwang House was built after the Revolution of 1911 (the Chinese bourgeois democratic revolution led by Dr. Sun Yat-sen which overthrew the Qing Dynasty). "Beiwang", meaning "looking to the North", represents Chen's loyalty to the Qing Dynasty and the wish of its restoration. The House once hung a huge picture of Pu Yi in the court and displayed things such as sacrificial vessels.

晞楼是陈氏五楼中最后建成的，名字取嵇康《养生论》中"晞以朝阳"的语意，坐西朝东，以迎朝曦。晞楼建成时已是民国时期，所以建筑形式与风格都偏西式，楼上有阳台，设水泥固定桌椅。陈宝琛晚年时常在此迎风听雨、观日赏月。

2009年，陈氏五楼被列为省级文物保护单位。游人在风格各异的小楼中观光穿行，便能一览福州百余年来的历史沧桑演变。

◎ 梁厝古民居群

福州民居的另一特色是呈曲线形。白墙黛瓦、曲线山墙、飞檐翘角，是福州古厝特色独显的形式与美感，也是闽派建筑的标志性元素。连绵的马鞍墙勾勒出千年闽都的人文肌理，也延续着这座古城的文化精髓。

马鞍墙是封火墙的一种。在建造过程中，墙体顶端随着穿斗式屋架的起伏做成"几"字型，翘角伸出宅外，形状如马鞍，故称为"马鞍墙"。细看可以发现马鞍墙两端的弧线是不同的，其中靠近正门一侧会飞扬翘起，形如燕尾，而靠后的一段则比较平缓。马鞍墙在民间有多种做法，大多采用生土夯筑，具有防火、防风、防御等功能。

三坊七巷马鞍墙
Saddle-shaped Walls in Three Lanes and Seven Alleys

The Dawn House was the last to complete, named after "welcoming the rising sun" in *Yangsheng Lun* (Essay on Nourishing Life) written by Ji Kang. Sitting west to east, the House adopts the Western design famous in the Republic of China, with balconies and concrete tables and chairs on the second floor. In his later life, Chen liked to spend time here admiring the changing seasons, sunrise or sunset, in peace and serenity.

In 2009, Chen Baochen's Former Residence was listed as the Provincial Cultural Relics Protection Unit.

◎ Ancient Residential Complex in Liangcuo

Another distinctive feature of Fuzhou's traditional dwellings is their curved design. With white walls, dark tiles, gracefully curved gable walls and upturned eaves, they showcase a unique form and aesthetic that is characteristic of Fuzhou's ancient houses and a defining element of Min-style architecture. The meandering horse saddle walls throughout the city outline the cultural fabric of Fuzhou, spanning centuries, and carry on the essence of this historic city's heritage.

The saddle-shaped wall was made into a "几" shape on its top, with both ends protruding to the sky. The end near the main entrance flies up like a swallow's tail, while the one at the back is gentler. Built from rammed earth, the wall is used to prevent fire, wind and outside attacks.

此外，马鞍墙还具有装饰功能。在福州马鞍墙的墙身、墙帽，特别是墀头处，往往会出现题材多样、风格多变的装饰。这些装饰凸显了福州的宗教信仰和吉祥文化。

福建是一个宗教信仰繁杂的省份。佛教在西晋时期就已传入闽地，道教在唐五代也有了很大的发展。另外，伊斯兰教传入闽地的时间也比较早。因此，在马鞍墙飞翘的脊角处灰雕上，可以看到源于佛教的如意纹、卷草纹、法轮纹，源于道教的神兽、福禄寿、祥云，源于阴阳五行的四灵兽等。

在福州，三坊七巷是欣赏马鞍墙的绝佳地点。此外，位于仓山区城门镇的梁厝古民居群也是很不错的选择。

梁厝地处闽江和乌龙江交汇处，背靠燕山。这个只有两千多常住人口的小村落却是有着深厚文化底蕴的历史名村。这里有始建于唐朝的千年古刹龙瑞寺；宋代理学大儒朱熹曾在梁厝村讲学，并留下墨宝"贻燕堂"；自宋以来，梁厝村名人辈出，如清代梁章钜、梁鸣谦，我国海防导弹事业的奠基人梁守槃都出自这里。如今，修复改造后的村庄保存了唐、元、清等朝代的古建筑共30多处。

梁厝的建筑很有特色，白墙灰瓦，木石结构，低矮方正。在梁厝随处可见闽派建筑中特有的马鞍墙，线条流畅，十分精致。

在梁厝现存的古建筑中，永盛梁氏宗祠最负盛名。它始建于南宋隆兴元年（1163年），元朝时经扩建形成今天的规模。

宗祠的大门两侧有一对用白瓷酒盏拼镶的白象，约3米高，据说象身拼镶的瓷盏都是当时由梁氏族人每家每户捐献的。大象脚踏八宝，背有象鞍以及插着画戟的花瓶、玉磬，寓意"吉祥如意、吉庆平安"。

梁厝村儒文鼎盛，理学儒家文化传承久远，也培育了无数文人名士。从宋至清共产生27位进士，历史上曾出现福州地区"无梁不开榜，开榜必有果"的盛况。如今，不少古厝被改造成茶馆、花房和书院，重新焕发出生机，这里也成为福州文化新地标之一。

◎ 九头马民居

福州古厝在装饰方面也很有特色。徽州的建筑以砖雕、木雕、石雕闻名，尤以砖雕最为出色，而浙江东阳则以木雕称奇。福州的古建筑没有砖雕，但其木雕、石雕、彩绘和堆塑特别精美。

The saddle-shaped wall also boasts a variety of decorative patterns that represent a diversity of religious beliefs in Fuzhou. For instance, on the flying ends of the wall are engraved the Buddhist Ruyi (如意, "as desired"), the Taoist divine beasts and auspicious clouds, the four great beasts risen from Five Elements, etc.

In Fuzhou, apart from Three Lanes and Seven Alleys, the ancient residential complex in Liangcuo is also known for its exquisite saddle-shaped walls.

Located at the intersection of Minjiang river and Wulong river, with Yanshan at its back, Liangcuo, with a population of just over 2,000, is a village with rich cultural heritage. There are more than 30 ancient buildings from the Tang, Yuan and Qing dynasties. The Longrui Temple, for instance, was built in the Tang Dynasty and refurbished several times. Zhu Xi, a prestigious scholar of the Song Dynasty, once lectured here and inscribed "Yi Yan Tang" on a lacquered board.

The dwellings in Liangcuo are characteristic of white walls and grey tiles, wooden structures and well-designed saddle-shaped walls.

Among them, Liang's family's ancestral temple in Yong Sheng enjoys the most popularity. It was built in the first year during the reign of Long Xing of the Southern Song Dynasty (1163 AD) and expanded during the Yuan Dynasty to its present size.

On both sides of the main entrance are a pair of 3 metres high elephants made of white porcelain glasses that are said to have been donated by each household of the Liang clan at the time. The elephants have eight treasures on their feet, saddled with vases with painted halberds and jade pans, signifying "auspiciousness, good fortune and peace".

Liangcuo has a rich Confucian heritage and is home to countless literary figures, including 27 jinshi over the time from the Song Dynasty to the Qing Dynasty. Today, many ancient dwellings are developed into teahouses, green houses and study halls, becoming one of Fuzhou's new cultural landmarks.

◎ Nine Horses Residential Complex

In terms of ornamentation, traditional dwellings in Fuzhou boast their delicate stone carvings, wood carvings, paintings and clay sculptures.

九头马民居位于福州市长乐区鹤上镇岐阳村，因建筑内围的九块岩石形似骏马而得名。民居由富商陈利焕于清嘉庆年间（1796—1820年）始建，子孙三代历经七十余年完工。

民居坐北朝南，占地面积约16800平方米，是福州地区面积最大、保存较为完整的古民居建筑群之一。其最大特点是建筑装饰十分考究，雕梁画栋，青瓦灰墙，彰显出当年的富足和繁荣。整个建筑由五列五进共22座主体建筑组成，中轴对称，前低后高。每逢红白大事，所有的屏门都打开，从一进直接通到五进，规模宏大，透视感很强。

五落之间以高耸的马鞍墙、冷巷相隔，内部井、院相连，门廊相通，既能防火，又有利于通风、防潮。马鞍墙线条起翘夸张，造型多变，比福州其地区民居的马鞍墙更有张力。

东尽头一落三进。一进花园已毁。二进院被称为"接官厅"，形制规格很高，面阔八扇七间，当心三间四梁扛井造，有衙署之风，是接待达官贵人的主要场所。三进坐东朝西，十扇九间，供下人居住和活动。西尽头一落建造晚，现存面阔七间的四合院。门厅正对朝厅，主座为米巢馆。五落之间既区隔又相连，正面组成一字型立面。中落墙头上开有悬挂13个宫灯的空窗，独具特色。

民居最令人印象深刻的是无处不在的雕刻艺术。福州地处沿海，台风频繁，因此九头马民居在结构上采用牢固的穿斗式。此外，因雨水多、天气潮湿，民居注重以雕工而非油漆来进行装饰。放眼四望，门窗、屏风、阁楼，础石、廊轩企篷、穿鼻、距花（雀替）、梁托、悬钟……几乎无处不雕花。

就雕刻的内容而言，有人物、动植物、民间故事、戏文典故等。而雕刻技法分浅雕、高浮雕、镂空雕、双面雕、阴刻、阳刻、镶刻等。木雕多保持木材本色，有的采用闽漆贴金，也有的采用彩色套板衬托。石刻大多用于柱础，砖雕用于门楼亭、墙头、窗格，泥塑用于墙头饰，壁画广泛用于内墙壁。多采用象征、寓意、谐音等民族传统手法，寄寓祥瑞吉利的美好意念，如"和合二仙"、"升平景象"、"吉庆有鱼（余）"、蝙蝠（福）、鹿（禄）、松鹤（寿）、梅雀（喜）……正可谓是用细节把人引入这场雕刻艺术的视觉盛宴，领略雕刻艺术之美，感叹匠人的匠心独具。

"古城两千两百岁，信乎今夕是盛年。"两千多年的历史岁月和人间烟火，以福州古厝为载体，携着过往、牵着未来，氤氲出人间岁月长。

Situated in Qiyang Village, Changle District, Fuzhou, the Nine Horses Residential Complex is named after the nine surrounding rocks that resemble steeds. It was built by a wealthy merchant, Chen Lihuan, during the reign of Emperor Jia Qing of the Qing Dynasty(1796-1820), and took over 70 years to complete.

Sitting north to south and covering an area of about 16, 800 square metres, it is one of the largest and best-preserved ancient residential complexes in Fuzhou. The complex comprises a quinary of courtyards, with a total of 22 buildings arranged along a central axis. When there is a celebration or a funeral, entrances of each courtyard will be opened and people can look directly to the end and appreciate its grandness. The buildings in the complex feature white walls and grey tiles, with beams and pillars decorated with elaborate carvings and paintings.

The five courtyards are separated by towering saddle-shaped walls, and at the same time connected by lengxiang (literally "cold alley"), a very narrow passage between two buildings that has little exposure to sunlight all year long. Once air passes through lengxiang, its speed will increase and its pressure will decrease so that the hotter air in the rooms will be brought out and the cooler air will enter to replenish it, thus achieving effective ventilation.

The outer courtyard has been destroyed. The second courtyard, with a width of seven rooms, is known as "Hall for Receiving Officials" and modeled after governmental agencies, with three rooms in the middle held by crisscrossed beams. The third courtyard, with a width of nine rooms, sits east to west and accommodates servants. The courtyard in the west was the last to complete. With a width of seven rooms, it is a traditional Siheyuan with a hall called "Duizhao" (meaning "facing the sun") and a master residence named "Mitiao" (meaning "selling rice"). Altogether, the five courtyards spread out in a line, with thirteen sunroofs opened in the middle courtyard and decorated with palace lanterns.

Fuzhou, located in the southeastern part of China, has a warm and humid weather, frequently hit by typhoons in summer. Therefore, dwellings in Fuzhou are mostly decorated with carvings rather than paintings. Look around the complex and you will see a diverse variety of carvings on doors, windows, attics, corridors, beams, roofs, bells, etc.

The carvings include figures, plants, animals, folk tales and literary works, most of which use symbol, allegory, and homophony to convey messages of auspiciousness. The techniques include shallow and high relief carving, yinke and yangke, openwork carving, double-sided carving, etc. Wood carvings keep their original colour, with some lacquered or gilded, and there are also coloured overlays to set them off. Stone carvings are used for columns; brick carvings for entrances and window panes; clay sculptures for exterior walls; murals for interior walls.

Fuzhou, the ancient city, with its rich history spanning over two thousand years, embodies the essence of time and the vibrancy of human existence. Fuzhou's ancient dwellings serve as a testament to the past and a bridge to the future, encapsulating the enduring spirit of the ages.

漫游：沉浸与品味

Rambling: Immersion and Taste

有福之州，城中有山，山中有城。而城中那些姿态各异的古老建筑承载着专属于福州的文化记忆与历史变迁，为中华民族传统文化注入了鲜活的生命力。福州古厝，以丰富多彩的建筑表达、深沉独特的历史记忆，书写了乡愁、乡情、乡恋。岁月匆匆，福州古厝见证了两千多年的沧海桑田，一砖一瓦都镌刻着岁月的痕迹，凝聚着前人的精巧构思，传承着关于家族的光辉荣耀。游览福州古厝，于闹市中寻觅一处"桃花源"，安享岁月风雅。

———————— · ◇ · ————————

Fuzhou is a blessed city with mountains inside and outside it. The distinctive ancient buildings in the city carry the cultural memories and record historical changes that belong exclusively to Fuzhou, breathing vibrant life into the Chinese nation's traditional culture. Utilizing colorful architectural expressions and unique historical memory, Fuzhou ancient dwellings have written nostalgia, affection and attachment. With time flyingby, ancient buildings in Fuzhou have witnesses vicissitudes for more than 2000 years. A single brick and tile inscribe the sign of age, conveys predecessors' ingenious conception and passes the family's glory on. While visiting ancient dwellings in Fuzhou, it seemed as if we were seeking " the Shangri-la--the land of idyllic beauty" in the downtown area and enjoying elegance and peace in our life.

第十三章　梦回闽都　岁月如歌

Chapter Thirteen
Dreaming back to Ancient Fuzhou City

◎ 屏山怀古：欧冶池

欧冶池位于今鼓楼区鼓屏路冶山路南的冶山春秋园内。

步入园区，映入眼帘的是欧冶池畔的石碑。此碑立于1328年，即元泰定五年。石碑曾裂为三段，移至于山九仙观碑廊保存，1998年重树于此。碑身由花岗岩筑成，圆首，通高2.65米、宽1.01米。碑文楷书，分三行竖刻："三皇庙五龙堂欧冶池官地　泰定五年岁次戊辰三月三日奉　福建闽海道肃政廉访司台旨立石"（福州老建筑百科，2022a）。这是景区三块石碑中唯一的元代真迹。碑文"三皇庙五龙堂欧冶池官地"昭示欧冶池自古以来就属于国有土地。岁月沧桑，当年的三皇庙与五龙堂早已不复存在。

后人在临池北侧分别建有剑光亭和喜雨轩，以示纪念。喜雨轩西侧并排立有两块石碑。正面镌刻"欧冶子铸剑古迹 光绪壬辰端阳节"的石碑并非原物。原碑立于光绪十八年（1892年）。背面书："春秋时期，越王允常聘铸剑名师欧冶子在此铸剑。池为淬剑处，故称欧冶池，是福州现存的最早古池。"碑文还说明："一九七六年前后碑失。为纪念福州建城两千两百年，据原照片重新刻制。"这是福州市政府1998年5月所立的复原石碑。

铸剑大师欧冶子雕像
The Sculpture of Ou Yezi，a Master Swordsman

◎ Reminiscence of the Past: Ouye Pond

Like a great hermit living in the city, Ouye Pond is located in the Garden of the Spring and Autumn Period Garden in the Mount Ye, the southern Yeshan Road and Guping Road, Gulou District.

When we step into the garden, we can see the monument near the bank of Ouye Pond. This monument was erected in 1328, the fifth year of Taiding Reign in the Yuan Dynasty. It was broken into three sections and moved to be treasured in the monument stele gallery in Nine Gods Taoist Temple on the Mount Yu. In 1998, it was erected here once again. It was made of granite. The top of it is round; it is 2.65 meters tall and 1.01 meters high. The inscription on the tablet is written in regular script and carved vertically in three lines. The inscription on the left read, "March 3rd in the fifth year of Taiding Reign."Inscriptions in the middle reads, "The tablet indicating the government ownership in Five Dragons Hall, Three Emperors' Temple" (Fuzhou Old Architecture Encyclopedia, 2022a). This is the only one authentic work of the Yuan Dynasty among the three tablets in this tourist attraction. The middle line of the inscription indicates that Ouye Pond belongs to government since ancient times. Time flies and the then Three Emperors' Temple and Five Dragons Hall have disappeared.

Sword Light Pavilion and Xiyu Veranda near the north side of the pond for commemoration have been built in the northern side of the pond by later generations. There are two stone tablets to the west side of Xiyu Veranda. On the obverse side of a stone tablet, there are inscriptions which read, "The site where Ou Yezi forged swords" and "the Duanwu Festival of Guangxu Reign". On the reverse side of it, inscriptions read, "In the Spring and Autumn Period, the King of Yue State, Yunchang ordered Master of swordmaking, Ou Yezi to forge swords here.This pond was used for quenching the swords. Therefore, the pond is called Oueye Pond. This is the earliest pond in Fuzhou". This stone tablet is not the original one which was erected in the 18th year of Guangxu Reign(1892 A.D.).

而另一块石碑则是福州市人民政府1983年8月所立，正面刻有"欧冶池 经本府于一九八三年八月公布为第二批市级文物保护单位 福州市人民政府"的字样。其背面文字除了介绍欧冶池的由来之外，还为世人展示了更多的珍贵史料：唐元和年间置剑院，浚池时出土有铜刀、刀环等遗物。宋郡守程师孟建欧冶亭，并作《欧冶亭序》，记述池广数里，上有亭阁，浮画舫可游宴。现存元泰定五年（1328年）石碑一方，一九八三年重浚。

综观三块石碑上的碑文，我们不难看出历代统治者以及当代政府对于承载着两千多年历史与文化的欧冶池之重视程度。

彼时，池塘周围数里，烟波浩渺，颇为壮观，后渐湮，现仅余方塘半亩（福州市政协文史资料和学习宣传委员会，2017）。可见，历经两千多年淘洗的欧冶池从往昔的浩瀚之湖变成了今日水草婆娑、幽深碧绿的半亩方塘。

省文史馆馆员、原福建省冶石山遗址博物馆馆长欧潭生认为："先秦时期的福州尚未经开发，人稀地广，山川险峻，原始森林资源丰富，树木是优良的冶炼燃料，然后因为当时的福州城还没有现在这么大，四周都是水，可以说是临海，海边有风，又是深山老林，选择这样的冶炼场所完全符合当时炼剑的环境。所以，在地理环境上，也能说明欧冶池就是当年欧冶子炼剑的地方。"（福州小鱼网，2018）

据《吴越春秋》记载，越王元常命欧冶子铸造了五把剑，而吴王则得到了越国进献的三把剑，分别为：鱼肠、磐郢与湛卢（赵晔，2019：79）。风胡子评价说："还有一把名叫湛卢，含有各种金属的精粹，蕴蓄了太阳的精华，拔出来便有烁烁神光，把它佩戴在身上显得威风凛凛，可以击退侵略，抵抗敌人。然而，人君如果有违背情理的阴谋，这把剑就会离他而去。"（赵晔，2019：80）尽管湛卢宝剑并非铸于欧冶池，然而从后人对其之珍视程度以及溢美之词可知大师的铸造技术出神入化，亦可窥见铸剑大师高贵的人格魅力。试想，欧冶子之所以选择在冶山的剑池淬剑，打造出流芳百世的名剑，除了技艺精湛外，必定是因冶山周边气候宜人，草木丰茂，生火便利，矿藏丰富，池水清冽，足见欧冶池是淬剑的风水宝地。

The other stone tablet was erected in August, 1983 by Fuzhou Municipal Government, with the obverse side of it carved inscriptions which read, "Ou Yechi was announced as the second batch of cultural site under municipal protection by Fuzhou People's Government." The inscriptions on the reverse side of it are relating the origin of the Ouye Pond and offering more historic records. It is known to us that in the Yuanhe Reign of the Tang Dynasty, the sword court was constructed; when the pond was dredged, there were some unearthed remains such as bronze knives and knife rings. It is also found from the inscription that the magistrate of Fuzhou Prefecture, Cheng Shimeng took the charge of Ouye Pavilion and wrote an article entitled "A Preface to Ouye Pavilion" which relates that with pavilions and halls, the area of Ouye Pong stretched for several li and there were even gaily-painted pleasure-boat on the pond; there remains a stone tablet erected in the fifth year of Taiding Reign(1328 A.D.); and the pond was redredged in 1983.

Reading inscriptions on the three stone tablets, it is not difficult to find that rulers in the past and the contemporary government places a high value on the Ouye Pond which carries more than two thousand years' history and cultural vein.

According to *Mount Ye History*, "In the beginning, miles around the pond, mists and waves stretched far into the distance, which was magnificent; however, gradually, the vast expanse of waters shrank and the western part of the pond neighboring to the local examination office was encroached by vernacular residences; hence there only remains a pond covering an area of half a mu." (Cultural and Historical Literature, Study and Publicity Committee of Fuzhou Municipal Committee of Chinese People's Political Consultative Conference, *Mount Ye History*) Over two thousand years witnessed the then vast Ouye Pond changed into a pond with half a mu at present.

Ou Tansheng, a member of the Provincial Research Institute of Culture and History, the former curator of Mount Tanshi Remains of Fukien Province maintained, "With precipitous mountains, fast flowing rivers, sparsely populated people, before Qin Dynasty Fuzhou hadn't been developed. However, it was rich in resources of primordial forests and timbers were excellent smelting fuels. In addition, since the then coastal Fuzhou City which was surrounded by water was not so big as it is at present, this melting site was suitable for forging swords. Therefore, geographically, it indicates that Ouye Pond is the place where Ou Yezi forged the sword."(Fuzhou Little Fish Network, 2018)

According to *The History of the Wu State and the Chu State,* the King of Yue ordered Ou Yesi make five swords. And the King of Chu was presented three of them, which were known as Yuchang, Pancheng and Zhanlu(Zhao Ye, 2019: 79). Feng Huzi commented that, "There is a sword named Zhanlu, which includes the cream of different kinds of metals and stores the sun's quintessence. It glitters when it is drawn from its sheath. When it worn, it will make the owner look commanding and help him repel the invasion and resist the enemy's attack. However, if the king has a plot which goes against the reason, this sword will stay away from him.(Zhao Ye, 2019: 80)." Although the sword named Zhanlu was not forged in the Ouye Pond, we can find that the master attains perfection in the technique in forging the sword and his noble personality since his work is highly valued and acclaimed by his contemporaries and later generations. As for the reason why Ou Yezi chose to forge the sword near the pond in the Mount Ye and produced immortal swords, it is obvious that around the Mount Ye, there are many a superior condition. For example, the climate is pleasant; the vegetation is luxuriant; it is convenient to start a fire; it is rich in mineral resources and clear water. In a word, Ouye Pond is a place with auspicious geomantic omens to gorge swords.

往昔的淬剑圣地今日已成为深藏于闹市区的怀古与游览的胜地。游人或倚坐在剑光亭的美人靠上，凝望偶尔随风飘落在静谧古池上的落叶，或驻足池畔，领略并感知不同节气下古池的时令之美，或让思绪穿越千年，梦回刀光剑影的春秋时期，一睹大师的风采。冷兵器时代的名剑，或随诗文传世至今，或被后人珍藏于各大博物馆内，闽越国古人的坚韧不拔、锐意进取、勇于创新的精神早已融入闽人血脉。今日的福州人秉承了先人的优良品质，敢为人先，为城市的建设播洒汗水与热血。

时值清明，春日融融，微风轻拂，树影斑驳，游人如织。古老的欧冶池恍若一位慈祥的老者，在天光云影间波澜不惊，娓娓讲述着一代宗师淬火成钢、铸就名剑的不朽传奇，无声吟唱着闽越先民筚路蓝缕、开疆拓土的辉煌史诗，安享这人间岁月静好。

◎ 坊巷寻踪：小黄楼

晋代永嘉年间"衣冠南渡"时，黄氏人家入闽聚居福州一巷中，此巷后便被称作黄巷，成为福州三坊七巷中最古老的一条巷子。黄巷中最出名的建筑莫过于位于中段北侧36号的小黄楼，得名于唐代进士、崇文阁校书郎、晚唐律赋三大家之一黄璞。清初，小黄楼毁于一场火灾，幸而遇到了一位匠心与赤子之心兼备的能人。道光年间，祖籍福州长乐的梁章钜（1775—1849年）返回福州养病，20岁中举、28岁登进士第的他此时已近花甲。他曾在江苏任职八年，参与修葺过可园、沧浪亭，这些经历使他对苏州古典园林之雅致深有感受，对修建工作得心应手。梁章钜集江南古典园林艺术与福州地方建筑风格之大成，对黄璞旧居进行了全面的修葺。亭台楼阁的秀美与小桥流水的温婉相映成趣，构成如今我们所见到的清幽雅致的古代私家花园"小黄楼"。

置身小黄楼西园，首先映入眼帘的是主体花厅建筑——雕刻精美的两层木构建筑"芝南山馆"。二层是主人的藏书阁，内部宽敞。走廊两侧对称分布，露台的屋檐两角上挑，气势不凡。垂下的木构件称悬钟，悬钟四周可以看到清晰雕刻的松鼠、燕雀、蜻蜓、谷穗、玉米等动植物，象征百子千孙、多子多福。亭周12个悬钟，各尽其致。

The sacred site of quenching the sword in the past has been a resort hidden in the downtown area. Some tourists lean on the bench in the Sword Light Pavilion, gazing at the leaves which occasionally fall on the tranquil ancient pond or stand at the bank of pond, appreciating the beauty of various Jieqi, or recalling the Spring and Autumn Period, the turmoil times thousands of years ago, witnessing the demeanor of the master swordsman. The renowned sword in cold steel era has been kept up to now or treasured in various museums. Today's Fuzhou people inherit the excellent quality of ancient Minyue people, who are firm, indomitable, enterprising and innovative, devote themselves to building the city heart and soul.

On this Qingming Festival, visitors flocked to the scenic spot where the breeze rustled and tree shadow mottled. Like an amiable senior citizen, the ancient Ouye Pond is tranquil in the sunshine, telling an immortal legend concerning a master swordsman, singing the splendid epic of Minyue ancestors' pioneering spirit, leading a peaceful life.

◎ Traces in the Lanes and Alleys: The Little Yellow Building

During the Yongjia Riot in the Jin Dynasty, some scholars were forced to move southward and the Huang's Family from Central China settled down in a lane which is called Huang Alley later on. It is the oldest lane in the Three Lanes and Seven Alleys in Fuzhou. The most famous architecture is the Little Yellow Building located at No.36 of the northern side of the middle part of the block. The name of Huang Alley derives from Huang Pu in Tang Dynasty, the presented scholar, the Historic Record Rectifier in charge of proofreading in the Chongwen Pavilion, the Imperial Library. He is one of the three artists skilled in metrical poetry and Fu which is a literary style. In the early Qing Dynasty, the Little Yellow Building was destroyed by fire. Luckily, a competent and ingenious celebrity bought and renovated it. In the Daoguang Years, when he was about 60 years old, Liang Zhangju who came from Changle, Fuzhou returned to his hometown to recuperate. At the age of 20, he passed the imperial examination at the provincial level. At the age of 28, he became Jinshi. He worked in Jiangsu Province for six years. Since he was involved in renovation of the Ke Garden and Canglang Pavilion, he was impressed by the elegance of classical landscape gardens in Suzhou and in his element in the garden renovation. After the comprehensive renovation under the direction of Liang Zhangju, the Little Yellow Building displays a style with a brilliant pastiche of classical garden art in Jiangsu Province and that in Fuzhou. With dainty pavilions and gentle streams and bridge blending together perfectly, the Little Yellow Building, the private landscape garden looks tranquil and exquisite at present.

In the western garden of the ancient architecture, the main building—delicately-carved two-storyed Mount Zhinan Hall made of wood came into view first. The spacious library occupies the second storey. The two sides of the corridor are symmetric.The corners of the terrace eaves title upwards, which is splendid.The pendulous woodwork is called pendants. Around them, there are 12 clearly-carved animals and vegetables such as squirrels, swallows, dragonflies, grain ears and corns, which symbolizes fertility.

　　楼南面为层峦叠嶂的假山，本着因地制宜、就近取材的原则，小黄楼西园多采用珊瑚礁、海蚀岩塑山，曲径盘旋，直通藏书阁。假山依邻碧波悠悠的鱼池，鱼池面积不大，为方形和半圆形。池上架着一座玲珑别致的拱桥，桥栏一侧刻有"知鱼乐处"四个大字，出自《庄子·秋水》中庄子和惠子的对话："子非鱼，安知鱼之乐？"桥题"知鱼乐处"，表明园林主人欣赏老庄的物我同化、旷达乐观的思想。除此之外，梁章钜曾作一楹联："历中外廿年身，宦海扁舟，万顷惊涛神尚悚；就高低数弓地，儒宫环堵，三竿晓日梦初醒。"联系此楹联，可见梁章钜宦海沉浮多年，身心俱疲，尔时归隐此处，在自然中寻找到生活的逸趣，自在非常。桥栏另一侧效仿扬州瘦西湖，镌刻着"廿网桥"。"廿网桥"中的"廿"即"二十"，"网"字内有四笔，寓意"四"，故"廿网桥"就是隐喻"二十四桥"。"二十四桥"自古便受到文人的青睐，在文学作品中常被引用。杜牧《寄扬州韩绰判官》诗云："二十四桥明月夜，玉人何处教吹箫"，表达了作者对扬州生活的深情怀念。姜夔在《扬州慢》中写道："二十四桥仍在，波心荡，冷月无声"，控诉了金朝统治者发动战争所造成的灾难，以及对南宋王朝偏安政策的谴责。那么梁章钜题写"廿网桥"又是为何呢？是对任职八年的江苏的深切怀念？抑或是因抱病而不得不告老还乡的惆怅？

　　楼东侧有小巧精美的半边亭，亭子只建一半，三面悬空，一面靠墙，精致美观，节约空间。宝珠结顶，四檐翘角。凉亭占据小黄楼最佳位置，由此凭栏坐憩、极目远眺，整个小黄楼的美景尽收眼底。

　　小黄楼内还有怪石嶙峋的雪洞。雪洞体现了明清时期典型的民居特点，主要用糯米、红糖、石灰等材料调制筑成。洞内如云海浮沉，又遍布峥嵘怪石。炎炎夏日，置身洞内，凉气扑面而来，可谓园中避暑胜地。其秘诀就在于气流通过凹凸的石壁产生回旋。

To the south of the building, there are towering rockeries. Based on the principle of acting according to local conditions and drawing on the local resources, rockeries were mainly made of coral reefs and marine erosion rocks in the western garden. And a winding path is leading to the library. Rockeries are along the small crystal clear fish pond which is square or semi-circle. An elegant arch bridge is over the pond, with four Chinese characters "知鱼乐处" which refers to the place where one knows the reason why the fish is happy on one side of the railing. These four Chinese characters are derived from the conversation that says, "If you are not the one, how can you figure out the happiness of fish?" (Zhuang Zhou, "Qiushui" of *Zhuangzi*) between Zhuangzi and Huizi, which is recorded in *Qiushui of Zhuangzi*. The inscriptions convey the Taoism notion of assimilation of creature and self and being optimistic and broad-minded, which was appreciated by the master. Besides, he once wrote a couplet, "At the official sea for twenty years, in the vast expanse of terrifying waves, I am just like a tiny boat. How I wish I could retire and live in a peaceful place surrounded by academy of classical learning and sleep like a log until 12 o'clock at noon." (Liang Zhangju, *Chinese Couplets' Stories*) From this couplet, it is obvious that having experienced ups and downs in the official circles, Liang Zhangju was exhausted mentally and physically. Fortunately, after his retirement, he found ease and pleasure in life. On the other side of the railing, three Chinese characters "廿网桥" have been inscribed, which is an imitation of that of the "廿四桥" in the Slender West Lake in Yangzhou. The Chinese character "廿" symbolizes "twenty" while inside the radical of "网" there are four strokes, which stands for "four". Hence "廿网桥" is the metaphor of "二十四桥", "Bridge Twenty-Four ", which is favored by men of letters from ancient times and frequently quoted in literary works. In Du Mu's poem entitled "To Han Chuo, Magistrate of Yangzhou", the lines which read, "Along Bridge Twenty-Four, at bright moon-lit nights, does the jadelike beauty still provide instruction on the flute?"(Du Mu, "To Han Chuo, Magitrate of Yangzhou"), expressing his unforgettable affection for the life in Yangzhou. A Southern Song Dynasty(1127-1279) writer, Jiang Kui wrote, "The Twenty-Four Bridges can still be seen, but the cold moon floating among the waves would no more sing a song." in the "Slow Tune of Yangzhou". The author accused the rulers of the Jin Dynasty of launching the war and causing disaster and condemned South Song Dynasty rulers' policy of being content to retain sovereignty over a part of the country. Why did Liang Zhangju name the bridge in the building "廿网桥" ? Does the naming convey his strong surges of nostalgia for Jiangsu Province where he worked for eight years or his melancholy of retiring from office and returning to private life due to his illness?

To the western side of the building, there is a small and exquisite one-sided pavilion with three overhanging sides and one side leaning against the wall, which is intended to save space. With the jewel on the top of it and the four tilted eaves, the pavilion is situated in the strategic point of the Little Yellow Building. When you take a rest against the railing and gaze into the distance, you will have a wonderful view of the building.

In the Little Yellow Building, there is a rockery snow cave, which is the typical characteristic dwelling house in the Ming Dynasty and Qing Dynasty. It is mainly constructed by materials such as glutinous rice, brown sugar and lime. In the snow cave, it seems as if sea of clouds floated and sank and strange rocks were lofty and towering. During the scorching summer, cold air blows against your face when you enter the cave. It is really a summer resort in the garden. Its secret lies in the fact that the airflow can produce gyration through the concave and convex stone wall.

西园虽小，但"五脏俱全"，这得益于其合理的布局和适宜的尺寸。幽深的雪洞与傲耸的半边亭位于同一视线，增强了园子的延伸感。从雪洞入口处往里望，半边亭恰如其分地被框进其中，营造出一种层次感。假山层层叠叠，踏上一层更有一层。假山东西的路径，东接半边亭，西接小黄楼，使得整个西园脉络相连、畅通无阻。此外，园中的鱼池、拱桥、植物、假山、天井都严格按照比例而设，在视觉上给人舒适自然之感，毫无人工雕琢的痕迹。

梁章钜不仅是一位官员，更是一位大文人，被称为"楹联学开山鼻祖"。楹联是"福"文化的重要载体，有吉祥、喜庆、祝福的寓意。在藤花吟馆前悬挂有梁章钜亲自创作的楹联："诗敲梅下月，醉卧柳边风"，彰显了中国传统文人的闲情雅致和豁达心态。此外，小黄楼内有各种各样的匾额。大门内悬挂的"选魁"匾文出自林则徐女婿沈葆桢的手笔。"选魁"是恭贺岁科或恩科选中的贡生。第一进大厅前面悬挂的牌匾"文炳球琳"为萨镇冰所题。古代的"球"指美玉，"文炳球琳"是称赞青年文章写得好。"义冠古今"为林则徐所题，"桓雅"为纪晓岚所题，"俊髦胪欢"为姚启圣所题……置身小黄楼，不仅可以看到建筑和园林之美，还能体会到古人的人文雅韵。

小黄楼现为福州市保存较为完整的明清古式花厅园林，2006年被公布为全国重点文物保护单位。小黄楼历经百年历史，见证了三坊七巷的变迁，一代又一代文人墨客聚集此处挥斥方遒。真可谓，"谈笑有鸿儒，往来无白丁"（刘禹锡《陋室铭》）。小黄楼的魅力，不只在于其精巧的建筑风格，也在于其一代又一代的文化积淀。

◎ 宗祠余韵：闽王祠

行走在人声鼎沸、旺铺林立的庆城路上，往日的庆城寺已随时光流逝而了无踪迹。然而，历经一千余年的风风雨雨，一座古色古香的祠堂依然矗立在福州闹市的一隅。它的一砖一瓦、一碑一亭无一不铭刻着历史的记忆。

这座位于福州市鼓楼区庆城路22号的祠庙，是有着"开闽王"之誉的王审知的祠堂，也称忠懿闽王祠、闽王庙。它地理位置优越，毗邻福州名校十九中，即如今福州三中的初中部。

Although the western garden is small, its structure is complete which benefits from its reasonable layout and suitable size. The deep snow cave and lofty one-sided pavilion are located at the same sight line, which contributes to the optical stretch of the garden. Look into the inside from the entrance to the snow cave, you will find that the one-sided pavilion is enclosed, creating a clear gradation. The path to the eastern and western side of the tiered rockeries is connected the one-sided pavilion in the east and the Little Yellow Building in the west. In this way, the western garden is connected and unblocked. Besides, fish ponds, vegetables, rockeries, small yards are constructed according to proportion strictly, which seems to be natural and comfortable visually without any trace of artificial carving.

Liang Zhangju who is not only an official but also a great man of letters is acclaimed as "the founder of Chinese couplets". Chinese couplets hung on the columns of a hall are vehicles of "福" (Blessing and Happiness) culture, connotating auspiciousness, happiness and blessing. In the front of the Vine Flower Chanting Hall, there is a couplet writter by Liang Zhangju which reads, " Knock at the moon under the plum with poems and lie drunkenly against the willow in the wind ", which reflects ease, elegance and open-mindedness of Chinese traditional men of literature and writing. Besides, there are a great variety of plaques in the building. The two Chinese characters "选魁" written by Shen Baochen (Lin Zexu's Son-in-Law) meaning "Selecting Talents" refers to congratulations on the gongsheng (a scholar of recommended by the provincial government to go to the Imperial College in the capital city for further studies in the Ming and Qing Dynasties) in suike (imperial examinations) or enke (special imperial examinations held on auspicious occasions). Written by Sa Zhenbing, the four Chinese characters "文炳球琳" meaning outstanding talent for writing on the plaque hung on the hall in the first row are meant to praise the youth who are good at writing. Other Chinese characters on the plaque such as "义冠古今" meaning unprecedented loyalty and righteousness, "桓雅" meaning elegance, and "俊髦胪欢" meaning singing and rejoicing of extraordinary talents were written by Lin Zexue, Ji Xiaolan and Yao Qisheng respectively. In the Little Yellow Building, not only can we taste the beauty of the architecture and landscape gardens but also the humane charm of writers and scholars in ancient times.

The Little Yellow Building, which was announced as the cultural site under state protection, is a well-preserved ancient landscape garden with parlor of the Ming Dynasty and Qing Dynasty style. Having experienced hundreds of years, it witnessed the vicissitudes of the Three Lanes and Seven Alleys and writers generation after generation who gathered here gushed enthusiasm and felt fresh and positive. As Liu Yuxi wrote, "The guests who gather here are renowned scholars and writers instead of illiterate people." (Liu Yuxi, "An Epigraph on Ode to My Humble Home") The charm of the Little Yellow Building not only consists in its quaint architectural style, but in the cultural accumulation generation after generation.

◎ Aftertaste of the Ancestral Temple: The Ancestral Temple of Wang Shenzhi

Walking across the Qingcheng Road which is crowded and bustling with a number of prosperous stores, the Qingcheng Temple of the bygone days disappeared with the passage of time. However, after over one thousand years ups and downs, a quaint ancestral temple still stands at the corner of downtown area of Fuzhou. The brick, tile, tablet and pavilion carry historical memory.

This ancient building, which is the ancestral temple of Wang Shenzhi reputed as "the king of the Min State" is called the Zhongyi King Temple as well. Adjacent to the renowned high school, then No. 19 Middle School boasts a superior geographical location.

闽王祠外观
The Exterior of Wang Shenzhi's Ancestral Temple

　　王审知（862—925年）是河南光州固始人，字信通，又字祥卿。五代后梁开平三年（909年）受封为闽王。王审知治理福建期间，政局稳定，经济、文化各方面都得到充分发展，深得民心，闽国一派祥和，人称"世外桃源"。王审知在开发闽地中做出了杰出贡献，后世尊其为"开闽第一人"（潘逸群，2013）。后晋开运三年（946），王审知的故居被改立为祠庙，福州百姓连年举行祀典。北宋至清，祠庙曾五度修复（施晓宇，2013：44）。

　　公元909年，因在闽主政期间社会经济、文化教育等事业取得卓著政绩，王审知被梁太祖朱温加封为"闽王"。他于公元925年去世，同年，被后唐庄宗赐谥"忠懿王"。这便是忠懿闽王祠得名的由来。

　　1961年，闽王祠被福州市人民委员会公布为第一批市级文物保护单位，闽王庙附属碑刻则由福建省人民委员会公布为福建省第一批省级文保单位（福州老建筑百科，2020c）。

Wang Shenzhi(862-925), who came from Gushi County, Guangzhou, Henan Province styled himself as " xintong" and "xiangqing". In 909, the second year of Kaiping Reign of Liang Dynasty during the Five Periods, he was crowned as the king of the Min State. During Wang Shenzhi's administration in the Min State, the political situation was stable and the economy, culture developed fully, which earned him praise among people. The Min State assumed a scene of peace and harmony. And it was called Shangri-la, a sacred land of idyllic beauty. He was acclaimed as " The first founder of the Min State" by later generations due to his outstanding contribution in developing the Min State(Pan Yiqun, 2013). In the third year during the Kaiyun Reign in Post-Jin Dynasty(946), Wang Shenzhi's former residence was converted to an ancestral temple where the common people in Fuzhou practiced sacrificial rites in successive years. From the Northern Song Dynasty to the Qing Dynasty, the compound had been renovated for five times(Shi Xiaoyu, 2013: 44).

In 909, owing to his excellent political achievements in the domain such as social economy, culture and education in the Min State, Wang Shenzhi was crowned as "the king of the Min State"by Zhu Wen, Taizu of Liang Dynasty. In 925, he passed away. In the same year, he was posthumously titled "Zhongyi King" by Zhuangzong of the Later Tang Dynasty. And this is the origin of the name, Zhongyi King's Temple .

In 1961, the Ancestral Temple of King of the Min State was announced the first batch of cultural site under municipal protection. The inscriptions on the tablet were announced as the first batch of the cultural site under provincial protection(Fuzhou Old Architecture Encyclopedia, 2022c).

公元 946 年，即后晋开运三年，南唐灭闽，福州并入吴越版图，吴越国国君钱俶下令在王审知故第改庙祀之，这是建庙之始，迄今已逾千年。宋、明、清历代重修，并在春、秋二季祭祀。解放后，人民政府数次拨款重修，雕梁画栋，焕然一新。如今的闽王祠为明代重建（曾意丹，1983）。

具有明代建筑风格的闽王祠，外墙为牌楼式，主体颜色为绛朱红色。在传统的中国建筑中，红色是帝王建筑或者庙堂建筑的色彩，一般平民百姓的居所等是不能使用的，以表示对皇帝权威的认可，或者显示出皇家建筑的威严（靳凤华，2019：137）。

从规模来看，这座由王审知故居改建而成的祠堂历经一千多年的风风雨雨，从历史上的甲第连云演变为如今的具有福州地方特色的三进院落。闽王祠坐北朝南，沿中轴线依次为庄严肃穆的朱色门墙、宽敞通透的前厅、祀门、天井和正殿。

祠堂的朱色门墙上开有三个圆拱形门洞。门前立着两尊高达 2 米的明代石狮，默默地守护着历经沧桑的祠庙。3 米多高的中门前那一对抱鼓石，表明祠主身份与地位较高。门上正中嵌竖碑，上书"奉旨祀典"，黄碑上则刻有"忠懿闽王祠"。左右边门上镶嵌的石额分别为"崇德"和"报国"。

步入前厅，赫然出现在眼前的是一座古朴典雅的碑亭。亭中竖立的石碑名为"恩赐琅琊郡王德政碑"。这座碑为圭形，立在莲花座上。它立于唐天祐三年（906 年），长 4.9 米、宽 1.87 米、厚 0.29 米。碑文由礼部侍郎于竞所撰，共 2600 多字，文采斐然，由弘文馆王倜书写。碑文记述了王审知的家世及政绩，肯定了他在闽期间的丰功伟绩。因其卓越功勋，朝廷给王审知加官晋爵，钦赐"琅琊郡王"。碑文是研究开闽王在建设闽国过程中的贡献，以及闽国史和五代史的重要文物资料。这方石碑十分珍贵，无怪乎清代著名学者郭柏苍称它为"天下四大碑之一"。它也是我国现存的四大唐碑之一。

In 946, the third year of Kuaiyun Reign in the Post-Jin Dynasty, the Southern Tang Dynasty conquered the Min State and Fuzhou was included in the map of the Wuyue State. The king Qian Liu ordered that Wang Shenzhi's former residence be converted to the ancestral temple, which boasts more than one thousand years history. It was reconstructed in the Song, Ming, and Qing Dynasties and offer sacrifices to gods or ancestors in spring and summer. After the founding of the People's Republic of China, government renovated it for several times.With carved beams and painted rafters, it takes on a new look. Today's Ancestral Temple of Wang Shenzhi was reconstructed in the Ming Dynasty(Zeng Yidan, 1983).

The external walls of the ancestral temple with the architectural style of the Ming Dynasty are the decorated-archway ones, with vermilion as the main color. Among Traditional Chinese architecture, red is the color for the emperor or temple and it is forbidden for the common people's dwellings. Hence, it indicates the recognition of emperors' authority or the dignity of royal architecture(Ji Fenghua, 2019: 137).

Having witnessed ups and downs for over one thousand years, this ancestral temple's size ranges from the original large-scale compound to a building in three rows with local characteristics in Fuzhou. The ancestral temple faces south. There is an existence of the axis in the main complex of the building. If you walk along the axis, you will pass the solemn vermilion door wall, spacious and bright front hall, the sacrifice gate, the patio and the main hall.

There are three circular arch doorways on the vermilion door wall. A couple of two-meter-high stone lions in the Ming Dynasty stand in front of the front door, safeguarding the ancestral temple which has witness turbulent times in silence. The pair of drum-shaped bearing stones which are three-meter-high in front of the middle door indicate the superior identity and social status of the master of the grand house. In the center, the gate has been set with a vertical tablet which is inscribed four Chinese characters which reads, "奉旨祀典" meaning holding memorial ceremonies under the emperor's order. On the yellow tablet, inscriptions consisting of the five Chinese characters which read, "忠懿闽王祠" indicate "Ancestral Temple of the king of the Min State". Inscriptions on the stone plaque set on the left and right side doors are "崇德" meaning advocating morality and "报国" meaning serving the country respectively.

Step into the front hall, a classical and elegant tablet pavilion came into view. The stone tablet in the pavilion is named "恩赐琅琊郡王德政碑" which means"A Bestowed Stele Commemorating the Merit of the Good Official, Langya King". This Gui-shaped tablet is erected on the lotus throne. Erected in the third year of Tianyou Reign in the Tang Dynasty(906), it is 4.9 meters long; 1.87 meters wide and 0.29 meters thick. With sophisticated literary grace, the passage of over 2, 600 words on the stele were produced by Yu Jing, the vice minister of rites and the calligraphy was written by Wang Chou from the Hongwen Center. In the passage, Wang Shenzhi's family background and his remarkable political achievement in the Min State have been related and affirmed. Due to his extraordinary accomplishment, he was promoted and granted the title, the Langya King. The article on the tablet is significant data concerning the research on his contribution in developing and constructing the Min State and the History of the Min State and Five Periods. This stone tablet is of great importance. It is not surprising that Guo Baicang, the famous scholar in the Qing Dynasty called it "one of the four tablets in the nation". It is one of the four existing tablets in the Tang Dynasty in China.

闽王王审知塑像
The Sculpture of Wang Shenzhi,
the King of the Min State

　　祀墙横立亭后，墙上镌有"绍越开疆"四个大字，赞誉之情尽在其中。墙后即为后庭，庭两侧设厢房。正殿为硬山顶土木结构建筑，面阔三间，进深三间。祀门上横挂一块"功垂闽峤"木匾。殿中俨然而坐者，正是祀主闽王王审知塑像，神貌怡然。对于这位有功于闽的先达，八闽子弟自然不会忘却，进而尊崇有加（佚名，2020a）。

　　三进为一双层阁楼。楼后有巨碑一方，有宋开宝七年（974年）刺史钱昱撰写的《重修忠懿王庙碑铭》（曾意丹，1983）。右墙上嵌"乞土胜地"碑，为福建人民纪念闽王开疆功勋而立。每年立春，由郡守率群僚来祠中致祭，在此碑前乞取一丸泥土捏制成春牛，发动春耕。自宋迄清，相沿成风俗（央视《海峡两岸行》，2006）。

　　闽王祠西墙外的大坪原是拜剑台，可惜被毁于"文革"之中。如今的拜剑台是重建的。大坪后方有一座一进三开间的殿堂，奉祀闽王的母亲太夫人董氏。王氏三兄弟都极为孝顺母亲。"竹林兵变"就是因兄弟三人保护母亲而起：光州固始的王家三龙加入安徽寿州王绪的起义军后，在漳浦境内王绪找借口要杀王家老母，王审知兄弟才不得不发动兵变。

　　王审知治闽期间，修好邻近，轻徭薄赋，省刑惜费，鼓励垦荒，倡修水利，兴办学校，发展海外贸易，招纳中原名士前来共同开发闽地，对闽地经济、文化的发展起了积极作用，使闽地成为当时全国比较稳定繁荣的地方，被喻为"海滨邹鲁"、"文儒之乡"。王审知也因此被后世誉为"开闽王"（福州老建筑百科，2022c）。

In the back of the pavilion, there is a wall on which four Chinese characters, "绍越开疆" are inscribed. The inscriptions in praise of Wang Shenzhi mean inheriting the achievement of Minyue people and developing the territory. The rear of the wall is the back yard where two wing rooms are set on either side of it. The main hall which is three rooms wide and deep is an architecture made of earth and wood. A wooden plaque which is inscribed four Chinese characters "功垂闽峤" paying tribute to Wang Shenzhi's great contribution to the Min State is hung on the sacrifice gate. Wang Shenzhi's sculptor which seems to be pleasant and contented sits solemnly in the hall. The people in Fukien Province will memorize and respect this well-known and successful ancestor(Anonymous, 2022a).

A two-story attic is situated in the third section of the compound. There is a big tablet which named "The Tablet Commemorating Renovation of Zhongyi King Temple" writter by Qian Yu, the prefectural governor in the seventh year of kaibao reign(1974)(Zeng Yidan, 1983) A tablet with inscriptions "乞土胜地"meaning "resort of taking soil" is set in the right wall. It was erected to commemorate Wang Shenzhi's distinguished service in the Min State. At the beginning of Spring(lichun), every year, the magistrate would lead the officials to practice memorial service. He would take soil to make a spring ox and launch plowing in spring. From the Song Dynasty to the Qing Dynasty, this practices lasted and became a local custom ("Journey Across the Taiwan Strait" by CCTV, 2006).

The large open space out of the western wall of the ancestral temple was originally the Sword Worship Platform which was unfortunately destroyed in the Cultural Revolution in 1960s. Today's Sword Worship Platform has been renovated. In the rear of the clearing, there is a three-room wide building which is used to offer sacrifices to Wang Shenzhi's mother, Mrs. Dong. The King of the Min State and his two brothers were filial to their mother. "Bamboo Forest Mutiny" resulted from the fact that three of them desired to protect their mother. After three tigers in the Wang Family from Gushi, Guangzhou joined in the army led by Wang Xu who came from Xuzhou, Anhui Province, in order to get rid of dissidents, Wang Xu found an excuse to kill their mother in Zhangpu. Hence they had to stage a mutiny.

While Wang Shenzhi governed the Min State, he not only fostered cordial relations between states, reduced corvee, taxes, and punishments, encouraged reclamation, advocated construction of water conservancy facilities but also built classical schools, developed overseas trade, recruited celebrities from the Central Plains in China to develop the Min State. What he did played a positive role in the development of economy and culture of the state and made it a place which was stable and prosperous nationwide. It is no wonder that it is named as a " Coastal State with Prosperous Culture" or "hometown of literacy and Confucianism". As a result, Wang Shenzhi has been acclaimed as "King of the Min State"(Fuzhou Old Architecture Encyclopedia, 2022c).

王审知宁可担任合法开明的地方官，也不愿意做小国寡民的国君。他在闽理政期间殚精竭虑、鞠躬尽瘁。王审知治闽功勋卓越。他的诸多事迹已在八闽大地传为佳话，对福建发展的影响是极为深远的。比如，王审知宅心仁厚，笃信佛教，在他主政福建的二十多年间，兴建和修复了260座寺庙和六座塔，包括于山多宝定光塔、乌山神光寺神光塔和鼓山涌泉寺。更加令人叹服的是，福州的名片之一——三坊七巷的雏形也形成于他治理福建之际，即在那遥远的一千多年前。

台江地名的由来也与王审知有关。唐末，王审知入闽，在福州筑"夹城"。筑毕，王审知登南城翘望，见有台临江——乃当年无诸在惠泽山（即大庙山）修筑的迎接汉王朝册封使者的"越王台"。于是，台江与南台的地名由此得来。（施晓宇，2013：44）。

总之，被尊为"八闽始祖"的王审知为后世留下了丰富的物质与非物质文化遗产。因王审知在闽的巨大贡献，宋太祖赵匡胤对其评价极高，封他为"八闽人祖"。王审知入闽之后，追随他的农民军将士在八闽大地安居乐业、繁衍发展，他的后裔有不少迁居台湾地区及海外。因此，今日的福州闽王祠也是海峡两岸乃至全球王审知后裔共同祭祀和缅怀的重要场所。闽王祠已然成为传播中原文化的象征。

◎ 书院留香：正谊书院

早在唐玄宗时期，书院这种有别于官学的教育系统就已经出现，作为聚徒讲授、研究学问的场所。发展至清朝，福建的书院建设早已初具规模，鳌峰书院、凤池书院、正谊书院和致用书院有"福州四大书院"的美名，享誉八闽。如今，穿过人潮拥挤的东街口，正谊书院就静静屹立在白墙青瓦之后，保留着独属于它的一段记忆。

During his governance in the Min State, he " preferred to be a governor rather than an emperor" and bent his back to the task, so his distinguished service is outstanding. His heroic deeds are continually on the lips of the local inhabitants in the state and his influence on Fukien's development is far-reaching. For example, since he was on the side of angels and a devout believer in Buddhism, during his more than twenty years' governance in the state, 260 temples and six pagodas including the White Pagoda in the Mount Yu, the Divine Light Pagoda in the Mount Wu and the Spring Temple in the Drum Mountain had been constructed and renovated.

When it comes to the naming of Taijiang, it has some connection with Wang Shenzhi as well. At the end of the Tang Dynasty, Wang Shenzhi arrived in Fukien Province. He ordered craftsmen to build semicircular enclosures between external and inner city gates to protect the city. After the completion of the project, Wang Shenzhi climbed the southern city, seeing a distant terrace overlooking the Minjiang River which was called " Minyue King Terrace" built in the Mount Huize(the Mount Damiao)to welcome the emissary for crowning from the Han Dynasty. Hence the naming of Taijiang and Nantai derives from it. (Shi Xiaoyu, 2013: 44).

In a word, Wang Shenzhi, who is reputed as the founder of Min State left a rich tangible and intangible cultural heritage to later generations. Because of his great contribution to Min State, Zhao Kuangyin, Emperor Taizu of the Song Dynasty sang high praise of him and called him "the ancestor of the Min State." After Wang Shenzhi's arrival, the soldiers and generals who followed him led a prosperous and contented life and multiple in the state. Quite a few of his descendants emigrated to Taiwan Province and foreign countries. Hence, nowadays, the Ancestral Temple of Wang Shenzhi is a paramount venue where the descendants of Wang Shenzhi across the Taiwan Straits offer sacrifices to gods and ancestors to cherish the memory of the past and forefathers.

◎ The Fragrance of the Academy of Classical Learning: Zhengyi Academy of Classical Learning

As early as the reign of Emperor Xuanzong in the Tang Dynasty, emerged an educational system named the academy of classical learning which is different from the official academy. It functions as the location of giving lessons to students and doing research. In the Qing Dynasty, the construction of this kind of academy began to take shape. The academy of classical learning named Aofeng, Zhengyi and Fengchi respectively are so renowned that in Fukien Province they enjoy the reputation of "four famous academies of classical learning in Fuzhou". At present, going across the congested Dongjiekou, Zhengyi Academy of Classical Learning stands quietly at the back of the white wall and black tiles, retaining its exclusive memory.

正谊书院的前身是正谊书局，同治五年（1866年）由时任闽浙总督左宗棠在新美里（今南后街黄巷）创设，最初只是为了安排举人和五贡入局工作。书局得名于清康熙年间曾任福建巡抚的理学大师、藏书家张伯行搜集前代文人文集刊印的《正谊堂丛书》。后在左宗棠的主持下，对原本有所增删。正谊书局先后刻印书籍五百余卷，整合为《正谊堂全书》。随后，地方绅士杨庆琛和首任船政大臣沈葆桢上书镇闽将军兼署闽浙总督英桂，希望将书局改为书院，致力于福州十郡的举人和贡生的教育。英桂采纳了二人的意见，出资买下骆舍铺（现东街省立图书馆旧址）的民宅并改建为书院，同治九年（1870年）正谊书院正式建成。书院名取"正其谊不谋其利，明其道不计其功"之意，又因为前身是正谊书局，故沿用"正谊"二字。书院建成后，左宗棠还特意写了一副楹联："青眼高歌，异日应多天下士；华阴回首，当年共读古人书。"并为此联作序，交代了书院建成的缘由和过程（江荣基、官桂铨，2003：422-423）。

在当时的福州，已经有鳌峰书院和凤池书院扬名在外，而正谊书院作为后起之秀，建筑风格和这两所书院截然不同，其整体风格可以用朴素大方来形容。正门上挂

正谊书院牌匾
The Plaque of Zhengyi Classical Learning Academy

一块用青石刻镌的、写有"正谊书院"几个大字的横匾，由当时著名的闽籍书法家郑世恭所写，现仍旧嵌于福建省图书馆的后进正门上，而另一块复制的匾额则镶嵌在福州一中的校园碑廊里。彼时的书院设有大讲堂而并无学舍，后进五间排是山长的住宅。客厅悬挂的是首任山长林鸿年亲题的对联："客皆当代要津，到此地只谈风月；我本昔年都讲，愿诸生共筮云雷。"可见，别的高官来此地是谈风月的，而林山长是来教学子成才济世的。典故出自《易经》："云雷，屯。君子以经纶。"谓有才以经世，用来勉励入院研学的众人。

1902年，正谊书院和凤池书院正式合并，改名"全闽大学堂"。1913年，省立图书馆迁入正谊书院旧址，并被福州市人民政府公布为市级文物保护单位。2009年，正谊书院计划于原址进行修复。2011年正式竣工后的书院占地约400平方米，它保留了原有的基本框架和一部分书院旧物。2015年起，正谊书院恢复对外开放。

Zhengyi Academy of Classical Learning grew out of Zhengyi Publishing House which was established by Zuo Zongtang, the governor of Fukien and Zhejiang Provinces in the fifth year of Tongzhi Reign(1866)in Xinmeili(Huang Alley in Nanhou Street at present). The intention of founding the publishing house was to offer jobs to juren (a successful can didate in imperial examinations at the provincial level)and five kinds of gongsheng(scholars recommended by local governments to study in the Imperial College). Zhengyi Academy of Classical Learning was named after *Zhengyi Hall Series* in which a collection of writers' works in previous dynasties was collected by Zhang Boxing, who was a master of Neo-confucianism and book collector. Zuo Zongtang was in charge of amending this book by m aking some additions and deletions and printed more than 500 volumes which were entitled *Zhengyi Hall Pandect* successively. Subsequently, the local gentleman, Yang Qingchen and Shen Baozhen, the first ship-building minister submitted a written statement to Ying Gui, the General of Fukien Province, suggested transforming the publishing house into an academy of classical learning, which was dedicated to giving lessons to juren and gongsheng in ten counties in Fuzhou. Ying Gui accepted their proposal and purchased the vernacular residence in Luoshepu(the site of the Provincial Library in East Street). Later on, it was converted into an academy of classical learning in 1870, the ninth year of Tongzhi's reign in the Qing Dynasty. It is named after the statement which reads, "Strive for morality and justice without personal gain and utilitarian concern". Since originally it was Zhengyi Publishing House, the two Chinese characters" 正谊 "(Zhengyi)retain. After its completion, Zuo Zhongtang made it a point to create a couplet which conveys his hope that more scholars would appear to contribute to the nation. He also wrote an introduction in which he related the cause and process concerning the establishment of this classical learning academy(Jiang Rongji, Guan Guishuan, 2003: 422 - 423).

In the then Fuzhou, there were well-known Aofeng Academy and Fengchi Academy while Zhengyi Academy of Classical Learning is just a rising star, which possessed simple and grand architecture style different from the other two. There is a bluestone plaque with inscriptions " Zhengyi Classical Learning Academy", which were written by the then Fukien calligrapher ----Zheng Shigong and embedded at the back door of the Fukien Provincial Library. A copy of the plaque has been embedded in the stele gallery in No. One Fuzhou High School. There was a spacious lecture hall in the then academy and the fives room at the back of it were quarters for the the principal. In the sitting room, there is a couplet written by the first principal----Lin Hongnian. It reads, "Those high official only talk about love here, but I impart knowledge and cultivate talents to contribute to our nation." It is apparent that other high officials talked about love and sex, but Lin aimed at giving lessons to students and motivating them to succeed and benefit the society. The allusion derives from *Yi Jing*, aiming at encouraging students to study hard .

In 1902, Zhengyi and Fengchi Classical Learning Academies merged formally and became "Fukien Provincial School". In 1913, Provincial Library was moved into the former site of Zhengyi Academy and was announced as a cultural site under municipal protection. In 2009, in the former site, Zhengyi Academy of Classical Learning was planned to be renovated. In 2011, the completed academy covered an area about 400 square meters and the original framework and some old objects of the academy retain. From 2015 on, reopened to the public.

推开书院厚重的木门，扑面而来的便是书香气息。虽没有华丽的雕梁画栋，整体的布局也像从前那般朴素简单，却能让到访者在这份干净整洁中寻得些许当年的印记。大门正对着的屏风上写着表明"正谊"二字的两句古文："正其谊不谋其利，明其道不计其功。"再往后走便进入另一个略小一些的院落，正中央分成三间敞亮的堂屋，高悬"博学堂"的匾额。室内添置了不少桌椅板凳，俨然现代课堂的模样。历经时光打磨，变化的是正谊书院的样貌，不变的却是其中无法割断的文脉传承。

作为后起书院，具有鲜明特色的正谊书院自然也延续了书局的特色，其录取的对象以举人和贡生为主。显然，作为课士的书院，对生源水平的要求不可谓不高。与之相比，鳌峰和凤池书院录取的学生是生员和童生。而致用书院专门研究经史，并为举贡和生员授课。值得一提的是，正谊书院的考试时间定于每年二月上旬，虽极为严格，但免收试卷费用。每年的报考人数可达四五百人。每年二月十五日以前，总督和巡抚会亲自来到书院（最初在今鼓楼前的贡院）主持考试，考试结束后评定等级，录取15名内课，每人给予四两膏火银；录取85名外课，每人给予三两膏火银；录取100名附课，但不给予膏火。每月要考课两次，初二是师课，十六日是官课，山长主持师课。

既建书院，就必须要有讲学之人，方能招纳举人、贡生前来研学。正谊书院的首任山长林鸿年，字勿村，原就是福建侯官（今福建福州）人，道光十六年（1836年）的状元。他的一生颇具传奇色彩，被誉为"清朝闽中第一位状元"。道光十八年（1838年）被任命为册封使出使琉球，在当地留下了不少诗篇、墨宝与佳话。随后，他历任广东琼州知府、云南临安知府、云南按察使、云南布政使、云南巡抚等职务。同治五年（1866年）正月，在镇压太平军的过程中，以"畏寇逗留"等罪名被革职查办。虽获正名，但他义无反顾地返回家乡，不久后便受聘为正谊书院的首任山长。一代大儒林鸿年在正谊书院主讲长达十九年，培养出不少杰出的人才，叶大焯、陈宝琛、林纾、陈衍、吴曾祺皆出自他的门下，对晚清文学的发展起到积极的推动作用。

Open the thick and heavy wooden door of the academy, the air seems to smell of the book's fragrance. Although it is far from the richly ornamented building, the layout is still plain and simple as it used to be and the visitor can find some traces of the past. On the screen across the front door, there are quotations which read, "Strive for morality and justice without personal gain and utilitarian concern."And then, we step forward and enter a relatively smaller courtyard. With a plaque written "Erudition Hall", there are three spacious and bright rooms and quite a lot of desks and chairs, which look as if it were modern class. With the passing time, what has changed is the appearance of the academy and what hasn't changed is the heritage of cultural veins which can't be severed.

Naturally, as an up-and-comer, Zhengyi Academy with salient characteristics retained the feature of Zhengyi Publishing House, mainly recruiting Juren and Gongsheng. Obviously, as an academy aiming at cultivating scholars, the admission standard was relatively strict compared with that of the other academy. In contrast, Aofeng and Fengchi Classical Learning Academy recruited Shengyuan(the intellectual who passed the Imperial examinations at the county level and Tongsheng(the intellectual who failed in the imperial examinations). Zhiyong Academy focused on research on Confucian classics and history and recruited juren, Gongsheng and Shengyuan. It is noteworthy that the entrance examination was set in the first ten-days period of February according to the lunar calender. Although examination regulations were strict, there also existed humanized actions, such as the examination paper was free of charge. The number of intellectuals who applied to enter the examination were approximately 400-500 annually.Before February 25th every year, the provincial governor would come to the academy to preside over the examination. In the beginning, the examination room was set in the Examination Institution where the imperial exam at the provincial and national level. The remains of it exist in Gulouqian. After the examination, candidates would be graded according to their performance. In the end, 200 scholars were admitted into the academy. Among them, 15 superb scholars were granted 4 silver as; and 85 star scholars were granted 3 silver as tuition. As for 100 first-class intellectuals, they had no allowance.These scholars took two examinations every lunar month. On the second and sixteenth days of the lunar month, they were tested by the principal of the academy and the local authorities respectively.

Since the academy was established, learned lecturers were indispensable so as to attract juren and gongsheng to study. The first lecturer of Zhengyi Academy is Lin Hongnian, styled Wucun, whose hometown is Fuzhou. In the 16th year of Daoguang's reign(1836), he became "状元"(zhuangyuan), which means the Number One Scholar, title conferred on the one who came first in the highest imperial examination. His life is legendary. And he is reputed as the "first zhuangyuan in Fukien province in the Qing Dynasty". Two years later, he made a voyage to Ryukyu as an envoy. He had left numerous pieces of poetry, some precious calligraphy works and moving stories there. Subsequently, he was appointed as Qiongzhou Magistrate in Guangdong Province, Lin'an Magistrate, the Chief Justice, commissioner and governor in Yunnan Province in succession. In the first month of the lunar year in the fifth year of Tongzhi Reign(1866), he was removed from his position because he failed to fight against the Taiping troops bravely. After that, he returned to Fuzhou, his hometown and became the first principal of Zhengyi Classical Learning Academy. He had been in charge of the academy for 19 years and cultivated a good many talents, such as Ye Dazhuo, Chen Baochen, Chen Yan and Wu Zengqi. He made great contribution to the development of literature in the late Qing Dynasty.

如今，随着现代化社会的快速发展，正谊书院依托福建省图书馆中丰富的馆藏资源，推动实现职能的逐步转变。书院以"文化、传统、经典"为内容定位，成为普及国学和弘扬优秀传统文化的课堂，以及举办高端学术研讨、进行学术引领的重要平台。正谊书院也凭借着独特的地理优势，融入台湾地区文创内容，以书院文化为主轴，改造书院的整体文化环境和文创内容，并推动文化旅游规划建设，让更多的人能够走进书院，传承优秀文化。

"窗外日光弹指过，席间花影坐前移。"（施耐庵《水浒传》）悠悠中华文化留存几千年，润泽百家，离不开书院的讲授研学之功。尤其是处在当下科技化的快节奏生活中，正谊书院得以保留实属不易。当你被俗世之事困扰时，不妨暂且将其搁置一旁，走进这所书院。或许，它会告诉你答案。

Currently, with the rapid development of modernized society, relying on rich resources in Fukien Library, Zhengyi Classical Learning Academy has gradually transformed its functions. The academy which is oriented on culture, tradition and classics has become the class to popularize Sinology and carry forward excellent traditional culture. Besides, it also has been a significant platform for high level symposiums and academic guidance. Definitely, depending on the academy peculiar geographical advantage, it integrates Taiwan's cultural creativity, with the classical academy as the core, transforming the cultural environment and cultural creativity, pushing the design and construction of culture and tourism. It is hoped that more and more visitors can enter the academy and inherit traditional culture.

"Time is transient, with the sunshine fleeting and the floral shadow moving" (Shi Naian, *Water Margin*). The education offered by the academy contributes to a long-standing Chinese culture and numerous families.Especially at present, in a fast-paced life, it is challenging to retain Zhengyi Academy of Classical Learning. When you are plagued by worldly problems, you might as well let it be and enter this academy. Maybe, you will find the key.

福州
古曆

第十四章　览胜三山　回味悠长

Chapter Fourteen
Enjoying the Beauty of Fuzhou
with a Lingering Finish

◎ 古刹传音：屏山华林寺、于山白塔寺

屏山华林寺

山门外，华林路车流如织，马路上匆匆忙忙；山门里，庙堂悄无声息，屋瓦层层叠叠。千年间，苔藓从时空里逃脱，尽数洒落，染出嫩绿的星星点点。绿植点缀其间，枝丫四处乱窜，在墙上缝编，织成鲜亮的花边。朱红、殷红、橙红……建筑的颜色褪去不少，它们静静地立在屏山脚下，宁静而安详，和华林路区隔成两个不同的时空。

日升月落，沧海桑田，时光倒流回公元前202年，闽越王无诸在屏山脚下建造了福州历史上最早的城池——冶城。此后，以此为核心，经历数次扩城，才发展成今天这样的繁华都市。华林寺前身是越山吉祥禅院，建造于五代十国时期。当时，吴越国国王钱镠割据闽浙等地，派驻福州的守将鲍修让为祈求佛祖保佑郡境的安宁拆除闽王宫殿，利用拆下来的材料在屏山南麓修建越山吉祥禅院。到宋代，吉祥禅院已是福州的著名寺院。明代初年，福建施行汰僧废寺，越山吉祥禅院也被列入废汰之列。正统九年（1444年），经福建参政司右参政宋彰奏请朝廷，禅院获得御赐匾额"华林寺"（鹿野，2014：85）。华林寺是我国长江以南最古老的木构建筑物，是全国重点文物保护单位。

游客稀少的华林寺，似乎更像这偌大城市中一段被定格的历史。静立于门外，已然可感受到穿越千年古朴而又静谧的华林寺。跨过山门，迎面所见的精巧大殿，与随处可见的高大雄伟的寺院大殿迥异，既不见人头攒动和鼎盛的香火，也不见信众虔诚供奉的佛像。整座殿堂建在台基之上，面阔三间，进深四间，呈正方形，有点儿类似唐朝和五代时期山西小寺庙的建筑风格。大殿正中只陈列一座华林寺模型，四周的墙上还有许多关于福州古建筑的介绍。

古朴而静谧的华林寺
Tranquil, Simple and Sophisticated Hualin Temple

◎ Ancient Temples: Hualin Temple in the Mount Ping and White Pagoda Temple in the Mount Yu

Hualin Temple in the Mount Ping

Outside the temple gate, the traffic is congested in the Hualin Road; inside it, it is silent with the roof tile layer upon layer. Over a thousand years passed. Mosses escape from the cleft of time and space, scattered and dyed light green everywhere. The lawn is dotted with green plants whose branches scatter everywhere and weave shining races on the wall. Vermilion, dark red and orange red....The color of the ancient building faded away. Pacific and serene, they stand at the food of Moun Ping motionlessly, separating themselves from Hualin Road and creating two different time and space.

The sun rises and the moon sets. Dating back to 202 B.C., Wuzhu, the Minyue King built the earliest city---Ye City in Fuzhou at the foot of the Mount Ping. Afterwords, based on it, after widening the city for several times, the city has developed into a prosperous currently. The precursor of Hualin Temple is Auspicious Buddhist Temple in the Mount Yue which was built in Five Periods and Ten States. At that time, Qianliu, the king of Wuyue State ruled areas such as today's Fukien Province and Zhejiang Province. Bao Xiurang, the general in Fuzhou demolished the Palace of Wang Shenzhi and employed the materials to construct the Auspicious Buddha Temple in the south part of Mount Ping in order to pray the Buddha for peace in the prefecture. In Song Dynasty, Auspicious Buddha Temple became a renounced temple in Fuzhou. During the early years of Min Dynasty, monks were eliminated and temples abolished. The Auspicious Buddha Temple was one of them. In the ninth year of Zhengtong Reign(1444 A.D.)in the Ming Dynasty, after the vice Resident Councillor, Song Zhang reported to the throne, the temple was bestowed the pique which read Hualin Temple by the emperor(Lu Ye, 2014: 85). It is the oldest wooden architecture in the south of Yangtze River and the cultural site under state protection.

With few tourists, it seems that Hualin Temple is a frozen history in this city. Standing outside the gate, the tranquility, simplicity and sophistication of Hualin Temple boasting over two thousand years history can be felt. Going across the gate, the delicate main hall differs from that in other magnificent temples. Neither do we see the incense smoke curling around in the crowded temple, nor the Buddhist image worshiped by devout believers. Three rooms wide and four rooms deep, the square temple is constructed on a base. The architectural style is somewhat similar to that of the small temple in the Tang Dynasty and Five Dynasties in Shanxi Province. In the middle of the main hall, there is only a model of Hualin Temple. On the wall, there are many pictures concerning introductions to Fuzhou ancient buildings.

古朴的红色大殿，没有什么色彩艳丽的装饰，屋顶灰瓦以及鸱尾也很朴素，屋脊的吻兽很简单，也无蹲兽。廊前的四根柱子没有想象中那么高，屋檐压得很低，但特别宽大，柱子头有一层一层粗大的斗拱支撑着屋檐。这是一座非常有特色的建筑（LAZY，2022）。

整座大殿为八架椽屋，一共使用18根柱子支撑，在梁架结构中未用到一颗铁钉。据说，华林寺这种建筑风格常见于南北朝时期，到了隋唐就不流行了，可见华林寺的风格在中国早期木构中可谓是别具一格。尤其是稳定的中国古建筑结构，使大殿千年后依然屹立不倒，更是难能可贵。

步入华林寺大雄宝殿内部，细品其建筑特色：梁、栿、前檐阑额均为月梁造。这些建筑结构全部采用粗大的原木，不对称曲线的云形驼峰让华林寺的木构看起来灵动不少。这种粗犷和简练的木构组合，在中国古建筑中并不多见。

在前廊和脊檩中还可以看到不少题刻，其中有清康熙三十六年（1697年）、道光四年（1824年）等重修大殿时刻下的文字，同时还可以看到更古老的宋代以来祈求保佑的"国界安宁"、"皇图巩固"等题记（马且停，2022）。这些宋代以来的祥瑞语题刻保存完好，极为珍贵。

据百度百科，千百年前的工匠们没有用到一颗铁钉，所有木构均采用榫卯工艺，构筑成如此磅礴大气的华林寺。而中国长江以南地区多雨、潮湿，古代木构建筑很难保留下来，在宋代木构建筑本来就保存很少的南方地区，此殿尤显珍贵，是研究古建筑的珍贵实物。在潮湿多雨的东南闽地，经受过台风等自然灾害的侵蚀以及朝代更迭中动荡不安局势的影响，这座木构的古老建筑居然神奇地保留下来，真可谓一个奇迹，这也是古人留给我们的弥足珍贵的文化遗产。

时过境迁，物易人非。"文革"期间，华林寺毁于"破四旧"。令人遗憾的是，寺内的文物荡然无存。数年后，在华林寺原址，东移10多米、往北内缩约4米重修了一座寺院。重修的华林寺，其主要构件虽是千年原物，却难复以往的繁华。

现今的华林寺如古朴雄茂的巨玺，静静地钤印在闽越古城的发端处，星移斗转，不朽不腐。虽然它难以再现昔日的鼎盛辉煌，但那寺院、那古木，都承载着一个族群跨越山海的记忆。

In the simple and sophisticated red main hall, neither are there any splendid decorations, nor squatting animals in the ridge. The grey tile on the roof and even the tail are plain. Four pillars in front of the corridor are not as high as imagined. The eave is relatively low but particularly wide. There are layers of dougong/brackets supporting the eave. In general, it is a charming temple(anonymous, 2022).

The main hall is an eight-rafter house supported by 18 pillars without a single nail in the frame structure. It is said that this architecture is commonly found in Northern and Southern Dynasties. However, it is not popular in the Sui Dynasty and the Tang Dynasty. Hence, the style of Huanlin Temple is unique in the early Chinese wooden structure. It is praiseworthy that it is the stable ancient Chinese building structure that leaves the main hall still stand after thousands of years.

Step into the Mahavira Hall of Hualin Temple, we can appreciate its architectural features. It is obvious that the beam, and the forehead of the front eave are made of the moon beam. These wooden raw materials are thick logs. The clouded hump with asymmetric curve makes the wooden structure more resilient. It is safe to say that the combination of the rough and concise wooden structure, which is rare in Chinese ancient architecture.

In the front corridor and backbone, we can find a lot of precious inscriptions which were carved in the 36th year of Kangxi Reign and Daoguang Reign of in the Qing Dynasty when the main hall was under renovation. Meanwhile, inscriptions which read, "National boundaries are peaceful" and "The empire is eternal." in the Song Dynasty and the following dynasties(Ma Qieting, 2022). These auspicious inscriptions which appeared as early as in the Song Dynasty are well-preserved and highly prized.

More than one thousand years ago, craftsmen never used a nail to construct a majestic Hualin Temple. Instead, all the wooden structures have been constructed by mortise and tenon. It is different to preserve ancient wooden buildings in the area to the south of Yangtze River owing to the rain and dampness. In the southern China, wooden buildings in Song Dynasty have rarely been preserved, so this building which is the priceless object for ancient architecture research is quite valuable(Anonymous, 2022). In the southeast part of Fukien Province, having experienced/undergone natural disasters such as typhoon and turbulent situations during the changes of dynasties, it is really a wonder that this ancient wooden building can survive miraculously. It is the priceless cultural heritage left by our ancestors.

Circumstances change with the passage of time. During the Cultural Revolution, the Hualin Temple was destroyed due to destruction of Four Olds. It is shame that the cultural relics in the temple disappeared. After many years, over ten meters away from the original site of Hualin Temple in the east, retracting four meters inward northward, a temple was renovated. Although principal the components of the temple are the original ones boasting over one thousand years history, it is difficult to restore its prosperity in the past.

Hualin Temple is like a classic and magnificent jade seal, standing silently at the starting point of the ancient city of the Minyue State with the seasons changing fast. Although it is not as brilliant and splendid as it used to be, the temple and the ancient wood are carrying the memory of a group of ethnic climbing the mountain and sailing across the sea.

于山白塔寺

福州"三山两塔一条江"中的"两塔"，指的是白塔和乌塔。白塔矗立在于山之麓，与乌山乌塔遥遥相对。置身白塔脚下，仰头望去，只见那笔直坚挺的塔身直入云霄，塔之洁白与天之湛蓝相得益彰，宛如天成。那庄严肃穆、巍峨壮观之景反衬出人的渺小，使人不禁产生崇敬之感。

于山位于福州市五一广场北侧，最高处海拔 58.6 米，占地面积 11.9 平方千米。相传，战国时有一支"于越族"迁居于此，由此得名"于山"。

定光塔在于山西麓的白塔寺内，白塔寺也叫定光塔寺。定光塔全名"报恩定光多宝塔"，初建于唐天祐元年（904 年）。传说在奠基时发现了一颗光芒四射的宝珠，所以取名"报恩定光多宝塔"。因塔身为白色，俗称白塔。

关于白塔建造的缘由，还有一个脍炙人口的故事。唐代福建文人黄滔曾专门写过一篇《大唐福州报恩定光多宝塔碑记》，详述了建塔的缘由："于兹九仙山造塔……为先君司空、先秦国太夫人、元昆故司空荐祉于幽阴也。"（转引自郭进邵，2022）其中先君司空、先秦国太夫人、元昆故司空分别指的是王审知的父亲、母亲和兄长，司空为追赠的官衔，秦国太夫人为封号。王审知的长兄即王审潮，五代十国时期闽国的奠基人。王审潮、王审邦、王审知兄弟三人并称"三龙"，攻占福建，开创闽国。按照惯例，王审潮完全可以将位子名正言顺地传给自己的儿子。但他出于稳定政局的考虑，将私心抛之脑后，临死前将大权交给了更具才干与威望的弟弟王审知。中国人崇尚"长兄如父"，王审知素来对兄长十分尊重，又受此传位大恩，故在几年之后建造宝塔，给兄长及父母祈求冥福、报答恩情。由此可见，白塔的修建是中国古代兄友弟恭、父慈子孝的最佳见证。

定光塔初建时模仿苏州的北寺塔，高 66.7 米，为七层砖心外檐木塔。内部砌砖，外部则为木构楼阁，斗拱重叠，颇为壮观。据文献记载，仅塔的轴心就用砖 40 万块。"每层的梁柱、斗拱、栏杆都经过了精雕细刻，塔壁和门扉还绘有佛像。"（孙群，2015：299）

White Pagoda Temple in the Mount Yu

The poetic statement that "three mountains, two pagodas and one river " indicates the salient feature in Fuzhou City geographically. Two pagodas in the statement refer to the White Pagoda and the Black Pagoda. Standing at the foot of the Mount Yu, the White Pagoda and the Black Pagoda in the Mount Wu face each other across a long distance. Standing at the foot of the White Pagoda, the upright pagoda seems to be close against the sky. The clean white pagoda and azure blue sky are complementary. Facing the solemn and majestic scenery makes visitors feel insignificant and reverent.

Located in the north side of the Wuyi Square, with the highest altitude of 58.6 meters, Mount Yu covers an area of 11.9 square kilometers. Tradition has it that Yuyue people settled here during the Warring Period, so it is named Mount Yu.

Dingguang Pagoda is inside the White Temple at the west foot of the Mount Yu, so the White Pagoda Temple is called Dingguang Pagoda Temple. Dingguang Pagoda's full name is Gratitude Dingguang Jewel Pagoda, which was built in the first year of Taiyou Reign in the Dang Dynasty(904 A.D.). According to the legend, a radiate jewel was found during the period of foundation. Since it is white, it is commonly called the White Pagoda.

As to the reason for construction of the White Pagoda, a popular story circulates among people. Huang Tao, a Fukien writer in the Tang Dynoasty wrote an article entitled "The Tablet of Fuzhou Gratitude Dingguang Jewel Pagoda in the Tang Dynasty", which elaborates the reason for building the pagoda. Huang Tao wrote, " In Mount Nine Immortals, the pagoda was built to present happiness and welfare to Wang Shenzhi's father, mother and eldest brother" (cited in Guo Jinshao, 2022). In the passage, the late Mr. Sikong, the diseased Lady of Qin State, the dead Si Kong refer to Wang Shenzhi's parents and the eldest brother respectively. Sikong is the official title presented after one's death and Lady of Qin State is a title. Wang Shenzhi's eldest brother is Wang Shenchao, the founder of Min State during the Five Periods and Ten States. Wang Shenchao, Wang Shenbang and Wang Shenzhi are called Three Dragons. They occupied Fukien Province and founded the Min State. According to the practice, Wang Shenchao's son could inherit his position justifiably, but in order to stabilize the political situation, when he was dying, he unselfishly transferred the power to his youngest brother, Wang Shenzhi, who was more capable and more prestigious. Since Chinese uphold the notion that the elder brother is like one's father and Wang Shenzhi always respected his eldest brother, several years later, he constructed the pagoda to pray for blessings for his late parents and the eldest brother and repay his debt of gratitude to them. Thus it can be seen that the construction of the White Pagoda perfectly conveys the essence of the notion that brothers in a family love and respect each other; the father is affectionate and the sons are filial.

Modeled on Northern Temple Pagoda, the original Dingguang Pagoda, a seven-story wooden pagoda was 66.7 meters high. The interior was made of bricks and the spectacular outer part was the wooden pavilion with dougong overlapping. According to historical records, the axis was made of 400, 000 bricks. " In every storey, the beam and column, dougong and railings have been carved elaborately. Craftsmen even drew Buddha images on the wall and door"(Sun Qun, 2015: 299).

明嘉靖十三年（1534年），该塔不幸被雷火焚毁，只剩下内部由砖块砌成的塔心。人们发现这样高大的木塔容易成为雷击的目标，恐难久存于世。于是，嘉靖二十七年（1548年）乡绅集资重建时，利用原有塔轴做塔身，建成七层八角楼阁式塔。从此白塔坚强地屹立在于山之巅，见证福州数百年来的沉浮。白塔的建造也反映出福州明代时期制砖业的发达。

白塔的设计还体现了古代福州建塔技术的进步。"福州古塔塔身平面以八边形居多，此外还有六边形塔、四边形塔和圆形塔。"（孙群，2015）白塔即是一座八边形塔。工匠们在长期的筑塔实践中，逐渐积累和摸索出一些经验，认识到八边形塔平面不仅可以扩大视野，还能抗震，削弱风力对塔身的冲击。福州处于地震带，又是沿海城市，台风侵袭可谓家常便饭。八边形白塔在抗震防风以及塔身的整体稳定性方面都有可圈可点之处。

"白衣佛面泪朝天，古寺凝恩举世颜。最是塔尖风骨浸，千年孝义染岚烟。"（搜狐网，2019）古往今来，多少文人骚客都曾作诗讴歌古塔之雄伟壮观。1962年9月，白塔被福州市人民委员会公布为市级文物保护单位，1991年，被福建省人民委员会公布为省级文物保护单位。

◎ 会馆集萃：永德会馆

福州市的上下杭文化历史街区被研究福州的学者们称为"福州传统商业博物馆"。作为闽商的主要发祥地，从清末至民初，这一带曾经行栈林立，商帮会馆云集。会馆是商业经济繁荣发展到一定阶段的必然产物。它如同今日省内外在福州设立的"办事处"，主要以乡谊为纽带，联络感情、互通信息，减少摩擦、协调纠纷，促进商业活动规范有序地开展（叶红，2012：72）。

大名鼎鼎的永德会馆坐落于上下杭文化历史街区的星安河畔。它的建筑风格独特，是这一街区的地标性建筑之一。作为众多会馆中的一家，它地处台江区田垱社区硋埕里20号。而其所在街道的命名也颇具地方特色，带有闽商文化的烙印。"硋"在福州方言中意指"瓷"。"埕"指房子正门前的空地。"硋埕"则指瓷器专卖市场。斗转星移，岁月悠悠，始建于清朝雍正年间的永德会馆，经历过光绪年间与民国20年（1931年）的两次重建。这两次重建均由永春、德化两县在榕的商帮慷慨解囊。

In the thirteenth year of Jiajing Reign in the Ming Dynasty(1534), unfortunately, the pagoda was destroyed by thunder and fire, with the center which was made by bricks left. It was found that it is easy for this kind of high wooden pagoda to be attacked by thunder and lightning. Therefore, in the 27th year of Jiajing Reign(1548), when the country gentlemen raised funds to renovate it, the original axis was employed to make the body of the pagoda and a seven-storeyed octagonal pavilion pagoda was completed. From then on, the White Pagoda stands on the summit of the Mount Yu, witnessing the ups and downs of Fuzhou for hundreds of years. The Construction of the White Pagoda reflects the flourishing of Fuzhou's brick-making industry in the Ming Dynasty.

The design of the White Pagoda reflects the advancement with regard to the pagoda construction technique in ancient Fuzhou. "Among Fuzhou ancient pagodas, most of them are octagonal ones. Besides, there are hexagonal, quadrilateral and round ones"(Sun Qun, 2015). The White Pagoda is a typical octagonal one. During the long period of pagoda construction, craftsmen accumulated and groped for some experiences. They realized that plane of the pagoda could not only widen the scope, but also fight against the earthquake, and lessen the attack from the wind. Located in the earthquake belt, Fuzhou is a coastal city, where typhoon is common occurrence, so octagonal White Pagoda is worth noting in fighting against the earthquake and typhoon and preserving the stability of the pagoda.

For centuries, numerous men of letters wrote poems in praise of the grandeur of the ancient pagoda. In September, 1962, it was announced as the first batch of cultural site under municipal protection by Fuzhou People's Committee. In 1991, the White Pagoda was announced as the first batch of the cultural site under provincial protection by Fukien People's Committee.

◎ A Collection of Guild Halls: Yongde Guild Hall

Shangxiahang Cultural and Historic Block in Fuzhou is acclaimed as "traditional commercial museums". As the major place of birthplace, there were a myriad of broker's storehouses, business groups and guild halls from the late period of Qin Dynasty to the early years of the Republic of China. When commercial economy is prosperous, the guild hall inevitably arises. It functions as today's office set up in Fuzhou. With the fellow villagers mutual affection as the bond, the guild hall aims at contact, communication, reducing conflicts, reconciling disputes, which promote the canonical and orderly development of commercial activity (Ye Hong, 2012: 72).

The renowned Yongde Guild Hall is located near the Xingan River in Shangxiahang Cultural and Historic Block. It boasts apeculiar architectural style and has become one of the landmark buildings in this area. As one of guild halls, it is on No. 20, Hechengli, Tiandang Community, Taijiang District. The street name is rich in local colors and Min Merchants' culture. In Fuzhou dialect, "he" means "porcelain" and "cheng" refers to the open space in front of the front gate. Thus, "hecheng" indicates the market which specializes in porcelains. In advancing years, the guild hall which was built in the reign of Yongzheng in Qing Dynasty was reconstructed in the Guangxu reign and the 20th year of the Republic of China(1931 A.D.). The reconstruction was funded by the merchant group from Yongchun County and Dehua County generously.

永德会馆中的"永德"为永春、德化两县的简称。名称的由来与福建省区域建置沿革相关。清初沿袭明制，永春、德化两县均隶属泉州府。雍正十二年（1734年）升永春县为福建布政使司直隶州，德化县归永春州管辖。两县地域毗邻，且所产陶瓷（同二县相邻的部分乡村也产陶瓷）成为福建对外贸易的大宗商品。共同的经济利益把两县商贾紧密联系在一起，"永德堂会"、"永德会馆"、"永德同乡会"先后建立。不仅福州建有永德会馆，境外如马来西亚、新加坡等地也建有永德会馆（福州老建筑百科，2022c）。

永德会馆地理位置优越，地处星安桥与三通桥之间，门前便是三捷河，也名星安河。自古以来，此地交通便利、四通八达。还设有道头，沿着大樟溪上溯便可以抵达德化等地。第一次鸦片战争后，根据中英《南京条约》，福州于1844年6月开埠。19世纪后半叶，陆续有外商光顾这里的瓷器批发市场，采购闻名遐迩的德化瓷器。

清朝建立后，星安桥畔的永德会馆便一直作为福州永德商帮堂会、商会、同乡会的活动场所。民国档案记载，永德同乡会筹备处主任林青山提交至福州市政府及福建省政府的报告中提及："永德地域系本省辖内永春县与德化县。自清业已在福州成立永德会馆，并建筑壮丽堂皇馆址壹座于南台硋埕里门牌三十九号，藉以联络同乡感情，增进桑梓福利，倡办公益事业等。"（福州老建筑百科，2022c）从前，会馆内还设有戏台，每逢节日都会上演高甲戏、闽剧等地方剧种，不仅增添了节日的喜庆，还能借此联络同乡的感情，促进交流。

因独特的建筑风格和文化价值，永德会馆于2019年7月25日被列为台江区第三批区级文物保护单位。会馆属于中西合璧式建筑，是一座具有我国闽南地域特色与西方建筑风格的古厝。它融入旋转楼梯与铁制门窗等诸多西洋建筑元素。这座古建筑坐东南朝西北，占地面积为1224平方米，东西宽36米。会馆共三层，总高约为15米。其中，第一层和第二层的高度均为4.5米，西式建筑元素占比较多。值得一提的是，第三层建筑匠心独运，采用我国传统的单檐歇山顶。且这一层比第一层和第二层足足高了1米。这一层体现清代建筑风格，是因为1931年重建时工匠们按清代福州会馆的厅堂样式而建。

"Yongde" is the abbreviation for Yongchun County and Dehua County. The origin is connected with the evolution of the Regional Organizational System in Fukien Province. The system was inherited from Ming Dynasty in the early Qing Dynasty, with Yongchun County and Dehua County under the jurisdiction of Quanzhou Prefecture. In the twelfth year of Yongzheng reign(1739), Yongchun County became a prefecture under the jurisdiction of Fukien commissioner. Dehua County had been under the jurisdiction Yongchun Prefecture. In these two neighboring counties, since some villages in Yongchun County also produced pottery and porcelian, ceramics was the bulk commodity in foreign trade in Fukien Province. The common economic interest connected the merchants in two counties closely, Yongde Tanghui, Yongde Guild Hall and Yongde Townsmen Association was constructed in succession. Not only dia Yongde Guild Hall exist in Fuzhou, but also in the southeastern Asia countries, such as Malaysia and Singapore (Fuzhou Old Architecture Encyclopedia, 2022c).

Yongde Guild Hall, which is located between Xing'an Bridge and Santong Bridge boasts advantageous geographical location Sanjie River(Xing'an River)in front of it. From ancient times, convenient traffic conditions stretch in all directions. With the unsophisticated wharf/quay, the boat can reach Dehua and other places down the Dazhang River. After the First Opium War, according to The Treaty of Nanking, in June, 1844, Fuzhou was opened up as a commercial port, starting trades officially. During the late 19th century, foreign merchants frequented the porcelain wholesale market to purchase the well-known Dehua porcelain.

After its construction in the Qing Dynasty, the guild hall which is near the Xing'an River has been a venue for the commercial group's tanghui, entertainment party with hired performers held at home on auspicious occasions, chamber of commerce and association of fellow provincials from Yongchun and Dehua County. According to the archive during the Republic of China, the director of preparatory office of Yongde fellow provincial association, Lin Qingshan, in the report submitted to Fuzhou Municipal Government and Fukien Provincial Government mentioned that, " Yongde includes Yonhun County and Dehua County in Fukien Province since Qing Dynasty. As a magnificent building, Yongde Guild Hall which is located at No.39 Hechengli in Nantai has been constructed in Fuzhou. It aims at promoting communication among townsmen, improving welfare in the hometown and devoting to charity, etc"(Fuzhou Old Architecture Encyclopedia,2022c). In the past, there was a stage for performance, where local operas such as Gaojia Opera and Min Opera were shown, which added to the holiday's happiness and helped to communicate with the townspeople.

Due to its unique architectural style and cultural value, Yongde Guild Hall was announced as the third batch of the cultural site under the protection in Taijiang District on June 25, 2019. The guild hall nowadays boasts its style mingling the traditional Chinese one with Western one. It is an ancient mansion which combines Southern Fukien style and Western style. It integrates many a western architectural factors, such as spiral stairs, steel doors and windows. It is situated in southeast, facing south and covering an area of 1224 square meters, with 36 meters wide in the east and west. As a three-story mansion, it is about 15 meters high. With the western style to a great extent, the first floor and the second one in the compound are both 4.5 meters high. It is worth mentioning that the architecture which is called gable and hip roof with single eave on the third floor follows the Chinese tradition. In addition, this floor is one meter higher than the other two floors. The architecture in this floor is characterized by the style of Qing Dynasty because in 1931, it was reconstructed by the craftsmen according to style of the hall in the guild hall with Fuzhou style in the Qing Dynasty.

移步正门，傲然挺立着两根罗马式石柱，门楣上嵌刻鎏金牌匾，榜书"永德会馆"。步入会馆内部，映入眼帘的是一副石刻楹联："永命肇基盛典桃源昭奕祀 德星耀彩华轩榕会焕祥辉"，寓意是希冀在榕的两县商帮能传承闽商精神，并将其发扬光大。

一方名为《桃源翁李立斋先生传赞》的石碑至今还保存于永德会馆内，这在上下杭文化历史街区的所有现存会馆中是绝无仅有的。碑文不仅记载了永春五里街商人、新加坡华侨李继如（字立斋）及其子李俊承前往南洋艰苦创业等史实，还高度评价了他们乐善好施的高风亮节。李氏父子致力于家乡公益事业，为报效社会、回馈桑梓，捐巨资重建福州永德会馆。作为华侨抗日领袖的李俊承，不仅热心慈善事业，还慷慨捐资支持祖国抗击日本侵略者。

福州永德会馆见证了永春籍商人的辉煌。实际上，永春人不畏艰险、远涉重洋经商的历史可追溯到五代后周（951—960年）时期。直到今天，因永春籍商人曾在海内外创造了众多商业奇迹，在东南亚一带仍然流传着"无永不开市"一说。清朝末年和民国年间，社会动荡不安，永春的老百姓为了生存不得不"下南洋"讨生活。他们吃苦耐劳、勇于拼搏，在异国他乡艰苦创业，不仅促进了当地经济的发展，也使"无永不开市"的精神在东南亚地区发扬光大。

会馆的橱窗内还陈列了一些珍贵的文物。永春和德化两县在榕商会特地从泉州收集了手风琴、时钟、皮箱、望远镜、相机、算盘等老物件进行现场展示。

在会馆中，市民还可以参观各种现代瓷器工艺品。其中，出自国家级非遗传承人、中国陶瓷艺术大师许瑞峰之手，用百个瓷壶打造的百福墙是"镇馆之宝"（石磊磊、包华，2020）。

文物是历史的见证者，永德会馆的老物件承载了久远的历史记忆，向我们诉说着过往的故事。永德会馆是一个不可忽视的、体现了当地历史文化尤其是闽商文化风韵的标志性建筑，其中不仅有文物的汇集与并置，同时也是文化与历史的盛宴。在风和日丽的日子里，我们徜徉在永德会馆中，沉浸在历史的怀抱里，犹如行走在时光隧道中。与此同时，这也是一场心灵的洗礼，先辈的敢为人先、勇于拼搏的精神引领新时代的我们不忘初心、砥砺前行。

Two Roman pillars stand proudly at the front door. On the lintel gilded plaque, Chinese characters which read "Yongde Guild Hall" has been carved. When we step into the ancient mansion, we can appreciate the couplet carved on the stone pillar. This couplet indicates that the merchant groups in Yongchun County and Dehua County can inherit and develop Min merchants' spirit generation after generation.

A stone tablet carved a passage entitled "The Biography and Paean of Mr. Li Lizhai from Taoyuan County" has been treasured in the guild hall, which is unique in the remaining guild halls in this cultural and historical block. The article not only records the struggling story concerning the overseas Chinese Li Jiru whose style is lizhai and his son Li Chengjun who came from Singapore in the Southeast Asian countries. They are devoted to charity in their hometown. In order to contribute to society and benefit their native place, they donate a large amount of money to reconstruct Yongde Guild Hall in Fuzhou. Apart from showing great e nthusiasm for philanthropy, as an overseas Chinese of the War of Resistance Against Japan, he made generous donation to the native country to fight against the Japanese aggressors as well.

Yongde Guild Hall in Fuzhou has witnessed the Yongchun merchant's glory in business circles.In reality, the Yongchun people's foreign trade history can date back to the Houzhou Dynasty during the Five Periods(951--960). Up to now, because of numerous business miracles created worldwide by Yongchun merchants, the saying, " Without Yongchun merchants, there don't exist markets." still circulates in the southeast Asian countries. In the late Qing Dynasty and the Republic of China, since the society was in chaos, in order to make a living, some people in Yongchun County had to make a voyage to Nanyang. They are hard-working, strenuous and enterprising, contributing to the local economic development and promoting the arduous and pioneering spirit in the southeast Asia area.

There are some precious cultural relics on display in the ancient building. In the window, we can see the suitcase, telescope, and clock and so on.They are collected by the commerce chamber of Yongchun and Dehua.

In the guild hall, citizens can appreciate a great variety of modern porcelain handicrafts. Among them, a wall with one hundred 'Fu' made of one hundred teapots is the highlight of the collections. This original artifact is created by Xu Ruifeng, China's master of ceramics artist. Mr. Xu is also a national inheritor of intangible cultural heritage (Shi Leilei, Baohua, 2020).

Cultural relics are the witnesses of history and the old objects in Yongde Guild Hall are invested with distant historic memory, telling us the passing story. It is a location which cannot be overlooked because it presents local cultural and historical flavour and Min merchant culture. It displays not only the collection and juxtaposition but also a cultural and historical feast. In a sunny day, we walked in this ancient mansion, it looked as if we had been immersed in history's embrace. At the same time, the visit is like a mental baptism as well. The ancestor's pioneering and dedicated spirit will lead us in the new era to stay true to the mission and forge ahead.

◎ 商号林立：咸康参号、罗氏绸布庄

咸康参号

敲开上下杭青石瓦砾的大门，沿着旧时的"金融街"一路向前，"咸康参号"的金字招牌赫然映入眼帘，斑驳古老的招牌隐匿了昔日的繁华。咸康参号坐落于福州市台江区下杭路219号，是福州现存最完整的民国大药房之一（福州新闻网，2021b）。

这是一幢朴素而庄重的老建筑，具有典型的清末民初建筑风格。由1920年民国时期的广告可知，咸康参号原为两层，抗日战争结束后，经历第一次重建，招牌与外立面保留原貌，主体则改建为三层。咸康参号南邻一座清代木制建筑——倪文彬故居，二者内部互通。专家推测，咸康参号过去可能是倪文彬故居的一部分。咸康参号是一栋砖木混搭的建筑，它的墙壁只有一部分砌砖，主墙体则是采用中式木构的方法。其装修风格中西合璧。门面主要使用青石和花岗岩，用水泥与铁艺装饰。至于内部，它的地砖、窗户甚至屋顶的天窗都是西式风格，大厅的花砖则是国外进口的。

咸康参号外观
The Appearance of Xiankang Pharmacy

◎ Numerous Stores: Xiankang Pharmacy and Luo Family Silk and Satin Store

Xiankang Pharmacy

Knocking down at the door made of bluestone, going down the "Wall Street" in the past, a signboard in gold letters which reads "Xiankang Pharmacy" came into view. The mottled and ancient sign conceals the prosperity in those days. Located at No. 219, Shangxiahang Road, Taijiang District, Fuzhou. Xiankang Pharmacy is one of the best-preserved pharmacies during the Republic of China in Fuzhou(Fuzhou News Website, 2021b).

It is a simple and solemn ancient building with typical architectural style in the early Qing Dynasty. According to the advertisement in 1920 during the Republic of China, it was found that the building was two-storeyed originally. After the anti-Japanese War, it was reconstructed, with the sign and facade retaining the original appearance and the bulk of the building transformed into three floors. Near the south of the pharmacy, there was a timber-structured building—Ni Wenbin's Former Residence. These two buildings are interconnected inside. Experts conjecture that Xiankang Pharmacy might well be a part of Ni Wenbin's Former Residence in the past. It is a building made of bricks and timber, including a part of the brick wall. Most parts of the wall were constructed by the method of Chinese timer-structured architecture. The renovation combines Chinese style with Western one, with a facade made of bluestones and granite, which was decorated with cement and iron art. As for the style of the interior, the tile, window, and the skylight in the roof is western. And the tile in the hall was imported from foreign countries.

今天呈现在我们眼前的这栋古厝，占地面积约为263.8平方米，坐南朝北，共有三层。店面装修精致，外观美轮美奂。修缮之初，施工人员仔细勘测，认真绘制图纸，使用传统的材料装修，最大限度地复原咸康参号。同时，考虑到建筑对采光和通风的要求，施工人员保留了咸康参号内部的众多窗户，还在三层的屋顶增加了一面玻璃天窗。天气晴朗时，和煦的阳光透过玻璃照在大厅里。这种补充采光的方法同样被运用于上下杭的罗氏绸缎庄。

"咸康"最初是兴化人创办的药行。我国近代著名政治家、书法家郑孝胥（1860—1938年）为其书写牌匾，并配有对联："咸宁资上药，康乐晋同胞"。20世纪30年代初，闽侯县上街銮浦乡人张桂荣（1894—1950年）接手了这家经营不善的药行。他虽出身农家，年少时却也读过私塾，在福州南街"大生春"药店当了五年学徒，之后便自立门户。张桂荣在制药上小有天赋，而且他做工的同时苦读医书，积极练习丸、散、丹、膏及饮片的制造技术。天道酬勤，他的生意从上杭路起步，先是开设了"张乾泰中药材批发栈"，从川、滇、黔等省老产区进货，追求地道的良药。同时，他发现日本向中国倾销大量价廉质优的"太极参"。他抓住商机，靠代销"太极参"发财致富。抗日战争期间，张桂荣不再代销日货，而是拥护国货，恢复做中药材批发和零售生意。他又在毗邻的隆平路开设了"华大医药商店"，但因为隆平路药店过多，明争暗斗的竞争让张桂荣疲于应付，他才辗转接手了下杭路口的"咸康国药行"。"咸康"这个招牌名蕴含着美好的寓意，即祈愿国人身体健康、平安吉祥。或许，这也是这家看似普通的药行吸引张桂荣的原因吧。

Currently, facing the north, this three-story ancient building covers an area about 263.8 square meters, with delicately-decorated facade and beautiful appearance. At the beginning of renovation, workers explored this architecture scrutinously, drew the blueprint carefully, used traditional materials to renovate it, which was conducive to restoring the pharmacy to the greatest extent. Meanwhile, having taken the requirements of the light and rejuvenation, workers retained many a windows in the inside of the building. A glass skylight has been added to the roof in the third floor. In a sunny day, the warm sunshine can penetrate the glass, shine on the hall. This method of adding light has been used in the renovation of The Luo Family Silk Store.

At first, it was a pharmacy established by Xinghua people. Zheng Xiaoxu (1860-1938), a famous politician and calligrapher was invited to inscribe four Chinese characters on the plaque and write down a couplet which sang high praise of the shop. In the early 1930, Zhang Guirong(1894--1905), who came from Luanpu Township, Shangjie, Minhou County took over this shop which performed poorly. Although he was born into a peasant family, he studied in an old-style private school when he was young. After apprenticing in "Dashengchun" Pharmacy in Nanjie, Fuzhou for five years, he started a business Talented for making medicine, he studied medical books diligently and actively practiced the techniques in the field of making the pill, powder, alchemical medicine/potions, plaster and decoction pieces. He started his business in the Shanghang Road. At first, he set up a "Zhang Qiantai Chinese Medicinal Material Warehouse", stocking good commodities from old production areas in the provinces such as Sichuan Province, Yunnan Province and Guizhou Province. Meanwhile, he found that Japanese merchants sold a large quantity of "Taiji Jingsen" with low price and high quality. He seized the opportunity to be commissioned to sell it and made a fortune. During the anti-Japanese war, instead of selling Japanese goods on a commission basis, he supported domestic products and specialized in wholesale and retail of Chinese medicinal materials again. He founded " the Huada Medicine Store" on the neighbouring Rongping Road. However, since there were too many pharmacies there, it was challenging and tiresome for him to deal with the ruthless competition, he took over Xiankang Traditional Chinese Medicine Pharmacy in the intersection of Xiahang Road eventually."Xiankang" indicates a sincere wish that people will lead a healthy, safe and auspicious life. Maybe, that is why this seemingly ordinary-looking store caught the eye of its later owner.

咸康参号的成就不仅仅缘于其有口皆碑的产品质量，更离不开经营有方。首先，张桂荣重视宣传。他选取良辰吉日按时开张，放鞭炮、宰活鹿，宾客如云，热闹非凡；所有药品的包装纸上皆醒目地印上了"咸康"字样，人参、鹿茸等名贵药材的包装更是华丽大方；药行的橱窗里摆放着独家秘制的"周公百岁酒"、"虎骨木瓜酒"以及各地的滋补品。其次，咸康参号遵循古法，严格按照传统秘方的投料比例制作药酒、饮片等。而对这些方子则是守口如瓶，一般人接触不到。同时，药房人员在操作过程中遵循严格的步骤，所有药材必须分类摆放，滋补品则按照等级定价，旨在让前来求取药品及补品的患者能够买得放心、吃得安心。最后，咸康参号始终秉持着先进的经营理念，十分重视售前和售后服务。一方面，他们将购入的原药分散成一个个小包装，从而降低批发价与单价，使得更多的中小药店能够前来进货，以此加快自身的资金周转速度，同时也有利于百姓购买药品。另一方面，参号大厅定期安排名医坐堂问诊，病人在此可享受把脉、开处方、配方、抓药、煎药、送药等"一条龙"服务。咸康参号规模之大，在国内都有知名度。

《本草纲目》记载，人参能"补中益气，厚肠胃"，服用后能补充气血，使人身强体健。而医者父母心，圣手为苍生。这正是咸康参号得以在众多药铺中脱颖而出并传承下来的原因。福州有着悠久的中医药文化历史，东汉时期名医董奉的祖籍便是福州长乐。民国时期福州药行林立，在上下杭地区近40家中药房中，咸康参号凭借地道的药材与优质的服务业务拓展迅速，不仅覆盖了闽江上下游，还在上海、香港开设了代办机构。民间将咸康与回春、四省、华来并列为"福州四大药店"。咸康的店主张桂荣不仅在药学方面资质颇高，同时为人诚恳、不弄虚作假。更重要的是，他还善于管理生意，其经营理念也得到不少业内人士的推崇。

新中国成立后，咸康参号经营有方，劳资关系融洽，企业发展欣欣向荣。1956年公私合营后，张桂荣的弟弟张震华相继担任咸康参号副主任、市工商联执委。张桂荣之子张希珊更是在土改中主动将田产献给农会，还在抗美援朝时期主动带头捐献。他先后担任小桥区工商联主委、市食品进出口公司副经理、市工商联副主委、省政协委员。改革开放时期，他又竭尽全力引进资金、技术、人才。今天，张家后代在海外定居者在200人以上（林精华，2006）。

Xiankang Pharmacy's accomplishments lie not only in its proverbial high quality but also in its excellent management. Above all, Zhang Guirong attached importance to publicizing. When the pharmacy opened on an auspicious day, with fireworks set off and a live deer killed, it was jammed with a noisy crowd of buyers and sellers. Two Chinese characters "Xiankang", the name of the drugstore were emblazoned on all the wrapping paper. The packaging of rare medicinal materials such as ginseng and pilose antlers was magnificent and stunning. Tonics such as "Longevity Liquor" and "Tiger Bone Liquor" which were exclusive products in the pharmacy or came from different corners of China were placed in the shop window. Second, the products like medicinal liquor and decoction pieces were made according to ratio in the traditional recipe which was kept as a secret. Meanwhile, employers followed the operating procedure strictly. All medicinal materials should be classified and put in the proper place. As to tonics, they were priced by grade, aiming at offering patients convenience and having them building up confidence in the medicine. Finally, Xiankang Pharmacy consistently upheld advanced management notions, attaching great importance to the pre-sale and after-sale services. On one hand, employers were asked to use small packages instead of big ones, which could reduce the retail price and unit price and attract more small or medium-sized drugstores to purchase goods. Therefore, this method not only accelerated turnover of the capital but also facilitated ordinary people to buy medicine. On the other hand, renowned doctors were employed to see patients regularly in the hall. Patients could enjoy one-stop service, including taking the pulse, prescribing, measuring out herbal medicine, filling a prescription, delivering the medicine, etc. The pharmacy is a large-scaled and well-known nationwide.

According to *Compendium of Materia Medica,* gingsen can "Buzhong Yiqi(tonifying middle-Jiao and Qi)and strengthen the stomach and intestines". Having taken it, nutrition can be supplemented and blood cycle taken good care of, which will be conducive to making people strong. That is the reason why this store stands out from is many competitsrs. From the ancient times, Fuzhou boasts of a long culture of Chinese traditional medicine. In the West Han Dynasty, the famous doctor, Dong Feng came from then Changle County, Fuzhou. In the Republic of China Period, a lot of drugstore sprang up, with about 40 ones in Shangxiahang Area. Among them, relying on its high-quality herbal medicine and first-class service, Xiankang Pharmacy developed rapidly. Its business not only covered the uprstream and downstream of Minjiang River, but also set up agencies in Shanghai and Hong Kong. Xian Kang Pharmacy and the other three pharmacies entitled, Huichuan, Sisheng, Hualai are reputed as "Four Grand Pharmacies in Fuzhou". The owner, Zhang Guirong is not only talented in pharmacy but also sincere and upright.More importantly, he was good at business management and his notion was acclaimed by a lot of insiders.

After liberation, due to superb management and harmonious labor relations, the development of the enterprise was flourishing. After joint state-private ownership in 1956, Zhang Guirong's younger brother Zhang Zhenghua successively held the post of Vice Director of Xiankang Pharmacy and an executive committee member of Municipal Association of Industry and Commerce. Zhang Guirong's son, Zhang Xishan seized the initiative to donate real estate to the peasant association during the period of land reform and took the lead in donations during the War to Resist U.S. Aggression and Aid Korea. He successively took the post of. In the period of reform and opening, he made great efforts to introduce capital, techniques and talents. Today, over 200 posterity of Zhang Family resided in foreign countries(Lin Jinghua, 2006).

今日，当我们再次步入修旧如旧的咸康参号，仿佛还能闻到扑面而来的药草清香，想象着药铺中的坐堂医生捻须把脉、问诊开方，厅内学徒抓药、递药来往匆忙；亦可想见，百年前的枪林弹雨中，又有多少救死扶伤的故事在这里上演。

罗氏绸布庄

昔日绸缎庄，今朝非遗馆。

罗氏绸布庄旧址位于下杭路181号，占地面积约1120平方米，建筑面积则达到1500多平方米。这座清朝建筑坐南朝北，一头连着下杭路，一头挨着星河巷，是一座四进的大宅子，由外而内依次为店面、仓库、住家、厨房和花园。由于紧邻星河巷，货物走水路，上岸后即可直接搬至第二进的仓库中。

绸布庄外墙由青砖砌成，石砌门框上部是民国初年增设的石质券顶。第一进的左右前披舍被改建为二层砖混建筑，主座面阔五间、进深五柱，上面的木构梁架都还在，只是增设了吊顶。穿过天井就是第二进，主座前后同样有天井、披舍，主座也是面阔五间、进深五柱。第三进主座面阔三间、进深七柱，朝向与前两进相反，高堂大厦，装饰华美。古厝第三进有一根"镇厝之宝"——闽楠木长梁，长度约13米，直径有60多厘米。在天然状态下，要生长百年以上。如果放在一百多年前，这种楠木算是御用的木材。另外，这座古厝还有一处独特的设计，就是第一进的后天井，其露天处却不露天，而是在上方装玻璃窗。据国家文物局古建筑专家库成员陈木霖介绍，罗氏绸缎庄的货物从星安河进出，绸缎本身特别怕湿，而福州的天气又难免淫雨霏霏、连月不开。因此，天井的上部就安装了玻璃窗，既保证阳光照射以防绸缎霉变，又能为它遮风挡雨。又因为罗氏绸缎庄是清末建筑，可以断定，这扇玻璃窗是民国初年罗翼庭买下古厝后加装的。

在时间的长河中，上下杭历史文化街区涌现出一大批优秀的闽商，罗氏绸缎庄的创始人罗翼庭就是其中的一员，同时他也是闽商中"江西帮"的代表人物。罗翼庭祖籍江西南城县。民国初年，上下杭的"绸布业一条街"上出现了一家名为"罗恒隆绸缎庄"的绸布店，即为罗翼庭所创办，主营业务为批发、售卖绸缎、纱罗、棉布等。此外，罗翼庭在上海市福州路还设了分号"永隆布庄"，将上海、杭州、苏州等地的绸布买入，再运到福州销售。

Today, when we enter this ancient building which has been reconstructed as it used to be, it seems as if we could smell the herbal fragrance, imagining the doctors twisting the beard and feeling the pulse, inquiring and prescribing. It looks as if the apprentice was busy filling a prescription and delivering the medicine. In the mind's eye, numerous stories concerning healing the wounded and rescuing the dying were on shown here about a hundred years ago.

Luo Family Silk and Satin Store

The silk and satin store in the past has become the Intangible Cultural Heritage Museum.

Luo Family Mercer's Shop, covering an area about 1120 square meters is located at No. 181, Xiahang Road. Its architectural area is more than 1500 square meters. This building which was constructed in the Qing Dynasty faces the north, with one end connecting with the Xiahang Road and the other end connecting with the Xinghe Alley. It is a mansion with four connected sections, which include the facade, storehouse, residence, kitchen and garden from the outside to the interior. Since it is neighboring to Xinghe Alley, cargoes could be shipped on the river and moved into the storehouse in the second section of the compound after the workers went ashore.

The external wall was made of blue bricks, with the upper part of the stone doorframe which had stone top coupons added in the early years of the Republic of China. The left and right rooms beside the principal room in the first section have been converted into a two-story brick-concrete building. The main building is five rooms wide and five pillars deep. The wooden beamframe in the main room is the original one apart from an added suspended ceiling. Going through the patio, we arrive at the second section of the architecture with five rooms wide and five pillars deep in the main building. There is also a patio and the wing in the front and back of the main room. With three rooms wide and seven pillars deep and inverse orientation as the other two sections, the third section is magnificent and gorgeously-decorated. There is a Fukien nanmu beam which is about 13 meters long and more than 60 centimeters in diameter in the third section. In general, it is taken from a tree which lived more than 100 years. In over 100 years ago, the nanmu was employed for the emperor exclusively (Fuzhou Evening's Newspaper, 2019). Besides, the design of the back patio in the first courtyard is unique. In the upper part of it, the glass window is installed. The ancient building expert, Chen Mulin said that since cargoes were moved in and out of Xing'an River, and silk should avoid dampness in Fuzhou where it often rains. Hence, the glass window was installed to protect the silk and satin against the sunshine and mildew and keep out wind and rain. The Luo Family Silk Store is the building in the late Qing Dynasty. It can be concluded that the glass window was installed in the early years during the Republic of China after Luo Yiting purchased this ancient mansion. (*Fuzhou Evening's Newspaper*, 2019)

In the time river, a great many excellent Fukien merchants emerged in Shangxiahang Historical and Cultural Block. The founder of Luo Family Silk Store, Luo Yiting is one of them. Meanwhile, he is also the representative of Jiangxi Group among Fukien merchants. Luo Yiting came from Nancheng County, Jiangxi province. In the early years of Republic of China, Luo Hengrong Silk Store which appeared in the textile street in Shangxiahang was founded by Luo Yiting. The store dealt in wholesaling and selling silk, leno and cotton, etc. Besides, in Fuzhou Road in Shanghai, Luo Yiting established a branch named Yongrong Cloth Shop, purchasing silk and satin from cities such Shanghai, Hangzhou and Suzhou and shipping them to Fuzhou to sell.

"罗恒隆绸缎庄"以信立店，遵循不怕吃亏、唯恐失信的理念，生意也越发红火，在抗日战争爆发前生意一度十分兴隆。1943年，罗翼庭在顺昌县洋口镇病逝，两年后，次子罗祖荫将"罗恒隆绸缎庄"更名为"罗恒隆布号"，1948年8月再次改称"联友布号"。从店名变化就可以看出，罗祖荫所关心的已然不仅是家族企业的发展，而是期望全国人民能够团结起来。

"棉纱大王"罗祖荫不仅生意场上应对自如，还心系教育事业与国家发展，是一个有担当的生意人。他曾捐资参与建设下杭路的"福州市私立南郡小学"（福州市下杭小学的前身），并持续捐建福州市"福商学校"（福州四中前身）直到1949年。抗美援朝期间，罗祖荫更是积极响应号召，主动参与福州市工商联发起的"福州市工商联工商界捐二架飞机"的活动并捐资。由于卓越的贡献，1956年他被任命为新成立的"福州市公私合营荣华棉布商店"的副主任，此后又当选为台江区人大代表、福州市政协委员及福州市工商联执委。他的贤内助王任华任职福州市工商联家属委员会副主任，出众的工作能力让她多次当选福州市人大代表，1956年更是代表福州市工商联家委会进京参加"全国工商联家属委员会代表大会"，有幸受到毛主席等国家领导人的接见。罗翼庭、罗祖荫父子两代创造了商界传奇，罗祖荫夫妇更是为社会做出了巨大贡献。

2013年1月，作为上下杭商号建筑群的一部分，罗氏绸布庄被列为第八批省级文物保护单位。经修缮保护，古厝重焕光彩，现已改造成福州市非物质文化遗产展示馆，隶属福州市文化馆（福州市非物质文化遗产保护中心），传扬历史文化。

福州市非物质文化遗产展示馆是一处公益性非遗展示场所，于2021年元旦揭牌。仅门楼上的匾额就和三项福州非遗有关——脱胎漆器髹饰技艺、福州金箔、茉莉花茶。馆内更是展示了诸多福州传统文化瑰宝。福州市非物质文化遗产展示馆内共有展品300余件，使用全息投影等新技术，打造出别具一格的沉浸式展览空间。这里游客如织，来此参观的民众都流连忘返。罗氏绸布庄这座上下杭的大宅院，历经百年变迁，"前世今生"都令人惊叹。而今，它风貌不改，功用却得到升华，展现了闽都文化的今日与昔时。罗氏后人罗家驹重返古厝，心情激动。修缮能够做到"修旧如旧"，保留了古厝的风貌，也让更多人欣赏到它的美。罗氏绸缎庄，正以福州市非遗展示馆的面貌开启新征程，诉说新传奇。

The owner of Luo Hengrong Silk and Satin Store holds the notion that honesty is the fist policy, so the business was more and more flourishing. Before the anti-Japanese war, the store was prosperous. In 1943, Luo Yiting passed away in Yangkou Town, Zhunchang County. Two years later, his second son Luo Zuyin changed the name of Luo Hengrong Silk Store into Luo Hengrong Textile Store. In August, 1948, it was changed into Unified Friends Textile Store, which indicates he attached importance not only to the development of his family enterprise, but also hoping Chinese nationwide could unite together.

As a responsible businessman, the king of cotton was not only good at doing business, he also cared about the education cause and nation's development. Not only did he donate money to build Fuzhou Private Nanjun Primary School(the former Xiahang Primary School) in Xiahang Road but also contributed money to the construction of Fuzhou Commercial School(former Fuzhou No. Four High School)successively until 1949. During the War to Resist US Aggression and Aid Korea, Luo Zuyin responded to the call actively. He participated in the campaign which launched by Fuzhou Federation of Industry and Commerce for donations. Due to his remarkable contribution, he was appointed as the deputy director of the newly-founded Fuzhou Ronghua Cotton Store with joint state-private ownership. Later, he was elected deputy to the People's Congress in Taijiang District, the member of Fuzhou CCPPCC and executive member of Fuzhou Federation of Industry and Commerce. His wife, Wang Renhua was appointed the deputy director of the Family Committee of Fuzhou Federation of Industry and Commerce and elected as the deputy to Fuzhou People's Congress because of her outstanding capacity for work. In 1956, she obtained the chance to attend conference of the Family Committee of National Federation of Industry and Commerce and received by national leaders such as Chairman Mao. Luo Yiting and Luo Zuyin worked a commercial wonder and made a great contribution to society.

In January 2013, as a part of " Shangxiahang Commercial Architecture", Luo Family Silk and Satin Store" was announced as the eighth batch of cultural relics under provincial protection. After renovation, the ancient building has taken on a new look and been transformed into a museum of intangible cultural heritage site which is affiliated to Fuzhou Cuttural Center(Fuzhou Preservation Center of Intangible Cultural Heritage).

Currently, the museum is a commonweal intangible cultural heritage exhibition site, which was open on the New Year's Day in 2021. The pique on the arch has connection with three Fuzhou intangible cultural heritage, including lacquering art of the bodiless lacquerware, Fuzhou gold foil and Jasmine Tea. Many a Fuzhou traditional cultural treasures are exhibited. There are more than 300 exhibits. Some new techniques such as holographic projection have been employed to create a unique immersive exhibition space so that visitors flock there and linger on without a thought of leaving.

Luo Family Silk and Satin Store boasts a hundred years of vicissitude and its past and present are really amazing. Today, the ancient building's style remains unchanged but the function is sublimated, and it presents the past and present of Fuzhou culture. Luo Jiaju, the posterity of Luo Family was excited after he returned to the old building. The renovation retains the original style of the old mansion and helps more people to appreciate its beauty. Luo Family Silk and Satin Store, Fuzhou Intangible Cultural Heritage Museum has started a new journey and relates a new legend.

罗氏一族由布业批发发迹，经两代人宵衣旰食，成就了一位"棉纱大王"。罗祖荫人如其名，不仅自己是"人生赢家"，还为福州的发展做出了不可磨灭的贡献，今天众多学子仍在享受他带来的福荫。位卑不敢忘忧国，罗祖荫不仅是纺织业的大王，更将永远成为商人的楷模。罗氏绸缎庄承载了一代人的记忆，而今改头换面，以福州市非遗展示馆的身份向世人讲述这些年的风雨沧桑。斯人已远，罗氏永续。

◎ 桥梁凌波：三通桥

名城福州的建筑文化是辉煌的，其中桥梁谱写了极具特色、极为精彩的一章。不少文人墨客都留下过咏桥的名句。唐宋八大家之一的曾巩在福州担任过知州，他写过一首诗《夜出过利涉门》，传神地描摹了安泰河畔的独特风情。陆游也写过一首名为《度浮桥至南台》的诗，其中，"浮渡桥"指的便是福州人所说的旧大桥（万寿桥与江南桥）。福州城内多河，城外郊县有山川溪涧。福州盆地是由闽江冲积而成的，有许多河、池、港湾，都需要借助桥梁来解决交通问题，所以福州多桥。南屿、上街一带有古桥百座以上（曾意丹，2019：25–26）。

Luo family made a fortune by dealing in textile retailing business. After two generations hard work, Luo Zuyin was reputed as the "King of Cotton".He resembled his namesake. He has become a "winner in life" and made immortal contributions to the development of Fuzhou. Numerous students are still enjoying his benevolence. Even in the low social status, he was concerned about the nation in his lifetime. Luo Zuyin is not only the king in textile industry, but also the model of merchants. Luo Family Silk Store carries a generation's memory. At present, it has been converted in to a museum of intangible cultural heritage, telling its ups and downs to the visitors. Although the King of Cotton passed away, his spirit will be eternal.

◎ **The Bridge over the River: The Santong Bridge**

Architectural culture is splendid and the bridge is a unique and wonderful chapter. Quite a few men of letters wrote famous poems about the bridge. Zeng Gong, one of the Eight Great Writers of the Tang and Song Dynasties, was once appointed as a prefectural magistrate/ a Magistrate of prefecture in Fuzhou. He wrote a poem entitled "Crossing the Lishe Door at Night" in which vividly portrayed the unique scenery on the bank of Antai River. In Lu You's poem "Crossing the Fu Bridge to Nantai Island", the Fu Bridge refers to the old bridge(Longevity Bridge and Jiangnan Bridge). There are a great many rivers in Fuzhou City and streams in the mountains in the countryside. Since the Fuzhou Basin is coursed by Minjiang River, there are a good many rivers, ponds and harbors which needs bridges for transportation. More than one hundred ancient bridges in Nanyu and Shangjie (Zeng Yidan, 2019: 25 - 26).

　　上下杭的正门牌坊旁边、三捷河古河道上矗立着一座斑驳古桥——三通古桥，它静静地注视着上下杭这片土地上的沧海桑田变迁。三通桥原位于福州市台江区中亭街以西的小河上，曾是福州一景。自古以来，周围居民的饮用水都取自桥下的河水。三通桥始建于清嘉庆十一年（1806年），即丙寅年间，距今已有二百多年的历史。这是一座石构拱桥，二墩三孔，不等跨。桥墩为船形，造型古朴，颇具气势，外观沉稳结实。该桥全长36.7米，宽3.1米，跨长30米，桥梁石板上有"嘉庆丙寅年仲秋吉旦造"题刻。三通桥并非指桥通三方，而是指福州城内的三条小河均流经此桥。三通桥往东通小桥（达道河），往西通三保（三捷河），往南通新桥仔（新桥仔河）。河流、水位未改变之前，三条小河同时在桥下涨潮、退潮的奇观令人拍手叫绝。古河道自唐以来就是福州的重要航运通道，历史上这一带就是交通便捷、物流通畅的地方。三通桥斑驳的身躯见证了上下杭从兴盛到衰落再到复兴的过程。两百多年前，三坊七巷是福州钟鸣鼎食之地，上下杭则是福州繁华汇聚之所。当时，贯通上下杭的古河道是福州重要的航运通道之一，放眼看去，三通桥下百舸争流、桥上行旅络绎，热闹非凡（佚名，2020b）。如今福州市人民政府立的石碑上刻着："保护范围：桥两端五十米及两岸河床"。这座历尽沧桑的老桥见证了上下杭的繁华、落寂与复兴。岁月荏苒，尽管老桥历经劫难，但在人民与政府的关心下已然离开原地，劫后余生，它依然默默地横卧在三捷河古河道上，敞开博大的胸怀接纳着如织的游人与暖心的市民。

三通桥
The Santong Bridge

Near the memorial archway of the front gate, a mottled ancient bridge ancienst santong Bridge stands over ancient river course of Sanjie River, focusing on the ups and downs of this land. Originally, as a scenic spot, Santong Bridge was over the river in the south of Zhongting Street in Taijiang District in Fuzhou. From the ancient times, the resident's drinking water comes from the river under the bridge. Boasting over 200 years' history, the bridge was built in the 11th year during the Jiaqing Reign in Qing Dynasty(1806 A.D.), Bingyin Year. This is an arch bridge made of stone, with two piers and three bridge openings. The piers are boat-shaped, classic, imposing, steady and sturdy. This is a stone arch bridge which consists of two piers and three boat-shaped opening bridges. The bridge is simple, sophisticated, stable in appearance. It is 36.7 meters long, 3.1 meters wide and 30 meters long in span. There are inscriptions which read, "Built in the auspicious morning on Mid-autumn Festival in Bingyin Year in Jiaqing Reign". The name of the Santong Bridge doesn't mean the people who cross the bridge can go to three directions. Santong indicates that three rivers in Fuzhou City flow under this bridge. The bridge can connect Datao River, Sanjie River and Xinqiaozai River. Before the river course and water level remained unchanged, the scenery of flood tide and ebb tide is marvelous. The old river course has been Fuzhou's leading shipping route Since the Tang Dynasty. Historically, transportation was convenient and logistics were smooth in this area. Beneath the bridge, countless boats sailed; pedestrians went to and fro in constant streams on the bridge. His mottled body witnessed the process of ups and downs and rejuvenation of Shangxiahang Block. Over 200 years ago, Three Lanes and Seven Alleys was once affluent and Shangxiahang was prosperous. In those days, the ancient river course which was penetrated by Shangxiahang is one of the paramount river lines in Fuzhou. Beneath the bridge, countless boats sailed; travelers came and went in an endless stream on the bridge, which was extraordinarily bustling(Anonymous, 2020b). Inscriptions on the tablet erected by Fuzhou Government read, " Protective range: 50 meters around the two ends and the riverbed on both sides". This long-tested old bridge witnessed the prosperity, loneliness and rejuvenation. How time flies. Although the old bridge suffered a lot, with the people and government's concern, it has left its original home and come back to life. He still stands over the old course of Santong Bridge, embracing streams of visitors and warm-hearted citizens.

涨潮时，三条小河的潮水汇聚到桥前，在三通桥北侧圣君殿（即张真君祖殿）前形成"河水两头涨"的独特汇潮景观。这也是福州谚语"圣君殿水两头涨，涌出黄金滚滚来"的由来，迎合了商人"财源滚滚"的吉利口彩。郊边货船竞相从这条水道入城，三通桥一带甚是繁忙。桥上人影绰动，栏作椅来阶作床。以前，桥头常有老艺人搭台讲福州评话，真可谓是：桥头搭台讲书场，桥上听书人如山。说到刀光剑影处，唯有桥下水潺潺（福州新闻网，2021a）。走过上下杭历史文化街区，古老的三通桥静静地立于绿荫之下。当我们缓缓踏上石桥，就会发现脚下的青石经过岁月的雨打风吹变得颇为光滑圆润。这古老而年轻的石桥仿佛在吟咏着如歌的岁月。试想，百年前这一带曾是商贾云集之地，多少腰缠万贯的巨贾曾行走于此，挖到人生的第一桶金，直至走上人生的巅峰；又有多少顾客光临这些鳞次栉比的商铺，悠然挑选心仪之物……

1992年，三通桥被公布为市级文物保护单位。然而，自从桥附近的中亭街地块进行房地产开发后，这里的历史风貌被彻底改变了。2000年，这处存在了近二百年的人文景观却在一夜之间被无情地毁灭。在"有关部门"的协调下，2004年，决定由该开发商承担修复三通桥的所有费用，按照原样、原材料重新修建。但此时，两条古河道已被填埋，仅存一条河，且东头三通桥原址的河道已被覆盖为涵洞，无法按原址、原貌修复古桥，原本是东西走向的桥却成了南北走向，且离开原址10米开外。又由于中亭街的新建筑已紧贴三通桥，达道河东段河道也已成为暗沟，三通桥被人为造成一座无水的旱桥（佚名，2015）。无奈之下，有关部门不得不将三通桥转向70度并位移47米，桥呈南北走向，架设于"水部尚书"陈文龙庙南侧的河道之上。现在，虽然当年的"市级文物保护单位"的石碑犹在，但旁边耸立的却是高楼大厦，三通古桥的历史环境早已被彻底改变。三通桥事件还直接影响了之后的万寿头陀寺的拆迁安置工作。

2004年底，对三通桥进行修复重建。修复后的三通桥采用原有的石构件，保留了原貌，保持原状向南扭转、移位，与移建的陈文龙尚书庙毗邻呼应。鉴于三捷河河道较窄，二墩三孔无法安放，有关部门还拓宽了河道，拆迁了周边的居民区。而迁建后的三通桥作为上下杭的"门面担当"，也成为网红打卡点。

桥身历经风雨沧桑，苔痕漶漫；桥下是静静流淌着的三捷河，河上有福船络绎穿过。如今，随着上下杭历史文化街区的重建，三通桥也带着过去的历史继续讲述着迈向未来的故事（福州新闻网，2021a）。

When the tide rises, three rivers gather in front of the bridge. In front of Sacred Temple of Zhang Zhenjun, the northern part of Santong Bridge, people would enjoy the unique scenery that "The two ends of the river tide rises". This is also the origin of the Fuzhou proverb which goes, "When the tide of two ends of the river near Shengjun Temple rise, treasure keeps rolling in."whose connotation caters to merchants' auspicious blessing speech that the source of wealth is billowing. The freighter from the suburbs and the neighboring counties sailed to the city from this water course. And the area around the bridge was a hectic traffic artery. The bridge railing is used as a chair and the step is used as a bed. In the past, in the bridgehead veteran folk artists often set up a stage, performing Fuzhou storytelling. It can be said: on the stage in the bridgehead, the audience was packed like sardines on the bridge. When the artist talked about glittering swords in the battlefield, we only heard the running water murmur under the bridge (Fuzhou News Website, 2021a). As we cross the Cultural and Historical Block in Shangxiahang, the old Santong Bridge still lies under the shade of trees, calm and silent. Stepping on the stone bridge slowly, we will find that the stone has become smooth and mellow. It looks as if this ancient and young stone bridge was singing a melodious song of passing years. Suppose hundreds of years ago, numerous businessmen gathered here and countless rich merchants frequented here. Some of them made great fortune and reached their life summit. Suppose customers like wave went to row upon row shops, picking up their favorite goods at will....

In 1992, Santong Bridge was announced as a cultural site under municipal protection. However, the scenery was destroyed cruelly overnight. With reconciliation from concerned department, in 2004, it was decided that the real estate developer bear the restoration cost with the original material according to the original appearance. However, at that time, with two ancient river courses had been covered and transformed into culverts, only one river still exists. Hence, the ancient bridge couldn't be restored to the original appearance at the original site. The Westeastern bridge has become the Northsouth one. It is not only moved 10 meters away from the initial site but also changed its direction. Since the new architecture in Zhongting Street is adjacent to Santong Bridge and the north river course becomes the hidden drain. Therefore, Santong Bridge has become a bridge without water (Anonymous, 2015). The concerned department had to have the bridge turn 70 angle and moved 47 meters and made it face the Northsouth direction. It stands over the river course to the south of the "prime minister of water resources", Chen Wenlong's Temple. Nowadays, although the stone tablet which reads "The cultural site under the municipal protection" exists, the historic environment has been undermined completely. The Santong Bridge incident influenced the demolition and resettlement of the Longevity Buddhist Temple later on.

At the end of 2004, Santong Bridge was renovated and reconstructed. The newly-renovated bridge made of the original stone construction parts and retairs the initial appearance, turning and moving towards the south. It is across the Chen Wenlong Temple near the bank. Since the Sanjie River is narrow, the concerned department widened the river and demolished the neighboring residential area. Today, the Santong Bridge is a resort.

The bridge has experienced hardships/yeas' of trials and vicissitudes, with the rampant moss trace scattering; under the bridge quietly flows the Sanjie River; over the bridge, the Fu Boat navigates slowly. Nowadays, with the reconstruction of the Shangxiahang Cultural and Historical Block, the Santong Bridge which boasts a long history, tells a story which is oriented toward the future (Fuzhou News Website, 2021a).

福州
古曆

第十五章

城南旧事　藤山余韵

Chapter Fifteen

The Old Memories of the Southern District of Cangshan

◎ 洋务旧梦：法国领事馆旧址、美国领事馆旧址

法国领事馆旧址

从烟台山著名景观石厝教堂漫步至乐群路23号，便来到法国领事馆旧址（Former site of the French Consulate）。站在阶下、廊前感受时光划过的痕迹，我们仍可以从如今的静穆中窥见一些曾经的喧嚣。

这座三层（含一层地下室）砖木结构的券廊式建筑始建于1882年，面积为1603.2平方米。主楼正面朝南，南北入口处均带有门楼，面阔七间，进深六间。外廊多采用拱券结构，少部分采用平梁结构。因圆弧状外形，拱券具有良好的承重作用，看上去也很美观。

法国领事馆是一座砖砌小楼，从外观来看，外立面为典型的殖民式平面，四面均有外廊，各房间砌有英式壁炉。站在外墙从远处看该建筑，还能望见一根砖砌深红色的烟囱。整座建筑表面用砂浆粉刷，中央开间为厅堂，底层南、北向均有门廊，砖柱，平顶，上为露台，台阶作八字，台阶向上通往门廊。

清光绪七年（1881年），法领事布得兰（Cte.de Pourtalè-Gorgier）委托多明我会李宏治主教在天安铺租地，次年开工建设，建设完毕便作为法国驻福州领事馆办公楼使用。民国7年到18年（1918—1929年）的某段时间美孚洋行租用了该建筑，但具体时间不详。美孚洋行很早就进入福州，并在番船浦设有行屋、仓库等。美孚洋行于光绪三十四年（1908年）开始在仓前山设立办公室。另据有关资料，民国18年（1929年）12月福建美丰银行倒闭后，其建筑（原同珍洋行）曾为美孚洋行租用。抗战胜利后，中华民国救灾总署于民国35年（1946年）3月到10月成立期间也曾短暂借用此楼。之后，婴德小修院、仓山区环卫所等亦借用过此楼。直到1981年，因落实宗教政策，仓前天主堂的产权归还给天主教会，现为教徒租住。

法国旧领事馆门廊
The Porch of the French Consulate

◎ Old Stories of Foreign Affairs: Former Site of the French Consulate and the Former Site of the American Consulate

The Former Site of the French Consulate

Embarking on a leisurely journey from the renowned Shicuo Church, also known as the Stone House Church, perched on Yantai Mountain to No.23 Lequn Road, one soon reaches the Former Site of the French Consulate. As we stand beneath the porch's steps, enveloped in today's quietude, the echoes of time reverberate, offering glimpses into the vibrant past.

This three-story architecture, encompassing a basement, Showcases a colonial corridor-style design. Constructed in 1882, this 1603.2 square meter brick and wood structure stands as a testament to its era. The primary facade of the building gazes southward, boasting gatehouses at both the north and south entrances, spreading seven rooms wide and six rooms deep. Most of the outer corridors feature the arch structure, while a select few adhere to the flat beam design, harmonizing both structural integrity and decorative allure.

The consulate itself, though modest in size, embodies the quintessential colonial architectural style. A striking feature is the encompassing verandas, and each room within is adorned with an English-style fireplace. Gazing from the exterior, one can still discern the presence of a dark red brick chimney, rising gracefully against the painted mortar surface. At the heart of the building lies the main hall, with porches gracing the ground floor in both the southern and northern directions. Flat roofs, supported by sturdy brick columns, cap these porches, with steps gracefully leading to the entrance from either side, forming the shape of the Chinese character of "eight".

In the seventh year of the Guangxu period during the Qing Dynasty, in 1881, French Consul Cte. de Pourtalè-Gorgier entrusted Dominican Bishop Li Hongzhi to rent a plot of land in Tiananpu. Construction commenced the following year, culminating in its use as the French Consulate's office building in Fuzhou. For a period spanning from the seventh year of the Republic of China (1918) to the eighteenth year (1929), the building was leased by the Mobil Firm. The Mobil Firm had established a foothold in Fuzhou early on, setting up firms and warehouses in Fanchuanpu. In the 34th year of the Guangxu period (1908), the Mobil Firm erected an office in Cangqian Mountain. Additional records indicate that following the closure of the Fukien American Oriental Bank in December of the 18th year of the Republic of China (1929) due to bankruptcy, the Mobil Firm temporarily rented the building, formerly occupied by the Tongzhen Firm. After the conclusion of the Anti-Japanese War, during the establishment of the General Administration from March to October in the 35th year of the Republic of China (1946), the Fuzhou Branch of the Chinese National Relief and Rehabilitation Administration also briefly borrowed and utilized this edifice. Subsequently, the Yingde Minor Seminary and Cangshan District Sanitation Institute made use of the building. It was not until 1981, a significant year marked by the implementation of revised religious policies, that the property rights of the Cangqian Catholic Church were formally restored to the Catholic Church. Presently, the building is leased by a community of faithful believers, serving as a testament to its diverse history and enduring significance.

　　而在这其中，在这座建筑里发生的最为著名的事件，莫过于被誉为"20世纪前半叶法国文坛杰出人物"的法国文豪、诗人、剧作家及外交官保罗·克洛代尔（Paul Claudel，1868—1955年，曾用中国名字"高乐待"）曾在此居住、办公。先后任法国驻福州副领事、领事的他，1898年至1905年于此度过了七年悠悠岁月。其影响一代法国人的散文诗集《认识东方》中的半数作品亦诞生于此。他在《认识东方》中写道："现在天色已晚；在我脚下，一点灯光冲破了夜晚和浓雾，我走过那条熟路，钻进了苍郁的松树浓荫。我到达我的住所……"读到此段，历史和现实重叠，脚下踏过的路也许就是当年保罗走过的"那条熟路"，而依旧郁郁葱葱的树木还在摇曳，或许它们也曾用荫庇带给保罗一抹清凉的慰藉。可以说，福州是他心目中的理想家园，在他的日记中更是多次以"家"称呼这里。而这座被他称颂有着"玫瑰和蜜的颜色"的城市，带给他太多难忘的回忆和灵感。保罗的作品让世人对福州这座城、烟台山这座山有了更多的了解，亦可以说是这城、这山滋养了他。时光流转，更迭的是这片土地上的人和事，而不变的是安静的岁月随着每天的日升月落日复一日地消逝，从那松树叶的缝隙里溜走。

　　而今再踏上覆有青苔及小草的石阶，昔日的浮华早已化为尘埃散落在各处。法国领事馆早已失去它原本的功用，既不是领事馆，也不是各机构的驻地。在被纳入烟台山街区改造后，这处让保罗·克洛代尔魂牵梦萦的住所，作为历经时代更迭依旧留存的古厝，就这样静静掩在烟台山领事馆旧址的一隅，留待一代又一代的人们驻足欣赏，聆听与书写它的故事。

美国领事馆旧址

　　沿着烟台山一路漫游，踏上爱国路，不久便会看到早期美国领事馆旧址。这座建筑经过复原和重修，呈现在世人面前的已是崭新的面貌。不过，因"修旧如旧"的复原原则，在推开那扇厚重的铁栅栏大门后，如今我们依旧能从细微处触摸到它被虚掩着的前世今生。

　　早期美国领事馆（Former Site of the early U.S. Consulate）位于爱国路2号，坐落于烟台山西侧，为仓山区第五批区级文物保护单位。此地环境幽静，建筑主体被绿植所环绕，只有不时经过的行人才能稍微打破这和谐的宁静。

Among the myriad tales etched within the walls of this edifice, one particularly stands out—the narrative of Paul Claudel (1868-1955, known in Chinese as "Gao Ledai"), the eminent French writer, poet, playwright, and diplomat, who once called this place home. Paul Claudel held the positions of vice-consul and consul of France in Fuzhou, residing within these very walls for a span of seven significant years, from 1898 to 1905. It was within these chambers that he penned a substantial portion of his prose and poetry collection, Connaissance de l'est, which wielded profound influence over a generation of French readers. In this book, Claudel shared poignant reflections: "It was getting late now; under my feet, a dim light broke through the night and the thick fog, and I walked along the familiar road and got into the shade of the lush pine trees. I arrived at my abode." As we read these words, we cannot help but sense the convergence of history and the present moment. The very road beneath our feet might well mirror the "familiar road" that Claudel once traversed, while the gentle sway of the verdant trees must have bestowed upon him a soothing, cool respite in their shade. Without a doubt, Fuzhou held a special place in his heart, as evidenced by his repeated mentions of the city as "home" in his diary, reaffirming the sentiment that Fuzhou was his cherished abode. This city, which he fondly described as being bathed in "the hues of roses and honey," evoked an abundance of memories and inspirations within him. Paul's works spurred extensive historical research on Fuzhou and Yantai Mountain, contributing to a deeper understanding of these places worldwide. Concurrently, both the city and Yantai Mountain served as a wellspring of nourishment for his creativity. As time has passed, despite the changing faces and dynamics of the locale, a constant remains—the silent, unceasing flow of time as the sun rises and sets each day, slipping through the gaps in the leaves of the flourishing pine trees.

Now, the stone steps lie concealed under layers of moss and grass, the former glory reduced to scattered remnants of dust. The present location of the former French consulate has relinquished its initial purpose; it no longer operates as a consulate or any other institution. Having been integrated into the Yantai Mountain restoration project, this ancient dwelling that once captivated Paul Claudel and weathered the sands of time now peacefully nestles in the corner of the former Yantai Mountain Consulate complex. Here, visitors can pause to appreciate its unique allure and listen to the whispers of its storied past, finding inspiration to retell its narrative.

The Former Site of the American Consulate

Wandering along Aiguo Road and ascending Yantai Mountain, one can swiftly reach the Former Site of the American Consulate. The structure has undergone meticulous restoration and renovation, unveiling a fresh visage to the world. Yet, adhering to the restoration principle of preserving the historical character, as one pushes open the gate secured by a weighty iron fence, remnants of the bygone era still imbue the air, offering a glimpse into the past.

Situated at No. 2 Aiguo Road, on the western flank of Yantai Mountain, lies the Former Site of the U.S. Consulate, also known as the early U.S. consulate. This historical site is proudly designated as one of the "fifth batch of district-level cultural relic protection units in Cangshan District." Nestled amidst a serene locale, the surroundings are adorned with lush greenery, enhancing the peaceful ambiance. Occasionally, the tranquil atmosphere is gently interrupted by the passing footsteps of pedestrians, harmoniously blending with the setting.

修缮后的早期美国领事馆，主体建筑外观为白色，在周围植被的衬托下显得更为大气庄严。它始建于1863年，面积为899.3平方米，主体立面运用折中主义（eclecticism）手法，融合了西方古典主义、巴洛克等多种建筑风格。折中主义是形而上学思维方式的一种表现形式，而在建筑上用该表现手法则是把各种不同的风格杂糅在一起，呈现出一种异域感十足的华丽之美。这是目前福州保存较为完好的近现代历史建筑之一，是在百年烟台山上先后设立的17国领事馆中最具代表性的西式建筑之一，在烟台山近代建筑群中更是独领风骚。

早期美国领事馆是典型的外廊式建筑，三层（含地下室）砖木结构，四面外廊，中央为过厅（即玄关，又称门厅，是从入门处到正厅之间的一段转折空间），左右各有四个房间，以内廊沟通。从正面来看，整体建筑呈规整的长方体造型，线条流畅平直。二层带有一个露台，能俯瞰周边景色。与烟台山上其他早期外廊式建筑相似，早期美国领事馆总体上也呈现维多利亚风格，并带有新古典主义和文艺复兴的样式细节。

回溯历史，该地最早为英商J·Forster&Co.洋行（天裕洋行）所有。天裕洋行经营茶叶生意，此地便作为经营地及住宅使用。后几经易主，先后为天祥洋行、怡和洋行、邮政部门等所有。1891—1928年该地租借给美国，作为美国驻福州领事馆早期办公场所，使用时间长达三十余年。

第一次鸦片战争后，1842年中英《南京条约》签订，福州被定为五个通商口岸之一，西方各国便先后于此设立领事馆，中外交往也愈发增多。在小小的福州市仓山区，这个岛屿面积不过1平方公里的区域内，先后有17个国家设立领事馆。

漫步于此，总能感受到来自异域文化的碰撞和中西合璧的氛围。现如今早期美国领事馆作为烟台山历史风貌区第一座经修缮开放的历史建筑，以烟台山历史博物馆的面貌展示在大家面前。回溯以往，它曾具有多种身份，承载了福州近代历史的变迁；再看如今，历史的大门已对众人敞开，过往与现今的界限已不再分明。推开厚重的大门，每个人都能徜徉在百年洋房里并体味它的过往，站在当世回看往昔。

The meticulously restored main building of the early US consulate graces the landscape, adorned in a resplendent white hue, standing in stark contrast to the lush green embrace of its surroundings. Erected in 1863, this architecture spans an area of 899.3 square meters. The main facade is a splendid testament to eclecticism, a style that seamlessly weaves together Western classicism, Baroque, colonial,and various architectural influences. Eclecticism serves as an embodiment of metaphysical thought, and in the case of the early US consulate, it manifests as an amalgamation of diverse styles, fashioning an exotic and opulent beauty. This edifice ranks among the relatively well-preserved modern historical buildings in Fuzhou and stands as an epitome of Western-style architecture among the consulates of 17 countries that successively dotted the Yantai Mountain over a century. It stands out prominently amidst the modern constructions on Yantai Mountain.

This early American consulate is a quintessential colonial-style veranda building, characterized by its three-story structure, including the basement, with verandas enveloping all four sides. At its core lies the central hall, a grand space connecting four rooms on each side through a corridor. When viewed from the front, the building presents a regular cuboid shape, characterized by sleek, unembellished lines. The second floor treats onlookers to a charming terrace offering sweeping views of the surrounding landscape. Much like its counterparts, the early American consulate predominantly boasts Victorian influences with nuanced details of neoclassical and Renaissance aesthetics.

Exploring its historical tapestry, this building's initial ownership and use were entrusted to J. Forster & Co. (Tianyu Foreign Firm), a prominent tea business firm of British origin. In succession, it was possessed by Intertek Firm, Jardine Firm, and the postal department, with ownership changing hands several times. Notably, for over three decades, spanning from 1891 to 1928, this property was leased to the United States, serving as the inaugural office space for the U.S. Consulate in Fuzhou.

The roots of this historical significance trace back to the signing of the Sino-British Treaty of Nanjing in 1842 during the First Opium War, designating Fuzhou as one of the five trading ports. This designation spurred a wave of Western countries to establish consulates in the city, fostering increased Sino-foreign exchanges. Within the confines of the small island of Cangshan District, Fuzhou City, encompassing an area of less than one square kilometer, 17 countries consecutively established consulates.

As you wander through these grounds, the interplay of foreign and Chinese cultures is palpable—sometimes in collision, and at other times, in harmony. Today, the initial American consulate, painstakingly restored and unveiled as the first historical edifice accessible to the public within the Yantai Mountain Historical Scenic Area, proudly stands as the Yantai Mountain History Museum in Fuzhou. Tracing back the annals of time, we witness the diverse roles the early American consulates played, intricately interwoven with the metamorphoses of Fuzhou's modern history. Now,history's portal stands wide open, inviting all to traverse its threshold, blurring the lines between bygone eras and the present. With a resolute push against the weighty door, one can instantly journey through this century-old mansion, embracing both its storied past and its vibrant present.

◎ 西式美宅：以园、梦园、可园、拓庐、忠庐

以园、梦园

穿过车水马龙的上三路，挂有"马厂街"三个字的拱门映入眼帘。这里曾是朱榨笔下的"世外桃源"，也是新贵云集的"洋界"。经过岁月的洗礼，曾经的辉煌如今掩藏于闹市中。马厂街是条不太长也不太宽的街巷，长约450米，最窄处不足3米，但它却承载了一代又一代老仓山人的生活与记忆。而在这其中的老洋房也蕴含了颇多滋味，值得人细细品读。

一头扎进康山里，路上经过几间小小的咖啡店，走不了几步便来到老洋房群里的第一站——以园。

这座位于马厂街支巷康山里12号的建筑建于1920—1930年间，具体时间不详。其为叶氏家族私宅，原主人叶嘉亨曾任三都澳福海关关长，为牧师叶颂林之子、梦园主人叶见元之弟。叶嘉亨以《圣经·创世纪》中"亚伯拉罕以子奉献神"的典故将宅子命名为"以园"。

该园占地面积为390平方米，主体建筑为二层砖木结构，长23米、宽19米、高7.6米，是具有朴素英式风格的近代建筑。砖木结构乃房屋的一种建筑结构，是指建筑物中竖向承重的墙、柱等用砌块砌筑，楼板、屋架等采用木结构。这样的结构使得材料易于准备，费用相对较低，建造起来也较为容易。以园的装饰极为简单，门窗均不采用发券，用木百叶门窗。顶部开有数个老虎窗，这是其一大特色。老虎窗是一种开在屋顶的天窗，也就是在斜屋面上凸出的窗，利于房屋采光和通风。以园带有院落，门楼上有"以园"匾额。

梦园大门
The Main Entrance of Meng Yuan

距以园不远有座梦园，位于马厂街支巷康山里13号。该建筑为福州近代著名华侨领袖叶见元（叶慰亨）先生的故居，建于1926年。叶见元出身于基督教世家，与孙中山先生私交很深。

◎ **Western-Style Old houses: Yi Yuan, Meng Yuan, Ke Yuan, Tuo Lu, Zhong Lu**

The Yi Yuan and the Meng Yuan

As we traverse the bustling Shangsan Road, our eyes are drawn to an arch overhead proudly displaying three Chinese characters — "Machang Street". This very place once embodied the poetic imagery of a "Xanadu" as described by Zhu Gao, a renowned Song Dynasty poet. It also served as a vibrant hub for the emerging elite — a "foreign world" where new forces converged. Despite the relentless march of time, remnants of its former grandeur still echo through the lively neighborhood today. Machang Street is a thoroughfare neither extensive nor broad, spanning approximately 450 meters in length and less than 3 meters in width at its narrowest points. Yet, within this limited expanse, it cradles the essence of countless lives and preserves the collective memories of generations of Cangshan's inhabitants. The antiquated dwellings concealed along its path hold stories steeped in history, awaiting our appreciation.

Turning into Kangshan Alley and passing by quaint coffee shops along the way, we soon reach our first destination within the old house cluster — the Yi Yuan, or the Yi Yuan.

Yi Yuan is situated at No. 12, Kangshan Alley, a branch lane of Machang Street. Its construction dates back to the period between 1920 and 1930, though the precise date remains elusive. This residence belonged to the Ye family, with Ye Jiaheng, the son of Pastor Ye Songlin and younger brother of Ye Jianyuan (owner of Meng Yuan, the Meng Yuan), serving as its original proprietor. Ye Jiaheng, who once held the position of head at Sandu Aofu Customs, named the estate "Yi Yuan" about the biblical allusion of "Abraham consecrated God with his son" found in the Book of Genesis. The choice of "Yi" stems from its meaning of "with" in Chinese.

Yi Yuan encompasses an area of 390 square meters and boasts a two-story brick and wood structure. It stretches 23 meters in length, 19 meters in width, and stands at a height of 7.6 meters. The primary house embodies a modern design with a simple English style. The construction blends vertical load-bearing walls and columns crafted from bricks or blocks, while the floors and roof trusses are constructed using wood. This combination allows for convenient acquisition of building materials, cost-effectiveness, and relatively straightforward construction processes. The architectural embellishments are minimal, characterized by non-arched doors and windows adorned with wooden shutters. One notable feature is the presence of dormer windows atop the structure. Dormer windows, and protruding skylights on the roof, serve the purpose of both illumination and ventilation. Yi Yuan is endowed with a charming courtyard, and the gatehouse still proudly bears a plaque displaying the name "Yi Yuan."

Not far from Yi Yuan lies Meng Yuan, the Meng Yuan, situated at No. 13, Kangshan Alley, a branch lane stemming from Machang Street. Erected in 1926, this splendid garden was once the abode of Mr. Ye Jianyuan (Ye Weiheng), a prominent overseas Chinese leader in modern Fuzhou. Hailing from a devout Christian family, Ye Jianyuan shared a deep personal bond with Sun Yat-sen, an important figure in Chinese history.

该园占地面积221平方米，由两座建筑组成。正座为两层带地下室的英式建筑，高8.8米，面阔三间。西侧为加建的三层斜角碉楼，高11.8米，小青瓦双坡顶，坡度极缓。小青瓦是一种弧形瓦，呈青灰色，故名小青瓦。院落正门有"梦园"匾额，后门有"梦园别径"匾额，字迹清晰可辨。因年代久远，匾额周围已被覆盖上厚厚一层青苔，但仍掩不住这幢拥有百年历史的老洋房的魅力。

此地环境清幽，院内有葱郁树木，映衬着红砖蓝窗，显得尤为美丽。历经百年岁月销蚀，高大的楼体并未遭到极大的毁损。

梦园不仅是叶见元的私宅，还是多次会议的举办地。

民国17年（1928年）叶见元任福建侨务委员会福州办事处主任，7月1日，福建省侨务委员会旅省名誉咨议会第一次讨论会就在梦园举行，此后又有多次民国福建侨务、政务系统会议相继在此举行。

据叶嘉亨之女、叶华娇回忆：

> 忘记了何年何月，我父亲买了一块很大的地，在仓前山对湖。听母亲说，是海关每七年有一年的红利，就利用这项款买了地。那时恰逢父亲的大哥（伯父）一家从南洋迁回福州，住在我家明月山馆。他见到我父亲所买的地，则想要之。后来我父亲分一半地给他，因此大家就起屋，伯父的屋名叫"梦园"，我父亲的屋名叫"以园"，意思就是以奉献与神。正如神试验亚伯拉罕，要他独生儿子以撒献为燔祭（《创世记》第22章），这是我父亲解释他之所以取此名的原因，我将之永铭于脑海中。我的母亲就是住在以园，直到过世。当屋完成之后，伯父则迁入新屋，祖母和他同住，我们屋因为父亲不在福州，所以全部出租。那时候我仍在毓英中学读初中，大哥、二哥已先后往上海读大学，只剩我一人在伯父家出入。

这段材料不仅说明了"以园"名字的由来，也证明叶氏家族对该房屋拥有所有权，还对"梦园"的所有权也进行了说明。

如今的以园，砌的白墙已经不再如初，覆上绒绒的青苔。门楼上匾额的字迹也已不再清晰。深红色的砖头更是由于日晒雨淋呈现斑斑驳驳的颜色。而在梦园的门口，刷成绿色的木门略有些斑驳，几盆绿植顺着石阶摆放齐整，绿油油的爬山虎顺势而上，长势颇好。

Spanning an area of 221 square meters, the garden encompasses two distinct structures. The primary building showcases a two-story English-style architecture, complete with a basement, standing at a height of 8.8 meters and spanning three rooms in width. Adjacent to it on the west side stands a three-story oblique-angle watchtower, soaring to a height of 11.8 meters. Crowned with a Xiaoqing tile roof, gently sloped, these tiles, known for their blue-gray hue, give the structure a distinctive appearance. Xiaoqing tiles, with their arc-shaped design, contribute to the distinct aesthetic of the building. Emblazoned with the characters "Meng Yuan," a prominent plaque adorns the front door of the courtyard. Similarly, the back door proudly displays a plaque inscribed with "The Path of Meng Yuan." Despite the passage of time, the plaques bear witness to the wear of age, veiled by a verdant layer of moss. Yet, this shroud of antiquity fails to diminish the enduring allure of this nearly century-old abode.

Nestled within a tranquil environment, the garden exudes a distinct beauty accentuated by the verdant trees gracing its courtyard, harmoniously juxtaposed against the backdrop of red brick walls and blue windows. Despite the passage of nearly a century, this towering structure has remarkably withstood the test of time, showing minimal signs of damage or decay.

Meng Yuan not only served as Ye Jianyuan's private residence but also played host to numerous pivotal meetings. In the seventeenth year of the Republic of China (AD 1928), Ye Jianyuan assumed the role of Director at the Fuzhou Office of the Fukien Overseas Chinese Affairs Committee. On July 1st of that year, the inaugural discussion meeting of the Fukien Provincial Overseas Chinese Affairs Committee's honorary council took place within the premises of Meng Yuan. Additionally, various significant meetings involving overseas Chinese affairs and government matters for the Republic of China's Fukien offices were convened in this very location.

Ye Huajiao, Ye Jiaheng's daughter, recalled:

"I can't recall the precise year or month, but I distinctly remember when my father acquired a sizable parcel of land on Duihu Road in Cangqian Mountain. According to my mother, the customs office yielded a dividend every seven years, and my father utilized this to purchase the land. Around that period, my eldest uncle had recently returned to Fuzhou from overseas, residing in our Moon Mountain Pavilion (Mingyue Mountain Pavilion). Intrigued by the land, he expressed his desire to share the ownership. Consequently, my father transferred half of the land's equity to him. The two brothers then proceeded to build houses on the property—my uncle named his residence 'Meng Yuan,' while my father chose 'Yi Yuan,' signifying an offering to God. This naming was inspired by the biblical tale where God tested Abraham by asking him to sacrifice his only son, Isaac (Genesis 22). My father's explanation for the garden's name has left an indelible mark on my memory. My mother spent her entire life at Yi Yuan. Upon completion of the new house, my uncle and grandmother relocated to the 'Meng Yuan.' Meanwhile, our house was leased out as my father was frequently away from Fuzhou. During this period, I was attending Yuying Junior High School in Fuzhou, and both of my elder brothers pursued their studies in Shanghai. As a result, I became the sole family member to visit my uncle intermittently. This account not only clarifies the genesis of the 'Yi Yuan' name but also substantiates the Ye family's rightful ownership of the house, providing supporting evidence for the ownership of the 'Meng Yuan.'"

In the present Yi Yuan, adorned with a gentle blanket of moss, the once pristine white walls have weathered, showcasing a transformation. The characters on the gatehouse plaque have faded over time, no longer as distinct as they once were. The red bricks, aged and seasoned, now exhibit a charming mottled hue. As we approach Meng Yuan, the green wooden door bears a similar weathered appearance, with a row of well-arranged green plants adorning the stone steps and lush ivy gracefully climbing the wall at its side.

这两座老洋房，不论是充满异国风情的整体建筑风格，还是精美的砖瓦细节，都仿佛在为我们讲述在这其间悠悠流转的岁月。我们站在门口往里张望，仿佛仍能看到那些老一辈的居民居住的痕迹和生活的身影，寻一丝过往，品一段人生。

可园

可园紧邻以园和梦园，且建筑风格也较为接近。可园院落呈哑铃形，大门为石库门式，位于外楼前院。走到门口便可见匾额"可园"二字，字迹分明，两边栽种绿植，显得优雅可爱。

可园位于仓山区康山里5号，始建于1928年左右，主体为英式建筑，由两座建筑组成，均为红砖砌筑的三层砖木结构公寓，建筑结构也与以园、梦园接近。其中西楼（内楼）占地540平方米，长27米、宽19.5米，底层有券廊，建筑时间有可能早于1928年。东楼（外楼）占地300平方米，长20米、宽15米，被分为四个公寓单元，每单元一个开间。

可园为钟氏民居，其早期的主人钟景竹为华侨，曾任清末至民国盐务系统官员。可园具有相当浓厚的文化氛围，福州近现代许多著名文化人都曾在可园居住。其中最有名的要数建筑学家、作家林徽因。1928年8月，林徽因回福州探母，曾寓居于此。另据载，福州基督教家庭聚会的创办人，也是福州教会的七位同工之一的王连俊，在可园亦有住处，并曾经在此传道。从可园走出的名人甚多，这也为可园增添了许多人文气息。

可园
Ke Yuan

The architectural style exudes a captivating exotic essence, and the intricate brick and tile details of these two historical residences seem to whisper tales of bygone years. Standing at the threshold and peering within, we catch glimpses of the imprints left by previous generations— their lives, their tales, and the essence of their existence.

The Ke Garden

Ke Yuan, or the Ke Garden, is adjacent to Yi Yuan and Meng Yuan, boasting similar architectural styles. The courtyard of Ke Yuan takes on the shape of a dumbbell, featuring a gate at the front yard designed in the classic Shikumen, or stone gate style. As you approach the entrance, the clear characters of "Ke Yuan" (Ke Garden) grace the plaque, flanked by greenery on both sides, lending an elegant and charming aura to the garden.

Located at No. 5 Kangshan Alley, Cangshan District, Ke Yuan was constructed in 1928. The garden comprises two English-style buildings, standing three stories tall and constructed with a brick and wooden framework. The building structure mirrors that of Yi Yuan and Meng Yuan. The west building (inner building) spans an area of 540 square meters, measuring 27 meters in length and 19.5 meters in width. The ground floor of the west building features an arched-roof gallery, hinting at a potential construction predating 1928. On the other hand, the east building (outer building) encompasses an area of 300 square meters, measuring 20 meters in length and 15 meters in width. This building is divided into four apartment units, each occupying all floors from the ground to the top.

Ke Yuan, presently the residence of the Zhong family, has a notable historical connection. Its previous owner, Zhong Jingzhu, was an overseas Chinese who held a position at the salt affairs office from the end of the Qing Dynasty to the Republic of China era. Reverberating with a rich cultural atmosphere, Ke Yuan holds a significant place in Fuzhou's modern history, having served as a residence for numerous renowned intellectuals. One of the most prominent figures associated with Ke Yuan is Lin Huiyin, a distinguished female architect and writer. In August 1928, she resided in Ke Yuan while visiting her mother in Fuzhou. Another notable inhabitant was Wang Lianjun, the founder of the Fuzhou Christian Family Meeting and one of the seven co-workers of the Fuzhou Church, who both resided and preached at Ke Yuan. The residence has hosted various distinguished personalities, further enriching its cultural significance and humanistic appeal.

伴随着参天古榕投射下来的绿荫，在可园里走一走、逛一逛，抬头看看独具特色的红砖洋房，读一读林徽因留下来的作品，逛可园大可称得上是一趟文化之旅了！

拓庐

从可园出发，再悠悠走上几步便来到拓庐。由此可见，在马厂街漫游，走几步便可遇到老洋房。马厂街的每个转角都承载着历史，诉说着老故事。

拓庐为金景松家族私宅，位于仓山区马厂街4号。门口有一棵葱郁绿植，周围以砖墙遮挡。有两个大门，一个看上去匾额的字迹较为清晰，而另一个大门及匾额则略显陈旧。后者位于坡下，需要沿一道小陡坡步行几步才能走到。

拓庐始建于民国时期，主体建筑为三层砖木结构，具有外廊式风格。占地面积300平方米，层数为两层，长18米、宽17米。一层窗发券。值得一提的是，拓庐的一层外廊采用的是木质仿铁艺工艺，木质仿铸铁拱廊保存完好，在仓山地区并不多见，是研究近现代历史街区风貌的重要载体。

拓庐原主人金文泳曾任职于大东电报局，在原对湖江南金氏茉莉花园旧址建造拓庐。1949年初，金文泳去台湾为儿子举办婚礼，其间因福州解放而滞留台湾。于是拓庐便由他的另一个在福州的儿子金章汉居住，并传承至今。

拓庐是一处能够很好反映近现代历史街区风貌的载体。虽它远不如可园那样具有丰厚的历史文化底蕴，也不像梦园一般拥有一段前尘往事，但作为马厂街老洋房的一部分，其存在本身便已极具价值和意义。

拓庐大门
The Main Entrance to
Tuo Lu

As you stroll along the shaded paths under the sprawling ancient banyan trees within Ke Yuan, you'll find yourself immersed in the ambiance of unique red-brick bungalows, where you can also peruse the literary works left behind by Lin Huiyin. A visit to Ke Yuan is, without a doubt, a cultural journey.

The Tuo House

Upon leaving Ke Yuan, a few steps lead to Tuo Lu, also known as the Tuo House, reaffirming the idea that a casual stroll through Machang Street might unexpectedly unveil an old house at any turn. Indeed, every corner of Machang Street is steeped in history, each with its own compelling story to tell.

Tuo Lu serves as the residence of the Jin Jingsong family and is situated at No. 4 Machang Street, Cangshan District. The entrance is adorned with lush greenery and surrounded by brick walls. The residence features two gates — the first displaying a relatively clear plaque, while the other gate and its corresponding plaque exhibit charming signs of weathering. The latter gate is situated at the base of a slight slope, requiring a few steps down its short descent.

Tuo Lu, constructed during the Republic of China era, represents a modern colonial-style building with verandas. The main structure stands as a two-story brick and wood edifice, covering an area of 300 square meters. It spans 18 meters in length and 17 meters in width, featuring arched windows on the ground floor. Notably, the outer corridor on the first floor imitates the appearance of cast iron using wood — a rare and well-preserved feature in the Cangshan area. This characteristic makes it an excellent subject for studying modern historical architecture.

Jin Wenyong, the original owner of Tuo Lu, was employed at the Dadong Telegraph Bureau. He commissioned the construction of Tuo Lu on the former site of Jin's Jasmine Garden in Duihu. In early 1949, Jin Wenyong traveled to Taiwan to celebrate his son's wedding but ended up staying there after the liberation of Fuzhou. Consequently, Tuo Lu has been occupied by Jin Zhanghan, his other son residing in Fuzhou, up to the present day.

Tuo Lu embodies the shifts and transformations of the area 's modern history, making it an ideal subject for the study of modern historical architecture. Although it may not possess the same rich historical and cultural heritage as Ke Yuan, nor a past as intriguing as Meng Yuan, being a part of the old houses on Machang Street lends it significant value and historical significance.

忠庐

忠庐位于马厂街11号，与拓庐分处道路两侧，遥遥相望。还未走近忠庐，我们便能感知到忠庐与其他几处洋房都大不相同。忠庐没有它们整体红砖的模样，而是整体呈石灰色，院内除了参天大树，更有几丛茂密的竹林笔直地生长。

忠庐是一处极具魅力的院落。远观便能感受到它庄严的气派，近看更是能细细品味那细致的木质窗户、小小的青绿花窗、精巧的建筑布局。

忠庐建造于1932年，占地面积为245平方米，共三层。院落较大，环境宁静清幽，从容淡雅。建筑主体为砖木结构，高9.6米、长22.4米、宽13米。底层带有外廊，用青砖砌筑。山墙有一组对称的烟囱，并挑出三层露台。建筑一层外廊发券，窗均做平过梁。建筑立面除腰线外未做过多装饰，檐口也没有采用福州近代建筑常见的叠涩线脚。由此可见，忠庐是福州市西洋建筑中艺术风格突出的典型，是福州近现代城市建筑发展的重要载体。

忠庐原为曾在"电光刘"家族开办的企业（光禄坊刘家开办的福州电气公司）任会计师的许世光先生建造的私宅。在忠庐西侧原另有一座"省庐"，木构，20世纪90年代已毁。许世光先生的女儿住忠庐，儿子住省庐。且从建立至今，忠庐始终为许氏家族居住。

忠庐外观
The Exterior of Zhong Lu

忠庐也承载了一段又一段历史和名人故事。初有革命志士黄展云子女、福建教育厅厅长黄翼云及女儿等黄家人租住于此，后曾住过毓英女校校长李淑仁、国民党财政专员吴漱真等人，之后又有辛泰银行福州分行入驻于此。最著名的当属"文革"之前，蒋介石和宋美龄的英文秘书吴漱真曾在此居住过十年，这座院落也因此拥有了一层更为神秘和迷人的色彩。20世纪50年代后忠庐被作为公房使用，而到了80年代末许家后人落实华侨政策拿回产权。这栋老宅今由许家后人应荣荣居住打理。

The Zhong House

Zhong Lu, or the Zhong House, situated at No. 11 Machang Street, stands across from Tuo Lu on the opposite side of the road. Observing Zhong Lu from a distance, one can immediately discern its distinction from other foreign-style houses. Unlike the predominant red brick appearance of neighboring houses. Zhong Lu boasts an overall lime-grey hue. The courtyard is adorned with towering trees, and along the high walls, clusters of dense bamboo shoot straight upwards.

Zhong Lu exudes a unique and captivating charm. At a distance, its dignified style is appreciable, and upon closer examination, the intricate green wooden windows reveal their small and delicate craftsmanship, showcasing an exquisite architectural layout.

Zhong Lu, constructed in 1932, spans an area of 245 square meters and encompasses three stories. Nestled in a tranquil environment, it boasts a spacious courtyard, exuding an aura of tranquility and elegance. The primary structure is a brick and wood edifice, standing at a height of 9.6 meters, with dimensions of 22.4 meters in length and 13 meters in width. The ground floor features a veranda crafted with gray bricks, adorned with symmetrical chimneys on the gable, and showcases three levels of terraces on both sides. The outer corridor on the first floor displays an arched structure, while the windows sport flat tops. The facade is relatively modest in ornamentation, with minimal decorative elements, except for the waistline. Unlike common modern Fuzhou buildings, Zhong Lu's cornices lack the typical folded moldings. Clearly, Zhong Lu epitomizes typical Western-style architecture, representing Fuzhou's modern urban architectural development.

Originally built by Mr. Xu Shiguang, the accountant of the family-run enterprise " Dianguang Liu" (Fuzhou Electric Company founded by the Liu family in the Guanglu Lane), Zhong Lu's history is rich with various occupants. On the west side, there once stood a wooden structured house named Xing Lu, or the Xing House, which was unfortunately destroyed in the 1990s. The daughters of Mr. Xu Shiguang resided in Zhong Lu, while his sons occupied Xing Lu. The Xu family has maintained ownership of Zhong Lu since its establishment.

Zhong Lu's historical significance is further augmented by its diverse array of past occupants. Notably, it was a residence for the Huang family, including the children of Huang Zhanyun, a renowned revolutionary hero, and Huang Yiyun, the director of the Fukien Education Department, along with his daughter. Later, it housed prominent figures like Li Shuren, the Principal of Yuying Girls ' School, and Wu Shuzhen, Kuomintang Finance Commissioner. Additionally, it served as the former site of the Fuzhou Branch of Xintai Bank. Among its notable tenants, Wu Shuzhen, the English secretary of Chiang Kai-shek and Soong Meiling, lived here for a decade until the Cultural Revolution. This courtyard exudes a mysterious and captivating allure. After the 1950s, Zhong Lu has designated a state-owned property and was eventually returned to the Xu family in the 1980s following the implementation of overseas Chinese policies. Presently, Ying Rongrong, one of the descendants of the original owner — the Xu family, resides there and oversees the maintenance of this historical abode.

从忠庐走出的许家后人，人才济济，成就斐然。在这充满文化气息的院落里成长，再从这里走出去，走向更为广阔的世界，这也许就是许世光先生建宅的初心吧。

◎ 沧桑古韵：橄榄五大厝、安澜会馆、罗宅

橄榄五大厝

离开马厂街，沿着仓前方向一路前行，穿过几条热闹的街区，便走到福州"橄榄大王"的宅院——橄榄五大厝（Ancient Residence of the Zheng Family）。这栋宅院安静地矗立在仓前路131号。若站在同侧，则无法看到该建筑的全貌，一定要穿过马路走到对侧道路才能一览它的全貌。

这是栋气派的宅院，高大且精美。它位于如今仓山区最热闹的地段之一，沿街的优势使它每天都吸引无数游人驻足欣赏。除地理条件优越之外，橄榄五大厝四周也被古树所掩映着，更显古朴素雅。行人就从它的旁边匆匆走过，来来往往的车辆也是疾驰而过。现在就让我们慢下脚步，静静聆听一段具有橄榄清香味道的历史故事。

橄榄五大厝始建于清光绪年间，由号称福州"橄榄大王"、有"橄榄五"之称的郑则铭家族兴建，宅内并供奉有橄榄神庙。坐落在仓前路131号沿街的这座老宅为三层砖木结构，是近代"洋门脸"、"柴栏厝"式建筑。柴栏厝是福州最老式的民居，构造简单。木构架、瓦屋面，四周木板为墙，屋为连排式柴楼，俗称"柴栏厝"。这种柴栏厝，一户占一开间，几户、十几户并列共建。它占地少，结构简单，节约用地，造价低，故易为平民百姓所接受。这类房子为框架式结构，栉比鳞次，排列紧密，相互依靠，泄水防风。即便楼身严重倾斜，也能维持不倒。底层临街，常作为店铺营业，后面做厨房兼饭厅。罗宅则为前店、中坊、后院的三进式宅院。据郑氏家族后人回忆，第一进为店面，第二进为工人宿舍及工厂，第三进为郑氏家族自己居住的房屋。第三进后还有晾晒橄榄的大埕，一部分橄榄加工工作也在大埕完成。因此，这种三进式宅院的设计很好地考虑到家族的职业特性，所有生活起居及工作皆能在宅院里完成，具有方便、高效的特点。橄榄五大厝1958年部分被改建为新村。

The descendants of the Xu family, raised and nurtured in Zhong Lu, have demonstrated remarkable talents and achieved significant milestones across various domains. Growing up in this culturally rich courtyard, they embarked on journeys beyond, venturing into the world. Undoubtedly, this was likely the initial aspiration of Mr. Xu Shiguang when he commissioned the construction of this house.

◎ A Glimpse into Ancient Chinese Grandeur: The Zheng Family Residence, Anlan Guild Hall, and Luo's Mansion

The Zheng Family Residence

Leaving Machang Street and venturing onto Cangqian Road, passing through vibrant blocks, we arrive at the Ancient Residence of the Zheng Family — the abode of the renowned "Olive King" in Fuzhou. Serenely standing at No. 129-131 Cangqian Road, this house unveils its full splendor only when viewed from the opposite side of the road.

From a distance, one can glimpse the grandeur of this magnificent, tall and elegant, mansion in the bustling heart of Cangshan District. Its location right by the street attracts countless tourists, prompting them to pause and marvel at its beauty daily. Surrounded by ancient trees, the Residence of the "Olive King" exudes a quaint and graceful ambiance. Though pedestrians and vehicles rush by daily, let us pause and immerse ourselves in the stories infused with the fragrance of olives.

The Ancient Residence of the Zheng Family was constructed during the Guangxu period of the Qing Dynasty. The mastermind behind this was the Zheng Zeming family, known as the " Olive King," referred to as "Olive Five" by the people of Fuzhou. The house features a temple dedicated to the god of olives within its walls. Nestled at No. 129, Cangqian Road, this ancient residence embodies modern Western-style architecture— a three-story brick and wood structure, adorned with the characteristic "Yangmenlian" or foreign-style facade and "Chailan Cuo" or wooden row houses. Chailan Cuo, an archaic residential style in Fuzhou, boasts a simple structure— a wooden frame and a tiled roof, encompassed by wooden walls. The row of wooden buildings, each unit for a household, hence earned the moniker "Chai Lan Cuo" or wooden row houses. This type of "Chailan Cuo" consists of one unit per household, with several households, even a dozen or more households, constructed side by side. This style, favored by the common people for its compact size, straightforward structure, land efficiency, and affordability, features a frame structure and closely connected rows, ensuring stability even if the building tilts. Moreover, it offers effective drainage and wind resistance. The ground floor of these houses typically serves as a shop front, with a kitchen and dining room in the rear. No. 131 Cangqian Road exemplifies a courtyard dwelling with three sections: a shop front, a middle workshop, and a backyard. The descendants of the Zheng family recalled that the first section housed the storefront, the second served as the workers' dormitory and workshop, while the third was the residence of the Zheng family. Behind the third section lay an open area where olives were air-dried and sometimes processed. This three-sectioned house design catered to the occupational dynamics of the family, efficiently accommodating daily life and work within the same premises. In 1958, segments of the residence were transformed into a "Xincun," a new village.

2013年1月30日，《福州晚报》登载了一篇《烟台山走出福州橄榄大王》，我们从中能了解郑氏家族与仓前路大厝的兴衰故事，也能从故事里听得几段有趣的轶事。

"橄榄五"是郑则铭的别号，他于1864年出生在仓山高湖，是家族的第五代传人。郑则铭作为福州橄榄研发、生产和销售领域的领军人物而闻名全国，因此被人们称为"橄榄五"。作为福州的第一位橄榄制品开发者，郑则铭还是第一位将福州橄榄生意拓展至海内外的大橄榄商。他也是第一个包销闽侯甘蔗、白沙以及闽清橄榄产区全部优质青橄榄的大橄榄商，是公认的"橄榄大王"。他经营的店号为"郑福记橄榄大王"。其中，檀香橄榄是"橄榄五"最著名的产品之一。从光绪年间到20世纪50年代，这种檀香橄榄一直是老上海人在春节款待和拜年时的必备佳品。

再说说这宅院内那座世界上唯一的橄榄神庙。橄榄神庙中，白姑娘神像绘于正中，两旁原为颂扬白姑娘保佑福州橄榄商生意兴隆、福州橄榄美名远扬的对联，现已被毁。神像下原为精美的木质供台，现已被水泥供台取代。要说起这"世界唯一"的庙，那可是大有来头。在准备建造第三进宅院时，遇到榕树该不该砍伐的难题。一天夜里，"橄榄五"的妻子江金枝做了一个奇怪的梦，梦里一名白衣女子与她对话，梦醒之后发现大榕树就倒在地上。后来，江金枝根据梦中记忆，为那位白衣女子绘像，并为其打造供台，称该女子为"白姑娘"。而这座橄榄神庙被认为是"橄榄五"的财富守护神。自此之后，家中每年加工檀香橄榄和每艘运输橄榄的船出发前，一定要先到橄榄神庙里祭祀。

随着仓前及烟台山街区改造工作逐步推进，仓前一带沿街的店铺也逐渐热闹兴旺起来。穿过繁忙的街区就能走到橄榄五大厝，似乎立刻又把人从现实拉回往昔。赶上哪天天气晴好时，嚼着橄榄果走在仓前街区，品一品橄榄的清香，逛一逛橄榄五大厝，实为一个不错的选择。

安澜会馆

离开橄榄五大厝，往前闲逛几步就能走到两尊威严的石狮子前。抬头看看匾额，上书四个金色的大字，便可知我们来到了安澜会馆。

细端详门口，两尊石狮子镇守门前，一扇木门紧闭，仿佛万千历史就藏于门后。匾额从右至左写着"安澜会馆"四个金色大字，气派且威严。墙上挂着两块牌子，左书"浙商总会福建商会"，右书"福建省浙江商会"。依此，对安澜会馆的前尘往事已能大概猜出几分，即它是作为浙商在福建经商、社交的场所在使用。

From an article titled "The Fuzhou Olive King of Yantai Mountain" published in the Fuzhou Evening News on January 30th, 2013, we can delve into the rise and fall of the Zheng family and their abode on Cangqian Road, accompanied by a few intriguing anecdotes.

"Olive Five," born Zheng Zeming, was the fifth child in his family in Gaohu, Cangshan District in 1864. Achieving national renown as a developer, producer, and seller of Fuzhou olives, Fuzhou locals affectionately referred to him as "Olive Five." Zheng Zeming pioneered various olive products in Fuzhou and was the first olive merchant to expand the olive business both locally and internationally. He secured exclusive sales rights for all high-quality olives produced in Ganzhe, Baisha in Minhou County, and Minqing County. He was recognized as the "Olive King," and his shop earned the name "Zheng Fook Kee Olive King." "Olive Five" was particularly renowned for its sandalwood olives. From the Guangxu period of the Qing Dynasty to the 1950s, even Shanghai residents incorporated "Olive Five" Fuzhou sandalwood olives into their Spring Festival guest entertainments.

Now, let's closely examine the world's only olive temple, enshrined within this house. Positioned at the shrine's center is a portrait of Bai Guniang, or the Bai Girl. Initially, there were couplets praising the white girl for blessing the prosperity of Fuzhou olive merchants and the fame of Fuzhou olives on both sides, but sadly, they were destroyed. Under the portrait, there used to be a finely crafted wooden altar, now replaced by a cement one. This unique olive temple has an intriguing backstory. During the residence's construction, a dilemma arose regarding whether or not to cut down a banyan tree. One night, Jiang Jinzhi, the wife of " Olive Five," had a peculiar dream where a woman in white conversed with her. Upon waking, she discovered that the giant banyan tree had fallen. Recalling her dream, Jiang Jinzhi painted a portrait of the woman in white and dedicated a shrine to her, naming her "White Girl." This olive temple is now regarded as the guardian of fortune for the "Olive Five" family. Since then, before processing sandalwood olives and embarking on olive transportation voyages, offerings are made to the shrine.

As the renovation work progressed in the Cangqian District and Yantai Mountain neighborhoods, the shops along Cangqian Road began to thrive. Wandering through this bustling neighborhood, you can find your way to Olive Five House after a few steps, where you'll be transported back in time. On pleasant days, exploring the Cangqian neighborhood and visiting the "Olive Five House" while savoring olives and their aroma is a delightful option.

Anlan Guild Hall

Upon leaving the Residence of "Olive Five" and taking a few steps forward, you 'll encounter two magnificent stone lions. Gazing at the plaque adorned with four golden characters, you'll know you've arrived at the Anlan Guild Hall.

Observing the door closely, you'll see two stone lions guarding the entrance and a securely shut wooden door, hinting at the mysteries concealed within. The plaque bears the inscription " Anlan Guild Hall" in four grand golden characters, presenting an imposing and majestic façade. Flanking the door, there are two vertical plaques — the left designates "Fukien Chamber of Commerce of Zhejiang Chamber of Commerce," and the right "Zhejiang Chamber of Commerce in Fukien Province"— revealing its historical role as a hub for Zhejiang businessmen to conduct business and socialize in Fukien.

安澜会馆大门
The Gate of Anlan Guild Hall

　　安澜会馆又名浙江会馆、上北馆，清乾隆四十年（1775年）始建，原为浙人在闽商人及官员、名人聚集之处。而将会馆命名作"安澜"，则含有希望在闽的浙商风平浪静、海不扬波、平安往返、生意兴旺的祈愿。该建筑占地面积约为2400平方米，坐南朝北，前后为两进三落的结构。建筑前跨街原有照壁、旗杆、香炉等，但早年间被毁，现已无法看到。大门为浙江风格，青砖外墙，八字大门，上下有砖雕装饰，绘有人物、植物等场景，栩栩如生，样式精美。大门内为戏台，歇山屋顶，内做藻井。天井两侧为双层看楼。

　　正殿面阔五间、进深七柱，副阶周匝，重檐歇山顶。正殿前再设一道外廊，外廊前檐原有浮雕盘龙柱，后被移往于山玉皇阁。第二进在大殿后高台之上，为双层木构，面阔九间、进深五柱，左右有双层厢房。建筑两侧还有附属用房若干。整个会馆以浙江风格为主。

　　安澜会馆和其他会馆一样，除了以商业功能为主，还有联谊、娱乐和文化教育的功能。且安澜会馆在1927年以后，各地商帮在福州建立的会馆逐渐式微的情况下还继续存在着。会馆经常邀约、集聚浙江籍在闽任职的官员、社会贤达和文化名人与会，参加馆庆或中国传统节日的民俗庆贺活动，以扩大影响力、增加知名度。20世纪30年代中后期，任福建省政府主席的陈仪和作家、文化名人郁达夫等都成为这里的常客。由此可见，安澜会馆在闽的地位极高，影响力是极大的。

The Anlan Guild Hall, also known as the Zhejiang Guild Hall and Shangbei Hall, was constructed in the 40th year of the Qianlong era during the Qing Dynasty, in 1775. It was initially established as a gathering place for merchants, government officials, and notable figures hailing from Zhejiang and residing in Fukien. The name "Anlan" symbolizes of calming turbulent waters, embodying the aspiration for the safety, prosperity, and well-being of Zhejiang's business community in Fukien. This impressive edifice faces north and encompasses an area of approximately 2,400 square meters. It comprises two courtyards and three grand halls. In its earlier days, the building featured screen walls, flagpoles, and incense burners at the front, but these were regrettably lost over time. The gate reflects the architectural style of Zhejiang, with its distinctive blue brick outer wall and an entrance shaped like the Chinese character for "eight." The gate is adorned with intricate brick carvings, portraying vibrant scenes of humans and nature. Just inside the gate, a theater stage with a gable and hip roof and a sunken panel was once a focal point. On either side of the yard, there are double-decked pavilions for spectators.

The primary hall is five rooms wide and extends seven pillars deep. It is surrounded by a covered corridor and features a gable and hip roof with multiple eaves. In front of the main hall, there is an outer porch that originally boasted a relief coiled dragon column on its front eaves, which was later relocated to Yuhuang Pavilion on Yushan Mountain. Behind the main hall, on a raised platform, stands the second hall. This is a two-story wooden structure spanning nine rooms in width and five columns in depth. Flanking the main building are double-decked wing rooms, along with auxiliary spaces. The overall architecture is predominantly influenced by the traditional Zhejiang style.

Much like other guild halls of its time, the Anlan Guild Hall served not only as a hub for commercial activities but also as a center for social gatherings, entertainment, and cultural enrichment. Unlike many other guild halls that saw a decline in the post-1927 era, the Anlan Guild Hall continued to thrive. It frequently hosted officials from Zhejiang Province working in Fukien, as well as esteemed scholars and cultural luminaries, who attended meetings and participated in the hall's folk celebrations and traditional Chinese festivals. This engagement was aimed at expanding the guild hall's influence and popularity. During the mid-to-late 1930s, notable figures such as Chen Yi, the chairman of the provincial government, and Yu Dafu, a celebrated writer and cultural figure, became regular patrons, underscoring the high status and significant influence of the Anlan Guild Hall in Fukien.

因其地位及影响力，安澜会馆历经二百多年风风雨雨至今仍保存完好，既雅致清幽，又堂皇壮观，实为难得，体现出闽浙两地建筑艺术融为一体的特色。只要走近安澜会馆，很难不被其气势所折服。安澜会馆的存在能够充分证明福州自古以来便是对内、对外贸易的集散中心，也是一块吸引国内外商人来此经商的宝地。途经于此，很难不被安澜会馆气派的外观所吸引而驻足，定要停下脚步，读一读纪念碑上的文字，抬头看一看匾额，品一品二百多年间的商海故事。

罗宅

距离安澜会馆不远有一座美丽的中式建筑，她坐落在烟台山公园脚下，与周围景色迥异却又融合得极好，这就是拥有四百余年历史的罗宅。

罗宅始建于明代万历年间，并于清代重建。它的占地面积约为800平方米，是一座三进七柱的中式庭院。这座中式合院民宅依山而建，高高的围墙使她免于尘世喧嚣。自罗氏后人在清光绪年间购买后，便一直作为罗氏族人的居所世代传承，故后世称为"罗宅"。五口通商后，烟台山上的西式建筑如雨后春笋般出现，而唯有这大气优雅的罗宅以纯粹的东方姿态优雅地立于烟台山下，面貌独具一格，极难让人忽视它的存在。

罗宅大门
The Gate of Luo Zhai

The enduring legacy of the Anlan Guild Hall, standing tall for over two centuries, attests to its enduring significance and impact. This venerable structure has weathered numerous challenges and stands as a testament to the fusion of Fukien and Zhejiang architectural traditions, exuding a rare blend of elegance and grandeur. As one approaches the Anlan Guild Hall, its majestic presence is truly awe-inspiring. The continued existence of the Anlan Guild Hall serves as a compelling reminder of Fuzhou's historical role as a bustling hub for domestic and international trade. It remains a magnetic beacon for both local and foreign entrepreneurs,offering an irresistible glimpse into its resplendent façade. Passing by, it's nearly impossible not to be captivated by the splendid visage of the Anlan Guild Hall. One instinctively halts to peruse the inscriptions on the stone tablet at its entrance, gazes up at the ornate plaque above, and indulges in the rich tapestry of two centuries of business history.

The Luo's Mansion

Nestled at the foot of Yantai Mountain Park, not far from the Anlan Guild Hall, one encounters a striking Chinese-style edifice. Its architectural style distinctly sets it apart from the surrounding structures, yet it harmoniously integrates with its environment. This is Luo Zhai, or the Luo 's Mansion, boasting a history spanning over four centuries.

Originally constructed during the Wanli era of the Ming Dynasty and later restored in the Qing Dynasty, Luo's Mansion is an exemplary Chinese-style courtyard dwelling, comprising three sections and seven columns, encompassing an area of approximately 800 square meters. Nestled against the mountainside, it shields itself from the outside commotion with towering walls. Purchased by the Luo family's descendants during the Guangxu period of the Qing Dynasty, it has been handed down through the generations, earning the name "Luo Zhai" (Luo's Mansion) among later generations. During the Qing Dynasty, as Western-style buildings mushroomed atop Yantai Mountain following the opening of the five trading ports, Luo Zhai stood resolutely at the mountain's base, maintaining its pure Oriental elegance, making it an unmissable, distinctive, and evocative presence.

罗宅的外观有中式建筑的淡然大气。简单的白墙，灰黑瓦片的墙沿，构成了类似中国画中"留白"的艺术风格，朴素内敛，低调庄严。其正门较高，中间压低，形成"凹"字形。且凹下部分的墙沿处设计有"墙堵"的装饰，图案是蝙蝠，中间为寿字，组合在一起取谐音"福寿"，寓意十分吉祥。正门下方由石头砌筑的部分称"花基"，蘑菇面凸起式样，工整精致。这样设计的用意是：古时候的建筑常因为上半部是土墙，导致洪水泛滥时容易浸水，故采用这样的设计能够起到防洪的作用。"花基"在明代常用，在清末逐渐消失。

进入宅院，身临其中便能够感受到何为三进式院落。其中"一进"为围绕着天井系统组成的"庭院"，"庭"为天井，"院"为围墙，同时还有一个比较大的厅堂。值得注意的是，天井四面瓦片的排水是由中间汇聚到天井，而不是朝外倾泻，其寓意乃为"四水归堂"，意思是四方聚财。

这类来自古时候的小巧思吉祥话，于罗宅的其他很多处皆有体现。例如罗宅屋顶的常见雕花（称"雀替"），运用一种"草"的元素，即"惹草"，其特点为不断生长、不断分枝，寓意家族繁荣、开枝散叶。又如罗宅整体墙面的造型"马鞍墙"，前半部翘角较高，后半部低且长，称为"尾长"，寓意子孙绵延。

罗氏祖先系近代福州巨贾罗金城，他出生于一个商人家庭。罗金城自幼聪明好学，后因父亲身患眼疾，便子承父业弃学从商。当时的他经营着三家钱庄，后又经营进出口商行，其业务远达上海、天津、大连等口岸，常往返于沿海各大商埠之间，生意盛极一时。同时他在台江、仓山两地布置房地产业，以增强经济实力，巩固商业根基。之后，罗金城之子罗勉侯更是将家业继续发扬光大，不仅创办多家商行，还与他人合资开办"延福泉汽车公司"，这是福建省首家公共交通汽车运输企业。

如今的罗宅已俨然成为闽文化的一部分，是来烟台山游玩的人必打卡之处。经修复，罗宅整体既保证了安全性和稳定性，又保持着精美度，具有极高的审美价值。在现代社会，被注入全新生命力的罗宅正以其独立之姿亭亭矗立在烟台山脚下，于喧闹之中呼唤大家返璞归真，寻找自己心目中的理想家园。

Luo Zhai, like all Chinese-style structures, emanates an air of grandeur, simultaneously detached and imposing. Its uncomplicated white walls, adorned with gray and black roofing tiles, evoke a kind of artistic minimalism akin to the "blank space" concept found in Chinese paintings. This aesthetic is marked by simplicity, restraint, and solemnity. The entrance walls stand tall, with a central section recessed, creating a concave shape. The edges of these concave portions are adorned with decorative "wall blocks" featuring patterns of bats and the Chinese character "Shou." Bats symbolize auspiciousness, as their Chinese pronunciation resembles that of good fortune, while " Shou" signifies longevity. Together, this combination conveys a sense of good fortune and propitiousness. Beneath the walls, a lower section is constructed using stones, known as "huaji" or " flower base," with the stone's surface gently bulging like mushrooms, presenting a tidy and delicate style. This method was adopted for flood protection, as walls made of earth were susceptible to water damage during floods. "Flower base" was commonly used in the Ming Dynasty but gradually faded during the late Qing Dynasty.

Upon entering the building, one can witness the concept of a "courtyard abode with three sections." The first section encircles the central courtyard, known as the "Ting Yuan," where "Ting" refers to the courtyard and "Yuan" signifies the wall. Additionally, a relatively spacious hall is attached to this area. It's worth noting that the roof tiles surrounding the patio are designed to channel water into the courtyard, symbolizing the convergence of all good fortunes toward the center.

This meticulous attention to auspicious details can be found throughout Luo Zhai. For instance, the roof carvings known as "Queti" or decorated brackets feature patterns of grass leaves, symbolizing growth and branching, signifying the prosperity of the Luo Family. The "saddle wall," a distinctive feature of the building's walls, is characterized by a raised front half and a lower, elongated back half, referred to as "Wei Chang" or " tail length," symbolizing the family's enduring prosperity over time.

Luo Jincheng is the ancestral figure of Luo's lineage, a prominent modern Fuzhou merchant who hailed from a family of traders. With an innate intelligence and a thirst for knowledge, Luo Jincheng assumed his father 's business due to his father's eye ailment, eventually managing three banks and an import and export firm. His commercial ventures extended to ports such as Shanghai, Tianjin, and Dalian, and he frequently journeyed between major coastal commercial hubs. Luo Jincheng also invested in real estate in Taijiang and Cangshan districts, further bolstering the family's economic standing and consolidating their business foundation. His son, Luo Mianhou, continued to advance the family's legacy by establishing multiple commercial banks and co-founding the "Yanfuquan Automobile Company," the first public vehicle enterprise in Fukien Province.

Today, Luo Zhai has become an integral part of Fukien's cultural heritage, an essential destination for visitors to Yantai Mountain. Following restoration, Luo Zhai has not only ensured its safety and stability but has also retained its exquisite aesthetics and enduring value. In the modern era, this rejuvenated Luo Zhai stands steadfast at the foot of Yantai Mountain, a solitary reminder for all to embrace a simpler way of life and discover the true essence of home.

◎ 西学东渐：陶淑女子学校旧址

福建师范大学仓山校区是一个具有深厚人文底蕴和历史气息的地方。漫步在百年老校的校园内，经过文科楼前的大榕树往右走，缓缓地沿着斜坡直上，到坡顶之后往右拐，行数十步就可以看见一片由几栋老洋房组成的建筑群掩映在苍翠的绿树丛中。这片建筑群就是一个多世纪以前福州陶淑女中的旧址，后为福建师范大学音乐系使用。音乐系搬去新校区以后，又为不同院系使用。

历经百年风霜洗礼，这几栋小楼已不复旧时模样，但半圆形拱门和落地大窗、如同教堂的尖顶、硕大的罗马柱等仍在。这片由一座平房、一座二层楼和一处礼堂连成的西式建筑群依旧雄伟，依稀透出过往的荣光。漫步在古老的走廊中，仿佛能听见百年前少女们的琅琅读书声、曾经音乐系的同学们在琴房里叮叮咚咚的琴声。安静的花窗任风吹拂，虔诚地映照出时光的变换。夕阳下建筑的侧影投射在地上，踏进去仿佛就能立刻回到旧时光里。

陶淑女子学校位于福州仓前山岭后路17号，建于1903年，原为英国圣公会在1864年创办的"安立间女学堂"。校园占地有10余亩，建筑布局紧凑，其中教室楼、宿舍楼、教堂通过半地下通道及走廊相连，形成一个整体的建筑群，呈现出浓厚的西洋建筑雄伟之风。教学楼对面为独立的办公楼，与教学楼形成一个三面围合的院落。

陶淑女子学校外观
The Exterior of Do-Seuk Girls' School

建筑大都是砖木结构，用材考究，木料多用进口红木、楠木等，门窗插销、把手等则均为铜制。建筑形式多样，有英国式、罗马式、哥特式和东欧式等。学校建筑群沿山势而建，背靠长安山，面朝闽江，绿树掩映，风景秀丽。在参天大树的映衬下，那红砖白墙格外优雅和华丽。

◎ The Spread of Western Learning to China: the Former Site of Fuzhou Do-seuk Girls' School

The Cangshan Campus of Fukien Normal University is steeped in rich cultural heritage and exudes a profound historical ambiance. A stroll through the century-old university's grounds leads you past the magnificent banyan tree gracing the front of the Liberal Arts Building. Ascending the slope beyond, then veering right at the summit, you'll soon encounter a cluster of venerable Western-style buildings nestled amid the verdant surroundings. This architectural ensemble is the former site of the Fuzhou Do- seuk Girls' School, a structure more than a century old. In later years, it served as the home of the Music Department of Fukien Normal University before being repurposed by several other institutes.

The passage of time has left its mark on these buildings, robbing them of their original luster. Nevertheless, with their semi-circular arches, towering windows, church-like spires, and imposing Roman columns, this Western-style complex, consisting of a bungalow, a two-story edifice, and an auditorium, still retains an air of grandeur, albeit now gently echoing the glories of days gone by. As you wander the aged corridors, it's almost as if you can still hear the voices of young women studying a century ago and the melodious notes of music students playing the piano. Gentle breezes sweep through the serene, stained -glass windows, serving as a poignant reminder of the relentless march of time. When the setting sun casts its silhouette upon the ground, simply stepping into the shadow can transport you back to old days.

Originally founded as the "Anritsu Girls' School" by the Anglican Church in 1864, the Do-Seuk Girls' School was established in 1903 at No. 17, Linghou Road, Cangqian District, Fuzhou. The campus, encompassing approximately 10 acres, boasts an architecturally compact layout where teaching buildings, dormitories, and a church are interconnected by semi-underground passages and corridors, forming an integrated architectural complex characterized by a resolute and majestic Western style. Facing the teaching building stands an independent office structure, which, together with the teaching building, forms a three-sided courtyard. Most of the buildings were constructed using high-quality materials, featuring wood predominantly imported — such as red sandalwood and nanmu. Even the door and window latches, handles, and doorknobs are meticulously crafted from copper. The architectural styles on display range from British and Roman to Gothic and Eastern European influences. Nestled against the Chang 'an Mountain backdrop, with the Minjiang River to the front, the campus is enveloped in lush greenery, creating a picturesque setting. Amidst the towering trees, the juxtaposition of red brick and white walls presents an exceptionally elegant and resplendent picture.

陶淑女子学校内正对校门的是教堂，巴西利卡式平面，这是古罗马的一种公共建筑形式。教堂正面山墙朝北，立面设计成两层，横向三开间，每开间设两个哥特式尖券窗。中央开间略大，下层出哥特式小抱厦，上层为两个哥特式尖券窗夹圆形玫瑰窗。教堂南侧突出为圣坛，设置彩色花窗。教堂东为宿舍，为两层带地下室砖木结构楼房，平面呈凸字形，中央有T字形中廊。教堂西面则为两栋教学楼，均为两层带地下室券廊式建筑，两栋教学楼以走廊相连，并与教堂大厅相连。教学楼对面为办公楼，单层砖木结构。办公楼以东、宿舍楼以南为操场，另外在宿舍楼以东有一座两层外廊式建筑。

陶淑女子学校作为一所福州本地的学校，却又如此具有异域风情。这是因为鸦片战争之后，随着福州作为通商口岸被迫对外开放，西方传教士随之纷纷涌入福州，并开设教会学堂。1862年英国传教士胡约翰（John Richard Wolfe）来榕筹建女校。1884年英国圣公会租用乌山弥陀寺部分房间创办女子小学校。后几经波折，英国差会于1889年通过募捐的形式筹得款项兴建新校舍，新校舍建成后定名为陶淑女子学校。

有意思的是，陶淑女子学校的英文名Do-Seuk Girls' School为福州话音译，并用"罗马字"拼音书写。这种命名方式在近代教会创办的学校中是很罕见的。其名字意思是读书，作为一所供女子读书的学校，这无疑打破了中国自古以来"女子无才便是德"的传统。

从社会角度来看，福州陶淑女子学校在解放妇女思想、挖掘妇女潜能、培养妇女成才，进而推进妇女解放运动的开展方面产生了深远的影响。她们中的许多人毕业后服务于教育、卫生等部门，成为文教、医务等各条战线的骨干力量，为新中国建设事业做出了卓越的贡献。而从历史角度来看，陶淑女子学校在福州地区教会中学中建筑保存最为完好。建筑协调统一，环境优美，是研究福州近现代城市发展的实物资料。

夕阳西下，踏上通往陶淑女子学校的小路，听脚下的落叶发出窸窸窣窣的响声，于肃穆中感受西洋古典建筑的风情。再欣赏一番夕阳透过繁密的树叶投影到花窗、白墙上，如此交错，形成一幅美妙的古典画卷。在这里，可以于建筑中了解历史，于历史中品味人文，于人文中细品建筑。福州陶淑女子学校大概就具有这样深远且深刻的意义和价值吧！

An architectural masterpiece awaits within the hallowed grounds of the Do-Seuk Girls ' School. As you pass through the gates, your gaze falls upon a basilica-style church, reminiscent of the grand public edifices of ancient Rome. The front gable wall of the church faces north, featuring a two-story facade with three bays, each adorned with graceful Gothic pointed arched windows. The central bay, slightly larger than its counterparts, showcases a charming Gothic-style covered porch on the lower floor and two elegant Gothic-style pointed windows, complemented by a circular rose window on the upper level. The church's southern side takes the role of the altar, its magnificence accentuated by colorful stained windows. Adjacent to the church, to the east, stands a dormitory, a two-story brick and wood structure, with a basement, a convex facade, and a central T-shaped corridor. To the west of the church, two teaching buildings rise, two stories in height, featuring arched galleries and basements. These teaching buildings are connected by a corridor and share a vital connection with the church hall. Across from the teaching building, a single-story brick and wood office building stands independently. To the east of the office building and the south of the dormitory building, you'll find the playground, while a two-story veranda - style building graces the eastern side of the dormitory.

While the Do-Seuk Girls ' School is a local institution in Fuzhou, it possesses an aura of exoticism. This peculiarity can be traced back to the aftermath of the Opium War when Fuzhou was compelled to open as a trading port, attracting Western missionaries who established church schools. In 1862, British missionary John Richard Wolfe arrived in Fuzhou and initiated a girls' school. By 1884, the Anglican Church had rented a few rooms within the Wushan Amitabha Temple to establish a girls ' primary school. Eventually, British Mission funding facilitated the construction of a new school building, christened the Do-Seuk Girls' School after its completion.

Remarkably, the English name "Do-Seuk Girls' School" is a transliteration from the Fuzhou dialect and is rendered in "Roman characters," a rarity in modern church nomenclature. The name signifies "reading," as a school dedicated to nurturing female literacy, it disrupts the traditional Chinese belief that "a lack of talent is a virtue."

From a societal perspective, the Fuzhou Do-Seuk Girls ' School has profoundly impacted emancipated women's minds, unearthing their potential, cultivating their talents, and advancing the cause of women's liberation. Many of the school's graduates went on to serve in education, healthcare, and various other sectors, becoming pillars of culture, education, and medical care while making significant contributions to the construction of New China. Historically, the Fuzhou Do-Seuk Girls' School stands as the most well-preserved architectural complex among the missionary middle schools in Fuzhou. The harmonious and integrated structures are nestled within a picturesque environment, serving as a valuable historical record for studying modern urban development in Fuzhou.

As the sun descends in the western sky, follow the path to Fuzhou 's Do-Seuk Girls ' School. Listen to the gentle rustle of fallen leaves underfoot and take in the dignified allure of Western classical architecture. Bask in the warm hues of the setting sun filtering through the dense leaves. The figures adorning the stained windows come to life against the backdrop of the pristine white walls, crafting a picture of classical beauty. Here, history unfolds in architecture, humanity reveals itself through history, and architecture becomes an embodiment of humanities— such is the profound significance of the Fuzhou Do-Seuk Girls' School.

第十六章

海丝觅踪：揽古察今

Chapter Sixteen

Traces of Maritime Route: A Look into

Past Gives Insight into Present

◎ 航海印迹：罗星塔、圣寿宝塔

罗星塔

在福州市马尾区南部的闽江之滨，静静矗立着一座古老又美丽的石塔。千百年来，它阅尽了马尾的沧海桑田，见证了船政文化的兴衰。中国有数不清的塔，但被称为"中国塔"的却只有这一座。它便是闻名中外的"罗星塔"，为第七批全国重点文物保护单位。

《闽都记》载，罗星塔为宋朝岭南柳七娘所建。关于这座古塔，流传着一个凄婉的爱情故事。据传，柳七娘有着一副贤婉俊美的相貌，被乡间豪强看中。于是豪强便设下了圈套，诬陷她的丈夫有罪。她力抗不过，只能眼睁睁地看着丈夫被冤枉并做苦役。即便如此，柳七娘也没有屈服，她一路跟随丈夫进入闽地。但不幸的是，她的丈夫没过多久便被折磨致死。于是她变卖全部家产，在丈夫服苦役之地建造了一座塔，为亡夫祈求冥福。由于塔所处的高阜突立于水中，江流与海水冲激于塔下，形成旋涡，如同"磨心"一般，所以这座塔也称"磨心塔"。

罗星塔最初为木塔，明代万历年间塔被海风摧毁。到了天启年间，当地著名学者徐渤等人以"塔毁福州文运不昌"为由，倡议在原来的地址上进行重建。重建的罗星塔改为石砌，塔身七层八角，高31.5米，塔座直径8.6米，每层均建拱门，可拾级而上。石塔外有石砌栏杆和泻水搪。檐角上镇有八佛，角下悬铃铎，海风吹来，叮当作响。故有诗云："舵楼风细听铃语，月近家园渐觉圆。"

塔前有清代楹联。清朝梁章钜所辑《楹联丛话 楹联续话》（梁章钜，2016：204）记载，福州城外由江达海之路，以罗星塔为关键。塔据山巅，四面皆波涛汹涌。其由闽县达长乐，则必以罗星塔山下为暂泊候潮之所。盖海潮由此而分也。塔上旧有七字联，不知何人所撰。其句云："朝朝朝朝朝朝夕，长长长长长长消。"过客皆不知所谓。康熙中有一道人到此，读而喜之。众请其说。道人笑曰："此山为海潮来往之区。……不过是言潮汐长消而已。"该联可以解读为："朝朝潮，朝潮朝汐；常常涨，常涨常消"，展现江水每天潮涨潮落的壮丽景象。

◎ Nautical Relics: Luoxing Pagoda, Shengshou Pagoda

Luoxing Pagoda

On the bank of the Minjiang River in the south of Mawei District, Fuzhou City, sits an ancient and beautiful stone pagoda, known as Luoxing Pagoda. For hundreds of years, it has witnessed the vicissitudes of Mawei and the naval administration culture. Of the countless towers in China, it is the only one popularly known as the "China Tower". Famous both at home and abroad, Luoxing Pagoda was listed in the seventh group of national key relics.

According to *the Records of Mindu*, Luoxing Pagoda was built by Liu Qiniang in Lingnan (Guangdong Province) of the Song Dynasty. About this ancient pagoda, there is a sad love story. Legend has it that a scoundrel in the country took a fancy to Liu Qiniang, who was a virtuous woman with pretty appearance. He set a trap and framed a case against her husband. Liu had no choice but to see her husband wronged and sent to penal servitude. Even so, Liu did not give in to her destiny and followed her husband to Min, the ancient Fukien Province. Unfortunately, her husband was tortured to death in the servitude. Sadly she sold out all her properties and with the money she built a pagoda to pray for good fortune for her deceased husband in the place where he had been subjected to hard labor. Because the pagoda is located in a high mound in the river mouth, the water of both the river and the sea converge under the pagoda and form powerful whirlpools, as if "grinding" a heart. It is therefore also called "Heart Grinding Pagoda".

Luoxing Pagoda was originally a wooden pagoda. During the reign of emperor Wanli in the Ming Dynasty about 500 years ago, the pagoda was destroyed by the sea wind. In the period of Tianqi in the Ming Dynasty about 400 years ago, Xu Bo, a renowned local scholar, along with some other scholars, proposed to rebuild the pagoda on the original site by arguing that "the destruction of the Pagoda would exert bad influence on the literary achievement of Fuzhou". Luoxing Pagoda was rebuilt and turned into a seven-floor stone pagoda with eight angles, measuring 31.5 meters high and 8.6 meters in diameter. Each floor has arches, stairs, stone railings and drainage openings. On the eaves' corners of each floor there are statues of eight Buddhas, and under the eaves' corners are small bells, which keep jingling in the sea breeze, hence the poem which roughly reads "while listening to the rudder tower jingle in the breeze, I find the moon rounding slowly with its closeness to home".

In front of the base of Luoxing Pagoda is a seven-character couplet dating back to the Qing Dynasty. According to the *Serial Introduction to Chinese Couplets: A Sequel* by Liang Zhangju of the Qing Dynasty, Luoxing Pagoda is situated at a critical junction connecting Fuzhou with the sea. It stands on the top of a hill, with rough waves raging at its foot. The waters below the pagoda are where vessels berth before they set off in sea tides from Min County to Changle County, two counties of Fuzhou in ancient times, for the possible reason that the place is a dividing line of river water and sea water. The seven-character couplet, written by someone anonymous, reads "Zhao Zhao Chao, Zhao Chao Zhao Xi; Chang Chang Zhang, Chang Zhang Chang Xiao" in Chinese Pinyin. With different pronunciations of the same Chinese character wisely used, they are descriptive of the spectacular view of the rise and fall of the river tides. The pronunciation is so tricky that no one can figure them out at the beginning. A Taoist priest happened to visit the place during the reign of Qing emperor Kangxi. He was amused at the ingenious couplet and explained to others happily that "the hill where the pagoda stands is the dividing line of river water and sea water, and the couplet describes the daily ebb and flow of tides. That's it."

石塔第二层有一方塔铭，是清乾隆时福州郡守李拔所撰。铭中把罗星塔的地势和作用概括为："中流砥柱，险要绝伦，以靖海疆，以御外侮"。

清光绪十年（1884年）的中法马江海战就在塔下开火，石塔损伤多处。战后，在塔顶安装一颗周长近7米的大铁球，以代替被炮火所毁之塔刹。1964年对该塔予以重修，因栏板和塔檐剥落，只好改用铁管栏杆。但建筑风貌犹在，仍存旧观。

第一次鸦片战争后清朝开放五口通商，福州于道光二十四年（1844年）开港，罗星塔见证了海上丝绸之路的繁华。蜂拥而至的各国商船，因吃水深多无法直接驶到福州城，而罗星塔一带水深江阔，于是商船皆停泊在此，罗星塔因而为欧洲人所熟悉。外国的船舶航行到福州马尾外海时，水手们远远望见此塔屹立于山顶，砥柱海天，欢呼道："China Tower! "慢慢地，罗星塔成为国际公认的航标、闽江门户的标志，在国际上有"中国塔"的美誉。清朝光绪二十三年（1897年），在福建海关内开办大清邮政福州邮务总局，并在营前海关内开设罗星塔分局。从此，罗星塔成为世界邮政地名之一，从世界各地邮寄到马尾的信，只要写上罗星塔的邮政地名"塔锚地"（Pagoda Anchorage）就能寄达。

罗星山北侧还有一个"罗零基准点"。当年，海上往来频繁，为避免商船触礁沉没，清政府请德国工程师对闽江下游的水位和流量进行系统观测，确定了以"罗星塔水准零点"作为闽江罗星塔段最低水位固定观测标记，这是近代中国第一个水位国际标准，即海拔原点。1992年，全国统一采用黄海零点，罗零基准点停止使用。

罗星塔现在是马尾船政文化遗址群的组成部分，塔下的高阜也已开辟为公园，西侧有溯江楼，南麓有望江亭，园中还有忠魂台、鸣潮阁、友谊轩等。石塔屹立于山顶，被几株郁郁葱葱的参天古榕环绕。从塔顶俯瞰，闽江出海处的港口码头尽在眼底，还可以看到江岸两旁的古炮台，以及当年硝烟弥漫的中法马江海战的古战场等。远眺巍巍古塔，犹如海天砥柱，似在静静聆听着三江奔流，凝视着古老中国的历史风云……

圣寿宝塔

在福州市长乐区吴航街道的南山（塔山）上，坐落着一座雄浑的石塔。它就是圣寿宝塔，又名三峰寺塔，是第六批全国重点文物保护单位，还入选海上丝绸之路中国世界文化遗产预备名录遗址地。

On the second floor of the pagoda, there is an inscription of pagoda introduction, which was written by Li Ba, the governor of Fuzhou during the reign of Qing emperor Qianlong. In the introduction the situation and role of Luoxing Pagoda is summarized as "a mainstay difficult to access and strategically located against foreign aggression".

In 1884 or the tenth year during the reign of Qing emperor Guangxu, a naval battle between China and France broke out nearby on the Ma River, causing much damage to the pagoda. After the war, a large iron ball with a circumference of nearly seven meters was installed on its top to replace the spire destroyed by gunfire. When the pagoda was rebuilt in 1964, the stone slabs in the railings were replaced with iron pipes because the coverings of the slabs and the projecting edges had come off in small pieces. But the artistic style of the pagoda still remains.

After the First Opium War, the Qing Regime was compelled to open five treaty ports including Fuzhou, which formally opened up in 1884, or the 24th year during the reign of Qing emperor Daoguang. Luoxing Pagoda has witnessed the prosperity of the Maritime Silk Route in Fuzhou since then. The foreign business ships that came in great numbers often had deep draughts due to heavy loads. They had to berth near the pagoda and wait for sea tides, as the part of the river where the pagoda is located is deep and wide. Luoxing Pagoda thus became well-known to Europeans. When foreign ships steered to the sea off Mawei, Fuzhou, the seamen could see the pagoda on the hill top in the distance. At the sight of it, they would jump joyfully shouting "China Tower!". Gradually, Luoxing Pagoda became an internationally recognized beacon of navigation and the gateway symbol of the Minjiang River. It also became popularly known as "China Tower" in the world. In 1897, or the 23rd year during the reign of Qing emperor Guangxu, Fuzhou General Bureau of Post was set up at Fukien Customs and its Luoxing Pagoda branch opened at Yingqian Customs. Since then, Luoxing Pagoda has become a well-known postal address. Letters sent to Mawei from other parts of the world can be received with the mail address "Pagoda Anchorage".

In the north of the Luoxing Hill lies the statue of "Luoxing Zero Datum Mark". Mawei saw a busy maritime trade at that time. To keep commercial vessels from being stranded, a German engineer was employed to conduct a systematic observation of the water level and flow quantity of the downstream Minjiang River. "Luoxing Zero Datum Mark" was recognized as the observation point of the lowest water level in the stretch of the Minjiang River near Luoxing Pagoda. It is the first mark of zero water level or altitude up to international standard in modern China. But it has not been in use since 1992, when the zero altitude mark in the Yellow Sea was introduced as the national standard.

Luoxing Pagoda has been listed as a heritage site of Mawei ship building culture. The hill where the pagoda stands has turned into a park. It includes Suojiang Pavilion in the west and Wangjiang Pavilion in the south as well as Zhonghun Sacrificial Altar, Mingchao Pavilion and Youyi Pavilion. Overlooking from the top of the pagoda, which stands on the hill top amid towering banyan trees, one can see wharfs beside the estuary of the Minjiang River, ancient fort barbettes on both banks, and the former site of the Sino-French naval war beside the Ma River, which is part of the downstream Minjiang River. Viewed from the distance, the towering ancient pagoda resembles a mainstay in the sea, as if listening to the racing current of the three rivers converging under the pagoda and reflecting upon the part of ancient Chinese history...

Shengshou Pagoda

On top of the Nanshan Hill (or Pagoda Hill) in Wuhang, Changle District, Fuzhou City, sits a majestic stone pagoda, named Shengshou Pagoda or Sanfeng Temple Pagoda. It is one of the sixth group of national key relics and is on the tentative list of World Maritime Silk Route Heritage Sites in China.

该石塔八角七层，为仿楼阁式建筑，极具我国东南沿海地方特色。塔身通高27.4米，建在近一丈高的平台上。塔基为大力士座，八面环饰狮子、牡丹等石刻图案。塔身中空，内有石阶，可盘旋登至塔顶。第一层门额上刻"雁塔"二字，塔壁上浮雕文殊、普贤、五十罗汉、十六飞天乐伎及佛教故事画面。塔身转角处各立一尊石雕护法天王，或执剑或按剑，戴盔披甲，足踏宝莲，顶护宝盖。第二层南面正门上悬挂"圣寿宝塔"石匾额。二至七层各开二门。第六层和第七层的塔壁上还刻有造塔记六条。各层的塔壁浮雕及壁龛内的圆雕，多取材于佛教故事，浮雕造型生动、风格古朴，是研究宋代建筑、石雕艺术的珍贵实物。

该塔于宋绍圣三年（1096年）始建，政和七年（1117年）竣工，距今已有九百余年历史，原是为宋徽宗祝寿而建，故名圣寿宝塔。明永乐年间郑和航海驻泊长乐，该塔成为其俯瞰停泊在太平港内的庞大船队的瞭望塔，也是郑和下西洋船队出入太平港的航标塔。据传，郑和登塔查看港口时知该塔为给宋徽宗祝寿而建，颇为不悦，说赵佶乃昏君，被金人所俘，丧身北国，遂题改塔名为"三峰寺塔"。据《长乐县志》记载，郑和下西洋中多次"奉施喜舍"修建该塔及塔旁的"三峰塔寺"。后来寺废塔存。明弘治三年（1490年）长乐知县潘府改塔名为雁塔。

说起圣寿宝塔，就不得不说一说太平港。太平港位于三峰寺塔的西侧，郑和七下西洋，每次出海前均在太平港停驻。太平港原名吴航头，别名河阳港。永乐七年（1409年），郑和为祈求往返航行太平安顺，奏改此地为"太平港"。

Shengshou Pagoda, which is pavilion-styled and octagonal-shaped, is typical of the pagodas in the coastal areas of Southeast China. The seven-floor pagoda, which measures 27.4 meters high, sits on a platform over 3.3 meters tall. The base of the pagoda features carvings of lions, peonies, and gods of great strength. The spirally arranged stone steps inside lead to the top. On the lintel of the first-floor gateway is a carving of "Yan Ta", two Chinese characters representing wild goose and pagoda respectively. On the walls there are relief sculptures of Buddhas including Wenshu, Puxian, 50 arhats, 16 flying apsaras musicians and dancers as well as Buddhist stories. In the corners of the outer walls there are carvings of dharma protectors in different styles. The protectors, who are in helmets and armor, either hold swords or put their hands on swords, with their feet resting on lotus flowers and canopies hanging over their heads. A stone tablet with the inscription of "Shengshou Pagoda" hangs on the southward second-floor gateway. There are two gateways on each of the floors except the first floor. On the walls of the sixth and seventh floors there are inscriptions of six pagoda building records. Most relief sculptures on the walls and the circular engravings in the niches on each floor are descriptive of Buddhist stories. Being lifelike with primitive simplicity, they are valuable objects for the study of the architecture and stone carving art of the Song Dynasty about 1, 000 years ago.

The construction of Shengshou Pagoda started in 1096 or the 3rd year during the reign of Emperor Shaosheng and completed in 1117 or the 7th year during the reign of emperor Zhenghe in the Song Dynasty. It was built to honor the birthday of emperor Huizong, hence the name Shengshou, two Chinese characters representing majesty and longevity respectively. During the reign of emperor Yongle in the Ming Dynasty about 600 years ago, the fleet led by the great navigator Zheng He berthed in Changle County for several times. The pagoda then became a watchtower as it overlooked the big fleet berthing in Taiping Harbor. It also became a marker tower for the fleet sailing into or out of the harbor. Legend has it that at one time when Zheng He made an inspection visit to the pagoda to observe the port, he was displeased to learn that the pagoda was built in honor of the longevity of emperor Huizong, saying that Zhao Ji or emperor Huizong had been a fatuous and self-indulgent ruler and he was killed in the State of Jin after being taken captive. Then he changed the name of the pagoda into Sanfeng Temple Pagoda. According to Changle County Annals, during his stay in Changle between his voyages to the West, Zheng He donated money several times for the repairing of the pagoda and the construction of Sanfeng Pagoda Temple, which was demolished many years later. In 1490 or the 3rd year during the reign of Ming emperor Hongzhi, Pan Fu, the county magistrate changed the name of the pagoda to Yan Pagoda.

Speaking of Shengshou Pagoda, we might also be interested in learning something about Taiping Harbor. Situated to the west of Sanfeng Temple Pagoda, the harbor was where the vessels berthed each time before the fleet set off during Zheng He's seven voyages to the West. It was initially named Wuhangtou or Heyang Harbor. In 1490 or the 7th year during the reign of Ming emperor Yongle, Zheng He proposed to the imperial court to change the name to Taiping Harbor with a wish for safe and smooth voyages.

圣寿宝塔原本并非孤零零的一处，在南山之上曾有一片恢宏的建筑群。郑和船队驻长乐太平港等待季风来临时，短则两个月，长则十个月。在漫长的等待中，船队没有闲着，而是招募水手、修造船舶、祭祀海神，伺风开洋。在第七次下西洋前，郑和组织整修三峰寺塔、天妃宫，并在天妃宫左侧修建一座三清宝殿。南山上塔、寺、宫、殿俱全，用郑和的话来说，便是"画栋连云，如翚如翼"。郑和修建的这组南山建筑，在历史更迭中仅留下一座三峰寺塔。

与圣寿宝塔交相辉映的是《天妃灵应之记》碑，俗称"郑和碑"，为圣寿宝塔的附属文物，今藏于长乐区郑和史迹陈列馆内。明宣德六年（1431年）郑和第七次奉使西洋，他统领船队又驻泊于太平港等候季风出海，立下该碑并亲自撰文。碑文详细记载了从明永乐三年至宣德六年（1405—1431年）前后二十六年间郑和六次下西洋的历程，以及又承担第七次下西洋的任务等，还褒扬了天妃（妈祖）的神力，记录之详尽绝无仅有。碑文阴刻楷书共计1176个字，除了有9个字磨损外，碑文至今基本完整可读。郑和碑与圣寿宝塔一同见证了郑和七下西洋的伟大壮举，是研究我国明代海外交通史及中外交往史的重要实物资料。

《天妃灵应之记》碑最早立于长乐南山天妃宫内，后天妃宫倒塌，埋于荒土之中。1930年，一位农民在天妃宫遗址挖土时发现了石碑。当时的长乐县县长吴鼎芬立即派人将碑移到县署中的"思善斋"侧。吴鼎芬离任后，这块碑又被荒草乱石掩盖。后来，时任长乐县县长王伯秋找到了这块碑。1937年抗日战争爆发后，为了不让石碑落入敌人手中，长乐人将其北运至南平。抗战胜利后，几经辗转，石碑又重回长乐，成为弥足珍贵的历史遗物。

《天妃灵应之记》碑1961年被福建省人民委员会公布为省级文物保护单位，2006年被国务院公布为全国重点文物保护单位（圣寿宝塔附属文物）。碑文记载了当年郑和下西洋贸易的盛况。据记载，永乐十五年（1417年）郑和下西洋时，"忽鲁谟斯国进狮子、金钱豹、大西马。……木骨都束国进花福禄并狮子。卜剌哇国进千里骆驼并驼鸡。爪哇、古里国进麋里羔兽"（林婧，2020：43）。从这段文字中可以看出，郑和七下西洋不仅带去了本国的奇珍异宝，也带回了各国的珍奇动物。

Shengshou Pagoda was not a solitary building on the Nanshan Hill. Instead it was part of a group of majestic buildings. Before the launching of each voyage, Zheng He's fleet would berth in Taiping Harbor for at least two months or even as long as ten months, waiting for the coming of the favorable monsoon. During the long stay in the harbor, Zheng He would recruit new sailors, organize the maintenance of vessels, and offer sacrifices to the sea goddess. Before setting off for the 7th voyage to the West, Zheng He organized the renovation of Sanfeng Temple Pagoda and Sea Goddess Palace as well as the construction of Sanqing Palace. The Nanshan Hill became a place featuring a combination of a pagoda, a temple, and two palaces. Zheng He was quoted as saying "The buildings are closely grouped and richly ornamented, resembling the brightly colored feathers of a pheasant." Of the different buildings, however, only Sanfeng Temple Pagoda has survived into the present after a long history.

Also well known as Shengshou Pagoda is the Stele Recording Efficacious Spiritual Response of Sea Goddess or Zheng He Stele, an attached part of the Pagoda relic. It is now kept in Changle Museum of Zheng He Relics. In 1431 or the 6th year during the reign of Ming emperor Xuande, before setting off the 7th voyage to the West, the fleet led by Zheng He berthed in Taiping Harbor, waiting for the coming of a monsoon. It was then that Zheng He had a stele bearing the inscription of a record written by himself set up. The inscription keeps a detailed record of the 6 voyages made during 26 years (1405-1431, or from the 3rd year in Yongle period to the 6th year in Xuande period of the Ming Dynasty), and the task to be fulfilled in the 7th voyage. Also included in the record is a compliment to Mazu or the Chinese sea goddess. The inscription is comprised of 1, 176 Chinese characters in standard script of handwriting. All the characters, except 9 damaged ones, are still complete and readable. Both the stele and Shengshou Pagoda are witnesses to the feat of Zheng He's seven voyages to the West. They are valuable physical objects for research on China's overseas transportation and exchange in the Ming Dynasty.

Zheng He Stele was originally placed in the Sea Goddess Palace on the Nanshan Hill but was buried up after the palace collapsed. In 1930 the stele was discovered by a farmer when he happened to scoop earth at the former site of the palace. On hearing the report, Wu Dingfen, the magistrate of the previous Changle County, had the stele carried to the side of Sishan House in the office compound of the county government. After Wu left his post, the stele was left unattended and covered up under weeds and stone pieces. Then it was rediscovered by Wang Boqiu, the succeeding county magistrate. In 1937 when the War of Resistance Against Japanese Aggression broke out, the stele was carried to Nanping City in northern Fukien to protect it from the Japanese troops. After the end of the War, with several attempts made, the stele was carried back to Changle. It is a precious relic still well preserved.

In 1961 Zheng He Stele was listed as a provincial relic by the People's Committee of Fukien Province. In 2006 it was listed as a national key relic and an attached relic of Shengshou Pagoda. The inscription of the stele keeps a detailed record of the overseas trade conducted by Zheng He during his voyages to the West. It notes that, in the 15th year during the reign of emperor Yongle, "lions, leopards ... were purchased in Hormuz, ... zebras and lions in Mogadishu, camels and ostriches in Brava, and blue bulls in Java and Calicut" (Lin Jing, 2020: 43). The record shows that in the seven voyages Zheng He not only brought rare treasures abroad but also brought back rare animals from abroad.

◎ 海贸之兴：迥龙桥、邢港古码头

迥龙桥

小木屋，石板路。炊烟飘出小木窗，绕过祥和静谧的村庄。漫步于狭窄的村道小巷，可以感受闽安村古朴的历史文化底蕴。回望过去，这个宁静的小村庄也见证了海贸的繁荣。

出了福州城，沿闽江向东至马尾亭江，就来到闽安村。这里古称闽安镇，是国家历史文化名村。它三面靠山，临江面海，从唐至清均为沟通福州与闽东地区及通向外海的重要门户。"两山如门，一水如线，而闽安镇缩其口"，明代董应举三言两语就道出了其地理位置的重要性。闽安取"安镇闽疆"之意。

闽安村的邢港古航道直通闽江闽安门。航道水深15米，港阔70米，港长约5公里，是天然的避风良港。自汉唐直至清代，所有进出福州港的外国船只都要先停留在闽安邢港古航道上，一为接受货物检验、缴纳课税，二为驻泊避风。由此可知其在当时的重要地位。

据文献记载，唐武则天时，闽安村邢港的海上贸易空前繁荣，作为福州海外贸易必经之路的通海大石桥迥龙桥就在此时开建。后来南宋丞相郑性之重修此桥，并题"飞盖桥"。迥龙桥呈南北走向，横跨邢港河，桥下就是当年海上丝绸之路的古航道。它历经千年依旧完好如初，是福州现存最古老的石桥，被列入《中国世界文化遗产预备名单》。

外观优美、造型别致的迥龙桥，全长66米，有四墩五孔，两墩间距为13米左右。最特别之处是四个桥墩均呈两头尖翘的船形，这样的构造能够有效地分水，防止因江水的冲击而导致桥体毁坏。墩与墩之间共架25根巨石梁，每根重达30吨，当年如何吊装上去的至今仍是个谜。石板横铺桥面，石栏护其两侧。石栏共有36根柱，柱顶雕刻有雄狮、猛豹等珍奇异兽，以及宝盒、珍果。这些柱雕虽然历经千年风雨已经有些风化和磨损，但仍然能看出当年的气韵，展示了唐宋时期石刻的精湛技艺。

◎ Prosperity of Maritime Trade: Jionglong Bridge, Ancient Xinggang Wharfs

Jionglong Bridge

Strolling in the narrow alleys paved with stone slabs alongside the wooden cottages, you can feel the historical and cultural touch of Min'an Village in simplicity. Walking by the tranquil houses, you can see smoke curling up out of small wooden windows and pervading the peaceful village. Peaceful as it is, the small village was a witness to the prosperity of maritime trade.

Travel eastward along the Minjiang River from downtown Fuzhou, and you will arrive at Min'an Village in Tingjiang, Mawei District. The village, known as Min'an Town in ancient times, is listed as a national village of historical and cultural interest. Lying on the riverside and facing seawards, with three mountains on its back, Min'an remained a hub connecting Fuzhou with eastern Fukien and the sea from the Tang to the Qing dynasties. Dong Yingju, a poet of the Ming Dynasty, was quoted as saying "here a river extends in between two mountains standing erect like doors, with its mouth tied up in Min'an." Dong's words well describe the strategic location of the town. The name Min'an, two Chinese characters representing Fukien Province and safety respectively, was adopted with a wish that the town could "safeguard the frontiers of Fukien".

The ancient waterway of the Xinggang River is directly connected with the part of the Minjiang River near Min'an. Measuring 15 meters deep, 70 meters wide and 5 kilometers long, the waterway has remained a natural shelter harbor since ancient times. From the Han to the Qing dynasties, the foreign vessels going in and out of Fuzhou port would berth in the waterway of the Xinggang River at first to have their cargo inspected and taxed or take shelter from storms. The importance of the waterway was indisputable.

Records show that during the reign of empress Wu Zetian in the Tang Dynasty, Xinggang saw an unprecedented prosperity of marine trade. The construction of Jionglong Bridge started then and it became a vital part of communications for the marine trade of Fuzhou City. In the Southern Song Dynasty more than 800 years ago, Zheng Xingzhi, the prime minister, organized the reconstruction of Jionglong Bridge and renamed it "Feigai Bridge". Running from north to south over the Xinggang River, the stone bridge crosses over the ancient waterway of the marine silk route. With a history of about one thousand years, the bridge still remains intact and has become the oldest existing stone bridge in Fuzhou. It is now on the tentative list of world cultural heritages in China.

The bridge is elegant in appearance and exquisite in structure. Stretching for 66 meters, it has four piers and five openings, with the gap between the tiers measuring 13 meters. The top of each pier is pointed and tip-tilted, as is the shape of a boat. The special design helps divert the water flow and keeps the bridge safe and sound in the constant impact force of the currents. There are a total of 25 big stone crossbeams on the top of the piers, with each beam weighing up to 30 tons. It remains unknown how such big stone pieces were lifted and set in place in ancient times. The bridge floor is paved with stone slabs and lined with stone railings that are supported by 36 columns. The top of each column is decorated with carvings of either animals such as lions and leopards or objects such as mirror cases and fruits. Being weathered and worn in some parts over about one thousand years, the column carvings still retain the artistic style and the exquisite craftsmanship of the Tang and Song dynasties.

迴龙桥
Jionglong Bridge

　　在这些柱雕中，宝奁石雕有独特的寓意。宝奁是唐代女子出嫁时盛放金银首饰的箱子，是唐代女权的象征，代表唐朝妇女的地位。公元690年武则天称帝，这位中国历史上唯一的女皇帝在位期间，出现了凤在上、龙在下的宫殿雕塑，标志着当时女性至高无上的地位。

　　武则天当权时闽安迴龙桥开始筹建，但当地官员与建桥者难以理清女权与政权的先后关系，便心生一计：桥南石雕先宝奁后官印，桥北石雕先官印后宝奁，而在桥中心多增一组宝奁石雕，从而巧妙地化解了石雕排序的困扰。

　　迴龙桥不是常见的独体桥梁，其巧妙处在于附带有玄帝亭、圣王庙及观音阁三个古建筑。玄帝亭位于桥南的引桥上，是桥亭结构，穿过桥亭方能步上石桥。圣王庙建造在北引桥驳岸上，跨街廊亭与古石桥的驳岸共用一连体基础。当年的能工巧匠在有限的空间内把跨街亭、圣王庙、观音阁与石桥融为一体，这种桥亭庙合一的格局在我国古桥中十分罕见，至今依然是居住在邢港河两岸的人们的必经之路。

It is noteworthy that the carvings of mirror cases have special meanings. Mirror cases were popularly used to keep jewelry or dowry of wedded women in the Tang Dynasty, and they were symbols of women's power and social status. In 690 A.D., Wu Zetian proclaimed herself the empress, the only one in Chinese history. During her reign as the empress, some statues of the phoenix were placed above statues of the dragon in the royal palace, an indication of women's supreme power at that time.

Preparations for the construction of Jionglong Bridge were made during the reign of the empress. The local officials and the bridge builders were struggling to find a way to arrange the images of women's power and political power harmoniously in the bridge design. They finally decided on a special order of the 36 column carvings, with the mirror case carvings placed in front of the official seal carvings on the southern part of the bridge and the order of the carvings reversed on the northern part. Meanwhile, they placed an extra pair of mirror case carvings in the middle of the bridge. This spared them trouble that might be caused by a wrong order of the carvings.

Jionglong Bridge is not independently structured, as it integrates with other three ancient buildings, namely Xuandi Pavilion, Monkey King Temple and Kwan-yin Temple. Xuandi Pavilion lies in the southern bridge approach while Monkey King Temple sits on the embankment alongside the northern bridge approach. The street-crossing pavilion and the embankment of the stone bridge are constructed on a shared foundation. The integration of the pavilion, the temple and the bridge is rare among the ancient bridges in China. They still remain a route that must be taken for people living on both sides of the Xinggang River.

邢港古码头

闽安村的邢港位于闽江峡谷内，因有旗盘山拦住海风，邢港便成为天然的避风港。再加上港深河阔，便于停泊大海船，因而成为古代海上丝绸之路上的商贸重镇。邢港古航道上的古码头是福州海上贸易的"见证者"。

马尾罗星塔上有乾隆时期福州郡守李拔题写的铭文："闽安镇海舶出入，为省会咽喉。"而邢港古航道便是进出福州港的外国商船必经之路，每艘船都要在闽安接受货物检验以及缴纳课税。循河道溯流而上，魁岐往福州方向沙洲多、吃水浅，大船无法行驶。所以从汉唐至清代，进出福州的大船只能停在闽安，货品分装至小船后运至福州城区。

邢港码头分布在迴龙桥南北两侧，呈内八字型排列，为福建省文物保护单位，同时也属于"海上丝绸之路"福州史迹的一部分。邢港沿岸共有三个古码头、六个古道头、八个古浦头。三个古码头分别为水门道码头、口头街码头（即海关埕码头）、员山码头；六个古道头比码头略小，分布在迴龙桥北岸和南岸，以及邢港与闽江交汇处等地；八个古浦头名义上称浦，实际上也是闽江口古代商贸交流中心和货物集散地。

目前，闽安遗留下来的最大古码头为水门道古码头，长约100米、宽3米许、高8米，一直延伸到闽江深水处。码头临江处与入水台阶呈丁字型，立有"闽安古渡"石碑。闽安古渡曾是北宋时期最早的粮食渡口，也是我国"海上丝绸之路"的起点之一。

优越的近海优势，使闽安自汉唐以来海上贸易一直很活跃。邢港河岸边曾经码头林立、舟楫相连，外国与内陆商船往来辐辏，商贾云集，是渔产、农产品、竹木材等的集散地。

唐朝在闽安邢港设立巡检司衙门，负责巡视海上贸易、缉私与巡捕海盗以及设关课税。唐武则天称帝时，闽安邢港的海上贸易空前繁荣。迴龙桥之下就是当年海上丝绸之路的古航道。

五代后梁开平三年（909年），王审知开辟甘棠港，由福州海运至辽东地区以及新罗国的大量商品货物都由邢港起航。

Ancient Xinggang Wharfs

Xinggang, a harbor in Min'an Village, is located in the valley of the Minjiang River. With the Qipan Mountain blocking the wind from the sea and the river water running deep and wide, Xinggang has been a natural shelter harbor for sizable sea vessels and was a major port in the maritime silk route in ancient times. The ancient wharves alongside the waterway of Xinggang are witnesses to the prosperity of marine trade in history in Fuzhou.

On Luoxing Pagoda in Mawei District, there is an epigraph written by Liba, the governor of Fuzhou during the reign of Qing emperor Qianlong. The epigraph reads "Min'an Town is situated where sea vessels arrive or depart and is the narrowest part of a vital communications route connected to the capital of the province". The ancient waterway in Min'an was the route to be taken for the foreign vessels steering into or out of Fuzhou port, and here the cargo on the vessels was inspected and taxed. The stretch of the Minjiang River between Min'an and Kuiqi or the further upstream wharves were not navigable for big vessels, because there were many sandbanks. From the Han to the Qing dynasties, big vessels would first berth at Xinggang of Min'an, where the cargo would be sorted and then re-loaded onto smaller vessels that could run upstream to downtown Fuzhou.

The ancient wharves in Xinggang are near both sides of Jionglong Bridge and are arranged in a pigeon-toe pattern. They are listed as both provincial relics and maritime-silk-route relics of Fuzhou. Along the riverside of Xinggang there are three ancient wharves, six ancient piers, and eight ship cargo yards. The three wharves are Shuimendao Wharf, Koutoujie Wharf (or Haiguancheng Wharf), and Yuanshan Wharf; The six ancient piers, which are a bit smaller, are located near both sides of Jionglong Bridge and the confluence of Xinggang River and the Minjiang River; The eight ship cargo yards or "Pu" were trade centers as well as cargo logistics in ancient times in the Minjiang River estuary.

Shuimendao Wharf is the biggest ancient wharf in Min'an. Measuring about 100 meters long, three meters wide, and eight meters high, the wharf runs all the way to the deep-water area of the Minjiang River. The out-reaching end of the wharf is joined in a "T" shape to a flight of stone steps reaching down to the river water. Standing by is a stele bearing the inscription "Ancient Wharf of Min'an". It is the grain cargo wharf constructed the earliest in the Northern Song Dynasty about 1, 000 years ago and was one of the starting points of the Maritime Silk Route in China.

With a favorable location in the coastal area, Min'an saw a prosperous marine trade since the Han and the Tang Dynasties: numerous business vessels from home and abroad sailed in and out in the Xinggang River, with their cargo loading or unloading at the densely distributed wharves. Xinggang of Min'an became a center of logistics for fishery products, farm produce, timber, bamboo wood, and so on.

In the Tang Dynasty (618-907 A.D.) an inspection bureau was established in Xinggang, Min'an, to inspect marine trade, suppress smuggling, combat pirates, and levy taxes. During the reign of Wu Zetian the empress, the marine trade in Xinggang was unprecedentedly prosperous, and the project of Jionglong Bridge, a vital route for the overseas trade in Fuzhou, was launched. The waterway below the bridge became an important part of the maritime silk route.

In 909 or the third year in the period of Kaiping of the Later Liang Dynasty, Wang Shenzhi, the king of Min, opened Gantang Port to expand marine trade. Many seagoing vessels set out from Xinggang on a route to the present eastern Liaoning Province and the Democratic People's Republic of Korea.

在宋代，邢港古码头是由福州至日本、大食诸国的重要出海口岸，朝廷在闽安常设关税机构。

在明清，各地生产的大量丝绸、陶瓷、茶叶等都在邢港码头装船并扬帆运往世界各地。来自日本、朝鲜以及美洲、欧洲等地的商品也汇集到闽安，在纵横交错的九街九铺交易，如口头街、桥头街、草尾街、万寿铺、保安铺、城隍顶、西山境等，真可谓是："八方商贾聚闽安，百货随潮船入镇。"郑和七下西洋的部分船队六次驻泊于闽安，当地至今有"三宝埕"、"三宝街"的地名。

邢港文化遗产形态多样，内涵丰富。尤其是多处港口古码头等，集中呈现了7世纪至10世纪福州古港的兴盛与空前繁荣的景象。

In the Song Dynasty, Xinggang became an important marine trade port connecting Fuzhou with Japan and Arabian countries. It was then that a tariff bureau was set up in Min'an.

In the Ming and the Qing dynasties, numerous products including silk, porcelain wares, and tea leaves would be loaded at Xinggang wharves and carried to different parts of the world; the commodities from Japan, the Democratic People's Republic of Korea, the Americas, and Europe would be unloaded at the wharves and transacted in the shops alongside the intertwined streets, such as Koutou Street, Qiaotou Street, Caowei Street, Wanshou Shop, Bao'an Shop, Chenghuangding, and Xishanjing. The prosperity is well depicted in the verse which roughly reads "business people from across Fukien would all meet here in Min'an, and vessels carrying all kinds of cargo would sail into the town when sea tides come in". For six times Min'an had been an anchorage of some vessels in the fleet led by Zheng He, who made seven voyages to the West in the Ming Dynasty. Some places in Min'an were named after the navigator, such as "Sanbao Cheng" and "Sanbao Street", and the names are still in use today.

The ancient wharves in Xinggang are relics featuring variety and historical richness. Together they reflect the unprecedented prosperity of Fuzhou port from the 7th to the 10th century.

第十七章 船政追昔：壮怀激越

Chapter Seventeen
Recollections of Mawei Shipbuilding Culture:
Tenacious Pursuit of National Rejuvenation

◎ 船政风华：总理船政衙门、船政轮机厂、绘事院、英国领事分馆

总理船政衙门

经福州江滨东大道往马尾方向行至马尾造船厂旧址，望北就可见船政格致园，其中有船政衙门景点，从中仍能窥见当年船政的辉煌。

清同治五年（1866年），闽浙总督左宗棠以"欲防海之害"奏请在福州马尾创建船政。于是，清政府在马尾设立总理船政衙门，直隶中央。后由沈葆桢接办船政，开设造船厂和船政学堂，建设海军，借鉴西学，制造与育才并重，使船政成为中国近代工业、航空业和近代海军之摇篮。

建于1867年的总理船政衙门是清朝船政的核心管理机构。其所辖事务涵盖造船、海军教育及舰队操练等多方面的内容，是近代中国最早进行海防、海军建设的国家部门。

总理船政衙门
Office Compound of Naval Administration Ministry

◎ Shipbuilding Culture Relics: Office Compound of Naval Administration Ministry, Engine Workshop of Naval Administration, Designing Institute of Naval Administration, and Branch Consulate of Great Britain

Office Compound of Naval Administration Ministry

Go along the East Riverside Avenue toward Mawei District until you arrive at the former site of Mawei Shipyard, and you can see the Naval Administration Museum in the north across the road. The replica of the Office Compound of Naval Administration Ministry still shows the glory of the shipyard in history.

In 1866 or the fifth year during the reign of Qing emperor Tongzhi, Zuo Zongtang the governor-general of Fukien and Zhejiang provinces proposed to the imperial court setting up a naval shipyard in Mawei, Fuzhou, with an aim to "prevent enemies from the sea". The Naval Administration Ministry, which was directly under the central government, was established in Mawei. Later Shen Baozhen, a renowned minister of the Qing Dynasty, took over the ministry from Zuo Zongtang. Under the leadership of Shen, the Ministry set up a naval shipyard and a navy academy and developed a new naval force. It laid equal stress on manufacturing and talent training, with Western technologies and ideas drawn on for reference. The establishment of the naval administration ministry led to the birth of a modern navy as well as modern manufacturing and aircraft sectors in China.

Established in 1867, the Naval Administration Ministry was the core department responsible for a wide range of naval affairs, covering shipbuilding, navy education, fleet drilling, etc. It was established the earliest in modern China as a national-level department of coast defense and navy development.

船政衙门原位于马尾莺脰山下，集办公、议事、休息功能于一体。抗战时遭轰炸，后期破败。1956年修福马铁路时被拆除。2013—2015年，择现址新建了"船政衙门"景点。

复建后的船政衙门突出了晚清特色，结构上融合衙门官府和福州官宦民居的特点，属合院式建筑群落。其主体采用清式大木构造，为三进建筑。主梁采用印尼的波萝格木材，十分坚硬且稳定性高，具有防火、防潮、防白蚁的特点。整体风格上体现庄重、威严、古朴和实用，成为南方明清府衙建筑的典范。

船政衙门正上方有一块竖匾，上书"总理船政"（当时冠以"总理"名义的国家机关只有两处，另一处为"总理各国事务衙门"，简称"总理衙门"，设在北京）。船政衙门落成时，首任船政大臣沈葆桢亲自撰写了多副楹联，用于激励船政人员。位于大门两侧的楹联写着："且漫道见所未见，闻所未闻，即此是格致关头，认真下手处；何以能精益求精，密益求密，定须从鬼神屋漏，仔细扪心来。"位于正门两侧的楹联写着："以一篑为始基，从古天下无难事；致九译之新法，于今中国有圣人。"

大堂是历任船政大臣办公的场所，正中间的屏风为仙鹤朝阳一品文官补子，是参照船政大臣沈葆桢的官级而设置的。两侧的执事牌陈列了历任船政大臣。任职的共有22位，其中专职的有8位，由福州将军和闽浙总督兼任的各有5位。大堂后方悬挂"天理国法人情"六个大字，即做事循天理、断案凭国法、处事合人情，以此警示总理船政衙门的官员们要秉公执法、廉政为民。

二堂包括卧室、书房、会客厅等。在船政大臣会见属僚的议事厅的正中央悬挂着匾额"开物成务"。这是出自《周易》中的一句话，寓意只要通晓万物之理，便能办好各种事情。

The former office compound of the Ministry was situated at the foot of the Yingdou Mountain. It was originally a place for office work, meetings and rest but was dilapidated after being bombarded in the War of Resistance against Japanese Aggression. The compound was dismantled in 1956 when Fuzhou-Mawei Railway was constructed. The replica of the office compound was built on the present site between 2013 and 2015.

The courtyard-centered compound highlights the architecture of the late Qing Dynasty by integrating the structure of an office compound and that of officials' residences. The main part of it is comprised of buildings in three rows. They are buildings with big wood structures, with the primary beams made of Indonesian merbau, a hard and stable wood resistant to fire, humidity and termites. Appearing in a style of solemn majesty with simplicity and practicality, the office compound well represents the buildings of its kind in the Ming and Qing dynasties in South China.

Over the front gate of the office compound hangs a vertical tablet bearing four Chinese characters representative of "Naval Administration Ministry" (There were two national-level departments of such kind in the late Qing Dynasty, the other being the Foreign Affairs Ministry, which was based in Beijing). When the office compound was completed, Shen Baozhen, the first naval administration minister, wrote several couplets to boost the morale of the staff. The couplet hanging on the two columns at the front gate roughly reads "Don't say you have never even seen or heard of something, because it offers a critical chance to closely study its nature; if you strive to achieve greater perfection, you should be scrupulous about every detail." And the couplet hanging on the two sides of the front gate roughly reads "Believe that the completion of a foundation starts with every basket of earth, and there are no difficulties in the world; devote yourself to studying the latest technologies of the West, and you will become pillars of the state."

The central hall of the compound was the office space for the naval administration minister. In the middle of the hall sits a big screen carrying the design of a red-crowned crane facing the red sun, a symbol of the highest-ranking civil officials in the Qing Dynasty. It was designed on the basis of the official ranking of Shen Baozhen, the first naval administration minister. On the two sides in front of the screen stand upright boards bearing the names of the original posts of the officials before he was appointed the minister. There were 22 officials holding the ministerial post, including eight full-time ministers, five part-time ones who were at the same time General of Fuzhou, and five part-time ones who were at the same time Governor-general of Fukien and Zhejiang Provinces. On the back wall of the hall there are six large-size Chinese characters, which are representative of "heavenly principles, national laws, and human ethics", with a reference to the principle of following heavenly principles, observing national laws, and conforming to human ethics. The slogan was posted to remind the officials in the Ministry to enforce laws impartially and be honest and clean officials in the service of civilians.

The second hall in the compound is comprised of bedrooms, studies, reception rooms, etc. Over the central meeting room where the minister often met his subordinates there is a horizontal board carrying the inscription of four Chinese characters, which roughly represent the idea that "understand thoroughly the truth of all things, and you can handle affairs successfully accordingly", a quote from the *Book of Changes*, a Chinese classic. The quotation was taken to remind the staff that a command of the principles of all things would lead to the achievement of all related goals.

走出衙门，在后门可以看到"官厅池"。它与轮机厂、绘事院、钟楼、一号船坞构成福建船政建筑群，为全国重点文物保护单位。官厅池占地面积700平方米，采用花岗石砌造而成。它集天水（雨水）、地水（泉水）、江水为一体，可谓集天地人和。池的沟渠和闽江水连通，水位受潮汐影响而涨落，水清景美，具有防火功能，还能存储造船所需的木料。

官厅池旁边的建筑是船政学堂，这是近代中国最先引入西方自然科学教材和教育制度设立的新式学堂，为中国近代造船、航海、航空等事业做出了巨大贡献。

虽然历史已经久远，但透过船政衙门景点，我们仿佛仍能看见一百年多前马尾船政的辉煌历程，还有中华民族图强逐梦的"我命由我不由天"精神。

船政轮机厂

位于福州市马尾区的福建船政建筑多建于船政创办初期，其中就包括轮机厂、绘事院等，是第五批全国重点文物保护单位，还被列入中国工业遗产保护名录。

当年中国在马尾设船政造轮船，是在没有任何工业基础上的创举。清朝首任船政大臣沈葆桢力主引进西方先进的技术、设备和人才，使马尾造船厂在两年左右的时间内快速形成规模，生产车间达到50多个。

走进船政文化城船厂车间片区，一座两层红砖大楼映入眼帘，这是现存的船政工业遗址中最古老的建筑，也是中国现存历史最悠久的近代红砖工业建筑。楼下是制造船用蒸汽机的车间，时称"轮机厂"（轮机车间）。楼上则是设计船体和蒸汽机样式、绘制图纸的场所，时称"绘事院"。这里是我国最早设立的工业设计所。

轮机厂始建于清同治六年（1867年）。光绪十年（1884年）甲申中法战役中，法船炮击船政局工厂，轮机厂中间的合拢厂（安装车间）中弹倒塌，而轮机厂幸免于难。民国30年（1941年），日寇以三个师团绕道攻入福州，船厂遭日寇洗劫，许多厂房被焚烧。民国33年（1944年），日寇再陷福州，船政局再次遭到破坏。经历了几次战火，轮机厂只剩一座楼保存至今。轮机车间外墙上残留的累累弹痕就是日军暴行留下的铁证。

Stroll out of the house, and you can see Guanting Pond, which is listed as a national key relic together with the Engine Workshop of Naval Administration, the Designing Institute of Naval Administration, the Bell Tower, and Dock No.1 in Mawei Shipyard. The pond, which covers 700 square meters, is built of granite flagstones. With rainwater, spring water, and river water stored together, the pond is seemingly an integration of all favorable natural conditions. As the drainage channels are connected to the Minjiang River, the water level in the pond rises and falls regularly with river tides, keeping the water fresh all the time and making a beautiful scene as well. The pond can also be used to provide water in fire fighting and space for the storage of shipbuilding timber when needed.

The building adjacent to Guanting Pond is the Navy School, a new-style school in modern China. Here text books on Western natural science were used and the Western education system adopted. It made a great contribution to the development of the shipbuilding, navigation and aviation sectors in modern China.

More than a century has elapsed since the founding of the Naval Administration Ministry in Mawei, but the office compound still reminds the visitors of its glory in the past and Chinese people's unyielding pursuit of national rejuvenation.

Engine Workshop of Naval Administration

Most of the Naval Administration buildings in Mawei District were constructed when the shipbuilding administration was established at its early stage. Among the oldest buildings are the Engine Workshop and the Designing Institute, both of which are listed as fifth-group national key relics and at the same time Chinese industrial heritages.

Mawei Shipyard was set up when an industrial foundation did not exist in China. Shen Baozhen the first Naval Administration Minister strongly advocated the introduction of advanced technologies and equipment as well as talents from the West. Due to his efforts, Mawei Shipyard developed into a sizable factory with up to over 50 workshops in approximately two years.

In the workshop section of the Naval Administration Culture Park, you can see a large red-brick building on two floors, the oldest building on the site of the shipyard heritages and the oldest red-brick factory building in China. On the ground floor lies the Engine Workshop, a place for manufacturing steam engines in vessels. On the second floor lies the Designing Institute, a place for designing vessels and steam engines as well as drawing blueprints. It was an industrial design institute established earliest in modern China.

The Engine Workshop was first constructed in 1867 or the 6th year during the reign of Qing emperor Tongzhi. In 1884 or the 10th year during the reign of emperor Guangxu when the Sino-France War broke out, Mawei Shipyard was bombarded by French warships. The assembly workshop in the middle of the original Engine Plant was hit and collapsed. Luckily, the Engine Workshop escaped the bombardment. In 1941 or the 30th year of the Republic of China, three divisions of the Japanese aggression army invaded Fuzhou City by taking a devious route. The shipyard was looted and many workshops were set on fire by the army. In 1944 or the 33rd year of the Republic of China, the Japanese army captured the city again and did great damage to the shipyard. Because of the wars, the original engine plant was ruined except the Engine Workshop, which has been preserved until today. The bullet and bomb holes left on the outer wall of the workshop are ironclad evidence of the atrocity of the Japanese aggression army.

轮机车间占地2000平方米，当年的整个造型和布局都是法国人设计的。轮机车间周围都是大落地窗，采光等方面考虑得非常周到。屋顶为双坡顶拼木屋架，在屋架处砌大砖柱承重。屋顶木梁每根长20余米，所用的木料都是从当时英国的属地泰国、缅甸进口的高级柚木，俗称铁木，相当坚固。据介绍，法国人按照同样的图纸建造的车间有两处，一处在法国，一处就在中国的马尾。法国的早已不在，马尾的这个也只剩下三分之二的建筑。除房顶和地面稍作修缮外，轮机厂其余部分均保持原样。轮机厂车间内还是原来的法式钢梁柱，120根实心铁柱上架设着由纯生铁铸造的吊车轨道，到现在还在使用。据说，有一批来自欧洲的外国朋友参观了轮机车间，不禁感慨道，像这样保留了当年风格的厂房，如今在欧洲也很难见到了。2006年12月，轮机车间厂房被辟为马尾造船历史陈列馆正式对外开放。

在中国近代工业史上，轮机厂有着举足轻重的地位。对于蒸汽时代的舰船而言，蒸汽机是核心部件，能否自行建造出实用的蒸汽机，决定着中国能否完全摆脱对西方工业的依赖。中国第一台大功率船用蒸汽机于1871年在这里诞生，而后被装在"安澜"号军舰上。到同治十三年（1874年），这里已生产出七台150匹马力船用蒸汽机。

绘事院

从轮机厂外墙沿铁梯到二楼，就是赫赫有名的绘事院旧址，占地1689平方米。绘事院始建于清同治六年（1867年），它是船政的生产设计和制图部门，负责测算、设计以及绘制船身构造图样、机器图样等工作，同时还是船政的工程制图教学机构。在清代的官方文件往来中一般被称为"画楼"。

船政创建时，通过雇佣洋人引进技术，同时也认识到培养人才的重要性。当时，船政招收了一批聪颖少年作为绘事院洋员的帮手（称"艺徒"），跟着洋员学习工程绘图。

从1868年到1873年底，从绘事院共毕业了22名学生。毕业之后，他们大多留在船政各厂和学堂任职。魏瀚、杨廉臣、陈兆翱等一批绘事院培育的英才就从这里起步，后来一起绘就了中国的船政历史。

一百多年前，一幅幅船舶设计图纸就是在这里绘制而成的，这里诞生了中国第一代船舶技术人才。1887年在马尾制造出中国第一艘近海防御铁甲舰——"平远"号，整个船体的甲板都是钢板构成的。当时北洋海军主力军舰有八艘，大部分是从德国、英国买来的，只有"平远"号是国产的，就是在马尾造出来的。1894年甲午战争爆发，"平远"号也参加了战斗，对日本海军构成了重大威胁。

The structure and layout of the Engine Workshop, which covers an area of 2,000 square meters, was designed by a French architect. It is bright with sunlight passing through big French windows on the four sides. The double-pitch roof on a wood-trussed structure is supported by large brick columns. The crossbeams in the roof support measure more than 20 meters long each. They are made of ironwood or teakwood imported from Thailand and Burma, two colonies of Britain at that time. Reports say that the blueprint of the Engine Workshop was used by the French architect for the construction of another workshop in France. Unfortunately, the workshop in France was dismantled long ago and only two thirds of the original workshop in Mawei still exists. But it has remained almost intact except for its roof and ground, which have undergone minor repairs. Inside the workshop, you can still see 120 solid French steel columns, and on top of the steel columns are the crane runways that are still in use today. It is reported that a group of European people who visited the workshop could not help but exclaim over its excellent state of preservation, because the workshop in the style of those years is rare even in Europe. In December, 2006, the workshop was turned into part of Mawei Shipyard History Exhibition Hall.

The Engine Workshop played a key role in the industrial development of modern China. With the steam engine being the vital part of a vessel, the ability to independently manufacture a steam engine of practical value determined the independence of China from the West in the shipbuilding sector. The first high-power steam engine for vessel use in China was manufactured here and installed in the Warship "Anlan". By 1874 or the 13th year during the reign of Qing emperor Tongzhi, a total of seven 150-horsepower steam engines for vessel use had been manufactured in this workshop.

Designing Institute of Naval Administration

Take a flight of iron steps adjoining the outer wall of the workshop, and you can reach the second floor, the former site of the prestigious Designing Institute, which covers 1, 689 square meters. Built in 1867 during the reign of Qing emperor Tongzhi, it was the production designing and blueprint drawing institute under the Naval Administration. Specifically, the Institute was responsible for designing and drawing up the plans for vessel body and machinery as well as measuring and calculating. It also served as an educational institute of engineering drawing. The office address of the Institute was usually referred to as the "Drawing House" in the official documents of the Qing Dynasty.

In the initial stages, the Naval Administration tried to introduce technologies from the West by recruiting foreign experts, but it was aware of the importance of training talents of its own. Therefore, it enlisted some gifted teenagers as helpers of foreign experts in the Designing Institute and, at the same time as, apprentices to them.

From 1868 to the end of 1873, 22 apprentices completed their training and most of them stayed in the Naval Administration factories or schools as employees. Of the many talents trained in the Designing Institute were Wei Han, Yang Liancheng, and Chen Zhao'ao. They made an important part of the history of the Naval Administration.

More than a century ago, lots of vessel plans were drawn up in the Institute, and the first generation of vessel manufacturing experts were also trained there. In 1887, the warship "Pingyuan", the first coastal defense iron vessel in China, was manufactured in Mawei, with its body including the deck all made of steel plates. There were eight main battleships in the Northern Navy of the Qing Dynasty. Except "Pingyuan", the battleships were all purchased from Germany and Britain. In 1894 the Sino-Japanese War broke out, "Pingyuan" was put into service in the battle, posing a big threat to the Japanese navy.

现在，船政绘事院成了马尾造船厂的厂史陈列馆。

英国领事分馆

在福州市马尾区马限山顶的昭忠祠景区内坐落着多处西式建筑，其中就包括英国领事分馆旧址。灰白的建筑、斑驳的墙体，诉说着福州沧桑的过去及其历史变迁。该馆为单层砖木结构，占地457平方米，由当时的英国工程处上海办公室设计建造。建筑物外观较朴素，但内部装修却颇为豪华。

第一次鸦片战争后，1842年中英《南京条约》签订，福州被定为五个通商口岸之一，被迫开放。英国殖民者最先踏上福州这片土地并设立领事馆。

当时经历了鸦片战争与赔款，中国民众尤其是士大夫阶层强烈抵制进城的洋人。此时英国人的到来可谓颇费周折。

和当时开埠的所有港口城市一样，福州城内的民众与进城的洋人摩擦不断，甚至发生了由林则徐带头驱逐洋人的大规模请愿活动。英国驻福州首任领事李太郭于1844年7月（清道光二十四年五月）到福州，最初只被准许在城外南台的鸭姆洲租赁民房办公。后几经周折，英国领事于1845年2月才迁到仓前山泛船浦设馆办公，此为各国在仓前山设驻领事馆的开始。

从1844年7月到1941年，英国先后派32位领事入驻福州。除了烟台山上的英国领事馆外，同治九年（1870年），又在马尾的马限山顶建了一座英国领事分馆，挂上英国副领事署的牌子，作为领事馆人员及英国海员的俱乐部，形成一地两馆的奇观。

这一副领事馆的设立与福建船政局的设立有关。同治年间清政府讨论设立船政的计划，选址马江。方案刚初步定下，英国便抢先购得马限山顶地面。待船政征地时，英方购地契约已经签订。虽然沈葆桢多次抗争，但英国始终不肯相让。同治九年（1870年），英国在该处建成副领事馆。因地势较高，此处可以俯瞰船政局，便于就近监视福建船政的动态，收集情报。时任船政大臣沈葆桢为了国家利益，在1874年不惜重金买回领事分馆的产权及周围土地。

The Designing Institute has turned into part of Mawei Shipyard History Exhibition Hall.

Branch Consulate of Great Britain

On the top of the Maxian Mountain in Mawei District is the scenic area of Zhaozhong Memorial Hall or Naval Martyrs Memorial Hall. In the scenic area are several western-style buildings, including the former site of the Branch Consulate of Great Britain. Covering 457 square meters, the single-storied brick-wood building was designed by H.B.M. Office of Works, Shanghai Office. It is simplistic in appearance but luxurious inside. The greyish white building with mottled walls embodies the vicissitudes of Fuzhou and the historical shifts of the city.

In 1842 after the first Opium War, the Sino-British Treaty of Nanking was signed, and Fuzhou was listed as one of the five ports opened up to foreign trade. The British colonists were among the first to set up consulates in Fuzhou.

Because of the Opium War and the indemnity imposed by the Western powers, the Chinese people especially the literati-official class had a strong aversion to Westerners. Therefore the arrival of the first group of English officials in Fuzhou was met with strong opposition.

As in the other port cities forced to be opened up, there were constant conflicts between the local residents and the foreigners who had just arrived in Fuzhou. A big petition demonstration against Western colonists was even organized in the city under the leadership of Lin Zexu, a Chinese national hero. In July of 1844 or in May of the 24th year during the reign of Qing emperor Daoguang, Li Taiguo, the first British consul in Fuzhou arrived but was only allowed to do office work in rented private residences. In February of 1845, after several attempts, the Consulate was finally relocated and officially set up in Fanchuanpu on the Cangqian Hill or the Yantai Hill. Since then many Western powers had set up their consulates on the Hill.

From July of 1844 to 1941, 32 consuls were dispatched to Fuzhou. In addition to the British Consulate on the Yantai Hill, a branch of the consulate was set up in 1870 or the 9th year during the reign of Qing emperor Tongzhi on the top of the Maxian Mountain in Mawei. It was the office place for the vice-consul and also a club for the consulate staff and British seamen. The co-existence of two office places of one consulate was seen as a unique phenomenon.

The Branch Consulate of Great Britain was set up due to the establishment of Fukien Naval Administration. Durng the reign of emperor Tongzhi, the Qing regime discussed the plan of setting up a naval shipyard and finally decided on a site near the Ma River in Mawei. The preliminary plan was hardly finalized when the British colonists rushed to purchase a piece of land on the top of the Maxian Mountain. The land purchase contract had already been signed before the Qing regime started land requisition for the construction of the shipyard. Although Shen Baozhen, the first Naval Administration minister, strongly opposed the land transaction for several times, the British colonists made no concessions. In 1870 or the 9th year during the reign of emperor Tongzhi, the construction of the branch consulate was completed on the piece of land. The high terrain of the office place gave a bird's-eye view of Mawei Shipyard and enabled the consulate staff to keep watch on its activities. In 1874, with a large sum of money Shen Baozhen managed to repurchase the property right of the branch consulate and the adjacent land.

领事馆外视野开阔、风景优美，但在领事分馆下方却是梅园监狱，即英国驻福州副领事馆附属监狱。该监狱分地面与地下两部分，立面较为讲究，呈维多利亚风格，外有围墙环绕。地下牢房的入口就在监狱的右侧，里面还有两道黑色铁栅栏"把守"。自1870年到1877年，数以千计无辜的中国民众被安上"海盗"的罪名送到地下牢房，不少人经受不住煎熬，在这里命丧黄泉。

时光荏苒，虽然物是人非，但历史却必须铭记。如今，英国领事分馆旧址成了"福州领事馆博物馆"，馆内的老照片和文字记录了外国列强在福州开埠后设立19个领事馆的情况。

◎ 海防雄风：昭忠祠、长门炮台、亭江炮台、琴江满族村

昭忠祠

巍巍昭忠祠，荡荡马江水。忠昭华夏，碧血千秋，娓娓述说着马江之伤。昭忠祠是中法马江海战796位烈士的埋骨处，位于福州市马尾区马限山东南麓，为全国重点文物保护单位。该祠是全国第一座海军专祠，民国时期又增祀在甲午战争中牺牲的海军烈士，是迄今为止全国仅存的且仍保留祭祀功能的近代海军祠堂。

清光绪十年（1884年）农历七月初三，下午1点56分，法国远东舰队闯入马尾港，袭击福建水师舰队，企图侵占福州，震惊中外的甲申中法马江海战爆发。马江海战是中国近代海军初建后参与的第一次大规模战役。由于清政府初次卷入现代战争，毫无经验，加之受李鸿章"虽胜亦斩"命令牵制，福建水师舰队陷于被动挨打局面。参战舰艇大多遭法舰突袭而覆没，水陆官兵死难者达千余人。战后，闽江沿岸的军民自发组织打捞英烈遗体，并分九冢安葬于马限山沿江的东南麓。为纪念中法马江海战中牺牲的英烈，船政大臣张佩纶向朝廷提出兴建昭忠祠，光绪帝下旨由新任船政大臣裴荫森主持修建。

Outside the consulate you can enjoy a wide view and a beautiful scenery. Below the consulate, however, is the former site of Meiyuan Prison or the Affiliated Prison of the Branch Consulate of Great Britain. The prison, which is made up of the overground and the underground parts and encircled by a wall, features an exquisitely designed appearance in Victorian style. The entrance to the underground jail is on the right of the building and is "guarded" by two black iron fences. From 1870 to 1877, up to one thousand innocent Chinese people were condemned to jail as "pirates" and locked up here. Many of them could not bear the suffering and lost their lives in the jail.

The buildings of the branch consulate and the prison still stand despite the flight of time. Although the colonists no longer exist, the part of history is to be engraved in mind. The former site of the branch consulate has been turned into Fuzhou Consulates Museum. With old photos and written records displayed, the Museum introduces the 19 consulates established in Fuzhou after the city was forced open by Western powers.

◎ Recollections of Coastal Defence: Zhaozhong Memorial Hall (or Naval Martyrs Memorial Hall), Changmen Fort Barbette, Tingjiang Fort Barbette, and Qinjiang Manchu Ethnic Group Village

Zhaozhong Memorial Hall (or Naval Martyrs Memorial Hall)

The Naval Martyrs Memorial Hall and the Ma River are witnesses to the heroic fight of the Chinese navy in the Sino-France War, which broke out more than a century ago in Mawei, Fuzhou. Situated at the southeastern foot of the Maxian Mountain, the memorial hall is the burying place for the osseous remains of the 796 martyrs in the war. It was the first naval martyrs memorial hall in the country and is now a national key relic. In the era of the Republic of China, the naval martyrs in the Sino-Japanese War, which broke out between 1894 and 1895, were added to the list of martyrs worshipped in the hall. It is so far the only memorial hall still in use in China for the navy martyrs in modern times.

At 1: 56 p.m. in 1884 or the 10th year during the reign of Qing emperor Guangxu, the Far East Fleet of France intruded Mawei Port and assaulted the Naval Administration Fleet with an attempt to invade Fuzhou. The Sino-France War broke out to the surprise of the whole world. The modern Chinese navy did not have any experience in dealing with the first large-scale war that it had to go into. Worse still, a strict order was given by Li Hongzhang, a major minister of the Qing Dynasty and founder of the Northern Navy, to forbid the forces from fighting the enemy by saying that "those disobeying the order would be beheaded even if the war was won." The navy was put in the passive position of having to receive blows from the enemy. As a result, most battleships in the Naval Administration Fleet submerged under the attack of the French navy. The war caused a total of more than one thousand casualties in the Chinese navy and army. After the end of the war, many soldiers and civilians voluntarily salvaged the bodies of the martyrs from the Ma River and buried them in nine tombs along the riverside at the southeastern foot of the Maxian Mountain. To commemorate the martyrs, Zhang Peilun the Naval Administration Minister proposed to the imperial court building Zhaozhong Memorial Hall. An edict was then issued by the Qing emperor Guangxu to start building the memorial hall, the construction of which was later undertaken by Pei Yinsen the successor to Zhang Peilun.

昭忠祠"负山面江，广八丈有三尺，深减九尺，五楹并列"。正厅内置写有烈士姓名、职务的碑石，梁上高挂一方"碧血千秋"金字匾额，为萨镇冰题、沈觐寿书，两边回廊分立昭忠祠碑和记叙烈士战绩的碑刻。厅中陈列有马尾港地形沙盘，西厢及廊庑陈列大炮、炮弹及烈士的遗物、遗嘱等。

祠西有中法马江海战烈士墓，墓台总长49米、宽10.5米、高1.1米。环台三面各设五层台阶，台正中有一座圆顶雕花四柱石碑亭。昭忠祠后山岩壁有"仰止"、"铁石同心"等题刻。墓西有一条登山石道，拾级而上，便是马限山炮台遗址、英国福州领事馆分馆遗址和梅园监狱遗址等。

马江海战烈士陵园墓碑刻有"光绪十年七月初三日马江诸战士埋骨之处"字样。1920年修缮时，墓碑亭用舰板焊成，以石灰饰以花纹。1984年重修时，碑亭依原状改用花岗石，打造成须弥座雕花拱顶样式。

1922年，鉴于在甲午海战中牺牲的海军烈士没有专门的纪念场所，在海军界人士和烈士家属等的呼吁下，当时的民国政府批准将甲午海战中殉国的海军将士在马江昭忠祠合祀，史称"甲午合祀"。从此，马江昭忠祠成了近代海军英烈纪念专祠，是中国历史上第一座专门纪念海军烈士的国家祭祀场所。

1984年马江海战一百周年之际，昭忠祠、烈士陵园、马限山公园合辟为福州马江海战纪念馆并正式对外开放。

巍巍昭忠祠见证了福建船政的兴衰，也见证了一个富国强兵梦的悲壮演绎，是一段血与火铸就的荣辱历程。

长门炮台

闽江口炮台群是沿着入海口往上在河流两岸密集设置的炮台。这种海防炮台的纵深配置，在全国同类炮台中十分罕见。

"Lying at the foot of the Maxian Mountain and facing the Ma River, Zhaozhong Memorial Hall measures about 27.67 meters in horizontal length and 30 meters in longitudinal length. There are five front columns standing side by side in the central hall", depicts a written record. In the central hall you can see memorial steles right ahead bearing the inscriptions of the martyrs' names and titles. On the crossbeam over the memorial steles hangs a plaque bearing the golden-color inscription of four Chinese characters representative of "long live the heroic spirit", written by Sa Zhenbing, head of the navy in the late Qing Dynasty, and Shen Jinshou, a prestigious Chinese calligrapher. In the corridors on both sides of the central hall there are steles bearing inscribed records of the memorial hall and the heroic acts of the martyrs. In the left-wing rooms there is an exhibition of cannons, shells, and items left behind by some martyrs including their handwritten wills. There is also a sand table model of Mawei Port in the central hall.

To the west of the memorial hall lies the grave of the martyrs in the Sino-France War. The grave platform measures 49 meters long, 10.5 meters wide and 1.1 meters high, with a flight of five steps on each of the three sides. In the center of the platform is a four-column monument pavilion roofed with a dome featuring carved designs. On the rock face of the hill behind Zhaozhong Memorial Hall are inscriptions of some Chinese characters representative of "admired with awe" and "unwavering faith". To the west of the grave are stone steps leading to the mountain top, where you can see the relics of Maxian Mountain Fort Barbette, the Branch Consulate of Great Britain and Meiyuan Prison.

On the grave monument in honor of the martyrs is a Chinese inscription, which reads "This is the burying place for the osseous remains of the martyrs in the Sino-France War that broke out on 3rd of July on the lunar calendar in the 10th year during the reign of Emperor Guangxu". In 1920 a small pavilion was built to shelter the monument. The pavilion, which was roofed with a dome decorated with plaster carvings, was made of steel plates for building battleships. In 1984 the steel plates were replaced with granite pieces, but the original style of the pavilion was preserved. The new monument pavilion features a base in Buddhist style and a dome with carved designs.

For the martyrs in the Sino-Japanese War, which broke out between 1894 and 1895, there was originally no dedicated memorial place as Zhaozhong Memorial Hall. As a response to the call of public figures in the naval forces and family members of the martyrs, in 1922 the central government of the Republic of China approved of adding the martyrs in the Sino-Japanese War to the list of martyrs worshipped in Zhaozhong Memorial Hall. It then became a memorial place dedicated to all the country's navy martyrs in modern times and was the first national memorial place of such kind in the country.

In 1984 at the 100th anniversary of the outbreak of the Sino-France War, Zhaozhong Memorial Hall, the Martyrs Cemetery, and the Maxian Mountain Park were integrated and turned into Sino-France War Museum.

The majestic Zhaozhong Memorial Hall is a witness to the vicissitudes of Fukien Naval Administration and its solemn and stirring pursuit of building a prosperous country with a powerful navy. It is also an embodiment of the struggling spirit of Chinese people in history.

Changmen Fort Barbette

The fort barbettes in the estuary of the Minjiang River are densely distributed along both riversides from the coastal to the downstream stretch of the river mouth. The in-depth coastal defense system of such kind is rare in China.

闽江明清海防炮台群数量较多，包括位置最靠前的壶江炮台，互为犄角构成闽江第一道防线的长门炮台、金牌炮台，相互对峙构成闽江第二道防线的北岸炮台、南岸炮台，以及圆山水寨炮台、琴江炮台、马限山炮台，还有闽江最后一道防线魁岐炮台等。

长门炮台位于连江县琯头镇长门村东电光山。它是闽江口要塞的主炮台，北与射马、划鳅等系列炮位组成防御线，南与金牌、獭石、烟台诸炮台隔江对峙，共同扼守闽江口最狭窄的咽喉地带。江面"双龟把口"，江口"五虎守门"，形势十分险要，长期以来就是福建沿海的军事要地。

道光十四年（1834年）林则徐在此设置军事机构。初建时为土炮台龛位，后经改建重修才形成规模。炮台城堡内设有兵营宿舍、弹药库、活动室等。炮台后面设练兵场、议事厅。

1884年8月，孤拔率领法国远东舰队入侵闽江口，偷袭福建水师，马江海战爆发。在李鸿章"不可衅自我开"、"违者虽胜亦斩"的严令下，闽江沿岸炮台竟坐视法国军舰侵入闽江口。后来法国军舰发现闽江航道水浅，军舰无法上溯至省城福州，于是炮击船政局后便退出闽江口。由于各炮台均面向下游，射角有限，难以射击从上游向下游航行的法国军舰，所以多数被法国军舰从背后炮击摧毁。

1884年闽江口战役后，清朝当局担心法国舰队再来攻击，迅速启动了炮台的重建和增建工作。闽江口地区陆续增建了许多炮台，包括装备两门28厘米口径克虏伯巨炮的长门电光山炮台。

日本侵华战争时期，炮台屡遭日机轰炸。1941年4月，日本海陆军联合进攻福州。因国民党陆军战败放弃守城，长门炮台孤悬敌后，于是守军放弃炮台，并主动破坏了台上的火炮。后来经过陆续修复，基本保留原貌至今。

长门炮台是我国规模最大、保存较好的清代炮台，是清代海防历史的重要实物见证。1991年被公布为省级文物保护单位。

The coastal fort barbettes of the Ming and Qing dynasties are in large quantities in the estuary, with Hujiang Fort Barbette in the foremost position, the oppositely positioned Changmen and Jinpai fort barbettes as the first line of defense, the oppositely positioned Northern Bank, Southern Bank, Yuanshan Shuizhai, Qinjiang, Maxian Mountain fort barbettes as the second line of defense, and Kuiqi fort barbettes as the last line of defense.

Situated on the Dianguang Mountain to the east of Changmen Village in Guantou Town of Lianjiang County, Fuzhou, Changmen Fort Barbette was a major fort barbette in the estuary of the Minjiang River. It formed a line of defense with Shema and Huaqiu fort barbettes on the northern bank of the river, opposite Jinpai, Tashi and Yantai fort barbettes on the southern bank. Together they guard the narrowest part of the estuary. With two islets in the river and the five fort barbettes on the banks, this section of the estuary became strategically important in the coastal defense system and remained for a long time as a major military base along the coast of Fukien Province.

In 1834 or the 14th year during the reign of Qing Emperor Daoguang, Lin Zexuin, a high court official of the Qing regime, set up a military agency here. At first Changmen Fort Barbette was built on an earthen platform and later was renovated and expanded. The stronghold of the fort barbette was comprised of barracks, ammunition depots and houses for activities. Behind the fort barbette there was also a drill ground and a meeting hall.

In August 1884, under the leadership of Amédée Courbet, the Far East Fleet of France intruded the estuary of the Minjiang River and assaulted Fukien Navy, causing the outbreak of the Sino-France War. A strict order, however, was given by Li Hongzhang, a major minister of the Qing Dynasty and founder of the Northern Navy, to forbid Fukien Navy from combating the enemy by saying "shots are not allowed unless permitted" and "those disobeying the order would be beheaded even if the war was won". Unexpectedly, the fort barbettes fired no shot and the French battleships intruded the estuary unharmed. The French forces found that the waterway of the Minjiang River was not deep enough for their battleships and had to give up their plan to go upstream to Fuzhou City. Then they fired their guns upon Mawei Shipyard and withdrew from the estuary. Because most of the fort barbettes faced downstream with confined shooting angles, the station troops could not turn the guns toward the French battleships positioned further up the river. Consequently, most of the fort barbettes were destroyed after being bombarded from behind by the French battleships.

After the outbreak of the Sino-france War in 1884, the Qing regime quickly started rebuilding the destroyed fort barbettes as well as building new ones for fear that the French fleet would launch new attacks. As a result, new fort barbettes were built one after another in the estuary, including Changmen Dianguang Mountain Fort Barbette, which was equipped with two Krupp cannons each with a caliber of 28 cm.

During the Japanese invasion in China, Changmen Fort Barbette had been bombarded repeatedly by Japanese bombers. In April 1941, the Japanese ground and naval forces jointly attacked Fuzhou City. The defending troops of the Kuomintang government lost the battle and gave up the city. Changmen Fort Barbette was thus left on its own in the enemy-occupied areas. The station troops destroyed the cannons before withdrawing from the stronghold. After being restored for several times, the original features of the fort barbette have basically been preserved .

Changmen Fort Barbette is a well-preserved fort barbette of the Qing Dynasty and the largest one of its kind in China. It is an important material witness to the coastal defense history of the Qing Dynasty. In 1991 the fort barbette was listed as a provincial relic.

亭江炮台

闽江下游入海口自古以来就是福建海防的重点。位于马尾区亭江镇南般村的亭江炮台，素有"省府门户"之称。它前临闽江、背靠群山，所以又称北岸炮台，与长乐象屿村的南岸炮台隔江呼应，可形成交叉火力封锁闽安江峡，扼守闽江下游的咽喉地带，是闽江口近代海防体系的第二道防线。

亭江炮台始建于清顺治十四年（1657年），由山巅主炮台、山边突出部前沿炮台、临江岸炮台群及山后弹药库组成。炮台与弹药库、炮台与炮台之间有地道相通，地道里设有休息室。经历过鸦片战争、马江海战、抗日战争，现在亭江炮台公园存留的炮座、坑道和弹孔，是亭江炮台经受数百年风雨的印迹。

道光、光绪年间，炮台经历多次重修。1884年，中法马江海战爆发。法国舰队在马尾罗星塔锚地突袭福建水师后，在退出时沿途摧毁了闽江两岸的炮台，并派陆战队登岸包抄，毁坏亭江炮台。后来船政大臣裴荫森主持修复炮台，安装了部分新式克虏伯要塞炮。抗日战争中，亭江炮台遭日军破坏，不久再次重修。

新中国成立后，亭江炮台受到较多关注和保护。2013年，亭江炮台被列为第七批全国重点文物保护单位。

沿着登山道而上，在半山腰的位置便是前沿炮台。这是两座相连的暗炮台，用于定向攻击近距离江面和江边目标，掩护主炮台。在炮位上，陈列着在这里出土的两门清代铁炮，它们铸于1841年鸦片战争期间。

在高约22米的山顶，有一个露天的主炮台炮位，炮口朝闽江，可攻击中远距离目标。炮台后下方设有三间营房、一间弹药库，均是根据当年的格局仿造的。在主炮台的位置安放着210毫米口径（也称"二十一生"）德国克虏伯大炮。这门大炮是目前国内唯一的精准复制品。虽然是仿制的，但其据守关隘的气势丝毫不减。

亭江炮台是我国现存少有的近代典型海防岸炮阵地，也是目前闽江下游炮台遗迹中保存最完整的一座。它有着数百年的历史，在这里可以同时看到炮房式、露炮台式等多种典型的近代炮台建筑形式，是研究我国近代海防体系及其演变的实物例证。

Tingjiang Fort Barbette

The estuary of the Minjiang River has remained an important area in the coastal defense system of Fukien. Tingjiang Fort Barbette, situated at Nanban Village of Tingjiang Town, Mawei District, was known as the "gateway to the capital city of Fukien". As the fort barbette lay on the northern bank of the Minjiang River, with mountains at its back, it was also called Northern Bank Fort Barbette. It was opposite the Southern Bank Fort Barbette at Xiangyu of Changle across the Minjiang River. The cross fire of the two fort barbettes could cover the Min'an Narrows and guard the narrowest part of the estuary. Together they formed the second defense line of the modern coastal defense system in the estuary.

Tingjiang Fort Barbette was built in 1657 or the 14th year during the reign of Qing emperor Shunzhi. It was comprised of a main barbette on a mountain top, front barbettes on the protruding part of the mountain, barbettes on the river bank, and an ammunition depot on the back of the mountain. Tunnels, complete with rest areas, were built to connect different barbettes and connect barbettes with the ammunition depot. The fort barbette is a witness to the Opium War, the Sino-France War, and the War of Resistance against Japanese Aggression. The cannon platforms, the tunnels and the craters preserved in the Tingjiang Fort Barbette Park are traces of the trials the fort barbette went through over several hundred years.

In the periods during the reign of emperors Daoguang and Guangxu, Tingjiang Fort Barbette was rebuilt for several times. In 1884 the Sino-France War broke out. The French fleet assaulted the navy of the Naval Administration in their anchorage points near Luoxing Pagoda in Mawei. When the fleet withdrew, it bombarded the fort barbettes on both banks of the river and sent land forces ashore to destroy Tingjiang Fort Barbette. Later it was rebuilt under the leadership of Pei Yinsen the Naval Adimination Minister, with new Krupp cannons installed. In the War of Resistance against Japanese Aggression, Tingjiang Fort Barbette was ruined by the Japanese forces but rebuilt afterwards.

After the founding of the People's Republic of China, great efforts have been made to preserve Tingjiang Fort Barbette. In 2013 it was listed in the 7th group of National Key Relics.

Go up along the mountain trail, and you will see two front barbettes half way on the mountainside. These two hidden barbettes, which are connected with each other, could shield the main barbette on the mountain top by attacking the targets on the river and the bank within a close range and a fixed angle. On the platforms there are two unearthed iron cannons cast by the Qing regime in 1841 during the Opium War.

In the open air on a mountaintop about 22 meters high is the main barbette, which is equipped with a replica of a 210-millimeter Krupp cannon facing the Minjiang River. A real cannon of such kind is said to have firepower covering a medium or long range. The replica is the only precisely reproduced cannon of the kind in the country. A replica as it is, it looks grand and majestic like a genuine one guarding a strategic post. In the lower area behind the barbette are barracks made up of three rooms and an ammunition depot reproduced and arranged in the original style.

Tingjiang Fort Barbette is one of the few typical modern platforms of coastal artillery well preserved in the country. It is also the best preserved one among the fort barbettes in the downstream areas of the Minjiang River. Here you can find coastal defense facilities that are several hundred years old; you can see modern barbettes of several types at the same time, including barbettes enclosed by walls and barbettes in open air. They are material proof of the modern coastal defense system in China and its evolution.

琴江满族村

走进琴江满族村，宛如进入了庞大的迷宫世界。这里特有的满族文化，沉淀了琴江村三百多年的历史。肃穆的官宅、兵房，古朴的民居建筑，处处彰显着满族文化的独特魅力。

琴江满族村是福州市长乐区航城街道下辖村，距长乐城区4公里，距闽江口15公里。流经这一段的闽江宛如一把古琴，故名琴江。这里曾是清朝镇守闽江、乌龙江、琴江三江口的水师旗营营地，也是马江海战的古战场，而今是中国历史文化名村以及中国东南地区唯一保存完整的满族村。

清雍正六年（1728年），为了加强对东南海疆的防守，镇闽将军阿尔赛奏请朝廷从老四旗中抽调513名官兵携眷进驻琴江，围地筑城，建立"福州三江口水师旗营"。这是当时全国沿海四大水师旗营之一，比马尾的福建水师的组建还早一百五十一年。三江口水师旗营的官兵几乎参与了中国近代史上有关海疆的所有重大军事行动，除了鸦片战争、中法马江海战外，还包括平定台湾林爽文之乱、歼灭海盗蔡牵等。辛亥革命后，该水师旗营逐渐演变成村落。

旗营建有公衙门（将军行辕）、军械库、炮台、校场、箭道场、演武厅等。营房按照诸葛亮八阵图建造，设十二条街、四条直巷、东西南北四个城门及城墙，街巷呈"T"或"L"型，没有断头巷。小街尽头看似是死胡同，两边却有小街横过。街道与街道连接处都有一座寺庙，庙前是较大的空地。外人进入如入迷魂阵，俗称"旗人八卦营"，是完全按照作战需要进行布局的。

这座清朝老兵营，街道上的建筑极其相似，房屋布局统一。旗人街是琴江村保存得相对完好的街道之一。街两旁的兵房全是单层木结构，既是营房又是民宅。兵房临街分为四扇门、六扇门，四扇门为普通人家，六扇门为官宦之家。各家正中的门上都统一套一扇矮木门，上端有几个镂空的小窗，这种门叫作"第喜门"。中法马江海战爆发后，东北旗兵奉命来闽，村里的家眷不敢上街，只能通过镂空的木格小窗观看街景。据说，"第喜门"只有在婚丧时才打开，平常紧闭着。"第喜门"对旗人来说意义非同一般，搬家时必须拆下来带走。

Qinjiang Manchu Ethnic Group Village

Stroll in Qinjiang Manchu Village, and you will feel as if you walked in a big maze. The unique Manchu culture of the village boasts a history of more than 300 years. The ancient office compounds and barracks, along with the civilian dwellings, are traces of the unigue life of the ethnic group.

Qinjiang Manchu Village is a village of Hangcheng subdistrict in Changle, Fuzhou City. It is situated four kilometers from downtown Changle and 15 kilometers from the estuary of the Minjiang River. The river course near the village is shaped like a Chinese lute, hence the name Qinjiang, two Chinese characters representative of "Chinese lute" and "river" respectively. It was originally the camp of a navy garrison responsible for defending the estuary of three rivers including the Minjiang River, the Wulong River, and the Qin River, with all the soldiers being Manchu ethnic groups. The village was also part of the battlefield of the Sino-France War, which broke out in the Ma River. It is a national historical and cultural village and the only well-preserved Manchu village in Southeast China.

In 1728 or the 6th year during the reign of Qing emperor Yongzheng, Arsai, a general stationed in Fukien Province, proposed to the imperial court dispatching 513 officers and soldiers along with their families from the troops of the original "four banners" to Qinjiang, Fuzhou and setting up the "Three-river-estuary Navy Garrison" there. As one of the four major Manchu navy garrisons in the coastal areas of the country, it was founded 151 years earlier than Fukien Navy in Mawei. The Manchu soldiers in the navy garrison participated in almost all the major military operations that took place in the coastal frontiers in modern times. Apart from the Opium War and the Sino-France War, which broke out in the Ma River, they also participated in the operations of cracking down on the rebellion of the forces led by Lin Shuangwen in Taiwan and annihilating a pirate gang headed by Cai Qian. After the Revolution of 1911, the Manchu navy garrison gradually developed into a village.

The garrison is made up of an administration office (or the Office of Fuzhou General), an armament depot, a fort barbette, a drill ground, an archery range, a martial arts hall, etc. It was constructed in an eight-diagram pattern, which was originally created by Zhu Geliang, a statesman and strategist in the period of the Three Kingdoms (220-265), with 12 streets, four straight lanes, four gates in the east, west, south and north respectively, and ramparts. The streets and the lanes are arranged in "T" or "L" patterns, so there are no dead-end routes: a seemingly dead-end small street would turn out to intersect another street. At each intersection of two streets there is a temple with a big open space in front of it. The unique layout, which was elaborately designed to defend the garrison in battles, makes itself a bewildering trap for outsiders. Thus the garrison is also popularly called the "Eight-diagram Barracks of Manchu Troops".

In the ancient barracks of the Qing Dynasty, the buildings on both sides of the streets are uniform in their layout and resemble each other closely. Manchu Street is one of the well preserved ancient streets in the village. On both sides of it are all single-storied wooden houses, which are both barracks and civilian dwellings. The houses facing the street have either four or six doors each. The four-door and six-door houses used to be the residences of soldiers and officers respectively. Outside the central doors at the entrance of each house is another specially designed door, which features a lower frame and several carved openings on its upper part. It is called "Dixi Door". When the Sino-France War broke out in the Ma River, Manchu troops from Northeast China were dispatched to Fukien and were stationed in the barracks. The women and the children didn't dare go to the street and they only watched what was happening outside through the carved openings of "Dixi Doors". It is said that "Dixi Doors" are normally closed and only open at weddings or funerals. They are extraordinarily meaningful to Manchu nationality and should be removed from their houses and taken along when they move to a new place.

旗营当时实行严格的军事管理，出城须有假条，离城 20 里算逃旗。晚上定时熄灯就寝，眷属皆是如此。旗营还分左、右两翼，平时训练极为严格，一翼留营演射，一翼前往三江口演习水务，互为轮换。福州驻防每年春秋两季按月分八拨轮流到三江口操演水务。将军、副都统每年春秋两季轮流来营巡查。

在琴江村口的八旗广场边，有一座花岗岩砌成的陵园矗立在山坡上，这是抗法烈士陵园，在中法马江海战中牺牲的琴江子弟长眠于此。

1884 年 8 月 23 日（农历七月初三），驻防三江口的水师佐领黄恩禄，以"将在外军令有所不受"为由，不顾清廷"无旨不得先行开炮……违者虽胜亦斩"的禁令，以大屿岛为屏障，在琴江水道上设下埋伏，待法舰经过时，命属下向敌舰开炮，打响了保卫马尾港口的战斗。这次战役中，水师旗营官兵阵亡 129 人。据村民介绍，旗营中有一条叫马家巷的小巷，原由姓马的旗营兄弟居住，中法马江海战中马家男丁全部上阵血战，无一人生还。从此，马家巷再无一人姓马。

在那之后，每年农历七月初三，琴江村人都举行马江海战公祭，自发来到江边放水灯祭奠先烈。

洋务运动后，水师旗营的子弟们纷纷投身海军学校。村中有许多海军世家，其中以贾、黄、许三家最为有名，贾家连续九代、黄家连续八代、许家连续七代均有人参加海军。在村中的孝友坊旁，有一座挂有"海军世家贾氏故居"牌子的宅院，正屋中堂上面挂着一块由陈绍宽题写的"海权至要"牌匾。

The garrison was managed following strict military rules. Anyone who wanted to go out of the garrison should produce an approved written request for leave and anyone who went 10 kilometers away from the garrison would be seen as a deserter. At night all people including children in the garrison should go to bed according to a fixed schedule and lights should be put out at the same time. The troops in the garrison were divided into two units. They trained very strictly in normal times. When one unit was practicing archery in the garrison, the other unit would practice combating skills in the Three-river Estuary, and they would do it in rotation. The general and the deputy commander-in-chief would inspect the garrison in turn every summer and autumn.

On a slope near the Eight Banners Square at the entrance to Jinjiang Village there is a cemetery built of granite slabs, a burying ground for some martyrs in the Sino-France War. The martyrs are all natives of Qinjiang Village.

On August 23rd or the third of July on the lunar calendar in 1884, led by Huang Enlu, the commander, a navy battalion stationed in the Three-river Estuary ambushed the French battleships in the Qin River waterway, using the Dayu Islet as a natural defense, and fired their cannons at the enemy. The attack was the first move in the battle defending Port Mawei located in the upstream stretch of the Minjiang River. Before the outbreak of the Sino-France War, however, the imperial court of the Qing regime issued a decree prohibiting firing first shot at the enemy. Those acting against the decree would be beheaded even if the war was won. The battalion commander launched a surprise attack in the Qin River on the grounds that a field commander must decide on the basis of actual situations. In the battle 129 soldiers and officers of the Manchu navy battalion lost their lives. According to the villagers, there is an alley called Ma's Alley where soldiers with the family name Ma used to live, but there have been no residents bearing that surname in the alley after the Sino-France War, because all the males died in battle.

Since then, on the third of every July on the lunar calendar, the villagers will worship the martyrs along the riverside by placing water lanterns in the Qin River.

After the Westernization Movement, which lasted between the 1860s and the 1890s, many young people in the garrison went to the navy school. There are many families holding navy posts for generations in the village. The most prestigious ones are Jia's family, Huang's family and Xu's family, holding navy posts for nine, eight and seven generations respectively. Near the Honorific Arch of Filial Piety and Fraternity in the village, you can see the former residence of Jia's Family. On the wall at the entrance is a plaque with the family's honorific name, "Former Residence of Jia's Family, Which Holds Navy Posts for Generations". Up in the central hall of the compound hangs a plaque with the inscription written by Chen Shaokuan, head of the admiralty of the Republic of China. The plaque bears the inscription of four Chinese characters representative of "the pursuit of maritime power is of vital importance."

福州
古历

第十八章

古居探幽：体味静好

Chapter Eighteen

Ancient Residences:
Experience of Peaceful Life

◎ 古韵悠悠：三落厝、"九头马"古民居

三落厝

"山泉入宅，宅中有河，河中有房。"巧妙的设计营造出古厝的静谧与古朴。青石、木板，流水、小草，见证着古厝的历史。啁啾鸟鸣和潺潺流水相映成趣，共同鸣奏欢快的古厝赞歌。

三落厝古民居位于连江县丹阳镇坂顶村杜棠自然村，距离县城有30分钟左右车程。三落厝原为"七星台"，始建于唐末，是连江县第一位进士、官至礼部尚书的张莹的故居。明朝时，古厝被大火烧毁。嘉靖年间，郑氏族人在原地重建了这座有大唐遗风的三落大厝。它是连江迄今为止发现的规模最大、保存最完整的古民居群落。

三落厝为木石结构，依山傍水，坐东朝西，建筑面积达3000多平方米。它由三座水平三进并以过雨亭相连的四合院组成，建筑风格与福州南后街、闽清宏琳厝等明清古建筑大为不同，后者均是纵深分布三进格局。

三落厝共有正房、后正房、前书院、后书院、僻舍、边房等大小房间共200多间，每座四合院有上下两层房、中间一口天井。虽历经四百多年的风雨洗礼，古民居内的美人靠、观景阁、纳凉凳、练武石、石磨、石舂等依旧保存完好。令人称奇的是，每个四合院之间均有过水渠相连，穿院而过的水渠清澈见底，生长有很多鱼虾田螺，给古民居增添了一份自然乐趣。

三落厝
Sanluocuo Compound

◎ **Ancient Charm: Sanluocuo Compound, Jiutouma Compound**

Sanluocuo Compound

Sanluocuo Compound is exquisitely designed. With mountain spring flow murmuring in the ditches in its courtyard, the house gives an atmosphere of tranquility and simplicity. The blue stone slabs, the wooden boards, the running stream and the weeds add beauty by mutual reflection. Together they are witnesses to the history of the compound. The chirping of birds and the murmuring of running water echo each other harmoniously as if playing a concerto of happiness.

Located in Dutang of Banding Village, Danyang Town, Lianjiang County, Sanluocuo Compound is approximately 30-minute drive to downtown Lianjiang. Built in the late Tang Dynasty (618-907 A.D.) and called "Seven-star Platform" originally, the compound was the residence of Zhang Ying, a successful candidate in the highest imperial examinations and the Minister of Rites during the reign of Tang emperor Dashun. But it was burnt down in the Ming Dynasty (1368-1644 A.D.). In the period during the reign of Ming emperor Jiajing, Zheng's Clan rebuilt the compound on the original site and erected three rows of buildings in the style of Tang Dynasty. It is the largest and the best preserved ancient compound discovered so far in Lianjiang County.

Sanluocuo Compound is mainly built of wood and stone, with a floor space of more than 3, 000 square meters. The west-facing compound lies at the foot of a mountain and is bordered by a river. It consists of three horizontally distributed quadrangle courtyards connected with roofed corridors. This is distinct from the layout of three longitudinally distributed courtyards, a spatial arrangement characterizing the ancient dwellings of the Ming and Qing dynasties in the Three Lanes and Seven Alleys in downtown Fuzhou and Honglincuo Compound in Minqing County.

Sanluocuo Compound is made up of more than 200 rooms, including principal rooms, back principal rooms, front studies, back studies, corner rooms, side rooms, etc. It also includes three quadrangle courtyards, each with an open space in the middle surrounded by two-storied buildings. Despite a long history of over 400 years, the long armchairs, pavilions, benches, stone dumbbells for martial arts exercising, stone mills, and big stone mortars in the compound are all well-preserved. To the surprise of the visitors, the quadrangle courtyards are linked by shallow ditches, where crystal clear water flows peacefully and fish, shrimps and river snails thrive, adding the joy of nature to the ancient residence.

明朝连江籍名臣吴文华有诗描写三落厝：

"桥通流水出青林，与客寻幽古径深。占象有台迷草色，砌花无主漫春阴。"（《题张莹宅》）

最能体现三落厝唐朝风格的地方是水榭平台。在这里抬头望去，能看到房顶的脊梁两尾翘起的挑檐，被称为"龙舌燕尾翘"，还有平缓舒展的小瓦屋面。屋脊上悬挂的木质装饰"悬鱼"雕刻了四种吉祥图案：双鱼，有人丁兴旺、连年有余的美好寓意；梅花，象征"福禄财喜寿"五福，又有"喜上眉梢"之意；双喜，表达喜庆的美好祝愿；阴阳太极，表示天人合一、融合协调。

整座古厝结构自然、古朴纯美，近有错落有致的屋檐，远有黛青色的山峰，耳畔是浅溪潺潺的流水声，充满了宁静与诗意。院子外还有中鹄桥、望星台、采风阁、八仙屏、下马桥等景观。

进士张莹是地地道道在三落厝生长的历史名人。在所居住的中座后书院里，他常常夜以继日地挑灯夜读、伏案著述。科举中进士后，他一路平步青云，直至成为礼部尚书，因而彼时的三落厝人称"尚书房"。后因不愿与奸臣佞幸同流合污，他毅然退居故里，居住在杜棠望星台。他深居简出，潜心学问，著书立说，在这里安度晚年。

据介绍，郑氏后人在每年的农历七月会择吉日大祭三天，各家各户都要献上自家精心制作的米糕、糍粑等美食进行祭祀。这个习俗被称作"祀食"，四百多年来代代传承至今，成为当地民俗的一大景观。

2018年，第十六届威尼斯国际建筑双年展中国国家馆巡展落地于此。2019年，"福州古厝保护与文化传承论坛"系列活动之一的"延续·新生"传统聚落保护与活化专题论坛也在此举办。

"九头马"古民居

在长乐市鹤上镇岐阳村福庭自然村，有一组保存完整的清代民居建筑群。因宅地中及周边有九块巨石，俗称"九头马"。它是福州地区清代传统民居建筑的典范，为第七批全国重点文物保护单位。

Wu Wenhua, a prestigious official native to Lianjiang County in the Ming Dynasty about 400 years ago, wrote a poem titled "About Former Residence of Zhang Ying" to sing the praises of Sanluocuo Compound. It roughly reads:

"Bridges span the ditches where water flows in peacefully from the green mountain nearby. In the company of my guest, I explore the secluded places by the ancient passageways leading to the depth of the compound. Here we find green grass enchanting and flowers unattended on the steps thriving in full bloom."

The waterside pavilion is where you can enjoy the most typical style of the Tang Dynasty in the compound. Raise your head, and you can see on the roof ridge ends upturned and pointed eaves, called the "dragon tongues or swallow tails". You can also see the gently stretched roofs covered with small tiles. Hanging from the roof ridge ends are wooden ornaments called "hanging fish", which feature carvings of four propitious patterns, including double fish representative of a growing family and prosperous life, a plum flower representative of five blessings (i.e. fortune, promotion, wealth, joy and longevity), a Chinese character representative of double happiness, and the diagram of Yin and Yang representative of the harmony of man and nature.

The compound is characterized by its layout with natural beauty and ancient simplicity. The well spaced roofs against the setting of bluish mountains, in the company of the murmuring of the small streams in the ditches, give a feeling of tranquility and poetic flavor. Outside the compound are Zhonghu Bridge, Wangxingtai (or Star Observation Platform), Caifeng Pavilion, Eight-immortal Screen, Xiama Bridge and other scenic spots.

Zhang Ying, a prestigious historical figure in the Tang Dynasty and also a native of the compound, often read books or wrote scholarly works late into the night in the back study of the central quadrangle courtyard. After he succeeded in the highest imperial examination, Zhang was promoted rapidly to the post as Minister of Rites. Thus Sanluocuo Compound was also called "Minister's Residence" at that time. But he was unwilling to go along with the treacherous court officials in their dishonest schemes. Then he resolutely resigned from the post and returned to his hometown. He spent his remaining years at Wangxingtai in Dutang, the place where Sanluocuo is situated. There he lived a secluded life in comfort, devoting himself to the study and writing of scholarly works.

It is said that the later generations of Zheng's Clan members in Sanluocuo hold a three-day worshipping ceremony in every July on the lunar calendar. At the ceremony, they offer sacrifices prepared by themselves, such as cakes made of ordinary or glutinous rice. The custom has been passed on from generation to generation for more than 400 years, which is rare for a local custom of its kind.

The compound has also been a place for important activities, including the 2018 touring exhibition of 16th Venice Architecture Biennale China Pavilion and the 2019 forum on the "Protection and Utilization" of traditional settlements, a special session of Fuzhou Ancient Building Protection and Cultural Inheritance Forum.

Jiutouma Compound

Situated in Futing of Qiyang Village, Heshang Town, Changle District, Nine-horse Compound is a group of well preserved dwellings of Qing Dynasty. There are nine big rocks on the house site and in its vicinity, hence the popular name Nine-horse Compound. It is a typical residential building of the Qing Dynasty in Fuzhou and one of the 7th group of national key relics.

　　"九头马"民居依山坡而建，是陈利焕和他四个儿子历经数十载匠心构筑的。第一座建于清嘉庆年间（1796—1820年），大部分建于道光年间（1821—1850年），最迟一座竣工于1872年前后。

　　"九头马"建筑群坐北朝南，平面基本呈正方形，占地1.5万平方米，规模宏大，彰显出当年的富足和繁荣。东西宽、南北深各120米，房屋分五列，主体建筑有22座。四周有6米高的围墙，开放十多个门洞，设有望楼、枪眼。五列房屋间隔着防火墙、夹弄，有框门相通。

　　每列南面正中各设大门一扇，逢红白喜事，大门、屏门、厅门一路洞开，呈现"五落透后"的景象，一望到底，十分壮观。南面中列墙额上开设了13个灯窗，可以悬挂宫灯照明。"九头马"四周台础高筑，前面还有广场。

　　"九头马"的设计体现了建筑艺术与便利生活的完美结合。这里的建筑形式有亭、台、楼、阁、轩、榭、厢等，按功能不同划分为祖厅、接官厅、客厅、议事厅、喜事厅、仓库、钱库、米粿馆、书斋、健身房、武术馆、闺阁、守节楼等；还可分为五柱厅、七柱厅、九柱厅、出游廊厅等。

　　"九头马"的建筑材料以木材为主，使用的木料有杉木、柯木、楠木、樟木、红木、檀香木、铁梨木、黄杨木……最长的楠木梁达10米。

　　走进古民居，可看见建筑部分保存较完整，木雕、藻井、壁画、书法、浮雕、青石柱础，还有门窗、户扇，都带有原汁原味的古韵。

　　"九头马"的小木作精巧别致，达到一流的艺术水准。有形式多样的藻井：单层、双层、多层，方形、圆形、多角形等。斗拱、插屏、门窗户扇……几乎无处不雕。雕刻形式有浅雕、浮雕、镂空雕、双面雕，阴刻、阳刻、镶刻；内容有自然物、民间戏文典故、三教九流故事。雕刻的动物、昆虫、人物、花草树木形象逼真，还采用谐音、象征、寄寓等传统表现手法，带有祥瑞吉利的美好寓意，如福（蝙蝠）、禄（鹿）、寿（松鹤）、喜（梅雀）等。

Nine-horse Compound was erected at the foot of a mountain by Chen Lihuan and his four sons, with the construction work taking several decades. The first section of the compound was built during the reign of Qing emperor Jiaqing (1795-1820 A.D.), the largest proportion of it during the reign of emperor Daoguang (1821-1850 A.D.), and the last section around 1872.

The southward compound is basically square-shaped, measuring about 120 meters on each side, with a total area of 15,000 square meters. The size of the compound is a display of wealth and prosperity of the owner at the time when it was constructed. The buildings in the compound, including 22 major ones, are in five rows, which are separated by fire walls and alleys but connected with exits. The buildings are enclosed by a wall measuring six meters high with about a dozen door openings, holes for shooting, and watch towers in the corners.

There is an entrance to each row of the buildings right in the middle of the front. At weddings or funerals, the doors of the entrance, the screen, and the halls will all open. Stand in front of the entrance, and you can see the farthest back of the compound through these doors and enjoy a spectacular view. Up the entrance of the central row are 13 wall openings for lanterns. Apart from the wall, which is built on a high base, the compound also eatures a big square to the south of it.

Nine-horse Compound is a perfect integration of architecture and life. The buildings are in a variety of patterns, including pavilions, terraces, open halls, verandas with windows, wing-rooms, etc.; they are of multiple purposes, including ancestral halls, official reception halls, living rooms, meeting rooms, festivity rooms, storerooms, treasuries, rice shops, studies, gyms, martial arts halls, boudoirs, chastity houses, etc.; the halls are also manifold: there are five-pillar halls, seven-pillar halls, nine-pillar halls, veranda halls, etc.

The compound is mainly built of stone and wood. And the wood used is of many different kinds, including China fir, Chinese oak, Phoebe nanmu, camphorwood, mahogany, sandalwood, lignum vitae, boxwood, etc. The longest Phoebe nanmu beam measures up to 10 meters.

Stroll into the compound, and you can find the ancient parts of the buildings fairly well preserved. Here wood carvings, caisson ceilings, frescoes, calligraphy works, relief carvings, bluestone plinths, doors, and windows are still in their original styles.

The wood craftwork in the compound is ingeniously made up to first-class standards. The caisson ceilings, for example, are in various patterns: there are single-layer, double-layer, or multiple-layer caisson ceilings; there are also square, round, or polygonal-shaped ones. Carvings are everywhere: in the bucket arches, table plaques, doors, windows and so on and so forth. They are of multiple types: in low or normal relief, hollowed-out, double-faced, intaglio, tessellated, etc.; they are on different themes: natural objects, folklore in operas, and stories about people in various trades. The carvings of animals, plants, insects, figures, flowers and trees are lifelike. They are representative of auspiciousness with an infusion of traditional techniques of expression, such as homophones, symbols and connotations. For example, the carvings of bats, deer, pine trees with cranes, and plum flowers with sparrows are representative of good fortune, high rank, longevity and festivity respectively, as their names are homophones of the Chinese characters representing these meanings.

这里的许多木雕作品把诗词歌赋、金石书法、绘画雕刻等诸多艺术形式有机融为一体。有的利用不同木材的不同颜色搭配成各种花窗图案，甚至把木头天然的蛀伤结疤融入构图，来表现瓜果虫眼或老藤枯木，妙趣天成。木雕作品大多保持木材本色，有的明漆贴金，也有用彩色套板衬托的。

"九头马"也有不少石刻、砖雕、泥塑和壁画。其中石刻大多用于柱础，砖雕用于门楼亭、墙饰、窗格，泥塑用于墙头饰，壁画则广泛用于内墙壁。

"九头马"的建筑与装饰风格蕴含着以人为中心的理念，体现了福州民居独特的审美文化特征。走进"九头马"，犹如置身一座民俗艺术博览馆。

◎ 岁月静好：黄氏父子三庄寨、宏琳厝

黄氏父子三庄寨

从永泰县城沿大樟溪西行，向戴云山深处探寻，便来到霞拔乡锦安村下辖的长万自然村，可以看见两座规模宏大的庄寨静静地坐落在穿山而下的小溪沿岸的山坡上，它们就是谷贻堂、积善堂。这两座庄寨连同东洋乡的绍安庄，有一个共同的主人——锦安黄氏家族。

与永泰的大多数庄寨一样，黄氏家族庄寨群长期隐于深山，罕为世人所知。直到2022年世界建筑文物保护基金会（WMF）发布《2022世界建筑文物观察名录》，"黄氏父子三庄寨"成为全国唯一入选的建筑文物，并从此一朝闻名全球知。

"父子三庄寨"所在的区域地处戴云山脉深处，平均海拔近700米。这里山势连绵不断，离永泰城关较远，且交通不便。许多到访的人不禁好奇，锦安黄氏家族何以能在这里繁衍生息、发展壮大，并在深山之中起造如此大规模的复杂建筑？

据黄氏族人回忆，黄氏家族第十五代黄孟钢及其子主要从事茶油的生产和销售。黄孟钢在周坑与长万开设油坊，利用上和村的锦安溪水力带动油坊水车榨油。当地因此流传一句俗话："上和出水流，到此变成油。"黄孟钢不仅自家有好几处油茶林，而且还从周边村落的油茶户手中收购茶籽。每年农历十月至来年三四月，油坊事务最为繁忙，茶籽烘焙工作每日从天刚破晓就开始了。

Many of the wood carvings feature an integration of different artistic forms such as poetry, seal cutting, calligraphy, painting, and engraving. The wood pieces in various colors are harmoniously arranged to form designs on lattice windows; even the scars of insect holes on the wood are smartly integrated with other parts of the images to mimic old vines, dead wood, or insect holes on fruits. The carvings are mostly in the natural color of wood, and some of the rest are varnished, gilded, or set off by colorful boards underneath.

In Nine-horse Compound there are also stone or brick carvings, clay sculptures and frescoes. Most of the stone carvings are on the plinths, and brick carvings are on the walls, the window lattices, and the arches over the gateways. Clay sculptures can be found on the top of walls, and frescoes can be seen here and there on the inner side of the walls.

The architecture and decoration of Nine-horse Compound embody human-centered philosophy and the unique aesthetic features of traditional residences in Fuzhou. A tour in the compound is almost like a visit to a museum of folk art.

◎ Peaceful Life: Three Fortified Manors of Huang Family, Honglincuo Compound

Three Fortified Manors of Huang Family

Start from downtown Yongtai County and go westward along the riverside of the Dazhangxi River, and you will access the depth of the Daiyun Mountain and find Changwan natural village in Jin'an, Xiaba Township. Lying on the slope along the bank of a brook running down from the mountain are two manors named Guyitang and Jishantang respectively. They, along with Shao'anzhuang in Dongyang Township, belong to the same Huang family.

Like the owners of most manors in Yongtai County, Huang's family has long stayed in seclusion in remote mountains and remained unknown to the outside world. But it rose to fame overnight across the world when the "Three Fortified Manors of Huang Family" were designated by WMF (or World Monuments Fund) a heritage on the list of 2022 World Monuments Watch. They are the only Chinese heritage included on the list so far.

The three manors were situated in the remote areas of the Daiyun Mountain at an average altitude of about 700 meters. Being distant from downtown Yongtai County and surrounded by rolling hills, they are not easily accessible. Many visitors can not help but wonder how the Huang family has developed in this place and managed to build structures as large and complicated as the three manors.

According to Huang's family members, Huang Menggang, a descendant in 15th generation, and his sons conducted business mainly in the production and sale of tea oil. Huang Menggang set up oil mills in Zhoukeng and Changwan villages, using the water power of the Jin'an Rivulet running down from Shanghe Village to drive the seed-pressing waterwheels. There was a saying spread locally, that is, "the rivulet water running down from Shanghe Village changes into oil in the mill." Huang not only possessed several farms of tea-oil trees but also purchased tea seeds from the growers in the neighboring villages. Between October and the following March or April on the lunar calendar, Huang's oil mills were the busiest, with tea seed baking starting at dawn every day.

黄氏家族依靠茶油生意积累了大量财富。黄孟钢与其子接二连三地营建了一系列大规模的兼具居住与防御功能的庄寨建筑。对于黄氏家族而言，其生存策略就是"寸积尺累，幸获羡余之裕，多增山林田地，多盖屋宇土堡"。其生计模式不仅推动了庄寨的建设与使用，亦推动了其家族的发展与壮大。

"父子三庄寨"不仅具有防御性乡土建筑的特色，同时也留存了农耕社会家族聚落的生存记忆，体现了中国传统家族的生存智慧和家文化。

谷贻堂

咸丰十年（1860年），锦安黄氏家族第十五代黄孟钢修建的谷贻堂在长万村落成，筑在半山，占地面积1727平方米，建筑面积2650平方米。据传，当年黄孟钢"花了大本钱"，学得"赣州真风水术"悉心打造。而黄家的富庶更是四乡皆知，有人说黄家的茶油多得可以用来带动水车春米，正如那句形容——富得流油。

绍安庄

光绪二十一年（1895年），黄孟钢长子黄学书在隔壁周坑村起造绍安庄。绍安庄依坡而建，平面呈长方形，占地面积3708平方米，建筑面积2790平方米，有大小房间186间。前后三进，最高处与最低处落差竟达16.5米，颇有布达拉宫式的风情。绍安庄根基深厚、规模庞大，整体风格简朴端庄，可谓是那位人到中年的主人稳重、周全性格的投射。

积善堂

光绪三十一年（1905年）黄孟钢三子黄学猷于谷贻堂对面起造积善堂，平面呈少有的八角形，其中多有风水讲究，其占地面积1610平方米，建筑面积3117平方米。黄学猷少年聪颖，13岁就开始替父亲记账管家。但他后来染上了鸦片瘾，未经几时，就将祖业败尽，导致积善堂的后期装饰无力为继。

宏琳厝

宏琳厝位于闽清县坂东平原南部的演溪之畔，在坂东镇新壶村，是我国保存完好的最大单体古民居建筑。

Huang's family accumulated a big fortune in tea oil business. With the money earned Huang and his sons built fortified manors one after another. The survival strategy of the family is to "accumulate wealth little by little, purchase mountain forests or farmlands with spare money, and build more houses or fortified manors with accumulated wealth". The family's survival strategy led to the construction and the use of the three manors. It also helped the family go from strength to strength.

The "Three Fortified Manors of Huang Family", which are representative of defensive rural dwellings, still retain the memory of family settlements in the era of agricultural society. They are an embodiment of family culture and the survival wisdom of traditional families in China in ancient times.

Guyitang

In 1860 or 10th year during the reign of Qing emperor Xianfeng, the construction of Guyitang was completed. Situated on a slope in Changwan Village, the manor covers an area of 1, 727 square meters, with a total floor space of 2, 650 square meters. Legend has it that Huang Menggang "spent a big sum of money" on the construction of the manor and arranged the buildings in a pattern based on "genuine geomancy that originated in Ganzhou, Jiangxi Province", a fengshui theory he had grasped. The wealth of Huang family was well known. Some locals jokingly said the tea oil owned by the family was even enough to drive a waterwheel to husk rice in a mortar. Its affluence is like that depicted in the Chinese saying "one is so wealthy as if oil is even flowing out of his home."

Shao'anzhuang

In 1895 or 21st year during the reign of Qing emperor Guangxu, Huang Xueshu, the oldest son of Huang Menggang, built Shao'anzhuang in Zhoukeng Village next to Changwan. Also situated on a slope, the rectangular-shaped manor covers an area of 3, 708 square meters. It has 186 rooms of different sizes and a total floor space of 2, 790 square meters. The manor features buildings in three rows, with a height gap of up to 16.5 meters between the first and the last row, very much in the style of the Potala Palace. Founded on a deep and thick base, the manor is large in size and simplistic and elegant in appearance. The design of it is a reflection of the character of its middle-aged owner who was sensible and considerate.

Jishantang

In 1905 or 31st year during the reign of Qing emperor Guangxu, Huang Xueyou, the third son of Huang Menggang, built Jishantang opposite Guyitang. The manor features an octagonal-shaped layout, which is rarely seen among the houses of its kind and is said to be based on geomancy. It covers an area of 1, 610 square meters and a floor space of 3, 117 square meters. Being smart in his boyhood, Huang Xueyou was entrusted with account keeping for his father at the age of 13! But later he became addicted to opium and dissipated all his family fortune. Consequently, there was no money left for the decoration of the manor after it was completed.

Honglincuo Compound

Situated by the Yanxi River in southern Bandong Plains in Xinhu Village of Bandong Town, Minqing County, Honglincuo Compound is the biggest individual ancient residence still well preserved in China.

宏琳厝
Honglincuo Compound

位于梅溪上游的演溪在这里形成一个深湾，宏琳厝就在河湾内的平原之地。隔河而望，从近到远是由低到高的五重平行山脊，被称为"五重案"。宏琳厝就这样背靠着柯洋仙峰，"门迎五重案，前有玉带环"，山环水抱、藏风聚气，广受山水灵气之润泽。无论从哪个角度来看，这里都是非常理想的居住之处。

宏琳厝始建于清乾隆六十年（1795年），始建者据说是药材商黄作宾、黄宏琳父子。黄作宾当时从闽清六都一个地主手中购得地皮，用去优质木材7万多根才建成。

古厝占地面积17832.28平方米，共有大小厅堂35间、房屋666间。据记载，规模宏大的宏琳厝为一次性设计、一次性施工，耗时二十八载完成。它的设计给人们很多启示。

整个建筑按纵向中轴线对称建造，厅堂、住房、天井、花圃等都对称分布。厝内廊回路转，纵横有序。古厝分为三进，依从长幼有序的礼法，第一进由家中的小字辈居住，第二进由家中的中字辈居住，第三进由家中的老字辈居住。第三进的建筑要比第一、第二进高大雄伟，厅堂宽敞明亮，装饰更考究。正屋两翼的"横厝"是女仆生活的地方，向外扩展的"外横厝"则是供男家丁居住的。

The compound lies on the plains cradled in a bend of the Yanxi River, the upstream stretch of the Meixi River. Viewed from opposite the Yanxi River, the compound is set against the background of five parallel mountain ridges, which gradually rise from the near to the distant. With the five ridges of the Keyang Mountain behind and the river bend in front, it is in a favorable position to take in all the essence of its surroundings. From any perspective, the compound is an ideal place to dwell in.

The construction of Honglincuo Compound started in 1795 or 60th year during the reign of Qing emperor Qianlong. It is said that the compound was first built by Huang Zuobin and his son Huang Honglin, both being herbal medicine dealers, on a piece of land purchased from a landlord in the previous Liudu (or the present Bandong Town). A total of over 70, 000 logs of high quality were used in the construction of the compound.

Occupying an area of more than 17, 832 square meters, the compound is comprised of 35 halls and 666 rooms of different sizes. Records show that the construction of the grand compound lasted uninterruptedly for 28 years on the basis of a one-time design, which still gives inspiration to architects today.

The compound is longitudinally symmetrical, and so are its different sections, including the halls, the rooms, the courtyards, and the flower beds. It is criss-crossed with corridors smoothly joined and well aligned. The buildings in the compound are in three rows, which are arranged following the code of respect for seniority, with the first row of buildings allotted to the junior generation of the family, the second to the intermediate generation, and the third to the older generation. The buildings in the third row are larger and taller with a grand appearance, the halls being more spacious and the decoration being of higher quality. In the two inner wings and the two outer wings of the compound there are rooms for female and male servants respectively.

宏琳厝设计上特别重视防火功能，体现了建筑师的独具匠心。进与进之间隔着一条横街，由过雨亭相连。过雨亭平时作挡雨的过道，而万一遇到房子起火，可以立即拆除过雨亭，宽大的横街能使火势得到控制，不会蔓延至后院。同时，厝内有三十六面"几"字形封火墙，墙下是方便人员疏散的火墙弄。据说，历史上宏琳厝曾发生过一场不小的火灾，在族人奋力扑救的同时，封火墙也有效地阻止火势向边上的建筑蔓延。此外，古厝南边还开引了一条水沟，把水导入厝内纵横交错的沟网和众多的窨井，保证有充足的水源灭火。

宏琳厝的防匪设计也颇为严密。古厝东南角和西北角各建一座"兔耳"（铳楼），可以窥视整座大厝四个方向高墙以外的动静。外横厝的外墙顶与屋檐之间留有"城槛"，用于射箭、打枪、投石。万一大门被攻破，内部还有道道防线，墙根布满备用绊脚绳和突袭的洞孔，横街里还安置了从葡萄牙进口的"佛郎机炮"，炮眼正对街口。

宏琳厝窗台的设计也特别人性化。为了保证室内生活的隐蔽性，窗设计在离地较高的位置。窗屉可以上下左右推拉，窗屉板活动的空间仅限于墙体内部，尽可能压缩窗扇的活动空间。大家族里人口众多，窗扇向室内外开启过大难免会造成碰撞伤害。这种窗扇设计在给生活起居带来方便的同时，还保证了人员安全，这也使得厝内的窗二百余年来依然如故。

宏琳厝黄氏先祖十分重视子女教育，于清乾隆四十八年（1783年）建崇文学堂，后更名为文泉书院。文泉书院石框大门的门楣上镶嵌"文泉书院"的青石横额，为宣统太傅陈宝琛题。后来书院又先后发展改名为文泉中学、闽清中学，如今是闽清二中，这所学校培养出侨领黄乃裳等许多知名人士。

宏琳厝已历风雨二百余年，文化积淀深厚，厝内子孙繁衍了十一代，人口有两千多，遍布海内外。2000—2001年，中央电视台和福建电视台以宏琳厝的人情风俗为素材，联合录制了纪录片《祖屋》，将古厝文化向世界传播。

When the compound was constructed, great importance was attached to fire prevention designs. The different rows of buildings are separated by wide horizontal streets connected with roofed corridors, which can normally be used as rain shelters and immediately be dismantled in case of house fire. Once the corridors are disconnected from the houses, fire can be stopped from spreading to the next courtyard. Meanwhile, 36 saddle-shaped fire walls have been erected in the compound, and below each fire wall there is an evacuation passage. A big fire is said to have broken out somewhere in the compound. As the residents struggled to put it out, the fire walls effectively helped stop it from spreading to the adjoining buildings. In addition to the fire walls, a ditch has been excavated in the south of the compound to channel water from the outside to the criss-crossed drainage and the numerous inspection wells so that there would be abundant water to put out a fire.

The compound also features tight security designs. In the southeastern and northwestern corners there are two blockhouses, which are also called "rabbit ears". They are towers with loopholes through which shotguns could be fired. In the blockhouses, people could observe what is going on in the vicinity of the high wall on the four sides of the compound. Up the wall under the eaves of the outer wings there are lots of small openings, through which arrows or bullets could be shot and stones be hurled. Inside the compound there are still several lines of defence: at the foot of the wall there are numerous holes, through which people can make surprise attacks or set stumbling ropes; in the horizontal streets there are Farangi cannons imported from Portugal, with their muzzles directed at the intersections.

The windows in the compound are characterized by human-centered designs. They are set in a position higher than ordinary ones to ensure privacy inside the houses. The windows are opened and closed by sliding them up and down or by pushing and pulling them on hinges at the side. As the windows are specially designed, they can not open further than the external wall, and the movement of them is thus confined to a minimum space. The unique design helps prevent the windows from hitting passers-by in the populous compound. With an integration of such convenience and safety designs, the windows in the compound remain intact even after more than 200 years.

The early residents of the compound attached great importance to the education of children. In 1783 or 48th year during the reign of Qing emperor Qianlong, they set up Chongwen School, which was later renamed Wenquan School. Over the stone door frame at the entrance to Wenquan School hangs a blue-stone tablet bearing an inscription of the school name in Chinese characters, which was written by Chen Baochen, the teacher of Qing emperor Xuantong. The school was renamed Wenquan Middle School, and then Minqing County Middle School, the predecessor of the present Minqing County No. 2 Middle School. It is the old school of many renowned figures including Huang Naishang, an overseas Chinese leader.

The two-century old Honglincuo Compound boasts long standing and well established culture of its own. It has been home to more than 2, 000 people of 11 generations at home and abroad. Between 2000 and 2001, a documentary named "Ancestral House" was jointly produced by China Central Television and Fukien Television to record the life and customs of the compound. It helps spread the culture of the compound to the rest of the world.

参考文献
Reference

（春秋）孔子，2016，《论语》，陈晓芬译注，北京：中华书局。

（西汉）司马迁，1959，《史记》，北京：中华书局。

——，2005，《史记》，裴骃集解，长春：吉林大学出版社。

（东汉）赵晔，2019，《吴越春秋》，崔冶译注，北京：中华书局。

（明）何乔远，1995，《闽书》，厦门大学古籍整理研究所《闽书》校点组校点，福州：福建人民出版社。

（明）王应山，2001，《闽都记》，福州：海风出版社。

（清）梁章钜，1996，《楹联丛话全编》，北京：北京出版社。

——辑，2016，《楹联丛话 楹联续话》（子海精华编），王承略、布吉帅点校，南京：凤凰出版社。

（宋）梁克家，2003，《三山志》，陈叔侗校注，福建省地方志编纂委员会整理，北京：方志出版社。

〔日〕高良仓吉，1993，《琉球王国》：东京：岩波书店。

〔英〕毛里斯·柯立斯，1979，《汇丰—香港上海银行：汇丰银行百年史》，李周英等译，北京：中华书局。

〔法〕保尔·克洛代尔，2007，《认识东方》，徐知免译，上海：上海人民出版社。

《福州日报》，2022，《今天！人民日报连赞永泰庄寨！》，微信公众号，7月12日，https://mp.weixin.qq.com/s/P6S-iCBjF2mqqe24R3sWJA。

《孟子》，2008，王常则译注，太原：三晋出版社。

《亲历者》编辑部编，2015，《寻找中国最美古建筑》，北京：中国铁道出版社。

安然，2020，《福州古景观，探访柔远驿——追忆辉煌500年的国宾馆》，安然聊景观微信公众号，https://mp.weixin.qq.com/s/x1H_FuQyH4otHgIRi4rA4g。

鲍爱明，2017，《爱荆庄，古代村落女绅文化载体的孤本》，永泰县同安镇人民政府微信公众号，https://mp.weixin.qq.com/s/UCnb3P1bqOfa_6Xp_cx37g。

蔡人奇，2002，《藤山志》，福州：海峡摄影艺术出版社。

仓山旅游，2022，《陈氏五楼：五幢建筑复刻出的传奇人生》，微信公众号，2月16日，https: // mp.weixin.qq.com/s/jX7UB1FXEkg57CKCN7z7sQ。

仓山区文化体育和旅游局，2021，《一曲漫步烟台山，一起寻觅老时光》，搜狐网，https: //www. sohu.com/a/450526923_120207622。

陈晋、包华，2021，《唤醒老建筑，"秀"出文艺范》，《海峡都市报》7月21日。

陈敏灵，2014，《福建闽安迥龙桥建于唐代 至今保存完好》，《福州日报》5月6日。

陈楠，2022，《〈船政1986〉：岁月钩沉 见证船政衙门向史而新》，百家号，1月21日，https: // baijiahao.baidu.com/s?id=1722577905224596215&wfr=spider&for=pc。

陈炘、陈弓，2006，《福州地区孔庙建筑文化》，《闽都文化研究》第2期。

陈奕森，2018，《浅论福州"三坊七巷"传统街区各历史时期建筑的有机融合》，《中外建筑》第8期。

陈瑷，2014，《行走上下杭：重拾老福州商业记忆》，《闽商》1月刊。

带娃去旅行，2020，《福建沿海的第一门户，被誉为"闽南小上海"，藏着福州最古老石桥》，百家号，8月26日，https: //www.163.com/dy/article/H61IR9PE0553276Y.html

东南网，2022，《福州这座塔与祖国同名——"中国塔"》，百家号，https: //baijiahao.baidu.com/ s?id=1678034048963980705&wfr=spider&for=pc。

董思思，2021，《锦安黄氏家族与"父子三庄寨"》，厦门大学历史文献研究中心，https: //crlhd. xmu.edu.cn/2021/1207/c11914a445089/page.htm。

福建纪检监察，2022，《马江昭忠祠，两场海战铭就不朽精神》，清风福州微信公众号，5月9日，https: //view.inews.qq.com/a/20220524A06FYM00。

福建侨网，2021，《杜棠三落厝》，5月26日，http: //qb.fujian.gov.cn/jsxs/202105/ t20210526_5602073.htm。

福建省工信厅，2020，《第四批国家工业遗产，福建船政入选啦》，百家号，12月23日，https: // baijiahao.baidu.com/s?id=1686867071610412581&wfr=spider&for=pc。

福建省炎黄文化研究会、福建省作家协会编，2016a，《走进鼓楼：山水福地 人文名区》，福州：海峡书局。

——，2016b，《走进马尾：船政福地 活力新城》，福州：海峡书局。

福建省炎黄文化研究会编，2018，《闽台文化大辞典》，北京：商务印书馆。

——，2019，《八闽地名要览·山水篇》，福州：海峡文艺出版社。

福建省政协文史委员会编，1998，《福建名祠》，北京：台海出版社。

福建省政协文史资料委员会编，2007，《福州名人故居》，福州：福建人民出版社。

福州开元寺主办，2020，《21 世纪禅文明》第 2 期，（闽）内资准字 K 第 191 号。

福州老建筑百科，2019a，《鼓岭疗养院（宜夏别墅）》，10 月 17 日，https：//www.fzcuo.com/?doc-innerlink-%E5%AE%9C%E5%A4%8F%E5%88%AB%E5%A2%85。

——，2019b，《陶淑女子学校旧址》，10 月 20 日，https：//www.fzcuo.com/?doc-innerlink-%E9%99%B6%E6%B7%91%E5%A5%B3%E4%B8%AD。

——，2020a，《橄榄五大厝》，2 月 25 日，http：//www.fzcuo.com/index.php?doc-innerlink-%E6%A9%84%E6%A6%84%E4%BA%94%E5%A4%A7%E5%8E%9D。

——，2020b，《梦园》，4 月 23 日，https：//www.fzcuo.com/index.php?doc-view-102.html。

——，2020c，《闽王祠》，10 月 9 日，http：//fzcuo.com/index.php?doc-view-477.html。

——，2021a，《以园》，5 月 5 日，https：//www.fzcuo.com/index.php?doc-view-104.html。

——，2021b，《忠庐》，5 月 6 日，http：//www.fzcuo.com/index.php?doc-view-101.html。

——，2021c，《法国驻福州领事馆旧址》，5 月 31 日，http：//www.fzcuo.com/index.php?doc-view-273.html。

——，2021d，《鹤龄英华书院》，8 月 3 日，http：//www.fzcuo.com/index.php?doc-view-2222。

——，2021e，《美志楼》，8 月 6 日，https：//www.fzcuo.com/index.php?doc-view-61.html。

——，2022a，《三皇庙五龙堂欧冶池官地碑》，3 月 3 日，http：//www.fzcuo.com/index.php/index.php?doc-view-1397.html。

——，2022b，《拓庐》，5 月 6 日，https：//www.fzcuo.com/index.php?doc-view-100.html。

——，2022c，《永德会馆》，8 月 15 日，https：//www.fzcuo.com/index.php?doc-view-534.html。

——，2023a，《鼓岭万国公益社》，6 月 16 日，https：//www.fzcuo.com/index.php?doc-view-796.html。

——，2023b，《可园》，10 月 21 日，https：//www.fzcuo.com/index.php?doc-view-105.html。

——，2024a，《闽江口海防炮台群》，5 月 16 日，http：//www.fzcuo.com/index.php?doc-view-745.html。

——，2024b，《安澜会馆》，4 月 23 日，https：//www.fzcuo.com/index.php?doc-view-518.html。

——，2024c，《下杭路曾氏祠堂》，3 月 11 日，http：//www.fzcuo.com/index.php?doc-view-513.html。

福州日报社，2021，《贵在精神，闽江边的"最美大学"》，《家园》第 3 期。

福州市博物馆，2019，《福州古厝系列（19）螺洲天后宫》，微信公众号，12 月 4 日，https：//mp.weixin.qq.com/s/vEMRwdoS2d12VTXa-YC99g。

——, 2022,《古田会馆》, 微信公众号, 3月3日, https: //mp.weixin.qq.com/s/OAYIxcT-iQvKT3MiqrJC1g。

福州市仓山区政协委员会编, 2003,《仓山历史文化景观萃编》, 福州: 福州市仓山区政协委员会。

福州市档案馆编, 2014,《福州古村镇历史与文化》, 福州: 海峡文艺出版社。

福州市纪委监委、连江县纪委监委, 2021,《连江杜棠三落厝: "山泉入宅、宅内有河、河中有房"》, 百家号, 12月27日, https: //baijiahao.baidu.com/s?id=1720202804994189046&wfr=spider&for=pc。

福州市人民政府名城委, 2020,《海丝史迹点——长乐区圣寿宝塔及天妃灵应之记碑》, 福州市人民政府网, 9月10日。

福州市政协文史资料和学习宣传委员会编, 2017,《冶山史话》, 福州: 福建人民出版社.

福州市政协文史资料委员会编, 2014,《烟台山史话》, 福州: 海峡书局、海潮摄影艺术出版社。

福州市自然资源和规划局, 2012,《大福话福州 (二十九) | 罗星塔: 在马尾的"中国塔"》, 3月14日, http: //zygh.fuzhou.gov.cn/zz/ztzl/fzcssx/202203/t20220314_4325196.htm。

福州小鱼网, 2018,《福州这口2400多年的池塘, 曾经被一位神匠级别的男人承包……》, 搜狐网, 3月19日, https: //www.sohu.com/a/225846840_254088。

——, 2021,《福州这一"万国建筑博物馆"中, 竟曾有这4国领事馆! 它们的历史你了解吗?》, 搜狐, 12月15日, https: //www.sohu.com/a/508359350_254088。

——, 2022,《这家银行跨越世纪, 竟还被誉为福州城里的"小欧洲"!》, 网易, 3月30日, https: //www.163.com/dy/article/H3NB24F60525I8S7.html。

福州新闻网, 2019,《大美宏琳厝　风雨两百年》, 福州市人民政府网, 6月23日, http: //daj.fuzhou.gov.cn/zz/wszt/ztzl/201909/t20190906_3032980.htm。

——, 2021a,《"三通桥"究竟"通"哪了》, 百家号, https: //baijiahao.baidu.com/s?id=1713085764515692810&wfr=spider&for=pc。

——, 2021b,《福州最完整的民国大药店! 咸康参号将对市民开放》, 百家号, https: //baijiahao.baidu.com/s?id=1719025676728895314。

关瑞明、吴智顺, 2022,《福州会馆的类型及其建筑特色研究》,《HA》第6期。

光明网, 2020,《九头马 长乐建筑史上的辉煌篇章》, 9月18日, https: //m.gmw.cn/baijia/2020-09/18/1301577678.html。

郭进绍, 2022,《说说于山白塔的原名》,《福州晚报》5月23日。

哈雷, 2015,《六都平原上的风雨古厝》,《文艺报》12月11日。

何绵山，2016，《闽文化通论》，北京：北京大学出版社。

胡阔，2011，《福州地区教会大学建筑艺术研究》，硕士学位论文，福州：福建师范大学。

黄金钟，1985，《福州四大书院》，《教育评论》第3期。

黄荣春，2009，《福州市郊区文物志》，福州：福建人民出版社。

黄守明，2019，《福州正谊书院：融入台湾文创，活化书院文化》，AM 585东南广播微信公众号，2月27日，https: //mp.weixin.qq.com/s/rWe5Wj6wz1bVFvGBCQ_d1Q。

黄新宪，1990，《从华南女子大学到华南女子文理学院——对旧中国一所著名教会女子大学的考察》，《教育科学》第3期。

家园Homeland编，2021，《古厝故事》，《家园》第3期。

江荣基、官桂铨，2003，《左宗棠在福州的遗迹》，《船政文化研究》第6期。

江秀山、邹元昊，2022，《上下杭历史街区的保护更新研究》，《中外建筑》第2期。

金银珍、凌宇，2010，《书院·福建》，上海：同济大学出版社。

靳凤华，2019，《闽王祠文化与艺术装饰审美探究》，《艺术与设计》(理论)，第7期。

蓝瑜萍、余少林，2021，《圣寿宝塔：见证郑和七下西洋》，《福州晚报·海外版》7月12日。

李莉，2002，《明清福州琉球馆考》，《福建师范大学学报》第4期。

李升宝，2004，《冰心故里散记》，《福建乡土》第1期。

李夕汐，2015，《福州美国领事馆旧址的修复设计研究》，硕士学位论文，泉州：华侨大学。

李熙慧，2012，《福州乐群路曾住着法国文豪保罗·克洛代尔》，福州新闻网，4月7日，http: //news.fznews.com.cn/shehui/2012-4-7/201247c7Ti6Vco43101657_2.shtml。

连江县人民政府办公室，2018，《长门炮台》，福州市连江县人民政府网，10月11日，http: //www.fzlj.gov.cn/xjwz/zwgk/zfxxgkzdgz/ggwhty/whycbh/201810/t20181011_2632065.htm。

林精华，2006，《"咸康"国药行及其老板张桂荣》，福州新闻网，http: //news.fznews.com.cn/sfqx/2006-7-25/2006725-9Ud8W-k55162731.shtml。

林婧，2020，《长乐太平港〈天妃灵应之记碑〉的史学价值》，《福建文博》第3期。

林凯，2021《福州长乐九头马古民居 百年建筑古韵悠长》，新华社，2月20日。

林凯、吴念，2021，《昭忠祠：马江的"碧血千秋"》，新华社，1月24日。

林仁川，1992，《中国租界史》，上海：上海社会科学院出版社。

林诗羽，2020，《福州烟台山历史文化风貌区建筑价值评价研究》，硕士学位论文，福州：福建农林大学。

林晓捷，2014，《基于平衡因素的福州泛船浦教堂景观空间设计》，《福建建筑》第5期。

林旭昕，2008，《福州"三坊七巷"明清传统民居地域特点及其历史渊源研究》，硕士学位论文，西安：西安建筑科技大学。

刘可耕、吴旭涛，2021，《守护"万国建筑博物馆"福州烟台山欲申遗》，中国侨网，http：//www.chinaqw.com/zhwh/2021/11-09/313146.shtml。

刘林丰，2020，《基于百度POI数据的福州市宗教建筑分布特点》，《四川建筑》第6期。

卢美松主编，2017，《福州通史简编》，福州：福建人民出版社。

卢美松，2022，《闽中稽古》，厦门：厦门大学出版社。

鹿野，2014，《华林寺，大隐于世的千年古刹》，《闽都文化》第5期。

马丽清，2021a，《福州"国保"亭江炮台：研究近代海防的活教材》，《福州晚报》6月18日。

——，2021b，福建船政建筑：百年遗产变"锈"为"秀"，《福州晚报·海外版》12月27日。

——，2022，《马江昭忠祠：忆碧血千秋 传船政精神》，《福州晚报·海外版》1月3日。

马且停，2022，《福建有座古寺，面积不大却跻身中国木构建筑top10，就藏在省会福州》，百家号，https：//baijiahao.baidu.com/s?id=1726980947998244097&wfr=spider&for=pc。

马尾区委党史和地方志研究室，2022，《走进马尾船政格致园，感受船政文化的魅力》，搜狐网，3月14日，https：//www.sohu.com/a/529762345_121106994。

马尾区文体局，2021，《打卡马尾造船厂旧址》，福州市马尾区人民政府网站，10月9日，http：//www.mawei.gov.cn/xjwz/zwgk/zfxxgkzdgz/ggtywh/wtssml/202110/t20211009_4202612.htm。

宓盈婷，2021，《来这座塔，一起眺望郑和曾经眺望过的远方》，新华社，7月29日。

闽声传媒，2020，《福州烟台山：遇见凝固的近代史》，腾讯网，https：//new.qq.com/rain/a/20201118A02J1900。

欧阳进权，2020，《"国保"亭江炮台长假迎客》，百家号，10月5日。

——，2021，《迥龙桥邢港码头诉说千年"海丝"史》，《福州日报》7月9日。

潘宏，2012，《革命者的大爱情怀——林觉民〈与妻书〉赏析》，《语言建设》第9期。

潘逸群，2013，《王审知开闽第一人》，《福建人》第11期。

澎湃新闻，2020，《船坚炮利丨惨败中的亮色：1884年闽江口之战中的长门炮台》，搜狐网，12月11日，https：//www.sohu.com/a/437595164_260616。

钱嘉宜、吴晖，2016，《谷颐堂：藏在深山的建筑明珠》，《福州日报》6月21日。

钱江、涂洪长、王成，2021，《福州：古城两千两百岁，信乎今夕是盛年》，《新华每日电讯》7月16日。

任继愈主编，2002，《佛教大辞典》，南京：江苏古籍出版社。

三坊七巷社区学习促进会，2016，《福州四大书院系列之三——正谊书院》，微信公众号，7月21
    日，https：//mp.weixin.qq.com/s/DgHI2g-RUQEa7iUOhOV6rQ。

施晓宇，2013，《福州第一人：王审知》，《文化广角》第8期。

石磊磊、包华，2020，《福州上下杭永德会馆开馆！百个瓷壶打造"镇馆之宝"》，《海峡都市报》12
    月16日。

树红霞，2014，《长乐琴江满族村：昔日旗营今犹在》，《福建日报》4月24日。

搜狐网，2019，《东阳诗词微刊》，9月16日，https：//m.sohu.com/coo/sg/341384273_785801。

孙群，2015，《福州古塔的建筑类型与造型特征探析》，《福建工程学院学报》第3期。

汪敬虞，1983，《十九世纪西方资本主义对中国的经济侵略》，北京：人民出版社。

汪晓东，2012，《福州马鞍墙装饰图式特点及其成因探析》，《设计艺术研究》第4期。

王刚，2018，《福州螺洲古镇的这座孔庙，七百多年的历史告诉了我们什么？》，搜狐网，https：//
    www.sohu.com/a/230582718_402295。

王晓霞，2020，《福州迥龙桥及邢港码头、罗星塔被列为海丝史迹遗产点》，新浪网，6月7日，http：//
    fj.sina.com.cn/news/b/2020-06-07/detail-iircuyvi7139491.shtml。

——，2021，《福州罗星塔：屹立江口数百年 见证沧桑巨变》，《福州晚报》7月21日。

——，2022，《千年前，中国女性是什么地位？福州这座石桥印证了……》，《海峡都市报》3月8日。

网易，2022，《船政轮机厂、绘事院——浓缩百年船政荣耀》，1月7日，https：//www.163.com/dy/
    article/GT3VFMAQ0525B2ES.html。

吴安钦，2021，《杜棠三落厝的前世今生》，《福州晚报·海外版》5月24日。

吴丹红，2021，《马尾古港古塔 诉说千年"海丝"史》，《海峡日报》7月22日。

伍媛媛，2021，《清宫档案里的柔远驿》，《清史论丛》第1期。

谢必震，2024，《香飘魁岐村：福建协和大学》，石家庄：河北教育出版社。

谢承平、关瑞明，2014，《19世纪福州基督教教堂建筑研究》，《福建建筑》第12期。

谢海潮，2022，《"美国驻福州领事馆"旧址新探》，《福建日报》1月4日。

岫云，2020，《柔远驿：福州古代"国宾馆"》，《福州晚报》12月21日，第6版。

许山，2021，《古厝深深深几许》，央广网，http：//www.cnr.cn/fj/wh/20210706/
    t20210706_525528139.shtml。

寻文颖，2013，《浅谈中西文化的交融与碰撞—以鼓岭老街保护规划为例》，《福建建筑》第5期。

闫茂辉、朱永春，2011，《福州仓山近代领事馆遗存考述》，《华中建筑》第4期。

央视《海峡两岸行》，2006，《福建名祠之闽王祠》，新浪网，https：//news.sina.com.cn/c/2006-08-

28/143110850220.shtml。

杨成和，2013，《邢港古航道揭示闽安海上丝绸之路的起源》，《海峡日报》7月4日。

——，2016，《港口古码头：闽安"海上丝绸之路"兴盛的见证》，个人图书馆，6月19日，http：//
www.360doc.com/content/22/0625/22/80006572_1037431125.shtml。

杨琼，2017，《福州古田会馆的建筑艺术理念及其表征》，《艺术与设计》第8期。

叶红，2012，《台江区上下杭历史文化街区——台江商贸的发源地》，《海峡科学》第11期。

佚名，2015，《台江区后洲街道三通桥》，老百晓集桥，http：//www.china-qiao.com/ql19/fzql/
fzql054.htm。

——，2017，《美国领事馆旧址，福州烟台山复兴样本》，搜狐焦点，5月19日，https：//m.focus.
cn/fz/zixun/7f26e9d623815727.html。

——，2020a，《你可知，闽侯洋里深山里竟隐匿着一座闽越王庙》，微信公众号，https：//
mp.weixin.qq.com/s/gZZiKPVMGHARscps0Uowsg。

——，2020b，《上下行三通桥的来历》，星哥奇闻趣事网，http：//www.soubct.com/info/20200130-
dp3pnr.html。

——，2020c，《中国四大进士之乡，福州、苏州、杭州、吉安，福州进士全国第一》，百家号，
https：//baijiahao.baidu.com/s?id=1681769141879838797&wfr=spider&for=pc。

——，2021a，《福州鼓岭资源情形》，百度文库，https：//wenku.baidu.com/view/
a9fc8c6227d3240c8447ef94.html。

——，2021b，《曾长兴溪纸行曾氏：经营纸行，福州之首》，网易，https：//www.163.com/dy/
article/GR5U4BR20514FJJE.html。

于亚娟，2013，《宋代福建孔庙建筑布局初探》，《福建史志》第5期。

余少林，2020，《圣寿宝塔：昔看郑和七下西洋 今见海丝再创辉煌》，《吴航乡情报》5月27日。

悦迪，2022，《小众古建筑列入世界级名录永泰庄寨：深山里的"超级民居"》，齐鲁壹点，https：//
baijiahao.baidu.com/s?id=1727709875469112532&wfr=spider&for=pc。

云仙，2004，《汇丰银行与近代中国金融发展研究（1865-1949）》，博士学位论文，北京：中国人
民大学。

云游长东，2022，《邂逅百年建筑，感受古韵悠长——九头马古民居》，微信公众号，4月23日，
https：//mp.weixin.qq.com/s/5pRvLCdz9zsksZa9aRlnjA。

曾意丹，1983，《闽忠懿王庙》，《福建论坛》第3期。

——，2019，《福州古厝》，福州：福建人民出版社。

张建设，2022，《梦幻绍安庄：福建永泰的"小布达拉宫"》，《中华民居》第189期。

张培奋，2016，《永泰庄寨》，福州：海峡世纪影视文化有限公司。

张维璟、赵莹、翁宇民，2017，《积善堂——世事变迁溯初心》，《福州晚报》11月9日。

赵君尧，2011，《琉球馆：尘封一百三十多年的历史记忆》，《历史文献研究》第30期。

——，2014，《由封闭走向开放——福州城中轴线上的朱紫坊、上下杭、烟台山》，《政协天地》第
    4期。

赵晔：《吴越春秋》，长沙：岳麓书社，1996。

郑振满，2020，《庄寨密码：永泰文书与山区开发史研究》，福州：福建人民出版社。

中国第一历史档案馆编，1993—2002，《清代中琉关系档案选编》，北京：中国档案出版社。

朱楠楠，2011，《宗族文化下的祠堂建筑研究—以徽州宗祠为例》，硕士学位论文，厦门：厦门大学。

LAZY，2022，《有福之州——华林寺，江南最古老的木构建筑》，厦航福州航旅圈微信公众号，5月
    22日，https：//mp.weixin.qq.com/s/m3vmjofTPd_ZDp5Efgs-Ug。

Frank H. H. King with Catherine E. King and David J. S. King, 1987, The Hongkong Bank in Late
    Imperial China, 1864-1902on an even koel. The History of the Hongkong and Shanghai
    Banking Corporation, Volume 1. Cambridge: Cambridge University Press.

World Monuments Fund: Fortified Manors of Yongtai, https://www.wmf.org/project/fortified-
    manors-yongtai.

图书在版编目（CIP）数据

福州古厝：汉文、英文 / 林明金主编 . -- 北京：
社会科学文献出版社，2024.6. --（福建历史文化双语
丛书）. -- ISBN 978-7-5228-3695-9

I. K928.71

中国国家版本馆 CIP 数据核字第 2024GV2538 号

· 福建历史文化双语丛书 ·

福州古厝（中英双语版）

主　　编 / 林明金

出 版 人 / 冀祥德
责任编辑 / 赵晶华　刘学谦
责任印制 / 王京美

出　　版 / 社会科学文献出版社 · 文化传媒分社（010）59367004
　　　　　　地址：北京市北三环中路甲 29 号院华龙大厦　邮编：100029
　　　　　　网址：www.ssap.com.cn
发　　行 / 社会科学文献出版社（010）59367028
印　　装 / 北京联兴盛业印刷股份有限公司

规　　格 / 开本：787mm×1092mm　1/16
　　　　　　印张：27　字数：605 千字
版　　次 / 2024 年 6 月第 1 版　2024 年 6 月第 1 次印刷
书　　号 / ISBN 978-7-5228-3695-9
定　　价 / 158.00 元

读者服务电话：4008918866